T.M.C. ASSER INSTITUUT
The Hague

The European Union and Its Neighbours

A Legal Appraisal of the EU's Policies of Stabilisation, Partnership and Integration

Edited by

Steven Blockmans
and
Adam Łazowski

T·M·C·ASSER PRESS

Published by T·M·C·ASSER PRESS
P.O.Box 16163, 2500 BD The Hague, The Netherlands
<www.asserpress.nl>

T·M·C·ASSER PRESS English language books are distributed exclusively by:

Cambridge University Press, The Edinburgh Building, Shaftesbury Road,
Cambridge CB2 2RU, UK,
or
for customers in the USA, Canada and Mexico:
Cambridge University Press, 100 Brook Hill Drive, West Nyack, NY 10994-2133, USA

<www.cambridge.org>

ISBN 90-6704-201-3
ISBN 978-90-6704-201-7

T.M.C. Asser Instituut - Institute for Private and Public International Law, International Commercial Arbitration and European Law
Institute Address: R.J. Schimmelpennincklaan 20-22, 2517 JN The Hague, The Netherlands; P.O. Box 30461, 2500 GL The Hague, The Netherlands; Tel.: (31-70)3420300; Fax: (31-70)3420359; URL: <www.asser.nl>.
Over forty years, the T.M.C. Asser Institute has developed into a leading scientific research institute in the field of international law. It covers private international law, public international law, including international humanitarian law, the law of the European Union, the law of international commercial arbitration and increasingly, also, international economic law, the law of international commerce and international sports law. Conducting scientific research either fundamental or applied, in the aforementioned domains, is the main activity of the Institute. In addition, the Institute organizes congresses and postgraduate courses, undertakes contract-research and operates its own publishing house, T.M.C.ASSER PRESS. Because of its inter-university background, the Institute often cooperates with Dutch law faculties as well as with various national and foreign institutions. The Institute organizes Asser College Europe, a project in cooperation with East and Central European countries whereby research and educational projects are organized and implemented.

FOREWORD

The relations between the European Union and its neighbouring countries have been at the heart of the T.M.C. Asser Institute's activities for more than twenty-five years. In the 1970s, the T.M.C. Asser Institute was one of the first academic institutions in Western Europe to establish close contacts with universities in Central and Eastern Europe: first with the so-called Hague-Zagreb-Ghent Colloquia on the Law of International Trade, and later, at the end of the eighties, when the political divide between the two blocks in Europe began to fade away, with a post-graduate training and research programme called 'Asser College Europe'. This programme brought intensive academic cooperation between universities from almost all the European Union's neighbouring countries in Central and Eastern Europe.

Furthermore, since the nineties, the Institute has been active in consultancy and legal advice activities in these countries, under the auspices of such programmes as Matra, Phare, Tacis, OBNOVA and CARDS. Experts from the Institute have been advising governments as well as the European Commission on various issues, including problems relating to the adoption and implementation of the *acquis* in the European Union's neighbouring countries, especially those countries with a membership perspective. In the growing tradition of its EU enlargement publications, with *EU Enlargement: The Constitutional Impact at EU and National Level* (edited by Alfred Kellermann, Jaap de Zwaan and Jenö Czuczai) and *Handbook on European Enlargement: A Commentary on the Enlargement Process* (edited by Andrea Ott and Kirstyn Inglis) as the most prominent exponents, the T.M.C. Asser Institute has now published *The European Union and its Neighbours: A Legal Appraisal of the EU's Policies of Stabilisation, Partnership and Integration*, edited by Steven Blockmans and Adam Łazowski.

Both editors have built up extensive experience in consulting and teaching EU law in the countries of Central and Eastern Europe. As representatives of one of the 'old' and one of the 'new' Member States, they share the vision of a strong European Union which is currently redefining its position in a wider Europe, indeed the world. With the support of a multinational team of experts drawn from the Institute's extensive network of contacts, the editors have compiled a comprehensive and well-structured overview of the political and legal developments of the relations between the European Union and each of its current neighbours. By choosing a methodology which holds the middle ground between a handbook, which necessarily implies precision and simplicity, and a critical academic analysis, Blockmans and Łazowski have made sure that this book will continue to be useful, despite the constant developments on the international scene which render any book on the external relations of the European Union outdated before it is even published. *The European Union and its Neighbours* should prove a valuable tool for anyone seeking a better legal and political understanding of both the overall and the specific relations between the Union and its neighbours.

I congratulate both editors with the publication of this highly interesting book, which forms a perfect addition to the Asser Institute's enlargement publication 'series'.

I recommend it with pleasure to anyone interested in the legal and political relations between the European Union and its neighbours.

Prof. Dr Frans A. Nelissen
Director T.M.C. Asser Institute
The Hague, June 2006

PREFACE AND ACKNOWLEDGEMENTS

The relations between the European Union and its geographical neighbours are not a new topic on the research agenda. On the contrary, it is a theme with a deep historical background covered by many discussions and publications. It is striking to note that the current legal and political academic literature has a tendency of compartmentalising the neighbouring countries according to the type of (contractual) relations that exist with the European Union. As such, the (potential) candidate countries, the states covered by the European Neighbourhood Policy, the members of the European Economic Area, the micro-states and Russia are dealt with separately.[1] This approach denies a more holistic understanding of the European Union's actions and ambitions on the European continent, indeed internationally. It is our view that, in the wake of its biggest expansion ever, the European Union will have to adapt its neighbourhood policies to the new legal, (geo)political, economic and social environment in order to secure its international position. Hence, after the 'big bang' enlargement of the Union in 2004, it is useful to re-evaluate the European Union's policies of stabilisation, partnership and integration as applied to its neighbours. It is only by studying the relations between the European Union and all of its geographical neighbours that one is able to offer insights into the linkages that exist between the different neighbourhood policies and the contractual relations that underpin them and to make suggestions on how to better organise them.

[1] See, *inter alia*, M. Maresceau, *Enlarging the European Union* (London, Longman 1997); A. Mayhew, *Recreating Europe: The European Union's Policy towards Central and Eastern Europe* (Cambridge, Cambridge University Press 1998); K. Smith, *The Making of EU Foreign Policy: The Case of Eastern Europe* (Basingstoke, Palgrave 1999); P.-Ch. Müller-Graff and E. Selvig, eds., *EEA-EU Relations* (Berlin, Berlin Verlag Arno Spitz GmbH 1999); R. Dwan, ed., *Building Security in Europe's New Borderlands: Subregional Cooperation in the Wider Europe* (Brussels, EWI 1999); T. de Wilde and L. Spetschinsky, eds., *Les relations entre l'Union européenne et la Fédération de Russie* (Louvain-la-Neuve, IEE 2000); M. Maresceau and E. Lannon, eds., *The EU's Enlargement and Mediterranean Strategies* (Basingstoke, Palgrave 2001); A. Ott and K. Inglis, eds., *Handbook on European Enlargement – A Commentary on the Enlargement Process* (The Hague, T.M.C. Asser Press 2002); W. Jacoby, *The Enlargement of the European Union and NATO. Ordering from the Menu in Central Europe* (Cambridge, Cambridge University Press 2004); R. Dannreuther, ed., *European Union Foreign and Security Policy: Towards a Neighbourhood Strategy* (London, Routledge 2004); C. Hillion, ed., *EU Enlargement: A Legal Approach* (Oxford, Hart Publishing 2004); M. Emerson, *The Wider Europe Matrix* (Brussels, CEPS 2004). For literature on the European Union's external relations in general, see, *inter alia*, I. Macleod, I.D. Hendry and S. Hyett, *The External Relations of the European Communities* (Oxford, Clarendon Press 1996); A. Dashwood and Ch. Hillion, *The General Law of EC External Relations* (London, Sweet & Maxwell 2000); P. Eeckhout, *External Relations of the European Union* (Oxford, Oxford University Press 2004); and P. Koutrakos, *EU International Relations Law* (Oxford/Portland, Oregon, Hart Publishing 2006).

While the objective of this volume is to give a legal appraisal of the European Union's relations with its neighbours, the contributors have enriched their chapters with insights and perspectives from other disciplines. As such, the book contributes to a legal and policy-relevant assessment of the European Union's external relations. Rather than providing new theoretical or conceptual constructs for understanding the European Union's external policies, this study builds upon existing constructs and offers new insights into them. The book offers an academic analysis of the relations between the European Union and its neighbours, primarily from an EU perspective. It should appeal to academics because of its comprehensive scope and because it allows for a comparative analysis of the European Union's legal relations with the neighbouring countries. Practitioners will find this publication useful as a tool that identifies and examines the legal framework for cooperation with each of the European Union's neighbours.

The anthology starts out with a general section devoted to the European Union's historical, political and legal approach to its relations with its neighbours. In this section, the 'European' identity and the main types of relationships between the European Union and its neighbours are questioned (chapter 1), the multi-level complexity of the European Union's external relations regime is analysed (chapter 2) and the evolving nature of EU membership conditionality applied to future and potential Member States is studied (chapter 3). In the second part of the book, fifteen chapters are devoted to the European Union's relations with specific countries or groups of countries (chapters 4 to 18). Each of these chapters starts with a schematic overview of the most important legal documents which currently define the relationship(s) in question. Furthermore, the chapters have all been composed along similar lines and contain:

(i) a brief historical and political account of the European Union's relations with its neighbours;
(ii) an analysis of the structure and contents of the main legal documents which define those relations;
(iii) a more in-depth analysis of specific legal, political, economic and/or social issues that define the nature of those relations; and
(iv) some concluding remarks on the impact of enlargement on those relations and an outlook of where those relations might go in the near future.

Through an inductive, bottom-up and cross-pillar approach, the linkages and overlaps between the Union's bilateral and multilateral relations with all of its geographical neighbours are exposed. This focus contributes to a more holistic understanding of the European Union's external policies and has led us to formulate some ideas and concrete proposals to improve the consistency and coherence of the Union's neighbourhood policies (chapter 19).

The editing and content management of this book, as well as the coordination of a group of sixteen authors from eleven different countries would not have been possible without the help of many committed colleagues. We would like to thank the individual authors for producing excellent chapters in accordance with the overall brief of the book. We would like to express our gratitude to the Director of the T.M.C. Asser Institute, Professor Dr Frans Nelissen, for providing financial and logistical support for this project. Special thanks go to the staff at T.M.C. Asser Press, Philip van Tongeren and Marjolijn Bastiaans, for their enthusiasm and continued support when this book proved to become much bigger than anticipated. We are also grateful to Anna Łabędzka for her assistance in the compilation of the index. Much credit lies with the core editing team. For their excellent language revision, sub-editing and – above all – patience and understanding, we would like to extend our warmest gratitude to Daniel Stephens and Inge van Dun-van den Bosch.

Steven Blockmans and Adam Łazowski
Brussels/London, July 2006

SUMMARY TABLE OF CONTENTS

DETAILED TABLE OF CONTENTS

ABBREVIATIONS

AA	Association Agreement
ACG	Azeri-Chirag-Guneshli
ADD	Addendum
AEPLAC	Armenian-European Policy and Legal Advice Centre
AFSJ	Area of Freedom, Security and Justice
AG	Advocate General
AII	Adriatic-Ionian Initiative
ALE	Alliance libre européenne
AMG	OSCE Advisory and Monitoring Group
APuZ	Aus Politik und Zeitgeschichte
BBC	British Broadcasting Corporation
BiH	Bosnia-Herzegovina
BSEC	Black Sea Economic Cooperation
BTC	Baku-Tbilisi-Ceyhan
Bull. EC	Bulletin of the European Communities
Bull. EU	Bulletin of the European Union
BVerfGE	Entscheidungen des Bundesverfassungsgerichts
CAP	Common Agricultural Policy
CARDS	Community Assistance for Reconstruction, Development and Stabilisation
CBC	Cross-Border Cooperation
CC	Constitutional Court
CDDRL	Center on Democracy, Development and the Rule of Law
CDU	Christlich Demokratische Union Deutschlands
CEE	Communauté économique européenne
CEEC	Central and Eastern European Countries
CEES	Common European Economic Space
CEFTA	Central European Free Trade Association
CEI	Central European Initiative
CEPS	Centre for European Policy Studies
CES	Center for Eastern Studies
CES	Common Economic Space
CFE	Conventional Armed Forces in Europe
CFI	Court of First Instance
CFSP	Common Foreign and Security Policy
CIA	Central Intelligence Agency
CiO	OSCE Chairman-in-Office
CIS	Commonwealth of Independent States
CISR	Center for Strategic Studies and Reforms
CMLRev.	Common Market Law Review
CoE	Council of Europe
COM	European Commission document
Comecon	Council for Mutual Economic Assistance
CONV	Convention

COPPS	EU Coordinating Office for Palestinian Police Support
CPT	European Committee for the Prevention of Torture and Inhuman or Degrading Treatment or Punishment
CREST	Scientific and Technical Research Committee
CS	Common Strategy
CSCE	Conference on Security and Cooperation in Europe
CSES	Common Space of External Security
CSFSJ	Common Space of Freedom, Security and Justice
CSO	Committee of Senior Officials
CSP	Country Strategy Paper
CSRE	Common Space of Research and Education
CSU	EU Common Strategy on Ukraine
CUP	Cambridge University Press
DCMT	Danube-Cris-Mures-Tisza
DG	Directorate General
DSP	Directorate of Strategic Planning
EA	Europe Agreement
EAEC	European Atomic Energy Community
EAGGF	European Agricultural Guidance and Guarantee Fund
EAPC	Euro-Atlantic Partnership Council
EAR	European Agency for Reconstruction
EAW	European Arrest Warrant
EBRD	European Bank for Reconstruction and Development
EC	European Community
ECB	European Central Bank
ECHO	European Community Humanitarian Aid Office
ECHR	European Convention for the Protection of Human Rights and Fundamental Freedoms
ECJ	European Court of Justice
ECMI	European Centre for Minority Issues
ECOSOC	UN Economic and Social Council
ECR	European Court Reports
ECSA	European Community Studies Association
ECSC	European Coal and Steel Community
ECSEE	Energy Community of South-Eastern Europe
ECU	European Currency Unit
EDIS	Extended Decentralisation Implementation System
EDRC	European Documentation and Research Centre
EEA	European Economic Area
EEC	European Economic Community
EFA Rev.	European Foreign Affairs Review
EFTA	European Free Trade Association
EG	Europäische Gemeinschaft
EGV	Vertrag zur Gründung der Europäischen Gemeinschaft
EIB	European Investment Bank
EIDHR	European Initiative for Democracy and Human Rights
EJIL	European Journal of International Law
EJML	European Journal of Migration and Law

ELJ	European Law Journal
ELR	European Law Review
EMA	Euro-Mediterranean Agreement
EMDB	Euro-Mediterranean Development Bank
EMEA	Euro-Mediterranean Economic Area
EMFTA	Euro-Mediterranean Free Trade Area
EMP	Euro-Mediterranean Partnership
EMPA	Euro-Mediterranean Parliamentary Assembly
EMU	Economic and Monetary Union
ENP	European Neighbourhood Policy
ENPI	European Neighbourhood and Partnership Instrument
EP	European Parliament
EPL	European Public Law
EPP	European People's Party
ESDP	European Security and Defence Policy
ESS	European Security Strategy
ETS	European Treaties Series
EU	European Union
EU BAM	EU Border Assistance Mission
EuConst	European Constitutional Law Review
EU COPPS	EU Coordinating Office for Palestinian Police Support
EUF	European Union-led Forces
EUFOR	European Union Force in Bosnia and Herzegovina
EuGH	Europäischer Gerichtshof
EUI	European University Institute
EUISS	European Union Institute for Security Studies
EUJUST	EU Rule of Law Mission
EUMM	European Union Monitoring Mission
EUPM	European Union Police Mission in Bosnia and Herzegovina
EUPOL	European Union Police Mission
EuR	Europarecht
Euratom	European Atomic Energy Community
Euromed	Euro-Mediterranean Partnership
Europol	European Police Office
EUV	Vertrag über die Europäische Union
EuZW	Europäische Zeitschrift für Wirtschaftsrecht
EWG	Europäische Wirtschaftsgemeinschaft
EWR	Europäischer Wirtschaftsraum
EWS	Europäisches Wirtschafts- und Steuerrecht
FAO	Food and Agriculture Organisation
FEMIP	Facility for Euro-Mediterranean Investment and Partnership
FEOGA	Fondo Europeo de Orientación y de Garantía Agrícola
FRTD	Facilitated Rail Transit Document
FRY	Federal Republic of Yugoslavia
FSP	Food Security Programme
FTA	Free Trade Area
FTD	Facilitated Transit Document
FTE	Full Time Equivalent
FYROM	Former Yugoslav Republic of Macedonia

G-5	France, Germany, Italy, Spain and the United Kingdom
G-7	Canada, France, Germany, Italy, Japan, the United Kingdom and the United States of America
G-8	G-7 plus Russia
GA	General Assembly
GAERC	General Affairs and External Relations Council
GATS	General Agreement on Trade in Services
GATT	General Agreement on Tariffs and Trade
GCC	Gulf Cooperation Council
GDP	gross domestic product
GEPLAC	Georgian-European Policy and Legal Advice Centre
GFAP	General Framework Agreement for Peace in Bosnia and Herzegovina
GMP	Global Mediterranean Policy
GNI	gross national income
GSP	Generalised System of Preferences
GTZ	Deutsche Gesellschaft für Technische Zusammenarbeit
GUUAM	Georgia, Ukraine, Uzbekistan, Azerbaijan and Moldova
HCJ	High Court of Justice
HDZ	Hrvatska Demokratska Zajednica [Croatian Democratic Union]
HLG	high-level group
HLPG	High-Level Planning Group
HQ	headquarters
HR	Human Resources
HR CFSP	EU High Representative for the CFSP
HRLJ	Human Rights Law Journal
HS	Harmonised System
IBRD	International Bank for Reconstruction and Development
ICG	International Crisis Group
ICJ	International Court of Justice
ICTY	International Criminal Tribunal for the former Yugoslavia
IDF	Israel Defense Forces
IDP	internally displaced persons
IFOR	Implementation Force
IGC	Intergovernmental Conference
IHT	International Herald Tribune
IISEPS	Independent Institute of Socio-Economic and Political Studies
ILC	UN International Law Commission
ILM	International Legal Materials
IMF	International Monetary Fund
INOGATE	Interstate Oil and Gas Transport to Europe
INTAS	International Association for the Promotion of Cooperation with Scientists from the New Independent States of the former Soviet Union
Interpol	Commission Internationale de Police Criminelle
INTERREG	Interregional Cooperation Programme
IntRes	Interim Resolution
IPTF	International Police Task Force (UN)

ISPA	Instrument for Structural Policies for Pre-Accession
ITAR-TASS	Information Telegraph Agency of Russia – Telegranoe Agentsvo Sovetskogo Soyuza
JCMS	Journal of Common Market Studies
JHA	Justice and Home Affairs (EU)
JNA	Jugoslovenska narodna armija [Yugoslav People's Army]
JO	Journal officiel de l'Union européenne
JPC	Joint Parliamentary Committee
KGB	Komitet Gosudarstvennoy Bezopasnosti [Committee for State Security]
LIEI	Legal Issues of European Integration
LNTS	League of Nations Treaty Series
MDE	Middle East (as used by Amnesty International)
MEDA	financial instrument of the Euro-Mediterranean Partnership
MEP	Member of the European Parliament
MEPP	Middle East Peace Process
MFN	most favoured nation
MIP	Multi-annual Indicative Programme
MoU	Memorandum of Understanding
MP	Member of Parliament
NACC	North Atlantic Cooperation Council
NATO	North Atlantic Treaty Organisation
NGO	non-governmental organisation
NIP	National Indicative Programme
NIS	Newly Independent States
NJ	Nederlandse Jurisprudentie
NMP	New Mediterranean Policy
NMS	National Market System
NPAA	National Programme for the Adoption of the Acquis
NQHR	Netherlands Quarterly of Human Rights
NSC	National Security Council
NTER	Nederlands Tijdschrift voor Europees Recht
NUTS	Nomenclature of Territorial Units for Statistics
NVwZ	Neue Zeitschrift für Verwaltungsrecht
NYIL	Netherlands Yearbook of International Law
nyp	not yet published
nyr	not yet reported
ODIHR	OSCE Office for Democratic Institutions and Human Rights
OECD	Organisation for Economic Cooperation and Development
OHR	Office of the High Representative in Bosnia and Herzegovina
OIC	Organisation of the Islamic Conference
OJ	Official Journal of the European Communities/Union
OLAF	European Anti-Fraud Office
OMC	Organisation Mondiale du Commerce (WTO)

OMON	Otryad Militsii Osobogo Naznacheniya [Special Operations State Militia]
OSCE	Organisation for Security and Cooperation in Europe
OUP	Oxford University Press
PA	Palestinian Authority
PCA	Partnership and Cooperation Agreement
PES	Party of European Socialists
PfP	NATO Partnership for Peace
Phare	originally: Poland Hungary Assistance for the Reconstruction of the Economy
PISG	Provisional Institutions of Self-Government in Kosovo
PJCC	Police and Judicial Cooperation in Criminal Matters
PLO	Palestine Liberation Organisation
PM	Prime Minister
PolYIL	Polish Yearbook of International Law
PPC	Permanent Partnership Council
PPP	purchasing power parity
PR	Personal Representative
PSC	Political and Security Committee
PSE	Parti Socialiste Européen
R&D	Research and Development
RAE-LEA	Revue des Affaires Européennes – Law and European Affairs
RAPEX	Community Rapid Information System
RECEP	Russian-European Centre for Economic Policy
RIW	Recht der internationalen Wirtschaft
RIZ	Rechtszentrum für europäische und internationale Zusammenarbeit
RM	Republic of Moldova
RMC	Revue du Marché Commun
RMCU	Revue du Marché Commun et de l'Union Européenne
RRM	Rapid Reaction Mechanism
RSP	Regional Strategy Paper
SAA	Stabilisation and Association Agreement
SAC	Stabilisation and Association Council
SAC	Supreme Administrative Court
SaM	Serbia and Montenegro
SAP	Stabilisation and Association Process
SAPARD	Special Accession Programme for Agriculture and Rural Development
SCA	Surveillance and Court Agreement
SCAD	South Caucasus Anti-Drug Programme
SEC	Commission Staff Working Paper
SECI	Southeast European Cooperative Initiative
SEECP	South East Europe Cooperation Process
SEESP	South East European Studies Programme at Oxford University
SEI	Sussex European Institute
SFOR	Stabilisation Force in Bosnia and Herzegovina
SFRY	Socialist Federal Republic of Yugoslavia

SG	Secretary-General
SG	State Gazette
SIS	Schengen Information System
SME	small and medium-sized enterprises
SPF	CBC Small Projects Facility
START	Strategic Arms Reduction Treaty
STCU	Science and Technology Center in Ukraine
STM	SAP Tracking Mechanism
SWP	Stiftung Wissenschaft und Politik
Tacis	Technical Assistance to the Commonwealth of Independent States
TAIEX	Technical Assistance and Information Exchange Unit of the Directorate-General for Enlargement of the European Commission
TCA	Trade and Cooperation Agreement
TCE	Treaty establishing a Constitution for Europe
TEC	Treaty establishing the European Community
TEEC	Treaty establishing the European Economic Community
Tempus	Trans-European Mobility Scheme for University Studies
TEU	Treaty on European Union
TK	Tweede Kamer der Staten-Generaal [House of Representatives of the Dutch Parliament]
ToA	Treaty of Amsterdam
TRACECA	Transport Corridor Europe Caucasus Asia
TRIPS	WTO's Agreement on Trade-Related Aspects of Intellectual Property Rights
TRNC	Turkish Republic of Northern Cyprus
UCITS	Undertakings for Collective Investment in Transferable Securities
UDHR	Universal Declaration of Human Rights
UE	l'Union européenne
UK	United Kingdom
UKRPOLBAT	Ukrainian-Polish Battalion
UN	United Nations
UNCTAD	United Nations Conference on Trade and Development
UNDPI	United Nations Department of Public Information
UNGA	United Nations General Assembly
UNMIK	United Nations Interim Administration Mission in Kosovo
UNOMIG	United Nations Observer Mission in Georgia
UNRWA	United Nations Relief and Works Agency for Palestine Refugees in the Near East
UNSCOP	United Nations Special Committee on Palestine
UNTAES	United Nations Transitional Authority in Eastern Slovenia
UPFM	Unified Police Force Mostar
US	United States
USA	United States of America
USAID	US Agency for International Development
USD	US dollar
USIA	United States Information Agency
USSR	Union of Soviet Socialist Republics

VAT	value-added tax
VCLT	Vienna Convention on the Law of Treaties
WB	World Bank
WEU	Western European Union
WHO	World Health Organisation
WMD	weapons of mass destruction
WTO	World Trade Organisation
YPES	Yearbook of Polish European Studies
ZaöRV	Zeitschrift für ausländisches öffentliches Recht und Völkerrecht
ZEuS	Zeitschrift für Europarechtliche Studien

Part I

General Aspects

CHAPTER 1

THE EUROPEAN UNION AND ITS NEIGHBOURS: QUESTIONING IDENTITY AND RELATIONSHIPS

Steven Blockmans* and Adam Łazowski**

1. THE DISCOVERY OF EUROPE

An old story recounts that Phoenician seafarers – who controlled the Aegean Sea in the second millennium BC – introduced the difference between *asu* and *ereb*. For them, *asu* was the land or the direction of the rising sun, and *ereb* the land or direction of the setting sun. *Erev* is also Hebrew for evening. *Asu* and *ereb* may therefore be the oldest terms for East and West, described by ancient Greek historian Herodotus as the morning land and the evening land, the *Levant* and the *Ponant*. It is from *asu* that the term Asia was probably derived, and from *ereb* the term Europe.[1]

For the Greeks and the Romans, however, Europe never had a continental meaning. Greeks and Romans were born universalists, whose world centred around the Mediterranean Sea and was not limited to its European shores. Never did the Greeks or Romans call themselves Europeans. Northern Africa, the Middle East, Asia Minor and the Black Sea were as dear to them as their European territories or trading posts. Europe was a vague geographical notion, definitely not a border. If there was a border in the Mediterranean world, then it existed between Greeks, Romans and 'barbarians', but its exact location could be anywhere. It was defined by way of colonies and legions, not by continents.

Likewise, the spiritual *heimat* of Europe is to be found not on the European continent, but on the island of Crete, and later on the eastern shores of the Aegean

* Researcher in European Union Law, T.M.C. Asser Institute, The Hague.

** Senior Lecturer in Law, School of Law, University of Westminster, London.

[1] See, e.g., O. Wattel-de Croizant, 'Echoes of Antiquity: The Rape of Europe', in E. Bussière, M. Dumoulin and G. Trausch, eds., *Europe: The European Idea and Identity from Greek Antiquity to the 21st Century* (Antwerp, Yuste 2001) pp. 1-22. For the mythological story of the birth of Europe, see also M.-L. von Plessen, ed., *Idee Europa: Entwürfe zum 'Ewigen Frieden'. Ordnungen und Utopien für die Gestaltung Europas von der pax romana zum Europäischen Union* (Berlin, Henschel 2003) at pp. 47-53.

S. Blockmans and A. Łazowski (eds.), The European Union and Its Neighbours

Sea, in Asia Minor.[2] That is where the oldest Greek colonies blossomed after the beginning of the first millennium BC, and where Europe's oldest thinkers lived. In the fifth century BC, Herodotus was probably the first to use the adjective 'European' – *Europèios* – to denote a people that used to live on the Western shores of the Aegean Sea but settled in Asia Minor. When the Roman citizens of Byzantium talked about Europeans – *Europaioi* – they meant to distinguish themselves from the barbarians, including followers of Western Christianity. But the Catholic Church never called itself European. It defined itself on the basis of belief, contrasting its members with pagans, heathens, Muslims and Jews. For fourteen centuries, it dreamt of a Christian world, not a Christian Europe. This changed in the fifteenth century, when the Byzantine Empire collapsed and new continents were discovered. The fall of Constantinople in 1453 took away Europe's last barrier against the pending threat of Ottoman aggression. Perhaps it was this threat that led Christianity as a whole to defend not only itself but also Europe. The great discoveries and the colonisation of America and of African and Asian coasts did the rest. Faced with such big new contrasts, Europe's biggest discovery was the belated discovery of Europe itself.[3]

However, it took many centuries before the geographical entity of the European continent began to take shape and assume its own cultural identity.[4] The loss of religious unity during the Reformation and the subsequent rise of secular nation states delayed the idea of Europe immensely. What added to the divisions was that the explorers were not Europeans, but Spaniards or Portuguese, English or French, Dutch or Russians, who fought each other harder than that they fought their common enemies. The same happened in the east, where the Polish-Lithuanian empire was torn to pieces by series of partitions at the end of the eighteenth century.[5] These divisions remained very outspoken until well into the twentieth century and were only overcome after nation states had plunged almost the entire continent into two world wars, and when secularisation had progressed to such levels that it was able to neutralise religious differences. Seen through this prism, the discovery of Europe is a very recent phenomenon: for Western Europe the discovery is not older than 1945; Eastern Europe even had to wait until 1989. The fall of the Berlin Wall and the accession of eight post-Communist countries to the European Union in 2004 brought an end to a division in Europe that was much older than the wall itself.

---

[2] See M. Heirman, *De ontdekking van Europa: een geschiedenis van de toekomst* (Antwerp, Houtekiet 2003) at pp. 7-10, from whom the title of this section is borrowed.

[3] Ibid.

[4] See W. Blockmans, *A History of Power in Europe* (Antwerp, Fonds Mercator 1997); and more recently W. Blockmans, 'Europe's History of Integration and Diversity', 14 *European Review* (2006) pp. 241-256.

[5] See N. Davies, *God's Playground. A History of Poland*, Volumes I-II, revised edn. (Oxford, Oxford University Press 2005).

With the creation of the European Coal and Steel Community (ECSC) in 1951 and the European Economic Community (EEC) in 1957, memories of Charlemagne were never far off. Geographically speaking, the common territory of the six founding states of the ECSC, the EEC and Euratom overlapped to a large extent with the Holy Roman Empire that Charlemagne united by fire and sword in the eighth century. But while his empire was the largest – but at the same time the weakest – that medieval Europe could produce, the European Communities of the 1950s have gradually expanded to cover almost the entire continent and have been granted the powers to potentially form the strongest union of free and prosperous states that Europe has ever seen, albeit one in which diversity continues to be the dominant feature. Over a period of fifty years, the progressive and peaceful spread of the rule of law and democracy has seen authoritarian regimes change into secure, stable and dynamic democracies. Successive enlargements of the European Union are making a reality of Robert Schuman's vision of a united and peaceful continent.

After five rounds of enlargement, the European Union now has twenty-five members and provides a common roof not only for a Catholic, Protestant and Orthodox Europe, but also for a Latin, Germanic, Slavic and Celtic Europe. And this is not the end of the road for EU enlargement. Bulgaria and Romania will accede to the European Union on 1 January 2007 or 1 January 2008 at the latest.[6] Turkey, Croatia, Macedonia and the rest of the Western Balkans have also been promised a membership perspective. And according to the Union's own rule book, 'European' countries such as Belarus, Ukraine, Moldova, Switzerland, Norway and Iceland could in the future also be considered for membership. A Union of such size, depth and unity has no predecessor in Europe's turbulent history.

2. EUROPE'S FINAL FRONTIER

The €1 million question in the success story of EU enlargement is where one has to draw the line. According to Article 49 TEU, 'any European state' which respects the principles set out in Article 6(1) TEU (liberty, democracy, respect for human rights and fundamental freedoms and the rule of law) may apply to become a member of the Union. But what is Europe and where lies its final frontier?

In geographical terms, Europe is a continent that is hard to define. In the north, south and west, this is still relatively easy. The Arctic Ocean, the Mediterranean Sea and the Atlantic Ocean roughly form Europe's 'natural' borders. However, Europe's eastern frontier is difficult to discern, because Europe and Asia form

[6] See chapters 7 and 8 in this volume.

one single land mass. Before the publication in 1730 of an influential book that suggested pushing the border between Europe and Asia eastwards to the Urals, because this mountain range divided the Ural language group (which includes Finnish and Hungarian) and the Altaj language group (which includes Turkish, Mongolian and even Korean), the river Don long constituted the 'naturally' accepted border between 'European' and 'Asian' societies.[7] The 'enlargement' of 'Europe' from the Don to the Urals had everything to do with the rise of the Russian Empire and its orientation towards the West under Peter the Great. At present, the Don – *grosso modo* – forms the border between Ukraine and the Russian Federation. By those who are heavily in doubt about the European credentials of a country that stretches all the way to Vladivostok, the Don should be regarded as Europe's final frontier. Yet, in political terms, the question whether Russia is European and thus eligible to apply for EU membership is a purely hypothetical one. Today's political leaders in the Kremlin would no doubt prefer to approach this matter in terms of the European Union's accession to Russia rather than *vice versa*.

Nevertheless, whereas normative history has somehow accepted that Russia – with its Indo-European, Slavic and Orthodox roots – is historically anchored in Europe, the bloody legacy of four centuries of Ottoman rule in Europe has shaped a widely accepted 'European' point of view to deny the legitimacy of the Ottoman past.[8] The pressing question of EU enlargement with secular but overwhelmingly Islamic Turkey has intensified the ongoing debate on Europe's identity and final frontier. In objective terms, the arguments of those who claim that Turkey is not European are not very convincing. Like Russia, the westernmost part of the country geographically belongs to Europe. Moreover, its Islamic identity is no different from that of Albania, Bosnia-Herzegovina and Macedonia, whose European credentials have not been questioned on this ground. By analogy, the decision to grant candidate country status to Turkey is therefore justified. Of course the consequences of this decision are not just limited to the interpretation of the foggy term 'European'. They are potentially grave in view of the functioning of the EU institutions and in view of the instability that might result from pushing the Union's borders to countries with volatile regimes such as Syria, Iraq and Iran. The geopolitical situation will in the end define the future size of the European Union and relations with its neighbours. Hence, '[e]ven in an era of globalisation, geography is still important.'[9]

---

7 P.J. von Strahlenberg, *Das Nord- und Östliche Theil von Europa und Asia* (Stockholm 1730), reproduced under the same title by J. Papp (Szeged, Universitas Szegediensis de Attila József 1975).

8 See M. Mazower, *The Balkans: From the End of Byzantium to the Present Day*, 4th edn. (London, Phoenix Press 2003) at pp. 1-18.

9 European Security Strategy (ESS), A Secure Europe in a Better World. European Security Strategy, 12 December 2003, at p. 7. On the ESS, see, e.g., R. Kissack, 'The European Security

3. THREATS AND CHALLENGES POSED BY THE EUROPEAN UNION'S 'NEIGHBOURHOOD'

At the beginning of the new millennium, large-scale aggression against any EU Member State is improbable. Instead, the European Union faces a multitude of security threats which are more diverse, less visible and less predictable: violent or frozen conflicts (Middle East, Kosovo, Transnistria, Abkhazia, Nagorno Karabach), terrorism, the proliferation of weapons of mass destruction (Middle East), mass illegal migration (Africa), cross-border illegal trafficking of various kinds (Balkans), trans-boundary ecological hazards (Ukraine), the disruption of the flow of vital energy sources (Russia, Southern Caucasus) and so forth.[10] The European Union's 'big bang' enlargement of May 2004 has forced it to deal more directly with a number of these threats and challenges, simply because the eastward push of its borders has brought it closer to some of the troubled areas mentioned above.

It is in the European Union's interest that the countries on its borders are well-governed. Neighbours who are engaged in conflict, weak states where organised crime flourishes, dysfunctional societies and exploding population growth on its borders all pose problems for the European Union: the influx of refugees, the importation of organised crime, the fall-out of environmental disasters and so forth. Hence the need for the European Union to prevent conflicts, spread good governance, support social and political reform, deal with corruption and abuse of power, and establish the rule of law and protect human rights in the neighbouring countries. Arguably, extending reform to a Europe wider than that represented by the Member States of the European Union and its candidate countries is the best way of strengthening the European order, among other reasons because it prevents the creation of new dividing lines in Europe after each new enlargement. Hence the European Union's self-assigned[11] task to promote a 'ring of friends',[12] a circle of well-governed neighbouring countries to the east and on the borders of the Mediterranean with which it can enjoy close and cooperative relations. The creation of the European Neighbourhood Policy (ENP) was the European Commission's

---

Strategy: A First Appraisal', 2 *CFSP Forum* (2004) pp. 19-20; and S. Duke, 'The European Security Strategy in a Comparative Framework: Does it Make for Secure Alliances in a Better World?', 9 *EFA Rev.* (2004) pp. 459-481.

[10] For an official overview of the global challenges and key threats that Europe faces, see the ESS, op. cit. n. 9, at pp. 2-5.

[11] This was also expected by the United States (which wants a stronger Europe so that it can disengage from the Balkans, for example) and the European Union's neighbours. Great power comes with great responsibilities and generates great expectations.

[12] Dixit Romano Prodi, President of the European Commission, in a speech to the Sixth ECSA-World Conference, 'A Wider Europe – A Proximity Policy as the Key to Stability', SPEECH/02/619, 6 December 2002. The term 'ring of friends' is repeated in the ESS, op. cit. n. 9, at p. 8.

response to the wish of Member States to develop a new strategy ahead of the European Union's enlargement of May 2004, to mitigate the exclusion effects for countries like Ukraine, Belarus and Moldova and to prevent the Mediterranean countries pooled together in the so-called 'Barcelona Process', plus the three countries from the Southern Caucasus, from being disadvantaged by the new initiative.[13]

The official use of the term 'neighbourhood' – which may have abhorred those familiar with the negative connotations attached to similar concepts like Russia's 'Near Abroad' or America's 'backyard' – seems to have gone down relatively well with the fifteen eastern and Mediterranean neighbours that are included in the ENP.[14] From a geographical point of view, however, it seems strange for the European Union to use the term only to denote its neighbours in the east and on the Mediterranean, since it has many more direct neighbours than those covered by the ENP: Switzerland, the EEA countries (Iceland, Norway and Liechtenstein), the micro-states (Andorra, Monaco, San Marino and the Vatican City), the acceding states (Bulgaria and Romania), the candidate countries (Turkey, Croatia and Macedonia), the rest of the Western Balkans (Albania, Bosnia-Herzegovina, Serbia (including Kosovo) and Montenegro) and Russia.[15] Yet, as will become clear from this overview, the European Union operates different external policies towards each of these groups of neighbours. Through differentiation and diversification, the Union arguably tries to establish ways and means to better accommodate its own interests and desires within the opportunities raised and threats and/or challenges posed by specific countries or groupings of neighbouring countries.[16] Central to this book is the question whether the new organisation of the European Union's neighbourhood policies helps it to assert its position on the European – indeed international – scene and build peace and security on the continent.

---

[13] The ENP was first outlined on 11 March 2003 in Communication from the Commission to the Council and the European Parliament, Wider Europe – Neighbourhood: A New Framework for Relations with our Eastern and Southern Neighbours, COM (2003) 104 final. A more developed strategy paper was published on 12 May 2004 as Communication from the Commission, European Neighbourhood Policy, COM (2004) 373 final. On the origins and development of the ENP, see, *inter alia*, M. Emerson, 'The European Neighbourhood Policy: Strategy or Placebo?', 215 *CEPS Working Document* (2004) at pp. 6-8.

[14] Algeria, Armenia, Azerbaijan, Belarus, Egypt, Georgia, Israel, Jordan, Lebanon, Moldova, Morocco, Palestine, Syria, Tunisia and Ukraine, with a total population of roughly 400 million. Libya, though being geographically eligible, does not take part in the ENP at present.

[15] Russia dismissed the whole ENP as misconceived because it would create the wrong kind of competition for influence in the European CIS states.

[16] The impact of neighbouring countries on the formulation of their (contractual) relations with the European Union, let alone the Union's policies towards them, is rather limited. On the implicit assumptions of EU conditionality and the risks and potential consequences involved in the promotion of democracy, human rights and market economy in Central and Eastern Europe, see the contributions to J. Zielonka and A. Pravda, eds., *Democratic Consolidation in Eastern Europe, Volume 2: International and Transnational Factors* (Oxford, Oxford University Press 2001).

4. A MIXTURE OF POLICIES

4.1 **Introduction**

The European integration process remains first and foremost a peace project. In its preamble, the Treaty on European Union refers directly to the role of the European Union as a promoter of 'peace, security and progress in Europe and in the world'. The determinants of security stabilisation on the European continent are numerous. In some areas of the periphery, a strategy for lasting peace and security has to aim at the creation of an opposite logic to that of (armed) conflict (e.g., Israel and Palestine, Kosovo and the Southern Caucasus). This not only implies international and European efforts geared at protecting the right of external self-determination of peoples and the enforcement of the principle of non-intervention and the prohibition on the use of force, but also requires the creation of new or reformed administrative structures which guarantee the rule of law instead of the 'law of the ruler'. The establishment of effective democratic structures (internal self-determination) is a *conditio sine qua non* for administrative reform in a wider group of the European Union's neighbouring countries than the ones torn apart by (frozen) conflict (e.g., Syria, Egypt and Libya). Administrative, economic and social reform extends to practically all of the Union's eastern and southern neighbours. Hence, what is needed is a flexible, multi-layered approach that recognises local and regional specificities and provides a mixture of instruments designed to encourage political, economic and social reform in Europe. In the Council's humble opinion, 'the European Union is particularly well equipped to respond to such multi-faceted situations.'[17] If this is really so, then the follow-up question is of course whether the European Union is also effectively using its tools to tear down barriers and build peace, security and progress on the European continent.

4.2 **Stabilisation**

Since the entry into force of the Treaty of Amsterdam, the Member States have actively used the *diplomatic* structures with which they have endowed their Union in the field of the Common Foreign and Security Policy (CFSP). Much to his credit, Javier Solana, Secretary General/High Representative for the CFSP (SG/HR), supported by his staff at the Council, has made the most of the cautious wording of his tasks in Article 26 TEU.[18] To a large extent, the Union's success in

---

[17] See ESS, op. cit. n. 9, at p. 7.

[18] 'The Secretary-General of the Council, High Representative for the common foreign and security policy, shall assist the Council in matters coming within the scope of the common foreign and

preventing the eruption or escalation of violence in a number of regions and defusing tensions is due to the leading diplomatic role played by Javier Solana. The SG/HR frequently travels to problem regions, sometimes accompanied by the Commissioner for External Relations and European Neighbourhood Policy or the Commissioner for Enlargement. Supported on the ground by the EU (Special) Representatives (See Box 1) and the heads of the Commission's delegations, the SG/HR can put considerable pressure on all relevant parties to engage in dialogue and arrive at an agreement by political means. To this end, economic and financial sanctions, the prospect of negotiating or concluding a trade and/or cooperation accord and the launching of funding programmes are some of the

Box 1: EU (Special) Representatives in the neighbouring countries (Art. 18 TEU)

Federal Republic of Yugoslavia	June 1998 - October 1999	Felipe González
Kosovo	October 1998 - July 1999	Wolfgang Petritsch
Royaumont Process (Balkans)	May 1999	Panagiotis Roumilotis
Stability Pact for South-Eastern Europe	July 1999 December 2001	Bodo Hombach Erhard Busek
Macedonia	June 2001 October 2001 September 2002 January 2004 July 2004 October 2005	François Léotard Alain Le Roy Alexis Brouhns Søren Jessen Pettersen Michael Sahlin Erwan Fouéré
Bosnia-Herzegovina	March 2002 January 2006	Paddy Ashdown Christian Schwarz-Schilling
Kosovo future status process	November 2005	Stefan Lehne
Montenegro independence process	December 2005	Miroslav Lajčák
Southern Caucasus	July 2003 February 2006	Heikki Talvitie Peter Semneby
Moldova	May 2005	Adriaan Jacobovits de Szeged
Middle East peace process	November 1996 July 2003	Miguel Ángel Moratinos Marc Otte
Palestinian counter-terrorism	April 1997 - May 2002	Nils Eriksson

security policy, in particular through contributing to the formulation, preparation and implementation of policy decisions, and, when appropriate and acting on behalf of the Council at the request of the Presidency, through conducting political dialogue with third parties.'

tools that can be used. It is thanks to the combination of first pillar (dis)incentives and second pillar pressure that the European Union managed, for example, to broker a peace deal between the government and the Albanian separatists in Macedonia, to prevent the destabilisation of Kosovo by forcing the Montenegrins to accept a three-year 'cooling off' period before organising a referendum on independence from Serbia, and to launch a Border Assistance Mission (BAM) to Moldova and Ukraine to prevent smuggling and trafficking through the renegade province of Transnistria.

History has shown that rogue leaders with bad intentions only understand the language of diplomacy backed by force.[19] For long it has been clear that the European Union is in need of other, more persuasive machinery to force parties (that have the intention of) fighting each other in an armed conflict not to commit heinous crimes such as ethnic cleansing and religious persecution and to settle their differences in a peaceful manner. The need to move beyond the paper security structures which were introduced in the Treaty on European Union during the 1991 IGC quickly became apparent from the violent disintegration of the Socialist Federal Republic of Yugoslavia. Frustration at its inability to contribute to the prevention and 'management' of conflicts on its doorstep throughout the 1990s has led the European Union to take its *military* emancipation more seriously. In subsequent steps, dedicated structures and procedures aimed at realising the full range of conflict prevention and crisis management tasks defined in Article 17 TEU (the so-called 'Petersberg tasks') have been put in place within the institutions; the principles for consultation and cooperation with non-European allies and NATO in crisis management have been agreed; and measures to enhance the Union's military and civilian capabilities in the area of crisis management have been adopted, as has the European Security Strategy, the first comprehensive approach to security issues.[20] The European Security and Defence Policy was – somewhat prematurely – declared operational at the European Council of Laeken on 14 and 15 December 2001.[21] The most striking manifestation – and *raison d'être* – of this policy is the Union's capacity to back its diplomatic efforts by action on the ground, i.e., its crisis management operations. Since 2001, the European Union has affirmed its operational capability by launching seventeen

---

19 See, e.g., R. Holbrooke, *To End a War* (New York, Random House 1998) at p. 146.

20 For an overview of the Union's efforts to build an ESDP, see, e.g., N. Gnesotto, ed., *EU Security and Defence Policy: The First Five Years (1999-2004)* (Paris, EUISS 2004). On the so-called 'Berlin Plus' Agreement of 16 December 2002, which allows the European Union to draw on some of NATO's military assets in its own peacekeeping operations, see M. Reichard, *A Shifting Balance: Legal and Political Aspects of the EU-NATO Relationship* (Aldershot, Ashgate 2006). On the ESS, see *supra* n. 9.

21 *Bull. EU* 12-2001, points I.5.6 and I.28.

ESDP operations, of which nine, so more than half of all missions, either took or are still taking place in the European Union's neighbourhood (see Box 2).[22]

Box 2: ESDP operations (Art. 17 TEU)

Bosnia-Herzegovina	EU Police Mission (EUPM)	Since 1 January 2003
Bosnia-Herzegovina	EUFOR 'Althea'	Since 2 December 2004
Macedonia	EUFOR 'Concordia'	31 March 2003 - 15 December 2003
Macedonia	EUPOL 'Proxima'	15 December 2003 - 14 December 2005
Macedonia	EU Police Advisory Team	15 December 2005 - 14 June 2006
Georgia	EUJUST 'Themis'	16 July 2004 - 14 July 2005
Transnistria	EU BAM to Moldova and Ukraine	Since 1 December 2005
Palestinian territories	EU BAM Rafah	Since 30 November 2005
Palestinian territories	EUPOL COPPS	Since 1 January 2006

Maintaining the 'negative peace' (absence of hostilities) is a necessary condition for establishing and maintaining a 'positive peace'. However, it does not, on its own, deal with the underlying causes and conditions of the symptoms of violent conflict. Arguably, the European Union is far better equipped for this latter task because it can capitalise on its greatest assets, i.e., giving the associate countries a stake in the internal market, possibly even a membership perspective, in return for sustained political, administrative, economic and social reforms.

4.3 Partnership and association

The European Community has a long-standing tradition of contractual trade relations with its neighbours.[23] On the basis of Article 238 TEEC, the Community negotiated its first Association Agreements with Greece and Turkey in the early

[22] For an up-to-date list of ESDP operations, see: <http://www.consilium.europa.eu/cms3_fo/showPage.asp?id=268&lang=EN&mode=g>.

[23] For a quick, although somewhat broader overview, see S. Peers, 'EC Frameworks of International Relations: Co-operation, Partnership and Association', in A. Dashwood and C. Hillion, eds., *The General Law of EC External Relations* (London, Sweet & Maxwell 2000) at pp. 160-176. More generally, see I. Macleod, I.D. Hendry and S. Hyett, *The External Relations of the European Communities* (Oxford, Clarendon Press 1996); and P. Eeckhout, *External Relations of the European Union* (Oxford, Oxford University Press 2004).

1960s.[24] These neighbouring countries were offered an association which provided for a future customs union with the Community, as well as future free movement of goods, services and workers, freedom of establishment, limited free movement of capital, the adoption of the Common Agricultural Policy and competition and state aids provisions. The so-called 'mixed' agreements with Greece and Turkey also provided for potential future membership.[25] The comprehensive scope of these early agreements was soon restricted, however.[26] Subsequent Association Agreements with Malta (1971) and Cyprus (1973), which were concluded by the Community alone, and the mixed 'Cooperation Agreements' with almost all of the states on the south of the Mediterranean Sea – Morocco, Algeria, Tunisia, Egypt, Lebanon, Jordan and Syria (all from 1978) – only provided for a freer movement of goods, sometimes adding protocols on financial and technical cooperation to trade preferences and the inclusion in EC programmes.[27]

With its so-called 'second generation' Cooperation Agreements, the Community pursued a closer form of partnership with its eastern neighbouring countries – Hungary (1988), Poland (1989), Bulgaria (1990), Czechoslovakia (1990), the Soviet Union (1990) and Romania (1991) – by including references to economic cooperation in the fields of, *inter alia*, agriculture, energy, environmental issues, industry, science and transport. With its eyes set on the completion of the internal market, and in the wake of the democratic awakening in the former Communist states, the Community and its Member States widened the scope of the trade agreements with the neighbouring countries even further, but in a differentiated way. Firstly, they concluded the European Economic Area (EEA) with the EFTA states (1994), ultimately without Switzerland (1995), offering unprecedented integration into the EC legal system. Secondly, they agreed Europe Agreements (EAs) with ten states in Central and Eastern Europe – Poland (1993), Hungary (1993), Romania (1994), Bulgaria (1994), Czech Republic (1994), Slovak Republic (1994), Estonia (1998), Latvia (1998), Lithuania (1998) and Slovenia (1999) – which included free trade areas, competition provisions, political dialogue and a

24 Agreement of 9 July 1961 establishing an Association between the European Economic Community and Greece, *OJ* 1963 L 26/294; Agreement of 12 September 1963 establishing an Association between the European Economic Community and Turkey, *OJ* 1964 L 27/3685.

25 See D. O'Keeffe and H.G. Schermers, eds., *Mixed Agreements* (Deventer, Kluwer 1983).

26 For more on the Association Agreement with Turkey, see chapter 9 in this volume. See also N. Rogers, *A Practitioners' Guide to the EC-Turkey Association Agreement* (The Hague/London/Boston, Kluwer Law International 2000).

27 Much like the FTAs concluded on the basis of Art. 113 TEEC with the EFTA states (Switzerland (1972), Sweden (1972), Norway (1973), Iceland (1972), Finland (1973), Portugal (1972), Austria (1972), Israel (1975), Spain (1970), the Socialist Federal Republic of Yugoslavia (1973), Portugal (1978), Romania (1980) and Czechoslovakia (1989)).

wide range of cooperation.[28] Thirdly, they agreed so-called 'Euro-Mediterranean Agreements' (EMAs) with the majority of countries participating in the so-called 'Barcelona Process' – Tunisia (1998), Morocco (2000), Israel (2000), Jordan (2002), Egypt (2004), Algeria (2005), Lebanon (2006)[29] – which proposed a lesser form of integration. Fourthly, the Community and its Member States signed so-called 'Partnership and Cooperation Agreements' (PCAs) with Russia (1997), Ukraine (1998), Moldova (1998), Armenia (1999), Azerbaijan (1999) and Georgia (1999).[30] And finally, they took to negotiating so-called 'Stabilisation and Association Agreements' (SAAs) with the countries of the Western Balkans: FYROM (2004) and Croatia (2005).[31]

In sum, the Community has a long record of promoting economic reform by exporting its internal market legislation. Conversely, the Community has a relatively short history of extending non-economic reform through classic external relations instruments. The standard inclusion of human rights and democracy clauses in the European Community's trade agreements and Community aid regulations, the infringement of which could lead to the partial or full suspension or denunciation of the agreement and/or aid, dates back only from the early 1990s.[32] Arguably, this mechanism has not been very effective up until now. To induce voluntary democratic and administrative reforms in the neighbouring countries in the east and south through increased political dialogue, exchange and cooperation, the European Union couched its contractual relations in multilateral policies. Throughout the 1990s, the Union experimented with the so-called 'Northern Dimension' aimed at the Baltic countries, and since 1995 with the so-called 'Barcelona Process' for Israel and the Muslim countries of North Africa

---

[28] For an overview see, *inter alia*, A. Ott and K. Inglis, eds., *Handbook on European Enlargement. A Commentary on the Enlargement Process* (The Hague, T.M.C. Asser Press 2002). Europe Agreements with the new Member States of the European Union terminated upon their accession on 1 May 2004. The only EAs remaining in force are with Bulgaria and Romania. See chapters 7 and 8 in this volume.

[29] EMAs are still to be concluded with Libya, Syria and Palestine.

[30] The ratification of the PCA with Belarus has been suspended following political developments in the country. See chapter 16 in this volume.

[31] At the time of writing, an SAA with Albania had been signed but had not yet entered into force. Separate SAAs were being negotiated with Bosnia-Herzegovina and, after the peaceful dismantling of the state union in June 2006, with both Serbia and Montenegro. See chapter 10 in this volume.

[32] See M. Cremona, 'Human Rights and Democracy Clauses in the EC's Trade Agreements', in N. Emiliou and D. O'Keeffe, eds., *The European Union and World Trade Law: After the GATT Uruguay Round* (London, Wiley 1996) p. 62; F. Hoffmeister, *Menschenrechts- und Demokratieklauseln in den vertraglichen Außenbeziehungen der Europäischen Gemeinschaft* (Berlin, Springer 1998) pp. 117-175; E. Riedel and M. Will, 'Human Rights Clauses in External Agreements of the European Communities', in P. Alston, ed., *The European Union and Human Rights* (Oxford, Oxford University Press 1999) pp. 723-754; M. Bulterman, *Human Rights in the Treaty Relations of the European Community* (Antwerp, Intersentia 2001).

and the Middle East. The results have been mixed.[33] The European Neighbourhood Policy is the European Union's newest foreign policy instrument geared towards expanding the zone of prosperity, stability and security on the European continent.[34] While, at first sight, it is true that some of the neighbouring countries involved (e.g., Armenia, Azerbaijan, Georgia, Morocco and Tunisia) seem attracted to the idea of converging more closely on European identity and standards, the whole package of conditionality hardly looks like a credible balance of obligations and incentives. For all the comprehensive lists of would-be obligations laid down in the bilateral Action Plans, the ENP does not strike one as particularly strong leverage for a sustained process of all-encompassing transformation of the European Union's outer periphery. On the one hand, this is due to the fact that the ENP does not offer the prospect of EU membership, the 'pull' needed in European countries like Ukraine and Moldova that wish to accede. On the other hand, it is because the disincentives the Union applies are not strong enough to force long-ruling political elites into the tracks of progressive democratic reform (e.g., Belarus, Egypt and Syria).[35] The question is whether the European Union can go further in developing links with its partners that go beyond the current ENP yet fall short of accession agreements? By looking more closely at the relations between the Union and the ENP countries, it is hoped that proposals can be made to render greater force to the ENP.

4.4 Integration

Membership conditionality is the key instrument geared towards the reform and integration of EU candidate countries.[36] Overall, this multi-dimensional instrument

---

33 On the Northern Dimension, see C. Archer, 'The Northern Dimension as a Soft Option for the Baltic States' Security', in H. Ojanen, ed., *The Northern Dimension: Fuel for the EU?* (Helsinki, The Finnish Institute of International Affairs 2001) pp. 188-209; and H. Haukkala, 'The Northern Dimension: A Presence and Four Liabilities?', in R. Dannreuther, ed., *European Union Foreign and Security Policy: Towards a Neighbourhood Strategy* (London, Routledge 2004) pp. 98-118. On the Barcelona Process and the ENP, see E. Lannon and P. van Elsuwege, 'The EU's Emerging Neighbourhood Policy and its Potential Impact on the Euro-Mediterranean Partnership', in P. Xuereb, ed., *Euro-Med Integration and the 'Ring of Friends': the Mediterranean's European Challenge*, Vol. IV (Valetta, EDRC of University of Malta 2003) pp. 21-84; and R. Del Sarto and T. Schumacher, 'From EMP to ENP: What's at Stake with the European Neighbourhood Policy towards the Southern Mediterranean?', 10 *EFA Rev.* (2005) pp. 17-38.

34 See B. Ferrero-Waldner, 'The European Neighbourhood Policy: The EU's Newest Foreign Policy Instrument', 11 *EFA Rev.* (2006) pp. 139-142; and *supra* nn. 11-14 and accompanying text.

35 See Emerson, loc. cit. n. 13, at pp. 6-8.

36 See, e.g., F. Hoffmeister, 'Changing Requirements for Membership', in Ott and Inglis, op. cit. n. 28, at pp. 90-102; K. Smith, 'The Evolution and Application of EU Membership Conditionality', in M. Cremona, ed., *The Enlargement of the European Union* (Oxford, Oxford University Press 2003) pp. 105-139; and M. Cremona, 'EU Enlargement: Solidarity and Conditionality', 30 *ELR* (2005) pp. 3-22.

is established by the membership conditions of Articles 49 and 6(1) TEU and the 1993 Copenhagen criteria.[37] The content of EU membership conditionality develops in parallel with the evolution of the *acquis*.[38] In addition, special requirements reflect the distinct historical development and peculiar problems of the candidate countries. In its annual reports, the European Commission closely monitors progress regarding the fulfilment of an ever-increasing body of conditions for eventual membership. Through the screening process and the accession negotiations, the Commission identifies the main weaknesses and the technical adaptations needed by the candidate countries, sets out priorities and benchmarks accordingly and directs EU funds towards relevant projects.

On top of all the conditions and (dis)incentives that apply to candidate countries, the Copenhagen European Council of June 1993 gave the Union the responsibility of ensuring its own 'capacity to absorb new members, while maintaining the momentum of European integration.'[39] Institutional reform has been a constant in the EC/EU's history, as each enlargement since 1973 has emphasised the strain that widening puts on the deepening of the European integration process. The need to reform the institutional architecture of the Union became increasingly pressing with the prospect of the accession of ten new Member States in 2004. Although the pre-Nice IGC did not effectively deal with the so-called 'Amsterdam left-overs' (the size of the Commission, voting weights in the Council and further moves towards qualified majority voting),[40] enlargement went ahead as scheduled. The 'big bang' enlargement of 1 May 2004 has stretched the operational capacity of the EU institutions to the maximum. Further enlargements will certainly aggravate this situation, because the current legal framework, as provided for by the Treaty of Nice, does not cater for the absorption of any states other than those with which accession negotiations had already started prior to the Nice summit, i.e., Bulgaria and Romania.[41]

The Treaty establishing a Constitution for Europe (TCE), which was signed on 29 October 2004 in Rome by the Heads of State and Heads of Government of the twenty-five Member States, as well as Bulgaria, Romania and Turkey in their

---

[37] *Bull. EU* 6-1993, point 13. See also E. Lannon, K. Inglis and T. Haenebalcke, 'The Many Faces of EU Conditionality in Pan-Euro-Mediterranean Relations', in M. Maresceau and E. Lannon, eds., *The EU's Enlargement and Mediterranean Strategies – A Comparative Analysis* (London, Palgrave 2001) pp. 97-138.

[38] See C. Hillion, e.g., 'The Copenhagen Criteria and their Progeny', in C. Hillion, ed., *EU Enlargement: A Legal Approach* (Oxford/Portland, Oregon, Hart Publishing 2004) pp. 1-22.

[39] *Bull. EU* 6-1993, point 13.

[40] See G. Edwards, 'Reforming the Union's Institutional Framework: A New EU Obligation?', in Hillion, op. cit. n. 38, at pp. 23-43.

[41] Treaty of Nice amending the Treaty on European Union, the Treaties establishing the European Communities and Certain Related Acts, *OJ* 2001 C 80/1, Declaration No. 20 on the enlargement of the European Union.

capacity as candidate countries and observers to the IGC, was intended to improve the democracy, transparency and efficiency of the European Union's decision-making process, in the light of, *inter alia*, the ongoing enlargement process.[42] At the moment of writing, the Constitutional Treaty has been ratified by fourteen Member States.[43] According to Article IV-447 TCE, the Constitutional Treaty can only enter into force when it has been ratified by each of the twenty-five high contracting parties in accordance with their own constitutional procedures and the ratification has been officially notified. The entry into force of the Constitutional Treaty has been thrown into doubt after voters in France and the Netherlands rejected the text of the treaty in referenda held on 29 May 2005 and 1 June 2005, respectively.[44] Since the 'no' votes in France and the Netherlands, the European Union's enlargement plans got snarled up in a much bigger argument between rival groups of Member States that disagree about the long-term objectives of the Union, its shape and final borders. On several occasions, certain political leaders have insisted that the Union should pause for breath, consolidate and grant a 'privileged partnership' instead of full EU membership to big neighbouring countries such as Turkey and Ukraine, even though no-one really seems to agree on what is understood by the term.[45] In short, the institutional arrangements needed to take in today's candidate countries, as well as the (timing of the) accession of Croatia, Macedonia and Turkey, are up in the air.

From this quick scan of legal and political realities, the conclusion re-emerges that the European Union can neither integrate all of its neighbours nor exclude all of them on principle. The question is, if not through enlargement, how the Union

42 Treaty establishing a Constitution for Europe, *OJ* 2004 C 310/1. For backgrounds and analysis on the Constitutional Treaty, see, *inter alia*, D. Curtin, A.E. Kellermann and S. Blockmans, eds., *The EU Constitution: The Best Way Forward?* (The Hague, T.M.C. Asser Press 2005); and J-C. Piris, *The Constitution for Europe. A Legal Analysis* (Cambridge, Cambridge University Press 2006).

43 Austria, Belgium, Cyprus, Estonia, Finland, Greece, Hungary, Italy, Latvia, Lithuania, Luxembourg, Malta, Slovenia and Spain. Germany's President said on 15 June 2005 that he would not complete ratification of the TCE until the *Bundesverfassungsgericht* ruled on the treaty's conformity with Germany's Constitution. The Slovak Constitutional Court has asked the President not to sign off on the ratification of the TCE until judges decide if there should have been a referendum on the new document. An updated state of affairs is available at: <http://europa.eu.int/constitution/index_en.htm>.

44 By 54.68 per cent and 61.6 per cent of the voters respectively (turnout 69.3 per cent and 62.8 per cent respectively).

45 See, e.g., L. Harding and N. Watt, 'Turkey's EU dream dealt double blow as Chirac and Merkel raise doubts', *The Guardian*, 27 August 2005; L. Kubosova, 'Sarkozy calls for definition of "borders of Europe"', *EUObserver.com*, 31 March 2006; V. Giscard d'Estaing, 'A better European bridge to Turkey', *Financial Times*, 25 November 2004; and A. Leparmentier, 'UE: les turcosceptiques durcissent leurs positions', *Le Monde*, 16 November 2004. Austrian Chancellor Wolfgang Schüssel used the argument as *ultimum remedium* to block a unanimous decision on the opening of accession talks with Turkey until the other Member States agreed to do the same for Croatia. See A. Browne, 'Turkey left out in cold as Austria digs in heels over EU entry talks', *The Times*, 3 October 2005. See also chapter 19 in this volume.

can best use its soft power to leverage the kind of reforms needed to expand the zone of prosperity, stability and security on the European continent. For many years, the answer has been to give associates a stake in the internal market.

5. INTERIM CONCLUSION

The picture that emerges from this quick scan of neighbourhood policies is that the European Union, through bilateral and multilateral policies, assistance programmes, targeted (trade) measures and (membership) conditionality, is trying to contribute to better governance in its neighbouring countries. Add to this the gradual establishment of a real and credible Common Foreign and Security Policy and the launching of the first-ever EU missions in the framework of the European Security and Defence Policy, and every self-declared Europhile would be tempted to conclude that what we are witnessing today is nothing less than the emergence of the first international organisation that is able to single-handedly adopt a comprehensive strategy to create a secure, stable and prosperous environment on the European continent. If this is really the case, then it is both a tribute to the soft power of the European Union and a welcome development in the improvement of the European hardware security architecture.

CHAPTER 2

THE EU'S EXTERNAL RELATIONS REGIME: MULTILEVEL COMPLEXITY IN AN EXPANDING UNION

Andrea Ott and Ramses Wessel*

1. INTRODUCTION: DEFINITION OF THE EU'S EXTERNAL RELATIONS

The external relations law of the European Union is generally considered to cover all relations between the European Union (and the European Communities) and third states or other international organisations. It is concerned both with competences and procedures (the institutional dimension) and with the norms and rules laid down in agreements concluded with third parties (the substantive dimension). After the qualification in 1963 of the Community as constituting 'a new legal order of international law',[1] one year later the Court confirmed the Community's 'own legal capacity and capacity of representation on the international plane'.[2] Obviously, the Community was not merely meant to govern the relations between its Member States but also to partly replace these Member States in their relations with third states and other international organisations. In fact, the extent to which the Community can do the latter may very well be the most important question in the law of external relations.

Since, at least in the early days, the Treaty did not devote too much space to the division of external competences between the Community and its Member States, developments in this field are to a large extent driven by case law. Thus, the 'outside' of the European Community was placed under the spotlight every now and then. After a boom in the 1970s, following judgments or opinions of the European Court of Justice like *ERTA*, *Kramer*, *Haegeman*, *International Fruit Company* and Opinion 1/76, and in the 1990s,[3] as a reaction to Opinions 1/91 and

---

* Dr Andrea Ott, Lecturer in European Law, University Maastricht, The Netherlands; Prof. Dr Ramses Wessel, Professor of the Law of the European Union and other International Organisations, Centre for European Studies, University of Twente, The Netherlands.

[1] ECJ, Case 26/62 *Van Gend en Loos* [1963] *ECR* 1.

[2] ECJ, Case 6/64 *Costa* v. *ENEL* [1964] *ECR* 585 at 593.

[3] ECJ, Case 22/70 *Commission* v. *Council (ERTA)* [1971] *ECR* 263; ECJ, Case 181/73 *Haegeman* v. *Belgium* [1974] *ECR* 449, at 460, paras. 2-6; ECJ, Case 21-24/72 *International Fruit Company NV et al.* v. *Produktschap voor Groenten en Fruit* [1972] *ECR* 1219; ECJ, Opinion 1/76 *Draft Agreement establishing a European laying-up fund for inland waterway vessels* [1977] *ECR* 741, paras. 3-4.

S. Blockmans and A. Łazowski (eds.), The European Union and Its Neighbours

1/92 (EEA), 2/91 (OECD) and especially 1/94 on the WTO Agreement,[4] the beginning of the new millennium seemed to herald yet another period in which the external dimension of the European Community received abundant attention. This may have been triggered by some new case law, in which the Court addressed the relationship between Community law and international law proper (e.g., *Racke*, *Opel Austria* and *Portugal* v. *Council*),[5] but also reflects the problems resulting from the establishment of the European Union (introducing external relations in separate but connected areas) and the subsequent modification treaties, as well as from the conclusion of the Treaty establishing a Constitution for Europe.

If nothing else, the external relations regime of the European Union reflects the tension that is apparent in the constitutional debate as well. It is in this area, in particular, that the complex relationship between the Union and its Member States presents itself in all its dimensions.[6] One way of making sense of this complex development is not to focus on an emerging constitution at the EU level, but instead to take account of the complex relationship with the Member States, as well as the unity of national and supranational legal orders, and to try and see a constitution made up of the constitutions of the Member States bound together by a complementary constitutional body consisting of the European Treaties.[7] Pernice describes this *Verfassungsverband* – as he calls it – as a multilevel constitution.[8] This approach acknowledges that one cannot simply place the

---

[4] ECJ, Opinion 2/92 *OECD* [1995] *ECR* I-521; ECJ, Opinion 1/92 *EEA* [1992] *ECR* I-2821; ECJ, Opinion 1/94 *WTO* [1994] *ECR* I-5267.

[5] ECJ, Case C-162/96 *Racke GmbH & Co.* v. *Hauptzollamt Mainz* [1998] *ECR* I-3655, para. 45; CFI, Case T-115/94 *Opel Austria GmbH* v. *Council* [1997] *ECR* II-39, para. 77.

[6] This is not to say that this phenomenon is not more general. In the words of Joerges: '*De facto*, the dependence of European governance on the collaboration of the Member States is drastically perceptible everywhere one looks. This dependence determines the EU's shaping of political programmes which are then transposed with the help of the committee system; the inclusion of non-governmental organisations, and the preference for "soft law" and information policy measures. Equally important is the fact that the freedoms that European law guarantees are exercised outwith, or away from one's own Member State and, at the same time, can be upheld against one's own "sovereign".' Ch. Joerges, 'The law in the process of constitutionalizing Europe', paper presented at the ARENA Conference on Democracy and European Governance (4-5 March 2002) p. 33, available at: <http://www.arena.uio.no/events/Conference2002/documents/Joerges.doc>. The same line of thought can be discovered in A. Milward, *The European Rescue of the Nation State* (London, Routledge 1992).

[7] Cf., K. Lenaerts and M. Desomer, 'New models of constitution-making in Europe: The quest for legitimacy', 39 *CMLRev.* (2002) pp. 1217-1253 at p. 1219: 'There are no convincing legal arguments why a Constitution may not be made up of a variety of interconnected Treaty texts founding the legal order.'

[8] I. Pernice, 'Multilevel Constitutionalism and the Treaty of Amsterdam: European Constitution-Making Revisited?', 36 *CMLRev.* (1999) pp. 703-750 at pp. 706-707 and 715: 'This perspective views the Member States' constitutions and the treaties constituting the European Union, despite their formal distinction, as a unity in substance and as a coherent institutional system, within which competence for action, public authority or, as one may also say, the power to exercise sovereign rights is divided among two or more levels. … This concept treats European integration as a dynamic

different issue areas of the Union (such as the internal market or foreign policy) under either the heading of supranationalism or intergovernmentalism, but that competences related to these issue areas are allocated between the different levels of decision making.[9] The evolution of the external relations regime reveals its (need for) flexibility. According to the Court's judgment in *ERTA*, 'the system of internal Community measures may not ... be separated from that of external relations',[10] which means that variations in the allocation of competences between the Union and its Member States will have an impact on the external relations regime. And indeed, as one observer holds, 'the EU should be seen not as a static model, but as a dynamic experiment, a process or a laboratory in which new methods of integration, multi-level and multi-centred governance and a new constitutionalism are being worked on and bargained, and are evolving.'[11]

While keeping in mind the more specific focus of this book on the European Union and its neighbours, the present contribution aims to shed some light on the current legal and institutional framework of the European Union's external relations and on the problems related to the complex division of powers between the Union and its Member States in this area. A key question will be whether and to what extent the current twenty-five Member States still have powers to formulate and implement an external policy – including a neighbourhood policy – of their own. In the expanding European Union, the law and politics of external relations are characterised by a complexity of different levels of decision making, policy making and law-making that results in a major challenge for a coherent and effective EU foreign policy. Most of the legal analyses provided by the literature and cases brought before the ECJ concentrate on the division of external competences, in particular among the European Community and its Member States, as well as on the consequences of this division, *inter alia*, in the form of

process of constitution-making instead of a sequence of international treaties which establish and develop an organisation of international cooperation. The question "Does Europe need a Constitution?" is not relevant, because Europe already has a "multilevel constitution"... According to the concept of "multilevel constitutionalism", the Treaties are the constitution of the Community – or, together with the national constitutions, the constitution of the European Union – made by the peoples of the Member States through their treaty-making institutions and procedures.' The notion finds its source in the multi-level governance literature, popular in some political science approaches. See, for instance, L. Hooghe and G. Marks, *Multi-level Governance and European Integration*, (Lanham, MD, Rowan & Little Field Publishers 2001). In legal studies the notion has been picked up and applied, *inter alia*, by N. Bernard, *Multilevel Governance in the European Union* (The Hague, Kluwer Law International 2002).

9 On this issue, see U. Di Fabio, 'Some Remarks on the Allocation of Competences between the European Union and its Member States', 39 *CMLRev.* (2002) pp. 1289-1301; G. de Búrca and B. de Witte, 'The Delimitation of Powers Between the EU and its Member States', in A. Arnull and D. Wincott, eds., *Accountability and Legitimacy in the European Union* (Oxford, Oxford University Press, 2002) pp. 201-222.

10 ECJ, Case 22/70 *Commission* v. *Council (ERTA)* [1971] *ECR* 263, para. 19.

11 M. Cremona, 'The Union as a Global Actor: Rules, Models and Identity', 41 *CMLRev.* (2004) pp. 553-573 at p. 554.

the mixed agreements (international agreements in which Member States and European Community participate and share competences).[12] This is without doubt an important and complex subject which explains not only the dynamic nature of the entity that is the European Community/Union but also the complexity of external relations, with different actors and concrete legal questions relating to the impact of external relations on internal law, liability and legality. However, the overall complexity in the external policy field goes beyond law-making and concerns the internal management of external relations and its appearance towards third countries. The parallelism of competencesm[13] thus translates into a parallelism of complexities.

In an enlarged European Union, the division of competences to engage in international legal relations thus deserves renewed attention. What are the legal parameters on the basis of which the Community and the Union are competent to implement the so-called Wider Europe – Neighbourhood policy? In addition, is it possible to point to trends concerning the division of competences between the European Community/Union and its Member States? Before entering into the complexity of the second question (on the 'exclusivity' of competences), the following section starts by examining the state of affairs regarding the competences of the Community and the Union on the basis of the relevant treaties and case law (the 'existence' question).[14]

2. EXTERNAL COMPETENCES: BETWEEN ATTRIBUTED AND IMPLIED POWERS

2.1 Competences based on the EC Treaty

From the outset, the capacity of the Community to enter into legal relations with third states or other international organisations has been undisputed. In *Costa/ENEL*, the Court already referred to 'its own personality, its own legal capacity and capacity of representation on the international plane'.[15] The status enjoyed by the Community as a 'legal person' was already established by Article

[12] On mixity, see A. Dashwood, 'Why continue to have mixed agreements at all?', in J.H.J. Bourgeois, J.-L. Dewost and M.-A. Gaiffe, eds., *La Communauté européenne et les accords mixtes* (Brussels, Presses Interuniversitaires Européennes 1997) pp. 93-99; N.A. Neuwahl, 'Joint Participation in International Treaties and the Exercise of Power by the EEC and its Member States: Mixed Agreements', 28 *CMLRev.* (1991) pp. 717-740.

[13] On the doctrine of parallelism, see, for instance, M. Cremona, 'External Relations and External Competence: The Emergence of an Integrated Policy', in P. Craig and G. de Búrca, *The Evolution of EU Law* (Oxford, Oxford University Press 1999) pp. 137-176 at p. 139.

[14] The distinction is borrowed from A. Dashwood, 'Implied External Competence of the EC', in M. Koskenniemi, ed., *International Law Aspects of the European Union* (The Hague, Kluwer Law International 1998) pp. 113-124.

[15] ECJ, Case 6/64 *Costa* v. *ENEL* [1964] *ECR* 585.

281 TEC, which simply states that '[t]he Community shall have legal personality.' The same provision makes clear that a number of legal capacities are connected to this status: 'In each of the Member States, the Community shall enjoy the most extensive legal capacity accorded to legal persons under their laws…'.[16] However, two questions were not completely answered at that time. First, does the Community also enjoy objective legal personality, that is to say, can it enter into legal arrangements with non-Member States? Second, if so, does Article 281 constitute a general legal basis for international action by the Community?

Regarding the first question, the Court confirmed the earlier observation that the Community is competent to enter into international agreements with third states in its *ERTA* judgment of 1971. After all, the Treaty explicitly allowed the Community to do so with regard to some issue areas (e.g., Article 133 concerning trade relations). However, in *ERTA*, the Court also acknowledged the treaty-making capacity of the Community in cases where this was not explicitly provided for in the Treaty: 'Such authority arises not only from an express conferment by the Treaty … but may equally flow from other provisions of the Treaty and from measures adopted, within the framework of those provisions, by the Community institutions.' In fact, 'regard must be had to the whole scheme of the Treaty no less than to its substantive provisions.'[17]

Following this line of reasoning, one could come to the conclusion that the capacity to enter into international agreements could be used across the board. Based on the place of Article 281 in the 'General and Final Provisions', the Court held 'that in its external relations the Community enjoys the capacity to establish contractual links with third countries over the whole field of objectives defined in Part One of the Treaty.'[18] Nevertheless, the Court made clear that 'capacity' should not be interpreted as a 'competence' to enter into every international agreement. Account should be taken of the 'attribution principle' (now in Article 5, first paragraph, TEC), which implies that the Community must be specifically authorised to deal with a particular issue.[19]

One could thus argue, on the basis of an interpretation of the *ERTA* case, that the Community has a general capacity to enter into international agreements, as long as authorisation follows either from explicit attribution of that competence or from other provisions implying an international competence. Since then, the link between the international competence and existing provisions has become more

---

16 On the distinction between 'personality' and 'capacity', see R.A. Wessel, 'Revisiting the International Legal Status of the EU', 5 *EFA Rev.* (2000) pp. 507-537.

17 ECJ, Case 22/70 *Commission* v. *Council (ERTA)* [1971] *ECR* 263, paras. 15-16.

18 Ibid., para. 14.

19 See more extensively A. Dashwood and J. Heliskoski, 'The Classic Authorities Revisited', in A. Dashwood and C. Hillion, *The General Law of E.C. External Relations* (London, Sweet & Maxwell 2000) pp. 3-19 at pp. 6-7.

loose. In Opinion 1/76, the Court seemed to place the 'attribution principle' into perspective by holding that 'authority to enter into international commitments may not only arise from an express attribution by the Treaty, but may equally flow implicitly from its provisions.'[20] Here, the argument was that external competence was needed for the Community to attain its objectives. The (implied) powers were thus related to the so-called 'complementarity principle':[21] an external competence exists as a necessary corollary of an existing internal competence. Or, as generally phrased in Opinion 1/76:

> The Court has concluded *inter alia* that whenever Community law has created for the institutions of the Community powers within its internal system for the purpose of attaining a specific objective, the Community has authority to enter into the international commitments necessary for the attainment of that objective even in the absence of an express provision in that connexion. …
>
> Although the internal Community measures are only adopted when the international agreement is concluded and made enforceable … the power to bind the Community *vis-à-vis* third countries nevertheless flows by implication from the provisions of the Treaty creating the internal power and in so far as the participation of the Community in the international agreement is … necessary for the attainment of one of the objectives of the Community.[22]

Nevertheless, subsequent case law made clear that, although the principle of complementarity was clearly upheld, this also implied that no division could be made in the application of the attribution principle in relation to internal and external competences. After all, if the Community would enjoy a general power to enter into international agreements in furtherance of any objective whatsoever, the attribution principle would be undermined.[23] And, indeed, in Opinion 2/94, the Court clearly stated that 'the principle of conferred powers must be respected in both the internal action and the international action of the Community.'[24] Implied powers thus have their limits.

---

[20] ECJ, Opinion 1/76 *Draft Agreement establishing a European laying-up fund for inland waterway vessels* [1977] *ECR* 741, para. 3.

[21] Dashwood and Heliskoski, loc. cit. n. 19, at pp. 12-13, seem to have a point in arguing that this label describes the relationship between internal and external competences better than the more widely used term 'parallelism'. After all, 'things which are parallel, run alongside each other without ever meeting'.

[22] ECJ, Opinion 1/76 *Draft Agreement establishing a European laying-up fund for inland waterway vessels* [1977] *ECR* 741, paras. 3-4. Also in the *Kramer* judgment, Joined Cases 3, 4, and 6/76 *Cornelis Kramer and others* [1976] *ECR* 1279.

[23] Cf., A. Dashwood, 'The Attribution of External Relations Competence', in Dashwood and Hillion, op. cit. n. 19, pp. 115-138 at p. 117.

[24] ECJ, Opinion 2/94 *Accession by the European Community to the European Convention for the Protection of Human Rights and Fundamental Freedoms* [1996] *ECR* I-1759.

Express references to external action were rare in the original EC Treaty, and were limited to what are now known as Article 133 (on the implementation of the Common Commercial Policy),[25] Article 310 (on the conclusion of Association Agreements) and three provisions on other international cooperation: Article 302 (on the duty of the Commission to maintain appropriate relations with the United Nations, the GATT organs and other international organisations), Article 303 (on cooperation with the Council of Europe) and Article 304 (on cooperation with the OECD). The general procedural arrangements were – and although amended are – laid down in (current) Article 300(1):

> Where this Treaty provides for the conclusion of agreements between the Community and one or more States or international organisations, the Commission shall make recommendations to the Council, which shall authorise the Commission to open the necessary negotiations. The Commission shall conduct these negotiations in consultation with special committees appointed by the Council to assist it in this task and within the framework of such directives as the Council may issue to it.

The Single European Act (1986) extended the Community's explicit external competences to other fields that were thought to form part of the newly introduced concept of the 'internal market': agriculture and fisheries (Article 37),[26] transport (Article 71), competition (Article 83), the harmonisation of indirect taxation (Article 93) and the general approximation of legislation and administrative practices (Article 94). In addition, the SEA introduced the possibility of international action in furtherance of internal Community policy in some areas. Even before the establishment of the European Union, we have thus been able to witness an evolution in the express external powers of the Community from commercial policy and the conclusion of Association Agree-ments to research and technology (Article 170) and environmental policy (Articles 174(4) and 175).[27] The Treaties of Maastricht, Amsterdam and Nice subsequently provided not only for a broadening of the scope of the Common Commercial Policy, but also for external powers in development policy (Article 181), monetary matters, cooperation powers with third states (related to education, culture, health and

---

25 Originally Article 113 TEC. Article 114 concerned the conclusion of agreements by the Council and has been repealed. For an application, see Council Decision of 2 June 1997 concerning the conclusion of the Euromed Interim Association Agreement on trade and cooperation between the EC and the Palestine Liberation Organisation for the benefit of the Palestinian Authority of the West Bank and the Gaza Strip, *OJ* 1997 L 187/1. This Council Decision refers to Articles 133 and 181 EC.

26 See, for instance, Council Decision of 25 July 1983 on the accession of the Community to the Convention on fishing and conservation of the living resources in the Baltic Sea and the Belts, *OJ* 1983 L 237/4.

27 Council Decision of 25 April 2002 concerning the approval, on behalf of the European Community, of the Kyoto Protocol to the United Nations Framework Convention on Climate Change and the joint fulfilment of commitments thereunder, *OJ* 2002 L 130/1.

trans-European networks), including a new legal basis for economic, financial and technical cooperation with third countries (Article 181a).

Special attention should be devoted to Title IV TEC, the communitarised part of the Justice and Home Affairs domain, which deals with visas, asylum, immigration and other policies related to the free movement of persons. As no explicit external competences can be found in this title, the competences of the Community in this area depend on the existence of implied powers. Indeed, complementary external action can be envisaged in relation to a number of internal competences in the fields of asylum, immigration and civil law cooperation, including more concrete powers related to illegal immigration and the residence and repatriation of illegal residents (Article 63(3)(b) TEC). Practice has revealed the use of these competences, for instance, in the conclusion of readmission agreements with a number of third countries as well as in readmission clauses in Political Dialogue and Cooperation Agreements and Association Agreements.[28]

The external competences – and more specifically their division – have been subject to dispute from the outset. Irrespective of the limited number of explicit provisions in the original Treaty, the Community was already involved in so many agreements by the end of the 1960s that the question of how to justify its treaty-making power and how to define its scope in relation to the remaining treaty-making powers of its Member States arose. We have already referred to the landmark *ERTA* case, in which the ECJ developed the doctrine of parallelism in such a way that competences flow not only from the express conferral of competences but also from implicit competences, such as the other Treaty provisions, the Act of Accession and the measures adopted.[29] Matters were further complicated when the Court ruled that the Community can rely on its implicit competences even when they have not yet been used for internal measures. These implicit competences may, in turn, lead to exclusive external competences. This very broad interpretation was refined in later judgments as a special exemption, which is only to be used when it is necessary to achieve Treaty objectives that cannot be attained by the adoption of autonomous Community rules,[30] or in the words of the ECJ:

[28] Cf., Council Decision of 17 December 2003 concerning the conclusion of the Agreement between the European Community and the Government of the Hong Kong Special Administrative Region of the People's Republic of China on the readmission of persons residing without authorisation, *OJ* 2004 L 17/23. See more extensively J. Monar, 'The EU as an International Actor in the Domain of Justice and Home Affairs', 9 *EFA Rev* (2004) pp. 395-415.

[29] ECJ, Case 22/70 *Commission* v. *Council (ERTA)* [1971] *ECR* 263. See also these other judgments: ECJ, Joined Cases 3, 4 and 6/76 *Cornelis Kramer and others* [1976] *ECR* 1279; ECJ, Opinion 1/76 *Draft Agreement establishing a European laying-up fund for inland waterway vessels* [1977] *ECR* 741, paras. 3-4.

[30] ECJ, Opinion 2/92 *OECD* [1995] *ECR* I-521, at 559, para. 32; ECJ, Opinion 1/94 *WTO* [1994] *ECR* I-5267, at 5413.

> [W]henever the Community has included in its internal legislative acts provisions relating to the treatment of nationals of non-member countries or expressly conferred on its institutions powers to negotiate with non-member countries, it acquires an exclusive external competence in the spheres covered by those acts (Opinion 1/94, paragraph 95; Opinion 2/92, paragraph 33).
>
> The same applies, even in the absence of any express provision authorising its institutions to negotiate with non-member countries, where the Community has achieved complete harmonisation in a given area, because the common rules thus adopted could be affected within the meaning of the *ERTA* judgment if the Member States retained freedom to negotiate with non-member countries (Opinion 1/94, paragraph 96; Opinion 2/92, paragraph 33).[31]

In most of the agreements concluded, except for trade agreements, the Commission and the Council decided to involve the Member States and conclude so-called mixed agreements. Parallel to this pragmatic inclusion of Member States for reasons of legal liability and blurred lines of competences, the ECJ has at least established that the areas of the Common Commercial Policy,[32] the Common Fisheries Policy[33] and competition policy[34] belong to the exclusive competences of the European Communities. This external relations *acquis* is confirmed in Part I of the Constitutional Treaty, specifically in Article I-13(1), which also includes a codified *ERTA* doctrine.[35]

The evolution of the Community's external powers is further proof of the fact that Community policy – in the words of Cremona – 'emerges within an international context and increasingly that international context is helping to define the content of that policy, while Community policy and institutions contribute to the development of international norms and standards.'[36]

---

31 Open Skies judgments: ECJ, Case C-467/98 *Commission* v. *Denmark* [2002] *ECR* I-9519.

32 ECJ, Case 41/76 *Donckerwolke and Schou* v. *Procureur de la République* [1976] *ECR* 1921; the scope of the Common Commercial Policy in relation to services and intellectual property was only defined by the WTO opinion, see ECJ, Opinion 1/94 *WTO* [1994] *ECR* I-5267.

33 More precisely the conservation of the biological resources of the sea: ECJ, Joined Cases 3, 4 and 6/76 *Cornelis Kramer and others* [1976] *ECR* 1279; ECJ, Case 804/97 *Commission* v. *UK* [1981] *ECR* 1045, para. 20.

34 ECJ, Opinion 1/92 *EEA* [1992] *ECR* I-2821, paras. 40-41; I. MacLeod, I.D. Hendry and S. Hyett, *The External Relations of the European Communities* (Oxford, Clarendon Press 1996) pp. 56-57.

35 Article I-13(2): 'The Union shall also have exclusive competence for the conclusion of an international agreement when its conclusion is provided for in a legislative act of the Union or is necessary to enable the Union to exercise its internal competence, or insofar as its conclusion may affect common rules or alter their scope.'

36 Cremona, loc. cit. n. 13, at p. 148.

2.2 Competences based on the Treaty on European Union

The introduction of the Common Foreign and Security Policy (in Title V of the 1992 Maastricht Treaty) and the more recent European Security and Defence Policy extended the external competences of the Community/Union beyond economy-related issues. The same increasingly holds true for Police and Judicial Cooperation in Criminal Matters (Title VI TEU). The main instruments to be used in implementing the CFSP are enumerated in Article 12 TEU, which outlines the means to achieve the objectives listed in Article 11:

> The Union shall pursue the objectives set out in Article 11 by:
> - defining the principles of and general guidelines for the common foreign and security policy;
> - deciding on common strategies;
> - adopting joint actions;
> - adopting common positions;
> - strengthening systematic cooperation between Member States in the conduct of policy.

An interesting new development is that apart from these means in Article 12 TEU, the CFSP objectives may also serve to establish an external *Community* competence. In two judgments of September 2005, the Court of First Instance held that in the area of sanctions the Community is competent to impose financial sanctions on individuals (irrespective of Article 60 TEC indicating otherwise) because this is covered by the objectives of the *Union*.[37]

In general, however, CFSP objectives are to be attained through CFSP means. Apart from the instruments listed in Article 12, which all find their basis in different provisions (Articles 14 and 15 in particular), other legal bases can be found in Article 17 (concerning defence issues) and Article 18(5) (concerning the appointment of special representatives).[38] Furthermore, practice has revealed the frequent use of the instrument of declarations.[39] This implies that there are different

---

[37] CFI, Cases T-306/01 *Ahmed Ali Yusuf and Al Barakaat International Foundation* v. *Council and Commission* and T-315/01 *Yassin Abdullah Kadi* v. *Council and Commission* [2005] *ECR*, nyr.

[38] Practice revealed the possibility of using Article 18(5) as an autonomous legal basis. See, for instance, Council Decision 1999/361/CFSP of 31 May 1999 implementing Common Position 98/633/CFSP defined by the Council on the basis of Article J.2 of the Treaty on European Union concerning the process on stability and good-neighbourliness in South-East Europe, *OJ* 1999 L 141/1.

[39] For example: Declaration by the Presidency on behalf of the European Union on the situation in Togo, 6 June 2005, 9750/05; Declaration by the Presidency on behalf of the European Union on Belarus, 27 September 2004, 12735/04; Declaration by the Presidency on behalf of the European Union on the parliamentary elections and the referendum of 17 October 2004 in Belarus, 20 October 2004, 13728/04.

instruments as well as different legal bases at the disposal of the Union to shape its policy, while at the same time the enumeration of means in Article 12 must be considered non-limitative.[40]

The competences relating to Police and Judicial Cooperation in Criminal Matters can be found in Article 34(2) which allows the Council to:

> … take measures and promote cooperation, using the appropriate form and procedures as set out in this title, contributing to the pursuit of the objectives of the Union. To that end, acting unanimously on the initiative of any Member State or of the Commission, the Council may:
>
> (a) adopt common positions defining the approach of the Union to a particular matter;
> (b) adopt framework decisions for the purpose of approximation of the laws and regulations of the Member States. Framework decisions shall be binding upon the Member States as to the result to be achieved but shall leave to the national authorities the choice of form and methods. They shall not entail direct effect;
> (c) adopt decisions for any other purpose consistent with the objectives of this title, excluding any approximation of the laws and regulations of the Member States. These decisions shall be binding and shall not entail direct effect; the Council, acting by a qualified majority, shall adopt measures necessary to implement those decisions at the level of the Union;
> (d) establish conventions which it shall recommend to the Member States for adoption in accordance with their respective constitutional requirements. Member States shall begin the procedures applicable within a time limit to be set by the Council.

Although the external dimension of these competences in Title V and VI TEU is obvious, it is ironic to note that – once again – they basically relate to the relationship between the Union and its Member States rather than its relationship with third states and other international organisations. This means that explicit external competences are largely absent in these areas as well and that external action should be connected to the internal competences, ranging from the representation of the Union by the High Representative or the Presidency in CFSP matters to the emerging defence dimension.[41] The only explicit competence concerns the treaty-making power of the Union (see below).

---

[40] This would seem to be confirmed by Article 23(2), first indent, which refers to joint actions, common positions or any other decision taken on the basis of a common strategy.

[41] See more extensively Wessel, loc. cit. n. 16, at pp. 533-536.

The question of the division of competences between the Union and the Member States (or the possible exclusivity of Union competences) is more difficult to answer. The EU Treaty is silent on this issue and case law is obviously absent. Most probably, the answer is to be found in the nature of the legal regime governing the non-Community parts of the Union. The CFSP obligations are largely procedural in nature and only foresee a common policy (read: Union policy) to the extent that this is supported by the Member States. The key principle underlying the CFSP is Article 16, which provides enough leeway to the Member States to prevent issues from being placed on the Union's agenda in the first place. Irrespective of the obligation in Article 16 for Member States to 'inform and consult one another within the Council on any matter of foreign and security policy', the subsequent words 'of general interest' indicate a large margin of discretion on the side of (individual) Member States. And although there is an obligation to try and reach a common policy, in the case of a failure to do so the Member States remain free to pursue their own national policies.[42] A similar starting point may be found in Article 34(1) in relation to Police and Judicial Cooperation in Criminal Matters.

3. THE CONCLUSION OF INTERNATIONAL AGREEMENTS AND THEIR STATUS IN THE UNION

3.1 The EC Treaty

In the Community, international agreements are concluded according to the procedural provisions of Article 300 TEC, with derogations for agreements on the exchange-rate system for the ECU, monetary or foreign exchange regime matters relating to Article 111(1) and (3) TEC and the Common Commercial Policy in Article 133 TEC.[43] Article 300 TEC clarifies the division between external and internal competences. It does not constitute a competence norm but implies external competences without specifying them.[44] It addresses the internal division of competencies among the Community institutions and the procedural dimension of treaty making. Negotiations are conducted by the Commission according to the guidelines set by the Council; the conclusion and implementation of agreements

---

42 One may argue, however, that at one moment this may conflict with Article 11(2), which provides that 'The Member States shall support the Union's external and security policy actively and unreservedly in a spirit of loyalty and mutual solidarity.' On the other hand, there must first be something to support in that case. In the absence of any Union policy, this provision seems less relevant.

43 Article 101 of the outdated but still applicable Euratom Treaty contains a separate provision on the conclusion of international agreements with third states.

44 See, for instance, A. Wünschmann, *Geltung und gerichtliche Geltendmachung völkerrechtlicher Verträge im Europäischen Gemeinschaftsrecht* (Berlin, Duncker & Humblot 2003) p. 31.

fall under the responsibility of the Council. Nevertheless, the Commission, on the basis of Article 302 TEC, is responsible for the relations with international organisations. The legal question of whether and to what extent the Commission is allowed to conclude international agreements, especially executive agreements, on its own initiative has already been addressed. Article 300(1) TEC provides the Commission's mandate to conduct negotiations.[45] The Court clarified that the expression 'agreement' in Article 300 TEC (then Article 228 TEC) was to be understood in a broad sense. On the other hand, Article 300(2) sets the boundary ('subject to the powers vested in the Commission in this field…') and the Commission's powers are clearly limited to administrative or working agreements, which implement the working relations with international organisations in accordance with Article 302.[46] Consequently, the role of the Commission is strictly limited to the management of external relations under the auspices of the Council, and negotiations take place on the basis of a mandate given by the Council. Recent case law reveals that this mandate may also include the negotiation of guidelines that create no legally binding effect and have a clearly defined scope.[47]

Compared to national parliaments and their classical pivotal role in the ratification process of international treaties, the role of the European Parliament is restricted, although it has evolved over the years thanks to successive treaty reforms.[48] Particularly striking is the limited role of the European Parliament in the important field of the Common Commercial Policy on the basis of Article 133 TEC. Contrary to the wording of Article 300(3), the European Parliament is at least consulted in practice. In other areas – in particular those having important budgetary implications – the collaboration of the European Parliament in the form of assent is necessary. This is the case also for Association Agreements on the basis of Article 310 and agreements that entail amendments to an act adopted under the procedure outlined in Article 251 TEC. This list reflects the parallelism of internal-external competences, which was addressed above. Adding to the complexity, the European Court of Justice not only assesses the legality of international agreements through the preliminary rulings procedure outlined in Article 234 TEC but may also render an opinion on the legality of an envisaged agreement

45 ECJ, Case C-327/91 *French Republic* v. *Commission* [1994] *ECR* I-3641. See also W. Hummer, 'Enge und Weite des "Treaty making Power" der Kommission der EG nach dem EWG-Vertrag', in A. Randelzhofer, R. Scholz and D. Wilke, eds., *Gedächtnisschrift für E. Grabitz* (Munich, Beck Verlag 1995) pp. 195-226.

46 ECJ, Case C-327/91 *French Republic* v. *Commission* [1994] *ECR* I-3641, paras. 24-37; C. Tietje, 'Artikeln 302-304 EGV Absatz 7', in E. Grabitz and M. Hilf, eds., *Das Recht der Europäischen Union* (Munich, Beck 2000).

47 On the Guidelines negotiated between the Commission and the United States of America, which were based on an Action Plan for the Transatlantic Economic Partnership between the European Union and the United States, see ECJ, Case C-233/02 *France* v. *Commission* [2004] *ECR* I-2759.

48 See S. Krauss, 'The European Parliament in External Relations: The Customs Union with Turkey', 5 *EFA Rev* (2000) pp. 215-237.

before it comes into force on the basis of Article 300(6). This legal instrument of compliance control before ratification has been used quite frequently ever since the European Community resorted to mixed agreements, with the conclusion of extensive Association Agreements in different policy fields, involving both the European Community and Member States to bridge competence conflicts internally.[49]

As a final observation in this section, it should be noted that the treaty-making capacity is not restricted to the European Community as such. Apart from the capacity of the European Central Bank to enter into legal relations with third actors (on the basis of Article 23 of the ECB Statute),[50] it could be argued, on the basis of the general legal personality of most of the agencies in the Community, that they are meant to be able to act in the international public sphere as well.[51]

3.2 The Treaty on European Union

With regard to international agreements concluded by the Union, Article 24 TEU is the applicable provision. This provision is modelled after Article 300 TEC, as indicated for instance by its paragraph 6,[52] and has undergone changes with the Nice Treaty revision.[53] However, as will be shown below, there are clear differences between the Community and Union procedures. Article 24 TEU provides:

> When it is necessary to conclude an agreement with one or more States or international organisations in implementation of this Title, the Council, acting unanimously, may authorise the Presidency, assisted by the Commission as appropriate, to open negotiations to that effect. Such agreements shall be concluded by the Council acting unanimously on a recommendation from the Presidency.

The scope of this provision extends to Police and Judicial Cooperation in Criminal Matters, as the cross-references in Articles 24 (CFSP) and 38 (PJCC) indicate. This turns the provision into the general legal basis for the Union's treaty-making. The debate on whether such agreements are concluded by the

---

[49] See, for instance, the following legal opinions: ECJ, Opinion 2/92 *OECD* [1995] *ECR* I-521; ECJ, Opinion 1/92 *EEA* [1992] *ECR* I-2821.

[50] See D.-C. Horng, 'The European Central Bank's External Relations with Third Countries and the IMF', 9 *EFA Rev.* (2004) pp. 323-346.

[51] R. van Ooik, 'The Growing Importance of Agencies in the EU: Shifting Governance and the Institutional Balance', in D.M. Curtin and R.A. Wessel, eds., *Good Governance and the European Union: Reflections of Concepts, Institutions and Substance* (Antwerp, Intersentia 2005) pp. 125-152.

[52] Compare with Article 300(7) TEC.

[53] Namely the inclusion of paragraph 6 and an extension of qualified majority voting. See E. Regelsberger and D. Kugelmann, 'Artikel 24 EUV Absatz 1', in R. Streinz, *EUV/EGV* (Munich, Beck 2003).

Council on behalf of the Union or on behalf of the Member States[54] seems to be superseded by practice now that the Union has become a party to a number of international agreements on the basis of Article 24.[55] The regime of Article 24 and the connected Declaration No. 4 adopted by the Amsterdam IGC[56] reflects the multilevel character of the external relations regime. Article 24 provides that the Council concludes international agreements after its members (the Member States) have unanimously agreed that it can do so.[57] The above-mentioned Declaration does not seem to conflict with Article 24 TEU. Since the right to conclude treaties is an original power of the Union itself, the treaty-making power of the Member States remains unfettered. The Declaration can only mean that this right of the Union must not be understood as creating new substantive competences for it.[58] The Nice Treaty underlined the separate competence of the Union to conclude treaties. According to modified paragraphs 2 and 3 of Article 24, the Council shall still act unanimously when the agreement covers an issue for which unanimity is required for the adoption of internal decisions, but it will act

54 See, in particular, N. Neuwahl, 'A Partner with a Troubled Personality: EU Treaty-Making in Matters of CFSP and JHA after Amsterdam', 3 *EFA Rev.* (1998) pp. 177-196; Cremona, loc. cit. n. 13, at p. 168. Cf., also J.W. de Zwaan, 'Community Dimensions of the Second Pillar', in T. Heukels, et al., *The European Union after Amsterdam: A Legal Analysis* (The Hague, Kluwer Law International 1998) p. 182. See also J.W. de Zwaan, 'The Legal Personality of the European Communities and the European Union', 30 *NYIL* (1999) pp. 75-113. It has even been argued that Article 24 agreements are 'not legally binding' and not to be viewed as treaties. See the opinion of the Dutch Government in the documents of the Second Chamber, TK 1997-1998, 25 922 (R 1613), No. 5, at p. 51.

55 The first treaties were concluded in 2001 and concerned agreements with the Federal Republic of Yugoslavia and Macedonia concerning the activities of the EU observer mission in that country. Agreement between the European Union and the Federal Republic of Yugoslavia, *OJ* 2001 L 125/2. The agreement with Macedonia can be found in *OJ* 2001 L 241/2. Subsequent treaties include the participation of third states in operations in the framework of the Union's security and defence policy. Apart from agreements with states, the Union may also engage in a legal relationship with another international organisation, as shown by the agreements concluded with NATO on defence cooperation in 2003. See Council Decision 2003/211/CFSP of 24 February 2003 concerning the conclusion of the Agreement between the European Union and the North Atlantic Treaty Organisation on the Security of Information, *OJ* 2003 L 80/35, which includes the text of the Agreement. See further R.A. Wessel, 'The State of Affairs in EU Security and Defence Policy: The Breakthrough in the Treaty of Nice', 8 *Journal of Conflict & Security Law* (2003) pp. 265-288.

56 Declaration No. 4 reads: 'The Provisions of Article J.14 and K.10 [now Articles 24 and 38 TEU] of the Treaty on European Union and any agreements resulting from them shall not imply any transfer of competence from the Member States to the European Union.'

57 The explicit reference to the unanimity rule (as a *lex specialis*) seems to exclude the applicability of the general regime of constructive abstention in cases where unanimity is required as foreseen in Article 23 TEU. Furthermore, as indicated by G. Hafner, 'The Amsterdam Treaty and the Treaty-Making Power of the European Union: Some Critical Comments', in G. Hafner, et al., *Liber Amicorum Professor Seidl-Hohenveldern – in Honour of his 80th Birthday* (The Hague, Kluwer Law International 1998) p. 279, the application of the constructive abstention to Article 24 would make little sense, since Article 24 already provides the possibility of achieving precisely the same effect insofar as Member States, by referring to their constitutional requirements, are entitled to exclude, in relation to themselves, the legal effect of agreements concluded by the Council.

58 As also submitted by Hafner, op. cit. n. 57, at p. 272.

by a qualified majority whenever the agreement is envisaged to implement a joint action or common position. Finally, paragraph 6 sets out that the agreements concluded by the Council shall also be binding on the institutions of the Union. This explicitly answers the question of whether the Union may have obligations under international law apart from the obligations of the Member States.

According to its second paragraph, and in conjunction with Article 38 TEU, Article 24 also applies to international agreements concluded in the area of Police and Judicial Cooperation in Criminal Matters.[59] The Council has so far made use of the treaty-making capacity of the Union in this area in a number of cases.[60] However, Article 24 TEU displays obvious differences to the structure of Article 300 TEC.[61] The Commission has a subordinate role in assisting the Presidency in negotiations, where appropriate, and the Council decides unanimously in cases where the internal adoption would require unanimity. In other cases, qualified majority voting is possible. The same holds true when an agreement is envisaged in order to implement a joint action or common position. Qualified majority voting takes place in accordance with the special procedure laid down in either Article 23(2) (CFSP) or Article 34(3) (PJCC) TEU. Neither the European Parliament nor the European Court of Justice has a role in the conclusion or control of agreements concluded by the Union.

A maybe somewhat confusing provision can be found in Article 34(2)(d), which authorises the Council to establish 'conventions' in the field of Police and Judicial Cooperation in Criminal Matters, which it shall recommend to the Member States for adoption in accordance with their respective constitutional requirements. However, this provision only applies to agreements among Member States and not to agreements between Member States and third countries.[62] They are part of the Union's primary law, which defines their interpretation.[63] Nevertheless external effects are not completely absent. Thus, the Convention on Mutual

---

[59] On this issue, see Monar, loc cit. n. 28.

[60] See the EU-US Agreement on Extradition, *OJ* 2003 L 181/27, the EU-US Agreement on Mutual Legal Assistance, *OJ* 2003 L 181/34, and the Agreement between the European Union and Iceland and Norway on the application of certain provisions of the EU Convention on Mutual Assistance in Criminal Matters, *OJ* 2004 L 26/3.

[61] For example, the Agreement between the European Union and the Federal Republic of Yugoslavia on the activities of the European Union Monitoring Mission (EUMM) in the Federal Republic of Yugoslavia, *OJ* 2001 L 125/2-4. On Article 24 TEU, see S. Marquardt, 'The Conclusion of International Agreements under Article 24 of the Treaty of the European Union', in V. Kronenberger, *The European Union and the International Legal Order: Discord or Harmony?* (The Hague, T.M.C. Asser Press 2001) p. 333.

[62] See further W. Brechmann, 'Artikel 34 Absatz 11', in C. Calliess and M. Ruffert, eds., *Kommentar zu EU-Vertrag und EG-Vertrag* (Neuwied, Luchterhand 1999). Since the entry into force of the Amsterdam Treaty in 1999, the use of conventions has become less popular. The further integration in this policy area called for more decisions of the Council rather than agreements between the Member States. See also P.J. Kuijper, 'The Evolution of the Third Pillar from Maastricht to the European Constitution: Institutional Aspects', 41 *CMLRev.* (2004) pp. 609-626.

[63] H. Satzger, 'Artikel 34 EUV Absatz 12', in Streinz, op. cit. n. 53.

Assistance in Criminal Matters between the Member States, for instance, forms the basis for the agreement between the European Union, Iceland and Norway on the application of certain provisions of this Convention between them.[64]

The difference with treaties concluded on the basis of the EC Treaty is further relevant in relation to the role of the Court. While the Court currently has no control over the CFSP, Article 35 TEU, in conjunction with Article 46 TEU, enables some legal control by the ECJ when it comes to aspects of Police and Judicial Cooperation in Criminal Matters. The limits and tasks of the ECJ in this area are under-explored, and it was only in a 1998 case concerning air transit visas that the judges emphasised that the jurisdiction of the Court extends to ensure that acts concluded on the basis of former Article K.3 TEU (now Article 30 TEU) do not affect the provisions of the EC Treaty.[65] In principle, both areas – the Common Foreign and Security Policy and Police and Judicial Cooperation in Criminal Matters – can come under scrutiny by the ECJ when legal acts have implications for first pillar matters. A second pillar example can be found in the case concerning a sanctions measure relating to the Federal Republic of Yugoslavia which also found its legal base in the EC Treaty (Article 301).[66]

Furthermore, external effects can be found on the basis of what is probably the Union's most famous convention, namely the Europol Convention. It is particularly striking that Europol can negotiate and sign agreements with non-EU countries or bodies in its own right, but with approval by the Council. Article 42(2) of the Europol Convention enables the organisation to establish and maintain relations with third states and third bodies. Ever since 2001, Europol has made full use of this competence.[67]

Finally, Article 49 TEU deserves to be mentioned, as it refers to Accession Treaties concluded between current and new Member States. This type of treaty is characterised by the ECJ as an international agreement and is also to be regarded as forming part of the Union's primary law.[68] It needs to be ratified by all parties,

---

[64] Agreement between the European Union and Iceland and Norway on the application of certain provisions of the Convention on Mutual Assistance in Criminal Matters, *OJ* 2004 L 26/3-9. See chapter 4 on the EEA countries in this volume.

[65] ECJ, Case C-170/96 *Commission* v. *Council* [1998] *ECR* I-2763.

[66] See, for instance, ECJ, Case C-317/00 P *'Invest' Import und Export GmbH and Invest Commerce* v. *Commission* [2000] *ECR* I-9541. On this topic, see more extensively R.A. Wessel, 'Fragmentation in the Governance of EU External Relations: Legal Institutional Dilemmas and the New Constitution for Europe', in J.W. de Zwaan, et al., eds., *The European Union – An Ongoing Process of Integration – Liber Amicorum Alfred E. Kellermann* (The Hague, T.M.C. Asser Press 2004) pp. 123-140.

[67] The first agreement was signed on 6 December 2001 and concerned an exchange of information in the fight against international crime between Europol and the United States (Council Doc. 14586/01). For an extensive survey, see S. Peers, 'Governance and the Third Pillar: The Accountability of Europol', in Curtin and Wessel, op. cit. n. 51, at pp. 253-276.

[68] ECJ, Case C-171/96 *Rui Alberto Pereira Roque* v. *His Excellency the Lieutenant Governor of Jersey* [1998] *ECR* 4607; ECJ, Case C-445/00 *Republic of Austria* v. *Council* [2003] *ECR* I-8549, para. 62.

but not by the Union. The complex relationship (or coexistence) between primary European law and international law among the current and new Member States simultaneously has consequences for legal review.[69] In the *LAISA* case, the Court denied legal review – on the basis of an annulment procedure – on the grounds that the Act of Accession would not fall under the broad definition of a binding act with legal effect.[70] This was further refined by *Republic of Austria* v. *Council* in 2003, in the sense that the protocols and annexes to an act of accession constitute primary law which, unless that act provides otherwise, may not be suspended, amended or repealed otherwise than in accordance with the procedure established for review of the original Treaties.[71] In other cases, however, the Act of Accession came under scrutiny in line with the legal proceedings at stake.[72] Therefore, the Act of Accession and the Accession Treaty came under legal review only when a preliminary ruling was given on their scope,[73] when the Act of Accession had been infringed or when the Court examined secondary law that had been modified by the Act of Accession. These conditions have to be seen in the context of procedural Community law and the subject under review. Article 234 TEC is meant, *inter alia*, for the interpretation of the Treaty, including the Accession Treaties,[74] whereas the annulment procedure of Article 230 TEC reviews the legality of acts[75] on the grounds of an infringement of the EC Treaty, including the Accession Treaties.[76]

3.3 The status of international law in the Union and its Member States

The ECJ has regularly been confronted with international agreements and their legal consequences, in particular through preliminary questions on the basis of Article 234 TEC, when EU citizens, companies or third-country nationals residing in a Member States have invoked provisions of international agreements such as free trade agreements and Association Agreements. Depending on the

---

[69] ECJ, Joined Cases 194 and 241/85 *Commission* v. *Greece* [1988] *ECR* 1037.

[70] ECJ, Joined Cases 31 and 35/86 *LAISA* [1988] *ECR* 2285, para. 15. It has to be pointed out that in this case the Advocate General came to the opposite conclusion based on the reasoning that it results from an adjustment of secondary law that is of immediate concern to the applicant. See Opinion AG Lenz, *LAISA* v. *Council* [1988] *ECR* 2285.

[71] ECJ, Case C-445/00 *Republic of Austria* v. *Council* [2003] *ECR* I-8549, para. 62.

[72] CFI, Case T-187/99 *Agrana Zucker und Stärke AG* v. *Commission* [2001] *ECR* II-1589; ECJ, Case C-30/00 *Hinton Ltd.* v. *Fazenda Publica* [2001] *ECR* I-7511; ECJ, Case C-27/96 *Danisco Sugar* [1997] *ECR* I-6653; ECJ, Case C-3/87 *The Queen* v. *Ministry of Agriculture* [1989] *ECR* 4459.

[73] ECJ, Case C-233/97 *KappAhl Oy* [1998] *ECR* I-8069.

[74] This is not so clear in K. Lenaerts and D. Arts, *Procedural Law of the European Union* (London, Sweet & Maxwell 1999) p. 116, but see B. Wegener, 'Artikel 234 Absatz 5', in Calliess and Ruffert, op. cit. n. 62.

[75] This excludes primary law but includes all measures which intend to have legal effect.

[76] Lenaerts and Arts, op. cit. n. 74, at p. 197.

direct effect of these provisions, the facts of the case were considered. In cases involving Member States, Article 230 TEC (the annulment procedure) has been used to establish the invalidity of secondary law that infringes international agreements. In the famous *Banana* case involving the WTO Agreement, the Court even required proof of the direct effect of these provisions in relation to the privileged applicant Member State.[77]

There is no coherent picture of the legal impact of international agreements in the legal order of the Community/Union and its Member States. It is not even addressed in Article 300 TEC. While paragraph 7 provides that agreements concluded under the conditions of this article shall be binding on the institutions of the Community and on Member States, it does not say anything on its legal effect in Community or Member State law. It has been stated that this phrase cannot be seen as a mere repetition of international treaty law, because it also mentions the Member States and consequently means that they are also bound by international agreements that fall under the exclusive competence of the Community.[78] The question of legal effect was addressed by the *Haegeman* decision of the ECJ in 1974, in which the judges explained that international agreements form an integral part of the EC legal order.[79] Consequently, international agreements share the 'legal destiny' of European Community law in the form of primary and secondary law. Their legal destiny and special characteristics are defined by their direct effect and the supremacy of EC/EU law.[80] These findings have been extended to principles of international law that the European Communities must respect.[81] In the *Kadi* and *Yusuf* cases, the CFI recently emphasised the primacy of UN obligations under the UN Charter, which prevail over obligations of domestic law or the ECHR but also obligations arising from the EC Treaty. The Court even confirmed the fact that the Community is bound by the UN Charter – not on the basis of public international law but through its own constituting document.[82] However, the fundamental Community principle of direct effect – providing enforceable rights for the individual *vis-à-vis* the European Community and its Member States – cannot automatically be extended to international agreements. The direct effect of international agreement

---

[77] ECJ, Case C-280/93 *Germany* v. *Council* [1994] *ECR* I-4973. This was later refined in Case C-149/96 *Portugal* v. *Council* [1999] *ECR* I-8395, by referring to the general political and economic argument of the lack of reciprocity.

[78] See further W. Weiss, 'International Agreements in the European Community Legal Order and in the Legal Orders of the Member States', in A. Ott and K. Inglis, eds., *Handbook on European Enlargement* (The Hague, T.M.C. Asser Press 2002) pp. 201-204.

[79] ECJ, Case 181/73 *Haegeman* v. *Belgian State* [1974] *ECR* 449.

[80] See A. Ott, 'Fundamental and Basic Principles of the EC and the EU', in Ott and Inglis, op. cit. n. 78, at p. 17.

[81] ECJ, Case C-162/96 *Racke* [1998] *ECR* I-3655, para. 45.

[82] CFI, Case T-315/01 *Yassin Abdullah Kadi* v. *Council and Commission*, nyr, para. 181; Case T-306/01 *Ahmed Ali Yusuf and Al Barakaat International Foundation* v. *Council and Commission*, [2002] *ECR* II-2387, para. 243.

provisions, including Association Council decisions, is evaluated by interpreting the wording, purpose and nature of the agreement, as well as the preciseness and clarity of the obligation.[83] The Court has developed a two-step approach in which it starts by analysing whether and to what extent a provision could be considered directly effective. Subsequently, it examines whether the directly effective provisions of an international agreement can be interpreted in the same way as provisions of the EC Treaty. The Court does not opt for a simple analogy with other Community law, but instead claims that the direct effect of international agreements depends on the aim pursued by each provision of the agreement in comparison with the aims pursued by the EC Treaty.[84] Once the direct effect of an international law provision is established, the hierarchy of norms becomes relevant. In the Community perspective, Community law ranks above national law, and international agreements concluded by the Community rank above secondary but below primary law.[85]

The interpretation of international agreements thus depends on their context and wording. It is questionable whether international agreements, which form part of the Community legal order as a result of their integration, retain their characteristics as international law or whether they are transformed into Community law. As we have seen, they can have the same effect as other Community law, albeit subject to some limitations. One legal principle which has to be considered when interpreting international law is the principle of good faith, which derives from common international law principles and forms part of the general legal order of Community law. The principle that Community law is to be interpreted in conformity with international law is reflected in several decisions of the ECJ.[86] Another pivotal and important principle is the loyalty principle laid down in Article 10 TEC, which gains special importance in relation to the conclusion, implementation and even interpretation of mixed agreements.[87] This also extends to mixed agreements that are concluded on the basis of mixed competences,

---

[83] ECJ, Case C-87/95 *Bresciani* v. *Amministrazione Italiana delle Finanze* [1976] *ECR* 129, para. 16; ECJ, Case C-192/89 *Sevince* v. *Staatsecretaris van Justitie* [1990] *ECR* I-3461, para. 15; ECJ, Case C-469/93 *Chiquita Italia* [1995] *ECR* I-4533, para. 25; CFI, Case T-115/94 *Opel Austria* v. *Council* [1997] *ECR* II-39, para. 101; ECJ, Case C-162/96 *Racke* v. *Hauptzollamt Mainz* [1998] *ECR* I-3655, para. 31.

[84] ECJ, Case 225/78 *Procureur de la République de Besançon* v. *Bouhelier* [1979] *ECR* 3151, para. 6; ECJ, Case 104/81 *Hauptzollamt Mainz* v. *Kupferberg & Cie KG* [1982] *ECR* 3641, para. 30; ECJ, Case C-312/91 *Metalsa* [1993] *ECR* I-3751, paras. 10-11; ECJ, Case C-469/93 *Amministrazione delle Finanze dello Stato* v. *Chiquita Italia* [1995] *ECR* I-4533, para. 52; ECJ, Opinion 1/91 *EEA* [1991] *ECR* I-6079, para. 14; ECJ, Cases C-114 and 115/95 *Texaco et al.* v. *Middelfart havn et al.* [1997] *ECR* I-4263, para. 28.

[85] Clarified in ECJ, Case C-179/97 *Spain* v. *Commission* [1999] *ECR* I-1251, para. 11.

[86] ECJ, Case C-162/96 *Racke GmbH & Co.* v. *Hauptzollamt Mainz* [1998] *ECR* I-3655; ECJ, Case C-69/89 *Nakajima* [1991] *ECR* I-2069; ECJ, Case 70/87 *Fediol III* [1989] *ECR* 1805.

[87] See, for instance, ECJ, Opinion 1/94 *WTO* [1994] *ECR* I-5267, para. 108; ECJ, Case C-25/94 *Commission* v. *Council* [1996] *ECR* I-1469 para. 48.

cross-pillar effects and – in the case of parallel international agreements concluded by Member States – in areas of remaining competences. It is open to debate to what extent the general principle of reciprocity also finds its way into Community law. In any event, the Court has stated clearly – again referring to good faith – that legal reciprocity cannot by itself exclude the direct effect of international agreements in the Community legal order.[88] This does not seem to be contradicted *a priori* by the Court's decision in *Portugal* v. *Council*, in which the judges emphasised that, due to the principle of reciprocity, the lack of direct effect in the interpretation of the WTO Agreement by the main trading partners of the European Community would lead to a denial of the direct effect of WTO law in the Community legal order.[89] This judgment should be seen in the light of judgments on GATT/WTO law in which the Court consistently held that GATT and WTO law is not capable of conferring rights on the individual due to its lack of direct effect. Instead, it emphasised a form of political reciprocity that restrains the ECJ when ruling on the legal impact of these agreements, with the justification that otherwise the Community's and Member States' negotiating powers within the WTO forum would be reduced and such trade policy instruments as the Trade Barriers Regulation put at risk.[90]

The status of international agreements that were not concluded by the European Community but by the European Union will remain somewhat unclear until the ECJ has the competence to scrutinise these agreements. As far as the Member States are concerned, it may be assumed that they do not have any direct rights or obligations on the basis of Union agreements *vis-à-vis* third parties. After all, and perhaps ironically, the agreements are concluded exclusively by the Union; no mixed agreements have yet been concluded. This means that the legal relationship exists between the Union and the Member States and not directly between the Member States and the contracting third party. On the other hand, it is clear that the agreements form an integral part of the Union's legal order and that they bind the institutions (cf., Article 24(6) TEU). In this respect, the principle of consistency as reflected in Articles 1, 3 and 11 TEU should be mentioned.[91] The notion that '[t]he Union shall in particular ensure the consistency of its external activities as a whole' (Article 3 TEU) could link the Union agreements to agreements or other external actions based on the EC Treaty. It is disputed whether we are

---

[88] ECJ, Case 104/81 *Hauptzollamt Mainz* v. *Kupferberg* [1982] *ECR* 3641.

[89] ECJ, Case C-149/96 *Portugal* v. *Council* [1999] *ECR* I-8395. See also A. Ott, 'Der EuGH und das WTO-Recht: Die Entdeckung der politischen Gegenseitigkeit – altes Phänomen oder neuer Ansatz?', 38 *Europarecht* (2003) p. 504.

[90] Ott, loc. cit. n. 89. On these issues, see in general R. Leal-Arcas, 'The European Court of Justice and the EC External Trade Relations: A Legal Analysis of the Court's Problems with Regard to International Agreements', 72 *Nordic Journal of International Law* (2003) pp. 215-251.

[91] See more extensively R.A. Wessel, 'The Inside Looking Out: Consistency and Delimitation in EU External Relations', 37 *CMLRev.* (2000) pp. 1135-1171.

dealing with a judiciable principle.[92] The principle of consistency may be regarded as a special form of the loyalty principle laid down in Article 10 TEC, as it emphasises institutional coordination and the coordination of actions among institutions and Member States.[93]

3.4 Case law on the European Community/Union's neighbours

Since the 1960s, the Community has created an intricate web of trade agreements and Association Agreements with its neighbours.[94] This has resulted in extensive case law on the provisions of some of these international agreements and their legal consequences in the Community legal order.[95] In particular, the so-called Accession Association Agreement with Turkey, the Europe Agreements with the candidate countries from Central and Eastern Europe and the special Association Agreement with the EEA have raised interesting legal questions on the effect and scope of these agreements. Extensive case law was developed by the ECJ on the legal effects of the Ankara Agreement and Association Council Decisions 2/76, 1/80 and 3/80 for Turkish nationals and their family dependents residing in one of the Member States. It was concluded, *inter alia*, that certain provisions may have direct effect and that specific employment rights also imply the existence of a corresponding right of residence.[96]

---

[92] See, for instance, B. Weidel, 'The Impact of the Pillar Construction on External Policy', in S. Griller and B. Weidel, eds., *External Economic Relations and Foreign Policy in the European Union* (Vienna, Springer Verlag 2002) p. 23 at p. 34.

[93] See C. Calliess, 'Artikel 1 EU Absatz 43', in Calliess and Ruffert, op. cit. n. 62. In addition, its influence is reflected in the context of the unity of law, which is generally seen as a guiding obligation in relation to the interpretation of Community law rather than] overall Union law. On this issue, see especially T. Oppermann, 'Die Dritte Gewalt in der Europäischen Union', 109 *Deutsche Verwaltungsblatt* (1994) p. 901; and further A. Hatje, 'Europäische Rechtseinheit durch einheitliche Rechtsdurchsetzung', in J. Schwarze and P-C. Müller-Graff, eds., 'Europäische Rechtseinheit durch einheitliche Rechtsdurchsetzung', *Europarecht*, Beiheft 1/1998, p. 7; U. Becker, 'Differenzierungen der Rechtseinheit durch "abgestufte Integration"', in Schwarze and Müller-Graff, ibid., p. 29.

[94] The so-called 1963 Athens Agreement with Greece and the still applicable 1964 Ankara Agreement with Turkey are examples of early Association Agreements that were concluded with neighbouring countries (Agreement establishing an association between the European Economic Community and Greece, *OJ* 1963 L 26/294; Agreement establishing an Association between the European Economic Community and Turkey, *OJ* 1973 C 113/1).

[95] The free trade agreements with Portugal and Spain and the free trade agreements with former EFTA countries Austria and Sweden have thus come under scrutiny.

[96] Article 2(1)(b) of Decision No. 2/76 has direct effect: ECJ, Case C-192/89 *Sevince* [1990] *ECR* I-3461, para. 26; Article 7 of Decision 2/76: ECJ, Case C-192/89 *Sevince* [1990] *ECR* I-3461, para. 26; Article 6 of the Decision 1/80 has direct effect: ECJ, Case C-192/89 *Sevince* [1990] *ECR* I-3461, para. 26; ECJ, Case C-355/93 *Eroglu* v. *Land Baden-Württemberg* [1994] *ECR* I-5113, para. 11; ECJ, Case C-171/95 *Tetik* v. *Land Berlin* [1997] *ECR* I-329, para. 24; ECJ, Case C-386/95 *Eker* v. *Land Baden-Württemberg* [1997] *ECR* I-2697, para. 18; ECJ, Case C-36/96 *Giinaydin* v. *Freistaat Bayern* [1997] *ECR*, para. 61; ECJ, Case C-98/96 *Ertanir* v. *Land Hessen* [1997] *ECR* I-5179; ECJ, Case C-1/97 *Birden* [19981 *ECR* I-7747, para. 67; ECJ, Case C-340/97 *Nazli* v. *Stadt Nürnberg* [2000] *ECR* I-937, para. 28; Article 7 of Association Council Decision 1/80 has direct effect: ECJ, Case

Another generation of accession Association Agreements, the Europe Agreements, first became subject to review in relation to their establishment provisions and later in relation to their provisions on workers, which are not only directly effective but also provide a right of non-discrimination and residence to the respective third-country nationals once they are legally established or legally employed in one of the EU Member States.[97]

3.5 An integrated external policy?

Irrespective of the function of the principle of consistency, the fragmentation of EU external relations is striking. This situation is rooted in many causes, one obviously being the current pillar structure.[98] In the first pillar, the external economic or Common Commercial Policy forms one of the core responsibilities of the European Community. Ever since 1968, the European Community constitutes a customs union and has been actively involved in the most important trade regime to be established since the 1960s, namely the GATT.[99] In 1995, the European Community – as the only regional trade arrangement – became a member of the WTO.[100] The Common Commercial Policy in Article 133 TEC falls within the scope of the exclusive competences of the Community,[101] and the European Commission is endowed with extensive functions for the management of this important external policy field, including monitoring the market access strategy[102] and concluding and negotiating trade agreements with third countries.

C-355/93 *Eroglu* v. *Land Baden Ulm* [2000] *ECR* I-1487, para. 34; ECJ, Case C-65/98 *Eyüp* v. *Landesgeschaftsstelle des Arbeitsmarktservice Vorarlberg* [2000] *ECR* I-4747; Article 13 of Decision No. 1/80: ECJ, Case C-192/89 *Sevince* [1990] *ECR* I-3461, para. 26, Article 3(1) of Decision No. 3/80 establishes a precise and unconditional principle: ECJ, Case C-262/96 *Sürül* v. *Bundesanstalt für Arbeit* [1999] *ECR* I-2685, para. 74, ECJ, Joined Cases C-102 and C-211/98 *Kocak* v. *Landesversicherungsanstalt Oberfranken und Mittelfranken* [2000] *ECR* I-1287, para. 35.

97 ECJ, Case C-63/99 *The Queen* v. *Secretary of State for the Home Department, ex parte Wieslaw Gloszczuk and Elzbieta Gloszczuk* [2001] *ECR* I-6369; ECJ, Case C-235/99 *The Queen* v. *Secretary of State for the Home Department, ex parte Eleanora Ivanova Kondova* [2001] *ECR* I-6427; ECJ, Case C-257/99 *The Queen* v. *Secretary of State for the Home Department, ex parte Julius Barkoci and Marcel Malik* [2001] *ECR* I-6557; ECJ, Case C-268/99 *Aldona Malgorzata Jany and Others* v. *Staatssecretaris van Justitie* [2001] *ECR* I-8615.

98 And the various forms of decision making and law-making in the first pillar.

99 Since the successful establishment of the customs union in 1968, the European Community had a *de facto* institutional status in the *de facto* international organisation known as the GATT. See, for instance, A. Ott, *GATT und WTO im Gemeinschaftsrecht* (Cologne, Carl Heymanns Publisher 1997) p. 111.

100 For regional trade arrangements in the form of a customs union or free trade area, the relevant provision is Article XXIV of the GATT Agreement. See Article XI of the Agreement establishing the WTO. On this issue, see A. ter Heegde, 'The EC and Member States in International Organisations: GATT and WTO', in Ott and Inglis, op. cit. n. 78, at p. 61.

101 ECJ, Case 41/76 *Donckerwolke and Schou* v. *Procureur de la République* [1976] *ECR* 1921.

102 On the market access strategy, see G.M. Berrisch and H-G. Kamann, 'The European Community's Trade Barriers Regulation and the new Market Access Strategy of the European Commission', *EWS* (2001) p. 461.

The current management of external relations in the European Commission is divided between four different Directorates General – Trade, External Relations, Development and Enlargement – with overlapping responsibilities.[103] DG Development is responsible for development policy and has direct responsibilities for Community relations with sub-Saharan Africa, the Caribbean, the Pacific and the Indian Ocean; DG Trade defines its mission as conducting the Union's commercial policy; DG Enlargement is responsible for the enlargement process and its financial instruments; and DG External Relations is responsible for managing bilateral relations with third countries that do not form part of the wider enlargement process such as the EEA countries and Switzerland and for the new European Neighbourhood Policy.

As we have seen, other aspects of external relations relate to the European Union's Common Foreign and Security Policy (the 'second pillar'), which hands a leading role to the Council of the European Union and its High Representative Javier Solana rather than to the Commission. To complicate matters, other examples such as the European Union's reaction to the Helms-Burton Act,[104] legislation on dual-use goods[105] and legislation on terrorism[106] demonstrate the cross-pillar effects of certain measures by combining legal instruments from the different pillars, which further complicates decision making and law-making and threatens coherent implementation.[107] A solution is mostly found in a combination of two governance regimes, as in the case of the Union's reaction to extraterritorial application of legislation on the basis of the Helms-Burton Act. The classic example is of course the case of economic sanctions, where the CFSP and EC measures are presented as complementary. Despite the obvious differences in the separate decision-making procedures needed – the most striking ones being the need for a Commission proposal under Article 301 TEC,[108] the possibility of qualified majority voting under the same provision and the requirement of unanimity under Article 23(1) TEU – this combination of legal bases is still the way

---

103 See the website of the Commission, available at: <http://europa.eu.int/comm/world>.

104 Council Regulation (EC) No. 2271/96 of 22 November 1996 protecting against the effects of the extra-territorial application of legislation adopted by a third country, and actions based thereon or resulting therefrom, *OJ* 1996 L 309/1-6; Joint Action of 22 November 1996 adopted by the Council on the basis of Articles J.3 and K.3 of the Treaty on European Union concerning measures protecting against the effects of the extra-territorial application of legislation adopted by a third country, and actions based thereon or resulting therefrom, *OJ* 1996 L 309/7.

105 Council Regulation (EC) No. 1504/2004 of 19 July 2004 amending and updating Regulation (EC) No 1334/2000 setting up a Community regime for the control of exports of dual-use items and technology. On this issue, see P. Koutrakos, *Trade, Foreign Policy and Defense in EU Constitutional Law* (Oxford, Hart Publishing 2001).

106 See, for instance, Council Common Positions 2001/930/CFSP and 2001/931/CFSP of 27 December 2001, *OJ* 2001 L 344.

107 See more extensively Wessel, loc. cit. n. 66; Koutrakos, op. cit. n. 105; P. Gauttier, 'Horizontal Coherence and the External Competences of the European Union', 10 *ELJ* (2004) pp. 23-41.

108 On this issue, see K. Osteneck, 'Artikel 301 EG', in J. Schwarze, ed., *EU-Kommentar* (Baden-Baden, Nomos 2000).

in which the legal institutional dilemma is being approached, apart from the possibility of using either a single CFSP legal basis (arms embargoes)[109] or a single EC legal basis (many sanctions regimes based on UN resolutions). As pointed out above, the consequences of the current pillarisation on economic and financial sanctions imposed on individuals or entities are somewhat softened by the *Yusuf* and *Kadi* cases, in which the CFI accepted the recourse to the cumulative legal bases of Articles 60, 301 and 308 TEC for a regulation fighting international terrorism and freezing the funds and financial resources of certain persons and entities associated with the Al Qaeda network and the Taliban. The Court exceptionally extended the conservative reading of Article 308 EC to supplement the Union's powers to adapt 'to those new threats'.[110]

The same complexity occurs with regard to unilateral measures adopted by the Union in the case of a violation of international obligations by a third state (e.g., withdrawal of benefits, suspension of development assistance or flight bans) or in the case of a suspension of treaty obligations (e.g., suspending a Cooperation Agreement because of a fundamental change in circumstances or invoking the human rights clauses in bilateral cooperation or trade agreements).[111] Whereas the latter may only be based on the EC Treaty (Article 300(2), second subparagraph), in the former case one may come across single CFSP or EC decisions, or combinations of the two, on the basis of Article 301 TEC and Articles 14 or 15 TEU. In the Union's formative years, a similar example could be found in the regime concerning the export of dual-use goods: the economic decision on the export ban was taken on the basis of Article 133 TEC, whereas the actual list of goods falling under the regime, as well as their destinations, was established on the basis of Article 14 TEU.[112] In 2000, this situation largely came to an end with the introduction of a new regulation, bringing the CFSP parts of the regime within the Community field of competence.[113] Nevertheless, the tension between the Common Commercial Policy (EC) and national security measures (CFSP) continues to exist as the control of technical assistance related to certain military end-uses continues to be based on the second pillar.[114]

---

[109] The rationale for not using Article 301 TEC in this situation is to be found in Article 296(1)(b), which permits Member States to take the necessary measures for the protection of their essential security interests connected with the trade in arms.

[110] CFI, Case T-315/01 *Yassin Abdullah Kadi* v. *Council and Commission*, nyr, paras. 130-132.

[111] See more extensively E. Paasivirta and A. Rosas, 'Sanctions, Countermeasures and Related Actions in the External Relations of the EU', in E. Cannizzaro, *The European Union as an Actor in International Relations* (The Hague, Kluwer Law International 2002) pp. 207-218.

[112] For an overview, see P. Koutrakos, 'Inter-Pillar Approaches to the European Security and Defence Policy: The Economic Aspects of Security', in Kronenberger, op. cit. n. 61, at pp. 435-480.

[113] Council Regulation (EC) No. 1334/2000 of 22 June 2000 setting up a Community regime for the control of exports of dual-use items and technology, *OJ* 2000 L 159.

[114] See Council Joint Action 2000/401/CFSP of 22 June 2000 concerning the control of technical assistance relating to certain military end-uses, *OJ* 2000 L 159.

As we have seen, external relations in the area of Police and Judicial Cooperation in Criminal Matters (the 'third pillar') are booming as well. An obvious reason for this is the fast development of the Justice and Home Affairs domain in general. Over the past few years, the Council has adopted almost ten texts per month on JHA issues.[115] Since 2001, external relations in the JHA domain can be found in the so-called 'multi-presidency programmes',[116] and a number of agreements have been concluded on the basis of Article 38 TEU as well as on the basis of Article 42(2) of the Europol Convention.[117] These agreements reveal a serious shortcoming in the treaty-making procedure of Articles 24 and 38 TEU, as it does not include consultation of the European Parliament, irrespective of the potentially major implications for citizens' rights and freedoms. The fact that different procedures are used in the third pillar, as compared to the Community, adds to the fragmentation of the Union's external relations, as Article 300 TEC does call for consultation of the Parliament. But cross-pillar problems are not limited to parliamentary control. The competences of the Community on the basis of Title IV TEC (asylum, immigration, border controls and judicial cooperation in civil matters) have a clear relationship with EU competences under Title VI TEU.

Community competences on the basis of Title IV TEC occasionally overlap with EU competences in the third pillar. Obvious examples may be found in relation to the Schengen *acquis*. Agreements have been concluded or are under negotiation with Switzerland, Norway and Iceland regarding the free movement of persons, covering both Community and third pillar issues. Switzerland has concluded an international agreement associating itself with the implementation, application and development of the Schengen *acquis*, which involved the participation of the European Community and the European Union. Modelled after similar agreements concluded with Norway and Iceland in 2001,[118] it differs in that the agreement needs to be adopted by two Council decisions based on the EC Treaty and the Treaty on European Union (Arts. 24 and 38 TEU and Arts. 63, 66 and 95 TEC)[119] and consequently constitutes a special type of 'internal' mixed

[115] On this issue and on the external relations of the third pillar in general, see Monar, loc. cit. n. 28.

[116] For a recent update, see Council of the European Union, JHA External Relations Multi-Presidency Programme, Council Doc. 5001/05 of 3 January 2005.

[117] See also Council Act of 8 November 1998 laying down rules governing Europol's external relations with third States and non-European Union related bodies, *OJ* 1999 C 26/19, providing for an explicit treaty-making power of Europol. See also H.G. Nilsson, 'Organs and Bodies of the Third Pillar as Instruments of External Relations of the European Union', in G. De Kerckhove and A. Weyembergh, *Sécurité et justice: enjeu de la politique extérieure de l'Union européenne* (Brussels, Éditions de l'Université de Bruxelles 2003) p. 201 at pp. 205-209.

[118] Agreement concluded by the Council of the European Union and the Republic of Iceland and the Kingdom of Norway concerning the latters' association with the implementation, application and development of the Schengen acquis – Final Act, *OJ* 1999 L 176/35. See chapter 4 on the EEA countries in this volume.

[119] European Commission, Proposal for a Council Decision, 14 September 2004, COM (2004) 593 final. See also Council Decision of 25 October 2004 on the signing, on behalf of the European

agreement. Monar but also the Commission point to the fact that this has the effect that, in one and the same article of an international agreement, one aspect falls under Title IV TEC and another under Title VI TEU. This necessitates an enormous effort to coordinate between the Commission, the Presidency and the Member States,[120] as well as between the different legal natures of Community and Union law, which are subject to the ECJ's jurisdiction to different degrees.[121] Nevertheless, recent case law reveals that the separation between the first and the third pillars may not be as strict as one might have thought. The Court accepted a Community competence in the area of criminal law once this is necessary to make use of an explicit Community competence, in this case Article 175 on environmental protection measures.[122]

After the terrorist attacks of 11 September 2001, in particular, the relationship between the second and the third pillar has grown closer as well. At present, third pillar anti-terrorism issues are part and parcel of 'political dialogue' meetings, which generally take place on the basis of the CFSP and agreements with third states, and combine policies on the basis of both (or even all three) pillars.[123]

With regard to the participation of Member States and the European Community/Union in international agreements, one may thus differentiate between international agreements involving only the European Community (such as trade agreements) or the European Union (on CFSP matters), agreements involving all Member States and the European Community (such as the GATS and TRIPS Agreements) and agreements involving some or all of the Member States that are concluded either within or outside the framework of the European Community/ Union. The latter are the so-called partial or parallel agreements.[124] They may also include third countries. The original Schengen Agreement and its follow-up serve as an example of this,[125] as the Member State of Denmark and non-members Iceland and Norway participate in the Schengen regime on the basis of international

---

Community, and on the provisional application of certain provisions of the Agreement between the European Union, the European Community and the Swiss Confederation, concerning the Swiss Confederation's association with the implementation, application and development of the Schengen acquis, *OJ* 2004 L 386/26 and 370/78. For the text of the agreement, see <http://www.europa.admin.ch/nbv/off/abkommen/e/schengen.pdf>. See also chapter 5 in this volume.

120 Monar, loc. cit. n. 28. See also E. Barbe, 'L'influence de l'Union européenne dans les enceintes internationals', in De Kerckhove and Weyembergh, op. cit. n. 117, p. 211 at p. 213.

121 European Commission, Proposal for a Council Decision, 14 September 2004, COM (2004) 593 final.

122 ECJ, Case C-176/03 *Commission* v. *Council*, nyr.

123 See, for example, the Political Dialogue and Cooperation Agreements, available at: <http://europa.eu.int/comm/external_relations>.

124 See B. de Witte, 'Chameleonic Member States: Differentiation by means of partial and parallel international agreements', in B. de Witte, D. Hanf and E. Vos, eds., *The Many Faces of Differentiation in EU Law* (Antwerp, Intersentia 2001) p. 231 at p. 232.

125 Agreement between the Governments of the States of the Benelux Economic Union, the Federal Republic of Germany and the French Republic on the gradual abolition of checks at their common borders, *OJ* 2000 L 239/13.

law.[126] Part of the fragmentation in this field flows from the fact that the European Community and the European Union still have separate legal personalities. Nevertheless, theoretical as well as empirical evidence of the Union's legal personality (as based on the large number of international agreements to which the Union as such is now a party) seems to have paved the way to an explicit recognition of the Union's international legal personality in the Treaty establishing a Constitution for Europe.[127]

4. REDEFINING EXTERNAL RELATIONS IN THE EXPANDING EUROPEAN UNION

4.1 The impact of enlargement

The impact of enlargement on external relations has a legal as well as a political dimension. With respect to the legal consequences, the European Union already tried to make sure that the new Member States would bring their international obligations in line with the requirements of EU membership before accession. From the perspective of Community law, primary EC law ranks above international law and the EC Treaty emphasises that Member States are obliged to eliminate incompatibilities between international agreements and the EC Treaty (Article 307, second paragraph). The *pacta sunt servanda* principle, reflected in the first paragraph of this provision, neither creates direct effect, which works to the advantage of EU citizens by enabling them to rely on favourable international agreements,[128] nor does it give Member States a right to refer to existing international law obligations, which works to their advantage. After all, it does not apply to intra-Community relations, and Community law in principle takes preference over international law and obligations towards third countries.[129] This paragraph only confirms the existing rights of third countries under international

[126] Agreement concluded by the Council of the European Union and the Republic of Iceland and the Kingdom of Norway concerning the latters' association with the implementation, application and development of the Schengen acquis, *OJ* 1999 L 176/36; Agreement between the European Community and the Republic of Iceland and the Kingdom of Norway concerning the criteria and mechanisms for establishing the State responsible for examining a request for asylum lodged in a Member State or in Iceland or Norway, *OJ* 2001 L 93/40; Agreement between the European Union and the Republic of Turkey on the participation of the Republic of Turkey in the European Union-led forces in the Former Yugoslav Republic of Macedonia, *OJ* 2003 L 234/ 23.

[127] There was a broad consensus in the Working Group on Legal Personality established by the Convention that the European Union is endowed with legal personality. See the result in Article I-7 TCE.

[128] ECJ, Case 812/79 *Burgoa* [1980] *ECR* 2787.

[129] ECJ, Case 121/85 *Conegate Limited* [1986] *ECR* 1007, para. 25; ECJ, Case C-473/93 *Commission* v. *Luxembourg* [1996] *ECR* I-3207; ECJ, Case C-62/98 *Commission* v. *Portuguese Republic* [2000] *ECR* I-5171.

law (see also Article 30 of the Vienna Convention on the Law of Treaties), namely that existing treaty obligations shall not be breached, and Article 307, second paragraph, is a special expression of the loyalty principle laid down in Article 10 TEC.[130] In addition, both the European Community and its Member States are members of the WTO and need to coordinate their trade policies in this forum.[131] With the accession of Bulgaria and the Baltic States to the WTO in 1996, 1999 and 2001, the institutional need to coordinate Community trade policy in the WTO has been strengthened.[132]

The accession of the new EU Member States in 2004 has also had consequences for their external relations. Article 6(1) of the Act of Accession refers to the principles of law applicable in Community law[133] and underlines that new Member States are bound by international agreements concluded in accordance with Article 300 TEC or Articles 24 or 38 TEU and that they undertake to accede to these agreements or conventions. The subsequent paragraphs list agreements that form part of the external relations *acquis*, such as the Cotonou Agreement, the EEA Agreement and association and trade agreements with countries such as Algeria, Georgia and South Korea.[134] Article 6(10), second paragraph, of the Act of Accession paraphrases Article 307, second paragraph, TEC. Going one step further, in accordance with the result of the accession negotiations, the Act of Accession forces the new Member States to withdraw from any free trade agreements with third countries, including the Central European Free Trade Association.

Politically, the success of the enlargement and the related policies can be seen as a role model for a more structured approach to the Union's policies towards its neighbours. As one observer notes, it was, after all, the 'most successful ever instrument of the EU foreign policy'.[135] Setting clear targets and priorities and giving incentives seems to be a recipe for having a sustainable influence on third countries in their policy making. It remains to be seen whether this concept will succeed in the long run without the 'accession incentive' but with financial

---

130 On this issue, see M. Cremona, 'The Impact of Enlargement: External Policy and External Relations', in M. Cremona, ed., *The Enlargement of the European Union* (Oxford, Oxford University Press 2003) p. 161 at p. 170.

131 See Article XI of the Agreement establishing the WTO.

132 On this issue, see A. ter Heegde, 'The Candidate Countries in International Organisations: GATT and WTO', in Ott and Inglis, op. cit. n. 78, at p. 75.

133 On Article 6 of the Act of Accession, see also K. Inglis, 'The Union's Fifth Accession Treaty: New Means to Make Enlargement Possible', 41 *CMLRev* (2004) p. 940.

134 Act concerning the conditions of accession of the Czech Republic, the Republic of Estonia, the Republic of Cyprus, the Republic of Latvia, the Republic of Lithuania, the Republic of Hungary, the Republic of Malta, the Republic of Poland, the Republic of Slovenia and the Slovak Republic and the adjustments to the Treaties on which the European Union is founded, *OJ* 2003 L 236/33.

135 M. Cremona, 'Enlargement: A Successful Instrument of Foreign Policy?', in T. Tridimas and P. Nebbia, *European Union Law for the Twenty-First Century*, Vol. I (Oxford, Hart Publishing 2004) p. 397, citing Wim Kok.

support and an extension of the internal market principles. Much will also depend on the individual countries and their interest in the European integration process. Enlargement formed an important part of the external relations of the Union and the successful strategies tested during the pre-accession process are now being used to structure the relations with third countries in the Wider Europe and beyond.[136]

4.2 The European Neighbourhood Policy: new policy making after enlargement?

Enlargement and its impact are regularly viewed through the prism of the Copenhagen criteria, including the Union's institutional ability to accept new members. At first sight, this inward-looking criterion lacks external relations aspects, but the whole pre-accession process with its legally binding Association Agreements structured by Accession Partnerships and the bundling of the financial and political aid for the new members, has shaped the future planning of external relations beyond the first wave of enlargement in May 2004.

The new European Neighbourhood Policy (ENP)[137] attempts to follow the pre-accession path and uses its flexible but nevertheless structured approach. The Treaty establishing a Constitution for Europe puts it as follows in Article I-57:

1. The Union shall develop a special relationship with neighbouring countries, aiming to establish an area of prosperity and good neighbourliness, founded on the values of the Union and characterised by close and peaceful relations based on cooperation.
2. For the purposes of paragraph 1, the Union may conclude specific agreements with the countries concerned. These agreements may contain reciprocal rights and obligations as well as the possibility of undertaking activities jointly. Their implementation shall be the subject of periodic consultation.

This approach was tested in practice over a period of many years and certainly paved the way for the successful accession of an initial group of ten countries into the European Union.[138] The pre-accession strategy, with its 'multi-coloured bundle'

---

[136] See generally Cremona, loc. cit. n. 130.

[137] The Commission defines the scope of this policy very broadly – or even vaguely – as a region which, due to its geographical proximity, should not be completely included but also not excluded because of geopolitical interests. On the ENP, see M. Cremona, 'The European Neighbourhood Policy: Legal and Institutional Issues', CDDRL Working Papers (2 November 2004); E. Lannon and P. van Elsuwege, 'The EU's Emerging Neighbourhood Policy and its Potential Impact on the Euro-Mediterranean Partnership', in P.G. Xuereb, ed., *The Mediterranean's European Challenge*, Vol. 4 (Malta, European Documentation and Research Centre, University of Malta 1998); M. Emerson, 'The Shaping of a Policy Framework for the Wider Europe', CEPS Policy Brief No. 39 (September 2003).

[138] See also Cremona, op. cit. n. 137, p. 4.

of strategy papers, partnership regulations and progress reports, seems to have found its resurrection in the ENP. The Commission initiated the ENP in March 2003 and produced a strategy paper in May 2004, a number of individual country reports and action plans.[139] Currently, these mutually agreed instruments need to be monitored through the existing Partnership and Cooperation Agreements and Association Agreements (and their joint institutional structures) and will be supplemented by a European Neighbourhood and Partnership Instrument to structure the financial assistance.[140]

In 1997, the European Union already became aware of the need to address the relationship with its future neighbours, but specific policies or measures were not yet adopted. This only changed with the development of a proximity policy through the Council in 2002 and developed a more definite shape through the proposed framework for relations with the European Union's eastern and southern neighbours in 2003 and the adoption of a report by the European Parliament.[141] Following the successful enlargement in May 2004, the Commission started to concentrate on including all its new neighbours in Eastern Europe (Russia, Ukraine, Belarus, Moldova, Georgia, Armenia and Azerbaijan) and on integrating the existing Euromed cooperation with the countries of Southern Europe and beyond (Algeria, Egypt, Israel, Jordan, Lebanon, Libya, Morocco, Syria, Tunisia and Palestine) into the ENP.[142]

One major difference with the enlargement process is that its conditionality is not built around accession but around the long-term plan of extending the internal market *acquis* to these neighbouring countries. However, what has worked with countries such as Norway, Iceland and Liechtenstein in the European Economic Area and, with minor differences, with Switzerland[143] will not necessarily succeed with countries such as Azerbaijan, Ukraine or Egypt. The two groups, consisting of the EEA and Switzerland on the one hand and the wider Europe countries on the other, could not be further apart. The European Union has never disputed the rights and the place of the former in the Union, and due to their economic

139 Communication from the Commission, European Neighbourhood Policy – Strategy Paper, COM (2004) 373 final; Cremona, op. cit. n. 137, p. 1.

140 Proposal for a Regulation of the European Parliament and of the Council laying down general provisions establishing a European Neighbourhood and Partnership Instrument, COM (2004) 628 final.

141 European Parliament, Report on 'Wider Europe – Neighbourhood: A New Framework for Relations with our Eastern and Southern Neighbours' (Napoletano Report), 20 November 2003; Communication from the Commission to the Council and the European Parliament, 'Wider Europe – Neighbourhood': A New Framework for Relations with our Eastern and Southern Neighbours, Brussels 11 March 2003, COM (2003) 104 final.

142 G. Harpaz, 'Enhanced Relations between the European Union and the State of Israel under the European Neighbourhood Policy: Some Legal and Economic Implications', 31 *LIEI* (2004) pp. 257-274.

143 On Switzerland, see S. Breitenmoser, 'Sectoral Agreements between the EC and Switzerland: Contents and Context', 40 *CMLRev* (2003) pp. 1137-1186. See also chapter 5 in this volume.

strength they have been contributing to the Union's budget and are willing to voluntarily adapt to EU law. A mutual interest exists between the EU and the EFTA countries to contribute to further European integration and harmonise their interests. The internal market is exported to these countries in order to give them a fair share of the benefits of the Union while accepting their reservations against paying into the budget for all the policies or participating in new ones, including the Common Foreign and Security Policy and Police and Judicial Cooperation in Criminal Matters.[144]

In contrast, the candidates for Wider Europe are presented with an abstract perspective of participation in the internal market and a promise on the part of the Union to bring stability and prosperity to the region, but with a clear mix of advantages and disadvantages. And while the four EFTA countries clearly belong to Europe and have even been applying for membership (but for political and economic reasons have 'frozen' their application for accession),[145] only some of the Wider Europe countries – such as Ukraine – geographically belong to Europe, but their membership is not (yet) seriously being considered by the European Union.[146] It should be noted however, that the European Parliament has voted overwhelmingly in favour of Ukraine's accession.[147] Despite these caveats, something seems to be encouraging the Commission to stick to a mix of legal, political and financial instruments and to use the instruments of conditionality and funding to influence the internal policies and reforms of its new neighbours in a peaceful manner.[148] From the experience gained during ten years of pre-accession strategy, it is clear that some flexibility can be added to more static and legally binding instruments such as Association Agreements by means of additional financial and political tools. In addition, by using the action plans and the future European Neighbourhood Policy Instrument (ENPI), the former modelled on the Accession Partnerships for the Central and Eastern European countries, the ever-

---

[144] In practice, Norway or Switzerland participate in certain CSFP or PJCC cooperation schemes on a voluntary and international law basis: Agreement concluded by the Council of the European Union and the Republic of Iceland and the Kingdom of Norway concerning the latters' association with the implementation, application and development of the Schengen acquis – Final Act, *OJ* 1999 L 176/36-62; Agreement between the European Union and the Government of the Swiss Confederation, represented by the Federal Department of Foreign Affairs, on the participation of Switzerland in the European Union Police Mission (EUPM) in Bosnia and Herzegovina (BiH), *OJ* 2003 L 239/14-16.

[145] In Norway, the population turned down membership twice. Its causes seem to be a mix of political, cultural and economic reasons. Switzerland has not pursued its membership application since the Swiss population rejected EEA participation.

[146] On Ukraine's policy intention to join the European Union, see 'Ukraine wants to join the European Union', 26 January 2005, available at: <http://www.euobserver.com>; 'Ukraine reinforces its commitment to EU', 24 January 2005, available at: <http://www.euractiv.com>.

[147] European Parliament resolution on the results of the Ukraine elections, P6_TA (2005) 0009 adopted on 13 January 2005.

[148] Cremona describes this as 'to repeat the perceived success of the accession process by setting some of same targets and by using similar instruments and methodologies, including conditionality and differentiation, but without the goal of accession to provide the incentive.'

changing process of approximation and the mix of policy, financial and legal instruments[149] can be given some structure. With the conditionality tool, a convincing incentive is created to steer these countries in the direction intended by the European Union. Another appealing aspect is the role of the European Commission in policy making in this area. As in the case of the enlargement process, the Member States have assigned the Commission an active role in the guiding and monitoring of the ENP, which in turn enables the Commission to represent the Union's interests as an independent 'broker' in the region, thereby preventing the individual Member States' different interests in the neighbouring regions from prevailing and creating anxieties and envies among the participating third countries.

4.3 The Constitution for Europe and external relations: new law-making after enlargement?

It can be claimed that one of the prominent goals of the mission to draft a Constitutional Treaty was the consolidation of external relations. This is reflected in the Laeken Declaration and in the establishment of two working groups by the European Convention to address the issue of legal personality and external relations.[150] Indeed, as discussed above, the Union's external relations have been strongly influenced by the case law of the ECJ and therefore reflect a piecemeal approach. In addition, external relations have been the main representative of incoherence in the current structure of the European Union/Communities, with legal personalities assigned to the different European Communities, the European Union (implicitly) and even some of the sub-organisations of the Community and the Union.[151] The different legal characteristics of the three pillars, as well as their diverging instruments and decision-making procedures, add immensely to the complexity of the Union's external relations. In that respect, the abolishment of the pillar structure and the merger of the Communities and the current European Union could only be welcomed, as it would leave us with a single international organisation – the Union – with competences in the former Community areas as well as in the areas of the CFSP and PJCC. In the Constitutional Treaty, in the area of external relations, no division is made between economic and political (foreign affairs) issues. Title V of Part III of the EU Constitution is labelled 'The Union's External Action' and covers all the Union's external policies. In addition,

---

149 The ENP is characterised by international agreements, financial instruments MEDA and TACIS, the Barcelona Process policy instrument and new instruments including the planned ENP Regulation and ENP strategy papers and country reports.

150 See further C. Herrmann, 'Die Außenhandelsdimension des Binnenmarktes im Verfassungsentwurf von der Zoll- und zur Weltordnungspolitik', in A. Hatje and J.P. Terhechte, eds., 'Das Binnenmarktziel in der europäischen Verfassung', *Europarecht* Beiheft 3/2004, p. 186.

151 On this subject, see D.M. Curtin and I.F. Dekker, 'The EU as a "Layered" International Organization: Institutional Unity in Disguise', in Craig and de Búrca, op. cit. n. 13, at pp. 83-136.

the external objectives of the Union are no longer scattered over different treaties. Instead Article I-3(4) provides:

> In its relations with the wider world, the Union shall uphold and promote its values and interests. It shall contribute to peace, security, the sustainable development of the earth, solidarity and mutual respect among peoples, free and fair trade, eradication of poverty and protection of human rights and in particular children's rights, as well as to strict observance and development of international law, including respect for the principles of the United Nations Charter.

Other provisions add to the idea of the integration of the different external policies as well. Firstly, Article III-194 codifies the existing practice according to which the former 'common strategies' (the term is no longer used) may cover all aspects of the Unions' external action: they are no longer restricted to the CFSP. Secondly, consistency is being pursued with the introduction of a Union Minister for Foreign Affairs, who not only chairs the Foreign Affairs Council but also serves as Vice-President of the Commission and is supported by a European External Action Service in accordance with Article III-296(3).[152] Thirdly, the legal personalities of the Community and the European Union are merged into one legal personality of the new Union. This certainly simplifies matters in relation to the conclusion of treaties and questions of accountability and responsibility. Article III-227 applies to all agreements concluded by the Union and no distinction is made, either in procedure or in legal nature, between the different external policies. Finally, the Constitutional Treaty puts an end to the different types of instruments for the CFSP aspect of external relations. Common strategies, joint actions and common positions make way for the European decision, an instrument which may also be used in other (former Community) areas of external relations.

Another improvement is that the fundamental principles of external relations law, which have slowly evolved from the case law of the ECJ over the past thirty years, have been included in Part I of the Constitutional Treaty. This can be considered the most obvious part of the process of tidying-up and consolidating the external relations provisions.[153] Article I-12 defines the categories of competences in such a way that only the Union may adopt legally binding acts in areas where it has exclusive competence, the Member States being competent only if so empowered by the Union or for the implementation of Union acts. According to Article I-13, these exclusive competences relate to the customs union, the establishing of the competition rules necessary for the functioning of the internal

[152] For a critical view on this double-hatting, see A. Dashwood, 'The Impact of Enlargement on the Union's Institutions', in C. Hillion, ed., *EU Enlargement* (Oxford, Hart Publishing 2004) p. 45 at p. 52.

[153] On this exercise, see generally B. de Witte, 'Simplification and Reorganisation of the European Treaties', 39 *CMLRev* (2002) pp. 1255-1287.

market, monetary policy for the Member States whose currency is the euro, the conservation of marine biological resources under the Common Fisheries Policy and the Common Commercial Policy. Paragraph 2 of this provision may be seen as a codification of the *ERTA* doctrine.[154] The Union's external action is defined in Part III of the Constitutional Treaty. Article III-292 clarifies the guiding principles of external relations, namely democracy, the rule of law, the universality and indivisibility of human rights and fundamental freedoms, respect for human dignity, the principles of equality and solidarity and respect for the principles of the UN Charter and international law. More specifically, paragraph 2 states that the Union shall pursue common policies and actions in this area, in order to:

(a) safeguard its values, fundamental interests, security, independence and integrity;
(b) consolidate and support democracy, the rule of law, human rights and the principles of international law;
(c) preserve peace, prevent conflicts and strengthen international security, in accordance with the purposes and principles of the United Nations Charter, with the principles of the Helsinki Final Act and with the aims of the Charter of Paris, including those relating to external borders;
(d) foster the sustainable economic, social and environmental development of developing countries, with the primary aim of eradicating poverty;
(e) encourage the integration of all countries into the world economy, including through the progressive abolition of restrictions on international trade;
(f) help develop international measures to preserve and improve the quality of the environment and the sustainable management of global natural resources, in order to ensure sustainable development;
(g) assist populations, countries and regions confronting natural or man-made disasters;
(h) promote an international system based on stronger multilateral cooperation and good global governance.

The most important provision in external relations, Article 133 TEC, has been revised since the Treaty of Amsterdam, when the Member States decided to codify bits and pieces defined by the ECJ's case law. Further refinements by the Treaty of Nice, however, have resulted in substantial legal uncertainty.[155] A new and necessary revision is found in Article III-315 of the Constitutional Treaty.

---

154 'The Union shall also have exclusive competence for the conclusion of an international agreement when its conclusion is provided for in the legislative act of the Union or is necessary to enable the Union to exercise its internal competence, or insofar as its conclusion may affect common rules or alter their scope.'

155 See C. Herrmann, 'Common Commercial Policy after Nice: Sisyphus Would Have Done a Better Job', 40 *CMLRev.* (2003) p. 1315; P. Eeckhout, *External Relations of the European Union* (Oxford, Oxford University Press 2004).

Next to agreements relating to trade in goods and services, the first paragraph now includes the commercial aspects of intellectual property and foreign direct investment. The unclear text of paragraph 6 of Article 133 on shared competences with regard to certain agreements and the misleading reference to paragraph 5 will be substituted by a new version. New paragraph 4 expressly mentions the conclusion of agreements in the field of trade in cultural and audiovisual services and in the field of trade in social, education and health services, which require unanimity, while agreements in the field of trade in services and the commercial aspects of intellectual property and foreign investment require unanimity when the adoption of internal rules requires this. It could be argued that the scope of objectives and principles of the Common Commercial Policy is broadened through its linkage to Article III-292, which specifies the general principles guiding external actions and thereby includes new aspects of trade policy such as the protection of human rights, sustainable development and environmental development.[156]

As stated before, one achievement of the Constitutional Treaty is that it codifies the external relations *acquis*. This intention to structure and simplify the existing bits and pieces spread out over the EC Treaty and the Treaty on European Union and defined in the ECJ's case law becomes particularly visible when the provisions regarding treaty making are compared. Articles III-323, III-325 and III-326 will substitute the treaty-making provision of Articles 300, 111[157] and 310[158] TEC. The mixture in Article 300 TEC of procedures (paras. 1 to 5), division of competences (paras. 1 to 3), legal consequences (paragraph 7) and legal review (paragraph 6) is unravelled by splitting it up into two provisions: Articles III-323 and III-325. Article III-323 specifies the competence of the Union to conclude international agreements in line with the *ERTA* doctrine when either the Constitutional Treaty or a legally binding Union act provides for it or is likely to affect common rules or alter their scope. Identical to Article 300(7), Article III-323(2) repeats that international agreements concluded by the Union are binding on the Union and its Member States. Article III-325 lays down the procedure for concluding international agreements. Paragraph 1 refers to the successor of current Article 133 TEC, Article III-315, which specifies the treaty-making procedure in the area of the Common Commercial Policy. The first seven paragraphs of Article III-325 list the division of competences between the Union's institutions. The confusing second paragraph of Article 300 TEC ('subject to the powers vested in the Commission in this field') is replaced by

156 See M. Krajewski, 'External Trade and the Constitution Treaty: Towards a Federal and More Democratic Common Commercial Policy', 42 *CMLRev.* (2005) p. 91 at p. 107.

157 Article 111 TEC is the specific provision on the conclusion of international agreements involving formal agreements on an exchange rate system for the euro in relation to non-Community currencies.

158 Provision establishing association policy cooperation.

paragraph 3 of Article III-325, according to which the Commission submits recommendations to the Council. The Council's central role in the management of external relations is confirmed by paragraphs 2 and 3 of Article III-325. The Council mandates the opening of negotiations and the respective negotiating directives, authorises the signing of agreements and finally concludes them. When the subject of the international agreement concerns the Common Foreign and Security Policy, the new Union Minister for Foreign Affairs submits recommendations to the Council. The choice between the Commission or the Foreign Minister seems to depend on the gravity of the issue: the Foreign Minister takes the lead on issues that exclusively or principally relate to the CFSP. If and when the Constitutional Treaty enters into force, this division will no doubt lead to questions about how to define the demarcation line between 'principally' and 'marginally'.

The participation of the European Parliament is regulated in Article III-325(6) and simplifies the structure in comparison to Article 300(3) TEC. It unites the participatory rights of the European Parliament in one paragraph stating that its consent is required in cases involving Association Agreements or agreements with budgetary implications. Paragraph 9 concerns the procedural process for the suspension of an international agreement. Finally, paragraph 11 facilitates the legal review of international agreements before they become legally binding by requesting a legal opinion from the European Court of Justice.

It is difficult to assess whether these overall changes infuse more coherence or consistency into the external relations *acquis*. Some changes, such as giving the Union explicit legal personality and codifying the medley of external relations competences and procedures, form a necessary exercise that is long overdue. In other matters, such as the merging of the pillars and policies, more coherence is not necessarily created in cases where differences in the decision-making process prevail and legal review by the European Court of Justice is still restricted. In contrast to Police and Judicial Cooperation in Criminal Matters, the Common Foreign and Security Policy partially remains a *domaine réservé*. According to Article III-376, the ECJ has no jurisdiction to rule on matters relating to Articles I-40, I-41 and III-293, which concern the formulation of strategy and objectives on external relations by the European Council. However, the exception applies that compliance control in regard to procedures and competences is enabled, in line with Articles I-13, I-15 and I-16. This means that, according to Articles III-376 and III-293, legal control is possible in regard to the procedural side of exercising competences (Article 308 TEC) and the legality of European decisions providing restrictive measures against natural or legal persons adopted by the Council on the basis of the Common Foreign and Security Policy. In practice, this distinction might turn out to be blurred. In certain other cases, the complexity is merely shifted from the different pillars into the individual provisions and procedures. Indeed, a number of provisions indicate that the drafters of the

Constitutional Treaty were not willing to go all the way as far as the integration of the pillars was concerned. The CFSP continues to have a distinct nature under the Constitutional Treaty.[159] One element concerns the categories of competence that exist in the CFSP area. Article I-12 describes the competences of the Union in different areas as exclusive, shared or supporting and supplementary. However, none of these competences relates to the CFSP, as Article I-12 includes a separate paragraph referring to a 'competence to define and implement a Common Foreign and Security Policy, including the progressive framing of a common defence policy.' As Cremona has already indicated, it is a little difficult to see what kind of competence this could be if it does not belong to one of the other categories.[160] However, the simple fact that once again a special status is introduced is striking.

Similar confusion results from the available instruments. Indeed, the CFSP is going to be developed on the basis of one type of instrument, the 'European decision', which is defined in Article I-32(1) as 'a non-legislative act, binding in its entirety'. However, the procedure for adopting European decisions in the area of the CFSP still differs from other areas of external relations and comes close to the current situation: a limited role for the Commission and the European Parliament and an important (even enhanced) role for the European Council and the Council of Ministers. The Court's jurisdiction continues to be excluded. In addition, despite the overall simplification of the instruments, the Treaty even seems to hold on to the former CFSP instruments, albeit disguised as European decisions. Thus, we can easily discover the common strategy ('European decisions on the strategic interests and objectives of the Union', Articles I-39 and III-194), the common position ('European decisions which shall define the approach of the Union to a particular matter of a geographical or thematic nature', Article III-199) and the joint action ('Where the international situation requires operational action by the Union, the Council of Ministers shall adopt the necessary European decisions', Article III-198(1)). The chances are high that, in practice, the current fragmentation of instruments will continue to exist.

Former Community and CFSP policies thus still occupy separate positions in the Constitutional Treaty. Title V of Part I contains a separate chapter (II), entitled 'Special Provisions', in which the institutional provisions and procedures in the area of the CFSP and the common defence and security policy are laid down. In addition, Article III-209 underlines the separation by providing that the implementation of the CFSP shall not affect the other competences of the Union, and vice versa. Finally, the fragmentation returns in the external representation of the Union. While it is a general task of the Commission to 'ensure the Union's external representation' (Article I-25), this role is excluded in the area of the

---

159 For an evaluation of the external relations under the Constitution, see in general M. Cremona, 'The Draft Constitutional Treaty: External Relations and External Action', 40 *CMLRev.* (2003) pp. 1347-1366.

160 Ibid., p. 1353.

CFSP, where the Union Minister for Foreign Affairs is to take the lead. One may argue that consistency is ensured by the 'double-hatting' construction (the Union Minister for Foreign Affairs is at the same time a member of the Commission). On the other hand, given the fact that the preparation of CFSP policies will continue to be distinct from other policies, there remains a potential for conflicting policies or even institutional conflicts of interests.[161] In addition, practice would have to reveal whether the Foreign Minister would be able to avoid schizophrenia while serving the Commission and the Council at the same time. However, the likelihood that the Constitutional Treaty as we know it today will ever enter into force has greatly decreased in the wake of the negative outcomes of the referenda in France and the Netherlands.[162]

5. CONCLUSION

The recent enlargement had an obvious impact on the external relations of the Union. It has even been considered the most successful tool of EU foreign policy. After all, many former neighbours now fall under the *internal* relations regime, which calls for a redefinition of both the Unions' relations with its immediate surroundings and its position on the international plane. In addition, the pre-accession strategy for these new members has been turned into a neighbourhood strategy for some of the European Union's new and old neighbours in order to promise the extension of policies and law (in the form of the internal market *acquis*) to these countries without completely integrating them.[163] The Union has simply become bigger and its external relations regime has further developed on the basis of both treaty modifications and case law. At the same time, in practice, it has had to cope with a fragmented external policy. To the traditional problems of vertical consistency and delimitation (often resulting in 'mixity'), the pillar structure had added the problem of horizontal consistency and delimitation. Practice shows that, although competences are generally strictly divided, both vertically and horizontally, issues cannot always be handled within the safe boundaries of one pillar. Ironically, the legal institutional dilemmas caused by this situation seem to have resulted in a strengthening of the unity of the Union's legal order, as practice forced the Union to shoot holes in the dividing walls between the pillars as agreed upon in Maastricht. This, in turn, seems to have paved the way towards an integration and consolidation of the external policy elements of the Community and the Union in the Constitutional Treaty.

---

161 For this argument, see E. Denza, 'Lines in the Sand: Between Common Foreign Policy and Single Foreign Policy', in Tridimas and Nebbia, op. cit. n. 135, p. 259 at p. 271.

162 See chapters 1 and 19 in this volume.

163 Former Commission President Romano Prodi described this as 'sharing everything but institutions'. This description might be misleading because, as the example of the EEA shows, new joint institutions can be created. On this issue, see also Cremona, loc. cit. n. 135, at p. 410.

More prominently than ever before, the enlargement of the European Union has raised the question of whether and to what extent the current Member States still have powers to formulate and implement an external policy of their own and engage in relations with their immediate neighbours. After all, the complex division of competences between the Union and its Member States in this field has been extended from fifteen to twenty-five states. The main principles governing the multilevel regime of external relations have been codified in the Constitutional Treaty. Thus, Articles I-12 and I-13 clarify the division of competences in the case of exclusive powers. At the same time – and perhaps contrary to popular belief – it remains clear that external relations are the responsibility of both the Union and the Member States.[164] This means that even the new European Neighbourhood Policy is to be approached from a multilevel perspective. Irrespective of the provision in Article I-57(2), which states that 'the *Union* may conclude specific agreements with the countries concerned' (emphasis added), Member State participation seems to remain needed in the areas not falling under the Union's exclusive competence. Under the Constitutional Treaty, however, Member State action in this field would be restricted to areas not covered by a legislative act of the Union or to cases in which it does not harm the Union's ability to exercise its internal competence (Article I-13(2)). With the further development of the external relations of the new Union, for example triggered by the coming of age of the internal market, the introduction of the Union Minister for Foreign Affairs and the establishment of a diplomatic External Action Service,[165] a redefinition of the position of the Member States in the Union could be foreseen. Whether the Union should be regarded as 'a constitutional order of sovereign states' or even 'a federation of sovereign states'[166] is left open by the Constitutional Treaty, but so far the development of the external relations regime has revealed its limits whenever the issue of exclusivity or the invocability of international agreements has been at stake. The Constitutional Treaty codifies

---

[164] Ironically, no 'mixed' agreements have been concluded by the current European Union. Treaty-making in the area of the CFSP and PJCC is 'exclusively' in the hands of the Union.

[165] Cf., Article III-328 TCE and the Declaration on the External Action Service adopted by the European Convention: 'To assist the future Union Minister for Foreign Affairs, introduced in Article I-27 of the Constitution, to perform his or her duties, the Convention agrees on the need for the Council of Ministers and the Commission to agree, without prejudice to the rights of the European Parliament, to establish under the Minister's authority one joint service (European External Action Service) composed of officials from relevant departments of the General Secretariat of the Council of Ministers and of the Commission and staff seconded from national diplomatic services.

The staff of the Union's delegations, as defined in Article III-230, shall be provided from this joint service.

The Convention is of the view that the necessary arrangements for the establishment of the joint service should be made within the first year after entry into force of the Treaty establishing a Constitution for Europe.'

[166] A. Dashwood, 'The Relationship between the Member States and the European Union/European Community', 41 *CMLRev.* (2004) pp. 355-381 at p. 356.

major principles of the bits and pieces of the external relations *acquis* and simplifies provisions. However, when we combine this with the continuation of the separation in the Constitutional Treaty of the economic and foreign policy areas in terms of procedures and competences, the external relations domain is bound to remain a complex legal regime, which even makes acquaintance difficult for our new neighbours.

CHAPTER 3

EU ENLARGEMENT: MEMBERSHIP CONDITIONS APPLIED TO FUTURE AND POTENTIAL MEMBER STATES

Kirstyn Inglis*

1. INTRODUCTION

Nowhere in the Treaties is enlargement set out as an end-goal of the European Union. The Constitutional Treaty,[1] providing it enters into force,[2] will not change this fact.[3] However, enlargement as a means of uniting the peoples of Europe must be seen as a core goal of the Union in order to further peace, prosperity, stability and security on the European continent. This chapter[4] explores current and future pre-accession conditionality as it applies to current and future candidates for accession and is not concerned with the historical evolution of that pre-accession conditionality.[5] The evolving nature of pre-accession conditionality reflects the particular nature and circumstances of both the incoming countries as well as the Union itself. Pre-accession conditionality, the enlargement or membership

* Senior Researcher, European Institute, University of Ghent, Belgium. This study was prepared under the auspices of the project 'Pre-accession and accession: a legal appraisal of the EU enlargement strategy', funded by the Flemish Scientific Research Fund (Fonds voor Wetenschappelijk Onderzoek).

[1] The full title of the Constitution is 'Treaty establishing a Constitution for Europe', which can be found in *OJ* 2004 C 310/1. It is referred to in the body of this contribution as the Constitution and in the footnotes in the abbreviated form of 'TCE' for ease of reference.

[2] Art. IV-447 TCE.

[3] For an overview of the scenarios in the wake of a ratification crisis, see B. de Witte, 'The Process of Ratification and the Crisis Options: A Legal Perspective', in D. Curtin, A.E. Kellermann and S. Blockmans, eds., *The EU Constitution: The Best Way Forward?* (The Hague, T.M.C. Asser Press 2005) pp. 21-38.

[4] The content of this chapter is taken from the PhD thesis being drafted by the author under the title 'European enlargement: an analysis of pre-accession and transitional arrangements with case studies on agri-food and environment law' (forthcoming).

[5] See F. Hoffmeister, 'Earlier enlargements' and 'Changing requirements for membership', in A. Ott and K. Inglis, eds., *Handbook on European Enlargement. A Commentary on the Enlargement Process* (The Hague, T.M.C. Asser Press 2002) pp. 87-102. See also K.E. Smith, 'The Evolution and Application of EU Membership Conditionality', in M. Cremona, ed., *The Enlargement of the European Union* (Oxford/New York, Oxford University Press 2003) pp. 105-139. See also C. Hillion, 'The Copenhagen Criteria and their Progeny', in C. Hillion, ed., *EU Enlargement: A Legal Approach. Essays in European law* (Oregon/Oxford, Hart Publishing 2004) pp. 1-22.

S. Blockmans and A. Łazowski (eds.), The European Union and Its Neighbours

conditionality (including Article 49 TEU, the Copenhagen criteria and the instruments of the pre-accession strategy) that applies during a country's preparations for membership of the Union, is a distinct category of the conditionality that the Union applies in its external relations with third countries.

This chapter takes a snapshot of pre-accession conditionality as it stands at present and considers the direction that it has taken from the starting point, mostly, of the fifth enlargement. While doing so it is important to bear in mind that enlargement has always been a core aim of the Union. The preamble to the ECSC Treaty, signed in Paris on 18 April 1951, had little to say about coal and steel but rather spoke of safeguarding peace, establishing an economic community and substituting for age-old rivalries and bloody conflicts the merging of essential interests.[6] The premise of the later EEC Treaty was that of an ever closer union of the peoples of Europe. Indeed, enlargement was already under consideration not even three years after the entry into force of the EEC Treaty on 1 January 1958, with talk of bringing in Britain, Denmark, Ireland, Norway and Switzerland. The United Kingdom first applied for membership on 31 July 1961, while Ireland applied the day before (30 July 1961) and Denmark on 10 August of the same year. The accession negotiations that followed were soon to fail for a variety of reasons, but primarily because of what can only be described effectively as a veto by President de Gaulle at a press conference in Rambouillet on 14 January 1963.[7] Early deliberations of the first Member States and the Union institutions in that context clearly show early elements of pre-accession conditionality. Moreover, the summit of 1 and 2 December 1969 in The Hague, commonly known for the launch of the European Political Co-operation, set out a triptych for action:[8] completion (to lay down a definitive financial arrangement for the Common Agricultural Policy (CAP)), deepening (or consolidation) and widening (or enlargement).

Enlargement conditionality includes conditions, incentives and disincentives that apply to aspiring Member States, but it also includes a conditionality that applies to the receiving Member States. The current membership conditionality applicable to any country eligible to accede to the European Union officially began in 1993 with the adoption by the June 1993 Copenhagen European Council of the 'Copenhagen criteria'. These were the criteria that applied to the fifth enlargement of the European Union, which took place on 1 May 2004.[9] The Copenhagen criteria read as follows:

---

[6] See W. Nicoll and T.C. Salmon, eds., *Understanding the European Communities* (Worcester, Philip Allan 1990) p. 7.

[7] Ibid., at pp. 23-24.

[8] See *Bull. EC* 2-1970.

[9] Treaty between the Kingdom of Belgium, the Kingdom of Denmark, the Federal Republic of Germany, the Hellenic Republic, the Kingdom of Spain, the French Republic, Ireland, the Italian Republic, the Grand Duchy of Luxembourg, the Kingdom of the Netherlands, the Republic of

> The associated countries in Central and Eastern Europe that so desire shall become members of the Union. Accession will take place as soon as a country is able to assume the obligations of membership by satisfying the economic and political conditions. Membership requires:
> - that the candidate country has achieved stability of institutions guaranteeing democracy, the rule of law, human rights and respect for and protection of minorities;
> - the existence of a functioning market economy, as well as the capacity to cope with competitive pressures and market forces within the Union;
> - the ability to take on the obligations of membership, including adhering to the aims of political, economic and monetary union;
> - the Union's capacity to absorb new Members, while maintaining the momentum of European integration, is also an important consideration in the general interest of both the Union and the candidate countries.[10]

This chapter is concerned with pre-accession conditionality, current and future, insofar as it applies to aspiring and candidate countries. Section 2, however, begins by looking at the pre-accession conditionality that applies to the receiving Member States – the fourth Copenhagen criterion – and predicts the ways in which this criterion will grow in significance as a precondition to membership as the Union enlarges, especially since the fifth enlargement on 1 May 2004. Section 3 explores pre-accession conditionality compared to other forms of conditionality generally, taking as a starting point Article 49 TEU on eligibility for membership, which contains the legal basis for enlargement of the Union. The implications of the Constitutional Treaty are explored, as is the content of the Copenhagen criteria in practice. Some comments are made on the borders of the Union and the possibility of further enlargements. Section 4 gives an overview of the instruments of the pre-accession strategy that carry the current pre-accession conditionality. It is broken up into three sub-sections outlining the instruments of the pre-accession strategy insofar as it relates to those candidates with which accession negotiations have been closed (Bulgaria and Romania), those candidates with which accession negotiations have been opened (Croatia and Turkey) and potential candidates (the countries of the Western Balkans).

Austria, the Portuguese Republic, the Republic of Finland, the Kingdom of Sweden, the United Kingdom of Great Britain and Northern Ireland (Member States of the European Union) and the Czech Republic, the Republic of Estonia, the Republic of Cyprus, the Republic of Latvia, the Republic of Lithuania, the Republic of Hungary, the Republic of Malta, the Republic of Poland, the Republic of Slovenia, the Slovak Republic, concerning the accession of the Czech Republic, the Republic of Estonia, the Republic of Cyprus, the Republic of Latvia, the Republic of Lithuania, the Republic of Hungary, the Republic of Malta, the Republic of Poland, the Republic of Slovenia and the Slovak Republic to the European Union, signed in Athens on 16 April 2003, *OJ* 2003 L 236/17, hereinafter 'the Accession Treaty'.

[10] *Bull. EU* 6-1993, point 13.

2. THE IMPERATIVE OF THE FOURTH COPENHAGEN CRITERION AS A PRECURSOR TO FUTURE ENLARGEMENTS?

The fourth Copenhagen criterion is not the subject of this paper as such, but a few comments thereon are relevant to this introduction. It is, after all, the Union that enlarges and the candidate that accedes. Each enlargement of the Union has emphasised the dilemma of the strain that widening puts on the deepening of integration efforts: how will the Union function in decision making and how can such a complex diversity of countries integrate further? So far, the Member States have not reverted to the fourth Copenhagen criterion in order to prevent an enlargement from going ahead as planned in political negotiations between the European Council and the candidates. When such a possibility has been tendered, it has been pushed aside by the Council, the Commission and the European Parliament, in particular, as an excuse and a disincentive that contradicts the political commitments and promises of the Union and which would ridicule the Union not only before the candidate that has worked so hard in good faith to meet its membership conditionality but also before the international community.[11] But in a Union of twenty-five Member States, will the fourth Copenhagen criterion concerning the Union's capacity to absorb more countries and the matter of maintaining the momentum of European integration continue to take a back seat in pre-accession conditionality compared to the three Copenhagen criteria that are addressed to those aspiring to membership?

It is useful, therefore, to keep in mind the fourth Copenhagen criterion because further enlargements will emphasise and accentuate the problems facing the Union in terms of its capacity to absorb new members and the continued evolution, implementation and enforcement of the *acquis communautaire*. Indeed, the strain on further deepening integration efforts was already prevalent in the Union prior to the fifth enlargement. This can be seen in the various measures and policy tools developed by the Union as a means of allowing integration to proceed in a flexible way so that some Member States have been able to remain outside core Union activities or so that a majority of willing or able Member States are able to deepen their integration efforts without the full participation of the remainder of the Member States.[12] It is also the case that the Member States have repeatedly pushed ahead with their widening ambitions in a committed and determined way

---

[11] See, for example, the European Parliament resolution of 14 March 1985 on the deadlock in accession negotiations with Spain. Negotiations nearly failed because of an intractable dispute among Member States concerning access of Spanish boats to EC waters. The European Parliament pointed out that the failure to agree was 'not enough to justify the failure of the negotiations and postponement of enlargement' and that, if this were the outcome, it 'might constitute a mortal blow to the Community's credibility as regards its ability to respect its commitments and negotiate effectively with third countries', *OJ* 1985 C 94/77.

[12] Notably in the cases of Schengen and EMU.

while holding back – for whatever reason[13] – from undertaking the necessary internal reforms, with all the sacrifices and compromises that those reforms require.

While the incoming ten Member States of the fifth enlargement have been more rigorously prepared for membership than any previous entrant, the sheer number of Member States that have to be accommodated within unfamiliar (if not inadequate) structures, as well as the multitude of complicating factors, including layers of transitional arrangements introduced with consecutive enlargements and the matter of working languages, demand a far greater effort for deepening integration efforts. Already, one of the new Member States – Malta – is struggling to keep up with the language demands of integration,[14] a structural problem that is particularly demanding for any small Member State. In the coming years, the Union has to transform itself further while consecutive Accession Treaties will enter into force.[15] Even at the time of the signature of the fifth Accession Treaty on 16 April 2004,[16] the Union itself was not fully ready. Two examples stand out. First, it is not clear as yet how the European Central Bank will continue to function once the new Member States of the fifth enlargement are ready to enter the Eurozone.[17] Second, the fifth Accession Treaty was signed before the full package of reform measures in respect of the CAP had been agreed,[18] raising certain important (negative) implications for the new Member States, which as a result they were not able to negotiate in the Accession Treaty.[19]

---

13 Of the more recent literature considering the future context of the Constitutional Treaty, see G.A. Bermann and G. de Búrca, 'The Legal Foundations of the Enlarged European Union', in G.A. Bermann and K. Pistor, *Law and Governance in an Enlarged European Union* (Portland, Oregon, Hart Publishing 2004) pp. 141-151. See also B. de Witte, 'The Impact of Enlargement on the Constitution of the European Union', in Cremona, op. cit. n. 5, at pp. 209-252.

14 See Council Regulation (EC) No. 930/2004, *OJ* 2004 L 169/1. It provides for a temporary derogation to the effect that only regulations adopted jointly by the Parliament and the Council have to be translated into Maltese. English is the second official language of Malta, but, according to the Maltese Constitution, should any conflict arise between the Maltese and English language versions, the Maltese language should prevail. See ECJ, Case C-361/01 P *Kik* v. *Office for Harmonization in the Internal Market (Trade Marks and Designs)* [2003] *ECR* I-8283, with annotation by N. Nic Shuihbne, 41 *CMLRev.* (2004) at pp. 1093-1111.

15 Apart from the ratification and entry into force of the Constitutional Treaty, Bulgaria and Romania have recently signed and ratified their Accession Treaty (see below) and other candidates (actual and potential) are holding promises of accession, which in turn will require revised decision-making procedures and structures.

16 *OJ* 2003 L 236/1.

17 See M. Lelart, 'The Eurozone and the Single Currency in an Enlarging Union', in N. Neuwahl, ed., *European Union Enlargement: Law and Socio-Economic Changes* (Montreal, Les Editions Thémis 2004) pp. 133-162. See also K. Inglis, 'The Union's Fifth Accession Treaty: New Means to Make Enlargement Possible', 41 *CMLRev.* (2004) at pp. 948-949.

18 See Commission Press Release 'Enlargement and agriculture: Commission tables amendments to take account of CAP reform', IP/03/1454 of 27 October 2003.

19 It was presented as a sort of *fait accompli* and as such incited an outcry in the incoming countries, notably in Poland, even before they acceded. See Inglis, loc. cit. n. 17, at p. 951.

So has enlargement become an imperative over the Union's capacity to absorb new members and over deepening? If this is the case, possible scenarios are seemingly unending. If indeed enlargement has become an imperative over deepening, looking to future enlargements, can this continue? Would further enlargements be self-defeating in that they would threaten to weaken the fabric of the Union to such an extent that it would threaten the very aims of peace, prosperity, stability and security on the European continent that it set out to achieve? Or is it that in order to continue to meet these aims in the context of the European continent, the Union must live with a looser integration? Will the political will be as present in the future among the new Member States in the absence of the incentive that integration provided pre-accession? Should the Union push ahead with flexibility mechanisms among willing Member States, with all the risks of introducing political conflicts or jealousies and further weakening the links between Member States? Or would the extreme alternative of reverting to a more shallow integration generally speaking be the only true alternative if the Union is to function in an harmonious way as it enlarges?

If enlargement cannot be seen as an imperative over the Union's capacity to absorb new members and the deepening of integration, then it will be no surprise to see the fourth Copenhagen criterion being used in future accession negotiations to slow down the pace of negotiations, maybe even to postpone a candidate's accession or to impose even longer and/or more complicated transitional arrangements and safeguard clauses to the benefit of the receiving Member States.

It is too early, perhaps, to predict whether the ratification process of the sixth Accession Treaty for Bulgaria and Romania, which was signed on 25 April 2005[20] and ratified by Bulgaria on 11 May 2005 and by Romania on 17 May 2005,[21] will be a mere technical exercise. Certainly, however, the functioning of the Union will experience considerable pressures to extents that so far have not been experienced in the European Union's institutional structures. Bulgaria and Romania are already 'in', to all intents and purposes, albeit in a limited capacity, given their participation in the institutions and decision making as observers in the European Parliament[22] and in the Council of Ministers and its preparatory

---

20 Treaty between the Kingdom of Belgium, the Czech Republic, the Kingdom of Denmark, the Federal Republic of Germany, the Republic of Estonia, the Hellenic Republic, the Kingdom of Spain, the French Republic, Ireland, the Italian Republic, the Republic of Cyprus, the Republic of Latvia, the Republic of Lithuania, the Grand Duchy of Luxembourg, the Republic of Hungary, the Republic of Malta, the Kingdom of the Netherlands, the Republic of Austria, the Republic of Poland, the Portuguese Republic, the Republic of Slovenia, the Slovak Republic, the Republic of Finland, the Kingdom of Sweden, the United Kingdom of Great Britain and Northern Ireland (Member States of the European Union) and the Republic of Bulgaria and Romania, concerning the accession of the Republic of Bulgaria and Romania to the European Union, *OJ* 2005 L 157/11.

21 See 'Bulgaria ratifies EU Accession treaty' and 'Romania ratifies EU entry', available at: <http://www.euractiv.com> (visited on 18 May 2005). See also chapters 7 and 8 in this volume.

22 Since 26 April 2005, Bulgaria and Romania have sent observers to the European Parliament: eighteen in the case of Bulgaria and thirty-five in the case of Romania. Such observers can speak but

bodies.[23] As already noted, Bulgaria and Romania will accede before the entry into force of the Constitutional Treaty. Therefore, their accession, rather than the Constitutional Treaty, will be the starting point of the international reform of the Union.

Whether the fourth Copenhagen criterion will take on new significance in pre-accession conditionality thereafter can be expected to depend on a number of factors. Significant among them will be how smoothly the Union functions in the next few years in terms of decision making to continue to develop the *acquis communautaire* and in terms of its implementation and enforcement. The new devices in the fifth Accession Treaty to continue pre-accession conditionality in the first years after the new Member States' accessions are evidence of the Union's preoccupation with ensuring its capacity to function as well as its ability to continue to deepen its integration efforts as it enlarges. Equally significant will be the matter of maintaining the political commitment to enlarge as well as the outcome of national referendums in the receiving Member States.

3. PRE-ACCESSION CONDITIONALITY AS A SOPHISTICATED FORM OF CONDITIONALITY

Pre-accession conditionality is very different from the conditionality that the Union has generally incorporated into its external relations with third countries. The conditionality of the Union in its relations with third countries has grown in intensity, and the ends sought by the Union have been supplemented and become increasingly specific, especially since the Treaty on European Union, which gave rise to 'the Union's self-appointed mission to propagate human rights and democracy'.[24] The Union sought to foster development and consolidation of democracy and the rule of law, as well as respect for human rights and fundamental freedoms,

cannot vote. However, see 'EP changes mind over Bulgarian and Romanian observers', available at: <http://www.euractiv.com> (visited on 13 May 2005): 'On 4 May, the European Parliament, led by the two biggest parties, the Socialists (PES) and the Christian Democrats (EPP), had set an earliest date of January 2006 for admission of observers. However, negotiations between the EP groups and Bulgarian and Romanian political parties continued, leading to PES leaders dropping objections to an earlier date. This led to a proposal from EP President Josep Borrell on 12 May that the observers should be welcomed from September or October 2005. The observers will attend Parliament sessions in preparation for the admission of the two countries to the European Union in January 2007. Leaders of all the EP groups agreed. The Parliament's change of mind came the day after the Bulgarian Parliament voted to ratify the country's treaty of accession to the EU.'

23 As of 26 April 2005. See Press Release of the Council of the European Union, Press 100, 8418/05, 25 April 2005. An information and consultation procedure allows the acceding states to be kept adequately informed of proposals, communications, recommendations or initiatives that might lead to decisions by the institutions or bodies of the European Union.

24 See E. Lannon, K. Inglis, T. Haenebalcke, 'The many faces of EU conditionality in Pan-Euro-Mediterranean Relations', in M. Maresceau and E. Lannon, eds., *The EU's Enlargement and Mediterranean Strategies: A Comparative Analysis* (New York, Palgrave 2001) pp. 97-138 at p. 97.

in its development co-operation policy and Common Foreign and Security Policy (CFSP). More recently, the Union has been concerned with terrorism and migration under the heading of Justice and Home Affairs in order to promote its soft-security concerns in third countries.

The conditionality that is prevalent in the Union's external relations with non-candidate countries includes, generally speaking, human rights and democracy, good neighbourliness, democratic institutions, the rule of law, market economy principles and the promotion of sustainable development.[25] The nature and content of conditionality very much depends on its legal basis in the specific bilateral relationship concerned, as well as the political and economic context. Thus, 'conditionality' as a concept is hard to describe in exhaustive and concrete terms. Membership conditionality, however, is easier to describe because of the range of official documents and legal, political and economic instruments that contain and develop it within the pre-accession strategy.

The main reason for such a different approach to third countries that are 'in pre-accession', or even potentially so, is their future status as a Member State. Accession involves becoming a member of the European Union and a party to the Treaties on which the Union is founded, as amended or supplemented.[26] Acceding to the Union is to accept, without reserve, the Treaty on European Union and all its objectives, all decisions taken since the entry into force of the Treaties establishing the European Communities and the Treaty on European Union and the choices made in respect of the development and strengthening of those Communities and of the Union.[27] This has always been the case.[28] Moreover, accession necessarily involves recognising that Community law takes precedence over any national provisions that might conflict with it, it requires that procedures exist for ensuring the uniform interpretation of Community law and, finally, it implies recognition of the binding nature of these rules, observance of which is indispensable to guarantee the effectiveness and unity of Community law.[29]

In the case of the countries of the Western Balkans, which were only recognised as potential candidates in 2000, the Copenhagen criteria could be seen from the outset in the Union's approach to the entire region.[30]

---

[25] Ibid., at pp. 117-132.

[26] This typically appears in Art. 1 of an Accession Treaty.

[27] In the case of the fifth enlargement, see Recital 9 of the Commission Opinion of 19 February 2003 on the applications for accession to the European Union by Czech Republic, the Republic of Estonia, the Republic of Cyprus, the Republic of Latvia, the Republic of Lithuania, the Republic of Hungary, the Republic of Malta, the Republic of Poland, the Republic of Slovenia and the Slovak Republic, *OJ* 2003 L 236/3.

[28] See, for example, Commission Opinion of 19 January 1972 on the applications for accession to the European Communities by the Kingdom of Denmark, Ireland, the Kingdom of Norway and the United Kingdom of Great Britain and Northern Ireland, *OJ* 1972 L 73/3.

[29] See Recital 10 of the Commission Opinion of 19 February 2003, loc. cit. n. 27.

[30] Notably with the Stability Pact for South-Eastern Europe. See Smith, loc. cit. n. 5, at pp. 136-137. See also chapter 10 in this volume.

3.1 Eligibility for EU membership, admissibility and procedure

Article 49 TEU establishes the conditions of eligibility to apply for EU membership, as well as the procedure for becoming a member of the Union. Before an Accession Treaty may be signed, the aspiring country makes a membership application to the Council, which takes a unanimous decision after having received the opinion of the Commission and the assent of the European Parliament, acting by an absolute majority of its component members (for each application for membership where there is more than one). Parliamentary assent is not normally necessary for treaty revision.[31] These documents introduce the Accession Treaty (which incorporates the Act of Accession) and are also expressly referred to in its preamble. While no specific reference to the participation of the Community institutions is made – notably the European Commission – their participation is not excluded.[32] As for the conditions of admission and adjustments to the Treaties which might be required in the first years after a new member's accession, the second paragraph of Article 49 TEU leaves this to 'an agreement between the Member States and the applicant State' and provides that such 'agreement be submitted for ratification by all the contracting States in accordance with their respective constitutional requirements.'

None of the receiving Member States in any enlargement have rejected an Accession Treaty after its signature, and no national referendum has been used in the receiving Member States in any of the first five enlargements, whether before or after signature of an Accession Treaty. Of course, they have ratified the Accession Treaties in accordance with their own national constitutional requirements, which do not necessarily involve a referendum. As for future enlargements, however, discussion of the possibility of reverting to the use of a national referendum in one or more of the receiving twenty-five Member States is increasing in the popular press. Thus, for example, President Chirac has announced that France will hold a referendum on the accession of Turkey,[33] despite the fact that it did not hold a referendum on previous Accession Treaties, including the fifth, and that this would require the introduction of amendments to the French Constitution in order to do so. Moreover, as concerns future enlargements, it is also true that the new CEE Member States have more of a tradition of using referendums, and in some cases the 'souverainist' character of their constitutions requires a referendum in respect of any treaty amendment that is of primary relevance to their national constitutional procedures.[34] An Accession Treaty involves provisions of a

31 Art. 48 TEU.

32 See P.J.G. Kapteyn and P. VerLoren van Themaat, *Introduction to the Law of the European Communities*, 3rd edn. (Dordrecht, Kluwer Law International 1998) pp. 93-94.

33 See 'Chirac considering referendums on future EU enlargements', available at: <http://www.euobserver.com/?aid=17408> (visited on 4 October 2004).

34 See A. Albi, 'Referendums in Eastern Europe', RSC Working Paper No. 65 (Florence, European University Institute 2002).

fundamentally constitutional nature. In the case of the fifth enlargement, only one of the ten acceding countries – Malta – held a national referendum that was consultative rather than required by its Constitution, and every referendum was affirmative. For the rest of these countries, the result was positive and in some cases overwhelmingly so.

With regard to future enlargements, however, it remains to be seen whether the receiving Member States will revert to national referendums as a precondition to the ratification of an Accession Treaty, not only among the CEE Member States but potentially also among the fifteen 'old' Member States. The fact that Denmark, France, Ireland, Luxembourg, the Netherlands, Portugal, Spain and the United Kingdom – in addition to the new Member States of Poland and the Czech Republic – have held or will hold a referendum on the Constitutional Treaty indicates the political concerns of these countries (except Ireland, where every ratification of a new treaty has to be subjected to a referendum according to an explicit clause to this effect in the Irish Constitution). The political reasons for holding a referendum include, for example:[35] making a genuine commitment to the Constitutional Treaty and renewing the expression of its legitimacy; resolving splits between a national parliament and its electorate; acting as arbiter between national political parties of opposing view; and resolving divisions between anti- and pro-integrationist groups within one and the same political party.

In terms of eligibility to make an application for membership, Article 49 TEU specifies that '[a]ny European State which respects the principles set out in Article 6(1) may apply to become a member of the Union'. In this regard, 'European' remains undefined – neither the Commission nor Council have fixed the geographical boundaries of the Union.[36] For example, in the case of the countries of the European Economic Area (EEA) or Switzerland, as a member of the European Free Trade Area (EFTA), their 'Europeanness' was not questioned. In fact, it was these countries that chose not to participate for their own reasons.[37] The Union has never withdrawn its extended hand to these countries, and if they are able to overcome their own internal wranglings there is no reason to prevent them from acceding. So the debate as to the geographical, historical and cultural elements that constitute 'European' continues. The fact that the Association Agreements signed with the CEECs were called 'Europe Agreements' was certainly a

[35] See C. Closa, 'Ratifying the EU Constitution: referendums and their implications', US-Europe Analysis Series (November 2004) pp. 1-10, available at: <http://www.brookings.edu>.

[36] See Commission Communication, 'Europe and the Challenge of Enlargement', *Bull. EU*, Suppl. 3-1992, at p. 11. See M. Maresceau, 'Association, partnership, pre-accession and accession', in Maresceau, ed., *Enlarging the European Union. Relations between the EU and Central and Eastern Europe* (London/New York, Longman 1997) pp. 3-22 at p. 13. See also chapter 1 in this volume.

[37] For example, where national referendums resulted in a rejection of accession (Norway and Switzerland). In the case of Liechtenstein, it was so closely bound up with the Switzerland that it had no choice but to follow Switzerland's lead. See also chapter 5 in this volume.

recognition by the Union of their 'Europeanness'. Although eastward enlargement was not the Union's expressed intention[38] at the time of the first Europe Agreements, these Association Agreements did differ from ordinary or qualified trade agreements such as the Partnership and Co-operation Agreements concluded with Russia, Ukraine, Belarus and Moldova.[39]

It seems of little use to explore the meaning of 'European' in abstract terms in the context of today's pre-accession strategy. In concrete terms, included among the actual and potential candidates for accession to the Union are countries that do not fall wholly within the European continent (e.g., Turkey) and countries for which the very prospect of accession to the Union had not been contemplated in the early 1990s (e.g., Albania[40]). Turkey's inclusion in the pre-accession strategy is now a fact, while Morocco was expressly excluded on the basis of the geographical criterion alone.[41] In addition, in concrete terms, changes in the geopolitical situation have been accompanied by the inclusion of the Western Balkans as eligible,[42] and they are now even officially recognised as 'potential candidates' for accession to the Union, including Albania.[43] The Commission refers to the Western Balkans as having a 'European vocation',[44] and states clearly

---

[38] See M. Maresceau and I. Montaguti, 'The Relations between the European Union and Central and Eastern Europe: A Legal Appraisal', 32 *CMLRev.* (1995) at p. 1328.

[39] See P.C. Müller-Graff, 'Legal Framework for Relations between the European Union and Central and Eastern Europe: General Aspects', in Maresceau, op. cit. n. 36, at pp. 27-40.

[40] The June 2000 Feira European Council stated that all the SAP countries are 'potential candidates' for EU membership and the Thessaloniki Summit of June 2003 reconfirmed this prospect. Albania signed a trade and co-operation agreement with the Union in 1992 (see *OJ* 1992 L 343/1), but in 1996 the Union's approach still focused more on fostering a regional approach in its co-operation with and amongst the Balkans countries, namely Bosnia-Herzegovina, Croatia, the Federal Republic of Yugoslavia (prior to the launch of the regional approach the Union had no contractual links with these three countries), Albania and Macedonia. See two reports from the Commission to the Council and Parliament, the first on 'Prospects for the development of regional co-operation for the countries of the former Yugoslavia and what the Community could do to foster such co-operation', SEC (1996) 0252, and the second on 'Common principles for future contractual relations with certain countries in South-Eastern Europe', *Bull. EU* 1/2-1996, point 1.4.108. See also European Parliament Resolution A4-0127/97 on said reports, *OJ* 1997 C 167/143.

[41] Morocco's application was made in 1987. See also chapter 12 in this volume.

[42] See Maresceau, loc. cit. n. 36, at pp. 4-5. Indeed, in the later 1980s and early 1990s, Yugoslavia was 'usually regarded as an impossible applicant', see Nicoll and Salmon, op. cit. n. 6, at p. 36.

[43] Namely, Serbia and Montenegro (including Kosovo), the Former Yugoslav Republic of Macedonia, Bosnia-Herzegovina and Albania. See section 3.1 above in this chapter and footnote 39 in particular which refer to and cite the Presidency Conclusions of the June 2000 Feira European Council and of the December 2002 Copenhagen European Council, the March 2003 Brussels European Council and the June 2003 Thessaloniki European Council. Conclusion 40 of the Presidency Conclusions of the June 2003 Thessaloniki European Council reads: The European Council, recalling its conclusions in Copenhagen (December 2002) and Brussels (March 2003), reiterated its 'determination to fully and effectively support the European perspective of the Western Balkan countries, which will become an integral part of the EU, once they meet the established criteria'. See also chapter 10 in this volume.

[44] See M. Cremona, 'Enlargement: A Successful Instrument of Foreign Policy?', in T. Trimidas and P. Nebbia, eds., *European Union Law for the Twenty-First Century* (Oxford, Hart Publishing 2004)

that the June 2000 European Council's objective of enlargement to the south-east 'is a promise which the EU will honour when each country fulfils the criteria'. This seems logical from a geographical viewpoint alone: once Romania and Bulgaria join the Union, these Balkan countries will be entirely surrounded by EU Member States.

With the certainty of future enlargements, the debate on the geographical limits of the Union seems of minor relevance and would seem to have been sidelined by the political goal of enlargement. The geographical criterion would seem superfluous in the context of future (potential) applications from Ukraine and Moldova, as both of these countries are situated wholly on the continent of Europe. As concerns Ukraine, in particular, it is the political and economic factors that militate against the tentative approaches made by Ukraine concerning a possible application.[45] Following the dramatic re-run of the presidential elections in Ukraine in December 2004, the matter of whether Ukraine might join the Union has come to prominence and outright exclusion of Ukraine has been carefully avoided by the European Commissioner in charge of the enlargement dossier.[46]

Article 6(1) TEU requires that any aspiring Member State respect the principles upon which the Union 'is founded' and 'which are common to the Member States', namely, 'the principles of liberty, democracy, respect for human rights and fundamental freedoms and the rule of law.' But the reference to Article 6(1) TEU must be seen as no more than a codification of an unwritten constitutional principle common to all Member States.[47] The full range of principles and rights that make up the fabric of the Union are included in and even reach out to the terminology used in the European Convention on Human Rights and its Protocols, for example, or to the 1990 OSCE Copenhagen Declaration concerning minorities.

Under the Constitutional Treaty, in Title IX on Union membership, Article I-58(1) and (2) establishes 'conditions of eligibility and procedure for accession to the Union', which promise to introduce a few changes both in terms of the relevant conditions but also in terms of the procedure. The European Parliament and the Member States' national parliaments will be 'notified' of any application for membership and the European Parliament will only require a majority, as opposed to an absolute majority, of its MEPs voting in plenary in order to give its

pp. 396-413 at pp. 403-407. See also Report from the Commission, The Stabilisation and Association Process for South East Europe: Third Annual Report, COM (2004) 202, 30 March 2004, s. 1.1.

45 See Joost Lagendijk MEP and Marinus Wiersma MEP, 'The ultimate borders of the European Union', available at: <http://www.euobserver.com> (visited on 17 December 2001).

46 See, for example, the words of the Enlargement Commission: 'We should never say never. But first it is better to offer Ukraine economic and political support', speaking to Radio Free Europe/Radio Liberty on 10 December 2004, on the topic 'EU discusses Romania, Turkey, Ukraine', available at: <http://www.isn.ethz.ch/news/sw/details.cfm?id=10340>. See also chapter 16 in this volume.

47 See Hoffmeister, loc. cit. n. 5, at pp. 93-96.

assent to an application. As concerns conditions, Article I-58(1) will, by reference to Article I-2, add to the list of explicit values (which are no longer referred to as principles) upon which the Union is founded. However, it will also require that the newcomer be 'committed to promoting [these values] together'. The wording of the draft gives a more inclusive vision of the Union based on common values: 'The Union shall be open to *all* European States which respect the values … and are committed to promoting them together' [emphasis added]. Moreover, the fact that Article I-58(1) uses precisely the same wording as the very first article of the Constitutional Treaty emphasises this point. According to Article I-2, the list of values upon which the Union is founded includes

> respect for human dignity, liberty, democracy, equality, the rule of law and respect for human rights, including the rights of persons belonging to minorities. These values are common to the Member States in a society of pluralism, non-discrimination, tolerance, justice, solidarity and equality between men and women prevail.

The prospect of the entry into force of the Constitutional Treaty required a new formula for the structure and format for the incorporation of future Accession Treaties into the Constitutional Treaty once its enters into force. However, while there will be procedural changes and national referendums on the Constitutional Treaty, and even on future enlargements, the Constitutional Treaty will not change the eligibility test of any country aspiring to membership of the European Union.

3.2 The Copenhagen criteria as applied to actual or potential candidates and the pre-accession strategy

The Copenhagen criteria refer specifically to the countries of Central and Eastern Europe but today the Copenhagen criteria are the catch-all phrase for the pre-accession conditionality that applies to any country aspiring to membership of the Union. While the Copenhagen criteria are set out in four brief sentences, their content is vast, all-embracing[48] and even vague.[49] An impression of the enormity of the task of meeting the Copenhagen criteria emerges from the legal, financial and policy instruments of the pre-accession strategy dealt with in the next section.

While the core threads of the Copenhagen criteria can be traced back through the first four enlargements of the Union, the membership conditionality that has evolved since the end of the Cold War has had to be dynamic in order to cope effectively with the diversity of the incoming Member States among themselves

48 See Hoffmeister, loc. cit. n. 5.
49 See Smith, loc. cit. n. 5, at pp. 137-138.

as well as compared to the receiving Member States. The incentive of accession has driven vast and wholesale reforms in countries aspiring to membership, while other forms of conditionality incentives or conditions, combined with dialogue and interaction, are more effective in specific circumstances or to bring about specific goals.[50] Moreover, it is always understood that an acceding country adheres to the aims of the Union when it accedes.

The evolution of the current membership conditionality must be understood as an extension and a working-out of the pre-accession strategy that has grown up since the June 1993 Copenhagen European Council. The European Commission briefly presents the three sets of Copenhagen membership conditions in its opinion on the applications of the ten new Member States, which introduces the fifth Accession Treaty.[51]

The Commission's brief description can be supplemented by the so-called Essen and Madrid conditions. The criteria of good neighbourliness, formally established by the December 1994 Essen European Council, had an effect on CEE relations under the Europe Agreements and in the pre-accession strategy.[52] In the context of the Stabilisation and Association Process (SAP), regional conditionality takes on a whole new dimension and the EU's regional approach. This regional approach to conditionality is one of the very first building blocks even for meeting the Copenhagen criteria and opening negotiations for bilateral contractual relations as a basis for developing an association between the European Union and each country in turn. The December 1995 Madrid European Council requirement could be implied by reference to the Copenhagen criteria that applicants should have the 'ability to take on the obligations of membership, including adhering to the aims of political, economic and monetary union'. The conclusions stated simply that the applicants should 'adjust their administrative structures'. This requirement was made in the context of the broader reform and modernisation of public administrations that had to be undertaken in the transition economies as they emerged from the entirely different political, judicial and administrative structures of their Communist past.[53]

Compliance with the Copenhagen criteria is not only a precondition to membership. While a candidate's efforts to meet the Copenhagen criteria to the very letter typically continue throughout the accession negotiations up until the very moment of accession,[54] certain of the Copenhagen criteria must be complied with

---

50 Ibid., at p. 136.

51 At recital 3, op. cit. n. 9, at p. 3.

52 *Bull. EU* 12-1994. See Maresceau, 'Pre-accession', in Cremona, op. cit. n. 5, at p. 18. See also Smith, loc. cit. n. 5, at pp. 121-130.

53 *Bull. EU* 12-1995.

54 And even after accession, transitional arrangements in an Accession Treaty allow for limited temporary and exceptional situations in which a new Member State has time to fully comply with certain laws.

before accession negotiations can begin. At the time of its decision to endorse *Agenda 2000* and open the first round of accession negotiations with the CEECs in December 1997, the Luxembourg European Council stated categorically that

> Compliance with the Copenhagen political criteria is a prerequisite for the opening of any accession negotiations. Economic criteria and the ability to fulfil the obligations arising from membership have been and must be assessed in a forward-looking, dynamic way.[55]

3.2.1 *Preconditions for the opening of accession negotiations*

If one looks at the Commission's 1997 opinions on the ten CEE applicants as well as Malta and Cyprus, attached to the European Commission's *Agenda 2000* document,[56] the decisive factors in the Commission's recommendation to open accession negotiations were as follows. A candidate may not open accession negotiations:

- in the absence of having free and fair elections;
- without the opposition party playing a normal part in the operation of the institutions;
- without having stable institutions to enable public authorities to function properly and democracy to be consolidated and to guarantee the rule of law and human rights.[57]

Establishing conditions and attaching incentives guides the behaviour of the candidate and is in line with the inclusive nature of the Union's approach to candidate countries – all candidates are treated on an equal footing. At the same time, membership conditionality has had to be dynamic in order to differentiate between the states of readiness and the particular situations and problems or needs of the candidates. The matrix of political, legal and economic tools outlined in the next section, which were devised to prescribe pre-accession conditionality, reflect this inclusive-yet-differentiating approach to the region. The systematic approach adopted was designed to prevent the impression of any arbitrary discrimination between candidates in preparation for the negotiations or during the negotiations. Any perceived arbitrary discrimination would threaten the effectiveness of pre-accession conditionality in that it could heighten political jealousies between future members and destabilise relations between them and with the Member States.

---

[55] See Presidency Conclusions, *Bull. EU* 11-1997, at Conclusion 24.

[56] Commission Communication, *Agenda 2000: For a Stronger and Wider Union*, COM (1997) 2000 final, 15 July 1997.

[57] Slovakia failed to meet this political criterion. See *Agenda 2000*, loc. cit. n. 56, Part 2 at p. 45.

To begin accession negotiations does not require complete fulfilment of the entire breadth of the Copenhagen political criteria. For the purposes of carrying on accession negotiations, Bulgaria and Romania continued to fulfil the Copenhagen political criteria,[58] but it is also the case that they were still pushing on with reforming the judiciary, the fight against organised crime and anti-corruption efforts, while discrimination against the Roma persists. Each country has its own specific problems.[59] The Copenhagen political criteria include respect for and protection of minorities, but shortcomings in this regard were not considered an impediment to the opening of accession negotiations[60] with the twelve countries of the fifth and sixth enlargement waves.

3.2.2 *The Copenhagen political criteria*

3.2.2.1 Turkey and the political criteria[61]

Staying with the theme of actual candidates for the moment, Turkey was refused accession negotiations alongside the CEECs, Malta and Cyprus because of anomalies in the functioning of public authorities, persistent human rights violations and major shortcomings in the treatment of minorities.[62] The lack of civilian control over the army was also a cause for concern. The means of taking relations with Turkey forward were dealt with separately in order to take the relationship beyond the customs union in the light of the decision of the April 1997 Association Council.[63] In 1998, the Commission insisted that Turkey make a constructive contribution to the settlement of all disputes with its neighbouring countries by peaceful means in accordance with international law. The issue of good neighbourly relations is dealt with below.

---

58 Commission Communication, Strategy Paper of the European Commission on progress in the enlargement process, COM(2004) 657, 6 October 2004, at p. 3.

59 Bulgaria must address libel and defamation by journalists, the trafficking of human beings and prison conditions, the placement of mentally disabled people and inadequacies in child welfare. Romania must improve policy making, the management of court cases and judicial judgments and introduce standards for child protection services, as well as trafficking in human beings and prison overcrowding.

60 Hoffmeister, loc. cit. n. 5, refers to the minimum standard of Art. 27 of the International Covenant on Civil and Political Rights (1996) and the fact that Arts. 31 and 32 of the OSCE Copenhagen Declaration of 1990 specifies the sort of rights that a minority should enjoy in a candidate country. Since OSCE states that wanted to conclude a partnership agreement with the European Community had to accept these provisions as binding, that same standard must apply *a fortiori* for all candidate countries. Hoffmeister also refers to the Council of Europe Framework Convention for the Protection of National Minorities of 1995.

61 See also chapter 9 in this volume.

62 See *Agenda 2000*, loc. cit. n. 56, Part 2 at pp. 67-68.

63 See COM (1997) 394, 15 July 1997, *Bull. EC* 6-1993, point I.12.

There is now a distinction between Turkey and the other candidates as concerns political reforms. This is due to the different circumstances of Turkey. The political conditionality imposed on Turkey since December 2004 has become increasingly specific in terms of the actions that Turkey has to take. In its annual report on Turkey's progress towards accession of 6 October 2004, the Commission dedicated thirty-five pages to its evaluation of the political criteria and Turkey's track record in meeting the political criteria since the 1999 Helsinki summit, where Turkey was nominated as a candidate but was refused accession negotiations.[64] The Commission recommended starting negotiations with Turkey. It considered that Turkey had sufficiently fulfilled the political criteria by achieving significant progress in its political reform process, which included far-reaching constitutional and legislative changes, although certain essential laws still had to enter into force.[65] There has been talk of a projected date of entry of 2017 or later.[66]

The Commission also pointed out that the proper implementation of the reforms would require 'strong efforts'. The Commission's and the Member States' concern is to ensure that these reforms are sustainable and that they are not reversed during the negotiations or after the eventual accession of Turkey. The Commission has stated that, during the course of the pre-accession process after the negotiations have started, it will make use of the tools available to it to recommend the suspension of the negotiations in the case of a serious and persistent breach of the principles of liberty, democracy, respect for human rights and fundamental freedoms and the rule of law. The decisive December 2004 European Council spoke of a draft safeguard measure – perhaps even a permanent provision – to this effect concerning the movement of Turkish workers and access to regional policy funds, which would be adopted in the Council by qualified majority.[67] However, there are already certain clauses within the legal instruments of the pre-accession strategy that might also provide an additional means of keeping up the pressure on Turkey during the negotiations. Under Article 4 of Regulation 390/2001,[68] the Council has a legal basis for suspending assistance. It reads:

---

64 See *Bull. EU* 12-1999, points I.2. to 1.27.

65 Law on Associations, the new Penal Code and the Law on Intermediate Courts of Appeal. Other measures that still have to be adopted: Code on Criminal Procedure, legislation establishing the judicial police and the law on the enforcement of punishments and measures. See Commission, Commission recommends to start negotiations with Turkey under certain conditions, Press Release IP/04/1180, 6 October 2004.

66 In an interview with President Jacques Chirac of France for the TF1 news on Wednesday 15 December 2004 conducted by Patrick Poivre d'Arvor, President Chirac emphasised that the work to be undertaken by Turkey would take 'certainly no less than ten or fifteen years'.

67 See 'Turkey Could face permanent safeguard clause', available at: <http://www.euractiv.com> (visited on 30 November 2004).

68 *OJ* 2001 L 58/1.

> Where an element that is essential for continuing to grant pre-accession assistance is lacking, in particular when the commitments contained in the EC-Turkey Agreements are not respected and/or progress towards fulfilment of the Copenhagen criteria is insufficient, the Council, acting by a qualified majority on a proposal from the Commission, may take appropriate steps with regard to pre-accession assistance granted to Turkey.

The Commission's insistence on Turkey's contribution to the settlement of all disputes with its neighbouring countries is an example of the good neighbourly relations requirement first established by the 1994 Essen European Council and later reiterated in Helsinki in 1999. Turkey has been keen to emphasise its pursuit of a peaceful foreign policy. In its national plan for the adoption of the *acquis* (see below), it was keen to emphasise in the very first introductory paragraphs the significance of the principle of a peaceful foreign policy and how it intends to continue developing its relations with neighbouring countries on the basis of a peace-seeking foreign policy and to undertake initiatives and efforts towards settlement of its problems with Greece through bilateral dialogue.[69] In addition, the December 2004 Brussels European Council asked Turkey to sign the Protocol enlarging the customs union with Turkey to the new Member States; whether this implies recognition of Cyprus is highly debatable.[70]

3.2.2.2 The Western Balkans and the Copenhagen political criteria[71]

The 'pre-pre-accession strategy' that has been devised with a view to preparing for the accession of the Western Balkan countries has once again added a new dimension of differentiation to membership conditionality. The Union's regional approach to pre-accession conditionality is exceptional and specific to the region. A kind of 'pre-pre-accession' conditionality has emerged. The Union insists that the countries in the Stabilisation and Association Process (SAP) make 'credible headway' in complying with the general political criteria in order to conclude bilateral contractual relations with the Union in the form of a Stabilisation and Association Agreement (SAA).[72] A checklist of the elements that the Commission

---

69 See A. Sözen, 'Turkey – EU Enlargement at a Crossroads: Turkey's Democratisation in Light of its EU Candidate Status', in K. Inglis and A. Ott, *The Constitution for Europe and Enlargement of the European Union* (Groningen, European Law Publishers 2005) pp. 281-304.

70 After all, it is not clear how Turkey can secure resolution of the Cyprus issue. See 'Turkey accession and Cyprus', 18 April 2005, available at: <http://www.euractiv.com>.

71 See also chapter 10 in this volume.

72 Take the example of Croatia. It opened negotiations for an SAA with the European Union following the positive opinion of the Commission on its application of 24 May 2000 (See Report of the Commission on the feasibility of negotiating a Stabilisation and Association Agreement with the Republic of Croatia, COM (2000) 311, 24 May 2000). The Commission was satisfied in particular with the parliamentary and presidential elections. Rather than this being a rigid precondition to

takes into account when examining the level of compliance of SAP countries with the general political criteria was drafted by the April 1997 General Affairs Council.[73] It includes the following elements for the examination of compliance with:

Democratic principles:

- Representative government, accountable executive;
- Government and public authorities to act in a manner consistent with the constitution and the law;
- Separation of powers (government, administration, judiciary);
- Free and fair elections at reasonable intervals by secret ballot.

Human rights, rule of law:

- Freedom of expression, including independent media;
- Right of assembly and demonstration;
- Right of association;
- Right to privacy, family, home and correspondence;
- Right to property;
- Effective means of redress against administrative decisions;
- Access to courts and right to fair trial;
- Equality before the law and equal protection by the law;
- Freedom from inhuman or degrading treatment and arbitrary arrest.

Respect for and protection of minorities:

- Right to establish and maintain their own educational, cultural and religious institutions, organisations or associations;
- Adequate opportunities for these minorities to use their own language before courts and public authorities;
- Adequate protection of refugees and displaced persons returning to areas where they represent an ethnic minority.

---

opening negotiations on the SAA, the Commission was moved to its favourable opinion because of 'the encouraging steps undertaken by Croatia to fulfil the EU conditionality', and it was convinced Croatia 'has the capacity ultimately to fulfil the obligations of an SAA.' The benchmarks are the same as those identified in the Commission's positive opinion for opening accession negotiations with nine of the candidates of the fifth enlargement in its *Agenda 2000* country opinions. Following its signature and conclusion, the SAA Croatia entered into force on 1 February 2005. See Stabilisation and Association Agreement between the European Communities and their Member States , of the one part, and the Republic of Croatia, of the other part, *OJ* 2005 L 26/3.

[73] Council Conclusions of 29 April 1997 on the application of conditionality with a view to developing a coherent EU strategy for its relations with the countries in the region, *Bull. EU* 4-1997, point 1.4.67.

Market economy reform:

- Macroeconomic institutions and policies necessary to ensure a stable economic environment;
- Comprehensive liberalisation of prices, trade and current payments;
- Setting-up of a transparent and stable legal and regulatory framework;
- Demonopolisation and privatisation of State-owned or socially-owned enterprises;
- Establishment of a competitive and prudently managed banking sector.

The opening of accession negotiations is a matter for subsequent discussion. A lower level of compliance is insisted on for the start of negotiations on an SAA than for the conclusion of an SAA. This approach paves the way for reaching a higher level of compliance with the Copenhagen criteria and thus also paves the way for opening proper accession negotiations. The conclusion of an SAA in turn becomes an incentive for compliance with the Union's pre-accession conditionality and is the bilateral legal instrument of the pre-accession strategy for each country of the Western Balkans. The conditionality attaching to the conclusion of an SAA gives further legal shape to pre-accession conditionality.

As was seen recently in the case of Croatia, accession negotiations are not contemplated if a country cannot, for example, guarantee the rule of law. In Croatia's case, the fact that it was unable to deliver an indicted war criminal to the International Criminal Tribunal for the former Yugoslavia (ICTY) proved fatal for its anticipated date for beginning actual accession negotiations on 17 March 2005.[74]

The political conditionality attaching to good neighbourly relations and good neighbourliness takes on new significance in the regional conditionality applied to the Western Balkans. Good neighbourly relations have been established as a general principle in terms of ten universally recognised principles deriving from the UN Charter, the Helsinki Final Act and the Paris Charter for a New Europe.[75] Good neighbourliness can be said to encompass good neighbourly relations and the appropriate means of developing friendly relations – of mutual respect, of trust and confidence and of security and peace – among states. While regional cooperation and good neighbourliness was fostered by the Union during the pre-accession process of the CEECs, there was less demand for regional conditionality in comparison to that seen in the context of the SAP.

[74] See chapter 10 in this volume.

[75] Sovereign equality, respect for rights inherent in sovereignty, refraining from the threat or use of force, inviolability of frontiers, territorial integrity of states, peaceful settlement of disputes, non-interference in internal affairs, respect for human rights and fundamental freedoms, including freedom of thought, conscience, religion or belief, equal rights and self-determination of peoples, co-operation among states, fulfilment in good faith of obligations under international law.

Good neighbourly relations/good neighbourliness conditionality must be seen alongside the Copenhagen-plus criteria for pre-accession insofar as the countries of the Balkans are concerned. The general political criteria of the Copenhagen criteria specify democratic principles, human rights and the rule of law, respect for and protection of minorities and market economy reforms. The Union sets out these conditions 'broken down into operation, verifiable elements' in the Annex to the 1997 Council Conclusions (as listed above).

Certain additional and generally applicable political conditions are also specified for the region. In addition to the right to return for refugees and displaced persons and the readmission of any of their nationals that are illegally present in the Union, the general conditions in the regional approach require the implementation of the Dayton Peace Agreements and 'proven readiness to enter into good neighbourly and co-operative relations with … neighbours'.[76] In addition to the foregoing general conditions, each country must meet its own specific conditions, and these reflect the Union's concern to improve and secure better relations in the region.[77]

---

[76] See 35 *ILM* (1996) 75. These general conditions include: '1. Credible offer to and a visible implementation of real opportunities for displaced persons (including so called 'internal migrants') and refugees to return to their places of origin, and absence of harassment initiated or tolerated by public authorities; 2. Readmission of nationals of the States concerned who are present illegally in the territory of a Member State of the EU; 3. Compliance of the countries which are signatories of the GFAP with the obligations under the peace agreements, including those related to co-operation with the International Tribunal in bringing war criminals to justice; 4. A credible commitment to engage in democratic reforms and to comply with the generally recognised standards of human and minority rights; 5. Holding of free and fair elections at reasonable intervals on the basis of universal and equal suffrage of adult citizens by secret ballot, and full and proper implementation of the results of these elections; 6. Absence of generally discriminatory treatment and harassment of minorities by public authorities; 7. Absence of discriminatory treatment and harassment of independent media; 8. Implementation of first steps of economic reform (privatisation programme, abolition of certain price controls); 9. Proven readiness to enter into good neighbourly and co-operative relations with its neighbours; 10. Compatibility of RS/FRY as well as the Federation/Croatia agreements with the Dayton Peace Agreements.' See Council Conclusions of 29 April 1997, loc. cit. n. 73.

[77] See Council Conclusions of 29 April 1997, loc. cit. n. 73. Croatia: '1. Compliance with the obligations under the Basic Agreement on eastern Slavonia and co-operation with Untaes and OSCE; 2. Opening of the customs border between Croatia and Republika Srpska; 3. Evidence of credible pressure on the Bosnian Croats to dissolve Herceg-Bosna structures and to co-operate in the establishment and functioning of the Federation, as well as evidence of the implementation of a truly unified City Council in Mostar and of effective functioning of the Unified Police Force of Mostar (UPFM). Evidence that the Government of Croatia is using its influence in bringing Bosnian Croat war criminals to justice before the International Tribunal.' Bosnia and Herzegovina: '1. Establishment of functioning institutions as provided for in the constitution, and formulation of a foreign trade and customs policy for Bosnia and Herzegovina; 2. Beginning of a credible process towards free movement of persons, goods and capital within Bosnia and Herzegovina; 3. Co-operation with the High Representative including on Brcko; 4. Evidence of the implementation of a truly unified City Council in Mostar and of effective functioning of the UPFM, and co-operation in the establishment and functioning of the Federation. Dismantling of all structures which the OHR judges contrary to the spirit and letter of the GFAP. Evidence of co-operation with the International Tribunal, notably in bringing Bosnian war criminals to justice before the Tribunal.' FRY: '1. Credible pressure on the Bosnian Serbs to co-operate in the institution building and the implementation of the provisions of the constitution. Evidence that the government of FRY is using its influence in bringing Bosnian

The 'potential candidates' covered by the SAP have been working towards compliance with the political and economic membership criteria in all their relations with the Union, even in advance of establishing contractual relations. Moreover, the political and financial conditioning of the work of the SAP countries is far more detailed and rigorously applied than the pre-accession conditionality that applied to the initial technical and financial assistance provided by the Phare programme.[78] In the case of the SAP countries, these criteria have been rigorously specified in general, regional and country-specific terms and then prioritised according to the nature of the relationship in order to help them benefit from assistance and autonomous trade preferences in advance of the establishment of any bilateral contractual relations. Thus, the Stabilisation and Association Agreement between the European Union and Macedonia underlines the importance of the SAP in its preamble, stating that it is 'to be further developed by an EU Common Strategy for the region, in the establishment and consolidation of a stable European order based on co-operation, of which the European Union is a mainstay, as well as the framework of the Stability Pact.'

3.2.3 *The Copenhagen economic, legal and administrative capacity criteria*

The Copenhagen economic and legal criteria are more flexible than the political criteria in that accession negotiations may begin provided that a candidate has taken its first steps in this direction and can be expected to meet the requirements in advance of its accession. There is a political dimension to these criteria, as can be seen from the above-mentioned checklist relating to the countries in the SAP. As Hoffmeister points out, a functioning economy can be measured by several indicators:

- trade and prices must be liberalised;
- significant barriers to market entry (establishment of new firms) and exit (bankruptcy) are absent;
- economic rights and contracts are legally enforceable; and
- macroeconomic stability exists.[79]

These indicators must be present to prove that a country has the capacity to cope with competitive pressures and market forces once it becomes a member. Additionally, this sub-clause of the economic criterion requires that:

Serb war criminals to justice before the International Tribunal; 2. Existence of a real dialogue with the Kosovo Albanians on the status of the Kosovo within the borders of the FRY.'

[78] The Phare instrument was only later reoriented under the pre-accession strategy after the 1993 Copenhagen European Council and again – and in a more accession-driven manner – following the publication in 1997 of Commission's *Agenda 2000*, loc. cit. n. 56.

[79] See Hoffmeister, loc. cit. n. 5.

- infrastructures and the financial climate together with education and research are sufficiently developed; and
- the role of the state in the economy should be modest and trade integration with the Union should be advanced.[80]

Since the fifth enlargement, candidates must be willing to enter into EMU and adopt Stage II of EMU, which requires central bank independence, co-ordination of economic policies and compliance with the Stability and Growth Pact. However, it should also be noted that the need to meet the Maastricht convergence criteria and fulfil the Stability and Growth Pact objectives are not accession conditions.[81] To proceed to Stage III of EMU, a Member State needs to meet the convergence criteria in order to introduce the Euro, and the new Member States were thus not obliged to fulfil all their obligations under the EMU *acquis* upon accession.[82] In fact, this stage cannot be reached until after accession to the Union.

As for the legal criteria, this relates directly to the acceptance of the rights and obligations – both actual and potential – of the Community system and its institutional framework as described by the Commission in its preparations for the last enlargement.[83] Typically, an Association Agreement will include a clause providing for the approximation of the partner's laws to the laws of the Union, as was the case in the Europe Agreements and as is now also the case in the SAAs, for example.[84] The examples of the fifth and sixth enlargements provide useful templates and experience regarding approximation for the countries of the Western Balkans and Turkey. In the end, however, the transposition and implementation exercise is their own responsibility and must work in their own situations. For the Balkan countries there is a singular advantage in their approximation efforts, because their whole association is based upon the premise that they may well become candidates. From this perspective, their approximation efforts will be accession-driven even in advance of any formal declaration by the Union on their actual candidate status.

Nowadays, the word *'acquis'* is also used to denote European Union activities outside the EC Treaty proper, falling under the second and third pillars of the Treaty

---

80 See the Commission's opinions on all applicants contained in Part 3 of *Agenda 2000*, loc. cit. n. 56.

81 See B. Dziechciarz, 'Candidate countries and economic and monetary union', in Ott and Inglis, op. cit. n. 5, at p. 710.

82 See F. Amtenbrink, 'Economic and Monetary Policy in the Framework of EMU', in Ott and Inglis, op. cit. n. 5, at pp. 701-702.

83 See Europe and the challenge of enlargement, *Bull. EC*, Suppl. 3-1992, at p. 12.

84 On the obligations of the associate to approximate, see in particular A. Łazowski, 'Approximation of Laws', in Ott and Inglis, op. cit. n. 5, pp. 631-639. Łazowski considers the obligations of the candidates to approximate their legal systems to the *acquis communautaire* and explore the scope of the approximation work as well as the technical assistance made available to associated countries to this end.

on European Union. The obligations of membership extend to the application of the entirety of the *acquis* as it stands on the date of accession, regardless of whether or not a receiving Member State applies the entire *acquis*. It will be interesting to see how this criterion will be developed in future enlargements should the Member States of the European Union make use of the various mechanisms for enhanced co-operation. If a majority of the Member States should decide to push ahead with legislative measures, the question arises as to whether such a flexibility measure would be considered an obligation of membership. Leading on from this question is that of whether the flexibility measures would continue to be legitimate if, after an enlargement, there would no longer be a majority of Member States participating.

As for administrative capacity, the ability to take on the obligations of membership necessarily includes the ability to correctly transpose, implement and then enforce the *acquis communautaire*. In practical terms, institution building involves budgetary implementation, decentralisation of the management of Phare and other pre-accession funding and the long-term secondment of experts from ministries of the Member States.[85] Intimately linked with the Madrid criteria is the matter of trust between Member States. Trust and reciprocity are not specified. Nicolaides points out that the issue of the implementation of the *acquis*, while important to the enlargement process, also has the potential to obstruct it.[86] The Union has been criticised for its approach to capacity building, in the main because it has consistently recommended that the accession countries follow the so-called 'M&M solution' – meaning men and money[87] – which fails to take account of the willingness of those responsible for applying and enforcing the *acquis*. Nicolaides advocates an approach of 'credible commitments' in order to establish the core of integration and to do so by means of an institutional approach. This approach involves the accession countries demonstrating to the Union their commitment to apply the *acquis* and assign the task of implementation to sufficiently empowered and accountable institutions which will have considerable decision-making independence and also be subject to performance obligations. Trust and reciprocity become a 'radical challenge' to the system of co-operative regulatory relations and trust at the heart of the Common Market.[88]

With the fifth enlargement, the acceding countries have had both to prove that they have adequate administrative capacity and to guarantee their continued administrative capacity as Member States. The concerns of the fifteen on this point led to the insertion of the safeguard clauses into the fifth Accession Treaty,

---

85 See *Agenda 2000*, loc. cit. n. 56, Vol. 2 at pp. A-3 to A-5.

86 See P. Nicolaides, 'Preparing for Accession to the European Union: How to Establish Capacity for Effective and Credible Application of EU Rules', in Cremona, op. cit. n. 5, at p. 46.

87 Ibid., at p. 44.

88 See F. Bignami, 'The Challenge of Co-operative Regulatory Relations', in Bermann and Pistor, op. cit. n. 13, pp. 97-140 at p. 99.

so that in the event of the failure by the incoming Member States to maintain their compliance and enforcement of the *acquis*, 'appropriate measures' may be taken by the Union against the country concerned.[89]

4. AN OVERVIEW OF THE PRE-ACCESSION STRATEGY INSTRUMENTS THAT CARRY THE CURRENT PRE-ACCESSION CONDITIONALITY

A direct consequence of the Union's eagerness to diffuse the potential political fall-out of such a rigorous and demanding conditionality has been the general expansion of the role of the Union's executive institution, the European Commission, in the pre-accession strategy. The Commission's role in managing, monitoring and evaluating compliance of the candidates' pre-accession progress has been dramatically enhanced compared to previous enlargements, commensurate with the number of candidates and the complexity of the preparations. The political organs of the Union, the European Parliament and the Council, have of course been heavily involved, but the administration of the instruments of pre-accession conditionality have been held firmly in the grip of the European Commission, taking political heat out of the implementation and progress of the pre-accession strategy and bringing structure to the accession negotiations.

4.1 Candidates with which accession negotiations have been closed

Bulgaria and Romania began accession negotiations in February 2000.[90] Of course, these countries have since signed and ratified their Accession Treaty, so this section explores how the pre-accession strategy applied to them in advance of that date. It does not cover the provisions of the sixth Accession Treaty concerning Bulgaria and Romania in the months leading up to their accession on 1 January 2007.[91] While accession negotiations have already closed with Bulgaria and Romania, as experience in all previous enlargements shows, in the interim between signature of the Accession Treaty and its entry into force, the pre-accession conditionality that applied prior to the signature of the Accession Treaty outlined below will continue to apply as established during the negotiations. Under their Accession Treaty, Bulgaria and Romania are subject to a new type of safeguard clause that will enable the Union to delay their entry to the Union in the event that they fail to meet the commitments that they made during the negotiations.

---

89 See Inglis, loc. cit. n. 17, pp. 937-973.
90 See L. Maurer, 'Negotiations in progress', in Ott and Inglis, op. cit. n. 5, pp. 113-129.
91 See also chapters 7 and 8 in this volume.

The Accession Partnerships set out the short, medium and long-term priorities and objectives of the candidate. Contrary to the impression of joint agreement that the word 'partnership' implies, they are unilateral legal instruments of the European Council and take the form of Council decisions. The legal basis is contained in a 1998 Council regulation[92] and they are updated annually upon the advice of the European Commission after it has published its annual report[93] on the progress that each candidate has made towards meeting the accession conditions. The candidate responds by adopting its own national plan for the adoption of the *acquis* (NPAA) in order to meet the objectives of the Accession Partnership. It is more a mutually complementing and parallel process than one based on a bilateral contractual association.

Typically, an Accession Partnership will specify, for example, that the candidate must complete trade liberalisation measures under the Europe Agreement or make progress in approximation efforts under the Europe Agreement. However, the Accession Partnerships are more demanding than the Europe Agreements because they are purely accession-driven, in particular specifying the work to be done in order to implement the *acquis*. The Accession Partnerships form the basis for programming all pre-accession assistance from Community funds and international financing institutions. The Accession Partnerships will continue to guide Bulgaria and Romania in their activities until the date of their accession. The general objective of this strategy is to offer a coherent programme for preparing these countries for membership of the European Union, and more particularly

- to bring together the various forms of aid offered by the European Union within a single framework, the Accession Partnerships;
- to familiarise applicants with the European Union's procedures and policies by offering them the opportunity to participate in Community programmes.

Three financing instruments are used for both Bulgaria and Romania: Phare,[94] SAPARD[95] and ISPA.[96] The support provided by the Phare programme and the

---

[92] Council Regulation (EC) No. 622/98 of 16 March 1998 on assistance to the applicant States in the framework of the pre-accession strategy, and in particular on the establishment of Accession Partnerships, *OJ* 1998 L 85/1.

[93] The last Comprehensive Monitoring Report of the Commission for Romania is dated 25 October 2005, SEC (2005) 1354. The last Comprehensive Monitoring Report of the Commission for Bulgaria is also dated 25 October 2005, SEC (2005) 1352.

[94] Council Regulation (EEC) No. 3609/89 of 18 December 1989 on economic aid to the Republic of Hungary and the Polish People's Republic, *OJ* 1989 L 375/11-12.

[95] Council Regulation (EC) No. 1268/1999 of 21 June 1999 on Community support for pre-accession measures for agriculture and rural development in the applicant countries of central and eastern Europe in the pre-accession period, *OJ* 1999 L 161/87.

[96] Council Regulation (EC) No. 1267/1999 of 21 June 1999 establishing an Instrument for Structural Policies for Pre-Accession, *OJ* 1999 L 161/73.

other pre-accession instruments focuses on the priorities established in the Accession Partnership. These countries, as shown in the Commission's annual progress reports for Bulgaria and Romania, are also being included in the decision-making procedures of the EU institutions (not as full Member States as such but as observers) as well as in Community agencies and programmes.[97]

4.2 Candidates with which accession negotiations have been opened: Croatia and Turkey

Turkey signed an Association Agreement with the Union in 1964. The opening of accession negotiations with Turkey in October 2005 has brought Turkey within the overarching pre-accession strategy and instruments. However, Turkey was an official candidate for many years before accession negotiations were opened. In fact, this distinction had been specifically introduced in order to appease Turkey when it was not included in the negotiations for the fifth enlargement alongside the ten CEECs, Cyprus and Malta. Later, Croatia, too, became a candidate with which accession negotiations had not been opened, until the European Council decided to open negotiations in October 2005. Thus, the Association Agreement between the European Union and Turkey is the bilateral legal basis for the association but it is the Accession Partnership with Turkey that programmes the work, funding and assistance given to Turkey and determines the actions under the Association Agreement. There is a separate financing instrument for Turkey.

The operative Accession Partnership with Turkey is that of 2003.[98] Turkey's NPAA is available on the Union's 'Europa' website,[99] and Turkey is also being included in Community programmes and agencies. The most recent Commission report on the progress of Turkey in meeting its membership conditions is that of 9 November 2005.[100] In terms of financial assistance, the pre-accession facility for Turkey was adopted in December 2001,[101] and the procedures for programming and implementing it largely follow those of the Phare programme. Significantly, it may also be used to finance activities that the ISPA and SAPARD programmes finance for Bulgaria and Romania. Between 1995 and 2003, €1,098 million was committed to Turkey, while the programme for 2004 had an allocation of €235.6 million.

97 Protocols were adopted to the Europe Agreements to this end, and the incorporation of both Bulgaria and Romania within Community programmes and agencies is a central component of the pre-accession strategy.

98 2003/398/EC: Council decision of 19 May 2003 on the principles, priorities, intermediate objectives and conditions contained in the Accession Partnership with Turkey, *OJ* 2003 L 145/40.

99 See <http://www.europa.eu.int/comm/enlargement/turkey/pdf/npaa_full.pdf>.

100 Turkey – 2005 Progress Report, SEC (2005) 1426, 9 November 2005.

101 The Commission reports annually on the use of the funds available under this facility. See, for example, the Commission's 2005 Regular Report on Turkey's progress towards accession, SEC (2005) 1426, 9 November 2005.

The pre-accession strategy instruments for Croatia are dealt with in the next section, because the relevant conditionality is applied within the SAP for the countries of the Western Balkans. The SAA Croatia is the bilateral legal basis for the pre-accession strategy applicable to Croatia.

4.3 Potential candidates: the countries of the Western Balkans

The potential candidates in the SAP are referred to as such in the body of the SAA once the country has met the conditions required in order to negotiate an SAA. This is significant. Neither Bulgaria nor Romania had been recognised as a 'potential candidate' until the 1993 Copenhagen European Council reoriented the Europe Agreements. It was only the CEE partners that had expressed their accession aspirations.[102] Moreover, the SAAs are framed in such a way as to reflect the pre-accession strategy reorientation of the bilateral association. The SAP provides a framework that programmes the content and negotiations of the SAAs in a way that was not done for the Europe Agreements. So far, SAAs have only been signed and ratified with the Former Yugoslav Republic of Macedonia and Croatia.[103]

Instead of Accession Partnerships, the Council adopts 'European Partnerships'. They are similar in that they provide a single framework for the programming of EU funding and assistance in line with the conditionality set out by the Union, but they cannot be thought of as pre-accession instruments in the same way as the Accession Partnerships. In particular, they are used to programme the work of the countries of the Western Balkans even in advance of the existence of contractual relations. The equivalent of Regulation 622/98[104] is Regulation 533/2004, establishing the European Partnerships for the SAP countries.[105] However, these two Regulations take a different legal basis in the EC Treaty and the SAP Regulation contains no essential elements clause to allow for the suspension of pre-accession assistance in the event that essential elements are missing, as is the case in Regulation 622/98.

The European Partnerships are based on Article 181a(2) TEC rather than Article 308 TEC, which was the legal basis for Regulation 622/98. Article 181a(2) was used as opposed to Article 179 TEC, because a number of the beneficiary countries are considered countries in transition. Article 181a is the only provision

---

[102] See Maresceau, loc. cit. n. 36, at p. 9.

[103] See Stabilisation and Association Agreement between the European Communities and their Member States, of the one part, and the former Yugoslav Republic of Macedonia, of the other part, *OJ* 2004 L 84/13 and Stabilisation and Association Agreement between the European Communities and their Member States, of the one part, and the Republic of Croatia, of the other part, *OJ* 2005 L 26/3 respectively.

[104] *OJ* 1998 L 85/1.

[105] Council Regulation (EC) No. 533/2004 of 22 March 2004 on the establishment of European Partnerships in the framework of the stabilisation and association process, *OJ* 2004 L 86/1.

which is capable of referring to Association Agreements and agreements concluded with states which are candidates for membership of the Union. Thus, it is appropriate because the SAP countries either have already signed an Association Agreement or will do so in the future. The focus of the European Partnerships changes according to the country concerned, but the purpose is the same. European Partnerships[106] have been adopted for Albania, Bosnia and Herzegovina, Macedonia, Serbia and Montenegro and Croatia. However, as yet only Croatia has been formally recognised as a candidate for membership, and only Macedonia and Croatia have concluded SAAs.

Some €197 million in Community funding to promote regional co-operation in the Balkans is provided under the Community Assistance for Reconstruction, Development and Stabilisation (CARDS) programme.[107] The Commission decided on a strategic direction for regional financial assistance for the Western Balkans on 15 December 2004 in the Multi-annual Indicative Programme (MIP) 2005-2006. The Union is also planning for the incorporation of these countries in Community programmes and agencies.[108]

5. CONCLUSIONS

The Union's conditionality in pre-accession is contained within an inclusive-yet-differentiating approach. This is the approach that the Union followed in the case of the fifth enlargement: all candidates within the region are treated on an equal footing but they may progress faster in the negotiations if they have progressed faster in their preparations. To hold back one country that is ready to accede because of another's failure to reach the same level of progress would run against the grain of the Union's pre-accession conditionality. In the fifth Accession Treaty, the twenty-five Member States underscored the 'continuous, inclusive and irreversible enlargement process' in their Joint Declaration: One Europe,[109] declaring the accessions of Bulgaria and Romania in 2007 an 'objective' and 'welcoming' the next stage in Turkey's candidature.[110]

---

106 See Communication from the Commission to the Council and the European Parliament, The Western Balkans and European Integration, COM (2003) 285, 21 May 2003, at pp. 3-4.

107 Council Regulation (EC) No. 2666/2000 of 5 December 2000 on assistance for Albania, Bosnia and Herzegovina, Croatia, the Federal Republic of Yugoslavia and the Former Yugoslav Republic of Macedonia, repealing Regulation (EC) No. 1628/96 and amending Regulations (EEC) No. 3906/89 and (EEC) No. 1360/90 and Decisions 97/256/EC and 1999/311/EC, *OJ* 2000 L 306/1.

108 Communication from the Commission to the Council and Parliament, Preparing for the participation of the Western Balkan countries in Community programmes and agencies, COM (2003) 748 final, 3 December 2003.

109 See Declarations adopted by the Plenipotentiaries, annexed to the Final Act of the Accession Treaty, loc. cit. n. 9, at p. 971.

110 This confirmed the decisions taken by the Informal European Council in Athens on the same day as the signature of the fifth Accession Treaty on 16 April 2003.

As with the fifth Accession Treaty, the sixth Accession Treaty with Bulgaria and Romania also contains the safeguard clauses to protect the functioning of the internal market and the Justice and Home Affairs *acquis*. It also reproduces the general economic safeguard clause that has been contained in every act of accession so far. The Commission certainly raised doubts as to the readiness of the incoming countries of the fifth enlargement. In its Opinion of February 2003 on the applications for accession,[111] required under Article 49 TEU, unlike in the case of previous Accession Treaties, the Commission called

> on the acceding States to pursue vigorously the improvements that still [need] to be made in the context of the political and economic criteria for membership and in relation to the adoption, implementation and enforcement of the *acquis*; the Commission will continue to monitor the implementation of the commitments and obligations taken on by the acceding States, and will assist them with the available instruments.

The introduction of entirely new forms of safeguard clauses in the fifth Accession Treaty are an added conditionality tool, and these clauses are included in the Accession Treaty with Bulgaria and Romania. The fifth Accession Treaty also provides an example of how pre-accession conditionality is applied to new Member States in terms of maintaining and improving administrative capacity. For three years beginning on 1 May 2004, the new Member States must continue in their efforts (in particular as regards administrative capacity) and two financial instruments have been introduced to this end: the transition facility (Art. 34 of the Act of Accession) and the Schengen facility (Art. 35 of the Act of Accession). In the case of Bulgaria and Romania, an additional safeguard clause provides for the postponement of their accession for up to one year 'if there is a serious risk' that either of these countries is 'manifestly unprepared to meet the requirements of membership by the date of accession', the only qualification to this requirement being that it must be so in 'a number of important areas' (Art. 39 of the Act of Accession). This was because of the number of commitments undertaken in the course of the negotiations by Bulgaria and Romania to make progress and the amount of time remaining until the envisaged date of accession in January 2007, all of which the Commission has to monitor. While Bulgaria has made 'excellent progress', Romania is in a more doubtful position.[112]

---

[111] Commission opinion of 19 February 2003 on the applications for accession to the European Union by the Czech Republic, the Republic of Estonia, the Republic of Cyprus, the Republic of Latvia, the Republic of Lithuania, the Republic of Hungary, the Republic of Malta, the Republic of Poland, the Republic of Slovenia and the Slovak Republic, *OJ* 2003 L 236/3.

[112] See the words of Enlargement Commissioner Olli Rehn speaking before Members of the European Parliament on 29 March 2005 and reported in 'MEPs back Bulgaria and Romania to join the EU', available at: <http://www.euractiv.com> (visited on 31 March 2005).

On the one hand, the postponement clause is remarkable. It is an indication of the European Union's political commitment to enlargement in spite of remaining doubts. This clause enables the Union to meet its political commitment to the planned date of enlargement. If either Bulgaria or Romania fails to demonstrate their ability to fulfil their commitments made in the negotiations, there is no further possibility, beyond the one-year postponement clause, to introduce separate treaties and acts of accession for these two countries. This too would run counter to the inclusive-yet-differentiating approach of the pre-accession strategy that still applies to these two countries as it did in respect of their CEE counterparts that acceded on 1 May 2004.

The postponement clause is clearly more of a conditionality stick than other Accession Treaty safeguard clauses. The two safeguard clauses are dubious because of their potential to discriminate between the incoming Member States and the receiving Member States and to undermine the solidarity between Member States. The Commission has made clear that it does not intend to make use of them for these and other reasons.[113] The postponement clause by comparison is simple and categorical and applicable in any or all areas of the *acquis communautaire*; it continues pre-accession conditionality even after the signature of the treaty and it is not negotiated with the incoming Member State, being adopted by unanimity in the Council, acting on a proposal of the Commission. In the case of Romania, serious doubts have been raised as to its ability to meet the commitments that it gave in the negotiations in time for its accession, and it may well face the use of the postponement clause should it fail to make better progress, particularly as concerns the fight against corruption, public procurement legislation, state aid in its outsized steel sector and the preparedness of its judiciary.[114]

So, has enlargement become a political imperative even over candidates' readiness to accede? Has enlargement become a political imperative over the Union's readiness to enlarge? Is enlargement premature? To find answers to these questions, one must take into account the fact that such safeguard clauses in an Accession Treaty are tangible evidence of the importance that the Union attaches to the candidates' ability to meet the Copenhagen criteria both before and after their accession. Also relevant will be how the new Member States continue to meet their obligations as Member States and whether the safeguard clauses contained in the Accession Treaties are used against new Member States. If the pre-accession conditions applied to the country have no meaning after it becomes a member, the very purpose of EU enlargement would be negated. The thoroughness of the pre-accession strategy and the limited transitional arrangements in the Accession Treaties certainly limit the possibility of new members failing in their obligations as Member State.

---

113 See Inglis, loc. cit. n. 17, pp. 937-973 at p. 957.

114 See <http://www.euobserver.com> (visited on 24 January 2005).

The tension and uncertainty arising between the project of enlarging and the Union's own functioning and continued deepening has been apparent in all enlargements. However, for the first time in any enlargement, incoming members do not participate in areas such as the CAP, EMU and Schengen from the date of accession. This accentuates these tensions and uncertainties. It is in addition to the fact that the Union must further revise its decision-making structures and institutions so that it can enlarge again and acts as a restraint on future enlargements.

While accession negotiations have opened with Turkey,[115] the perspective of Turkey becoming a Member State will of course accentuate again the uncertainties facing the Union. In its Staff Working Document entitled 'Issues Arising from Turkey's Membership Perspective',[116] the Commission highlights the effects of Turkey's integration into the Union. The issues raised are central to the capacity of the Union to absorb new members – the fourth Copenhagen criterion. It is emphasised that the 'considerations in the present paper do not constitute additional criteria or conditions to be fulfilled'[117] by Turkey, but it is also clear that it is too early to reliably predict the problems likely to arise during the negotiations. Not least among the uncertainties is the possibility of earlier accessions of countries in the Western Balkans, further EU policy development, the special arrangements made for Turkey (including transitional arrangements) and the fact that the current financial perspectives will change. The ability of the Union to go on deepening integration among the Member States and even to continue with what has already been achieved is brought into question. The negative referendums on the Constitutional Treaty in France and the Netherlands are like red lights to both the deepening and widening ambitions of the Union. How the Union functions, how it sees itself, as much as the vision for an enlarging Union, such questions are becoming urgent. In this context, with every new candidate, enlargement become less a question of the ability of a candidate to meet the membership conditions set down by the Union and more one of the fourth Copenhagen criterion: the capacity of the Union to absorb new members, in terms of its functioning and its future vision for the European Union.

---

115 See Commission Communication, Recommendation of the European Commission on Turkey's progress towards accession, SEC (2004) 656, 6 October 2004, and Council Conclusions of 3 October 2005, Press Release 12514/1/05 REV I (Presse 241).

116 SEC (2004) 1202, 6 October 2004.

117 Ibid., at p. 1.

Part II

Country and Regional Analysis

CHAPTER 4

EEA COUNTRIES (ICELAND, LIECHTENSTEIN AND NORWAY)

Adam Łazowski*

Relevant legal documents:

- Agreement on the European Economic Area, *OJ* 1994 L 1/1.
- Protocol adjusting the Agreement on the European Economic Area, *OJ* 1994 L 1/572.
- Agreement on the participation of the Czech Republic, the Republic of Estonia, the Republic of Cyprus, the Republic of Hungary, the Republic of Latvia, the Republic of Lithuania, the Republic of Malta, the Republic of Poland, the Republic of Slovenia and the Slovak Republic in the European Economic Area, *OJ* 2004 L 130/11.
- Agreement between the EFTA States on the Establishment of a Surveillance Authority and a Court of Justice, *OJ* 1994 L 344/1 (as amended).
- Protocol adjusting the Agreement between the EFTA States on the establishment of a Surveillance Authority and a Court of Justice, *OJ* 1994 L 344/82.
- Agreement on a Standing Committee of the EFTA States, available at: <http://secretariat.efta.int/Web/legaldocuments/AgreementOnStandingCommittee.pdf>.
- Agreement between the Kingdom of Norway and the European Community on a Norwegian Financial Mechanism for the period 2004-2009, *OJ* 2004 L 130/81.
- Agreement in the form of an Exchange of Letters between the European Community and the Kingdom of Norway concerning certain agricultural products, *OJ* 2004 L 130/93.
- Agreement between the Kingdom of Norway and the European Union on security procedures for the exchange of classified information, *OJ* 2004 L 362/29.
- Agreement between the European Union and the Kingdom of Norway establishing a framework for the participation of the Kingdom of Norway in the European Union crisis-management operations, *OJ* 2005 L 67/8.
- Agreement between the European Union and the Republic of Iceland establishing a framework for the participation of the Republic of Iceland in the European Union crisis-management, *OJ* 2005 L 67/2.
- Agreement between the European Union and the Republic of Iceland and the Kingdom of Norway on the application of certain provisions of the Convention of 29 May

* Senior Lecturer in Law, School of Law, University of Westminster, London.

S. Blockmans and A. Łazowski (eds.), The European Union and Its Neighbours

2000 on Mutual Assistance in Criminal Matters between the Member States of the European Union and the 2001 Protocol thereto, *OJ* 2004 L 26/3.
- Agreement between the European Union and the Kingdom of Norway on the participation of the Kingdom of Norway in the European Union Police Mission (EUPM) in Bosnia and Herzegovina (BiH), *OJ* 2004 L 239/32.
- Agreement between the European Union and the Republic of Iceland on the participation of the Republic of Iceland in the European Union Police Mission (EUPM) in Bosnia and Herzegovina (BiH), *OJ* L 2003 L 239/5.
- Agreement between the European Community and the Republic of Iceland and the Kingdom of Norway concerning the criteria and mechanisms for establishing the State responsible for examining a request for asylum lodged in a Member State or in Iceland or Norway, *OJ* 2001 L 93/40.
- Agreement concluded by the Council of the European Union and the Republic of Iceland and the Kingdom of Norway on the establishment of rights and obligations between Ireland and the United Kingdom of Great Britain and Northern Ireland, on the one hand, and the Republic of Iceland and the Kingdom of Norway, on the other, in areas of the Schengen *acquis* which apply to these States, *OJ* 2000 L 15/2.
- Agreement concluded by the Council of the European Union and the Republic of Iceland and the Kingdom of Norway concerning the latter's association with the implementation, application and development of the Schengen *acquis*, *OJ* 1999 L 176/36.
- Agreement on customs cooperation between the European Community and the Kingdom of Norway, *OJ* 1997 L 105/17.
- Agreement between the European Economic Community and the Kingdom of Norway [Free Trade Agreement], *OJ* 1973 L 171/2 (as amended).
- Agreement between the European Economic Community and the Republic of Iceland [Free Trade Agreement], *OJ* 1973 L 301/2 (as amended).

1. INTRODUCTION

1.1 Background

In legal terms, Norway, Iceland and Liechtenstein are undoubtedly the most integrated neighbouring countries of the European Union. This has not always been the case. Their path towards integration can be characterised as a long road from rivalry to enhanced cooperation. Although, formally speaking, none of them is a member of the European Communities/European Union, they remain a vital part of the internal market under the umbrella of the Agreement on the European Economic Area,[1] which was drafted more than a decade ago in order to establish a

[1] Agreement on the European Economic Area, *OJ* 1994 L 1/1.

common economic space between the twelve Member States of the European Communities and seven EFTA countries.[2] Although its creation was preceded by numerous setbacks, including the rejection of the agreement by one of its signatories, the European Economic Area (EEA) has proved during its first decade to be a well-functioning hybrid.

It is argued that over the past decade the EEA has successfully played a double role. For some EFTA countries, it has served as the antechamber on their way to the EU membership. Complex sets of political and economic motives pushed Sweden, Finland and Austria towards EU membership in 1995. For the other EEA-EFTA countries, this framework has proved to be a long-term alternative, without at the same time formally excluding their potential future accession to the European Union.[3] Their decision to remain outside the European Union is driven by a combination of political and economic factors. This is especially the case in Norway and Iceland, where anti-EU movements enjoy ample public support. In the case of the latter, it is not the electorate but rather the political elites that are considered to be very eurosceptic.[4] One should not forget that Norwegians have already twice rejected membership of the European Communities/European Union in nationwide referenda.[5] At the same time, Iceland has never formally expressed a desire to accede. In economic terms, fisheries policy and energy resources are decisive factors in this regard.[6] Also, the 'loss of sovereignty' argument plays a considerable role in public debate. This is particularly astonishing, as EU accession would grant both countries access to the decision-making machinery, while within the EEA framework they are at present technically obliged to swallow a majority of the EC *acquis* without any real participation in its adoption. The key question is whether the EEA is a sustainable enterprise or whether the EFTA countries would benefit more from the Swiss model of arrangements based on a series of bilateral treaties. There are definitely numerous arguments supporting both scenarios. Some of them are presented in the final parts of this chapter, while others are approached from the broader European neighbourhood perspective in the conclusions to this book.

---

2 The EFTA members at that time were Sweden, Finland, Norway, Switzerland, Liechtenstein, Austria and Iceland.

3 It is explicitly spelled out in the Preamble to the EEA Agreement that it 'shall not prejudge in any way the possibility of any EFTA State to accede to the European Communities.'

4 See G.H. Kristinsson and B. Thorhallsson, 'The Euro-sceptical political elite', in B. Thorhallsson, ed., *Iceland and European Integration. On the Edge* (London/New York, Routledge 2004) p. 145.

5 The first referendum took place in September 1972, the second in November 1994. For a detailed account of both plebiscites, see C. Archer, *Norway outside the European Union. Norway and European integration from 1994 to 2004* (London/New York, Routledge 2005) pp. 41-64.

6 On the impact of the fisheries on Iceland's European policy, see B. Thorhallsson and H.T. Vignisson, 'Life is first and foremost saltfish', in Thorhallsson, op. cit. n. 4, at p. 67.

Bearing this in mind, it is important to look at the EEA framework as a potential model for the future relations of the European Union with its neighbours. One should acknowledge that it was already in the early 1990s that the EEA was regarded as a tempting scenario for the emerging Eastern European neighbourhood. With fall of the Iron Curtain, membership of the EEA was offered to the newly independent democracies of Central and Eastern Europe. However, this offer was turned down, as these countries expressed no interest in anything short of the EU membership.[7] In 2004, they eventually acceded to the EEA, but in the capacity of EEA-EU members. Following the two enlargements of the European Union, the EEA is currently composed of a total of twenty-eight countries, with three on the EFTA side and twenty-five on the EU side. Further accessions to the EEA are expected when Bulgaria and Romania join the European Union.[8]

The extent and degree of integration within the EEA Agreement mainly covers the fundamental freedoms of the internal market: the free movement of persons, services, goods and capital. These are supplemented by provisions on competition law (including state aid) and numerous flanking policies (i.e., on transport, the environment and consumer protection).[9] However extensive the substantive scope of the EEA, one should not be mislead into thinking that the cooperation between the European Union and the three EEA-EFTA countries is limited to the EEA only. On a bilateral – and in some cases trilateral – level, it also extends to the Common Foreign and Security Policy and cooperation in the field of Justice and Home Affairs. The focus of this analysis is mainly on the EEA, but other areas of cooperation will be elaborated on in the last part of the chapter.

1.2 From rivalry to free trade agreements

In the early years, relations between the EFTA countries and the European Communities were almost non-existent.[10] This was mainly due to strong feelings

---

[7] At that time, Peers argued that 'Although the EAs may serve well as an interim measure while the EA States become familiar with the EU legal system, a comparison of the EEA with EAs will demonstrate that membership of the EEA is the best way of preparing EA States for EU membership.' See S. Peers, 'An ever closer waiting room? The case for Eastern European accession to the European Economic Area', 32 *CMLRev.* (1995) p. 187 at p. 189.

[8] See chapters 7 and 8 (respectively) in this volume. Shortly after the signature of the EU Accession Treaty, both countries submitted their applications for membership of the European Economic Area.

[9] See, *inter alia*, Art. 78 EEA.

[10] It is argued in the academic literature that the evolution of the bilateral relationship can be divided into five phases. The first started with the creation of EFTA in 1960 and lasted until the signature of free trade agreements in 1972. The second covered the years following the entry into force of the FTAs and lasted until free trade was in fact achieved in 1983. The third phase started with the Luxembourg Declaration in 1984 and the brainstorming on the European Economic Space

of rivalry felt on the Communities' side. It has to be remembered that one of the reasons for the creation of EFTA was to make an appropriate response to the emerging European Communities.[11] It was in the 1960s, when 'repeated EFTA efforts and invitations to the EC to create a single European market were looked upon by the EC side as a challenge to the creation of the Communities and EFTA and its Member States were therefore treated as rivals to the Community.'[12] The mood changed in the wake of the first enlargement of the European Communities, when three EFTA countries (the United Kingdom, Denmark and Norway) as well as Ireland were expected to accede. Following the negative result of a referendum in Norway this number was reduced, but without undermining the importance of these historical developments. Bearing in mind the degree of trade liberalisation within EFTA, it was argued that 'it would not have been possible for the EEC to accept two new members from EFTA, without allowing them as well as the other EFTA counties to maintain the trade liberalisation already achieved in EFTA.'[13] Therefore, it is justified to say that accessions pushed the European Communities and the remaining EFTA countries to the negotiating table. The ice already started to melt at the end of 1969, when on the initiative of President Pompidou the EEC invited the EFTA countries to discuss options for future cooperation with the enlarged European Communities.[14] The negotiations were commenced in December 1971 and were formally completed with the initialling and signing of agreements on 22 July 1972.[15] The product of those negotiations was a series of free trade agreements tailored to provide an appropriate framework for bilateral trade. A batch of agreements (with Austria, Sweden, Switzerland and Portugal)

---

that followed until 1988. The fourth phase covered the years of negotiations and ratification of the EEA (1989-1993). The fifth phase started with the entry into force of the EEA Agreement on 1 January 1994. See S. Norberg, K. Hökborg, M. Johansson, D. Eliasson and L. Dedichen, *EEA Law. A Commentary on the EEA Agreement*, 1st edn. (Stockholm, Fritzes Wolters Kluwer Sweden 1993) p. 36.

[11] The European Free Trade Association (EFTA) was created in 1960 with Austria, Denmark, Norway, Portugal, Sweden, Switzerland and the United Kingdom as members. In 1961, Finland became an associate member and in 1970 Iceland joined the club. To this day, the EFTA Convention is applicable in some respects between the remaining four EFTA countries: Norway, Iceland, Switzerland and Liechtenstein. It was amended in 2001 in order to accommodate changes resulting from the EEA membership of its three members and the entry into force of the first bilateral package between the European Community and Switzerland (see more on this in chapter 5 in this volume). The amended version entered into force on 1 June 2002. See Norberg, et al., op. cit. n. 10, at pp. 39-43. See also information available at the official EFTA website at: <https://www.efta.int>.

[12] Norberg, et al., op. cit. n. 10, at p. 36.

[13] Norberg, et al., op. cit. n. 10, at p. 47.

[14] E.P. Wellenstein, 'The free trade agreements between the enlarged European Communities and the EFTA countries', 10 *CMLRev.* (1973) p. 137.

[15] Formally speaking, there were two agreements per country – one with the European Economic Community and one with the European Coal and Steel Community. Together with the interim agreements with Austria and the special arrangements for Liechtenstein, sixteen agreements were concluded in total. See Wellenstein, loc. cit. n. 14, at p. 144.

entered into force simultaneously with the first enlargement of the European Communities on 1 January 1973.[16] The agreement with Iceland entered into force on 1 April 1973,[17] the agreement with Norway (negotiated following the accession referendum fiasco) on 1 June 1973,[18] and the agreement with Finland on 1 January 1974.[19] For most of the EFTA countries, these agreements were terminated with their accession to the European Union. Agreements with Norway, Iceland and Switzerland remain in force, albeit that the scope of their application is very limited in the case of the EEA countries.[20]

The free trade agreements undoubtedly opened a new era in the EFTA-EEC/ECSC relationship and by the end of 1983 the parties had achieved their aims. Not only did all agreements have the same rationale behind them, but all were similar in structure and contents.[21] The FTA with Iceland serves as a good example. The aims of the agreements were threefold:

---

16 Agreement between the European Economic Community and the Republic of Austria, *OJ* 1972 L 300/2; Agreement between the Member States of the European Coal and Steel Community and the European Coal and Steel Community, of the one part, and the Republic of Austria, of the other part, *OJ* 1973 L 350/33; Agreement between the European Economic Community and the Kingdom of Sweden, *OJ* 1972 L 300/97; Agreement between the Member States of the European Coal and Steel Community and the European Coal and Steel Community, of the one part, and the Kingdom of Sweden, of the other part, *OJ* 1973 L 350/76; Agreement between the European Economic Community and the Swiss Confederation, *OJ* 1972 L 300/189; Agreement between the Member States of the European Coal and Steel Community and the Swiss Confederation, *OJ* 1973 L 350/13; Agreement between the European Economic Community and the Portuguese Republic, *OJ* 1972 L 301/165; Agreement between the Member States of the European Coal and Steel Community and the European Coal and Steel Community, of the one part, and the Portuguese Republic, of the other part, *OJ* 1973 L 350/53.

17 Agreement between the European Economic Community and the Republic of Iceland, *OJ* 1972 L 301/2; Agreement between the Member States of the European Coal and Steel Community and the Republic of Iceland, *OJ* 1973 L 350/2.

18 Agreement between the European Economic Community and the Kingdom of Norway, *OJ* 1973 L 171/2; Agreement between the Member States of the European Coal and Steel Community and the European Coal and Steel Community, of the one part, and the Kingdom of Norway, of the other part, *OJ* 1974 L 348/17.

19 Agreement between the European Economic Community and the Republic of Finland, *OJ* 1973 L 328/2; Agreement between the Member States of the European Coal and Steel Community and the European Coal and Steel Community, of the one part, and the Republic of Finland, of the other part, *OJ* 1974 L 348/1.

20 In this context, see Art. 120 EEA, which reads: 'Unless otherwise provided in this Agreement and in particular in Protocols 41 and 43, the application of the provisions of this Agreement shall prevail over provisions in existing bilateral and multilateral agreements binding the European Economic Community, on the one hand, and one or more EFTA States, on the other, to the extent that the same subject matter is governed by this Agreement.' For analysis of this provision, see Norberg, et al., op. cit. n. 10, at pp. 296-297. See also EFTA Court, Case E-2/03 *Ákæruvaldið (The Public Prosecutor)* v. *Ásgeir Logi Ásgeirsson, Axel Pétur Ásgeirsson and Helgi Már Reynisson*, EFTA Court Rep. [2003] 185.

21 Differences existed for instance in the agreement with Finland. See Wellenstein, loc. cit. n. 14, at p. 145.

- to promote through the expansions of reciprocal trade the harmonious development of economic relations between the European Economic Community and the Republic of Iceland the advance of economic activity, the improvement of living and employment conditions, and increased productivity and financial stability;
- to provide fair conditions of competition for trade between the contracting parties;
- to contribute in this way, by the removal of barriers to trade, to the harmonious development and expansion of world trade.[22]

The FTAs predominantly covered trade in industrial products, although further cooperation in agricultural products was not excluded. According to Article 15(1) FTA EEC-Iceland, the parties were declaring 'their readiness to foster, so far as their agricultural policies allow, the harmonious development of trade in agricultural products.' In order to fulfil the aims of the agreements, the introduction of new customs duties was prohibited, and the FTAs envisaged the progressive abolition of existing customs duties on imports and exports in accordance with the time framework provided therein. Similar prohibitions covered measures having equivalent effect to customs duties. Quantitative restrictions and measures having equivalent effect were also covered by the FTAs. For example, Article 13 FTA EEC-Iceland provided for the abolition of existing quantitative restrictions and measures having equivalent effect in the area of exports. In the case of the EEC, the dates were set at 1 January 1973 for the former and 1 January 1975 for the latter. Iceland had to abolish both types of measures by 1 January 1975. In both cases, the imposition of new quantitative restrictions and measures having equivalent effect in the area of imports was prohibited. The FTAs envisaged the creation of Joint Committees responsible for the administration of the agreements.[23] Although the FTAs proved to be a success story in mid-1980s, it became clear that a widening and deepening of cooperation was desired. This was one of the driving forces behind the ambitious concept of the European Economic Space, which saw the light of the day in 1984.

1.3 Towards the European Economic Area

Although the debates on the enhancement of EFTA-EEC relations had been going on for a number of years, the real turning point was the first EFTA-EEC summit held on 9 April 1984 in Luxembourg. It resulted in the Luxembourg Declaration

22 Art. 1 FTA EEC-Iceland.

23 See, for example, Arts. 30-33 FTA EEC-Iceland.

on the development of the European Economic Space (*Espace économique européen*) between the two sides.[24] It did not provide an extensive outline for future cooperation between both sides. However, it contained a list of key issues that would be addressed. This major development was followed by years of brainstorming at various levels.[25] Numerous working groups and specialists groups were established in order to analyse the substantive scope and mechanisms for the EES. The structural problems emerging on the horizon included methods of securing the legal homogeneity of the EES without a transfer of legislative powers on the EFTA side, surveillance and participation of the EFTA countries in decision making.[26]

A political boost to the negotiations came from Jacques Delors, who, as the President of the European Commission, presented the work plan of the newly appointed Commission to the European Parliament on 17 January 1989. One of the important issues addressed in this plan was the shape of future EEC-EFTA relations. The two alternatives were the continuation of the bilateral relationship or the creation of a unique and far-reaching association.[27]

The idea of the European Economic Space gained momentum from that moment onwards, and the parties officially opened negotiations on 20 June 1990. Following a linguistically motivated initiative of the EEC, the name of the joint project was changed to European Economic Area.[28] It is truism to say that the negotiations were far from easy. This was due to the complexity of the project and the numerous legal issues attached to it. Structural problems of pivotal importance appeared on both sides. For the EFTA countries, securing homogeneity without undermining their sovereignty was one of the issues. The internal challenges for the European Communities were highlighted in ECJ Opinion 1/91.[29] It was delivered at the last moment, as the parties were getting ready for the official initialling ceremony. The ECJ ruled that the judicial architecture proposed under the EEA was incompatible with the EEC and that the conclusion

---

24 'Luxembourg: Ministerial Meeting Between EFTA Countries and the EC and its Member States', *EFTA Bull.* 2/84, 6 (1984).

25 For a detailed account, see Norberg, et al., op. cit. n. 10, at pp. 49-53.

26 For an analysis of various concepts presented at that time, see, *inter alia*, J. Temple Lang, 'Institutional Aspects of EC-EFTA Relations', in M. Robinson and J. Findlater, eds., *Creating a European Economic Space: Legal Aspects of EC-EFTA Relations* (Dublin, Irish Centre for European Law 1990) p. 17.

27 On the Delors initiative and the follow-up, see Norberg, et al., op. cit. n. 10, at pp. 53-59.

28 See Norberg, et al., op. cit. n. 10, at p. 59.

29 ECJ, Opinion 1/91 of the Court of 14 December 1991. Opinion delivered pursuant to the second subparagraph of Art. 228(1) of the Treaty. Draft agreement between the Community, on the one hand, and the countries of the European Free Trade Association, on the other, relating to the creation of the European Economic Area [1991] *ECR* I-6079.

of the agreement was therefore precluded. In early 1992, the parties sat down at the negotiating table again and successfully developed a new surveillance system. A positive evaluation by the ECJ in Opinion 1/92[30] paved the way for the conclusion of the EEA Agreement,[31] which was finally signed on 2 May 1992 in Oporto. In the case of the European Communities, the decision was based on Article 238 in conjunction with Article 228(3) TEEC (Arts. 310 and 300(3) TEC following the Treaty of Amsterdam) and ECSC Treaty.[32] On the same day, two additional agreements were signed between the EFTA states: an agreement establishing a Surveillance Authority and an EFTA Court[33] and an agreement on a Standing Committee of the EFTA countries.[34] The plan was for the whole EEA package to enter into force simultaneously with the completion of the EEC internal market scheduled for 1 January 1993. However, this did not come to pass. A major blow came on 6 December 1992, when the Swiss voters rejected the EEA in a nationwide referendum.[35] Not only did the parties have to adopt an adjusting protocol,[36] but Liechtenstein's accession was also delayed to allow this microstate to accommodate its EEA membership with its close relationship with Switzerland.[37] The EEA Agreement finally entered into force on 1 January 1994, but Liechtenstein was only able to accede a year later (simultaneously with the departure of Sweden, Finland and Austria, which became members of the European Union).

---

[30] ECJ, Opinion 1/92 of the Court of 10 April 1992. Opinion pursuant to the second subparagraph of Art. 228(1) of the EEC Treaty. Draft agreement between the Community, on the one hand, and the countries of the European Free Trade Association, on the other, relating to the creation of the European Economic Area [1992] *ECR* I-2821.

[31] See also B. Brandtner, 'The "Drama" of the EEA. Comments on Opinions 1/91 and 1/92', 3 *EJIL* (1992) p. 300; H.G. Schermers, 'Opinion 1/91 of the Court of Justice, 14 December 1991; Opinion 1/92 of the Court of Justice, 10 April 1992', 29 *CMLRev.* (1992) p. 991.

[32] Decision 94/1/EC, ECSC of the Council and the Commission of 13 December 1993 on the conclusion of the Agreement on the European Economic Area between the European Communities, their Member States and the Republic of Austria, the Republic of Finland, the Republic of Iceland, the Principality of Liechtenstein, the Kingdom of Norway, the Kingdom of Sweden and the Swiss Confederation, *OJ* 1994 L 1/1.

[33] Agreement between the EFTA States on the establishment of a Surveillance Authority and a Court of Justice, *OJ* 1994 L 344/1 (as amended).

[34] Agreement on a Standing Committee of the EFTA States, available at: <http://secretariat.efta.int/Web/legaldocuments/AgreementOnStandingCommittee.pdf>.

[35] See chapter 5 in this volume.

[36] Protocol Adjusting the Agreement on the European Economic Area, *OJ* 1994 L 1/572.

[37] On ratification, see B. Cottier and A. Gerber, 'Some Problems Regarding Ratification and Implementation of the European Economic Area Agreement in the EFTA Member States', 20 *PolYIL* (1993) p. 253 at pp. 254-257.

2. THE EUROPEAN ECONOMIC AREA

2.1 **EEA membership**

The EEA is not a club with closed doors. Unlike the founding treaties of the European Communities/Union, the EEA Agreement not only contains rules on accession but also a withdrawal clause.[38] They are paradoxically positioned in a rather illogical way. The withdrawal clause comes first in Article 127 EEA, while the accession clause is only second in Article 128 EEA. One should also consider the intra-EEA consequences of the EFTA countries' accession to the European Union. They remain EEA members, but as countries of the European Union. This shifting of EEA pillars is resulting in numerous legal and institutional changes, which were experienced for the first time in 1995, when Austria, Sweden and Finland acceded to the European Union.[39]

The current wording of Article 128 EEA originates in the adjustment protocol, which followed the unsuccessful EEA accession referendum in Switzerland in 1992.[40] It reads that 'Any European State becoming a member of the Community shall, and the Swiss Confederation or any European State becoming a member of EFTA may, apply to become a party to this Agreement…'.[41] This implies that countries joining the European Union (which includes membership of the existing two European Communities) have an obligation to accede to the EEA as well. In the case of Switzerland or any European country becoming a member of EFTA, there is no such obligation but rather a right to become a member of the EEA. However, once an EFTA country expresses such a desire it has an obligation also to accede to the EFTA Surveillance Agreement and the Standing Committee Agreement.[42]

As already noted, the EEA Agreement contains an exit clause in Article 127. Each party is allowed to withdraw from the EEA; however, it has to give at least twelve months' notice to the other states. Upon notification, the other parties shall

---

38 The Treaty establishing a Constitution for Europe was the first in the EU framework to contain a voluntary withdrawal clause in Art. I-60. See Treaty establishing a Constitution for Europe, *OJ* 2004 C 340/1.

39 See H. Tichy and L. Dedichen, 'Securing a smooth shift between the two EEA pillars: prolonged competence of EFTA institutions with respect to former EFTA States after their accession to the European Union', 32 *CMLRev.* (1995) p. 131.

40 See chapter 5 in this volume.

41 The original version reads: 'Any European State becoming a member of the Community shall, or becoming a member of EFTA may, apply to become a Party to this Agreement. It shall address its application to the EEA Council.'

42 See Art. 51 of the EFTA Surveillance Agreement and Article 13 of the Standing Committee Agreement. Similarly, under Article 14, such a country has an obligation to accede to the Agreement on a Committee of Members of Parliament of the EFTA States (hereinafter referred to as the Parliament Agreement).

hold a diplomatic conference in order to agree on necessary modifications to the agreement. Withdrawal from the EEA *ipso facto* leads to a withdrawal from the EFTA Surveillance Agreement, the Standing Committee Agreement and the Parliament Agreement. The membership of an EEA-EFTA country in the European Union also has such consequences.[43]

So far, the EEA has witnessed two changes in the structure of its membership. The first followed the EU enlargement of 1995, when three EEA countries acceded the European Union and by the same token remained EEA members, although in a different capacity. The second was the consequence of the big bang enlargement of 2004.

The 1995 EU enlargement forced internal rearrangements within the EEA itself. There were a number of important legal issues that had to be addressed well in advance. They dealt not only with the institutional set-up but also with the division of surveillance jurisdiction in relation to the three (initially four) EFTA countries becoming EU members. The institutional adjustments were made by means of separate legal acts. The surveillance issues required more sophisticated arrangements since neither the EEA nor the EU legal frameworks contained explicit provisions in this respect. This led to a separate agreement between Austria, Finland, Iceland, Norway and Sweden, which was tailored in order to secure a smooth shift of pillars without undermining the effectiveness of the EEA legal framework.[44] The transitional issues were also discussed by the European Court of Justice. For instance, in *Andersson*,[45] the ECJ ruled that it had no jurisdiction to interpret EEA law applicable in the period preceding the membership of Sweden in the European Union. Due to its importance, it is worth reproducing that part of the judgment which clearly shows the Court's reasoning in this regard.

> Although the Court has jurisdiction in principle to give preliminary rulings concerning the interpretation of the Agreement on the European Economic Area (EEA) when a question arises before one of the national courts, since the provisions of that Agreement form an integral part of the Community legal system, that jurisdiction applies solely with regard to the Community, so that the Court has no jurisdiction to rule on the interpretation of the EEA Agreement as regards its application in the States belonging to the European Free Trade Association (EFTA).

---

43 See Art. 50(2) of the EFTA Surveillance Agreement and Article 12(2) of the Standing Committee Agreement. See also Article 15 *in fine* of the Parliament Agreement.

44 Agreement on transitional arrangements for a period after the accession of certain EFTA States to the European Union of 28 September 1994. For the text of the agreement, see Tichy and Dedichen, loc. cit. n. 39, at pp. 151-156.

45 ECJ, Case C-321/97 *Ulla-Brith Andersson and Susannne Wåkerås-Andersson* v. *Svenska staten (Swedish State)* [1999] *ECR* I-3551.

> The fact that the EFTA State in question subsequently became a Member State of the European Union, so that the question emanates from a court or tribunal of one of the Member States, cannot have the effect of attributing to the Court of Justice jurisdiction to interpret the EEA Agreement as regards its application to situations which do not come within the Community legal order. Thus, although the jurisdiction of the Court of Justice covers the interpretation of Community law, of which the EEA Agreement forms an integral part, as regards its application in the new Member States with effect from the date of their accession, the Court has no jurisdiction to rule on the effects of that Agreement within the national legal systems of the contracting States during the period prior to accession.

It has hard to disagree with the Court's strict approach declining its jurisdiction in relation to pre-accession issues. It is worth noting that this school of thought has been followed in the subsequent case law of the ECJ.[46]

The 2004 big bang enlargement of the European Union was followed by the first enlargement of the EEA. Conditions of accession were specified in the Accession Agreement concluded between the EEA contracting parties (including the European Community) and the candidate states. Although the EEA Accession Agreement was negotiated separately from the EU Accession Treaty, it draws heavily upon the latter, copying the majority of the transitional periods contained therein.[47] In the case of the 2004 enlargement, membership of the EEA was somehow wrongly expected to be a fairly simple and technical exercise. It was obvious from the very beginning that the enlargements of the European Union and the EEA should take place simultaneously in order to allow the smooth functioning of the internal market.[48] However, the negotiations of the EEA Accession Agreement, supplemented by a set of four additional treaties,[49] were

---

46 See also ECJ, Case C-140/97 *Walter Rechberger, Renate Greindl, Hermann Hofmeister and Others* v. *Republik Österreich* [1999] *ECR* I-3499; Case C-300/01 *Doris Salzmann* [2003] *ECR* I-4899.

47 See, *inter alia*, Ch. Hillion, 'The European Union is Dead. Long Live the European Union… A Commentary on the Treaty of Accession 2003', 29 *ELR* (2004) p. 583; K. Inglis, 'The Union's Fifth Accession Treaty: New Means to Make Enlargement Possible', 41 *CMLRev.* (2004) p. 937.

48 See, for instance, Resolution of the EEA Consultative Committee of 26 June 2002 on enlargement and the future of the EEA, *OJ* 2003 C 67/10; EEA Consultative Committee, Resolution on the 'Enlargement of the European Economic Area (EEA) – Institutional and Legal Issues', *OJ* 2003 C 308/16.

49 Agreement between the Kingdom of Norway and the European Community on a Norwegian Financial Mechanism for the period of 2004-2009, *OJ* 2004 L 130/81; Additional Protocol to the Agreement between the European Economic Community and the Republic of Iceland consequent on the accession of the Czech Republic, the Republic of Estonia, the Republic of Cyprus, the Republic of Latvia, the Republic of Lithuania, the Republic of Hungary, the Republic of Malta, the Republic of Poland, the Republic of Slovenia and the Slovak Republic to the European Union, *OJ* 2004 L 130/85; Additional Protocol to the Agreement between the European Economic Community and the Kingdom of Norway consequent on the accession of the Czech Republic, the Republic of Estonia,

delayed, and this led to disruptions in the ratification of the package. The main areas of concern were fisheries and EEA and Norwegian funds for the new Member States.[50] The official signing ceremony took place on 14 October 2003. Subsequent delays in the ratification process forced the parties to apply the EEA Accession Agreement on a provisional basis.[51] It eventually entered into force on 6 December 2005.

2.2 Aims of the EEA

It was clear from the very beginning that the set of aims prescribed for the EEA would be broad and ambitious. However, they were not as broad as in the case of the European Communities and the European Union. This factor has a direct influence on the application and interpretation of the EEA Agreement, as well as on the nature of the legal system established on its basis.

The aims of the EEA are outlined in general terms in Article 1 EEA; however, their interpretation is determined by the political goals spelled out in the Preamble. They include, *inter alia*, promotion of 'continuous and balanced strengthening of trade and economic relations' leading to the creation of a dynamic and homogeneous economic space. This, as explicit in Article 1(2) EEA read in conjunction with the fifth recital of the Preamble, involves the realisation of the free movement of goods, persons, services and capital combined with enhanced cooperation in so-called 'flanking and horizontal policies'. It also includes the participation of the EEA-EFTA countries in EC programmes. The fact that the EEA is to a considerable extent economically driven does not imply that other objectives are excluded. A simple reading of agreement's Preamble allows the conclusion that it was also tailored to contribute to a reduction in regional economic

the Republic of Cyprus, the Republic of Latvia, the Republic of Lithuania, the Republic of Hungary, the Republic of Malta, the Republic of Poland, the Republic of Slovenia and the Slovak Republic to the European Union, *OJ* 2004 L 130/89; Agreement in the form of an Exchange of Letters between the European Community and the Kingdom of Norway concerning certain agricultural products, *OJ* 2004 L 130/93.

50 For a Norwegian perspective see Archer, op. cit. n. 5, at pp. 173-176.

51 Council Decision of 30 March 2004 concerning the provisional application of the Agreement on the participation of the Czech Republic, the Republic of Estonia, the Republic of Cyprus, the Republic of Hungary, the Republic of Latvia, the Republic of Lithuania, the Republic of Malta, the Republic of Poland, the Republic of Slovenia and the Slovak Republic in the European Economic Area and the provisional application of four related agreements, *OJ* 2004 L 130/1; Agreements in the form of an exchange of letters concerning the provisional application of the Agreement on the participation of the Czech Republic, the Republic of Estonia, the Republic of Cyprus, the Republic of Hungary, the Republic of Latvia, the Republic of Lithuania, the Republic of Malta, the Republic of Poland, the Republic of Slovenia and the Slovak Republic in the European Economic Area and the provisional application of four related agreements, *OJ* 2004 L 130/3.

and social disparities;[52] protection of the environment, consumers and the health of humans; equality of men and women; and the strengthening of the scientific and technological basis for European industry.

The concept of a homogeneous legal space lies at the heart of the EEA. This is absolutely clear from the Preamble, which makes it explicit that the objective of the EEA is creation of the 'dynamic and homogeneous' area. To this end the provisions of the EEA Agreement reflect the wording of the relevant TEC articles. Moreover, the annexes containing lists of applicable secondary *acquis* are regularly updated by the Joint Committee and their implementation in the domestic law of EEA-EFTA countries follows. Both the EEA Agreement and the Surveillance Agreement create an obligation to interpret EEA provisions reflecting EC legislation in accordance with the case law of the European Court of Justice. Judging from the ten-year experience of the EEA, one is allowed to conclude that the objective of securing the homogeneous legal area belongs to the main legal challenges the Member States and institutions operating in the two-pillar EEA framework have to face.

2.3 Institutional framework of the EEA

2.3.1 *An overview of the institutional framework*

The fulfilment of the ambitious EEA aims required the creation of a sophisticated institutional set-up guaranteeing the effectiveness of the EEA without, at the same time, undermining the autonomy of the EC legal order and its decision making, on the one hand, and the sovereignty of the EFTA states, on the other. In order to evolve into a homogeneous area, the EEA needed broadly empowered institutions encompassing quasi-legislative, executive and judicial powers. Moreover, only the creation of institutions capable of reacting to the natural development of EC law could secure the dynamic legal regime envisaged by the EEA Agreement.[53] Before the negotiations were initiated various concepts already emerged, and it was clear that tailoring a functional institutional framework, which would be acceptable to all the parties, would pose a major challenge. Indeed, as Reymond rightly notes, during the negotiations it was 'mainly on the legal and institutional side that significant stumbling blocks appeared.'[54] The task was completed successfully,

[52] The EEA financial assistance programmes serve as an excellent example. See Protocol 38a on the EEA financial mechanism, *OJ* 2004 L 130/14. See also information available on the official website of the EEA funds, at: <http://www.eeagrants.org>.

[53] See M. Cremona, 'The "Dynamic and Homogeneous" EEA: Byzantine Structures and Variable Geometry', 19 *ELR* (1994) p. 508 at p. 509.

[54] Ch. Reymond, 'Institutions, decision-making procedure and settlement of disputes in the European Economic Area', 30 *CMLRev.* (1993) p. 449 at p. 451.

albeit with serious legal hurdles on the way. As previously noted, the original shape of the judicial architecture was challenged by the European Court of Justice in Opinion 1/91. This led to the creation of a separate EFTA Court for the EEA-EFTA countries.

The bulk of the institutional provisions regulating the organisation and functioning of joint decision-making bodies and relevant procedures was inserted into the main part of the agreement (Part VII). Rules on surveillance institutions for EEA-EFTA countries are dealt with therein to a limited extent. It was left to the EFTA countries to make all necessary arrangements separately. As noted earlier, two additional agreements were concluded and entered into force simultaneously with the EEA Agreement.

Graph 1: The two-pillar structure under the EEA-EFTA Agreement

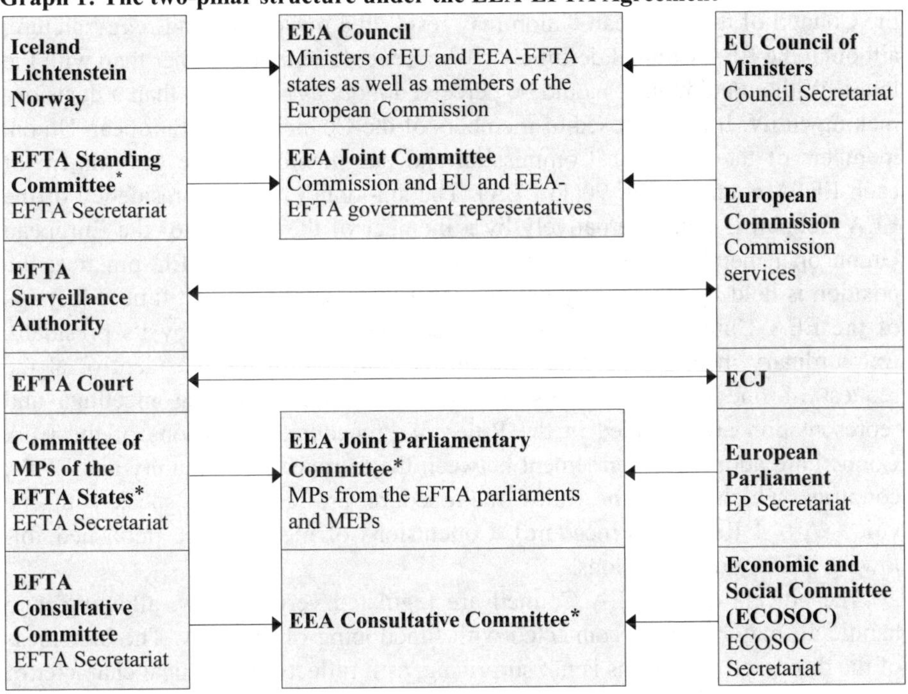

* Switzerland has observer status.

Source: <http://secretariat.efta.int/Web/EuropeanEconomicArea/institutions/TwoPillarSystem/2pillar_structure_under_EEA.jpg>.

The EEA is equipped with a so-called two-pillar institutional structure. It is composed of two kinds of bodies. The first are joint EFTA-EC institutions composed of representatives of both sides and the Member States. The second group consists of EFTA or EC institutions which were created to accommodate the needs of the EEA or which operated before within the respective institutional frameworks (see Graph 1). Due to its multi-layer complexity, the institutional set-up of the EEA has been referred to as a 'Byzantine structure.'[55] The joint institutions include the EEA Council, EEA Joint Committee, EEA Joint Parliamentary Committee and EEA Consultative Committee. Surveillance is conducted by the EFTA Surveillance Authority and the EFTA Court.[56] The EEA-EFTA countries also established a Standing Committee, which was envisaged to serve EFTA countries as a forum for consultation and shaping common positions. On the EU side, the relevant authorities equipped with surveillance powers are the European Commission and the European Court of Justice.

2.3.2 *EEA Council*

In political terms, it is correct to consider the EEA Council to be at the top of the institutional hierarchy of the EEA. Any comparison with the European Council or the Council of the European Union may result in a misleading and foggy picture, although the EEA Council definitely has more to do with the former than with the latter. Without a doubt, it should be perceived more as a political than a decision-making entity. It is composed of members of the Council of the European Union, members of the European Commission and one member of the government of each EFTA country (Art. 90(1) EEA). The six-month rotating presidency of the EEA Council is held alternatively by a member of the Council of the European Union or a member of the government of an EFTA state. In EU practice, the position is held by the country holding the EU presidency at that time. Meetings of the EEA Council are held twice a year and are convened by its president. Extraordinary meetings may be held on the initiative of the president or at the request of one of its members. Detailed rules on convening meetings and representation are included in the Rules of Procedure.[57] Decisions of the EEA Council are adopted by agreement between the European Community and EFTA countries, which, under the Rules of Procedure, are required to speak with one voice (Art. 4 Rules of Procedure). Conclusions of meetings are published following EEA Council sessions.

The powers of the EEA Council are regulated very vaguely, allowing it to handle all major matters connected with functioning of the EEA. The blurriness of the discussed provisions is not surprising, as it reflects the political character of the institution envisaged by the drafters. The EEA Council is mainly 'responsible for giving the political impetus in the implementation' of the EEA Agreement, as well as 'laying down the general guidelines for the EEA Joint Committee'. It shall 'assess the overall functioning and the development' of the EEA Agreement

---

55 Cremona, loc. cit. n. 53.

56 For a general overview, see Reymond, loc. cit. n. 54.

57 Decision of the EEA Council No. 1/94 of 17 May 1994 adopting the Rules of Procedure of the EEA Council, *OJ* 1994 L 138/39.

and shall 'take political decisions leading to' its amendment (Art. 89(1) EEA). When agreement on certain controversial or urgent matters is not possible at the lower level of the EEA Joint Committee, the EEA Council serves as an upper instance. In practice, the EEA Council serves as a forum for debate and the exchange of opinions on issues vital for the functioning of the EEA. For instance, during meetings held on 14 December 2004 and 15 June 2005, the dossiers included the EEA enlargement of 2004 and the impact of future EU accessions; the adoption of the Treaty establishing a Constitution for Europe; the Lisbon strategy, the adoption of the European Neighbourhood Policy and developments in the internal market.[58] So-called orientation debates are common in EEA Council meetings. As a matter of example, it is worth pointing out that during recent meetings such orientation debates were devoted to the European Neighbourhood Policy, future EU enlargements as well as developments regarding the WTO's Doha round.[59] It should be noted that the EEA Council is envisaged to play a central role in the revision procedure provided for in Article 118 EEA.

2.3.3 *EEA Joint Committee*

The EEA Joint Committee is at the heart of the institutional framework. As noted by the EFTA Court in *CIBA Speciality Chemical Waters Treatment Ltd. and Others* v. *Norway*,[60] 'the EEA Joint Committee is designed to function as an institution working in the pursuit of the common interest of the Community side and the EFTA side.'[61] In general terms, the EEA Joint Committee is equipped with competences to ensure the effective implementation and operation of the EEA Agreement. It is composed of representatives designated by the parties to the EEA Agreement, including ambassadors of the EEA-EFTA countries as well as representatives of the European Commission and the EU Member States. Moreover, the representatives of the EFTA Surveillance Authority and European Investment Bank are invited as observers.[62] The EEA Joint Committee meets at least once a month; however, extraordinary meetings may be convened by the president on his or her own initiative or at the request of the parties.[63] As practice

58 See Conclusions of the 22nd meeting of the EEA Council, Brussels, 14 December 2004, EEE 1610/04 (Presse 362); Conclusions of the 23rd meeting of the EEA Council. Luxembourg, 14 June 2005, EEE 1605/05 (Presse).

59 Ibid.

60 EFTA Court, Case E-6/01 *CIBA Speciality Chemicals Water Treatment Ltd and Others* v. *the Norwegian State*, EFTA Court Rep. [2002] 281.

61 Para. 33 of the judgment.

62 Art. 1(3) of the EEA Joint Committee Rules of Procedure, Decision of the EEA Joint Committee No. 1/94 adopting the Rules of Procedure of the EEA Joint Committee, *OJ* 1994 L 85/60 (as amended).

63 For procedural details, see Arts. 2-3 of the EEA Joint Committee Rules of Procedure.

proves, the EEA Joint Committee does not meet that often. For instance, in 2003 and 2004 there were eight meetings per year.[64] The six-month rotating presidency is held alternatively by a representative of the European Community and one of the EEA-EFTA countries. In its work, the EEA Joint Committee is assisted by permanent subcommittees, which in turn are supported by working groups.[65] Both are composed of representatives of the contracting parties and are chaired for six-month periods alternatively by an EFTA country or the European Commission.[66] At the time of writing, there are four subcommittees in operation, namely on the free movement of goods, the free movement of capital and services, the free movement of persons and one on flanking and horizontal issues.[67] There are also a number of active working groups. Decisions of the EEA Joint Committee are taken by agreement between the European Community and the EFTA states 'speaking with one voice' (Art. 93(2) EEA).

The extensive powers given to the Joint Committee allow it to perform legislative and dispute-settlement functions. As already noted, it is responsible for ensuring the proper functioning of the EEA. It serves as the main forum for consultations between the EFTA states, the EU Member States and the European Community (Art. 92(2) EEA). In order to fulfil its tasks, the EEA Joint Committee has the authority to 'take decisions in the cases provided for in this Agreement' (Art. 92(1) EEA).[68] This proviso was interpreted functionally by the EFTA Court in the above-mentioned *CIBA* case. The request for an advisory opinion on the interpretation of EEA law was made by the *Oslo byrett* (Oslo City Court) in connection with a litigation pending before it between a company operating in the chemical sector and the Norwegian state. As a matter of fact, it was a follow-up to an earlier reference and EFTA Court judgment in *Allied Colloids and Others* v. *Norwegian Government*.[69] The domestic dispute dealt with the obligation imposed on the plaintiff to label the substance polyacrylamide as carcinogenic when it contained very limited quantities of acrylamide. Derogation was granted to Norway in this respect in two subsequent joint statements of the

64 See Annual Report of the Joint Committee for the Year 2003 on the Functioning of the EEA Agreement, Ref. No. 1034120, para. 1; Annual Report of the Joint Committee for the Year 2004 on the Functioning of the EEA Agreement, Ref. No. 1051228, para. 1.

65 According to Art. 15 of the EEA Joint Committee Rules of Procedure the subcommittees are responsible for the preparation of EEA Joint Committee decisions. In addition, the latter may delegate further tasks to the subcommittees.

66 Arts. 16-17 of the EEA Joint Committee Rules of Procedure.

67 Art. 15 of the EEA Joint Committee Rules of Procedure envisaged the creation of five subcommittees, including the legal and institutional matters subcommittee.

68 EEA Joint Committee decisions are binding. Art. 104 EEA imposes an obligation on the parties to take 'necessary steps to ensure their implementation and application.'

69 EFTA Court, Case E-2/00 *Allied Colloids and Others* v. *The Government of Norway*, EFTA Court Rep. [2000-2001] 35.

EEA Joint Committee adopted in 1995 and 1999.[70] It was the legality of the latter that was challenged by the plaintiff in the Norwegian Court. It was argued that the EEA Joint Committee exceeded its powers in 1999 by amending the exceptions provided for in 1995 joint statement. Plaintiffs also submitted that the competences of the EEA Joint Committee regulated in Articles 98 and 102 EEA should be interpreted narrowly. The EFTA Court disagreed. It ruled that

> contrary to the Plaintiffs' contention, the wording of that provision must not be interpreted as constituting a narrow definition of the competence of the EEA Joint Committee. It cannot be assumed that the powers of the EEA Joint Committee are limited to those matters where specific powers or functions have been set out. The Court finds support for this finding, *inter alia*, in Article 102(3) EEA. The reference in that provision to 'matters relevant to this Agreement' must also cover matters that are not specifically dealt with in the texts of the EEA main Agreement, its Protocols and Annexes, but nevertheless are capable of affecting the good functioning of the EEA Agreement.[71]

The EFTA Court supported its position by arguing that maintenance of the homogeneity of the EEA and the protection of individuals remained 'the fundamental policy objectives' and that in order to achieve these objectives competences of the Joint Committee 'must not be overly restricted.' Of course, the operational freedom of the EEA Joint Committee is not unlimited and it must remain within 'the boundaries of the EEA Agreement'.[72] It is interesting to note that decisions of the EEA Joint Committee are not subject to judicial review. Neither in the case of actions for annulment based on Article 36 of the Surveillance Agreement nor in the advisory opinion procedure does the EFTA Court have the jurisdiction to rule on the validity of the Committee's decisions. In the above-mentioned case the attempts to challenge the jurisdiction of the EFTA Court failed. It was concluded that the questions related to the interpretation of the EEA Agreement and its provisions on the powers of the EEA Joint Committee (not validity of its statement).

The EEA Joint Committee plays a central role in securing the homogeneity of the EEA. In this regard, one of its main tasks is to adjust the EEA Agreement and its annexes to developments in EC law (Arts. 98 and 102 EEA). Practice proves

---

[70] Derogation was based on Annex II, Chapter XV, Part 1 of the EEA Agreement. It reads that 'The Contracting Parties agree on the objective that the provisions of the Community acts on dangerous substances and preparations should apply by 1 January 1995. ... If an EFTA State concludes that it will need any derogation from the Community acts relating to classification and labelling, the latter shall not apply to it unless the EEA Joint Committee agrees on another solution.'

[71] Para. 32 of the judgment.

[72] Para. 33 of the judgment.

that this remains one of its core activities. For example, in 2003 it adopted 179 decisions incorporating 297 EC acts; this was followed by 181 decisions incorporating 309 pieces of EC legislation in 2004.[73]

The EEA Joint Committee has been made responsible for setting up the information system facilitating the exchange of information between the EFTA Court and the EU Courts. Also, it has an obligation to keep under constant review the judicial developments in the European Court of Justice and the EFTA Court (Art. 105(2) EEA). Under Article 113 EEA, the EEA Joint Committee is at the heart of the safeguard measures procedure. These measures can be imposed by the parties, albeit only in extraordinary situations.

The Joint Committee also serves the EEA as a dispute-settlement authority. The key procedure is formulated in Article 111 EEA. Disputes concerning the interpretation or application of the EEA Agreement may be brought by the European Community or an EFTA state. Another example is the authority of the EEA Joint Committee to handle disputes between the EFTA Surveillance Authority and European Commission on complaints concerning the application of the EEA Agreement (Art. 109 EEA).

2.3.4 *EEA Joint Parliamentary Committee*

The EEA Agreement provides for the creation of parliamentary cooperation between the European Community and the EEA-EFTA countries (Art. 95 EEA). Detailed rules are included in the Statute inserted in Protocol 36 to the EEA Agreement[74] and in the Committee's Rules of Procedure.[75] The EEA Joint Parliamentary Committee is composed of twenty-four members[76] appointed in equal numbers by the European Parliament and the national assemblies of the EFTA states.[77] Meetings are also attended by observers from the Swiss Parliament. The ordinary sessions of the EEA Joint Parliamentary Committee are scheduled to take place twice a year. The Statute also facilitates extraordinary sessions when

---

[73] Annual Report of the Joint Committee for the Year 2003 on the Functioning of the EEA Agreement, loc. cit. n. 64, at pt. 1; Annual Report of the Joint Committee for the Year 2004 on the Functioning of the EEA Agreement, loc. cit. n. 64, at pt. 1.

[74] Protocol 36 to the EEA Agreement on the Statute of the EEA Joint Parliamentary Committee (as amended by the EEA Enlargement Agreement).

[75] European Economic Area Joint Parliamentary Committee Rules of Procedure, Doc. No. M/20/I/007 of 18 June 1996.

[76] Initially, the EEA Joint Parliamentary Committee was composed of sixty-six members (thirty-three MEPs and thirty-three EFTA MPs, but the number was reduced after the EU enlargement in 1995).

[77] See Art. 2 of the Statute. Interestingly enough, in April 2005, there were twenty-five members of the Committee. The prescribed number was exceeded on the EFTA side by five MPs from Iceland, two MPs from Liechtenstein and six MPs from Norway.

required by the Committee or its Bureau (Art. 4). The first meeting of the Committee took place in Brussels on 24-25 January 1994. By mid-2005, the total record of the Committee's gatherings stood at twenty-three meetings.[78]

The EEA Joint Parliamentary Committee is mainly tailored to perform political functions. As Article 95(3) EEA reads, it 'shall contribute, through dialogue and debate, to a better understanding between the Community and the EFTA States in the fields covered by this Agreement.' The voice of the Committee is formulated in resolutions and recommendations. In the course of recent years, it has adopted resolutions and reports on, *inter alia*, the functioning of the EEA; EEA decision shaping; the concept of Wider Europe; Internal Market Strategy 2003-2006; and the impact on the EEA of the Treaty establishing a Constitution for Europe.[79]

During its sessions, the EEA Joint Parliamentary Committee holds regular meetings with representatives of the EEA Council, the EEA Joint Committee and the EFTA Surveillance Authority.

2.3.5 *EEA Consultative Committee*

The EEA Consultative Committee is yet another joint body functioning within the EEA institutional framework. It is envisaged to facilitate cooperation between economic and social partners. The Committee is composed of members of the EC Economic and Social Committee and representatives of the EFTA Consultative Committee (in equal numbers). The Committees tasks are spelled out in Article 96 EEA, which provides that its members 'shall work to strengthen contacts between them and to cooperate in an organised and regular manner in order to enhance the awareness of the economic and social aspects of the growing interdependence of the economies of the Contracting Parties and of their interests within the context of the EEA.' The EEA Consultative Committee meets once a year. It is empowered to adopt reports and resolutions. For example, during its 2004 session the EEA Consultative Committee adopted a Report and Resolution on the Second Northern Dimension Action Plan[80] as well as a Report and Resolution on the European Neighbourhood Policy.[81]

---

[78] For an overview of the Committee's activities, see Information Note on the work of the EP-EFTA Parliamentary Relations and on the activities of the EEA JPC, PE 342.059.

[79] The text of the resolutions and reports is available at: <http://secretariat.efta.int/Web/EuropeanEconomicArea/institutions/EEAParliamentaryCommittee/eea_jpc_resolutions>.

[80] EEA Consultative Committee Report and Resolution on the Second Northern Dimension Action Plan, DI CESE 84/2004 – Ref. No. 1044051.

[81] EEA Consultative Committee Report and Resolution on the European Neighbourhood Policy and the EEA, DI CESE 83/2004 – Ref. No. 1043788.

2.3.6 *EFTA Surveillance Authority*

An absolutely pivotal role in the enforcement of the EEA Agreement in the EFTA countries is played by the EFTA Surveillance Authority. It was established on the basis of the EEA Agreement as well as the EFTA Surveillance Agreement. It is equipped with extensive powers, which to a considerable extent mirror the competences of the European Commission.

The EFTA Surveillance Authority is composed of three members who are chosen 'on the grounds of their general competence and whose independence is beyond doubt.' Article 7 of the Surveillance Agreement imposes the requirement that at least two of them shall be nationals of EFTA countries.[82] They are appointed for renewable four-year terms by common accord of the EFTA countries' governments (Art. 9 of the Surveillance Agreement). Vacancies resulting from normal replacement, resignation, death or compulsory retirement by the EFTA Court are filled only for the remaining time of the relevant member's term (Art. 10 of the Surveillance Agreement).[83] Similarly to Commissioners, the members of the EFTA Surveillance Authority have to be independent in their actions and should not seek or follow instructions from the governments of EEA-EFTA countries. In the case of serious misconduct, or when the conditions for appointment are no longer fulfilled, the members of the EFTA Surveillance Authority may be retired by the EFTA Court (Art. 11 of the Surveillance Agreement). This arrangement mirrors the compulsory retirement procedure envisaged by Article 216 TEC. The EFTA Surveillance Authority acts under the leadership of a president appointed from its members by the governments of the EFTA countries for a two-year term (Art. 12 of the Surveillance Agreement).[84] The Authority's staff is fairly limited. For example, in 2004 the permanent staff amounted to fifty-two persons, the majority coming from EFTA countries.[85] Like the members of the Commission, the staff members of the Authority must be independent in their actions.

The powers of the EFTA Surveillance Authority are extensively regulated in the Surveillance Agreement. They can be divided into two groups. The first can be defined as a general authority to ensure the fulfilment of membership obligations by the EEA-EFTA countries. To this end, Article 5 of the Surveillance Agreement specifies that it shall 'ensure the fulfilment by the EFTA States of their obligations

---

[82] At the time of writing, the EFTA Surveillance Authority is composed of Bjørn T. Grydeland (Norwegian) (President), Kurt Jaeger (Liechtenstein and Switzerland) and Kristján Andri Stefánsson (Iceland). See the website of the EFTA Surveillance Authority, at <http://www.eftasurv.int>.

[83] Since there is no parliamentary assembly in the EEA institutional structure, the EFTA Surveillance Authority may not be dismissed by a motion of censure as in the case of the European Commission.

[84] No alternations were made to the position of the President of the EFTA Surveillance Authority following the strengthening of European Commission President in the Treaty of Nice.

[85] See EFTA Surveillance Authority Annual Report 2004 (Brussels 2005) p. 11.

under the EEA Agreement and this Agreement [i.e., the EFTA Surveillance Agreement]'. The second group covers selected areas of EEA law where the EFTA Surveillance Authority has been granted considerable enforcement powers. These areas include public procurement, competition law and state aid. In all these fields, the powers of the EFTA Surveillance Authority reflect those of the European Commission under the EU legal framework. To this end, Protocol 2 to the EFTA Surveillance Agreement implements Council Directives 89/665/EEC and 92/13/EEC on public procurement remedies,[86] while Protocol 3 deals with state aid and implements Council Regulation 659/1999/EC on state aid procedures.[87] Similarly, rules on competition law enshrined in Protocol 4 reflect the EC *acquis* in this respect (including the concentration of undertakings). The powers of the EFTA Surveillance Authority are discussed in detail in section 2.5 of this chapter.

2.3.7 *EFTA Court*

The original draft of the EEA Agreement did not envisage the creation of a separate judicial authority for the EFTA countries only. On the contrary, the initial concept involved the creation of a joint EEC/ECSC-EFTA judicial architecture comprising the EEA Court as well as the EEA Court of First Instance. Such a potentially far-reaching arrangement was declared to be contrary to the EEC Treaty and eventually led to the creation of the EFTA Court.[88] The EEA Agreement itself only scarcely deals with the EFTA Court and its jurisdiction. Article 108(2) EEA merely creates an obligation for the EFTA countries to conclude a separate agreement on the Court. As a consequence, detailed rules on its composition and jurisdiction are thoroughly regulated in the EFTA Surveillance Agreement and the Statute annexed thereto.[89]

---

[86] Council Directive 89/665/EEC on the coordination of the laws, regulations and administrative provisions relating to the application of review procedures to the award of public supply and public works contracts, *OJ* 1989 L 395/33; Council Directive 92/13/EEC of 25 February 1992 coordinating the laws, regulations and administrative provisions relating to the application of Community rules on the procurement procedures of entities operating in the water, energy, transport and telecommunications sector, *OJ* 1992 L 76/14.

[87] Council Regulation (EC) No. 659/1999 of 22 March 1999 laying down detailed rules for the application of Art. 93 of the EC Treaty, *OJ* 1999 L 83/1.

[88] See, *inter alia*, C. Baudenbacher, et al., eds., *The EFTA Court. Ten Years On* (Oxford/Portland, Oregon, Hart Publishing 2005); P. Christiansen, 'The EFTA Court', 22 *ELR* (1997) p. 539; C. Baudenbacher, 'Between Homogeneity and Independence: The Legal Position of the EFTA Court in the European Economic Area', 3 *Columbia Journal of European Law* (1997) p. 169; C. Baudenbacher, 'The EFTA Court – an example of the judicialisation of international economic law', 28 *ELR* (2003) p. 880; C. Baudenbacher, 'The EFTA Court: An Actor in the European Judicial Dialogue', 28 *Fordham Int'l L.J* (2005) p. 353.

[89] See Protocol 5 on the Statute of the EFTA Court (hereinafter referred to as the Statute). See also Rules of Procedure of the EFTA Court available at the official website of the EFTA Court, at <http://www.eftacourt.lu/default.asp?layout=article&id=193>.

The Luxembourg-based EFTA Court is composed of three judges who are chosen on the grounds of their qualifications and undisputed independence. The appointment is effected by common accord of the EEA-EFTA states and covers a six-year term. Judges are eligible for reappointment.[90] There is also a possibility to appoint *ad hoc* judges, who may serve when an appointed judge cannot proceed.[91]

The jurisdiction of the EFTA Court draws considerably on the powers of the European Court of Justice in the first pillar of the European Union; however, its scope is much more limited. It includes:

- an infraction procedure (Art. 31 of the EFTA Surveillance Agreement),
- advisory opinions that are the equivalent of preliminary rulings (Art. 34 of the EFTA Surveillance Agreement),
- actions for annulment of EFTA Surveillance Authority decisions (Art. 36 of the EFTA Surveillance Agreement),
- actions for failure to act against the EFTA Surveillance Authority (Art. 37 of the EFTA Surveillance Agreement),
- actions for damages against the EFTA Surveillance Authority (Art. 39 of the EFTA Surveillance Agreement).

Details of these actions are discussed further in section 2.5 of this chapter, which is devoted to surveillance in the EEA. For the purposes of this part of the analysis, it is important to look at the legal nature of EFTA Court judgments. Formally they are not precedents within the meaning of common law. However, similarly to the ECJ and CFI, the EFTA Court itself 'treats its own judgments as precedents'.[92] Analysis of the first ten years of its activities leaves no doubt that, when it comes to the methodology of the interpretation of EEA law, the EFTA Court follows closely in the footsteps of the European Court of Justice. Teleological and functional interpretation of law is one of the key characteristics of its work.

2.3.8 *Standing Committee of the EFTA states*

The Standing Committee serves as an important platform for consultations between the EFTA states in the preparation of EEA Council Decisions or EEA Joint Committee Decisions. It operates on the basis of a separate agreement concluded

---

[90] For details on the appointment of judges and the organisation of the EFTA Court, see Arts. 28-30 of the EFTA Surveillance Agreement. See also Arts. 2-16 of the Statute.

[91] In February 2006, there were six *ad hoc* judges at the EFTA Court. See the information on the official website of the EFTA Court, at: <http://www.eftacourt.lu/default.asp?layout=article&id=128>.

[92] Baudenbacher (2003), loc. cit. n. 88, at p. 895.

between the EFTA countries.[93] Its detailed powers are specified in Article 3 of the Standing Committee Agreement. In the performance of its tasks, the Standing Committee is empowered to take binding decisions as well as to make soft law recommendations. Each EFTA country is represented on the Committee and is equipped with one vote. Unanimity is the rule, however in some cases majority voting is envisaged.

2.4 Decision shaping and decision making in the EEA

2.4.1 *Introduction*

A key issue connected with the functioning of the EEA is the participation of the EEA-EFTA states in EU decision-making procedures. Although these countries are not formally taking part in decision making on an equal footing with the EU Member States, they nevertheless have the right to participate in various committees and via this channel make attempts to influence negotiations at the 'pre-pipeline stage'. Moreover, so-called EEA-EFTA Comments adopted by the Standing Committee of the EFTA states may influence EU decision making. Due to the way in which the EEA-EFTA countries are influencing the EU decision-making process, their participation is often referred to as 'decision shaping'. The other important aspect of the EEA is its own decision making and in particular the incorporation of EC secondary legislation into the framework of the EEA by means of EEA Joint Committee decisions. This unique 'decision making' is one of the well-established ways of securing the homogeneity of the EEA. Both, decision shaping and decision making are discussed in this section.

2.4.2 *Participation of EFTA countries in EU decision-making procedures (decision shaping)*

One of the characteristics of the EEA is the very limited access of the EEA-EFTA countries to EU decision making, on the one hand, and their obligation to incorporate EC secondary law, on the other.[94] Representatives of the EEA-EFTA countries may participate in the European Commission's expert, comitology and

---

93 See also Decision of the Standing Committee of the EFTA States No. 1/94/SC of 10 January 1994 adopting the Rules of Procedure of the Standing Committee of the EFTA States, *OJ* 1994 L 85/72 (as amended), codified version of the text available at: <http://secretariat.efta.int/Web/EuropeanEconomicArea/institutions/EFTAStandingCommittee>.

94 Bearing in mind the association status of the EEA, one should distinguish this arrangement from voluntary harmonisation, which is at the heart of the Europe Agreements as well as the Stabilisation and Association Agreements.

non-comitology committees. Participation in the working groups of the Council of the European Union and the work of the European Parliament is excluded.

When it comes to decision shaping, Article 99 EEA is of pivotal importance. It creates an obligation for the European Commission to 'informally seek advice from experts of the EFTA states in the same way as it seeks advice from experts of the EC Member States for the elaboration of its proposals.' They are invited to participate in expert committees and do so on an equal footing with the experts from EU Member States. Due to the advisory character of these committees, no voting takes place. The effectiveness of EEA-EFTA experts in shaping the legislation varies; however, there are examples proving that their role has been of pivotal importance. In this context, EC legislation on maritime oil transport safety, which was influenced heavily by Norway, is worth mentioning.[95] In practice, experts from the EEA-EFTA countries participate in more than a hundred expert committees.[96]

Another channel which can be used by the EEA-EFTA countries to influence EC secondary legislation is through comitology committees. By this means, Iceland, Liechtenstein and Norway may participate in the adoption of the implementing legislation by the European Commission. The current comitology system is based on Council Decision 1999/468/EC,[97] which was adopted following a lively debate on the nature of the comitology procedures and their undemocratic and non-transparent character.[98] It provides for the creation of advisory, management and regulatory committees.[99] Based on Article 100 EEA, experts from the EFTA countries are granted 'as wide a participation as possible' in the comitology committees. They are also involved in the preparatory work leading up to the meetings of committees.[100] When it comes to voting, they do not have voting

[95] 'The European Economic Area: Decision Shaping and Participation in Committees', *EFTA Bull.* 1/2002, 14-15.

[96] In 2002, this number stood at 119. See *EFTA Bull.* 1/2002, 12.

[97] Council Decision 1999/468/EC of 28 June 1999 laying down the conditions for the exercise of implementing powers conferred on the Commission, *OJ* 1999 L 184/23. It replaced Council Decision 87/373/EEC of 13 July 1987 laying down the procedures for the exercise of implementing powers conferred on the Commission, *OJ* 1987 L 197/33. See also Agreement between the European Parliament and the Commission on procedures for implementing Council Decision 1999/468/EC of 28 June 1999 laying down the procedures for the exercise of implementing powers conferred on the Commission, *OJ* 2000 L 256/19.

[98] For an academic appraisal of comitology and its evolution, see, *inter alia*, G. Haibach, 'The History of Comitology', in M. Andenas and A. Türk, eds., *Delegated Legislation and the Role of Committees in the EC* (London, Kluwer Law International 2000) p. 185.

[99] For a list of Committees, see Information from the Commission – List of committees which assist the Commission in the exercise of its implementing powers, *OJ* 2000 L 225/2.

[100] The European Community declaration annexed to the EEA Final Act reads: 'The Commission of the European Communities confirms that in the application of the principles laid down in Art. 100, it is understood that each EFTA State will designate its own experts. Those experts will be involved on an equal footing together with national experts from the EC Member States in the work

rights and their presence may be denied. This undoubtedly limits the effectiveness of their involvement and emphasises the importance of their diplomatic skills and networking capabilities.

Representatives of the EEA-EFTA countries also attend meetings of committees involved in assisting the European Commission in the management and development of the EC programmes (including framework programmes). This possibility is granted under Article 81 EEA. Moreover, under Article 101 EEA, experts from EFTA countries may be associated with the activities of the committees listed in Protocol 37 when necessary for the good functioning of the EEA.

In the case of proposals, which require the consent of the Council of the European Union (with or without the participation of the European Parliament), the European Commission transfers legislative proposals upon completion of the pre-pipeline stage. At the same time, it has an obligation to submit copies of all proposals with EEA relevance to the EEA-EFTA states. At this stage, an information and consultation phase takes place, offering the EFTA countries a chance to express their views on the proposed legislation. This is facilitated within the framework of the EEA Joint Committee.[101] Article 99 EEA creates an obligation for the contracting parties to cooperate in good faith in this respect.

In areas of key interest, the Standing Committee of the EFTA states endorses official opinions of the EEA-EFTA countries. Recent examples include comments on proposals concerning the Media 2007 programme,[102] a proposed directive on energy[103] and a regulation on chemicals.[104]

The above-mentioned windows of opportunity facilitate access to the EU decision-making process, but at the same time pose challenges to the EEA-EFTA countries. Active participation requires appropriate administrative capacity as well as well-trained and experienced staff. It also has an impact on the national administrations of the EFTA countries.[105]

---

preparatory to the convening of the EC committees relevant to the *"acquis"* in question. The EC Commission will pursue consultations as long as deemed necessary, until the Commission submits its proposal at a formal meeting.'

101 Art. 99 EEA.

102 EEA-EFTA States' Comments on the Commission's Proposal Concerning the Implementation of a Programme of Support for the European Audiovisual Sector (Media 2007), Ref. No. 1053883.

103 EEA-EFTA States' Comments on the Proposal for a Directive on End Use Energy Efficiency and Energy Resources, Ref. No. 1051624.

104 EEA-EFTA States' Comments on the Proposal for a Regulation Concerning the Registration, Evaluation, Authorisation and Notification of Chemicals, Ref. No. 1054044.

105 For an empirical appraisal of the EEA's impact on Norwegian administration, see M. Egeberg and J. Trondal, 'Differentiated Integration in Europe: The Case of EEA Country, Norway', 37 *JCMS* (1999) p. 133.

2.4.3 *EEA decision-making procedures*

In purely political terms, the key decision-making authority is the EEA Council. Its composition and powers are thoroughly discussed in section 2.3.2 of this chapter. In legal terms, however, the decisive role is played by the EEA Joint Committee. This is especially the case when it comes to regular updates to the EEA legal framework securing the homogeneity of the area.

As already noted, the annexes to the EEA Agreement contain lists of EC legislation with EEA relevance and may be amended by decisions of the EEA Joint Committee. The relevant procedure is set forth in Articles 102-104 EEA. Following the adoption of the EC legislation, the relevant EU decision-making bodies have an obligation to transfer the new legislation to the relevant authorities of EFTA states. It is the task of the EEA Joint Committee to secure the homogeneity of the EEA legal space and amend the annexes as fast as possible in order to allow simultaneous entry into force of the legislation in the entire EEA.[106] The consent of all EEA-EFTA states is necessary and to this end an important role is played by the Standing Committee of the EFTA states. The decisions of the EEA Joint Committee are binding and require implementation by the EEA-EFTA countries.[107]

If the achievement of consent runs into difficulties, the EEA Joint Committee will take all possible measures in order to secure a compromise. If unsuccessful, it will 'examine all further possibilities to maintain the good functioning of this Agreement and take any decision necessary to this effect.'[108] The time limit is six months following the referral or date of entry into force of the relevant legislation (providing the latter date is the later one). If, following the expiry of the deadline, a compromise is still not within reach, the affected part of the EEA Agreement, as determined by the EEA Joint Committee, is suspended. The rights and obligations of individuals already acquired by individuals shall remain unaffected. In such cases, the EEA Joint Committee still has an obligation to take all measures possible to secure a compromise and bring the suspension to an end.

---

[106] On legal consequences of delays, see EFTA Court, Case E-3/97 *Jan and Kristian Jæger AS* v. *Opel Norge AS*, EFTA Court Rep. [1998] 1.

[107] See, for example, Decision of the EEA Joint Committee No. 130/2005 of 21 October 2005 amending Annex I (Veterinary and phytosanitary matters) to the EEA Agreement, *OJ* 2006 L 14/16; Decision of the EEA Joint Committee No. 134/2005 of 21 October 2005 amending Annex XVIII (Health and safety at work, labour law, and equal treatment for men and women) to the EEA Agreement; *OJ* 2006 L 14/22; Decision of the EEA Joint Committee No. 135/2005 of 21 October 2005 amending Protocol 31 to the EEA Agreement, on cooperation in specific fields outside the four freedoms, *OJ* 2006 L 14/24.

[108] Art. 102 EEA.

It should be recalled that, formally speaking, legislative powers have not been transferred to the EEA Joint Committee. Therefore, under certain circumstances, the implementation of its decisions may require decisions by national parliaments or even referenda. To this end, Article 103 EEA provides for a special procedure, which was tailored to facilitate the fulfilment of constitutional requirements by the EEA-EFTA states without simultaneously undermining the EEA decision-making procedure. The entry into force of EEA Joint Committee decisions may be conditional on the fulfilment of the relevant constitutional requirements. Under certain circumstances, EEA Joint Committee decisions may also apply on a temporary basis.

2.5 Surveillance machinery

The surveillance machinery of the EEA reflects its complex two-pillar structure and is characterised by a unique dichotomy. On the one hand, there is a set of surveillance institutions established especially for the EEA-EFTA countries. On the other hand, the powers of the existing bodies operating within the institutional system of the European Communities extend to the EEA. Under the EEA umbrella, all those institutions serve one and the same purpose – to secure the proper implementation and functioning of the area.[109] Both pillars will be discussed in this section, although the bulk of the analysis will concentrate on the EEA-EFTA pillar.

The EEA-EFTA surveillance institutions include the EFTA Surveillance Authority and the EFTA Court. As noted earlier, the powers and jurisdiction of both bodies are regulated thoroughly in the Surveillance Agreement. The provisions of this agreement draw heavily on EC arrangements relating to the European Commission and the European Court of Justice.

One of the main tasks of the EFTA Surveillance Authority is to ensure that EEA-EFTA countries fulfil all their obligations under the EEA. To this end, Article 31 of the Surveillance Agreement provides the EFTA Surveillance Authority with powers to initiate infraction procedures before the EFTA Court. The concept of this procedure originates in Article 226 TEC, but certain differences are clearly visible. Firstly, the wording in the Surveillance Agreement is less elaborate in comparison to the EC treaty. Secondly, the Surveillance Agreement does not include an equivalent to Article 228 TEC, which allows the European Court of Justice to impose financial penalties on states not implementing Article 226 TEC judgments. Similarly to its EC original, the infraction procedure is

---

109 Art. 58 EEA creates an obligation for both the European Commission and the EFTA Surveillance Authority to cooperate closely when it comes to competition law matters. Details of this cooperation are specified in Protocols 23 and 24 to the EEA Agreement (the latter dealing with concentrations).

formally initiated and conducted by the EFTA Surveillance Authority only. The non-judicial mechanism of individual complaints has been developed allowing individuals to participate actively in the enforcement of EEA law, on one hand, and improving the chances of detecting infringements, on the other. Like the European Commission under Article 226 TEC, the Surveillance Authority has a wide degree of discretion when it comes to submitting actions to the EFTA Court. They have to be preceded by a reasoned opinion. Similarly to the EC/Euratom frameworks, the EFTA Court will determine infringements by reference to the situation on the date set forth in the reasoned opinion.[110] Practice shows that infringements of provisions of the main body of the EEA Agreement as well as infringements of secondary law may lead to infraction procedures at the EFTA Court.

In the course of the past decade, the EFTA Surveillance Authority has taken the opportunity to initiate infraction procedures at the EFTA Court a number of times. One high-profile example is *EFTA Surveillance Authority* v. *The Kingdom of Norway*.[111] The EFTA Surveillance Authority submitted that Norwegian legislation allowing explicit restrictions limiting certain posts exclusively to women was contrary to Articles 7 and 70 EEA,[112] as well as selected provisions of Council Directive 76/207/EEC.[113] In its defence, the Norwegian Government argued that the contested measures were openly discriminating against men but that they were still justified in the light of the EC *acquis* and the case law of the European Court of Justice. The EFTA Court did not share this position and declared Norway to be in breach of EEA obligations. The free movement of services and Icelandic law on the taxation of intra-EEA flights was at stake in *EFTA Surveillance Authority* v. *Iceland*.[114] Icelandic legislation allowed for a differentiated tax on internal and external flights, with the latter incurring the higher rate. According to the plaintiff, this was in breach of EEA obligations. The EFTA Court rejected the argumentation of the Icelandic Government based on the specificity of the country's geographical position and distance separating it from the other EEA countries. Another interesting example is the EFTA Court's judgment in

---

110 EFTA Court, Case E-3/00 *EFTA Surveillance Authority* v. *The Kingdom of Norway*, EFTA Court Rep. [2000-2001] p. 73, at para. 39.

111 EFTA Court, Case E-1/02 *EFTA Surveillance Authority* v. *The Kingdom of Norway*, EFTA Court Rep. [2003] 1.

112 The first provision declares the secondary *acquis* listed in the annexes to EEA Agreement binding upon the contracting parties, while the latter creates an obligation to promote equality of genders.

113 Council Directive 76/207/EEC of 9 February 1976 on the implementation of the principle of equal treatment for men and women as regards access to employment, vocational training and promotion, and working conditions, *OJ* 1976 L 39/40.

114 EFTA Court, Case E-1/03 *EFTA Surveillance Authority* v. *The Republic of Iceland*, EFTA Court Rep. [2003] 143.

EFTA Surveillance Authority v. *Liechtenstein*.[115] This time, the EFTA Surveillance Authority submitted that Liechtenstein banking law was contrary to Article 31 EEA and the freedom of establishment enshrined therein. The legislation in question created a requirement that at least one member of the management board and the executive management should reside in Liechtenstein. This, according to the plaintiff, amounted to covert discrimination, not justifiable under Article 33 EEA or on the grounds of overriding public interests. Having analysed its earlier case law on the conformity of Liechtenstein's legislation with EEA law,[116] as well as the relevant ECJ case law on freedom of establishment, the EFTA Court declared that Liechtenstein was in breach of EEA law.

Article 36 of the Surveillance Agreement provides for an action for annulment of EFTA Surveillance Authority decisions.[117] *Locus standi* is given primarily to EFTA states; however, as already noted, individuals can also submit actions, albeit subject to severe limitations. Actions may be submitted against decisions addressed to applicants or decisions which although addressed to third parties remain of direct and individual concern to applicants. In this context, the position of individuals is similar to that under Article 230 TEC, and admissibility conditions have been interpreted accordingly by the EFTA Court. As a matter of fact, the EFTA Court has interpreted this provision in a very restrictive manner, reflecting the controversial *Plaumann* doctrine,[118] which is well established in the case law of the European Court of Justice.[119] The EEA's leading judicial authority is the EFTA Court's judgment in *Technologien Bau-und Wirtschaftsberatung GmbH and Bellona Foundation* v. *EFTA Surveillance Authority*.[120] The plaintiff requested the annulment of the EFTA Surveillance Authority's decision on state aid. The case dealt with a Norwegian Government decision to permit the development of a natural gas facility in the Barents Sea. Having received a complaint

[115] EFTA Court, Case E-8/04 *EFTA Surveillance Authority* v. *The Principality of Liechtenstein*, EFTA Court Rep. [2005] nyr.

[116] EFTA Court, Case E-3/98 *Herber Rainford-Towning*, EFTA Court Rep. [1998] 205; Case E-2/01 *Dr. Franz Martin Pucher*, EFTA Court Rep. [2002] 44.

[117] The term 'decision' has been interpreted broadly by the EFTA Court as also including letters rejecting state aid complaints submitted by natural and legal persons. See EFTA Court, Case E-2/94 *Scottish Salmon Growers Association Limited* v. *EFTA Surveillance Authority*, EFTA Court Rep. [1994-1995] 59.

[118] ECJ, Case 25/62 *Plaumann and Co.* v. *Commission of the European Communities* [1963] *ECR* 199.

[119] Examples of cases include: ECJ, Case 264/82 *Timex Corporation* v. *Council and Commission* [1985] *ECR* 849; Case 11/82 *A.E.Piraiki-Patraiki* v. *Commission of the European Communities* [1985] *ECR* 207; Case C-358/89 *Extramet Industrie SA* v. *Council* [1991] *ECR* I-2501; Case C-309/89 *Codorniu SA* v. *Council of the European Communities* [1994] *ECR* I-1853; Case C-263/02P *Commission of the European Communities* v. *Jégo-Quéré & Cie SA* [2004] *ECR* I-3425.

[120] EFTA Court, Case E-2/02 *Technologien Bau-und Wirtschaftsberatung GmbH and Bellona Foundation* v. *EFTA Surveillance Authority*, EFTA Court Rep. [2003] 52. See also case note on this judgment written by M. Varju, published in 42 *CMLRev.* (2005) p. 549.

from Bellona Foundation, the EFTA Surveillance Authority initiated a state aid procedure based on Article 61 EEA. In the contested decision, the defendant declared the proposal to be in conformity with the EEA Agreement and approved the project for regional aid. The admissibility point was raised and this led the EFTA Court to carry out an in-depth analysis of the *locus standi* of individuals in the action for annulment based on Article 36 of the Surveillance Agreement. Having analysed the controversial case law of the ECJ, the EFTA Court concluded that neither of the two applicants was individually concerned with the contested decision and hence that the action was not admissible.[121]

The grounds for annulment in actions based on Article 36 of the Surveillance Agreement include a general lack of competence, the infringement of an essential procedural requirement, the infringement of the EEA Agreement or any rule relating to its application and a misuse of powers. Like actions based on Article 230 TEC, the time-limit for the submission of actions for annulment under the Surveillance Agreement is two months counted from the publication or notification of the measure in question. In the case of well-founded actions, decisions of the EFTA Surveillance Authority are declared void. Actions for annulment are supplemented by the rarely used actions for failure to act, based on Article 37 of the Surveillance Agreement.[122] They may be submitted by EFTA states against the EFTA Surveillance Authority. Natural and legal persons also have *locus standi*, providing that the decision concerned was meant to be addressed to the applicant.

Another important aspect of the EEA surveillance system is advisory opinions, which may be delivered by the EFTA Court on the initiative of the national courts of EFTA countries.[123] The advisory opinions have their roots in the preliminary ruling procedure, which has a firm and well-developed standing in the law of the European Union.[124] However, there are two key features which make them distinct from preliminary rulings. The first is the non-binding character of advisory

---

[121] See also earlier judgments of EFTA Court, in Case E-2/94 *Scottish Salmon Growers Association Limited* v. *EFTA Surveillance Authority*, EFTA Court Rep. [1994-1995] 59; Case E-4/97 *The Norwegian Bankers' Association* v. *EFTA Surveillance Authority*, EFTA Court Rep. [1998] 38.

[122] EFTA Court, Case E-7/96 *Paul Inge Hansen* v. *EFTA Surveillance Authority*, EFTA Court Rep. [1997] 101.

[123] Domestic courts of EFTA countries may also request preliminary rulings from the European Court of Justice, providing that the state in question accepts the latter's jurisdiction (see Protocol 34 to the EEA Agreement on the possibility for courts and tribunals of EFTA States to request the Court of Justice of the European Communities to decide on the interpretation of EEA rules corresponding to EC rules). This has never taken place in practice, and the ECJ denied its jurisdiction without such notification in Case C-321/97 *Ulla-Brith Andersson and Susannne Wåkerås-Andersson* v. *Svenska staten (Swedish State)*, [1999] *ECR* I-3551 at para. 29.

[124] For the general regime, see Art. 234 TEC and Art. 150 Euratom. For the special regimes, see Art. 68 TEC and Art. 35 TEU. For a detailed account of the preliminary ruling procedure, see, *inter alia*, L.N. Brown and T. Kennedy, *The Court of Justice of the European Communities*, 5th edn. (London, Sweet & Maxwell 2000).

opinions.[125] The second is that it is a right and not an obligation to make references (as it is in some cases with preliminary rulings).[126]

Article 34 of the Surveillance Agreement reads as follows:

> The EFTA Court shall have jurisdiction to give advisory opinions on the interpretation of the EEA Agreement. Where such a question is raised before any court or tribunal in an EFTA State, that court or tribunal may, if it considers it necessary to enable it to give judgment, request the EFTA court to give such an opinion. An EFTA State may limit in its internal legislation the right to request such an advisory opinion to courts and tribunals against whose decisions there is no judicial remedy under national law.

As practice proves, advisory opinions are a very important part of the EFTA Court's jurisdiction. When it comes to procedural issues, it has followed the relevant case law of the European Court of Justice. This relates in particular to such issues as the definition of a court or a tribunal and the admissibility of references. As far as the first is concerned, the leading judicial authority is the *Restmark* case. The reference had been submitted by the Appeals Committee of the Finnish Board of Customs. The referring authority requested the interpretation of Articles 11 and 16 EEA (prohibition of quantitative restrictions and measures having equivalent effect, as well as rules on the adjustment of state monopolies, respectively). The Finnish and Norwegian Governments and the EFTA Surveillance Authority submitted that the reference was not admissible since it was submitted by the Appeals Committee, which could not be regarded as a court or a tribunal within the meaning of Article 34 of the EFTA Surveillance Agreement. The EFTA Court followed the reasoning of the ECJ and in a very casuistic way verified the nature of the referring body. This led to the conclusion that the Appeals Committee fulfilled all the necessary conditions and that the reference was admissible.[127]

Similarly to the preliminary ruling regime, references will only be admissible when the EFTA Court's opinion is necessary for the referring court to adjudicate in domestic litigation.[128] This point was recently highlighted in the EFTA Court's

---

125 It is noticeable that in the first years of its operation the EFTA Court had a tendency to describe its decisions delivered in response to the requests of national courts as 'advisory opinions.' This practice has subsequently changed and they are now described as 'judgments'.

126 Under the general preliminary ruling regime, the courts from which there is no further remedy have an obligation to make references, albeit under certain limitations arising from *acte clair* and *acte éclairé* principles.

127 See also EFTA Court, Case E-8/94 and E-9/94 *Forbrukerombudet* v. *Mattel Scandinavia A/S, Lego Norge A/S*, EFTA Court Rep. [1994-1995] 113; Case E-4/04 *Pedicel AS* v. *Sosial-og helsedirektoratet (Directorate for Health and Social Affairs)*, EFTA Court Rep. [2005] nyr.

128 Detailed guidelines for making reference have been published in a special note addressed to national courts. See Note for Guidance on Requests by national courts for advisory opinions, available at: <http://www.eftacourt.lu/default.asp?layout=article&id=129>.

judgment in *Paolo Piazza* v. *Paul Schurte AG*.[129] The reference from Liechtenstein's Princely Court of Justice dealt with the conformity of domestic legislation with the principles of free movement of services and free movement of capital (Arts. 36 and 40 EEA, respectively). Following the request of the EFTA Court, the referring court clarified procedural and factual issues. However, this did not stop the Government of Liechtenstein from claiming that the reference was not admissible due to the poor description of the facts and legal circumstances, as well as the potentially hypothetical nature of the reference. The EFTA Court emphasised that the advisory opinion procedure 'is a specially established means of judicial cooperation between the Court and national courts, with the aim of providing the national courts with the necessary elements of EEA law to decide the cases before them.' The EFTA Court then repeated the ECJ's reasoning and argued as follows:

> It is for the national court to determine, in light of the particular circumstances of the case, both the need for an advisory opinion in order to enable it to deliver judgment, and the relevance of the questions that it submits. Consequently, where the questions referred concern the interpretation of the EEA Agreement, the Court is in principle bound to give a ruling. However, the Court may not rule on a question, where it is quite obvious that the sought interpretation of EEA law bears no relation to the actual facts of the main action or its purpose, or where the issue is hypothetical.[130]

The scope of advisory rulings is formally limited to the interpretation of the EEA Agreement. However, following its judgment in *CIBA Speciality Chemicals Water Treatment Ltd. and others* v. *Norwegian State*,[131] it is clear that the EFTA Court will interpret this clause broadly as also covering the annexes to the EEA Agreement as well as the secondary legislation listed therein. However, this will not include the provisions of the FTAs which are formally not part of the EEA framework.[132]

---

[129] EFTA Court, Case E-10/04 *Paolo Pizza* v. *Paul Schurte AG*, EFTA Court Rep. [2005] nyr.

[130] Para. 21 of the judgment. See also EFTA Court, Case E-1/95 *Ulf Samuelsson* v. *Svenska staten*, EFTA Court Rep. [1994-1995] 145; Case E-5/96 *Ullensaker kommune and Others* v. *Nille AS*, EFTA Court Rep. [1997] 30; Case E-2/03 *Ákæruvaldið (The Public Prosecutor)* v. *Ásgeir Logi Ásgeirsson and others*, EFTA Court Rep. [2003] 185; Case E-6/96 *Tore Wilhelmsen AS* v. *Oslo commune*, EFTA Court Rep. [1997] 53. In the latter case, the EFTA Court concluded that some of the referred questions were not admissible due to their hypothetical character.

[131] EFTA Court, Case E-6/01 *CIBA Speciality Chemicals Water Treatment Ltd. and others* v. *Norwegian State*, EFTA Court Rep. [2003] loc. cit. n. 60.

[132] EFTA Court, Case E-2/03 *Ákæruvaldið (The Public Prosecutor) against Ásgeir Logi Ásgeirsson, Axel Pétur Ásgeirsson and Helgi Már Reynisson*, EFTA Court Rep. [2003] 185.

Although advisory opinions delivered by the EFTA Court are formally non-binding, they are followed by the referring courts. It should be added that, if the national court is not satisfied with the reference and requires further assistance from the EFTA Court, there are no formal obstacles against submitting further references. This arrangement follows developments relating to the ECJ and was officially confirmed by the EFTA Court in *CIBA Speciality Chemicals Water Treatment Ltd. and others* v. *Norwegian State.*[133] As already noted, advisory opinions have played an important role in the everyday application of EEA law in EFTA countries. They have served as a pivotal tool securing its uniform application and as an instrument for supporting the implementation of the principle of homogeneity (discussed in the following section). In lots of ways the EFTA Court is following in the footsteps of the European Court of Justice. A great example of its judicial activism, in which advisory opinions played a significant role, relates to the principle of state liability adopted for the purposes of EEA from the EU legal order.[134]

When it comes to EEA surveillance in the case of EU Member States, the first violin is played by the European Commission and European Court of Justice. Well-established procedures on infractions, the surveillance of competition law and state aid are also applicable to the obligations of Member States and individuals stemming from EEA law. For instance, an infringement of the EEA Agreement may lead to Commission action based on Article 226 TEC. The ECJ's judgment in *Commission* v. *Austria* may serve as an excellent example of the latter.[135] The plaintiff argued that Austrian legislation on electoral rights in workers' chambers and works councils were contrary to Article 39 TEC (as implemented by Article 8 of Regulation 1612/68/EEC[136]), Article 28 EEA and selected Association Agreements. The legislation contested in the first complaint linked passive voting rights to general assemblies with voting rights to national parliament. To this end, it excluded nationals of countries other than Austria and, as the ECJ concluded, was contrary to both EC and EEA legislation.[137]

---

133 Para. 12 of the judgment.

134 EFTA Court, Case E-9/97 *Erla Maria Sveinbjörnsdóttir* v. *Government of Iceland*, EFTA Court Rep. [1998] 95; Case E-4/01 *Karl K. Karlsson hf* v. *Icelandic States*, EFTA Court Rep. [2002] 240.

135 ECJ, Case C-465/01 *Commission of the European Communities* v. *Republic of Austria* [2004] *ECR* I-8291.

136 Regulation (EEC) No. 1612/68 of the Council of 15 October 1968 on freedom of movement for workers within the Community, *OJ* 1968 L 257/2.

137 The second complaint was related to the infringement of Association Agreements (including EEC-Turkey Association Council Decision 1/80). The ECJ held that Austrian legislation on voting rights in workers' councils was contrary to EC law.

2.6 Homogeneous legal space and the nature of the EEA legal order

In this section of the chapter, selected aspects of homogeneity are taken on board. The starting point will be the nature of the EEA legal order.

It is generally accepted that the European Communities have created a new legal order, different to classical public international law. As the ECJ held in Opinion 1/91, 'the Community treaties established a new legal order for the benefit of which the States have limited their sovereign rights, in ever wider fields, and the subjects of which comprise not only Member States but also their nationals.'[138] Following the judicial developments of the past fifty years, the principles of primacy, direct effect, indirect effect and state liability are at the heart of this unique legal system. None of them are regulated explicitly in the founding treaties; however, Article 10 TEC and the principle of loyal cooperation enshrined therein have served as a general legal basis for the judicial activism of the ECJ. Unlike the EEA, membership of the European Communities (now the European Union) involves the transfer of the right to exercise certain sovereign rights, allowing the European Union to legislate within its attributed powers. Discussion about the nature of the EEA and its homogeneity naturally turns the attention to the above-mentioned principles and focuses on their application to EEA-EFTA countries, which is questionable for variety of reasons. Firstly, the aims of the EEA are not as ambitious and widespread as in the case of the European Community. Secondly, membership of the EEA does not involve the transfer of legislative powers. Bearing this in mind, one cannot but agree with the European Court of Justice, which in Opinion 1/91 argued that it is due to those factors that full homogeneity will not be achieved. In the words of the ECJ,

> divergences which exist between the aims and context of the agreement, on the one hand, and the aims and context of Community law, on the other, stand in the way of the achievement of the objective of homogeneity in the interpretation and application of the law in the EEA.[139]

Those differences have been explicitly acknowledged in the EFTA Court's advisory opinion in *Sveinbjörnsdóttir* v. *Government of Iceland.* When justifying the application of the principle of state liability to the EEA Agreement, the EFTA Court argued that

---

[138] Para. 21 of the opinion. This conclusion draws upon the Court's earlier case law, starting from the early landmark cases of the 1960s. See ECJ, Case 26/62 *Van Gend en Loos* v. *Nederlandse Administratie der Belastingen* [1963] *ECR* 1 at 12; Case 6/64 *Flaminio Costa* v. *ENEL* [1964] *ECR* 585 at 593.

[139] Para. 29 of the opinion.

> the EEA Agreement is an international treaty *sui generis* which contains a distinct legal order of its own. The EEA Agreement does not establish a customs union but an enhanced free trade area... The depth of integration of the EEA Agreement is less far-reaching than under the EC Treaty, but the scope and the objective of the EEA Agreement goes beyond what is usual for an agreement under public international law.[140]

This line of reasoning was developed even further in the EFTA Court's judgment in *Ákæruvaldið (The Public Prosecutor)* v. *Ásgeir Logi Ásgeirsson, Axel Pétur Ásgeirsson and Helgi Már Reynisson.*[141] The EFTA Court argued that EEA legal order 'is characterised by the creation of an internal market ... the protection of the rights of individuals and economic operators and an institutional framework providing for effective surveillance and judicial review.'[142] By this means, the EFTA Court has argued for yet another new legal system, albeit placed about halfway between the European Communities and classical public international law.[143] This allowed the EFTA Court to search for a fair balance between the imperative of homogeneity and the different aims and lack of legislative powers of the EEA.

The EEA Agreement provides for a twofold set of tools tailored to serve as guarantors of homogeneity. In legal writing, they have been classified as legislative and judicial mechanisms.[144] The main element of the first mechanism is the decision-making machinery discussed in section 2.3.3 of this chapter. It has already been argued that the work of the Joint Committee has so far allowed the EEA to catch up successfully with the development of secondary legislation within the European Community. One of the drawbacks of this arrangement is its non-application to subsequent modifications of the EC Treaty. It should be recalled that the EEA Agreement was drafted back in early 1990s and that its main body has remained unchanged since then. At the same time, the EC Treaty has undergone a series of far-reaching revisions, including the Treaty of Maastricht, Treaty of Amsterdam and Treaty of Nice. Some of these involved the reformulation or even addition of new provisions considerably changing the substance of

---

140 Para. 59 of the opinion.

141 EFTA Court, Case E-2/03 *Ákæruvaldið (The Public Prosecutor)* v. *Ásgeir Logi Ásgeirsson, Axel Pétur Ásgeirsson and Helgi Már Reynisson*, EFTA Court Rep. [2003] 185.

142 Para. 28 of the judgment.

143 As Johansson and Sevon note 'Although there are differences in other respects between the Community legal order and the EEA Agreement, it is clear from the above that the latter is far from a standard agreement under public international law.' M. Johansson and L. Sevon, 'The Protection of the Rights of Individuals under the EEA Agreement', 24 *ELR* (1999) p. 373 at p. 380.

144 W. van Gerven, 'The Genesis of EEA Law and the Principles of Primacy and Direct Effect', 16 *Fordham International Law Journa*l (1992/1993) p. 955 at p. 962.

rights and obligations enshrined therein.[145] As proved by the EFTA court's judgment in *EFTA Surveillance Authority* v. *Norway*, this is not only an academic issue but also a problem with a practical relevance.[146]

Another important issue is the way in which the EEA-EFTA countries transpose EC legislation into their domestic legal systems.[147] Not surprisingly, it was one of the most controversial issues during the negotiations leading to the creation of the EEA. This was due, *inter alia*, to the fact that the majority of original EFTA-EEA states are so-called dualist countries.[148] As argued by Cottier and Gerber, 'During the negotiation of the EEA Agreement, the Nordic countries were not at all willing to give up their dualistic approach and to amend their constitutions so as to guarantee direct applicability and primacy of EEA law.'[149] This did not have such an influence on the position of directives with EEA relevance, as they anyhow require transposition into domestic law in the EC legal framework. But it did have an influence on those regulations which are directly applicable and in principle do not allow for domestic measures. The compromise reached provides for a degree of flexibility on the EFTA-EEA side. Article 7 EEA provides that legal acts listed in the annexes to the EEA Agreement (as regularly updated by the Joint Committee) are binding on the parties and 'acts corresponding to an EEC regulation shall as such be made part of the internal legal order of the Contracting Parties.' This excludes their direct application and at the same time narrows the discretion the states have when it comes to the transposition of directives. In this context, EEA-EFTA countries are basically left with two options.[150] Under the first option, they are allowed to make a regulation part of their domestic law albeit without amending its contents. The other option which remains is direct referencing in the domestic law to EC regulations. As far as directives are concerned, Article 7 EEA mirrors the wording of Article 249 TEC where it provides that 'an act corresponding to an EEC directive shall leave to the authorities of the Contracting Parties the choice of form and method of implementation.'[151]

---

145 On the impact of the Treaty of Amsterdam, see, *inter alia*, P.-Ch. Müller-Graff, 'The Treaty of Amsterdam: Content and Implications for the EEA-EU Relations', in P.-Ch. Müller-Graff and E. Selvig, eds., *EEA-EU Relations* (Berlin, Berlin Verlag Arno Spitz GmbH 1999) p. 11.

146 EFTA Court, Case E-1/02 *EFTA Surveillance Authority* v. *Norway*, EFTA Court Rep. [2003] 1. See also Ch. Tobler, 'Case E-1/02, *EFTA Surveillance Authority* v. *Norway*, judgment of 24 January 2003', 41 *CMLRev.* (2004) p. 245.

147 See, *inter alia*, S. Már Stefánsson, *The EEA Agreement and its Adoption into Icelandic Law* (Oslo, Centre for European Law, University of Oslo 1997).

148 See Cottier and Gerber, loc. cit. n. 37, at p. 257.

149 Ibid., at pp. 257-258.

150 Már Stefánsson, op. cit. n. 147, at p. 69.

151 See, *inter alia*, S. Prechal, *Directives in EC Law*, 2nd edn. (Oxford, Oxford University Press 2005).

The application of EEA provisions in the domestic legal systems of the EEA-EFTA countries is of pivotal importance, and the role of EFTA Court in this respect must be emphasised.[152] It is already clear from the fifteenth recital of the Preamble to the EEA Agreement that 'the objective of the Contracting Parties is to arrive at, and maintain, a uniform interpretation and application of this Agreement and those provisions of Community legislation which are substantially reproduced in this Agreement…'. To this end, Article 6 was tailored to secure the uniform interpretation of provisions originating in EC law throughout the whole EEA. It provides that

> Without prejudice to future developments of case law, the provisions of this Agreement, in so far as they are identical in substance to corresponding rules of the Treaty establishing the European Economic Community and the Treaty establishing the European Coal and Steel Community and to acts adopted in application of these two Treaties, shall, in their implementation and application, be interpreted in conformity with the relevant rulings of the Court of Justice of the European Communities given prior to the date of signature of this Agreement.

This obligation is reproduced in Article 3(1) of the Surveillance Agreement, but in the latter case its scope of application is limited to Protocols 1 to 4 and legislation listed in Annexes I and II to the Surveillance Agreement. It is interesting to note, however, that the EFTA Court has given this obligation a broad interpretation by also applying the case law of the European Court of Justice to procedural provisions to which this obligation does not formally extend. It was already in the very first judgment in *Restmark* that the EFTA Court interpreted the term 'court/tribunal in an EFTA state' for the purposes of the advisory opinion procedure. It relied heavily on the ECJ's case law on Article 234 TEC and the admissibility criteria for preliminary ruling references.[153] Another great example of such judicial activism is the EFTA Court's above-mentioned judgment in *Technologies Bau-und Wirtschaftsberatung GmbH and Bellona Foundation* v. *EFTA Surveillance Authority*.[154] The EFTA Court, when discussing the *locus standi* of individuals in an action for annulment relied heavily on the controversial ECJ case law. By the way of justification, the EFTA Court referred to its earlier judgments and concluded the following:

152 See, *inter alia*, Baudenbacher (1997), loc. cit. n. 88.

153 Para. 24 of the judgment.

154 See also EFTA Court, Case E 2/94 *Scottish Salmon Growers Association Limited* v. *EFTA Surveillance Authority*, EFTA Court Rep. [1994-1995] 59; Case E-1/95 *Ulf Samuelsson* v. *Svenska staten*, EFTA Court Rep. [1994-1995] 145.

> Although the Court is not required by Article 3(1) of the Surveillance and Court Agreement to follow the reasoning of the Court of Justice of the European Communities when interpreting the main part of that Agreement, the reasoning which led that Court to its interpretations of expressions in Community law is relevant when those expressions are identical in substance to those which fall to be interpreted by the Court. As stated in *Scottish Salmon Growers* v. *EFTA Surveillance Authority* ... this principle must apply equally to the issue of *locus standi* to bring an action for annulment.[155]

In both cases, the obligation extends to ECJ case law predating the signature of the EEA Agreement. For all subsequent case law developments, both the EFTA Surveillance Authority and the EFTA Court have an obligation to 'pay due account' to ECJ case law. However, the distinction should not be considered as a major practical challenge. As noted by Baudenbacher, 'the legally and politically important differentiation between old and new case law disappears to a large extent.'[156]

The EEA Agreement provides for the creation of an information exchange mechanism facilitating the transfer of new developments between the EC and EFTA courts. A central role is played by the EEA Joint Committee, which is also equipped with powers to keep under a constant review the relevant developments in EU judicature.[157] The EEA Agreement puts the EEA Joint Committee at the centre of the dispute-settlement mechanism, which can be used when difficulties arise in arriving at a homogeneous interpretation of the EEA Agreement. It is an interesting – albeit for the time being purely theoretical – example of the political procedure *par excellence*, which can be utilised in order to solve a legal dispute.

The right to take part in pending litigations is yet another tool created in order to secure the homogeneity of the EEA. To this end, for example, the European Commission and the EU Member States may present statements and observations to the EFTA Court. On the other side, the EEA-EFTA countries may proceed equally at the European Court of Justice. It is noteworthy that the European Commission has proved to be very active in this respect.[158]

With some minor exceptions of intellectual property law, the homogeneity of substantive provisions is not causing major difficulties. However, from the very beginning, the application of fundamental principles of supremacy, direct effect, indirect effect and state liability of EEA-EFTA countries has been a key issue not

155 Para. 39 of the judgment.

156 C. Baudenbacher, 'The EFTA Court and the European Court', in Müller-Graff and Selvig, op. cit. n. 145, p. 70 at p. 73.

157 See Arts. 105-106 EEA.

158 For a detailed account of cases, see EFTA Court, *Legal framework, case law and composition 1994-2003* (Luxembourg 2004) pp. 26-27.

only in academic discourse but also in legal practice. The debate is centred around the interpretation of Article 6 EEA, its exact meaning and the scope of its application. It is interesting to look at these issues from the perspective of Article 3 EEA, which contains the principle of loyal cooperation. Its wording is similar to Article 10 TEC, although the EEA limitations reduce the possibility of a homogeneous interpretation. One should also acknowledge the eighth recital of the Preamble to the EEA Agreement, which confirms the important role that individuals will play through the exercise of their rights envisaged by the EEA law. An important role is also played by Protocol 35 to EEA Agreement, which provides that 'for cases of possible conflicts between implemented EEA rules and other statutory provisions, the EFTA States undertake to introduce, if necessary, a statutory provision to the effect that EEA rules prevail in these cases.' This provision is implemented in both Nordic countries. For instance, section 2 of the Implementing Act in Norway reads as follows:

> Provisions of Acts of Parliament which serve to fulfil Norway's obligations under the Agreement shall in case of conflict prevail over other provisions which regulate the same matter. The same shall apply for a provision of an administrative regulation which serves to fulfil Norway's obligations under the Agreement [when it] conflicts with another such provision, or with a later Act of Parliament.[159]

This legislative jigsaw puzzle led to opinions touching both extremes. In the early 1990s, for example, Van Gerven already argued for a broad and generous interpretation of the provision in question.[160] He based his proposal around three major arguments. Firstly, Article 6 EEA is broad enough to cover both the principle of supremacy and direct effect (unless stated otherwise as in Protocol 35). Secondly, the differences in the aims and purposes of the European Community and the EEA do not contradict the broad meaning of Article 6. Last but not least, the reasoning of the ECJ only supports the broad meaning of the abovementioned provision.[161] The President of the EFTA Court, Carl Baudenbacher, takes a softer approach and argues on the basis of practical experience that 'the EFTA Court went for what may be called quasi-direct effect, quasi-primacy, and full state liability.'[162] It proves that the EFTA Court did not adopt as generous an approach as suggested by Van Gerven, but that numerous issues connected with the application of the EEA Agreement at the domestic level and with the enforcement of the rights of individuals are inherent in its judicial practice. Starting

159 Translation reproduced after Johansson and Sevon, loc. cit. n. 143, at p. 377.

160 Van Gerven, loc. cit. n. 144.

161 Ibid., at p. 971.

162 C. Baudenbacher, 'The Implementation of Decisions of the ECJ and of the EFTA Court in Member States' Domestic Legal Orders', *Texas International Law Journal* (2005) p. 383 at p. 386.

from its early judgment in *Restmark*, the EFTA Court has tried to accommodate the effectiveness of EEA law with the limitations discussed in this section.[163] In this judgment, the EFTA Court concluded that

> Protocol 35 EEA on the Implementation of EEA Rules stipulates that the EFTA States are under an obligation to ensure, if necessary by a separate statutory provision, that in cases of conflict between implemented EEA rules and other statutory provisions the implemented EEA rules prevail. It is inherent in the nature of such provision that individuals and economic operators in cases of conflict between implemented EEA rules and national statutory provisions must be entitled to invoke and to claim at the national level any rights that could be derived from provisions of the EEA Agreement, as being or having been made part of the respective national legal order, if they are unconditional and sufficiently precise.[164]

The EFTA Court developed its argumentation in the *Hördur Einarsson* v. *Icelandic State*.[165] In this context, it is particularly important to draw attention to the EFTA Court's judgments in *Erla Maria Sveinbjörnsdóttir* v. *Government of Iceland*[166] and *Karl K. Karlsson hf.* v. *Icelandic State*.[167] In both cases, the EFTA Court, drawing heavily on the case law of the European Court of Justice, took the opportunity to develop the principle of state liability for breach of EEA law.[168]

The objective of achieving a homogeneous EEA is not only fulfilled by the EFTA Court and the courts in the EEA-EFTA countries, but also by the European Court of Justice (and the Court of First Instance) and the domestic courts in the Member States. There are numerous examples of case law dealing with this issue, moreover, where reference is made to the case law of the EFTA Court.[169]

2.7 Overview of the EEA Agreement's substantive provisions

As noted in the introduction, the EEA was tailored to extend the benefits of the internal market to the EFTA countries. To this end, the EEA Agreement reproduces a majority of the substantive provisions of the EC Treaty and incorporates

---

163 EFTA Court, Case E-1/94 *Ravintoloitsijain Liiton Kustannus Oy Restmark*, EFTA Court Rep. [1994-1995] 15.

164 Para. 77 of the judgment.

165 EFTA Court, Case E-1/01 *Hördur Einarsson* v. *Icelandic State*, EFTA Court Rep. [2002] 1.

166 EFTA Court, Case E-9/97 *Erla Maria Sveinbjörnsdóttir* v. *Government of Iceland*, EFTA Court Rep. [1998] 95.

167 EFTA Court, Case E-4/01 *Karl K. Karlsson hf.* v. *Icelandic States*, EFTA Court Rep. [2002] 240.

168 See, *inter alia*, S.M. Stefánsson, 'State Liability in Community and EEA Law', in Baudenbacher, et al., op. cit. n. 88, at p. 145.

169 See, *inter alia*, Baudenbacher, loc. cit. n. 156, at pp. 81-95.

the vast majority of secondary legislation into the EEA framework.[170] In addition, numerous provisions contained in the main body of the EEA Agreement are supplemented by the annexes and protocols. Free movement of goods is covered in Part II of the EEA Agreement. The prohibition of customs duties and measures having equivalent effect is firmly established in Article 10 EEA. It is supplemented by prohibitions concerning quantitative restrictions on imports and exports as well as measures having equivalent effect (Arts. 11-12 EEA). A list of exceptions similar to Article 30 TEC is provided in Article 13 EEA. Article 14 EEA prohibits discriminatory taxation. Article 16 EEA deals with state monopolies and their necessary adjustment. Part III of the EEA Agreement is devoted to the free movement of workers, services and capital. Article 28 EEA is similarly worded to Article 39 TEC and contains basic rules on the free movement of workers. Provisions dealing with the right of establishment (Art. 31 EEA) and free movement of services (Art. 36 EEA) are also based on their equivalents in the EC Treaty. The situation is similar with regard to, *inter alia*, provisions on competition (Arts. 53-60 EEA) and state aid (Arts. 61-64 EEA).[171] The EEA Agreement also contains numerous provisions on so-called flanking policies. This includes environmental protection, transport, consumer protection and intellectual property.

---

[170] For example, the following pieces of secondary legislation listed in Annex V are applicable to the free movement of workers: Council Directive 64/221/EEC of 25 February 1964 on the coordination of special measures concerning the movement and residence of foreign nationals which are justified on grounds of public policy, public security or public health, *OJ* 1964 56/850; Regulation (EEC) No. 1612/68 of the Council of 15 October 1968 on freedom of movement for workers within the Community, *OJ* 1968 L 257/2; Council Directive 68/360/EEC of 15 October 1968 on the abolition of restrictions on movement and residence within the Community for workers of Member States and their families, *OJ* 1968 L 257/13; Regulation (EEC) No. 1251/70 of the Commission of 29 June 1970 on the right of workers to remain in the territory of a Member State after having been employed in that State, *OJ* 1970 L 142/24; Council Directive 72/194/EEC of 18 May 1972 extending to workers exercising the right to remain in the territory of a Member State after having been employed in that State the scope of the Directive of 25 February 1964 on coordination of special measures concerning the movement and residence of foreign nationals which are justified on grounds of public policy, public security or public health, *OJ* 1972 L 121/32; Council Directive 77/486/EEC of 25 July 1977 on the education of the children of migrant workers, *OJ* 1977 L 199/32; Commission Decision 2003/8/EC of 23 December 2002 implementing Council Regulation (EEC) No. 1612/68 as regards the clearance of vacancies and applications for employment, *OJ* 2003 L 5/16.

[171] See M.S. Rydelski, 'The EEA State Aid Regime', in A. Biondi, P. Eeckhout and J. Flyn, eds., *The Law of State Aid in the European Union* (Oxford, Oxford University Press 2004) p. 189.

3. RELATIONS OUTSIDE THE EEA FRAMEWORK

3.1 Introduction

However broad the scope of the EEA Agreement, it does not extend to all areas falling within the current powers and activities of the European Union. Whenever a desire to deepen and widen cooperation between the parties is expressed, they are left with a twofold choice. The first is the development of the EEA Agreement, and for this purpose a special 'evolutionary clause' is provided in Article 118 EEA. The second option is the development of relations beyond the EEA framework by means of separate arrangements.

Under the evolutionary clause, a special procedural mechanism may be initiated when 'it would be useful in the interests of all the Contracting Parties to develop the relations established by this Agreement by extending them to fields not covered thereby.'[172] To this end, requests are expected at the highest political level, which is the EEA Council. Details of such proposals are then discussed in the framework of the EEA Joint Committee. The latter is equipped with powers to produce reports in this respect. The political decision to initiate proper negotiations is in the hands of the EEA Council. In order to enter into force, the agreed amendments have to be ratified by all EEA Member States.

As a matter of fact, this procedure has not been used even once; hence it still remains a purely theoretical option. For the time being, it is the second of the two options that has proved its attractiveness and is used to some extent by the parties. In course of the past decade, we have witnessed the enhancement of relations in numerous areas of EU law which do not fall under the EEA framework. They extend to all three pillars of the European Union, including the Common Foreign and Security Policy (CFSP). Such closer cooperation is effected by treaties concluded between the European Communities and/or European Union and EFTA countries. Such agreements are usually concluded with Iceland and Norway only, due to the special microstate status of Liechtenstein.

For the purposes of this chapter, three leading examples of cooperation beyond the EEA framework are discussed. The starting point is the implementation of Schengen *acquis*, with which Iceland and Norway are associated. This is followed by an analysis of selected aspects of cooperation in criminal matters and in the framework of the CFSP.

---

[172] See Norberg, et al., op. cit. n. 10, at pp 292-294. The authors argue that this clause originates in the FTAs of the 1970s.

3.2 Schengen *acquis*

The first example of the developing relationship going beyond the borders of the EEA is the association of Iceland and Norway with the implementation of the Schengen *acquis*.[173] The arrangements in this respect follow the membership of Sweden and Finland in the European Union, on the one hand, and the changing status of the Schengen *acquis* following the entry into force of the Treaty of Amsterdam, on the other.[174] With regard to the former, the Nordic Passport Union that has existed between the five Nordic countries since the 1950s played a decisive role.[175] As acknowledged by Eiríksson, due to the EU membership of Sweden and Finland, those countries were left with a threefold choice. Firstly, they could have opted to stick to the Nordic Passport Union and refrain from acceding to Schengen. Secondly, those becoming members of the European Union could have accepted the Schengen *acquis* and imposed checks on their borders with the remaining Nordic countries. Last but not least, all Nordic countries could have acceded to the Schengen Agreement. The latter option was chosen, but due to the restriction of membership to EU countries, a special formula of association had to be developed for Iceland and Norway.[176]

The first agreement with Iceland and Norway was already concluded in 1996. The subsequent developments were directly connected to the changing status of the Schengen *acquis*. Both the Schengen Agreement of 1985 and the Schengen Implementing Convention of 1990 were concluded by a group of the Member States, albeit outside the scope of the European Communities.[177] It was only in the late 1990s when, on the basis of a special Protocol annexed to the Treaty of Amsterdam, the Schengen *acquis* was incorporated into the framework of the European Union. Article 6 of the Protocol envisaged the association of Iceland

---

173 For a comprehensive early analysis of the issue, see H. Bull, 'The Schengen Cooperation and Norway', in P.-Ch. Müller-Graff and E. Selvig, eds., *The European Economic Area – Norway's Basic Status in the Legal Construction of Europe*, (Berlin, Berlin Verlag 1997) p. 141. See also S. Eiríksson, 'Deeply involved in the European project. Membership of Schengen', in Thorhallsson, op. cit. n. 4, at p. 50.

174 For an academic appraisal of the Treaty of Amsterdam with special attention to the Schengen *acquis*, see, *inter alia*, D. O'Keeffe and P. Twomey, eds., *Legal Issues of the Amsterdam Treaty* (Oxford/Portland, Oregon, Hart Publishing 1999).

175 Convention on the Abolition of Passport Controls at Intra-Nordic Borders, signed in Copenhagen on 12 July 1957.

176 Eventually, Switzerland became another beneficiary of such an arrangement. See chapter 5 in this volume.

177 Agreement signed in Schengen on 14 June 1985 between the Governments of the States of the Benelux Economic Union, the Federal Republic of Germany and the French Republic on the gradual abolition of checks at their common borders, *OJ* 2000 L 239/13; Convention signed in Schengen on 19 June 1990 between the Kingdom of Belgium, the Federal Republic of Germany, the French Republic, the Grand Duchy of Luxembourg and the Kingdom of the Netherlands, implementing the Schengen Agreement of 14 June 1985, *OJ* 2000 L 239/19.

and Norway with the implementation of the Schengen *acquis*. Moreover, it created an obligation to conclude a separate agreement on rights and obligations in this respect between the United Kingdom and Ireland, on the one hand, and Iceland and Norway, on the other.[178]

These major developments in the EU arena were followed by the conclusion of another agreement with Iceland and Norway, which equipped the parties with a comprehensive framework for cooperation and replaced the earlier arrangements on the abolition of borders.[179] It is interesting to note that it was concluded formally by the Council of the European Union with Iceland and Norway on the basis of Article 6 of the Protocol.[180] Formally, both EFTA countries are associated with the implementation of the Schengen *acquis* as well as its future development. It is the latter element which makes this agreement particularly attractive for the purposes of this analysis. It shows how the parties have attempted to strike a balance between the uniformity and dynamism of the Schengen *acquis*, on the one hand, and the rights and obligations of both EFTA states, on the other. The *modus operandi* established therein is repeated in the second package of bilateral agreements with Switzerland.[181]

Article 2 of the agreement creates an obligation for Iceland and Norway to implement and apply the Schengen *acquis*. Two annexes were drafted in order to specify the scope of this obligation. The list of relevant instruments includes, *inter alia*, the Schengen Agreement of 1985 *in toto* and the Schengen Convention of 1990 (with the exception of provisions explicitly listed in Part 1 of Annex A), as well as numerous Executive Committee decisions.[182] A pivotal practical problem

---

178 Agreement of 28 June 1999 concluded by the Council of the European Union and the Republic of Iceland and the Kingdom of Norway on the establishment of rights and obligations between Ireland and the United Kingdom of Great Britain and Northern Ireland, on the one hand, and the Republic of Iceland and the Kingdom of Norway, on the other, in areas of the Schengen *acquis* which apply to these States, *OJ* 2000 L 15/1.

179 Agreement concluded by the Council of the European Union and the Republic of Iceland and the Kingdom of Norway concerning the latters' association with the implementation, application and development of the Schengen *acquis*, *OJ* 1999 L 176/36. It also required the conclusion of an agreement on requests for asylum (see Agreement between the European Community and the Republic of Iceland and the Kingdom of Norway concerning the criteria and mechanisms for establishing the State responsible for examining a request for asylum lodged in a Member State or in Iceland or Norway, *OJ* 2001 L 93/40).

180 See Council Decision 1999/439/EC of 17 May 1999 on the conclusion of the Agreement with the Republic of Iceland and the Kingdom of Norway concerning the latters' association with the implementation, application and development of the Schengen *acquis*, *OJ* 1999 L 176/35.

181 See chapter 5 in this volume.

182 See Council Decision 1999/435/EC of 20 May 1999 concerning the definition of the Schengen *acquis* for the purpose of determining, in conformity with the relevant provisions of the Treaty establishing the European Community and the Treaty on European Union, the legal basis for each of the provisions or decisions which constitute the *acquis*, *OJ* 1999 L 176/1; Council Decision 1999/436/EC of 20 May 1999 determining, in conformity with the relevant provisions of the Treaty

that had to be addressed by the parties was the relevance of subsequent developments at EU level to Iceland and Norway. The key questions were the level of engagement of both countries in EU decision making and the impact of new legislation on the agreement. A *modus operandi* was agreed in both cases. It is near to impossible not to notice that it draws heavily on the model known from the EEA framework.

When it comes to the adoption of new legislation, Article 6 of the agreement contains an obligation for the European Commission to informally seek advice from Icelandic and Norwegian experts, as it does in relation to experts from the Member States. This resembles the decision shaping that is well established in the EEA. The position of Iceland and Norway is considerably stronger, though. This is thanks to a special procedure available through a special Mixed Committee, which was created to ensure the effective application and development of the agreement.[183] According to Article 4, this committee 'shall ensure that any concern entertained by Iceland and Norway is duly considered.' In this forum, representatives of both countries shall have the opportunity:

- to explain problems they encounter in respect of a particular act or measure or to respond to the problems encountered by other delegations;
- to express themselves on any questions concerning the development of provisions of concern to them or the implementation thereof.

Moreover, they are authorised to make suggestions on the future development of the Schengen *acquis*, which may be taken on board by the EU Member States or the European Commission. This may eventually lead to the initiation of the legislative process.[184]

One of the interesting aspects of this agreement is the impact of the newly adopted *acquis* on Iceland and Norway. Bearing in mind the prerequisite of uniformity of the Schengen area, the parties decided to go for a dynamic model. Its key elements are specified in Article 8 of the agreement. In principle, new legislation shall enter into force simultaneously in the EU Member States and two EFTA countries. To this end, the adoption of such measures must be notified to

establishing the European Community and the Treaty on European Union, the legal basis for each of the provisions or decisions which constitute the Schengen *acquis*, *OJ* 1999 L 176/17.

183 The Mixed Committee is composed of representatives of Iceland and Norway as well as of Council of the European Union and the European Commission. There are a number of different personal settings in which it operates. These include ministerial level, senior official level and expert level (see Art. 3 of the agreement).

184 See also Council Decision 1999/437/EC of 17 May 1999 on certain arrangements for the application of the Agreement concluded by the Council of the European Union and the Republic of Iceland and the Kingdom of Norway concerning the association of those two States with the implementation, application and development of the Schengen *acquis*, *OJ* 1999 L 176/31.

Iceland and Norway immediately upon their adoption. The decisions of these countries shall be then notified to the European Commission and the Council of the European Union. In practice, longer transitional periods may be provided for either or both those countries if needed in order to accommodate constitutional constraints. A negative decision may lead to the termination of the agreement or, alternatively, a decision of the Mixed Committee on the continuation of the agreement.

Strong hints of the principle of homogeneity, which, as discussed above, is at the heart of the EEA, are clearly visible in Articles 9-10 of the agreement. Parties have an obligation to arrive at the same interpretation of Schengen *acquis*. In order to accommodate this imperative, the Mixed Committee shall keep under review judicial developments at the European Court of Justice as well as at courts in Iceland and Norway. Both EFTA countries are provided with the possibility of submitting statements in preliminary ruling cases pending before the ECJ. Both have also an obligation to submit reports to the Mixed Committee on the application of the Schengen *acquis* by national courts and administrative authorities. Differences in application and interpretation may lead to the initiation of the dispute settlement procedure, with a central role reserved for the Mixed Committee. Its powers in this respect add some quasi-judicial elements to its legal character. Lack of settlement may lead to termination of the agreement.

The Schengen *acquis* and its integration into the framework of the European Union is definitely a unique phenomenon itself.[185] The association of Iceland and Norway (subsequently also Switzerland) makes the whole arrangement even more sophisticated and calls for a legal appraisal. Looking from an EU perspective, one may argue that this very agreement may serve as a testing model for arrangements with third countries in cases where parties express a desire to introduce elements of EU law into their mutual relations. This bilateral model is well developed in relation to the Swiss Confederation; however, as seen from this example, it may also successfully serve relations with other countries. It is questionable whether in institutional terms Iceland and Norway are really better off in comparison with the EEA. On the one hand, they have gained greater access to the EU decision-making process and a quasi-right of initiative (leaving considerable discretion to EU Member States and the European Commission). On the other hand, non-acceptance of the new *acquis* may lead to termination of the whole agreement. Unlike in the EEA Agreement, such a blackmail clause is explicit in this

[185] Formally speaking, it is the first example of so-called closer cooperation between some of the Member States. Both the United Kingdom and Ireland have opt-outs in this respect, but may, at their request, participate in parts of Schengen cooperation (see, i.e., Council Decision 2000/366/EC of 29 May 2000 concerning the request of the United Kingdom of Great Britain and Northern Ireland to take part in some of the provisions of the Schengen *acquis*, *OJ* 2000 L 131/43). A special status has been granted to Denmark in order to accommodate its wishes to opt out from Title IV EC.

agreement (Art. 11). The same goes for the settlement of disputes, which may arise because of a differentiated interpretation of the Schengen *acquis*. One should remember that neither Icelandic nor Norwegian courts have the authority to submit preliminary ruling references to the European Court of Justice.

3.3 Cooperation in criminal matters

In the years following the conclusion of the Treaty of Maastricht, the European Union has provided a platform for an unprecedented coordination of Member State activities and harmonisation of national law in criminal matters. The third pillar of the European Union was established more than a decade ago to facilitate activities in numerous sensitive areas, under the general Justice and Home Affairs umbrella. In the years following the entry into force of the Treaty on European Union, practice required yet another reform in order to strengthen the treaty framework. Under the terms of the Treaty of Amsterdam numerous important steps were taken. First, a large chunk of the Justice and Home Affairs dossier was communitarised (albeit with some limitations) by transferring it to Title IV of the EC Treaty.[186] Secondly, the third pillar was not only rebranded as Police and Judicial Cooperation in Criminal Matters but was also considerably empowered by new legal instruments and the partial jurisdiction of the European Court of Justice.[187] Last but not least, the Schengen *acquis* was incorporated into EU law. All these developments remain of relatively limited direct relevance to the EEA and its EFTA Member States. In purely legal terms, cooperation under the third pillar does not fall within the scope of the 'internal market driven' EEA. So far, the EFTA countries have not expressed a desire to proceed with a revision of the EEA Agreement facilitating their deeper involvement in this rapidly developing area of EU law. Judging from the experiences so far, one can argue that they give preference to sectoral cooperation at EU level as well as cooperation within the framework of the Council of Europe. The participation of Iceland and Norway in the Convention on Mutual Assistance in Criminal Matters may serve as an excellent example of the former.[188] It is based on a separate agreement concluded

186 See, *inter alia*, P.J. Kuijper, 'Some legal problems associated with communitarisation of policy on visas, asylum and immigration under the Amsterdam Treaty and incorporation of the Schengen *acquis*', 37 *CMLRev.* (2000) p. 345.

187 See, *inter alia*, A. Albors-Llorens, 'Changes in the jurisdiction of the European Court of Justice under the Treaty of Amsterdam', 35 *CMLRev.* (1998) p. 1286.

188 Due to developments of the Schengen *acquis*, Norway and Iceland are associated with the 1995 Convention on simplified extradition procedure. See Council Decision 2003/169/JHA of 27 February 2003 determining which provisions of the 1995 Convention on simplified extradition procedure between the Member States of the European Union and of the 1996 Convention relating to extradition between the Member States of the European Union constitute developments of the Schengen *acquis* in accordance with the Agreement concerning the Republic of Iceland's and the

in 2003 between the European Union, on one side, and Iceland and Norway, on the other.[189]

The agreement provides for the application of an exhaustive list of provisions of the Convention[190] in relations between the European Union and Norway and Iceland, as well as between the latter two in their bilateral relations. Similarly, provisions of the Protocol listed in Article 1(2) of the agreement are applicable.[191] The scope of the agreement with Iceland and Norway therefore covers rules on formalities and procedures in the execution of requests for mutual assistance, restitution, temporary transfer of persons held in custody for the purpose of investigation, videoconference hearings, joint investigation teams and the interception of telecommunications. Parties have an obligation to apply and interpret the Convention uniformly. To this end, the agreement creates an obligation to set up a regular exchange mechanism covering both ECJ case law and judicial developments in Iceland and Norway. An interesting procedural tool is established under Article 3 of the agreement. If a request is refused, Norway or Iceland have the right to request the receiving state to report the problem to Eurojust in order to reach a solution. Any disputes arising out of the application or interpretation of the agreement shall be resolved by diplomatic means at meetings held at governmental level.

3.4 Common Foreign and Security Policy

Another area of enhanced cooperation between the European Union and EEA-EFTA countries is the CFSP. It was already during the early stages of European Political Cooperation that some of the EEA-EFTA countries expressed an interest in participation. This was particularly the case with regard to Iceland and Norway, which are both founding members of NATO and associate members of the WEU. Both continue with their own foreign policies, although it has become standard practice that each of them explicitly aligns itself with particular EU actions and activities.[192] To this end, a number of international agreements were concluded

Kingdom of Norway's association with the implementation, application and development of the Schengen *acquis*, *OJ* 2003 L 67/25.

[189] Agreement between the European Union and the Republic of Iceland and the Kingdom of Norway on the application of certain provisions of the Convention of 29 May 2000 on Mutual Assistance in Criminal Matters between the Member States of the European Union and the 2001 Protocol thereto, *OJ* 2004 L 26/3.

[190] According to Art. 1(1) these are 'Articles 4, 8-11, 13-22, 25 and 26, as well as Articles 1 and 24 to the extent they are relevant for any of those other Articles.'

[191] These are Arts. 1(1)-(5), 2-7, 9, 11 and 12.

[192] See, for example, Declaration by the Presidency on behalf of the European Union concerning Council Decision 2006/51/CFSP of 30 January 2006 implementing Common Position 2004/161/CFSP renewing restrictive measures against Zimbabwe, Council Doc. 6050/06 (Presse 36); Declaration by the Presidency on behalf of the European Union concerning Council Common

between the parties, including agreements on crisis management operations,[193] the exchange of classified information[194] and the participation of these countries in selected operations (i.e., EUPOL 'Proxima' and EUPM Bosnia-Herzegovina).[195] Moreover, CFSP issues are often debated in various EEA institutions (see the above-mentioned discussions on the ENP).

4. CONCLUSION

In the course of last decade, the EEA played a pivotal role in the economic and legal integration of EFTA countries into the internal market. In some cases, it was just a *prelude* to membership of the European Union; in others it proved to be an appropriate framework for a long-term relationship. Due to limited membership on the EFTA side, the EEA is quite often regarded as a redundant hybrid whose days are numbered. As this chapter proves, this very hybrid has considerable potential and has already proved its usefulness. It is near to impossible to consider the EEA in black and white terms. Some points may differ depending on the approach taken.

For EFTA countries which are not ready or interested in EU membership, the EEA may be an acceptable option guaranteeing access to the internal market and a considerable chunk of the *acquis* without real political involvement. It allows them to protect their sovereignty, at least theoretically, and facilitates protection of their vital economic interests. In the case of the latter, one shall remember that trade in fisheries products is not covered by the EEA and still remains primarily regulated by the FTAs. At the same time, the current *modus operandi* puts these

---

Position 2006/50/CFSP of 30 January 2006 extending and amending Common Position 2004/133/CFSP on restrictive measures against extremists in the former Yugoslav Republic of Macedonia (FYROM), Council Doc. 5939/06 (Presse 34); Declaration by the Presidency on behalf of the European Union on the application of specific measures to combat terrorism, Council Doc. 15725/05 (Presse 360).

193 Agreement between the European Union and the Kingdom of Norway establishing a framework for the participation of the Kingdom of Norway in the European Union crisis-management operations, *OJ* 2005 L 67/8; Agreement between the European Union and the Republic of Iceland establishing a framework for the participation of the Republic of Iceland in the European Union crisis-management, *OJ* 2005 L 67/2.

194 Agreement between the Kingdom of Norway and the European Union on security procedures for the exchange of classified information, *OJ* 2004 L 362/29.

195 Agreement between the European Union and the Kingdom of Norway on the participation of the Kingdom of Norway in the European Union Police Mission in the former Yugoslav Republic of Macedonia (EUPOL 'Proxima'), *OJ* 2004 L 354/86; Agreement between the European Union and the Kingdom of Norway on the participation of the Kingdom of Norway in the European Union Police Mission (EUPM) in Bosnia and Herzegovina (BiH), *OJ* 2004 L 239/32; Agreement between the European Union and the Republic of Iceland on the participation of the Republic of Iceland in the European Union Police Mission (EUPM) in Bosnia and Herzegovina (BiH), *OJ* L 2003 L 239/5.

countries in the position of 'prisoners in paradise'. In practice, their impact on EU decision making is fairly limited, but they remain under obligation and pressure to swallow large portions of secondary legislation.

The EU perspective is very different. In economic terms, the EEA facilitates the access of economic operators to an even bigger internal market. Thanks to the principle of homogeneity, effectively implemented by both sides, we are dealing with a market comprising twenty-eight Member States in which the fundamental freedoms of the internal market are guaranteed.

From the broader perspective of European integration and its future, one may argue that the EEA serves as an example of integration circles in which different groups of countries engage in cooperation in more limited areas than others. Bearing this in mind, the EEA should be considered in the light of the objectives of the European Union's emerging neighbourhood policy. It may be argued that the EEA has a potential to serve as a model arrangement for future relations with some of the European Union's neighbours that, for a variety of political, geographical and legal reasons, will not be able to benefit from EU membership in the decades to come.

CHAPTER 5

SWITZERLAND

Adam Łazowski*

Relevant legal documents:
(For a complete list, see <http://europa.eu.int/comm/external_relations/switzerland/doc/bilat.htm>.)

- Agreement between the European Economic Community and the Swiss Confederation, *OJ* 1972 L 300/191 (with subsequent amendments).
- Agreement between the European Economic Community and the Swiss Confederation on direct insurance other than life insurance, *OJ* 1991 L 205/3.
- Agreement between the European Community and its Member States, of the one part, and the Swiss Confederation, of the other, on the free movement of persons, *OJ* 2002 L 114/6 (with 2004 protocol extending application of the agreement to the new EU Member States).
- Agreement between the European Community and the Swiss Confederation on Air Transport, *OJ* 2002 L 114/73.
- Agreement between the European Community and the Swiss Confederation on the Carriage of Goods and Passengers by Rail and Road, *OJ* 2002 L 114/91.
- Agreement between the European Community and the Swiss Confederation on trade in agricultural products, *OJ* 2002 L 114/132.
- Agreement between the European Community and the Swiss Confederation on mutual recognition in relation to conformity assessment, *OJ* 2002 L 114/369.
- Agreement between the European Community and the Swiss Confederation on certain aspects of government procurement, *OJ* 2002 L 114/430.
- Agreement on Scientific and Technological Cooperation between the European Community and the European Atomic Energy Community, of the one part, and the Swiss Confederation, of the other part, *OJ* 2004 L 32/23.

* Senior Lecturer in Law, School of Law, University of Westminster, London. This chapter is partly based on the author's conference paper: 'Cooperation of Integration or Cooperation of Co-existence: The Union and Switzerland', presented at the seminar 'Enlargement and the Future of the European Union: Parallel Paths or Crossroads', which took place in Warsaw on 1-3 July 2004.

S. Blockmans and A. Łazowski (eds.), The European Union and Its Neighbours

- Agreement between the European Union, the European Community and the Swiss Confederation on the Swiss Confederation's association with the implementation, application and development of the Schengen *acquis*.*
- Agreement between the European Community and the Swiss Confederation concerning the criteria and mechanisms for establishing the state responsible for examining a request for asylum lodged in a Member State or in Switzerland.*
- Agreement between the European Community and the Swiss Confederation providing for measures equivalent to those laid down in Council Directive 2003/48/EC on taxation of savings income in the form of interest payments, *OJ* 2004 L 385/30.
- Cooperation Agreement between the European Community and its Member States, of the one part, and the Swiss Confederation, of the other part, to counter fraud and all other illegal activities to the detriment of their financial interests.*
- Agreement between the European Community and the Swiss Confederation concerning the participation of Switzerland in the European Environment Agency and the European Environment Information and Observation Network, *OJ* 2006 L 90/37.
- Agreement between the European Community and the Swiss Confederation on cooperation in the field of statistics, *OJ* 2006 L 90/2.
- Agreement between the European Community and the Swiss Confederation in the audiovisual field, establishing the terms and conditions for the participation of the Swiss Confederation in the Community programmes Media Plus and Media Training, *OJ* 2006 L 90/23.

* Not yet published in the *OJ*, text available at <http://www.europa.admin.ch/nbv/off/abkommen/e/index.htm>.

1. THE EVOLUTION OF EC/EU RELATIONS WITH THE SWISS CONFEDERATION

1.1 Introduction

The relations between the European Union and the Swiss Confederation are undoubtedly very peculiar and are characterised by a multiplicity of political and legal factors. In institutional terms, Switzerland remains on the outskirts of the main integration paths. It is neither a member of the European Union nor the European Economic Area (EEA). In economic terms, however, it can be regarded as one of the players in the integration process. As noted by Laurent Goetschel, it 'is economically more integrated within the European Union (EU) than many of the EU's own Member States.'[1] In legal terms, it is also harmonised to a

[1] L. Goetschel, 'Switzerland and European Integration: Change Through Distance', 8 *EFA Rev.* (2003) p. 313.

considerable degree. At this stage, it is enough to mention the ongoing voluntary approximation of its domestic legislation to EC law (often referred to as autonomous reconstruction),[2] as well as its obligation to apply selected parts of the *acquis communautaire* imposed by bilateral agreements. With the two recent packages of bilateral treaties, Switzerland has secured its participation in the key elements of the internal market, as well as certain aspects of the area of freedom, security and justice, albeit without political and institutional involvement in the decision making. On the basis of separate agreements with the European Union, Switzerland supports a select number of CFSP actions. All these factors facilitate and justify the argument that, over the years, the bilateral cooperation has evolved from a 'cooperation of coexistence' to a 'cooperation of integration'.[3] The question whether this is a short-term solution or rather a model for future cooperation remains unanswerable for the time being. At this stage, it is also questionable whether these developments open the door to potential membership of the European Union. The final decision on both sides will be influenced by a combination of political and legal factors. Notwithstanding the model of *finalité*, it leaves no doubt that after decades of troublesome relations the concept of enhanced bilateralism in EU-Swiss relations has continued to develop and can be regarded as operational and fruitful for both sides.

The EC/EU approach towards Switzerland has been subject to considerable changes over the years. Needless to say, it was driven by variety of different factors. These included, *inter alia*, developments in European integration, growing membership of the European Communities/European Union and the concept of a wider European economic space that eventually led to the creation of the EEA. The collapse of Switzerland's EEA accession in the 1992 referendum led to reorientation of the European Union's policy towards the Swiss Confederation. The initial Swiss request to open negotiations on bilateral agreements was not met with widespread enthusiasm, as the European Economic Community itself was still coping with the consequences of the EEA delays.[4] Although the European Commission still claimed that it was in the interests of the Community to have a good relationship with Switzerland, it argued that any future developments would have to be based on a fair balance of mutual advantages. In its 1993 Communication on relations with Switzerland, the

---

[2] F. Emmert, 'Switzerland and the EU: Partners, for Better or for Worse', 3 *EFA Rev.* (1998) p. 367 at p. 376.

[3] A. Łazowski, 'Unia Europejska i Konfederacja Szwajcarska – Współpraca współistnienia czy współpraca integracji?' [European Union and Swiss Confederation – Cooperation of Coexistence or Cooperation of Integration], in C. Mik, ed., *Unia Europejska i Świat. Aspekty prawne i polityczne* [The European Union and the World. Legal and Political Aspects] (Toruń, TNOiK 2005) p. 115.

[4] See B. Cottier and A. Gerber, 'Some Problems Regarding Ratification and Implementation of the European Economic Area Agreement in the EFTA Member States', 20 *Pol. YBIL* (1993) pp. 254-257.

European Commission argued that 'it would be inappropriate for Switzerland to obtain all the advantages of an Agreement which it has rejected.'[5] During the last decade, it has accepted this special relationship and refrained from putting it in the framework of a classic Association Agreement. Having seen some of the advantages of this enhanced bilateralism, both parties accepted the first package of bilateral treaties and soon afterwards engaged in the next round of negotiations leading to a second package of bilateral treaties.

From the early years, the Swiss approach to the institutionalised forms of European integration was characterised by a high degree of reluctance. Goetschel argues that the attitude can be described as 'a mixture of suspicion and attraction'.[6] It was mainly driven by the priorities of Swiss foreign policy and its neutrality in particular.[7] The Swiss internal political and constitutional system, which places a strong emphasis on participatory democracy, also played tremendous role in shaping Swiss relations with the European Communities/European Union.[8] Recent changes, including membership of the United Nations in 2002, participation in NATO's Partnership for Peace Programme (since 1996)[9] and ratification of the first package of bilateral treaties with the European

---

[5] Communication from the Commission, Future relations with Switzerland, COM (1993) 486 final.

[6] Goetschel, loc. cit. n. 1, at p. 313.

[7] Ibid.

[8] The Swiss Constitution of 18 April 1999 distinguishes between mandatory and optional referenda (Arts. 140 and 141 respectively). Within the first group, the following may be submitted for the vote of citizens as well as the Swiss cantons:

- revisions of the Federal Constitution;
- accession to international organisations of collective security or supranational organisations;
- Federal statutes which have no legal base in the Constitution, but which are urgent and the validity of which is longer that one year.

The vote of Swiss citizens is also required in cases of:

- 'popular initiatives for the total revision of the Federal Constitution';
- 'popular initiatives for partial revision of the Federal Constitution in the form of a general suggestion which were rejected by the Federal Parliament';
- 'the question whether a total revision of the Constitution should be carried out if both Chambers disagree'.

The optional referenda may be organised on the initiative of at least 50,000 citizens or eight cantons. The following, *inter alia*, may be subject to an optional referendum: Federal statutes, international treaties that provide for the membership of international organisations, treaties of unlimited duration that may not be terminated and treaties that involve a multilateral unification of law. Other international treaties may be submitted for a referendum on the initiative of the Federal Parliament. For a scientific political appraisal of the EU-connected referenda of the last decade, see L. Marquis, 'The Priming of Referendum Votes on Swiss European Policy', SEI Working Paper No. 82 (2004); L. Marquis and K.G. Lutz, 'Thinking About and Voting on Swiss Foreign Policy: Does Affective and Cognitive Involvement Play a Role?', SEI Working Paper No. 83 (2004); P. Sciarini and O. Listhaug, 'Single Cases or a Unique Pair? The Swiss and Norwegian "No" to Europe', 35 *JCMS* (1997) pp. 407-438.

[9] For an overview of Swiss activities within Partnership for Peace, see <http://www.pfp.admin.ch/internet/partnership_for_peace/en/home.html>.

Communities, are clear signs of changes within this multicultural society. The positive outcome of the referenda on Schengen (5 June 2005) and on the ratification of the Enlargement Protocol to the EC-Swiss Agreement on the Free Movement of Persons (25 September 2005) only support this argument.[10] It must be noted that euroscepticism is easily detectable among political elites and populist parties in particular. It was already in 1998 that Emmert noted that public debate on immigration, asylum and connected policies has become 'increasingly emotive' and 'ever less rational'.[11] No doubt the Schengen debate also followed this pattern.[12] It will undoubtedly have a strong impact on the results of any plebiscites and indirectly also on the shape of future EU-Swiss relations.[13]

The aim of this chapter is to take a closer look at the evolution of EU-Swiss relations and their current legal framework. Bearing in mind the complexity of the legal puzzle that binds both parties, this analysis will concentrate mainly on two sets of bilateral treaties, with particular emphasis on the EC-Swiss Agreement on the Free Movement of Persons. Due to its legal characteristics, this agreement may serve as a laboratory for numerous legal phenomena analysed throughout this book. These include, in particular, the external consequences of the European Union's three-pillar structure, the extension of EC legal concepts to relations with third countries and the multi-layered differentiation between the status of old and new Member States.

1.2 Three phases of the bilateral relationship

As acknowledged by the European Commission, EC/EU cooperation with Switzerland has been long-lasting and very intensive. As a matter of fact, no other third country has as many bilateral agreements with European Communities/ European Union as the Swiss Confederation.[14] The current state of affairs is of course the result of fifty years of cooperation. Its evolution can be divided into three main phases.

---

[10] Protocol to the Agreement between the European Community and its Member States, of the one part, and the Swiss Confederation, of the other, on the free movement of persons, regarding the participation, as contracting parties, of the Czech Republic, the Republic of Estonia, the Republic of Cyprus, the Republic of Latvia, the Republic of Lithuania, the Republic of Hungary, the Republic of Malta, the Republic of Poland, the Republic of Slovenia and the Slovak Republic, pursuant to their accession to the European Union, *OJ* 2006 L 89/30 (hereinafter referred to as the 'Enlargement Protocol').

[11] Emmert, loc. cit. n. 2, at p. 379.

[12] See, for example, *Financial Times*, 3-4 June 2005, p. 2.

[13] See C. Church, 'The Contexts of Swiss Opposition to Europe', SEI Working Paper No. 64 (2003).

[14] See comments on the European Commission external relations website, at: <http://europa.eu.int/comm/external_relations/switzerland/intro/index.htm>.

The first phase covers the period between 1956 and 1972. During these initial years, relations focused on the steel and coal sectors. The first notable agreement was signed in 1956 and dealt with general cooperation in those sectors between the High Authority and the Swiss Confederation.[15] It was followed by an agreement on the introduction of international railway tariffs for coal and steel transit through Swiss territory.[16] A number of bilateral treaties were signed during the 1960s, including agreements on products of the clock and watch industry,[17] an agreement on textiles[18] and a tariff agreement concerning cheese products[19] negotiated under Article XXVIII of GATT. In the meantime, Switzerland became one of the founding members of the European Free Trade Association (EFTA).

The real breakthrough came in the early 1970s. The accession of the United Kingdom and Denmark (both EFTA countries), as well as Ireland, to the European Communities undoubtedly changed the nature of EFTA and led its members to sign free trade agreements with the European Communities.[20] The Agreement between the European Economic Community and the Swiss Confederation was signed on 22 July 1972 and entered into force on 1 January 1973 pursuant to Article 36 of the agreement.[21] A separate free trade agreement with Switzerland was concluded by the European Steel and Coal Community.[22] With these developments, the relations between the European Communities and Switzerland entered into their second phase, lasting for almost two decades (1973-1992). It has to be acknowledged that a considerable number of agreements were concluded during those years.[23] Nevertheless, the intensity of bilateral relations

15 Accord de Consultation entre la Confédération Suisse et la Haute Autorité de la Communauté Européenne du Charbon et de l'Acier, *JO* 1957 7/85.

16 Accord relatif à l'établissement de tarifs directs internationaux ferroviaires pour les transports de charbon et d'acier en transit par le territoire Suisse, *JO* 1957 17/223.

17 Agreement concerning products of the clock and watch industry between the European Economic Community and its Member States and the Swiss Confederation, *OJ* 1974 L 118/12 (as amended).

18 Arrangement entre la Communauté économique européenne et la Suisse en vue de maintenir provisoirement des droits de douane réduits sur certains tissues, *JO* 1968 L 266/3.

19 Accord tarifaire avec la Suisse négocié au titre de l'article XXVIII du G.A.T.T. concernant certains fromages de la position ex 04.04 du tarif douanier commun, signé à Genève le 29 juin 1967, *JO* 1969 L 257/5.

20 See E.P. Wellenstein, 'The Free Trade Agreements between the Enlarged European Communities and the EFTA Countries', 10 *CMLRev.* (1973) pp. 137-149.

21 Agreement between the European Economic Community and the Swiss Confederation, *OJ* 1972 L 300/191 (with subsequent amendments).

22 Agreement between the Member States of the European Coal and Steel Community and the Swiss Confederation, *OJ* 1973 L 350/13.

23 See, *inter alia*, Cooperation Agreement between the European Atomic Energy Community and the Swiss Confederation in the field of controlled thermonuclear fusion and plasma physics, *OJ* 1978 L 242/2; Agreement in the form of an Exchange of Letters between the European Economic Community and the Swiss Confederation concerning non-agricultural and processed agricultural products not covered by the Agreement, *OJ* 1986 L 328/39; Framework Agreement for scientific and

was dictated by developments connected to the negotiation and conclusion of the Agreement on the European Economic Area.[24] As explained in chapter 4 of this book, the rationale behind the EEA was to extend the internal market to EFTA countries without their participation in decision making and their involvement in other areas of cooperation falling under the competences of three European Communities and the future European Union. Switzerland was one of the EFTA signatories to the EEA Agreement (along with Norway, Iceland, Finland, Liechtenstein, Sweden and Austria).[25] During this intensive period, it also submitted a formal application for membership of the European Economic Community[26] and concluded additional agreements with the European Communities.[27]

It may be argued that, at this point in time, Switzerland was clearly on a path leading to the enhancement of its relations with European Communities. However, this process was abruptly and effectively blocked by a referendum held on 6 December 1992.[28] Looking at its results and consequences from the perspective of more than ten years, it is easy to conclude that this plebiscite had a number of short and long-term implications for both sides. The referendum not only forced the Swiss Government to withdraw from the EEA but also led to the formal suspension of its EEC membership application. In addition, it forced the contracting parties to the EEA Agreement to adopt an additional protocol taking into account the fact Switzerland was not going to be the part of the European

---

technical cooperation between the European Communities and the Swiss Confederation, *OJ* 1985 L 313/6; Agreements in the form of exchanges of letters between the European Economic Community and the Swiss Confederation concerning agriculture and fisheries, *OJ* 1986 L 328/99; Convention between the European Economic Community, the Republic of Austria, the Republic of Finland, the Republic of Iceland, the Kingdom of Norway, the Kingdom of Sweden and the Swiss Confederation on a common transit procedure, *OJ* 1987 L 226/2; Convention between the European Economic Community, the Republic of Austria, the Republic of Finland, the Republic of Iceland, the Kingdom of Norway, the Kingdom of Sweden and the Swiss Confederation on the simplification of formalities in trade in goods, *OJ* 1987 L 134/2; Agreement between the European Economic Community and the Swiss Confederation on trade in electronic data interchange systems, *OJ* 1989 L 400/27; Agreement between the European Economic Community and the Swiss Confederation on the simplification of inspections and formalities in respect of the carriage of goods, *OJ* 1990 L 116/19; Agreement between the European Economic Community and the Swiss Confederation on direct insurance other than life assurance, *OJ* 1991 L 205/3; Agreement between the European Economic Community and the Swiss Confederation on the carriage of goods by road and rail, *OJ* 1992 L 373/28.

24 Agreement on the European Economic Area, *OJ* 1994 L 1/3.

25 On the potential implications of the EEA Agreement on Switzerland's legal system, see, for example, C. Alder, 'Zum Vorrang von EG und EWR-Recht vor schweizerischem Recht', 27 *EuR* (1992) p. 345; M. Haymann, 'Approaching Europe: Swiss Prospectives and Dilemmas', *LIEI* (1992) p. 71.

26 The formal document can be accessed at: <http://europa.eu.int/comm/external_relations/switzerland/doc/letter.pdf>.

27 See *supra* n. 23.

28 See Emmert, loc. cit. n. 2, at pp. 372-375.

Economic Area.[29] The referendum fiasco also had long-term implications. It became clear that Switzerland's membership in both organisations had to be removed from the agenda. As the European Commission noted in 1993: 'Switzerland, which applied for membership of the Community in May 1992, finds its road to close European integration effectively blocked.'[30] It also forced both parties to find a smart and effective way of bringing Switzerland closer to the developing and enlarging Union (to mutual benefit). With the enlargement of EFTA in 1995 and the 'big bang' enlargement slowly emerging on the horizon, Switzerland suddenly found itself in the potentially uncomfortable position of a blank spot on the map, surrounded by Member States of the European Union.

At the beginning of 1993, the concept of enhanced bilateralism found its place on the drawing board. By this means, EC/EU Swiss relations entered into their third phase (1993 to present). Officially, the concept of bilateral treaties covering selected aspects of the internal market was initiated by Switzerland during the meeting of the Joint Committee of the Free Trade Agreement in February 1993. The areas of interest of Switzerland covered a very broad range of topics and extended from rules of origin and public procurement to air and road transport, as well as cooperation on research. The initial EC response was positive, albeit backed by numerous reservations. The European Commission emphasised that the

> Swiss requests should … be considered on a strict basis of mutual advantage and without undermining the EEA. It would be inappropriate for Switzerland to obtain all the advantages of an Agreement, which it has rejected, and whose entry into force has been long delayed as a result.[31]

It was therefore proposed that the negotiations should concentrate on areas of mutual interest. Moreover, the Commission emphasised that agreements should be linked together. This set the scene for the introduction of the so-called 'guillotine clause' linking their entry into force and potential expiry/termination. Particular attention was paid to the implementation of the *acquis communautaire*, and the time framework for agreements was accepted. Finally, a reduction in the number of issue areas for the first wave of negotiations was suggested. It was followed by the Council, which in November 1993 gave the green light for the initiation of negotiations concerning agreements on the trade in agricultural products, the free movement of persons, research, road transport and – potentially – public

---

29 Protocol Adjusting the Agreement on the European Economic Area, *OJ* 1994 L 1/572.

30 Communication from the Commission, Future relations with Switzerland, COM (1993) 486 final, p. 1a.

31 Ibid., at p. 3.

procurement and technical barriers to trade. The negotiations took place during the years 1994-1999 and were far from easy. Although this conclusion may be regarded as a mere cliché, it is still true that there were number of controversial problems that negotiators had to approach. The most difficult was undoubtedly the free movement of persons and the connected rights of EU citizens in Switzerland. What may have initially looked like an attempt to accommodate two extremes ended with a rather complex compromise filled with transitional solutions extending beyond the initial term for which the agreement was concluded. The agreed transitional framework was a workable solution for the European Union's demand for full access to the Swiss labour market and Switzerland's aim to secure numerous restrictions and safeguard clauses. Other dossiers beset by political and legal difficulties included road transport and agriculture.[32] Following successful negotiations, a package of seven bilateral agreements bound by guillotine clauses was finally signed on 21 June 21 1999. Following a successful referendum in Switzerland and the completion of all necessary procedures, the agreements entered into force on 1 June 2002.[33]

While the ratification of Bilateral I was in progress, the parties decided to engage in yet another set of complex and difficult negotiations on the next batch of agreements (the so-called Bilateral II).[34] The first declaration of intent was already made by the time the first batch of treaties was signed.[35] The initial list of negotiation dossiers was already spelled out by the time of the signature of Bilateral I. It included amendments to the Free Trade Agreement of 1972 and the participation of Switzerland in various EC education, youth and environmental

32 See further Emmert, loc. cit. n. 2, at pp. 375-391.

33 Agreement between the European Community and its Member States, of the one part, and the Swiss Confederation, of the other, on the free movement of persons, *OJ* 2002 L 114/6 (hereinafter referred to as the 'EC-Swiss Agreement on the Free Movement of Persons'); Agreement between the European Community and the Swiss Confederation on Air Transport, *OJ* 2002 L 114/73 (hereinafter referred to as the 'EC-Swiss Agreement on Air Transport'); Agreement between the European Community and the Swiss Confederation on the Carriage of Goods and Passengers by Rail and Road, *OJ* 2002 L 114/91; Agreement between the European Community and the Swiss Confederation on trade in agricultural products, *OJ* 2002 L 114/132; Agreement between the European Community and the Swiss Confederation on mutual recognition in relation to conformity assessment, *OJ* 2002 L 114/369 (hereinafter referred to as the 'EC-Swiss Agreement on Conformity Assessment'); Agreement between the European Community and the Swiss Confederation on certain aspects of government procurement, *OJ* 2002 L 114/430 (hereinafter referred to as the 'EC-Swiss Agreement on Government Procurement'); Agreement on Scientific and Technological Cooperation between the European Communities and the Swiss Confederation, *OJ* 2002 L 114/468 (hereinafter referred to as the 'EC-Swiss Scientific and Technological Cooperation Agreement').

34 For a detailed chronology of Bilateral II, see the website of the Swiss European Integration Office at: <http://www.europa.admin.ch/nbv/expl/zeitplan/e/index.htm>.

35 See the joint declarations attached to final acts of every treaty constituting Bilateral I. See also Report from Presidency to Coreper II on EU-Switzerland relations, 18 June 2001, Council Doc. No. 9524/01.

programmes, including the European Environment Agency. In addition, it covered statistics and, most importantly, liberalisation of services. On the initiative of the European Union, further issues were included on the negotiation agenda. These were combating fraud and illegal activities affecting the European Union's financial interests and the adoption of measures equivalent to EC law in respect of the taxation of savings income.[36] It was a Swiss initiative to extend the negotiation dossiers to cooperation in justice, police, asylum and immigration matters (including Swiss participation in the Schengen and Dublin Agreements). The pre-negotiation meeting took place in early 2001 and, following the adoption of negotiating mandates, the talks started later that year. Initially, they covered four areas (prevention of fraud, amendment of the Free Trade Agreement, the environment and statistics). The remaining five dossiers were formally added in 2002. Due to differences between the parties, the troublesome agreement on services was removed from the Bilateral II agenda in 2003. In the meantime, the parties also engaged in difficult talks on the extension of the EC-Swiss Agreement on the Free Movement of Persons to nationals of the prospective new EU Member States. The negotiations of Bilateral II were completed with the adoption of political decisions during the first EU-Swiss summit on 19 May 2004.[37] This was followed by an official signing ceremony on 26 October 2004 after which the ratification procedure was opened.[38] On this occasion, the

---

[36] Negotiations of similar agreements were pursued with the United States, San Marino, Monaco and Andorra. See chapter 6 in this volume.

[37] The outstanding issues included Swiss association with Schengen, the fight against fraud and the extension of the Agreement on the Free Movement of People. All those matters were addressed and handled during the summit. Results were spelled out in the annexes to the summit conclusions. See <http://europa.eu.int/comm/external_relations/switzerland/doc/summit_0504.pdf>.

[38] Agreement between the European Union, the European Community and the Swiss Confederation on the Swiss Confederation's association with the implementation, application and development of the Schengen *acquis*, nyp (hereinafter referred to as the 'EC/EU-Swiss Agreement on Schengen'); Agreement between the European Community and the Swiss Confederation concerning the criteria and mechanisms for establishing the state responsible for examining a request for asylum lodged in a Member State or in Switzerland, nyp (hereinafter referred to as the 'EC-Swiss Agreement on Asylum'); Agreement between the European Community and the Swiss Confederation providing for measures equivalent to those laid down in Council Directive 2003/48/EC on taxation of savings income in the form of interest payments, *OJ* 2004 L 385/30 (hereinafter referred to as the 'EC-Swiss Agreement on Savings Income Taxation'); Cooperation Agreement between the European Community and its Member States, of the one part, and the Swiss Confederation, of the other part, to counter fraud and all other illegal activities to the detriment of their financial interests, nyp (hereinafter referred to as the 'EC-Swiss Antifraud Agreement'); Agreement between the European Community and the Swiss Confederation amending the Agreement between the European Economic Community and the Swiss Confederation of 22 July 1972 as regards the provisions applicable to processed agricultural products, *OJ* 2005 L 23/19 (hereinafter referred to as the 'EC-Swiss Agreement on Trade in Processed Agricultural Products'); Agreement between the European Community and the Swiss Confederation concerning the participation of Switzerland in the European Environment Agency and the European Environment Information and Observation Network, *OJ* 2006 L 90/37; Agreement between the European Community and the Swiss Confederation on

Enlargement Protocol to EC-Swiss Agreement on the Free Movement of Persons was also signed.

The developments of the last years do not only include two sets of bilateral treaties. Apart from the regular adaptation of the existing framework by means of joint committee decisions and the conclusion of agreements of relatively minor importance,[39] the parties also extended their cooperation to the second pillar. Although not fully aligned with the CFSP (as in the case of candidate and EEA countries), Switzerland has decided to participate in the European Union Police Mission (EUPM)[40] and military crisis management (ALTHEA) in Bosnia and Herzegovina.[41] Moreover, it was agreed that Switzerland will contribute to EU police mission in the Former Yugoslav Republic of Macedonia.[42] In mid-2005, the parties also concluded an agreement on the security procedures for the exchange of classified information.[43]

1.3 Institutional framework for EU-Swiss Cooperation

One of the important characteristics of the bilateral relations between the European Communities/European Union and Switzerland is the lack of a uniform and coherent institutional structure. Cooperation can be effected at various levels, mainly in the framework of joint committees established by the bilateral agreements or, in some cases, in the comitology committees.

The political dialogue is conducted at the highest political level, but its intensity and the rank of the meetings depends mainly on the dossiers occupying the

cooperation in the field of statistics, *OJ* 2006 L 90/2 (hereinafter referred to as the 'EC-Swiss Agreement on Statistics'); Agreement between the European Community and the Swiss Confederation in the audiovisual field, establishing the terms and conditions for the participation of the Swiss Confederation in the Community programmes MEDIA Plus and MEDIA Training, *OJ* 2006 L 90/23; Agreement between the Swiss Federal Council and the Commission of the European Communities with a view to avoiding the double taxation of retired officials of the institutions and agencies of the European Communities resident in Switzerland, nyp.

39 Administrative arrangement in the form of an Exchange of Letters between the European Community and the Swiss Confederation concerning the transitional points system applicable to heavy goods vehicles travelling through Austria, *OJ* 2004 L 57/17.

40 Agreement between the European Union and the Government of the Swiss Confederation, represented by the Federal Department of Foreign Affairs, on the participation of Switzerland in the European Union Police Mission (EUPM) in Bosnia and Herzegovina (BiH), *OJ* 2003 L 239/14.

41 Agreement between the European Union and the Swiss Confederation on the participation of the Swiss Confederation in the European Union military crisis management operation in Bosnia and Herzegovina (operation ALTHEA), *OJ* 2005 L 20/42.

42 Agreement between the European Union and the Swiss Confederation on the participation of the Swiss Confederation in the European Union police mission in the former Yugoslav Republic of Macedonia (EUPOL 'Proxima'), *OJ* 2004 L 354/78.

43 Agreement between the Swiss Confederation and the European Union on the Security Procedures for the Exchange of Classified Information, 29 April 2005, Council Doc. No. 8103/05.

bilateral agenda. During the past decade, most (but not all) of the contacts were obviously dominated by the negotiation of both sets of bilateral agreements. It should be noted that the first general EU-Swiss summit took place on 19 May 2004 and that it focused mainly on the completion of Bilateral II. It is hard to predict at this stage whether this model of governance at the highest political level will be practiced in the future (as it is for instance with Russia and Ukraine).[44]

The institutional framework of the bilateral agreements is highly fragmented and does not include a single set of bodies equipped with powers extending horizontally to all agreements. On the contrary, almost every treaty is administered by a separate joint committee[45] that is composed of representatives of both parties.[46] Analysis of these agreements leads to the inevitable conclusion that most of the committees have similar functions and powers. They may differ from one agreement to another, but it is easy to identify some common denominators. In principle, the main tasks of the joint committees include the administration of the relevant agreements. In the case of selected agreements, the competencies of the joint committees also include dispute settlement. In this context, it is particularly interesting to note the powers of the Mixed Committee acting in the framework of the EC/EU-Swiss Agreement on Schengen. Under Article 10 of this agreement, the Mixed Committee has the authority, *inter alia*, to settle disputes arising from substantially divergent interpretations of the Schengen *acquis* by the European Court of Justice and Swiss courts and administrative authorities. This permits the conclusion that the Mixed Committee has quasi-judicial powers. It must be remembered that, in the case of a failure to settle the dispute, the EC/EU-Swiss Agreement on Schengen will be terminated. Committees are equipped with decision-making powers and may also have the authority to adopt technical amendments to the existing treaty framework.[47] Detailed provisions on their operation and applicable procedures are included in the rules of procedure

---

44 See chapters 14 and 15 in this volume.

45 In the case of the EC/EU-Swiss Agreement on Schengen and the EC-Swiss Agreement on Asylum the joint body is called the 'Mixed Committee'.

46 Details of EC representation on those committees are regulated in Arts. 2-7 of Decision of the Council, and of the Commission as regards the Agreement on Scientific and Technological Cooperation, of 4 April 2002 on the conclusion of seven Agreements with the Swiss Confederation (2002/309/EC, Euratom), *OJ* 2002 L 114/1.

47 See, for example, Arts. 29-31 of the EEC-Swiss Free Trade Agreement; Arts. 15-18 of the EEC-Swiss Agreement on the simplification of inspections and formalities in respect of the carriage of goods; Arts. 37-38 of the EEC-Swiss Agreement on direct insurance other than life insurance; Art. 14 of the EC-Swiss Agreement on the Free Movement of Persons; Arts. 21-22 of the EC-Swiss Agreement on Air Transport; Art. 51 of the EC-Swiss Agreement on Carriage of Goods and Passengers by Rail and Road; Art. 6 of the EC-Swiss Agreement on Trade in Processed Agricultural Products; Art. 10 of the EC-Swiss Agreement on Conformity Assessment; Art. 11 of the EC-Swiss Agreement on Government Procurement; Arts. 3-10 of the EC/EU-Swiss Agreement on Schengen; Arts. 3-7 of the EC-Swiss Agreement on Asylum; Arts. 39-40 of the EC-Swiss Antifraud Agreement.

adopted by each committee.[48] Joint committees may also set up working groups.[49] Practice indicates that joint bodies play an essential role in the everyday administration of bilateral agreements. This is particularly visible in cases where they are responsible for the technical adaptation of the treaties. The Agreement on Mutual Recognition and Conformity Assessment serves as a perfect example in this respect.[50] Under Article 11 of this agreement, the Joint Committee is responsible for the inclusion or removal of conformity assessment bodies from the lists, and this has already occurred a considerable number of times.[51] In order to limit the practical burdens of this procedure, the parties have decided to revise the agreement.[52]

---

48 See, for example, Decision No. 1/2003 of the Joint Committee on Agriculture set up by the Agreement between the European Community and the Swiss Confederation on trade in agricultural products of 21 October 2003 concerning the adoption of its Rules of Procedure, *OJ* 2003 L 303/24; Decision No. 1/2003 of the Joint Veterinary Committee set up by the Agreement between the European Community and the Swiss Confederation on Trade in Agricultural Products of 29 July 2003 concerning the adoption of its Rules of Procedure, *OJ* 2003 L 254/35; Decision No. 1/2004 of the EU/Switzerland Mixed Committee established by the Agreement concluded between the European Union, the European Community and the Swiss Confederation concerning the latter's association in the implementation, application and development of the Schengen *acquis* of 26 October 2004 adopting its Rules of Procedure, *OJ* 2004 C 308/2.

49 See, for example, Decision No. 2/2003 of the Joint Committee on Agriculture set up by the Agreement between the European Community and the Swiss Confederation on trade in agricultural products of 21 October 2003 concerning the setting-up of the working groups and the adoption of the terms of reference of those groups, *OJ* 2003 L 303/27.

50 The EC-Swiss Agreement on the Free Movement of Persons may serve as another example. It is discussed thoroughly in part 3 of this chapter.

51 See, for example, Decision No. 2/2003 of 17 September 2003 of the Committee established under the Agreement between the European Community and the Swiss Confederation on mutual recognition in relation to conformity assessment on the listing of a conformity assessment body under the sectoral chapter for medical devices, *OJ* 2003 L 323/9; Decision No. 1/2004 of 16 January 2004 of the Committee established under the Agreement between the European Community and the Swiss Confederation on Mutual Recognition in relation to Conformity Assessment on the listing of a Conformity Assessment Body under the Sectoral Chapter for Toys, *OJ* 2004 L 34/72; Decision No. 2/2004 of 10 February 2004 of the Committee established under the Agreement between the European Community and the Swiss Confederation on Mutual Recognition in relation to Conformity Assessment on the removal of Conformity Assessment Bodies from the Chapter for measuring instruments and prepackages and from the Chapter for electrical equipment and electromagnetic compatibility, *OJ* 2004 L 74/23; Decision No. 3/2004 of 10 February 2004 of the Committee established under the Agreement between the European Community and the Swiss Confederation on mutual recognition in relation to conformity assessment, on the listing of a conformity assessment body under the sectoral chapter for equipment and protective systems intended for use in potentially explosive atmospheres, *OJ* 2004 L 63/67; Decision No. 2/2005 of 30 March 2005 of the Committee established under the Agreement on Mutual Recognition between the EC and the Swiss Confederation on amending Chapter 3 of Annex 1, *OJ* 2005 L 110/78.

52 Proposal for a Council decision concerning the conclusion of the Agreement between the European Community and the Swiss Confederation on the revision of the Agreement on mutual recognition in relation to conformity assessment between the European Community and the Swiss Confederation, COM (2005) 183 final.

On the basis of declarations attached to the final acts of all the treaties composing Bilateral I, Swiss representatives may attend the meetings of selected committees and working parties as observers. This includes meetings of:

- committees of research programmes (including the Committee for Scientific and Technical Research (CREST));
- the Administrative Commission on Social Security for Migrant Workers;
- the Coordinating Group on the Mutual Recognition of Higher-Education Diplomas; and
- advisory committees on air routes and the application of competition rules in the field of air transport.

The presence of these observers is not allowed during voting. Moreover, the procedure regulated in Article 100 EEA is applicable when other committees are dealing with aspects of the *acquis communautaire* that have been adopted by Switzerland (or in cases where it applies equivalent measures).[53] There is also a special arrangement for the EC/EU-Swiss Agreement on Schengen. In order to secure participation of Swiss officials in the committees, a separate agreement in the form of exchange of letters has been prepared.[54] Swiss experts will be also consulted when it comes to new legislation amending or replacing regulations covered by the EC-Swiss Agreement on Asylum.[55]

2. LEGAL ANALYSIS OF EC/EU RELATIONS WITH SWITZERLAND

2.1 The legal characteristics of the agreements

2.1.1 *The legal basis under EC/EU law*

The jigsaw puzzle of agreements creating the legal framework for EC/EU relations with Switzerland can serve as a laboratory for analysing the impact of European Union's three-pillar structure on its external policy and the conclusion of international treaties in particular. It is impossible and also pointless to analyse the legal basis of every single treaty concluded between the European Communities/

53 See chapter 4 in this volume.

54 Agreement in the form of an Exchange of Letters between the Council of the European Union and the Swiss Federation on the Committees that assist the European Commission in the exercise of its executive powers, nyp.

55 Art. 2 of the EC-Swiss Agreement on Asylum.

European Union and Switzerland over the last fifty years, and attention is therefore only devoted to selected instruments.

In most cases, the parties to the agreements are the European Economic Community (renamed the European Community by the Treaty of Maastricht) and the Swiss Confederation. However, there are also examples of treaties concluded between Switzerland and Euratom or the European Coal and Steel Community. Following the expiry of the latter, the agreements in principle remained in force, as the European Community became the successor of the ECSC under the Council Decision 2002/596/EC.[56] There are also very recent examples of mixed agreements with the European Community and its Member States, on one side, and Switzerland, on the other.[57] A real novelty comes with the agreement on Switzerland's association with the Schengen Agreement, which has the European Union and the European Community on one side.

The situation with the first major EEC-Swiss bilateral treaty was fairly straightforward. The Free Trade Agreement of 1972 was signed on the basis of Article 133 TEEC (now Article 130 TEC).[58] Since it fell within the exclusive powers of the European Economic Community, participation of the Member States was not necessary. On the contrary, both the Bilateral I and Bilateral II packages can be regarded as examples of a sophisticated and multiple, cross-pillar legal basis. In the first package, five of the seven agreements were concluded solely by the European Community, on one side, and the Swiss Confederation, on the other. The other two treaties were concluded by the Community and the Member States (on the free movement of persons) and by both remaining European Communities (on scientific and technological cooperation). The common legal basis for the whole package was Article 310 TEC, in conjunction with the second sentence of the first subparagraph of Article 300(2) TEC and the second subparagraph of Articles 300(3) and 300(4) TEC. In the case of the Scientific and Technological Cooperation Agreements, the legal base was also Article 101 Euratom.[59] Due to the cross-pillar nature of the Schengen *acquis*, the

---

[56] Council Decision 2002/596/EC of 19 July 2002 on the consequences of the expiry of the Treaty establishing the European Coal and Steel Community (ECSC) on the international agreements concluded by the ECSC, *OJ* 2002 L 194/36.

[57] This leads Breitenmoser to the argument that not all of the agreements are properly referred to as 'bilateral agreements'. See S. Breitenmoser, 'Sectoral agreements between the EC and Switzerland: contents and context', 40 *CMLRev.* (2003) pp. 1137-1168 at pp. 1142-1144.

[58] Regulation (EEC) No. 2840/72 of the Council of 19 December 1972 concluding an Agreement between the European Economic Community and the Swiss Confederation and adopting provisions for its implementation and concluding an additional Agreement concerning the validity, for the Principality of Liechtenstein of the Agreement between the European Economic Community and the Swiss Confederation of 22 July 1972, *OJ* 1972 L 300/190.

[59] Decision of the Council and of the Commission as regards the Agreement on Scientific and Technological Cooperation of 4 April 2002 on the conclusion of seven Agreements with the Swiss Confederation (2002/309/EC, Euratom), *OJ* 2002 L 114/1.

agreement on Swiss association had to be concluded by the European Union and the European Community, on one side, and the Swiss Confederation, on the other.[60] The legal bases for the relevant Council decision were Articles 24 and 38 TEU.[61] On the other hand, the Asylum Agreement was concluded by the European Community and the Swiss Confederation on the basis of Article 63(1)(a) TEC, in conjunction with Article 300(2) TEC. The remaining agreements constituting Bilateral II were also concluded by the European Community and the Swiss Confederation and had diversified legal bases. In all cases, these were sectoral provisions of the EC Treaty combined with Article 300(2) TEC.[62] Interestingly, the agreement on avoidance of double taxation of retired EC officials residing in Switzerland was concluded by the European Commission and the Swiss Federal Council. The 2004-2005 agreements dealing with second pillar cooperation are based on Article 24 TEU.

2.1.2 *Status of the agreements under the EC/EU legal framework*

The bilateral agreements with Switzerland are concluded by the European Communities/European Union. As a consequence, there is no doubt that they form part of the *acquis communautaire*. This is of pivotal importance when it comes to their application and enforcement at the domestic and EU level. Depending on their substance and importance, treaties are concluded in various procedures available under public international law. They include agreements in the simplified form of an exchange of letters but also treaties requiring ratification or acceptance. It is very rare that bilateral agreements with Switzerland are concluded as mixed agreements requiring ratification by all the EU Member States.

---

[60] See Council Decision 1999/435/EC of 20 May 1999 concerning the definition of the Schengen *acquis* for the purpose of determining, in conformity with the relevant provisions of the Treaty establishing the European Community and the Treaty on European Union, the legal basis for each of the provisions or decisions which constitute the *acquis*, *OJ* 1999 L 176/1; Council Decision 1999/436/EC of 20 May 1999 determining, in conformity with the relevant provisions of the Treaty establishing the European Community and the Treaty on European Union, the legal basis for each of the provisions or decisions which constitute the Schengen *acquis*, *OJ* 1999 L 176/17.

[61] Council Decision 2004/849/EC of 25 October 2004 on the signing, on behalf of the European Union, and on the provisional application of certain provisions of the Agreement between the European Union, the European Community and the Swiss Confederation concerning the Swiss Confederation's association with the implementation, application and development of the Schengen *acquis*, *OJ* 2004 L 368/26.

[62] The relevant provisions are Art. 94 TEC (EC-Swiss Agreement on Savings Income Taxation); Art. 175(1) TEC (EC-Swiss Agreement on Swiss participation in the European Environment Agency and European Environment Information and Observation Network); Art. 285 TEC (EC-Swiss Agreement on Statistics); Arts. 150(4) and 157(3) TEC (EC-Swiss Agreement on Swiss participation in MEDIA Plus and MEDIA Training programmes); Art. 133 TEC (EC-Swiss Agreement on Trade in Processed Agricultural Products'); Art. 280 TEC (EC-Swiss Antifraud Agreement).

Bearing in mind the legal basis for Bilateral I, it is interesting to take a closer look at the legal status of the agreements under EC law. Since all seven agreements are based on Article 310 TEC, it may be argued that they can be classified as Association Agreements.[63] Breitenmoser supports this opinion by mentioning the position of the European Parliament during the ratification procedure as well as the unanimous Council decision based on Article 300(2)(1) TEC.[64] Do those factors permit the conclusion that the Swiss Confederation is associated with the European Communities in a similar manner, for instance, to the eight Central and Eastern European countries before their accession to the European Union in 2004?[65] Or is this model of association closer to the European Economic Area? Analysis of Bilateral I leads to the conclusion that it is neither of the above and that we are dealing here with a very special kind of relationship.

The fact that the agreements are part of the *acquis communautaire* has serious implications for their application at the domestic level in the Member States as well as for the jurisdiction of domestic courts to make preliminary ruling references to the European Court of Justice. In the case of the EU Member States, EC-Swiss agreements must be applied in accordance with the principles of supremacy[66] and direct effect (providing that the provisions contained therein satisfy all the necessary conditions).[67] In the case of interpretation doubts, Member States' courts may submit preliminary ruling references to the European Court of Justice.[68] Depending on the substance of the agreement, they may be based on Article 234 TEC or Article 150 Euratom. Practical problems may arise in the case of the agreements concluded by the European Union as well as in the case of the EC/EU-Swiss Agreement on Schengen. In the case of the former, the European Court of Justice has no jurisdiction to hear the references. As far as the latter is concerned, the situation is more complicated, as the agreement reflecting the Schengen *acquis* has a cross-pillar dimension and falls partly under the first and third pillars of the European Union. Bearing this in mind, it is necessary to

---

63 See Breitenmoser, loc. cit n. 57, at pp. 1144-1145.

64 Ibid.

65 See, *inter alia*, A. Ott. and K. Inglis, eds., *Handbook on European Enlargement. A Commentary on the Enlargement Process* (The Hague, T.M.C. Asser Press 2002).

66 See ECJ, Case C-188/00 *Bülent Kurz, né Yüce* v. *Land Baden-Württemberg* [2002] *ECR* I-10691.

67 Recent examples include ECJ, Case C-63/99 *The Queen* v. *Secretary of State for the Home Department, ex parte Wieslaw Gloszczuk and Elzbieta Gloszczuk* [2001] *ECR* I-6369; ECJ, Case C-235/99 *The Queen* v. *Secretary of State for the Home Department, ex parte Eleanora Ivanova Kondova* [2001] *ECR* I-6427; ECJ, Case C-265/03 *Igor Simutenkov* v. *Ministerio de Educación y Cultura, Real Federación Española de Fútbol* [2005] *ECR* I-2579. See also chapter 2 in this volume.

68 In the case of courts from which there is no further remedy there is an obligation to refer. See L. Neville Brown and T. Kennedy, *The Court of Justice of the European Communities* (London, Sweet & Maxwell 2000) pp. 204-241.

remember that ECJ jurisdiction in the third pillar is optional (Article 35 TEU).[69] On a practical note, it is worth acknowledging that the ECJ has so far not had many opportunities to provide domestic courts with interpretations of the bilateral agreements with Switzerland. A handful of judgments deal with the Free Trade Agreement of 1972.[70]

In the Swiss legal order, all the agreements are applied in accordance with domestic principles on international law.[71] It must be remembered that Swiss courts have no jurisdiction to request preliminary rulings from the European Court of Justice. However, under the Swiss declaration to the Agreement on Air Transport, read in conjunction with Article 23 of the Statute of the European Court of Justice, Swiss lawyers may submit pleadings before the Court in relation to questions submitted on the basis of this agreement. Moreover, Article 8 of the EC/EU-Swiss Agreement on Schengen allows Switzerland to 'submit statements of case or written observations to the Court of Justice in cases where a court in a Member State has applied to the Court of Justice for a preliminary ruling concerning the interpretation' of the Schengen *acquis* defined in Article 2 of the agreement.

Direct actions before the Court of First Instance as well as European Court of Justice may also be of relevance. First of all, the European Commission may initiate infraction procedures against Member States that infringe the bilateral treaties. The ECJ's judgment in Case C-360/95 *Commission* v. *Spain* may serve as an excellent example.[72] The Commission claimed that Spain had failed to implement Council Directive 91/371/EEC on the implementation of the EEC-Swiss Agreement on direct insurance other than life insurance[73] or to inform the Commission about domestic measures. Having analysed the facts of the case, the European Court of Justice declared that Spain had indeed failed to implement the directive on time and, consequently, to adjust its domestic law to the agreement in question. In a fairly recent judgment in Case C-465/01 *Commission* v. *Austria*, the European Court of Justice emphasised that breaches of provisions of international agreements may lead to successful infractions. The case concerned Austrian

---

[69] See Art. 35 TEU. See also ECJ, Case C-105/03 *Criminal Proceedings against Maria Pupino* [2005] ECR I-5285.

[70] See ECJ, Case 65/79 *Procureur de la République* v. *René Chatain* [1980] *ECR* 1345; ECJ, Case 99/83 *Claudio Fioravanti* v. *Amministrazione delle finanze dello Stato* [1984] *ECR* 3939; ECJ, Case 218/83 *Les Rapides Savoyards Sàrl and others* v. *Directeur Général des Douanes et Droits Indirects* [1984] *ECR* 3105.

[71] For an overview, see Breitenmoser, loc. cit. n. 57, at pp. 1145-1151.

[72] ECJ, Case C-360/95 *Commission of the European Communities* v. *Kingdom of Spain* [1997] *ECR* I-7337.

[73] Council Directive 91/371/EEC of 20 June 1991 on the implementation of the Agreement between the European Economic Community and the Swiss Confederation concerning direct insurance other than life assurance, *OJ* 1991 L 205/48.

legislation which, contrary to the EEA Agreement and the Europe Agreement with Poland,[74] discriminated against workers legally admitted to the market in relation to their membership of workers' chambers and works councils.[75] Although this judgment did not deal with any of the EC-Swiss agreements, it may nevertheless be used as a very good example for potential infractions. Finally, one should not forget about actions for annulment, especially in the areas covered by the Agreement on Air Transport, where the European Commission has extensive powers, which are analysed later in this chapter. In this context, attention will be drawn to pending Case C-70/04 *Swiss Confederation* v. *Commission*.[76] The applicant has requested the annulment of a Commission Decision on approaches to Zurich airport.[77] Another pending litigation related to the EC-Swiss agreements is an action for annulment of the Council Decision on the conclusion of one of the Bilateral I agreements brought by *Commune de Champagne* (Case T-212/02).[78]

2.2 The characteristics of Bilateral I

The aim of this part of the chapter is to subject the agreements constituting Bilateral I to closer scrutiny. It is argued that they are characterised by features taking them far beyond the usual standard known in EU law. There are a number of elements that make them unique. The first consists of the guillotine clauses linking their entry into force and potential termination. The second is the far-reaching impact of EC law and, in some cases, the obligation to apply selected provisions in bilateral relations. The scope of this obligation is naturally not comparable to the scope of the European Economic Area. Nevertheless, it is considerable and goes beyond the model known from traditional associations.[79] It is particularly visible in the EC-Swiss Agreement on Air Transport, which due to

[74] Europe Agreement establishing an association between the European Communities and their Member States, of the one part, and the Republic of Poland, of the other part, *OJ* 1993 L 348/2.

[75] ECJ, Case C-465/01 *Commission of the European Communities* v. *Austria* [2004] *ECR* I-8291.

[76] *OJ* 2004 C 94/22.

[77] Commission Decision 2004/12/EC of 5 December 2003 on a procedure relating to the application of Article 18(2), first sentence, of the Agreement between the European Community and the Swiss Confederation on air transport and Council Regulation (EEC) No. 2408/92 (Case TREN/AMA/11/03 – German measures relating to the approaches to Zurich airport) (notified under document number C(2003) 4472), *OJ* 2004 L 4/13.

[78] *OJ* 2002 C 233/27.

[79] For instance, Europe Agreements or Stability and Association Agreements impose on associated countries an obligation to approximate their domestic legislation with the *acquis communautaire*. Only in exceptional cases do they require the application of EC law in bilateral relations and this usually applies to competition law. Art. 63(2) EA Poland may serve as an example in this respect. For more on the approximation of laws, see A. Łazowski, 'Approximation of Laws', in Ott and Inglis, op. cit. n. 65, at pp. 631-639.

its institutional arrangements is considered by Breitenmoser as a 'partial integration agreement'.[80]

The genesis of the guillotine clauses in Bilateral I has already been addressed in the first part of this chapter. Now it is the time discuss their content and functioning. They have been inserted equally into all agreements originally forming the package.[81] According to these clauses, all seven agreements could only have entered into force together, and *à la carte* choice was therefore excluded. The first six agreements were concluded for an initial period of seven years.[82] They will be renewed indefinitely unless the Swiss Confederation or European Community decide otherwise. Lack of prolongation or termination of one of the agreements will lead to the termination of the entire package six months later. As already noted, this sophisticated arrangement was aimed at securing the negotiating deal as a package and not giving Swiss voters too much choice following the unsuccessful 1992 EEA referendum. What might have been a tricky move may in fact lead to disaster when it comes to the vote on the Enlargement Protocol to the EC-Swiss Agreement on the Free Movement of Persons. It has already been indicated by the European Commission that rejection of the protocol will inevitably lead to the termination of Bilateral I and the suspension of the ratification procedures of the EC/EU-Swiss Agreement on Schengen.[83] Formally speaking, such an approach is contrary to Article 12 of the latter agreement.[84] However, from a substantive point of view, it is hard to imagine the functioning of the latter without rules on the free movement of people. Summing up, one may argue that, by inventing the guillotine clauses, the European Commission secured the entry into force of the whole package. In the long term, however, these clauses may bring more harm than benefits to bilateral relations.

---

80 Breitenmoser, loc. cit. n. 57, at p. 1171.

81 Art. 25 of the EC-Swiss Free Movement of People Agreement; Art. 36 of the EC-Swiss Agreement on Air Transport; Art. 58 of the EC-Swiss Agreement on Carriage of Goods and Passengers by Rail and Road; Art. 17 of the EC-Swiss Agreement on Trade in Agricultural Products; Art. 21 of the EC-Swiss Agreement on Conformity Assessment; Art. 18 of the EC-Swiss Agreement on Government Procurement; Art. 14 of the EC-Swiss Agreement on Scientific and Technological Cooperation.

82 Only in the case of the EC-Swiss Agreement on Scientific and Technological Cooperation was its duration linked to the duration of the relevant EC/Euratom framework programmes. Following the expiry of the existing framework programme, another agreement was signed in early 2004. See Agreement on Scientific and Technological Cooperation between the European Community and the European Atomic Energy Community, of the one part, and the Swiss Confederation, of the other part, *OJ* 2004 L 32/23.

83 See *Bulletin Quotidien Europe* No. 8962, p. 13.

84 'This Agreement shall not affect in any respect the agreements concluded between the European Community and Switzerland, or between the European Community and its Member States, of the one part, and Switzerland, of the other part.'

The aims and purposes of every agreement are specified in their preambles and opening provisions.[85] In addition, they had already been spelled out in a number of political declarations and documents presented in the aftermath of the referendum fiasco in 1992. In general terms, one may conclude that the rationale behind Bilateral I was to grant access for Switzerland to certain aspects of the internal market. This particularly includes facilitation of free movement of workers, liberalisation of civil aviation markets, access to road and rail transport markets, elimination of trade barriers relating to agricultural products, facilitation of trade by mutual recognition in relation to conformity assessment, scientific cooperation and, last but not least, liberalisation of public procurement markets. In the case of the latter, the aim of the agreement was formulated in the following way:

> The aim of this Agreement is to secure reciprocal, transparent and non-discriminatory access of the Parties' suppliers and service providers to purchases of products and services, including construction services, by telecommunications operators, railway operators, entities active in the field of energy other than electricity and private utilities of both Parties.[86]

Looking at the scope of the agreements, one may argue that, from a substantive viewpoint, we have witnessed a process of steady progress towards accession to the EEA through the back door. However exaggerated this statement is, it also partly reflects reality. Of course, the difference between the existing framework and the EEA lies in the decision-making machinery, formal structure, enforcement and nature of the legal order.[87]

One needs to note that some of the agreements contain a clause reflecting the principle of solidarity enshrined in Article 10 TEC. For instance, Article 17 of the EC-Swiss Agreement on Air Transport reads:

> The Contracting Parties shall take all appropriate measures, whether general or particular, to ensure fulfilment of the obligations arising out of this Agreement and shall refrain from any measures which would jeopardise attainment of the objectives of this Agreement.

---

[85] Art. 1 of the EC-Swiss Agreement on the Free Movement of Persons; Art. 1 of the EC-Swiss Agreement on Air Transport; Art. 1 of the EC-Swiss Agreement on Carriage of Goods and Passengers by Rail and Road; Art. 1 of the EC-Swiss Agreement on Trade in Agricultural Products; Art. of the 1 EC-Swiss Agreement on Mutual Recognition; Art. 1 of the EC-Swiss Agreement on Government Procurement; Art. 1 of the EC-Swiss Agreement on Scientific and Technological Cooperation.

[86] Art. 3 of the EC-Swiss Agreement on Government Procurement.

[87] See chapter 4 in this volume.

Notwithstanding this type of clause, the parties of course have a general obligation arising from the principle of *pacta sunt servanda*, which is generally considered to lie at the foundations of contemporary public international law.

The fulfilment of the agreements' ambitious aims requires at least partial application of the *acquis communautaire.*[88] Selected agreements therefore very often contain provisions that are similarly worded to EC law. Moreover, they make explicit references to regulations and directives that have to be applied. The impact of developments in EC law was one of the key issues that had to be addressed during the Bilateral I negotiations. The choice was twofold. The parties could have decided to give the agreements a dynamic character, comparable to the European Economic Area, or a static one, by not creating an obligation to automatically adopt every subsequent amendment to the EC legal framework that could potentially be relevant to the agreements. The decision was not only of legal importance but also carried a considerable political weight. Indeed, as Breitenmoser notes, the EEA's dynamic character was one of the reasons for the referendum fiasco in 1992.[89] Eventually, the parties decided to follow a less controversial, static model and placed the joint committees at the heart of the procedural machinery. In principle, the parties are bound by the relevant *acquis* existing at the time of signature, and the impact of every subsequent development in EC law may be determined by the joint committees. One should not forget, however, the different status of the EC-Swiss Agreement on Air Transport in this respect (which is discussed in the next paragraph). Another factor of pivotal importance is the impact of ECJ case law on the concepts of EC law falling under the agreements. Whenever this is relevant, parties shall take into account judicial developments predating the signature of Bilateral 1. This is the case, for instance, with regard to the EC-Swiss Agreement on the Free Movement of Persons. Its Article 16(2) read that 'account shall be taken of the relevant case-law of the Court of Justice of the European Communities prior to the date of signature.' Subsequent case law is brought to the attention of Switzerland, but its impact on the agreements may be determined by the joint committees.[90]

It was argued in the introduction to this chapter that Bilateral I is one of the fundamental elements adding an integration flavour to EC-Swiss cooperation. This is particularly visible when the Agreement on Air Transport is taken into account. The provisions on competition included in Articles 8 and 9 were clearly inspired by Articles 81-82 TEC. The enforcement machinery relies heavily on the EC institutional framework, with the European Commission at the heart of

[88] A similar issue, albeit on a much bigger scale, was one of the biggest obstacles on the path leading to the creation of the European Economic Area. For more information, see chapter 4 in this volume.

[89] Breitenmoser, loc. cit. n. 57, at p. 1159.

[90] Similarly, Art. 1 of the EC-Swiss Agreement on Air Transport.

enforcement machinery of antitrust and merger rules.[91] In the case of state aid, the enforcement of principles created by Articles 12 and 13 remains in the hands of the respective EC and Swiss authorities. It should be added that

> All questions concerning the validity of decisions of the institutions of the Community taken on the basis of their competences under this Agreement, shall be of the exclusive competence of the Court of Justice of the European Communities.[92]

In conclusion, it should be stressed that Bilateral I is an important political and legal arrangement granting the Swiss Confederation a privileged and unique status. It is important to note that it can easily serve the purposes of enhanced bilateralism and, at the same time, providing that this is desired, serve as a vehicle taking Switzerland closer to potential membership of the European Union.

2.3 The characteristics of Bilateral II

The second package of bilateral treaties adds a new dimension to the EU-Swiss enhanced bilateralism and substantially widens its scope. As indicated in the first part of this chapter, the dossiers cover a wide range of issues including, *inter alia*, the Schengen *acquis*, asylum, taxation and statistics. There are a number of fundamental differences between the two sets of agreements. Just a brief and general comparison proves that Bilateral II is more internally diversified and only formally constitutes a single package. The key elements of the new arrangements are discussed below.

The guillotine clause, which is at the heart of Bilateral 1 is almost non-existent in the 2004 package. The only exceptions are the EC/EU-Swiss Agreement on Schengen and the EC-Swiss Agreement on Asylum, which for substantive reasons are linked by the clause in question.[93] It is interesting to note that the application and implementation of both agreements are not only conditional on their ratification but also require the conclusion and implementation of separate agreements between the Swiss Confederation, Norway and Iceland as well as between the Swiss Confederation and Denmark.[94] The other agreements forming Bilateral II are not connected in a similar way. They may therefore enter into

---

91 Art. 11 of the EC-Swiss Agreement on Air Transport.

92 See the above-mentioned litigation in ECJ, Case C-70/04 *Swiss Confederation* v. *Commission of the European Communities* (based on an order of the ECJ of 14 July 2005, the case is pending before the CFI).

93 See Art. 15 of the EC/EU-Swiss Agreement on Schengen and Art. 14 of the EC-Swiss Agreement on Asylum.

94 See Art. 12, in conjunction with Art. 15, of the EC/EU-Swiss Agreement on Schengen and Art. 11, in conjunction with Art. 14, of the EC-Swiss Agreement on Asylum.

force and be terminated independently. Owing to their different subjects and importance, the agreements have diverse legal characters. Some of them require ratification or any equivalent form of acceptance, others have been concluded in the simplified form of an exchange of letters. Consequently, they do not enter into force simultaneously, and the periods for which they are concluded may differ. For instance, the Agreement on Trade in Processed Agricultural Products already entered into force on 30 March 2005. Moreover, selected provisions of the EC/EU-Swiss Agreement on Schengen[95] and the EC-Swiss Agreement on Asylum[96] are applicable on a provisional basis. The EC-Swiss Agreement on Savings Income Taxation entered into force on 1 July 2005,[97] and the EC-Swiss Agreement on Pensions of Retired EC Officials entered into force on 31 May 2005.

The majority of the agreements have been concluded for an unlimited period of time (EC/EU-Swiss Agreement on Schengen; EC-Swiss Agreement on Asylum; EC-Swiss Antifraud Agreement; EC-Swiss Agreement on Savings Income Taxation; Agreement on Trade in Processed Agricultural Products; EC-Swiss Agreement on Swiss Participation in the European Environment Agency and the European Environment Information and Observation Network; EC-Swiss Agreement on the Avoidance of Double Taxation of Retired EC Officials). The EC-Swiss Agreement on Statistics was signed for an initial period of five years, and the EC-Swiss Agreement on Participation in MEDIA Programmes is limited by the duration of the latter.

The general aim of Bilateral II is to deepen existing enhanced cooperation between the parties. The aims and purposes of particular agreements are specified therein. For instance, the purpose of the EC/EU-Swiss Agreement on Schengen and the EC-Swiss Agreement on Asylum is to associate Switzerland with the relevant EU *acquis*. Similar arrangements with Norway and Iceland served as a model in this regard.[98] The objective of the EC-Swiss Antifraud Agreement is to 'extend administrative and mutual legal assistance in criminal matters' between the parties so as to combat various illegal activities. These include, *inter alia*,

---

[95] Arts. 1, 3, 4, 5, 6 and 7(2)(a), first sentence, apply as of the time of signature of the Agreement (see Art. 14(2) of the EC/EU Swiss Agreement on Schengen).

[96] Arts. 2, 3 and Art. 4(2), first sentence, apply provisionally from the date of signature (see Art. 12(3) of the EC-Swiss Agreement on Asylum).

[97] See also Agreement in the form of an Exchange of Letters between the European Community and the Swiss Confederation on the date of application of the Agreement between the European Community and the Swiss Confederation providing for measures equivalent to those laid down in Council Directive 2003/48/EC of 3 June 2003 on taxation of savings income in the form of interest payments, nyp.

[98] The differences between the agreements with Norway and Iceland and the agreement with the Swiss Confederation have been outlined by the European Commission in the proposal for decisions on the signature and conclusion of the Agreement, COM (2004) 593 final. See also chapter 4 in this volume.

fraud, illegal trade in goods, trade contrary to tax legislation, and so forth.[99] The purpose of the EC-Swiss Agreement on Statistics has been defined in its Article 1. It aims 'to ensure the production and dissemination of coherent and comparable statistical information for describing and monitoring all economic, social and environmental policies relevant for the bilateral cooperation.' The purpose of the EC-Swiss Agreement on Savings Income Taxation is to secure the application of measures equivalent to Council Directive 2003/48/EC on the taxation of savings income in the form of interest payments.[100] Two agreements that are part of Bilateral II secure Swiss participation in the European Environment Agency and European Environment Information and Observation Network[101] and in the Community programmes MEDIA Plus and MEDIA Training.[102] The Agreement on Trade in Processed Agricultural Products has been tailored to the improvement of reciprocal market access for processed agricultural products.[103] Finally, the last agreement aims to avoid the double taxation of retired EC officials living in the Swiss Confederation.

Similarly to Bilateral I, some of the agreements falling under the umbrella of the second package require the application of the *acquis communautaire* in bilateral relations as well as the incorporation of some of its parts into the Swiss legal order. Relevant lists of legislation are included in the annexes or mentioned in the core text of the agreements. It is particularly worth taking a closer look at some of them.

Under the EC/EU-Swiss Agreement on Schengen, Switzerland has an obligation to implement and apply the Schengen *acquis* listed in Annex 1 to the agreement. This includes, *inter alia*, parts of the Schengen Agreement[104] as well as the Implementing Convention.[105] Moreover, it has an obligation to implement the listed decisions of the Executive Committee and directives and regulations listed in Annex B.[106] Unlike the 1999 package, the update machinery provided in

---

99 Arts. 1-2 of the EC-Swiss Antifraud Agreement.

100 This is already explicit in the title of the agreement.

101 Art. 1 of the EC-Swiss Agreement on participation in European Environment Agency and European Environment Information and Observation Network.

102 Art. 1 of the EC-Swiss Agreement on participation in Community programmes MEDIA Plus and MEDIA Training.

103 This is clearly spelled out in the preamble to the agreement.

104 Agreement signed in Schengen on 14 June 1985 between the Governments of the States of the Benelux Economic Union, the Federal Republic of Germany and the French Republic on the gradual abolition of checks at their common borders, *OJ* 2000 L 239/13.

105 Convention signed in Schengen on 19 June 1990 between the Kingdom of Belgium, the Federal Republic of Germany, the French Republic, the Grand Duchy of Luxembourg and the Kingdom of the Netherlands, implementing the Schengen Agreement of 14 June 1985, *OJ* 2000 L 239/19.

106 *Inter alia*, Council Regulation (EC) No. 1683/95 of 29 May 1995 laying down a uniform format for visas, *OJ* 1995 L 164/1 (as amended); Council Regulation (EC) No. 539/2001 of 15 March 2001 listing the third countries whose nationals must be in possession of visas when crossing

EC/EU-Swiss Agreement on Schengen has a dynamic character. By this means, even more integration elements are brought to the bilateral relationship. Article 7 of the EC/EU-Swiss Agreement on Schengen specifies that '[t]he adoption of new acts or measures related to the matters referred to in Article 2 shall be reserved to the competent institutions of the European Union.' Those measures shall enter into force simultaneously in the European Community, its Member States and Switzerland. This obligation may be compromised by a decision rejecting the legislation or by different transitional periods for the latter.[107] Article 7 provides for a special procedure that will be applied in order to secure the transposition of new legislation in Switzerland. It is worth mentioning that, in certain circumstances specified therein, the agreement may be terminated. Also, the parties have an obligation to keep under constant review the developments of ECJ case law. The agreements provide for the creation of a special mechanism to secure a regular mutual transmission of case law. Article 9 of the agreement creates an obligation for Switzerland to submit reports to the Mixed Committee on the application and interpretation of the Schengen *acquis*. In the case of serious divergences, the powers of dispute settlement are vested in the Mixed Committee.[108]

The EC-Swiss Agreement on Asylum obliges Switzerland to implement Council Regulation 343/2003/EC,[109] Commission Regulation 1560/2003/EC,[110] Council Regulation 2725/2000/EC[111] and Council Regulation 407/2002/EC.[112] It creates similar procedures to the EC/EU-Swiss Agreement on Schengen in relation to updates to the existing legislative framework and the determination of the relevance of ECJ case law.[113]

---

the external borders and those whose national are exempt from that requirement, *OJ* 1991 L 81/1 (as amended); Council Regulation (EC) No. 1091/2001 of 28 May 2001 on freedom of movement with a long-stay visa, *OJ* 2001 L 150/4.

107 It ought to be remembered that Swiss representatives may take part, albeit to a limited extent, in the decision-making process.

108 See section 1.3 of this chapter.

109 Council Regulation (EC) No. 343/2003 of 18 February 2003 establishing the criteria and mechanism for determining the Member State responsible for examining an asylum application lodged in one of the Member States by a third-country national, *OJ* 2003 L 50/1.

110 Commission Regulation (EC) No. 1560/2003 of 2 September 2003 laying down detailed rules for the application of Council Regulation (EC) No. 343/2003 establishing the criteria and mechanisms for determining the Member State responsible for examining an asylum application lodged in one of the Member States by a third-country national, *OJ* 2002 L 222/3.

111 Council Regulation (EC) No. 2725/2000 of 11 December 2000 concerning the establishment of 'Eurodac' for the comparison of fingerprints for the effective application of the Dublin Convention with a view of helping to determine the Contracting Party responsible for examining an asylum application in accordance with the Dublin Convention, *OJ* 2000 L 316/1.

112 Council Regulation (EC) No. 407/2002 of 28 February 2002 laying down certain rules to implement Regulation (EC) No. 2725/2000 concerning the establishment of 'Eurodac' for the comparison of fingerprints for the effective application of the Dublin Convention, *OJ* 2002 L 62/1.

113 See Arts. 4-7 of the EC-Swiss Agreement on Asylum.

It is also worth recalling the EC-Swiss Agreement on Statistics. A multiplicity of legal acts listed in Annex A to the agreement shall be binding upon the parties.[114] In the case of new EC legislation covered by the scope of the agreement, a static update procedure is foreseen. The procedure based on Article 4 of the agreement is similar to the Bilateral I machinery.

Finally, it should be mentioned that some of the agreements composing Bilateral II provide that Switzerland shall contribute to the administrative costs connected with the functioning of the agreements. This includes, for instance, the EC/EU-Swiss Agreement on Schengen, which requires an annual contribution to the EU budget of €8.1 million (subject to an annual inflation adjustment).[115]

This very general overview of Bilateral II leads to numerous conclusions. First of all, the agreements deepen the existing enhanced cooperation between the parties. Looking at their legal character and implications for Switzerland, one may also conclude that they strengthen the integration nature of relations. Due to a lack of general guillotine clauses, the agreements are more flexible and potentially more stable legal instruments. In many ways, the agreements falling under the umbrella of Bilateral II bring the Swiss Confederation closer to European Union.

3. THE FREE MOVEMENT OF PEOPLE BETWEEN THE EUROPEAN UNION AND SWITZERLAND

3.1 The EC-Swiss Agreement on the Free Movement of Persons

The EC-Swiss Agreement on the Free Movement of Persons is definitely the core of the Bilateral I package.[116] It creates a broad legal framework for the movement of persons covering the rights of both economically active and non-active nationals of the Contracting Parties. The main purpose of the agreement has already been outlined in a Commission Communication from 1993. Taking into account the number of EU citizens living in Switzerland, the Commission argued

114 For example, Council Regulation (EC, Euratom) No. 58/97 of 20 December 1996 concerning structural business statistics, *OJ* 1997 L 14/1 (as amended); Council Regulation (EC) No. 1172/98 of 25 May 1998 on statistical return in respect of the carriage of goods by road, *OJ* 1998 L 163/1 (as amended); Council Regulation (EC) No. 1172/95 of 22 May 1995 on the statistics relating to the trading of goods by the Community and its Member States with non-member countries, *OJ* 1995 L 118/10 (as amended); Council Regulation (EC, Euratom) No. 1287/2003 of 15 July 2003 on the harmonisation of gross national income at market prices (GNI Regulation), *OJ* 2003 L 181/1.

115 Art. 11 of the EC/EU-Swiss Agreement on Schengen.

116 See A. Łazowski, 'Swobodny przepływ osób między Unią Europejską a Konfederacją Szwajcarską' [Free Movement of People between the European Union and the Swiss Confederation], in A. Łazowski and R. Ostrihansky, eds., *Współczesne wyzwania europejskiej przestrzeni prawnej* [Contemporary Challenges of the European Legal Space] (Kraków, Zakamycze 2005) pp. 411-430.

that 'the objective of a new bilateral Agreement between the Community and Switzerland shall be the full implementation of the Community *acquis* in this area, as envisaged in the EEA Agreement.'[117] The broad objectives of the agreement have been set out in the Article 1. They are:

(a) to accord a right of entry, residence, access to work as employed persons, establishment on a self-employed basis and the right to stay in the territory of the Contracting Parties;
(b) to facilitate the provision of services in the territory of the Contracting Parties, and in particular to liberalise the provision of services of brief duration;
(c) to accord a right of entry into, and residence in, the territory of the Contracting Parties to persons without an economic activity in the host country;
(d) to accord the same living, employment and working conditions as those accorded to nationals.

General rules are specified in the main parts of the agreement, while detailed rules have been included in three annexes and a protocol. As already noted, Article 16 of the agreement is of pivotal importance. It creates an obligation to 'take all measures necessary to ensure that rights and obligations equivalent to those contained in the legal acts of the European Community to which reference is made are applied in relations between them.' References are made throughout the agreement, and lists of secondary legislation are included in the annexes. Moreover, concepts originating in EC law shall be interpreted in accordance with the case law of the European Court of Justice pre-dating the signature of the agreement.[118] The relevance of subsequent judicial developments to the application of the agreement may be determined by the Joint Committee.[119]

The agreement guarantees the right of entry into the territory of the other Contracting Party as well as the right of residence and access to economic activity (also including family members). The general principle of non-discrimination on the grounds of nationality is spelled out in Article 2 of the agreement.[120] Other rights included in Article 7 of the agreement include the right to equal treatment in respect of access to, and pursuit of, an economic activity, and living, employment and working conditions; the right to occupational and geographic mobility; and the right to acquire immovable property (as long as it is connected with the

[117] Communication from the Commission, Future relations with Switzerland, COM (1993) 486 final, p. 4.

[118] Art. 16 of the EC-Swiss Agreement on the Free Movement of Persons.

[119] Ibid.

[120] 'Nationals of one Contracting Party who are lawfully resident in the territory of another Contracting Party shall not, in application of and in accordance with the provisions of Annexes I, II and III to this Agreement, be the subject of any discrimination on grounds of nationality.'

exercise of rights conferred by the agreement). The agreement also extends to the right to stay in the territory of the host state following the end of an economic activity. Under the standstill clause laid down in Article 13 of the agreement the parties have an obligation not to adopt any further restrictive measures.

The personal scope of the agreement extends to nationals of the EU Member States as well as Swiss nationals. Similarly to the EC regime on the free movement of persons, family members are granted certain rights regardless of their nationality. The definition of family members is developed in Article 3 of Annex I. It encompasses the spouse of a person who has the right of residence, their relatives in the descending line (who are under the age of twenty-one or who are dependent) and his relatives in the ascending line (and those of the spouse who are dependant on him). In the case of students, family members include the student's spouse and dependant children. The Contracting Parties also have an obligation to facilitate the admission of other family members.[121] It remains open whether the adoption of European Parliament and Council Directive 2004/38/EC will have an impact on the interpretation of these provisions.[122] Article 2 of the directive gives the term 'family member' a brand new and much broader meaning.[123] Finally, it should be noted that the agreement's provisions on services also apply to legal persons.[124]

The EC-Swiss Agreement on the Free Movement of Persons differentiates between the status of beneficiaries depending on the nature of residence. There are separate regimes dealing with the rights of workers,[125] the self-employed,[126] service providers[127] and persons whose residence is not connected with economic activity.[128]

In principle, all workers are subject to a compulsory residence permit.[129] Exceptions include workers employed for a period shorter than three months and may also include frontier workers.[130] Workers benefit from the principle of equal

---

121 Art. 3 of Annex I to the EC-Swiss Agreement on the Free Movement of Persons.

122 Directive 2004/38/EC of the European Parliament and of the Council of 29 April 2004 on the right of citizens of the Union and their family members to move and reside freely within the territory of the Member States (amending Regulation (EEC) No. 1612/68 and repealing Directives 64/221/EEC, 68/360/EEC, 72/194/EEC, 73/148/EEC, 75/34/EEC, 75/35/EEC, 90/364/EEC, 90/365/EEC and 93/36/EEC), *OJ* 2004 L 158/77.

123 See Arts. 2-3 of Directive 2004/38/EC.

124 See Art. 18 of Annex I to the EC-Swiss Agreement on the Free Movement of Persons.

125 Arts. 6-11 of Annex I to the EC-Swiss Agreement on the Free Movement of Persons.

126 Arts. 12-16 of Annex I to the EC-Swiss Agreement on the Free Movement of Persons.

127 Arts. 17-23 of Annex I to the EC-Swiss Agreement on the Free Movement of Persons.

128 Art. 24 of Annex I to the EC-Swiss Agreement on the Free Movement of Persons.

129 See Art. 6 of Annex I to the EC-Swiss Agreement on the Free Movement of Persons.

130 The status of the latter is regulated in Art. 7 of Annex I to the EC-Swiss Agreement on the Free Movement of Persons. It applies to persons residing within the territory of one Contracting Party and working in the other, providing that they return to their place of the residence on a daily

treatment laid down in Article 9 of Annex I to the agreement. It extends to employment and work conditions,[131] tax and welfare benefits, access to vocational training, membership of trade unions and the exercise of rights resulting from this (including voting rights).

The obligation to obtain a residence permit extends also to nationals of the Contracting Parties who are engaged in self-employed activity. As in the case of workers, a special regime is created for self-employed frontier workers. Persons covered by the agreement are subject to the equal treatment clause of Article 15 of Annex I to the agreement. They shall be 'afforded no less favourable treatment in the host country than that accorded to its own nationals.' Article 9 of Annex I, as discussed above, applies *mutatis mutandis* to the self-employed.

As in EC law, the rights of individuals may be limited on the grounds of public order, public security or public health. Council Directive 64/221/EEC[132] as well as the relevant case law of the European Court of Justice are applicable in this regard.[133] Employment in the public service connected with the exercise of public power is excluded from the scope of the agreement. In this case, the *acquis*,[134] supplemented by ECJ case law, is also of the highest importance.[135]

The agreement also deals with the coordination of social security systems and the mutual recognition of diplomas. Detailed rules in this regard are included in Annexes II and III, respectively. A number of EC regulations are directly applicable to bilateral relations, including Council Regulation 1408/71/EEC on the coordination of social security schemes,[136] Council Regulation 574/72/EEC implementing Regulation 1408/71/EEC[137] and Council Directive 98/49/EC on

---

basis or at least one a week. The authorities of Member States may nevertheless decide to issue a special permit, the validity of which will depend on the length of employment.

[131] Particularly relating to payment, dismissal, reinstatement and re-employment.

[132] Council Directive 64/221/EEC of 25 February 1964 on the coordination of special measures concerning the movement and residence of foreign nationals which are justified on grounds of public policy, public security or public health, *OJ* 1963-64 English Special Edition, p. 117.

[133] See, for instance, ECJ, Case 41/74 *Van Duyn* v. *Home Office* [1974] *ECR* 1337. See C. Barnard, *The Substantive Law of the EU. The Four Freedoms* (Oxford, Oxford University Press 2004) pp. 373-399.

[134] Communication 88/C 72/02: Freedom of movement of workers and access to employment in the public service of the Member States – Commission action in respect of the application of Article 48(4) of the EEC Treaty, *OJ* 1988 C 72/2.

[135] See ECJ, Case 152/73 *Giovanni Maria Sotgiu* v. *Deutsche Bundespost* [1974] *ECR* 153; ECJ, Case 149/79 *Commission of the European Communities* v. *Kingdom of Belgium* [1982] *ECR* 1845; ECJ, Case 66/85 *Deborah Lawrie-Blum* v. *Land Baden-Württemberg* [1986] *ECR* 2121; ECJ, Case 2/74 *Jean Reyners* v. *Belgian State* [1974] *ECR* 631; ECJ, Case C-42/92 *Adrianus Thijssen* v. *Controledienst voor de verzekeringen* [1993] *ECR* I-4047.

[136] Council Regulation (EEC) No. 1408/71 of 14 June 1971 on the application of social security schemes to employed persons, to self-employed persons and to the members of their families moving within the Community, *OJ* 1971 L 149/2 (as amended).

[137] Council Regulation (EEC) No. 574/72 of 21 March 1972 fixing the procedure for implementing Regulation (EEC) No. 1408/71 on the application of social security schemes to employed

pension rights.[138] Moreover, the parties must also take into account a number of legal acts listed in the annexes.[139] The agreement extends the application of EC law on the mutual recognition of diplomas to relations with Switzerland. The relevant pieces of the secondary *acquis communautaire* relating to the general system of recognition as well as to particular professions apply. These include, *inter alia*, Council Directives 89/48/EEC[140] and 92/51/EEC[141] establishing the first and second general systems for the recognition of higher-education diplomas, respectively, as well as Council Directive 77/249/EEC[142] and European Parliament and Council Directive 98/5/EC on the legal profession.[143]

3.2 Transitional arrangements in the EC-Swiss Agreement on the Free Movement of Persons and the Enlargement Protocol

The EC-Swiss Agreement on the Free Movement of Persons is not fully applicable from the moment of its entry into force. Nationals of the EU Member States who wish to reside in Switzerland are subject to transitional periods established in Article 10 of the agreement. This article has been modified by the Enlargement Protocol and shall be considered as an example of the external face of differentiation (see Table 1). It has multi-layer dimension as it not only differentiates between the status of the old and new Member States but also creates differences between the latter.[144] It should be stressed at the outset that, in case of transitional

persons, to self-employed persons and to the members of their families moving within the Community, *OJ* 1972 L 74/1 (as amended).

138 Council Directive 98/49/EC of 29 June 1998 on safeguarding the supplementary pension rights of employed and self-employed persons moving within the Community, *OJ* 1998 L 209/46.

139 Annex I distinguishes between 'acts of which the Contracting Parties shall take due account' and 'acts of which Contracting Parties shall take note'. The first group is listed in Section B of Annex I, the second in Section C of Annex I.

140 Council Directive 89/48/EEC of 21 December 1988 on a general system for the recognition of higher-education diplomas awarded on completion of professional education and training of at least three years' duration, *OJ* 1989 L 19/16 (as amended).

141 Council Directive 92/51/EEC of 18 June 1992 of 18 June 1992 on a second general system for the recognition of professional education and training to supplement Directive 89/48/EEC, *OJ* 1992 L 209/25 (as amended).

142 Council Directive 77/249/EEC of 22 March 1977 to facilitate the effective exercise by lawyers of freedom to provide services, *OJ* 1977 L 78/17 (as amended).

143 Directive 98/5/EC of the European Parliament and of the Council of 16 February 1998 to facilitate practice of the profession of the lawyer on a permanent basis in a Member State other that in which the qualification was obtained, *OJ* 1998 L 77/36.

144 It somehow was inspired by a model adopted under the EU Accession Treaty regarding the restrictions on the free movement of workers. See M. Dougan, 'A Spectre is Haunting Europe… Free Movement of Persons and the Eastern Enlargement', in C. Hillion, ed., *EU Enlargement. A Legal Approach* (Oxford/Portland, Oregon, Hart Publishing 2004) pp. 111-141; A. Adinolfi, 'Free Movement and Access to Work of Citizens of the New Member States: The Transitional Measures', 42 *CMLRev.* (2005) pp. 469-498.

residence periods, Cyprus and Malta are treated as if they were old Member States. The differentiation of the rights and obligations of different groups of EU Member States is clearly visible in the scope and potential length of the transitional arrangements on access to the labour market and the acquisition of immovable property. Both groups of transitional arrangements will be discussed in the remaining part of this chapter.

As a general principle, there are no quantitative restrictions relating to short term-residence not exceeding four months of stay in the case of the nationals of the old and new Member States. Under the protocol, however, some additional qualification requirements for obtaining residence permits can be imposed on nationals of the eight new EU Member States. This exception is extended to service providers acting in the four sectors listed in Article 10(2a) (added by the protocol).[145] These restrictions can be maintained until 31 May 2007, with a possibility of prolongation until 31 May 2009.[146] The external face of differentiation is particularly visible when it comes to transitional arrangements for periods of residence exceeding four months. The first key difference is the right of the eight new Member States to impose quantitative restrictions on Swiss nationals. The old Member States, as well as Cyprus and Malta, are not entitled to impose such measures, although the latter is covered by a special regime laid down in Article 10(4b) of the EC-Swiss Agreement on the Free Movement of Persons (added by the protocol). In the case of both the old and new Member States, the general regime of quantitative restrictions can be used until 31 May 2007. The possibility of its prolongation in relation to the eight new Member States shows another aspect of differentiation. Upon notification to the Joint Committee, these restrictions can be maintained until 2009.[147] If this is the case, the eight new Member States are entitled to impose equal restrictions on Swiss nationals.

Another differentiating factor consists of the residence permits quotas that can be applied by Switzerland. In the case of old Member States, as well as Malta and Cyprus, a flat rate of quotas applies. Switzerland has an obligation to reserve at least 15,000 new residence permits for a period of residence equal to or exceeding one year. In the case of short-term residence lasting four to twelve months, the quota has been set at least 115,000 permits.[148] A progressive increase method is applied in relation to the nationals of the eight new Member States. The protocol also includes a safeguard clause allowing Switzerland and the eight new Member

---

[145] This includes horticultural service activities, construction, security and industrial cleaning.

[146] This is subject to notification to the Joint Committee by a party which has implemented the transitional regime. Lack of notification will lead to the expiration of the transitional arrangement on 31 May 2007.

[147] Lack of notification will lead to the expiration of the transitional arrangement on 31 May 2007.

[148] No additional numbers of residence permits will be added for Cyprus and Malta. In other words, they are restricted by limits imposed by Art. 10 of the EC-Swiss Agreement on the Free Movement of Persons.

States to introduce further transitional arrangements until 30 April 2011 (longer than in the case of the old Member States). This will only be possible in cases of serious disturbances on the labour market and will be subject to notification to the Joint Committee by 31 May 2009 at the latest.

Transitional arrangements under Article 10 of the EC-Swiss Agreement on the Free Movement of Persons (as amended by the Enlargement Protocol)

Until	No. of permits for a period equal to or exceeding 1 year		No. of permits for a period of more than 4 months and less than 1 year	
	Old Member States + Cyprus & Malta	Eight new Member States	Old Member States + Cyprus & Malta	Eight new Member States
31 May 2005	15,000	900	115,000	9,000
31 May 2006	15,000	1,300	115,000	12,400
31 May 2007	15,000	1,700	115,000	15,800
31 May 2008	Limitations possible under Art. 10(4) procedure	2,200 (subject to notification to Joint Committee)	Limitations possible under Art. 10(4) procedure	19,200 (subject to notification to Joint Committee)
31 May 2009	Limitations possible under Art. 10(4) procedure	2,600 (subject to notification to Joint Committee)	Limitations possible under Art. 10(4) procedure	22,600 (subject to notification to Joint Committee)
31 May 2010	Limitations possible under Art. 10(4) procedure	2,800 (safeguard clause) and also limitations possible under Art. 10(4) procedure	Limitations possible under Art. 10(4) procedure	26,000 (safeguard clause) and also limitations possible under Art. 10(4) procedure
30 April 2011*	Limitations possible under Art. 10(4) procedure	3,000 (safeguard clause) and also limitations possible under Art. 10(4) procedure	Limitations possible under Art. 10(4) procedure	29,000 (safeguard clause) and also limitations possible under Art. 10(4) procedure
31 May 2011	Limitations possible under Art. 10(4) procedure	Limitations possible under Art. 10(4) procedure	Limitations possible under Art. 10(4) procedure	Limitations possible under Art. 10(4) procedure
31 May 2012	Limitations possible under Art. 10(4) procedure	Limitations possible under Art. 10(4) procedure	Limitations possible under Art. 10(4) procedure	Limitations possible under Art. 10(4) procedure
31 May 2013	Limitations possible under Art. 10(4) procedure	Limitations possible under Art. 10(4) procedure	Limitations possible under Art. 10(4) procedure	Limitations possible under Art. 10(4) procedure
31 May 2014	Limitations possible under Art. 10(4) procedure	Limitations possible under Art. 10(4) procedure	Limitations possible under Art. 10(4) procedure	Limitations possible under Art. 10(4) procedure

* In the case of new Member States and restrictions under the safeguard clause.

The procedure laid down in Article 10(4) of the EC-Swiss Agreement on the Free Movement of Persons applies equally to the old and new Member States. In the period between five years and twelve years after entry into force of the agreement, Switzerland may impose quantitative restrictions on the number of residence permits in both categories. This may only take place if the number of permits in a particular year exceeds the annual average for the previous three years by more than 10 per cent. In such a case, the restriction shall be on the level of the average for the previous three years increased by 5 per cent. It is submitted that, in the case of the eight new Member States, the restrictions can be imposed alternatively on the basis of the safeguard clause or Article 10(4) of the agreement. However, if the latter is chosen by Swiss authorities, the limitations will apply equally to all Member States of the European Union.

As noted earlier, a special regime has been agreed in relation to Malta. In principle, Article 10(4b) of the EC-Swiss Agreement on the Free Movement of Persons (amended by the protocol) incorporates the safeguard clause from Annex XI of the Accession Treaty. In case of disturbances on the Maltese labour market seriously threatening the standard of living or level of employment in a particular region or occupation, Malta may request the European Commission to suspend partial or full application of Articles 1 to 6 of Regulation 1612/68/EEC[149] (and insofar as necessary Directive 68/360/EEC[150]). If this is the case, restrictive measures can also be applied to Switzerland, which in turn is entitled to adopt equivalent measures. This procedure can be used within the framework of the agreement until 30 April 2011.

Finally, Article 10(2) of the EC-Swiss Agreement on the Free Movement of Persons allows maintenance of the controls on the priority of workers integrated into the labour markets. In the case of the old Member States, the transitional period was two years from the entry into force of the agreement, with the possibility of extension for another two years. In the case of the eight new Member States, the transitional periods will last until 31 May 2007, with the possibility of extension for another two years.[151]

Another factor differentiating between the status of the old and new Member States consists of restrictions relating to the purchase of land and secondary residences. No such arrangements were made under the Article 25 of Annex I to the EC-Swiss Agreement on the Free Movement of Persons.[152] Annex I to the

---

149 Regulation (EEC) No. 1612/68 of the Council of 15 October 1968 on freedom of movement for workers within the Community, *OJ* 1968 English Special Edition, p. 475.

150 Council Directive 68/360/EEC of 15 October 1968 on the abolition of restrictions on movement and residence within the Community for workers of Member States and their families, *OJ* 1968 English Special Edition, p. 485.

151 Advance notification to the Joint Committee is required.

152 The only exception was granted to Denmark, as its Protocol I to the EC Treaty on Secondary Residences is also applicable to Swiss nationals.

protocol contains transitional measures relating to the Swiss nationals and their rights in all the new Member States (including Cyprus and Malta). It is interesting to note that in most of the cases they contain copies of the transitional arrangements established under the EU Accession Treaty.[153]

4. IMPACT OF EU ENLARGEMENT

One direct legal impact of the European Union's 'big bang' enlargement was the necessity to adopt the Enlargement Protocol to the EC-Swiss Agreement on the Free Movement of Persons. Its ratification could have had far-reaching consequences for the shape of future bilateral relations between the European Union and the Swiss Confederation. There are also indirect effects of enlargements which may potentially shape future relations between the parties. Geographically speaking Switzerland remains one of the few Western European countries that are not members of the European Union. Moreover, it is not a member of the European Economic Area either. This leaves this mountain country at the back of the class in terms of institutional forms of EU integration. The geopolitical changes that took place during the thirteen years following the unsuccessful EEA referendum have had a considerable impact on bilateral EU-Swiss relations. It remains to be seen to what extent the fifth and expected sixth enlargements will change the Swiss position towards the European Union.

5. THE FUTURE OF EU-SWISS RELATIONS

There are number of ways in which EU-Swiss relations may develop in the coming months and years. At the time of writing, there are plenty of question marks, and the direction of this development may be shift in one way or another. For the purpose of clarity, the following analysis is divided into two parts devoted to the short and long-term prospects for EU-Swiss bilateral relations.

---

153 Treaty between the Kingdom of Belgium, the Kingdom of Denmark, the Federal Republic of Germany, the Hellenic Republic, the Kingdom of Spain, the French Republic, Ireland, the Italian Republic, the Grand Duchy of Luxembourg, the Kingdom of the Netherlands, the Republic of Austria, the Portuguese Republic, the Republic of Finland, the Kingdom of Sweden, the United Kingdom of Great Britain and Northern Ireland (Member States of the European Union) and the Czech Republic, the Republic of Estonia, the Republic of Cyprus, the Republic of Latvia, the Republic of Lithuania, the Republic of Hungary, the Republic of Malta, the Republic of Poland, the Republic of Slovenia, the Slovak Republic, concerning the accession of the Czech Republic, the Republic of Estonia, the Republic of Cyprus, the Republic of Latvia, the Republic of Lithuania, the Republic of Hungary, the Republic of Malta, the Republic of Poland, the Republic of Slovenia and the Slovak Republic to the European Union, *OJ* 2003 L 236/17. See K. Inglis, 'The Union's Fifth Accession Treaty: New Means to Make Enlargement Possible', 41 *CMLRev.* (2004) pp. 937-973.

5.1 Short-term perspectives

There are a number of short-term factors and challenges that may potentially have a pivotal impact on the future shape of EU-Swiss relations. In that sense, it is fair to argue that they will also determine the long-term perspectives. In political terms, the next milestone was the referendum on the Enlargement Protocol to the EC-Swiss Agreement on the Free Movement of Persons. The positive outcome paved the way for its entry into force and application to all twenty-five Member States of the European Union. In political terms it also facilitated the conclusion of the ratification procedures for the EC/EU-Swiss Agreement on Schengen and the EC-Swiss Agreement on Asylum. Negotiations on yet another enlargement protocol will take place shortly, as Bulgaria and Romania get closer to membership of the European Union.

5.2 Long-term perspectives

The short-term prospects addressed above will to a large extent determine the long-term prospects of EC-Swiss relations. Church argues that, instead of the series of options that existed a while ago, the Swiss Confederation is now left with only two. These are further deepening of the bilateral framework or accession to the European Union.[154] It is hard to disagree with this argumentation as the number of options is clearly limited. This is due to a variety of political and legal factors connected to the Swiss rejection of the EEA as well as developments within the European Union itself. Over the past decade, the Swiss Confederation has literally become surrounded by EU Member States and their close neighbours. The first step was the EFTA enlargement of 1995 and the next one was the recent 'big bang' enlargement of 2004. This has put Switzerland in the position of a small dot on the map of the European Union. At the same time, the internal market has been implemented, along with economic and monetary union based on the Treaty of Maastricht.

The first option distinguished by Church is further development of the bilateral relations. Following the ratification of the Enlargement Protocol to the EC-Swiss Agreement on the Free Movement of Persons and the completion of all necessary procedures related to Bilateral II, negotiations will continue on the liberalisation of services. Without a doubt, new dossiers will subsequently enrich the bilateral agenda. As already noted, the upcoming accession of Bulgaria and Romania will require further negotiations and the adoption of yet another protocol to the EC-Swiss Agreement on the Free Movement of Persons. The initial seven-year term for the agreements forming Bilateral I will expire in 2009, a political

154 Church, loc. cit. n. 13, at p. 137.

decision concerning their future will therefore be needed. Two options seem to be available. The first option is the prolongation of the agreements (which according to the treaties will be for an indefinite period). The second option is their termination.

Analysis of the long-term perspectives of EU-Swiss relations inevitably leads to a consideration of Switzerland's' potential membership of the European Union. However speculative this argumentation may sound, accession has been formally acknowledged as a long-term foreign policy goal of the Swiss authorities.

Hypothetically speaking, Swiss membership would inevitably raise a number of pivotal procedural and substantive issues within the European Union itself. First of all, the Swiss application for membership of the European Economic Community [*sic*] has not been withdrawn but was only suspended in the aftermath of the EEA referendum fiasco. In the meantime, the European Union was created and Article 49 TEU was inserted into the legal framework. Therefore, it will be argued that the formal application should be renewed in order to initiate the procedure. Then the question of conditionality will inevitably arise.[155] Meeting the political and economic criteria will not constitute a major problem. Based on the experiences of the last enlargement, legal approximation should also not create additional problems. However, this does not allow the assumption that the negotiations would be trouble-free. The history of Bilateral I and II proves that there are a number of very sensitive dossiers for both sides that would potentially have to be addressed under such circumstances.

6. CONCLUSIONS

EU-Swiss relations are undoubtedly very peculiar and are organised in an unusual way. The same model of enhanced bilateralism is not followed in relations with any other geographical neighbour of the European Union. Switzerland is not connected to the European Community by a traditional Association Agreement or any variation thereof. For objective reasons already outlined in chapter 1 of this book, it is also not covered by the European Neighbourhood Policy. The existing jigsaw puzzle of bilateral agreements is a direct result of a decades-long evolution that is characterised by changing intensity. In the years following the rejection of the European Economic Area by the Swiss voters, the system of enhanced bilateralism has continued to develop. Through both packages of bilateral treaties, the Swiss Confederation is benefiting from a considerable number of internal market elements. Unlike the countries of the European Economic Area, it is not participating in the creation of a common economic and legal space. It is also not

155 See Hillion, op. cit. n. 144.

involved in complex decision making. This, at least formally, leaves Swiss sovereignty untouched. Either of the above-mentioned hypothetical scenarios may take place. Whatever happens, there is no doubt that Switzerland remains at the heart of Europe, as one of the closest geographical and economic neighbours of the European Union. This in itself is deserving of attention and will constitute a *leitmotif* for EU policy towards the Swiss Confederation.

CHAPTER 6

MICRO-STATES (ANDORRA, MONACO, SAN MARINO AND THE VATICAN CITY)

Fiona Murray*

Relevant legal documents:

Andorra

- Agreement between the European Economic Community and the Principality of Andorra (customs union agreement), *OJ* 1990 L 374/16.
- Decision No 1/2003 of the EC-Andorra Joint Committee of 3 September 2003 on the laws, regulations and administrative provisions necessary for the proper functioning of the Customs Union, *OJ* 2003 L 253/3.
- Protocol on veterinary matters supplementary to the agreement in the form of an exchange of letters between the European Economic Community and the Principality of Andorra, *OJ* 1997 L148/16.
- Agreement between the European Community and the Principality of Andorra providing for measures equivalent to those laid down in Council Directive 2003/48/EC on taxation of savings income in the form of interest payments (including a Memorandum of Understanding), *OJ* 2004 L 359/33.
- Cooperation Agreement between the European Community and the Principality of Andorra, *OJ* 2005 L 135/14.

Monaco

- Monetary Agreement between the Government of the French Republic, on behalf of the European Community, and the Government of His Serene Highness the Prince of Monaco, *OJ* 2002 L 142/59.
- Agreement between the European Community and the Principality of Monaco on the application of certain Community acts on the territory of the Principality of Monaco, *OJ* 2003 L 332/42.
- Agreement between the European Community and the Principality of Monaco providing for measures equivalent to those laid down in Council Directive 2003/48/EC, *OJ* L 2005 L 19/55.

* Manager of EU Public Affairs, Schuman Associates, Brussels.

S. Blockmans and A. Łazowski (eds.), The European Union and Its Neighbours

San Marino

- Agreement on Cooperation and Customs Union between the European Economic Community and the Republic of San Marino, *OJ* 2002 L 84/43.
- Monetary Agreement between the Italian Republic, on behalf of the European Community, and the Republic of San Marino, *OJ* 2001 C 209/1.
- Agreement between the European Community and the Republic of San Marino providing for measures equivalent to those laid down in Council Directive 2003/48/EC on taxation of savings income in the form of interest payments, *OJ* 2004 L 381/33.

Holy See/Vatican City

- Monetary Agreement between the Italian Republic, on behalf of the European Community, and the Vatican City State and, on its behalf, the Holy See, *OJ* 2001 C 299/1.

1. INTRODUCTION

Within Europe, there are a number of small, independent, internationally recognised states. Known collectively because of their size as the micro-states, they exist for various historical reasons but have a number of characteristics in common. They are Andorra, Monaco, San Marino and the Vatican City.[1]

All of these micro-states have close economic ties with particular Member States of the European Union,[2] but none of them are part of the European Union, nor aligned to the European Union's Common Foreign and Security Policy. With the notable exception of the Vatican City, the economies of the micro-states tend to rely on tourism and financial services.

Each of the micro-states has diplomatic relations with the European Community, and most have gradually stepped up their contacts and collaboration with the European Union. Although each has developed quite separate relations with the European Union, these relationships have developed along similar lines. For example, all four micro-states have entered into monetary agreements with the European Community. In most cases, formal relations with the European Community began with the signing of customs and cooperation agreements, and more recently most have entered into agreements with the European Community on the taxation of savings income of EU residents.

---

[1] The Principality of Liechtenstein, also classed as a micro-state, is covered in chapter 4 on the EEA Countries.

[2] Legally, each of the micro-states' formal relationships are with the European Community (EC). Throughout this chapter, the abbreviation 'EC' will be used to refer to the specific agreements and other legal texts forming the basis of this legal relationship. Elsewhere, the abbreviation 'EU' will be used to refer in a general sense to the European Union's relations with the micro-states.

In most cases, the micro-states are seeking to deepen their relations with the European Union. This deepening of relations will, for the foreseeable future, take place in the context of the various existing bilateral agreements between each of the micro-states and the European Community. Too small to support membership of the European Economic Area (EEA) or indeed full membership of the European Union, the micro-states and the Union are more likely to explore in the long term the possibility of a special association governing EU-micro-state relations.

2. ANDORRA

2.1 Summary of historical and political relations with the EU

The Principality of Andorra is situated in the eastern Pyrenees between France and Spain. The country has an area of 468 square kilometres and a population of approximately 70,000. The official language is Catalan, although French and Spanish are also spoken.

Andorra is a parliamentary democracy established by a Constitution that entered into force in March 1993. The Constitution vests sovereignty in the Andorran people and defines the office of the Co-Princes as that of head of state. Due to historic ties with both France and Spain, the principality has two official heads of state – Co-Princes – namely the President of France and the Bishop of Seo de Urgel in Spain. Both of these Co-Princes have representatives in Andorra. Whilst the Co-Princes have certain nominal powers, including the power to call general elections and give their consent for Andorra to bind itself under international treaties, the day-to-day work of the Principality is conducted by the Government and the country's legislative organ, the General Council of the Valleys (*Consell General de les Valls*).

Tourism accounts for around 80 per cent of Andorra's GDP. Financial services also make an important contribution to the economy.

Since the establishment of the sovereignty of the Andorran people with the 1993 Constitution, Andorra has become an active participant in the international community. In July 1993, Andorra set up its first international diplomatic mission at the United Nations. Andorra is now a member of several international organisations, including the Council of Europe (since 1994). In 1997, Andorra applied for membership of the World Trade Organisation (WTO). This application is still under review.

Formal EC-Andorra relations began with the entry into force on 1 July 1991 of a customs union agreement covering industrial products.[3]

---

[3] Agreement in the form of an Exchange of Letters between the European Economic Community and the Principality of Andorra, *OJ* 1990 L 374/14.

Negotiations on a Cooperation Agreement, complementing the Customs Union Agreement and covering various matters including the environment, communication, information, culture, education and transport, were finalised in January 1998. For a number of reasons however – notably the problem of tobacco smuggling from Andorra into the European Community – this agreement was only signed in November 2004 at the same time as the Savings Tax Agreement.

In October 2004, the EU Council adopted a decision opening negotiations on an agreement with Andorra on the use of euro banknotes and coins by Andorra, the legal status of the euro in Andorra and access to euro area payment.

Finally, Andorra has recently signed an agreement[4] with the European Community on measures equivalent to those laid down in Directive 2003/48/EC on the taxation of savings income[5] (hereinafter, the Savings Tax Directive).

2.2 General legal analysis of relations with the European Union

Prior to Spain's accession, Andorra had no formal relations with the European Communities. This was mainly because, without a constitution, Andorra had no formal legal recognition. Andorra's global engagement had consisted of two bilateral trade agreements dating back to the 19th century, one each with France and Spain. Whilst France's decision to become a founder member of the European Communities had little impact on Andorra, Spain's accession in 1986 had major repercussions. In particular, Spain was Andorra's main trading partner and Spanish accession had the effect of rendering its trade agreement with Andorra virtually obsolete.

2.2.1 *Customs union agreement*

Andorra's formal legal links to the European Community began in 1990 with a customs union agreement, signed in June 1990, effective from 1 July 1991. As Andorra was not then recognised by the international community, the agreement only took the form of an exchange of letters. The Community's legal base consisted of Articles 99 and 113 EEC (now Arts. 93 and 133 TEC). The agreement sets up a customs union between Andorra and the European Community for mainly industrial products. Specifically, Article 2 of the agreement provides for the customs union to be established for those products covered by chapters 25 to 97

[4] Agreement between the European Community and the Principality of Andorra providing for measures equivalent to those laid down in Council Directive 2003/48/EC on taxation of savings income in the form of interest payments and signature of the accompanying Memorandum of Understanding, *OJ* 2004 L 359/32.

[5] Council Directive 2003/48/EC of 3 June 2003 on the taxation of savings income in the form of interest payments, *OJ* 2003 L 157/38.

of the Harmonised System (HS). The agreement also includes provisions applicable to agricultural products falling under chapters 1 to 24 of the HS. The practical result of the agreement is that Andorra is treated as a member of the EC customs union for trade in manufactured products (to which no tariffs are applied) and as a non-EU member or third country in respect of agricultural goods. A joint committee is responsible for administering the agreement and ensuring that it is properly implemented. The Joint Committee is composed of representatives of both the European Union and the Principality of Andorra. Decisions are taken jointly by both parties by common accord on matters falling within the scope of the agreement. The Joint Committee meets at the request of either of the parties to the agreement. As specified in Article 18 of the agreement it also plays the role of a dispute settlement body.[6]

Under Article 7 of the agreement, Andorra has an obligation to adapt its legislation to selected parts of the EC customs *acquis*. The list of relevant legal acts was agreed by the EEC-Andorra Joint Committee and reproduced in Decision No. 2/91.[7] It included, *inter alia*, legislation on release for free circulation, customs obligations, valuation of goods for customs purposes, customs procedures with economic impact as well as rules of origin. It was subsequently repealed and updated by Decision No. 1/2003 of the Joint Committee.[8]

In 1997, Andorra applied to join the WTO and notified the latter of the EC-Andorra Customs Union Agreement, which was found to be contrary to WTO rules since it purported to exclude a complete area – agriculture – from its scope. The matter, which is still under review, may be resolved by including at least a percentage of agricultural products within the scope of the agreement.

2.2.2 *Protocol on veterinary matters*

In May 1997, Andorra and the European Community signed a protocol on veterinary matters supplementary to the Customs Union Agreement.[9] The principal aim of the protocol is to ensure that trade in live animals and animal products between

---

[6] If the Joint Committee is not successful in settling a dispute then the parties may refer to arbitration. Each has a right to appoint an arbiter. Formation of an arbitration panel is complete upon the designation of a third arbiter by the Joint Committee itself. The decisions of arbitration panels are taken by majority.

[7] Decision No. 2/91 of the EEC-Andorra Joint Committee of 12 July 1991 on the laws, regulations and administrative provisions applicable to customs matters in the Community to be adopted by the Principality of Andorra, *OJ* 1991 L 250/24.

[8] Decision No. 1/2003 of the EC-Andorra Joint Committee of 3 September 2003 on the laws, regulations and administrative provisions necessary for the proper functioning of the Customs Union, *OJ* 2003 L 253/3.

[9] Protocol on veterinary matters supplementary to the agreement in the form of an exchange of letters between the European Economic Community and the Principality of Andorra, *OJ* 1997 L 148/16.

Andorra and the European Community is carried out in compliance with EC veterinary legislation. There have been no amendments to the protocol, and discussions on the application of EC veterinary measures take place within joint veterinary committees. The principal driving force behind the protocol was the annual practice of transhumance of Andorran livestock – mainly sheep – to France, which could give rise to veterinary issues.

2.2.3 *Cooperation Agreement*

On 15 November 2004, Andorra and the European Community signed a Cooperation Agreement.[10] Intended to complement the Customs Union Agreement, it extends the scope of current EU-Andorra relations in various areas, including the environment, communication, information and culture, education, training and youth, social questions and health, transport, energy and trans-European communications, and regional policy. The Cooperation Agreement does not cover the free movement of persons and capital nor the freedom to provide cross-border services. The European Commission rejected Andorra's 2002 initiative to include the monetary sector in the agreement.

The agreement was in fact finalised in January 1998 but could not be signed until a satisfactory solution was reached on both sides on a number of issues, including that of cigarette smuggling from Andorra into the European Union. The issue of cigarette smuggling began in 1996, when Andorra was identified as one of the principal sources of cigarettes smuggled into the European Union. Specifically, it was revealed that large quantities of cigarettes were produced, imported and stored in Andorra, pending their eventual reshipment elsewhere, mainly for smuggling purposes. This resulted, according to estimates, in a loss to the European Union (both in terms of the European Union's own resources and Member State national duties) of approximately €4 million in 1997. Following a period of interchange with the European Union, Andorra adopted various measures to tackle cigarette smuggling. This action was viewed positively by the European Union and paved the way for a reopening of negotiations on the EC-Andorra Cooperation Agreement, which resumed in September 2002. They were completed in 2004 and the agreement entered into force on 1 July 2005.[11]

The Cooperation Agreement is intended to complement and enlarge the scope of present relations between Andorra and the European Community as set out in the Customs Union Agreement, but without replacing the latter. Under the agreement,

---

[10] Cooperation Agreement between the European Community and the Principality of Andorra, *OJ* 2005 L 135/14.

[11] Information relating to the entry into force of the Cooperation Agreement between the European Community and the Principality of Andorra, *OJ* 2005 L 138/17.

the European Community and Andorra undertake to cooperate on the broadest possible basis and particularly within a number of designated areas, including the following:

- Environment: for example, to reconcile conservation of the Pyrenean environment with economic development, addressing environmental problems facing Andorra and the Pyrenean regions of the European Union (Art. 2);
- Communications, information and culture: for example, undertaking joint projects such as exchanges of information on topics of mutual interest in the fields of culture and information, organisation of cultural events (Art. 3);
- Education, vocational training and youth: cooperation in these areas to help create a European Education Area (Art. 4); and
- Regional policy: stepping up regional cooperation in line with EU policies on cross-border, transnational and interregional cooperation (Art. 7).

Other areas of cooperation may also be included in the agreement by mutual consent of the two parties.

The Cooperation Agreement will be administered by a Cooperation Committee composed of representatives of the European Community (European Commission) and of the Principality of Andorra. Its decisions will be taken by common accord. The Cooperation Committee will also serve as a dispute settlement body (Art. 10).

2.2.4 *Savings tax agreement*

On 15 November 2004, in addition to signing a Cooperation Agreement, Andorra and the European Community also signed an agreement on the taxation of savings income[12] (hereinafter, the Savings Tax Agreement). This agreement (and parallel agreements with Switzerland, Liechtenstein, Monaco and San Marino) provide for the adoption of equivalent measures to those set out in the Savings Tax Directive. Under the agreement, Andorra has undertaken to apply a withholding tax to savings income in the form of interest payments made in Andorra to EU residents. In addition, the agreement provides for the exchange of information on request in cases of tax fraud and similar behaviour.

The agreement is accompanied by a Memorandum of Understanding (MoU) in which Andorra undertakes, *inter alia*, to introduce the concept of the crime of tax fraud into its legislation during the first year of application of the agreement for

[12] Agreement between the European Community and the Principality of Andorra providing for measures equivalent to those laid down in Council Directive 2003/48/EC on taxation of savings income in the form of interest payments, *OJ* 2004 L 359/33.

cases falling within the framework of the agreement. Specifically, this undertaking refers to the obligation in Article 12 of the Savings Tax Agreement itself, which provides that the European Union and Andorra shall exchange information on income covered by the agreement regarding 'conduct constituting a crime of tax fraud under the laws of the regulated state or the like'.[13] The MoU clarifies that the definition of tax fraud only relates to the taxation of savings within the framework of the agreement and is therefore without prejudice to developments relating to tax fraud under other circumstances.

The MoU also refers to other areas of closer cooperation, including discussions for a monetary agreement. The Savings Tax Directive is scheduled to apply from 1 July 2005, but the EU-Andorra Savings Tax Agreement will apply only if and when the same measures are adopted by the United States, Switzerland, Liechtenstein, Monaco, San Marino, the dependent and associated territories of the United Kingdom and the Netherlands and, of course, by the EU Member States. The ratification procedures were completed and the agreement entered into force on 1 June 2005.[14]

2.3 Some specific legal issues characterising the EU-Andorra relationship

2.3.1 *Monetary agreement*

Andorra has never had its own currency. Nor has it had a monetary issuing authority or a monetary law. Prior to the adoption of the euro in France and Spain, Andorra used both French francs and Spanish pesetas, though these currencies did not have legal tender status. No monetary agreement was concluded between Andorra and either France or Spain on the use of their currencies in Andorra. Therefore, when both France and Spain began circulating euro banknotes and coins in January 2002, Andorra introduced the euro without the need for any intervention by the European Union.

The signing of the EC-Andorra Savings Tax Agreement opened the way for negotiations by both sides on a monetary agreement for the use of the euro in Andorra. Negotiations officially started on 28 October 2004. Under the monetary agreement, Andorra is seeking to be able to mint euro coins and use the euro as its official currency. The monetary agreement will include provisions concerning the protection of the euro and against money laundering. Negotiations are likely to

13 Article 12(1) of the Savings Tax Agreement.

14 Information relating to the entry into force of the Agreement between the European Community and the Principality of Andorra providing for measures equivalent to those laid down in Council Directive 2003/48/EC on taxation of savings income in the form of interest payments, *OJ* 2005 C 119/1.

take some time due to the fact that Andorra – unlike Monaco and San Marino – has never had a monetary agreement with an EU Member State.

2.3.2 *Bilateral agreements on economic and fiscal cooperation*

In addition to a future monetary agreement, the MoU annexed to the Savings Tax Agreement provides for the opening of bilateral negotiations between Andorra and each of the EU Member States to define the administrative procedure for the exchange of information on tax-related issues. The MoU further calls for similar parallel bilateral negotiations to broaden economic and fiscal cooperation. The aim of bilateral economic programmes would be to promote the integration of the Andorran economy into the EU economy. The aim of bilateral cooperation in the area of taxation would be to examine the possible removal or reduction of withholding taxes currently imposed by EU Member States on the provision of services and financial products from Andorra.

2.3.3 *Free movement of Andorran citizens across external EU borders*

As Andorra has no airport and is completely surrounded by EU Member States, Andorran citizens are forced to cross external EU borders in order to reach their country. In order to make it easier for its citizens to pass through external EU frontiers, Andorra is seeking permission for Andorran citizens to be treated in the same manner as EU citizens, thereby avoiding the sometimes lengthy queues at such borders for non-EU citizens. This arrangement would of course only apply to those EU Member States within the Schengen area and would therefore not include the United Kingdom and Ireland. In the latter two cases, Andorra would like to negotiate bilaterally to agree similar arrangements for Andorran citizens passing through British and Irish borders.

3. MONACO

3.1 **Summary of historical and political relations with the European Union**

The Principality of Monaco is located on the Mediterranean coast surrounded by France. It has an area of just 1.95 square kilometres making it the smallest country in the world aside from the Vatican City. It has a population of around 32,000.

By charter of the French King, the independence of Monaco was recognised and guaranteed in 1489. The Protection Treaty with France of 1918 codified Monaco's relationship with France, securing its independence, with the country undertaking only to enter into international agreements with the consent of

France. Today, the Principality is a constitutional monarchy, the Constitution having been in place since 1962.[15] It was most recently amended in 2002.[16]

Monaco's main industries are tourism, financial services and property.

In 1993, Monaco became a member of the United Nations. Most recently, in October 2004, it became a member of the Council of Europe.

Much of Monaco's relationship with the European Union emanates from the Principality's special relations with France. For example, since 1968, Monaco has been part of the EU customs territory through its relationship with France, with which it has had a customs union since 1963. Likewise, although not a signatory in its own right to the Schengen Agreement on the Free Movement of Persons, Monaco benefits from the Schengen Agreement through its association with France.

EC value-added tax (VAT) applies in Monaco by virtue of Article 1 of Directive 92/111/EEC, as amended.[17] This arrangement is also based on a prior agreement with France on VAT and excise duties.

In December 2001, Monaco concluded an agreement with the European Community on the use of the euro as its official currency,[18] which required the renegotiation of a prior monetary agreement between Monaco and France.

An agreement on the application in Monaco of EC legislation on cosmetic, pharmaceutical and veterinary products was agreed in November 2003.[19]

In December 2004, as in the case of Andorra, an agreement was signed concerning the application by Monaco of measures equivalent to those set out in the Savings Tax Directive.[20]

3.2 General legal analysis of relations with the European Union

3.2.1 *EU common customs territory*

Monaco is part of the EC common customs territory. This relationship is defined by the Customs Convention between France and Monaco, signed in May 1963,[21]

---

15 *Journal de Monaco. Bulletin Officiel de la Principauté*, No. 7551.

16 Loi n° 1.249 du 2 avril 2002 portant révision de la Constitution du 17 décembre 1962, *Journal de Monaco. Bulletin Officiel de la Principauté*, No. 7541.

17 Council Directive of 14 December 1992 amending Directive 77/388/EC introducing simplification measures with regard to value added tax, *OJ* 1992 L 384/47.

18 Monetary Agreement between the Government of the French Republic, on behalf of the European Community, and the Government of His Serene Highness the Prince of Monaco, *OJ* 2002 L 142/59.

19 Council Decision of 17 November 2003 concerning the conclusion of the Agreement on the application of certain Community acts on the territory of the Principality of Monaco, *OJ* 2003 L 332/41.

20 Agreement between the European Community and the Principality of Monaco providing for measures equivalent to those laid down in Council Directive 2003/48/EC, *OJ* 2005 L 19/55.

21 *Official Journal of the French Republic*, 27 September 1963, p. 8679.

and stipulated in Article 3(2)(b) of the EU Customs Code.[22] Monaco's participation in the EU common customs territory does not, however, extend to external trade. Thus, preferential trade agreements concluded by the European Union apply only to goods originating in the territory of the Union. Goods produced in Monaco may not claim EU origin and are generally not included in an extended application of the protocol of origin with the trade partners of the European Union.

3.2.2 *Schengen Agreement*

Through its relationship with France, Monaco has become integrated into the Schengen area. However, Monaco is not a party to the Schengen Agreement. Rather, a decision of the Schengen Executive Committee in June 1998 recognised Monaco's seaport and heliport as French entry points to the EU territory.[23] In practical terms, this decision means that Monaco is part of the Schengen area and that those in possession of Monegasque residence permits may travel within the Schengen area in the same way as citizens of the Schengen area without being subject to border controls. However, as the arrangement depends on the recognition by France of the Monaco seaport and heliport as French entry points, Monaco could cease to be part of the Schengen area if France decided that Monaco was no longer to be regarded as a French entry point.

3.2.3 *EC VAT provisions*

Under Article 1(1) of Directive 92/111/EC, EC VAT rules apply to Monaco. Specifically, Article 1(1) provides, *inter alia*, that '… in view of the conventions and treaties which [they have] concluded … with the French Republic … the Principality of Monaco shall not be treated for the purposes of the application of this Directive as third territories.' EU VAT rules apply to Monaco on the basis of a prior Monaco-France agreement on VAT and excise duties. In essence, the arrangement assimilates Monaco traders and business with French traders and business, so that Monaco traders, for example, receive a French VAT number. The result is that neither Monaco traders nor their goods become EU traders or goods and, where no specific provision is made, Monaco traders and Monegasque goods are treated as third country traders or goods *vis-à-vis* the European Union.

---

22 Council Regulation (EEC) No. 2913/92 of 12 October 1992 establishing the Community Customs Code (as amended), *OJ* 1992 L 302/1.

23 The Schengen *acquis* – Decision of the Executive Committee of 23 June 1998 on Monegasque residence permits (SCH/Com-ex (98) 19), *OJ* 2000 L 239/199.

3.2.4 *Monetary agreement*

In December 2001, Monaco signed a monetary agreement with France (acting on behalf of the European Community).[24] Prior to the introduction of the euro in the European Union, Monaco already had a monetary agreement with France. According to Declaration No. 6 of the Maastricht Treaty, this agreement (and similar monetary agreements between Italy and San Marino and the Vatican City) remained valid until the introduction of the euro as the single currency in the European Union. Thereafter, the European Union would have to facilitate their renegotiation. Accordingly, on 31 December 1998, the Council adopted decisions on the position to be taken regarding monetary relations with Monaco (and San Marino and the Vatican City).[25] These decisions broadly provided that each of the three jurisdictions, including Monaco, could use the euro as its official currency, grant legal tender status to euro banknotes and coins, issue euro coins subject to certain conditions of issuance and issue euro collector coins also subject to certain conditions. In addition, all three jurisdictions undertook to cooperate with the European Union on measures against the counterfeiting of euro banknotes and coins. These provisions were subsequently reflected in the monetary agreements between Monaco, San Marino and the Vatican City and the relevant Member States.

The agreement places an obligation on Monaco to adopt measures reflecting the relevant EC law. For example, under Article 11 of the agreement, Monaco has an obligation to apply French law implementing EC legislation listed in Annex A[26] to the agreement.[27] Moreover, it shall adopt measures to implement the EC Directive on investment compensation schemes.[28] It shall also take measures that are equivalent to the EC law listed in Annex B[29] on the prevention of use of the

---

24 Monetary Agreement between the Government of the French Republic, on behalf of the European Community, and the Government of His Serene Highness the Prince of Monaco, *OJ* 2002 L 142/59.

25 Council Decision of 31 December 1998 on the position to be taken by the Community regarding an agreement concerning the monetary relations with the Principality of Monaco (1999/96/EC), San Marino (1999/97/EC) and the Vatican City (1999/98/EC), *OJ* 1999 L 30/31-36.

26 The legislation includes, *inter alia*, Directive of the European Parliament and of the Council of 4 April 2001 on the reorganisation and winding-up of credit institutions, *OJ* 2001 L 125/15; Directive of the European Parliament and of the Council of 27 January 1997 on cross-border credit transfers, *OJ* 1997 L 43/25; Directive of the European Parliament and of the Council of 30 May 1994 on deposit-guarantee schemes, *OJ* 1994 L 135/5.

27 The European Commission has an obligation to amend the list with every subsequent development of EC law.

28 Directive of the Parliament and of the Council of 3 March 1997 on investment compensation schemes, *OJ* 1997 L 84/22.

29 For the time being, the list includes only Directive of the Parliament and of the Council of 3 March 1997 on investment compensation schemes, *OJ* 1997 L 84/22.

financial system for the purpose of money laundering (Art. 11(6)).[30] All measures covered by the agreement shall be interpreted in accordance with ECJ jurisprudence.

A Joint Committee composed of a Monaco representative, the relevant Member State (France) and bodies party to the agreement (the European Commission and the European Central Bank) was set up. The aim of this Joint Committee is to facilitate implementation and operation of the agreement, to exchange views and to adopt decisions pursuant to the agreement (Art. 14). It also has powers to examine measures adopted by Monaco in implementation of the agreement.

3.2.5 *Cosmetics, pharmaceuticals and veterinary agreement*

An agreement on the application to Monaco of EC legislation on cosmetics, pharmaceutical and veterinary products was signed in December 2003 and entered into force in May 2004.[31] In particular, the agreement provides that EC legislation – listed in an annex to the agreement – covering medicinal products, cosmetics and medical devices shall also apply in the territory of Monaco (Art. 1).[32] The agreement clarifies that the relevant EC legislation applies in Monaco and that the French authorities can monitor the production in Monaco of those products against the particular standards outlined in the EU legislation. None of the other EU Member States, however, is similarly obliged to recognise the production of Monegasque goods.

A Joint Committee composed of representatives of the Community and Monaco is charged with managing and applying the agreement. To this end, the Joint Committee can formulate recommendations and take decisions. In order to keep the agreement in line with developments in EC law, the Joint Committee is empowered to amend the lists of legislation contained in the annexes to the agreement. It also serves as a dispute settlement body (also in case of divergent interpretation of EC law by courts in Monaco and the European Court of Justice). The Committee meets as and when necessary.

---

30 In the case of EC law developments, a decision on changes to Annex B is made either by the Joint Committee or by the Commission in accordance with the procedure set out in Article 11(5).

31 Agreement between the European Community and the Principality of Monaco on the application of certain Community acts on the territory of the Principality of Monaco, *OJ* 2003 L 332/42.

32 This includes, *inter alia*, Council Directive 78/25/EEC of 12 December 1977 on the approximation of the laws of the Member States relating to the colouring matters which may be added to medicinal products, *OJ* 1978 L 11/18 (as amended); Council Directive 89/105/EEC of 21 December 1998 relating to the transparency of measures regulating the pricing of medicinal products for human use and their inclusion in the scope of national health insurance systems, *OJ* 1989 L 40/8; Council Directive 76/768/EEC of 27 July 1976 on the approximation of the laws of the Member States relating to cosmetic products, *OJ* 1976 L 262/169 (as amended); Council Directive 93/42/EEC concerning medical devices, *OJ* 1993 L 169/1.

3.2.6 *Savings tax agreement*

On 7 December 2004, simultaneously with Liechtenstein and San Marino, Monaco signed an agreement on the Savings Tax Directive.[33] As in the case of Andorra, the central feature of the agreement is a provision for the imposition of a withholding tax on the interest paid in Monaco to EU residents. Likewise, the agreement is accompanied by a MoU concerning future cooperation between Monaco and the European Community, specifically in the area of financial services.

3.3 Some specific legal issues characterising the EU-Monaco relationship

3.3.1 *Access to the European Union of Monaco UCITS and insurance products*

The MoU attached to the EC-Monaco Savings Tax Agreement provides for the possibility of future negotiations between both parties on the access to the EU financial services market of certain Monegasque financial instruments, notably UCITS (undertakings for collective investment in transferable securities), and insurance products. Any future agreement in this area, however, will have to comply with WTO General Agreement on Trade in Services (GATS), which stipulates, *inter alia*, that trade agreements to which WTO members are party must cover a substantial part of trade. Any future EU-Monaco agreement that purports to cover only a limited part – rather than all – of the financial services sector might therefore be in conflict with the European Union's obligations under the GATS. The issue of compatibility with GATS of any future EC-Monaco agreement on financial services will obviously be a prime area for review, but at the time of writing there have been no formal discussions on such an agreement.

3.3.2 *Closer cooperation with the European Union on research*

Monaco is interested in developing closer ties with Europe in the area of research. Following Monaco's cooperation on the Savings Tax Directive, the European Union approved Monaco's application to become a member of EUREKA, the pan-European research and development initiative. Accordingly, on 21 March 2005, Monaco became the thirty-fifth member of EUREKA. Established in 1985, EUREKA broadly aims to raise the productivity and competitiveness of European industry by supporting businesses, research centres and universities that conduct

---

33 Agreement between the European Community and the Principality of Monaco providing for measures equivalent to those laid down in Council Directive 2003/48/EC, *OJ* 2005 L 19/55.

pan-European projects to develop innovative products, processes and services. The European Union is a full EUREKA member in its own right and its support for Monaco's application carries considerable weight. However, the European Union has linked its support for Monaco's membership of EUREKA to the Principality's commitment to applying the Savings Tax Directive, implying that any lack of commitment by Monaco regarding the latter might lead to a reconsideration by the European Union of its support for Monaco's membership of EUREKA.

4. SAN MARINO

4.1 Summary of historical and political relations with the European Union

Europe's third smallest country (after Monaco and the Vatican City), San Marino is located in north-central Italy, about 23 kilometres from the Adriatic coast. It has an area of just 61 square kilometres and a population of around 28,000. Italian is the official language.

Claiming to be the world's oldest democracy dating from the fourth century AD, San Marino's written constitution dates from 1600. Nevertheless, as a sovereign nation, it is strongly dependent on Italy.

Tourism is the country's main industry. Banking is also important.

San Marino has been a member of the Council of Europe since November 1988 and a member of the United Nations since March 1992.

Although official diplomatic relations between San Marino and the European Communities date from 1983, the relationship only formally got under way with the signing of a cooperation and customs union agreement in December 1991.[34] That agreement, however, took another decade to conclude and finally entered into force in May 2002.

Like Monaco and the Vatican City, San Marino also concluded a monetary agreement with the European Union, which allows San Marino to use the euro as its official currency.[35]

In December 2004, along with Liechtenstein and Monaco (and Andorra and Switzerland shortly before that), San Marino signed an agreement on the Savings Tax Directive.[36]

---

[34] Agreement on Cooperation and Customs Union between the European Economic Community and the Republic of San Marino, *OJ* 2002 L 84/43.

[35] Monetary Agreement between the Italian Republic, on behalf of the European Community, and the Republic of San Marino, *OJ* 2001 C 209/1.

[36] Agreement between the European Community and the Republic of San Marino providing for measures equivalent to those laid down in Council Directive 2003/48/EC on taxation of savings income in the form of interest payments, *OJ* 2004 L 381/33.

4.2 General legal analysis of relations with the European Union

4.2.1 *Cooperation and customs union agreement*

The EC-San Marino Cooperation and Customs Union Agreement establishes a customs union between both parties for both agricultural and industrial products, specifically those covered by chapters 1 to 97 of the HS. The provisions relating to customs applied provisionally from 1991, but the agreement (both in relation to customs and cooperation) entered into force only in 2002 when all EU Member States had finally ratified it.

The agreement provides for cooperation 'on as broad a basis as possible',[37] including, in particular, the following areas:

- Environment: environmental protection and improvement in order to resolve problems caused by the contamination of water, soil and air by erosion and deforestation (Art. 16);
- Tourism: supporting cooperation through operations such as exchanges of officials and experts on tourism, training in hotel management and administration. The parties will pay particular attention to the promotion of out-of-season tourism in San Marino (Art. 17); and
- Communications, information and culture: joint operations in these areas including exchanges of information on subjects of mutual interest in the fields of culture and information, cultural events and exchanges (Art. 18).

Aside from these specific areas mentioned in the agreement, Article 19 provides that the contracting parties may by mutual consent further extend the scope of the agreement to include cooperation on other specific sectors or activities.

A Cooperation Committee comprised of representatives of the parties to the agreement is responsible for administering both the customs and cooperation elements of the agreement. It also serves as a dispute settlement body (Art. 24).[38]

So far, as the agreement has only been in force for a relatively short period, cooperation between San Marino and the European Union has been rather limited. On 4 May 2005, the parties signed a protocol on the participation of the new Member States in the customs union with San Marino.[39]

---

[37] Article 14 of the Agreement on Cooperation and Customs Union between the European Economic Community and the Republic of San Marino, *OJ* 2002 L 84/43.

[38] Arbitration may be engaged if the dispute is not resolved by the Cooperation Committee (Art. 24(2)).

[39] Proposal for a Council Decision on the conclusion, on behalf of the European Community and its Member States, of a Protocol to the Agreement on Cooperation and Customs Union between the European Economic Community and the Republic of San Marino, regarding the participation, as

4.2.2 *Monetary agreement*

Like Monaco, San Marino signed a monetary agreement with the European Community[40] in December 2001, which entered into force on 1 January 2002 when the euro entered into circulation in the European Union. In the case of San Marino, Italy signed on behalf of the European Community because of its close historical links with San Marino. Prior to this, San Marino had a monetary agreement with Italy, which had to be renegotiated when the euro was introduced as the single currency of the European Union on 1 January 1999, including in Italy. On that date the European Community became competent for monetary matters relating to Member States (like Italy and France) that adopted the euro. The Monetary Agreement with San Marino contains similar provisions to the equivalent Monetary Agreement with Monaco. Therefore, it permits San Marino to use the euro as its official currency, to grant it legal tender status and to issue a limited quantity of euro coins according to specific guidelines on issuance and to issue euro collector coins also in line with certain conditions.

4.2.3 *Savings tax agreement*

San Marino signed an agreement with the European Community on the Savings Tax Directive on 7 December 2004. The agreement contains provisions similar to the savings tax agreements signed by Switzerland, Liechtenstein and Monaco, namely payment of a withholding tax on the interest income of EU individuals, voluntary disclosure of information as an alternative to withholding tax, a clause providing for a regular review of the agreement and exchange of information on request in cases of fraud or comparable behaviour. The San Marino agreement is also accompanied by a MoU concerning future cooperation with European Community. The agreement entered into force on 1 July 2005.[41]

---

contracting parties, of the Czech Republic, the Republic of Estonia, the Republic of Cyprus, the Republic of Latvia, the Republic of Lithuania, the Republic of Hungary, the Republic of Malta, the Republic of Poland, the Republic of Slovenia and the Slovak Republic, pursuant to their accession to the European Union, COM (2004) 258 final.

[40] Agreement between the European Community and the Republic of San Marino providing for measures equivalent to those laid down in Council Directive 2003/48/EC on taxation of savings income in the form of interest payments, *OJ* 2004 L 381/33.

[41] Information relating to the entry into force of the Agreement between the European Community and the Republic of San Marino providing for measures equivalent to those laid down in Council Directive 2003/48/EC on taxation of savings income in the form of interest payments, *OJ* 2005 C 119/1.

4.3 Some specific legal issues characterising the EU-San Marino relationship

4.3.1 *Mutual recognition of prudential measures on financial services*

The MoU attached to the EC-San Marino Savings Tax Agreement makes clear San Marino's wish to participate fully in the European Union's financial services market. To this end, the MoU provides that San Marino and the European Community will start consultations on achieving mutual recognition of both parties' prudential measures and systems of financial services, including insurance. San Marino further undertakes to adopt and implement the relevant existing EC legislation in this sector.

4.3.2 *Simplification of procedures under the EC-San Marino Cooperation and Customs Union Agreement*

The MoU to the Savings Tax Agreement further provides that San Marino and the European Community will discuss ways of simplifying procedures under the existing EC-San Marino Cooperation and Customs Union Agreement.

4.3.3 *Participation in EU research and development programmes*

Finally, the same MoU attached to the EC-San Marino Savings Tax Agreement opens the way for consultations between both sides on the possibilities for San Marino citizens and companies to take part in EC research and development programmes and activities.

5. THE VATICAN CITY/HOLY SEE

5.1 Summary of historical and political relations with the European Union

The Vatican City is located in Rome, Italy, but is an independent state. It has a total area of 0.44 square kilometres, making it the world's smallest state, and has a population of approximately 800.

The Vatican City is the ecclesiastical, governmental and administrative capital of the Roman Catholic church, headed by the Pope who exercises supreme, legislative, executive and judicial power. The Vatican City's independence and sovereignty was recognised in agreements signed with Italy in 1929.

The Holy See – the governing body of the Roman Catholic church – commenced formal diplomatic relations with the European Communities in November

1970. This followed the Second Vatican Council in the late 1960s, which included a decision to develop relations with international institutions with the broad aim of promoting peace and progress.

Unlike the other European micro-states, the Holy See has not sought to broaden its relationship with the European Union beyond a monetary agreement similar to those entered into by Monaco and San Marino.[42]

5.2 General legal analysis of relations with the European Union

5.2.1 *Monetary agreement*

Since a monetary agreement already existed between Italy and the Vatican City prior to the introduction of the euro, the European Union undertook to facilitate its renegotiation once the euro was introduced. As in the case of Italy and San Marino (and France and Monaco), Italy undertook to negotiate and conclude the Monetary Agreement with the Vatican City on behalf of the European Union because of its close economic ties to the Vatican City. The agreement, like its Monaco and San Marino counterparts, permits the Vatican City to use the euro as its official currency and provides for the limited issuance under certain conditions of euro coins, including euro collector coins.

5.3 Some specific legal issues characterising the EU-Vatican City relationship

One of the main reasons why the Holy See has not sought to broaden its relations with the European Union beyond a monetary agreement is because Italy is responsible for many matters touching on international relations with the Holy See, such as border controls, security and trade. As regards future relations between the Holy See and the European Union, the main focus will therefore be on spiritual matters and the promotion of human rights, particularly in the context of the new European Constitution. Article I-52 of the Constitution (status of churches and non-confessional organisations) provides, *inter alia*, for a regular dialogue between churches (including the Roman Catholic church) and the European Union.[43]

The Holy See was actively involved in the debate on the European Constitution, seeking a number of points for inclusion in the final Constitutional Treaty. These included:

42 Monetary Agreement between the Italian Republic, on behalf of the European Community, and the Vatican City State and, on its behalf, the Holy See, *OJ* 2001 C 299/1.

43 Treaty establishing a Constitution for Europe, *OJ* 2004 C 310/1.

1. The recognition of the 'institutional dimension' of religious freedom: namely, the constitutional recognition that religious communities are also political actors in their own right but in a form that is different from other actors in civil society. This point was generally acknowledged in Article I-52.
2. The recognition of an exemption from EU law for policies contrary to the church's teaching: for example, an exemption from EU rules on non-discrimination in the workplace. This request was acknowledged in Article I-52(1), which provides, 'The Union respects and does not prejudice the status under national law of churches and religious associations or communities in the Member States.'
3. Specific consultative status for the church: providing for the Catholic church to be consulted in the drafting of EC legislation on a broad range of matters of relevance for the church. This request was acknowledged in Article I-52(3) which reads: 'Recognising their identity and their specific contribution, the Union shall maintain an open, transparent and regular dialogue with these churches and organisations.'

The Holy See was unsuccessful in its efforts to have included in the European Constitution a specific reference to the Christian heritage of Europe, the final result being a general and non-specific mention of 'churches and religious associations in the Member States'.

6. GENERAL CONCLUSIONS: IMPACT OF ENLARGEMENT

In general, the micro-states recognise that it is less and less easy for small states to be outside the European Union but surrounded by EU Member States. There is the danger of becoming increasingly marginalised, particularly in an enlarged European Union of twenty-five Member States, which looks set to expand still further. In addition, because of their location within Europe and associations with particular EU Member States, EU policy and legislation is increasingly impacting on the micro-states. That said, however, the impact of the enlargement of the European Union to twenty-five Member States is not expected to be great, at least in the immediate future. The only short-term impact is extension of some of the existing agreements to the new Member States (see the Protocol to EC-San Marino Cooperation and Customs Union Agreement).

Nevertheless, EU enlargement has been partly responsible for the stepping-up of relations by the micro-states individually with the European Union. Thus, in general, the micro-states have sought to develop and broaden their existing bilateral agreements with the European Community, particularly in the context of their specific Cooperation Agreements. For example, although the EC *acquis* (i.e., the body of EC legislation) as such does not apply to the micro-states, Andorra and

San Marino have sought to extend, within the scope of their Cooperation Agreements with the European Community, the influence of the EC *acquis* in certain areas such as the environment, regional policy and tourism. The micro-states have also taken advantage of their negotiations with the European Community on the Savings Tax Directive to advance or initiate discussions in other areas of interest to them, including the euro (Andorra) and financial services (Monaco).

But what is the future for relations between the micro-states and the European Union? One option – that of full EU membership – is unlikely. Because of their small size, it would be extremely difficult for the micro-states to shoulder the administrative burden of full EU membership, and the latter is therefore not currently a realistic option.

A second option is membership of the EEA. In this way, like Liechtenstein (which is also a micro-state), the micro-states could benefit from the EU internal market without having to take on board the full responsibilities of EU membership. As with the first option, however, the micro-states would have great difficulty sustaining EEA membership on their own. Much of the administrative burden of Liechtenstein's membership of the organisation is currently supported by Switzerland. A further factor is that with only three members, two of which (Norway and Iceland) are considering full EU membership, the EEA may have a limited future.

The European Constitution includes a political declaration of intent to consider the specific position of the micro-states in the context of the European Union's relations with its neighbouring countries. Specifically, Declaration No. 11 on Article I-57 (The Union and its neighbours) provides: 'The Union will take into account the particular situation of small-sized countries which maintain specific relations of proximity with it.'

Acknowledging the growing impact of EU policy on the micro-states and the inadequacy of the current arrangement involving sectoral agreements, the European Commission has indicated its interest in exploring a new kind of association with the micro-states. The idea would be to negotiate a new framework arrangement between the European Union and micro-states under which, for example, EU legislation and policy would apply automatically to the micro-states unless the latter specifically requested otherwise. However, this new arrangement has not yet been formally discussed and is unlikely to be fully explored in the near future for lack of resources and also because of other more pressing priorities for the European Union generally. In the meantime, the present piecemeal relationship between the European Union and Andorra, Monaco, San Marino and the Vatican City is set to continue.

CHAPTER 7

BULGARIA

Adam Łazowski[*] and Svetla Yosifova[**]

Relevant legal documents:

- Treaty between the Kingdom of Belgium, the Czech Republic, the Kingdom of Denmark, the Federal Republic of Germany, the Republic of Estonia, the Hellenic Republic, the Kingdom of Spain, the French Republic, Ireland, the Italian Republic, the Republic of Cyprus, the Republic of Latvia, the Republic of Lithuania, the Grand Duchy of Luxembourg, the Republic of Hungary, the Republic of Malta, the Kingdom of the Netherlands, the Republic of Austria, the Republic of Poland, the Portuguese Republic, the Republic of Slovenia, the Slovak Republic, the Republic of Finland, the Kingdom of Sweden, the United Kingdom of Great Britain and Northern Ireland (Member States of the European Union) and the Republic of Bulgaria and Romania, concerning the accession of the Republic of Bulgaria and Romania to the European Union, *OJ* 2005 L 157/11.
- Europe Agreement establishing an association between the European Communities and their Member States, of the one part, and the Republic of Bulgaria, of the other part, *OJ* 1994 L 358/3.
- Additional Protocol to the Europe Agreement establishing an association between the European Communities and their Member States, of the one part, and the Republic of Bulgaria, of the other part, to take account of the accession of the Czech Republic, the Republic of Estonia, the Republic of Cyprus, the Republic of Latvia, the Republic of Lithuania, the Republic of Hungary, the Republic of Malta, the Republic of Poland, the Republic of Slovenia, and the Slovak Republic to the European Union, *OJ* 2005 L 155/5.
- Additional Protocol to the Europe Agreement on trade in textile products between the European Community and the Republic of Bulgaria, *OJ* 1997 L 127/2.
- Protocol adjusting trade aspects of the Europe Agreement between the European Communities and their Member States, of the one part, and the Republic of Bulgaria, of the other part, to take account of the accession of the Republic of Austria, the Republic of Finland and the Kingdom of Sweden to the European Union and the outcome of the

* Senior Lecturer in Law, School of Law, University of Westminster, London.
** Associate, PI Partners, Sofia, a law firm associated with Ernst & Young.

S. Blockmans and A. Łazowski (eds.), The European Union and Its Neighbours

Uruguay Round negotiations on agriculture, including improvements to the existing preferential arrangements, *OJ* 1999 L 112/3.

- Additional Protocol laying down the trade arrangements for fish and fishery products to the Europe Agreement establishing an association between the European Communities and their Member States, of the one part, and the Republic of Bulgaria, of the other part, *OJ* 2002 L 335/18.
- Protocol adjusting the trade aspects of the Europe Agreement establishing an association between the European Communities and their Member States, of the one part, and the Republic of Bulgaria, of the other part, to take account of the outcome of negotiations between the Parties on new mutual agricultural concessions, *OJ* 2003 L 102/65.
- Agreement between the European Community and the Republic of Bulgaria concerning the participation of the Republic of Bulgaria in the European Environment Agency and the European environment information and observation network, *OJ* 2001 L 213/66.
- Agreement between the European Community and the Republic of Bulgaria establishing certain conditions for the carriage of goods by road and the promotion of combined transport, *OJ* 2001 L 108/6.
- Agreement between the European Union and the Republic of Bulgaria establishing a framework for the participation of the Republic of Bulgaria in the EU crisis management operations, *OJ* 2005 L 46/50.
- Agreement between the European Union and the Republic of Bulgaria on the participation of the Republic of Bulgaria in the European Union Police Mission (EUPM) in Bosnia and Herzegovina (BiH), *OJ* L 2003 L 239/41.

1. THE EVOLUTION OF EU RELATIONS WITH BULGARIA

1.1 Introduction

After almost two decades of an ever-developing relationship, Bulgaria is standing on the doorstep of the European Union. Provided that everything goes according to plan, it will become a Member State on 1 January 2007. Even if the membership postponement in the Accession Treaty's safeguard clause is invoked by the Council, the European Union cannot delay the accession of Bulgaria by more than twelve months. From the Bulgarian perspective, membership seems to be a 'dream come true' scenario. With the country's weak economy, unstable political system and considerable poverty, many Bulgarians regard the accession as a magical panacea for all domestic problems. Following the signature of the Accession Treaty, the political elites are doing all they can to show their commitment to membership and by the same token to the fulfilment of the Copenhagen criteria. For the European Union, the accession of Bulgaria and Romania can be treated as a test of its capabilities and capacity. Will the European Union survive yet another enlargement? Does it have the capacity to swallow another two countries when it is itself suffering from a serious hiccup as a result of the impact of the big bang enlargement and the failure of the constitutional reform?

At the time of writing, one could argue that Bulgaria is already more of a member than a neighbour of the European Union. Indeed, this may be a very good legal and political argument, but there are a variety of reasons why the EU-Bulgaria relationship should be examined in this volume. Undoubtedly, it may serve as a basis for analysing numerous phenomena characterising the relations of the European Union with its neighbours. A closer look at the rocky road from association to membership will allow the reader to see the developing nature of the Europe Agreements from instruments for association to vital elements of the pre-accession strategy. Moreover, the EU-Bulgaria relationship may serve as a basis for the study of multidimensional conditionality and the role of financial and technical pre-accession assistance. The membership of Bulgaria and Romania should be also regarded as a testing ground for the effectiveness of various pre-accession instruments and tools supporting the fulfilment of the Copenhagen criteria. The experiences learned may be of great value when it comes to the introduction of pre-accession strategies towards the Western Balkans, where, for the time being, the European Union is a major player in the stabilisation and reconstruction of the region.[1]

This chapter is divided into three major parts. The first contains an historical overview of EU-Bulgaria relations, starting from the trade agreements of the late 1980s and ending with the signature of the Accession Treaty. This is followed by a thorough analysis of the Europe Agreement (part two) and other platforms of cooperation (part three). Last but not least, the Accession Treaty will be discussed in the fourth part of the chapter.

1.2 Association with the European Communities

In the decades preceding the fall of the Iron Curtain, the legal relations between the European Communities and Bulgaria were almost non-existent. The 1970s call of the EEC to set up a framework of general trade agreements with the countries of the Council of Mutual Economic Assistance (COMECON) remained unanswered or ignored.[2] The only international treaties bridging the gap between the two sides were a few short-lived sectoral trade agreements.[3] As was the case

---

[1] See chapter 10 in this volume.

[2] A. Mayhew, *Recreating Europe. The European Union's Policy towards Central and Eastern Europe* (Cambridge, Cambridge University Press 1998) p. 7.

[3] See, *inter alia*, Agreement between the European Economic Community and the People's Republic of Bulgaria on trade in textile products, *OJ* 1982 L 330/2; Exchange of letters between the European Economic Community and the People's Republic of Bulgaria on trade in the sheepmeat

with all the countries of Central and Eastern Europe, the ice started to melt by the end of 1980s.[4] Diplomatic relations between the EEC and Bulgaria were formally established on 9 August 1988. The conclusion of the first general bilateral trade agreement (the so-called first generation agreement) followed shortly afterwards.[5] With its entry into force on 1 November 1990, the parties received a proper legal framework for bilateral trade. Also, already in May 1990, a decision was made to extend the Phare programme beyond its initial borders and add Bulgaria to the list of beneficiaries.[6] The fall of the Communist dictatorships and the political and economic changes that rapidly started to emerge in the region forced the European Communities to adapt to this brand new geopolitical environment.[7] The trade agreements reached their limits in a very short amount of time and were soon after replaced by Europe Agreements, marking a new type of association.[8] The green light for the negotiations on the EA Bulgaria came from the European Council in April 1991.[9] In terms of its structure and contents, the agreement closely followed the earlier Europe Agreements signed with Poland, Hungary and Czechoslovakia (soon to be replaced by separate agreements with the Slovak and Czech Republics).[10] The EA Bulgaria was signed on 8 March 1993. Since it is a mixed agreement, it required ratification not only by the European Communities

and goatmeat sector, *OJ* 1982 L 43/13; Agreement between the European Economic Community and the People's Republic of Bulgaria on trade in textile products, *OJ* 1986 L 293/2.

4 For an analysis of the early years, see D. Horovitz, 'EC-Central/East European relations: New principles for a new era', 27 *CMLRev.* (1990) p. 259; D. Kennedy and D.E. Webb, 'The limits of integration: Eastern Europe and the European Communities', 30 *CMLRev.* (1993) p. 1095.

5 Agreement between the European Economic Community and the People's Republic of Bulgaria on trade and commercial and economic cooperation, *OJ* 1990 L 291/9. For an overview of the first generation agreements, see Horovitz, loc. cit. n. 4, at pp. 267-272.

6 Council Regulation (EEC) No. 2698/90 of 17 September 1990 amending Regulation (EEC) No. 3906/89 in order to extend economic aid to other countries of Central and Eastern Europe, *OJ* 1990 L 257/1.

7 See, *inter alia*, Communication from the Commission to the Council, Implications of recent changes in central and eastern Europe for the Community's relations with the countries concerned, SEC (1990) 111 final; Communication from the Commission to the Council and the Parliament, The development of Community's relations with the countries of central and eastern Europe, SEC (1990) 196 final; Communication from the Commission, The development of Community's relations with the countries of central and eastern Europe, SEC (1990) 717 final; Communication from the Commission to the Council and Parliament, Association agreements with countries of central and eastern Europe: a general outline, COM (1990) 398 final.

8 See, *inter alia*, M. Maresceau, '"Europe Agreements": A New Form of Cooperation between the European Community and Central and Eastern Europe', in P.-Ch. Müller-Graff, ed., *East Central European States and the European Communities: Legal Adaptation to the Market Economy* (Baden-Baden, Nomos 1993) p. 209; M. Maresceau and E. Montaguti, 'The relations between the European Union and Central and Eastern Europe: A legal appraisal', 32 *CMLRev.* (1995) p. 1327.

9 See Mayhew, op. cit. n. 2, at p. 21.

10 For a comparative overview of the Europe Agreements, see, *inter alia*, A. Ott and K. Inglis, eds., *Handbook on European Enlargement. A Commentary on the Enlargement Process* (The Hague, T.M.C. Asser Press 2002).

but also by its twelve Member States.[11] The ratification procedure in Bulgaria was completed smoothly on 15 April 1993. In order to speed up the entry into force of the agreement's vital trade section, an additional interim agreement was concluded.[12] It entered into force on 31 December 1993. Upon the completion of the various ratification procedures, the EA Bulgaria became operational on 1 February 1995. It was signed for an unlimited period of time, with a ten-year transitional period envisaged by Article 7(1) EA Bulgaria. The Europe Agreement will remain the key legal instrument connecting the parties up to the moment of the entry into force of the Accession Treaty of 2005. During the decade of its operation, the Europe Agreement was modified a number of times by means of additional protocols. Some of them were concluded to take account of the successive enlargements of the European Union.[13]

1.3 Towards EU membership

It was shortly after the fall of Communism that the newly independent states of Central and Eastern Europe started to express a strong desire to accede to the European Communities at the earliest possible opportunity. That being said, one should remember that the CEECs had generally rejected proposals for membership of the European Economic Area.[14] In the case of Bulgaria, it is notable that, already in December 1990, the Bulgarian Grand National Assembly had adopted a resolution placing membership on the list of priorities of Bulgarian foreign policy.[15] While the fall of Communism was met with widespread enthusiasm in

---

[11] See A. Rosas, 'The European Union and Mixed Agreements', in A. Dashwood and Ch. Hillion, eds., *The General Law of EC External Relations* (London, Sweet & Maxwell 2000) p. 200.

[12] Interim Agreement on trade and trade-related matters between the European Economic Community and the European Steel and Coal Community, of the one part, and the Republic of Bulgaria, of the other part, *OJ* 1993 L 323/1.

[13] Protocol adjusting trade aspects of the Europe Agreement between the European Communities and their Member States, of the one part, and the Republic of Bulgaria, of the other part, to take account of the accession of the Republic of Austria, the Republic of Finland and the Kingdom of Sweden to the European Union and the outcome of the Uruguay Round negotiations on agriculture, including improvements to the existing preferential arrangements, *OJ* 1999 L 112/3; Additional Protocol to the Europe Agreement establishing an association between the European Communities and their Member States, of the one part, and the Republic of Bulgaria, of the other part, to take account of the accession of the Czech Republic, the Republic of Estonia, the Republic of Cyprus, the Republic of Latvia, the Republic of Lithuania, the Republic of Hungary, the Republic of Malta, the Republic of Poland, the Republic of Slovenia, and the Slovak Republic to the European Union, *OJ* 2005 L 155/5.

[14] At that time, Peers argued that 'Although the EAs may serve well as an interim measure while the EA States become familiar with the EU legal system, a comparison of the EEA with the EAs will demonstrate that membership of the EEA is the best way of preparing EA States for EU membership'. See S. Peers, 'An ever closer waiting room?: The case for Eastern European accession to the European Economic Area', 32 *CMLRev.* (1995) p. 187 at p. 189.

[15] Source: <http://www.bulgaria.bg/Europe/EU/en/relationships/europeancommunity/default.htm>.

Western Europe, the membership aspirations of its Eastern neighbours were quite a different matter. The initial reaction of the twelve EC Member States was rather reserved, proving that the time had yet to come for this kind of commitment. In many ways, the Western European countries were taken by surprise by the rapid and unexpectedly peaceful developments behind the Iron Curtain. It turned that there was no strategy or clear plan for rearranging the relations of the European Communities with their close neighbours to the east.[16] It is only fair to mention that, in the years following the White Paper of 1985[17] and the Single European Act[18] (the first major treaty revision), the Communities were preoccupied with the implementation of the internal market programme. At the same time, the next IGC, filled with ambitious dossiers, was emerging on the horizon and the creation of the European Economic Area was pending.[19] This, together with the complex transformation that the newly born democracies had to face, meant that the EC Member States were quite reluctant to discuss the prospect of eastern enlargement. In this context, it should be stressed that 'originally, Europe Agreements were perceived by the EU more as an alternative to, rather than a preparatory instrument for, accession'.[20] Bulgaria followed the other countries of the region and decided to treat association as a step towards membership. This was mirrored in a unilateral declaration inserted into the preamble of the Europe Agreement. It read 'that Bulgaria's ultimate objective is to become a member of the Community, and that this association, in the view of the Parties, will help Bulgaria to achieve this objective.' As the ratification of the agreement progressed, the initial position of the European Communities changed, and it was ready to announce that the new democracies would have a chance to accede provided they fulfilled the membership criteria.[21] This landmark decision was taken during the Copenhagen European Council in June 1993.[22] Following a Governmental Declaration of 14 April 1994, Bulgaria submitted its formal application for membership on 14 December 1995.

---

[16] Mayhew, op. cit. n. 2, at pp. 12-14.

[17] Completing the Internal Market: White Paper from the Commission to the European Council, COM (1985) 310 final.

[18] Single European Act, *OJ* 1987 L 169/1.

[19] See chapter 4 in this volume.

[20] M. Maresceau, 'Pre-accession', in M. Cremona, ed., *The Enlargement of the European Union* (Oxford, Oxford University Press 2003) p. 9 at p. 15.

[21] See Ch. Hillion, 'The Copenhagen Criteria and Their Progeny', in Ch. Hillion, ed., *EU Enlargement. A Legal Approach* (Oxford and Portland Oregon, Hart Publishing 2004) p. 1; F. Hoffmeister, 'Changing requirements for membership', in Ott and Inglis, op. cit. n. 10, at p. 90.

[22] Presidency Conclusions, Copenhagen European Council of 21-22 June 1993, *Bull. EU* 6-1993, point 13.

The developments initiated by the Copenhagen European Council paved the way for the adoption of an unprecedented pre-accession strategy. Another important boost came from the Essen European Council in December 1994.[23] Due to the complexity of the process and the level of development of the applicant countries, the previous enlargements could not serve as a model. As noted by Kirstyn Inglis, 'No other enlargement has focused on so many and such a diversity of countries, nor indeed on countries so dramatically different from the Union in political and economic terms'.[24] A number of tools have been used as a part of this strategy. The main legal instruments have been the Europe Agreements, reoriented from mere association treaties into a pivotal pre-accession vehicle.[25] A patchwork of other instruments has included various policy instruments and, at a later stage, Accession Partnerships. The first major step was the European Commission's White Paper on the preparation of the CEECs for integration into the internal market,[26] which identified the internal market *acquis* that the aspiring countries were supposed to transpose and implement.

At the end of 1995, the European Council requested the European Commission to present its opinion on the membership applications that had by then been submitted by all the countries of Central and Eastern Europe. The batch of opinions was presented on 15 July 1997, together with a policy document entitled Agenda 2000. In terms of negotiations, it was suggested that the Czech Republic, Estonia, Hungary, Poland and Slovenia had achieved enough progress to start the negotiations.[27] In the case of Bulgaria, the opinion was negative.[28] Although the political criteria were generally satisfied, the European Commission identified numerous shortcomings in the fulfilment of the economic criteria and in the approximation of laws.[29] Moreover, Bulgaria did not have the necessary institutional capacity. In its conclusions, the Commission stated that

> Bulgaria's progress in the creation of a market economy has been limited by the absence of a commitment to market-oriented economic policies. Early liberalisation of trade and prices was partially reversed, and price controls were not removed

---

23 Presidency Conclusions, Essen European Council of 9-10 December 1994, *Bull. EU* 12-1994.

24 K. Inglis, 'The Europe Agreements compared in the light of their pre-accession reorientation', 37 *CMLRev.* (2000) p. 1173 at p. 1176.

25 Ibid.

26 White Paper – Preparation of the candidate countries of Central and Eastern Europe for integration into the Internal Market of the Union, COM (1995) 163 final.

27 Cyprus was also included on the list. At that time, the application for membership of Malta was frozen for internal political reasons.

28 Commission Opinion on Bulgaria's Application for Membership of the European Union, DOC/97/11.

29 See I. Shikova, 'Status and Tendencies in Bulgaria', in P.-Ch. Müller-Graff, ed., *East Central Europe and the European Union: From Europe Agreements to a Member Status* (Baden-Baden, Nomos 1997) p. 251.

> until this year. It is only since the crisis at the end of last year and the recent change of government that consensus about the desirability of economic reforms has began to develop.[30]

Bearing this in mind, the European Commission expressed doubts as to Bulgaria's capability of coping with competitive market forces in the European Union. The approximation of laws proved to be yet another major problem. Bulgaria not only had a considerable backlog with regard to the transposition of the *acquis*, but also suffered from a very limited capacity to implement newly adopted legislation. As the Commission noted, 'the weakness of public administration is a major problem, putting in question both the rate and the quality of approximation of legislation.'[31] In its final remarks, the European Commission argued that negotiations with Bulgaria could be opened as soon as the country made sufficient progress in its fulfilment of the Copenhagen criteria. This was considered to be the case two years later, and Bulgaria joined the group of negotiating countries following a decision by the Helsinki European Council in December 1999.[32] In the meantime, Bulgaria fell under the enhanced pre-accession strategy.[33] The Accession Partnerships – the main policy instruments of this strategy – are based on Council Regulation 622/98/EC[34] and are updated regularly,[35] allowing Bulgaria to respond with updates and adjustments of its own national plan for the adoption of the *acquis* (NPAA).[36] An important role has also been played by the European Commission's annual progress reports.[37] Shortly

---

30 Commission Opinion on Bulgaria's Application for Membership of the European Union, DOC/97/11, p. 119.

31 Ibid., at p. 120.

32 Presidency Conclusions, Helsinki European Council of 10-11 December 1999, *Bull. EU* 12-1999.

33 See, *inter alia*, K. Inglis, 'The Pre-accession Strategy and the Accession Partnerships', in Ott and Inglis, op. cit. n. 10, at p. 103.

34 Council Regulation (EC) No. 622/98 of 16 March 1998 on assistance to the applicant States in the framework of the pre-accession strategy, and in particular on the establishment of Accession Partnerships, *OJ* 1998 L 85/1.

35 Council Decision 1999/857/EC of 6 December 1999 on the principles, priorities, intermediate objectives and conditions contained in the Accession Partnership with the Republic of Bulgaria, *OJ* 1999 L 335/48; Council Decision 2002/83/EC of 28 January 2002 on the principles, priorities, intermediate objectives and conditions contained in the Accession Partnership with Bulgaria, *OJ* 2002 L 44/1; Council Decision 2003/396/EC of 19 May 2003 on the principles, priorities, intermediate objectives and conditions contained in the Accession Partnership with Bulgaria, *OJ* 2003 L 145/1.

36 See chapter 3 in this volume.

37 1998 Regular Report from the Commission on Bulgaria's progress towards accession, COM (1998) 707 final; 1999 Regular Report from the Commission on Bulgaria's progress towards accession, COM (1999) 501 final; 2000 Regular Report from the Commission on Bulgaria's progress towards accession, COM (2000) 701 final; 2001 Regular Report on Bulgaria's progress towards accession, SEC (2001) 1744; 2002 Regular Report on Bulgaria's progress towards accession, COM

before the Copenhagen European Council in 2002, the European Commission also published roadmaps for Bulgaria and Romania.[38] The latter were tailored to support the pre-accession efforts of both countries to meet the remaining criteria for membership by identifying the tasks ahead and providing increased financial assistance.[39] Following screening and a political decision in December 1999, the negotiations started in February 2000. The negotiation framework and underlying principles were the same as for the first group of countries.[40] Neither Bulgaria nor Romania managed to catch up with the other ten candidate countries, so they could not participate in the big bang enlargement. The Presidency Conclusions from the Copenhagen European Council explicitly stated that the 'successful conclusion of accession negotiations with ten candidates lends new dynamism to the accession of Bulgaria and Romania as a part of the same inclusive and irreversible enlargement process'.[41] Following their participation in the work of the European Convention, both countries were also invited to participate in the Intergovernmental Conference as observers. The accession negotiations were officially completed on 14 December 2004 and this was followed by the signature of the Accession Treaty on 25 April 2005. At the time of writing, the ratification procedure is pending.

2. EUROPE AGREEMENT

2.1 Introductory remarks

In this section, the EA Bulgaria will be analysed in detail. We will start with an overview of the aims and purposes of the agreement. This will be followed by a discussion on the substantive provisions of the agreement and its provisions on the approximation of laws in particular. Separate sections are devoted to the application of the agreement at domestic level by its contracting parties.

2.2 Aims of the association

The objectives of the association are spelled out in general terms in Article 1 EA Bulgaria. Taking into account the developments of the bilateral relationship, it is

---

(2002) 700 final; 2003 Regular Report on Bulgaria's progress towards accession, COM (2003) 676 final; 2004 Regular Report on Bulgaria's progress towards accession, COM (2004) 657 final.

38 Communication from the Commission to the Council and the European Parliament – Roadmaps for Bulgaria and Romania, COM (2002) 624 final.

39 Ibid., at p. 2.

40 See C. Banasiński, 'The Negotiations Decision-Making Machinery', 25 *PolYIL* (2001) p. 69.

41 Presidency Conclusions, Copenhagen European Council of 12-13 December 2002, *Bull. EU* 12-2002, point. 13.

submitted that this provision deserves a dynamic interpretation, bearing in mind the pre-accession reorientation of the Europe Agreement. The provision in question states that the objectives of the association are:

- to provide an appropriate framework for the political dialogue between the Parties allowing the developments of close political relations,
- to establish gradually a free trade area between the Community and Bulgaria covering substantially all trade between them,
- to promote the expansion of trade and the harmonious economic relations between the Parties and to foster the dynamic economic development and prosperity in Bulgaria,
- to provide a basis for economic, financial, cultural and social cooperation, as well as for the Community's assistance to Bulgaria,
- to support Bulgaria's efforts to develop its economy and to complete the transition into a market economy,
- to provide an appropriate framework for the gradual integration of Bulgaria into the Community. To this end new rules, policies and practices will be established in compliance with market mechanisms, and Bulgaria shall work towards fulfilling the necessary requirements in this respect,
- to set up institutions suitable to make the association effective.

It is questionable to what extent these broad and ambitious aims have been achieved. It is even more questionable to what extent they could have been achieved without the prospect of membership on the horizon and the transformation of the Europe Agreement into the pre-accession vehicle. On the other hand, it is beyond any doubt that the agreement played an important role in the last decade as a basic legal framework for the multidimensional bilateral relationship. One should particularly acknowledge its trade part, which has been the basis for the gradual creation of the free trade area. Also, the sixth *tiret* should not go unnoticed. It is quite astonishing to note that, on the one hand, the agreement has been envisaged as a framework for gradual integration,[42] while, on the other, the membership desire was only spelled out in a unilateral declaration. It is also interesting to note that the latter provision was interpreted dynamically by the European Court of Justice. For example, in its judgment in Case C-235/99 *The Queen and Secretary of State for the Home Department, ex parte: Eleanora Ivanova Kondova*,[43] the ECJ held that

[42] Moreover, Art. 2 EA Bulgaria is very clear in saying that the political dialogue conducted in the framework of the Europe Agreement 'will facilitate Bulgaria's full integration into the community of democratic nations and progressive rapprochement with the Community'.

[43] ECJ, Case C-235/99 *The Queen and Secretary of State for the Home Department, ex parte: Eleanora Ivanova Kondova* [2001] *ECR* I-6427.

according to the 17th recital in its preamble and Article 1(2), the objective of the Association Agreement is to establish an association designed to promote the expansion of trade and harmonious economic relations between the Contracting Parties, in order to foster dynamic economic development and prosperity in the Republic of Bulgaria, with a view to facilitating its accession to the Community.[44]

In institutional terms, the Europe Agreement proved to be a very good platform for the political dialogue, serving not only the association as such but also the implementation of the pre-accession strategy.

2.3 Substantive provisions

It has already been noted that the EA Bulgaria is very broad in terms of its content and that it therefore constitutes a comprehensive legal framework for bilateral relations. That being said, it will not have skipped readers' attention that the EA Bulgaria is similar to other Europe Agreements in many ways. For example, the opening provisions are devoted to the multilevel political dialogue and general principles (Arts. 2-7). The aims of the first are very considerable and include, *inter alia*, improving mutual understanding and increasing 'convergence of positions on international issues.' Article 6 makes respect of democratic principles and fundamental rights 'an essential element of the association'.

The economic part of the agreement is dominated by provisions on the free movement of goods (Arts. 8-37).[45] Article 8 envisages the creation of a free trade area within a ten-year transitional period. In common with the other Europe Agreements, no provision is made for the free movement of workers. However, Article 38 EA Bulgaria contains a non-discrimination clause guaranteeing that 'the treatment accorded to workers of Bulgarian nationality, legally employed in the territory of a Member State, shall be free from any discrimination based on nationality, as regards working conditions, remuneration or dismissal, as compared to its own nationals'.[46] As proved by the judgment of the ECJ in Case C-456/01 *Commission* v. *Austria*, a breach of this type of obligation may lead to an infraction procedure.[47] Article 45 EA Bulgaria deals with the right of establishment. It

---

44 Para. 36 of the judgment.

45 For a comparative overview, see P. Koutrakos, 'Free Movement of Goods under the Europe Agreements', in Ott and Inglis, op. cit. n. 10, at p. 369.

46 See ECJ, Case C-438/00 *Deutscher Handballbund eV* v. *Maros Kolpak* [2003] *ECR* I-4135. The case dealt with the EA Slovakia. However, due to the similarity of the wording, the ECJ's conclusions are applicable *mutatis mutandis* to the EA Bulgaria. For a comparative overview, see E. Guild, 'Workers', in Ott and Inglis, op. cit. n. 10, at p. 427.

47 ECJ, Case C-465/01 *Commission of the European Communities* v. *Republic of Austria* [2004] *ECR* I-8291.

creates an obligation for each Member State to grant, for the establishment and operation of Bulgarian nationals and companies in its territory, a treatment no less favourable than that accorded to its own companies and nationals.[48] In Case C-235/99 *The Queen and Secretary of State for the Home Department, ex parte: Eleanora Ivanova Kondova*, the ECJ ruled that the provision in question fulfils the requirements of the direct effect test. Other key provisions of the EA Bulgaria deal with the supply of services (Arts. 56-58), payments, capital, economic cooperation and public procurement (Arts. 60-97), cultural cooperation (Art. 98) and financial cooperation (Arts. 99-104). Articles 69-71 EA Bulgaria deal with the approximation of laws. Because of their importance, they are discussed separately in the next section.

2.4 Approximation of laws

The transposition and implementation of the *acquis communautaire* is definitely a *conditio sine qua non* for EU membership. In many areas of law, the transposition has been successfully completed, but it is the implementation that creates particular difficulties for Bulgaria. The country's internal problems and capacity limitations in this regard are not unique. On the contrary, similar problems have been witnessed in all the new Member States from Central and Eastern Europe. As Allan Mayhew has noted: 'while the problems of adapting the Community *acquis* are considerable, the problems of implementing the legislation are even more daunting.'[49] Legal approximation thus goes far beyond the mere transposition of the EU legislation into the domestic legal framework, and it is undoubtedly a time-consuming, complex and costly exercise that has a voluntary aspect.[50] In the case of countries like Bulgaria, the approximation activities are part of a wider process of legal reform related to the economic transition and Europeanisation of the domestic legal system. In numerous areas of law, the legal framework is being created from scratch.

Bearing the above in mind, it is worth taking a closer look at the EA Bulgaria's provisions on the approximation of laws and to consider them in the light of the agreement's pre-accession reorientation.[51] In the case of the EA Bulgaria, Articles 69-71 are relevant here. The first of these articles provides that

[48] For a comparative overview, see W. Weiß, 'Establishment', in Ott and Inglis, op. cit. n. 10, at p. 449.

[49] Mayhew, op. cit. n. 2, at p. 221.

[50] A. Evans, 'Voluntary Harmonization in Integration between the European Community and Eastern Europe', 22 *ELR* (1997) p. 207.

[51] For a comparative overview, see, *inter alia*, A. Łazowski, 'Approximation of Laws', in Ott and Inglis, op. cit. n. 10, at p. 631.

> The Parties recognise that an important condition for Bulgaria's economic integration into the Community is the approximation of Bulgaria's existing and future legislation to that of the Community. Bulgaria shall endeavour to ensure that its legislation will be gradually made compatible with that of the Community.

A literal interpretation of this provision may lead to the incorrect assumption that the obligation enshrined therein is a mere 'best endeavours' clause and that the negative consequences of non-compliance will therefore be limited. It is submitted here that approximation clause requires dynamic interpretation, taking into account Bulgaria's forthcoming membership of the European Union. The list of fields of law where approximation shall be given priority therefore exceeds the wording of Article 70 EA Bulgaria,[52] and covers the whole *acquis communautaire* as well as legislation from the second and third pillars of the European Union.[53] Moreover, in common with the other acceding countries, Bulgaria is required to adapt its international obligations to those of the European Union. In some cases, this will lead to the termination or amendment of international treaties that are binding on Bulgaria (including, for example, the Central European Free Trade Agreement).[54] Upon accession, Bulgaria will become a party to countless agreements concluded by the European Communities or the European Union (in some cases this will require the adoption of additional protocols).[55] Finally, it should be noted that, although Bulgaria has considerable freedom when it comes to the order and methods of approximation, it should follow the Accession Partnership and the roadmap, as mirrored in the national plan for adoption of the *acquis* (NPAA).

For objective and rather obvious reasons, approximation is mainly conducted by legislative means. In most cases, this leads to the adoption of normative acts, mainly acts of Parliament and executive acts adopted by the various branches of government. The list of sources of law in Bulgaria includes, *inter alia*, and in descending hierarchical order,[56] the Constitution, international treaties, acts of

---

52 Art. 70 EA Bulgaria reads: 'The approximation of laws shall extend to the following areas in particular: customs law, company law, banking law, company accounts and taxes, intellectual property, protection of workers at the workplace, financial services, rules on competition, protection of health and life of humans, animals and plants, consumer protection, indirect taxation, technical rules and standards, nuclear law and regulation, transport and the environment.'

53 On approximation in the third pillar, see A. Łazowski, 'Implementation of the Third Pillar Acquis. A Challenge for the Applicant Countries?', in G. de Kerchove and A. Weyembergh, eds., *Sécurité et justice: enjeu de la politique extérieure de l'Union européenne* (Brussels, Éditions de L'Université de Bruxelles 2003) p. 157.

54 The experiences of the new Member States of the European Union may serve as an excellent example in this respect. See, *inter alia*, E. Piontek, 'European Union Membership and Obligations under Bilateral and Multilateral Agreements to which Poland is a Party', 25 *PolYIL* (2001) p. 127.

55 Art. 6 of the Act.

56 D. Milkova, *General theory of law* [Обща теория на правото] (Sofia, Albatross Publishers 2000) pp. 167-188.

Parliament, acts of the Council of Ministers, acts of any of the Ministers and acts of local government.[57] Other sources include custom, the general principles of law and justice.[58] The dominance of legislative approximation was recently emphasised in a judgment of the Bulgarian Constitutional Tribunal, which noted that

> Today the supranational, direct, immediate and horizontal effect of the law of the EU on the territories of the Member States is a fundamental principle, established in the case law of the European Court of Justice more than four decades ago… However, here it is of importance to clarify that the supranational, direct, immediate and horizontal effect of the law of the EU, is inherent to the provisions contained in the founding treaties, and upon its ratification, to the provisions of the Treaty establishing a Constitution for Europe. With regard to the acts of secondary (institutional) law, it is only the regulations and as an exception to the principle for approximation of national legislation, some directives of the European Union that possess supranational, direct, immediate and horizontal effect.[59]

In the above-mentioned judgment, the Court acknowledged that although it is possible for secondary sources of EU law, and directives in particular, to possess direct effect, in the majority of cases they require transposition into national law. This is of particular importance when it comes to the implementation of directives, which, as evident from the case law of the European Court of Justice, are tools for the harmonisation of law. The cut-and-paste method is thus not necessarily the best *modus operandi*. We should not forget that the process of

[57] The Constitution of 1991 is the first to provide for the supremacy and direct effect of the Constitution and the primacy of international treaties over national law. Pursuant to Art. 5(4) of the Constitution, all international treaties that have been ratified by the Parliament, promulgated in the State Gazette and are in force for Bulgaria become part of domestic law and have primacy over colliding provisions of national law. However the Constitutional Court held that if a provision of the Constitution collides with a provision of an international treaty, the constitutional provision shall prevail. If any of the above prerequisites has not been fulfilled, the international treaty is in force for Bulgaria but does not become part of the legal order of the country and does not have primacy over conflicting national law. This creates a number of practical implications, as not all international treaties ratified in the course of last fifteen years have been duly promulgated in the State Gazette. In this regard, the Constitutional Tribunal ruled that in order to establish whether or not an international treaty has primacy over national law, it should be established whether at the time of the adoption of the treaty there existed a statutory obligation to promulgate it. If such an obligation did not exist, then the treaty is part of the national law of Bulgaria. Nowadays, there is a trend towards promulgating the treaties that have not been promulgated at the time of their ratification for the sake of legal certainty. However, this belated promulgation may not remedy the lack of due and timely promulgation and does not have retroactive effect.

[58] Art. 4 of the Code of Civil Procedure reads: 'The court shall decide on the case according to the exact meaning of the laws in force and when they [the laws] are incomplete, unclear or contradictory – according to their common sense. When there is no law the court shall base its judgments on the custom and the founding principles of law and the justice'.

[59] J-5/10.05.2005 of the CC on C-10/2004.

implementing the *acquis* should reflect the fact that approximation is not at all comparable to dressing up Bulgarian legislation in a new European garment. It is therefore regrettable that in many cases the transposition of secondary legislation is quite often carried out by copying directives into Bulgarian law. This is understandable when it comes to the transposition of directives, which harmonise technical standards,[60] but it is questionable in a majority of other cases. An instructive example is formed by a series of regulations, adopted jointly by the Minister of Labour and Social Policy and the Minister of Health, that implement the individual's safety and health at work directives within the meaning of Article 16(1) of Directive 89/391/EC.[61]

One should remember that Bulgaria has an obligation to approximate its domestic law to the third pillar *acquis*. A good example of such national legislation is the Extradition and European Arrest Warrant Act,[62] which implements Council Framework Decision 2002/584/JHA on the European Arrest Warrant (EAW).[63]

---

[60] For example, the approximation of the laws of the Member States with regard to technical requirements to two- and three-wheeled motor vehicles. In Bulgaria, the Minister of Transport and Telecommunications adopted eleven regulations *en bloc* on 10 January 2005, including, but not limited to: Regulation No. 121 of 10 January 2005 on stands for two-wheel motor vehicles, which implements Council Directive 93/31/EEC, *OJ* 1993 L 188/19; Regulation No. 122 of 10 January 2005 on passenger stand-holds on two-wheel motor vehicles, which implements Council Directive 93/32/EEC, *OJ* 1993 L 188/28; Regulation No. 123 of 10 January 2005 on protective devices intended to prevent the unauthorised use of two- or three-wheel motor vehicles, which implements Council Directive 93/33/EEC, *OJ* 1993 L 188/32; Regulation No. 124 of 10 January 2005 on statutory markings for two- or three-wheel vehicles, which implements Council Directive 93/34/EEC, *OJ* 1993 L 188/38; Regulation No. 125 of 10 January 2005 on the installation of lighting and light-signalling devices on two- or three-wheel motor vehicles, which implements Council Directive 93/92/EEC, *OJ* 1993 L 311/1; Regulation No. 126 of 10 January 2005 on the masses and dimensions of two- or three-wheel motor vehicles, which implements Council Directive 93/93/EEC, *OJ* 1993 L 311/76; Regulation No. 127 of 10 January 2005 relating to the space for mounting the rear registration plate of two- or three-wheel motor vehicles, which implements Council Directive 93/94/EEC, *OJ* 1993 L 311/83, etc.

[61] Regulation No. 3 of 5 May 2005 on minimum health and safety requirements regarding the exposure of workers to risks arising from vibration, which implements Directive 2002/44/EC, *OJ* 2002 L177/13; Regulation No. 6 of 15 August 2005 on minimum requirements of health and safety protection of workers from the risks related to noise exposure at work, which implements Directive 2003/10/EEC, *OJ* 2003 L 42/38; Regulation No. 7 of 15 August 2005 on the minimum health and safety requirements for work with display screens, which implements Directive 90/270/EEC, *OJ* 1990 L 156/14; Regulation No. 11 of 27 December 2004 on minimum requirements for improving the health and safety protection of workers potentially at risk from explosive atmospheres, which implements Directive 1999/92/EC, *OJ* 1999 L 23/57.

[62] Закон за екстрадицията и Европейската заповед за арест, ДВ бр. 46/03.06.2005 г. [Extradition and European Arrest Warrant Act, promulgated in State Gazette No. 46 of 3 June 2005].

[63] Council Framework Decision 2002/584/JHA of 13 June 2002 on the European arrest warrant, *OJ* 2002 L 190/1. On the EAW, see, *inter alia*, R. Blekxtoon and W. van Ballegooij, eds., *Handbook on the European Arrest Warrant* (The Hague, T.M.C. Asser Press 2004); M. Płachta, 'European Arrest Warrant: Revolution in Extradition?' 2 *European Journal of Crime, Criminal Law and Criminal Justice* (2003) p. 177; J. Wouters and F. Naert, 'Of arrest warrants, terrorist offences and

The parts of this act dealing with extradition entered into force on 4 July 2005, but its provisions on the EAW will only enter into force upon accession (Arts. 35-65).[64] In this context, one should note that the Bulgarian Constitution prohibits the extradition of own nationals, although a recent revision facilitates exceptions. No major constitutional problems (once EAW provisions enter into force), witnessed for example in Poland, are therefore expected.[65] The new legislation was tailored to fill the legal vacuum of domestic law with regard to extradition. Previously, the Code of Criminal Procedure made provision for extradition proceedings, but of a depth and detail that were insufficient for dealing with the increase in international organised crime and recent developments in EU law.[66] Articles 35-65 of the act set forth the legal framework of surrender based on the EAW. They deal with the scope of applicability, contents, exceptions to the principle of double criminality, and procedures under the EAW. The competent executing judicial authority is the regional court of the domicile or place of establishment of the person regarding whom execution of the EAW has been requested. The competent central authority is the Ministry of Justice.

Having presented some examples of approximated legislation, it is worth taking a closer look at the priorities listed in the last version of the Accession Partnership, based on Council Decision 2003/396/EC.[67] The 'to do' list is very long, running from reform of the judiciary to agricultural law. In some cases, it touches upon issues that are only indirectly connected to EU law and as such are not regulated by the latter. The prime example is reform of the judicial system. Priorities in this regard include the implementation of the National Reform Strategy for the Bulgarian Judicial System, the improvement of judicial proceedings in order to reduce the length of trials and the adoption of an appropriate financial framework for the judiciary. The fight against corruption has also found a place

extradition deals: An appraisal of the EU's main criminal law measures against terrorism after "11 September"', 41 *CMLRev.* (2004) p. 909.

64 Except for Arts. 35-65, which will enter into force on the date of entry into force of the Accession Treaty.

65 See A. Łazowski, 'Constitutional Tribunal on the Surrender of Polish Citizens under the European Arrest Warrant. Decision of 27 April 2005', 1 *EuConst* (2005) p. 569.

66 Art. 2 of the Act sets forth a definition of extradition: the surrender of a person established on the territory of Bulgaria against whom have been initiated criminal proceedings in the requesting state or before an international court of justice; the surrender of a person in order to execute a custodial sentence or detention order against him/her issued by the judicial authorities of the requesting state or an international court of justice. Art. 3 provides a definition of the European Arrest Warrant. Pursuant to Art. 4, the Act is applicable when there exists an international treaty, to which Bulgaria is a party. In cases where there is no such treaty, the Act is applicable on the basis of the principle of reciprocity. Arts. 5-8 lay down the requirements for the admission of extradition proceedings, e.g., the principle of double criminality. Arts. 9-34 set out the extradition procedure and the legal consequences of the admission of extradition.

67 Council Decision 2003/396/EC of 19 May 2003 on the principles, priorities, intermediate objectives and conditions contained in the Accession Partnership with Bulgaria, *OJ* 2003 L 145/1.

on the list of priorities. The areas of law in which the approximation of laws was found to be necessary include, *inter alia*, New Approach Directives, the *acquis* on chemical substances, motor vehicles, quality of foodstuffs, mutual recognition of diplomas and aliens law. It is interesting and astonishing to note that the Accession Partnership talks explicitly about the amendment of the Bulgarian Constitution to facilitate EU citizens' electoral rights enshrined in Article 19 TEC.[68] This is understandable when it comes to electoral rights in municipal elections, but it is rather questionable when it comes to elections to the European Parliament, since this is not required in relation to the existing Member States.

Other methods of approximation such as a 'pro-European interpretation of law' are very rarely used in the case law of the courts and in the practice of the regulatory authorities. One of the few examples of a judgment of the Supreme Administrative Court that refers to the EA Bulgaria is the judgment delivered in the *'168 HOURS' EOOD* v. *the Competition Protection Commission* case.[69] The claimant, a leading Bulgarian mass media company, submitted a motion for the judicial review of a decision in which the CPC imposed a penalty for a violation of Article 34(6) of the Competition Protection Act. In this case, the Court held that

> The concept of misleading advertising has been defined in the provisions of Article 2(3) of Council Directive 84/450/EEC.[70] The prescriptions of said Directive on protection against misleading advertising have been further developed in Directive 97/55/EC[71] of the European Parliament and the Council. Under the Competition Protection Act, the recommendations of the European Directives are fully taken into consideration by the Bulgarian legislator in the implementation of Articles 69-70 of the Europe Agreement … and in compliance with the undertaken obligation to approximate our legislation with that of the Community and to harmonise the measures granting administrative protection against misleading advertising and its prohibited effect on the consumers, competitors and the public interest.

---

[68] See also Council Directive 93/109/EC of 6 December 1993 laying down detailed arrangements for the exercise of the right to vote and stand as a candidate in elections to the European Parliament for citizens of the Union residing in a Member State of which they are not nationals, *OJ* 1993 L 329/34; Council Directive 94/80/EC of 19 December 1994 laying down detailed arrangements for the exercise of the right to vote and to stand as a candidate in municipal elections by citizens of the Union residing in a Member State of which they are not nationals, *OJ* 1994 L 368/38. For an academic appraisal, see, *inter alia*, P. Oliver, 'Electoral rights under article 8B of the Treaty of Rome', 33 *CMLRev.* (1996) p. 473.

[69] J-4420/30.07.1999 of the SAC on C-1257/1999.

[70] Council Directive 84/450/EEC of 10 September 1984 relating to the approximation of the laws, regulations and administrative provisions of the Member States concerning misleading advertising, *OJ* 1984 L 250/17.

[71] Directive 97/55/EC of European Parliament and of the Council of 6 October 1997 amending Directive 84/450/EEC concerning misleading advertising so as to include comparative advertising, *OJ* 1997 L 290/18.

There is an abundant case law of the Supreme Administrative Court in relation to the review of decisions of the Competition Protection Commission and, in particular, the review of penalties imposed under Article 34(6) of the Competition Protection Act. However, there are hardly any references to the case law of the Supreme Administrative Court and other Bulgarian courts. The main reason for this is that Bulgaria belongs to the family of civil law countries, and the case law of its courts is therefore not a source of law. This is the sole reason why this judgment delivered in the late 1990s has not been taken forward by the Bulgarian courts.

Another interesting judgment[72] of the Supreme Administrative Court was delivered, when a Bulgarian NGO seized the court with a claim regarding the compliance with Bulgarian legislation of a provision of an act of the Bulgarian Government,[73] which set forth the requirements for the photograph that should appear on the personal identification documents of Bulgarian citizens. Pursuant to this provision, a Bulgarian citizen may not use a photograph on which he or she wears a headscarf or hat on his or her identification document. The claimant maintained before the Court that this 'violated fundamental human rights and freedoms and facilitated indirect discrimination on the grounds of religion of those people whose traditional garments included wearing head or face scarves and hats.' The Court referred to Council Directive 2000/43/EC[74] and Council Directive 2000/78/EC[75] in order to substantiate its definition of the meaning of 'indirect discrimination'. It held that the limitation of fundamental human rights did not violate existing Bulgarian law or international legal instruments that are in force for Bulgaria, as the admissibility of this limitation of fundamental rights and freedoms was based on the priority of the public interest.

With regard to the case law of the Constitutional Court, it is worth mentioning the judgment delivered in May 2005 on the compliance with the Bulgarian Constitution of certain provisions of the Sea Spaces, Internal Waterways and Ports of Republic of Bulgaria Act.[76] By means of amendments to this act, the Bulgarian Parliament tried to establish a new state-owned enterprise with the power to

[72] J-11820/19.12.2002 of the SAC on C-7035/2002.

[73] Приложение No. 3 т.12 към Правилника за издаване на български документи за самоличност [Annex No. 3 i.12 to the Rules of Procedure for the issuance of Bulgarian identification documents].

[74] Council Directive 2000/43/EC of 29 June 2000 implementing the principle of equal treatment between persons irrespective of racial or ethnic origin, *OJ* 2000 L 180/22.

[75] Council Directive 2000/78/EC of 27 November 2000 establishing a general framework for equal treatment in employment and occupation, *OJ* 2000 L 303/16.

[76] J-5/10.05.2005 of the CC on C-10/2004. For the Act, see Закон за морските пространства, вътрешните водни пътища и пристанищата на Република България, обн. ДВ бр. 24/2004 г. [Sea Spaces, Internal Waterways and Ports of the Republic of Bulgaria Act, promulgated in State Gazette No. 24 of 2004].

perform functions previously falling within the competences of the executive ports agency of the Ministry of Transport. Under the amendment act, it was solely within the powers of the new enterprise to grant access to the Bulgarian ports, to collect port fees and decide on their disbursement, to implement port safety regulations, etc. The Court referred to a draft directive of the European Parliament and the Council on access to markets concerning the ports of the Member States.[77] In its judgment, the Court held that 'Art. 11(1) of the Draft Directive as an exception and subject to various limitations allows for the possibility that the managing body of the port may perform business activities, together with its state functions imposed by the national legislation.' Eventually, the Court declared some of the provisions of the act of Parliament unconstitutional.

2.5 Institutional framework of the association

The institutional framework created on the basis of the EA Bulgaria follows the pattern known from other Europe Agreements.[78] Three joint EC-Bulgaria institutions – the Association Council, the Association Committee and the Association Parliamentary Committee – have been equipped with powers to secure the proper implementation of the agreement. Moreover, Article 3 EA Bulgaria envisages a central role in the political dialogue for the Presidents of the Council, European Commission and Bulgaria. It should be noted that the role of these joint EC-Bulgaria bodies has developed in the course of the association and that they have been entrusted with an important role in implementing the enhanced pre-accession strategy. The political decision to this end was adopted by the Luxembourg European Council in 1997 and was inserted into the EU legal framework by Council Regulation 622/98/EC. The last recital of its preamble confirms that 'the role played by the bodies set up under the Europe Agreements is central to ensuring the proper implementation and follow-up of … Accession Partnerships'.

The Association Council is composed of members of the Council of the European Union and members of the European Commission, on the EU side, and persons appointed by the Bulgarian Government, on the other.[79] It has considerable decision-making powers, including the right to adopt binding decisions. Examples of the latter include Decision No. 1/2003, amending Protocol 4 to the Europe Agreement, concerning the definition of the concept of 'originating

---

[77] Proposal for a Directive of the European Parliament and of the Council on market access to port services, COM (2004) 654 final.

[78] See A. Evans, 'Institutions', in Ott and Inglis, op. cit. n. 10, at p. 1043.

[79] For an overview of procedural rules, see Decision No. 1/95 of the Association Council between the European Communities and their Member States, of the one part, and the Republic of Bulgaria, of the other part, of 29 May 1995 adopting its rules of procedure, *OJ* 1995 L 255/19.

products' and methods of administrative cooperation[80] and Decision No. 3/2002 adopting the terms and conditions for Bulgaria's participation in the Community Fiscalis programme.[81] The Association Council also plays a central role in the dispute settlement machinery.[82] The Association Council is assisted by an Association Committee.[83] It may also set up special committees. An important political role is also played by the Association Parliamentary Committee, which is composed of members of the Bulgarian Parliament and the European Parliament.

2.6 Application of the Europe Agreement in the EU legal system

So far, the European Court of Justice has not had many opportunities to deal with the EA Bulgaria.[84] However, because of their similar wording, the Court's case law based on other Europe Agreements is applicable *mutatis mutandis* to the EA Bulgaria.[85]

The leading judicial opinion on the EA Bulgaria is the ECJ's judgment in Case C-235/99 *The Queen and Secretary of State for the Home Department, ex parte: Eleanora Ivanova Kondova*. The reference for a preliminary ruling was submitted by the High Court of Justice of England and Wales and dealt with the interpretation of Articles 45 and 59 EA Bulgaria. The ECJ held that Article 45(1) EA

[80] Decision No. 1/2003 of the EU-Bulgaria Association Council of 4 June 2003 amending Protocol 4 to the Europe Agreement, concerning the definition of the concept of 'originating products' and methods of administrative cooperation, *OJ* 2003 L 191/1.

[81] Decision No. 3/2002 of the EU-Bulgaria Association Council of 20 November 2002 adopting the terms and conditions for Bulgaria's participation in the Community Fiscalis programme, *OJ* 2003 L 47/41.

[82] See J. Gomuła, 'Dispute Settlement under Association Agreements with Central and Eastern European States', 22 *PolYIL* (1995-1996) p. 107.

[83] The Association Committee is composed of representatives of the Council of the European Union, the European Commission and the Bulgarian Government (at senior civil servant level). See Art. 109 EA Bulgaria.

[84] For a general overview of the first judicial developments based on the Europe Agreements, see, *inter alia*, Ch. Hillion, 'Cases C-63/99 *Secretary of State for the Home Department* ex parte *Wiesław Głoszczuk and Elzbieta Głoszczuk*; C-235/99 *Secretary of State for the Home Department* ex parte *Eleanora Ivanova Kondova*; C-257/99 *Secretary of State for the Home Department* ex parte *Julius Barkoci and Marcel Malik*; judgments of the Full Court of 27 September 2001; Case C-268/99 *Aldona Małgorzata Jany* e.a v. *Staatssecretaris van Justitie*, judgment of the Full Court of 20 November 2001; Case C-162/00 *Land Nordrhein-Westfalen* v. *Beata Pokrzeptowicz-Meyer*, judgment of the Full Court of 29 January 2002', 40 *CMLRev.* (2003) p. 465; B. Bogusz, 'Regulating the Right of Establishment for Accession State Nationals: Reinforcing the "Buffer Zone" or Improving Labour Market Flexibility', 27 *ELR* (2002) p. 472; R. van Ooik, 'Free Movement of Self-Employed Persons and the Europe Agreements', 4 *EJML* (2002) p. 377.

[85] ECJ, Case C-63/99 *The Queen v Secretary of State for the Home Department, ex parte Wieslaw Gloszczuk and Elzbieta Gloszczuk* [2001] *ECR* I-6369; Case C-257/99 *The Queen v Secretary of State for the Home Department, ex parte Julius Barkoci and Marcel Malik* [2001] *ECR* I-6557; Case C-268/99 *Aldona Malgorzata Jany and Others* v. *Staatssecretaris van Justitie* [2001] *ECR* I-8615; Case C-162/00 *Land Nordrhein-Westfalen* v. *Beata Pokrzeptowicz-Meyer* [2002] *ECR* I-1049.

Bulgaria was directly effective and that this conferred the right of establishment as well as the corollary rights of entry and residence on Bulgarian nationals, albeit subject to limitations arising from the domestic law of the Member States.[86]

That being said, it should be emphasised that this was not the only judicial development based on the EA Bulgaria.[87] In November 2004, the ECJ delivered a judgment in Case C-327/02 *Panayotova and Others* v. *Minister voor Vreemdelingenzaken en Integratie*.[88] The reference for a preliminary ruling from the District Court of The Hague dealt with the interpretation of the similarly drafted provisions of three Europe Agreements (EA Bulgaria, EA Poland and EA Slovakia) on the right of establishment. The ECJ concluded, *inter alia*, that Articles 45(1) and 59(1) EA Bulgaria (as well as the relevant provisions of the other two EAs)

> do not in principle preclude legislation of a Member State involving a system of prior control which makes entry into the territory of that Member State with a view to establishment as a self-employed person conditional on the issue of a temporary residence permit by the diplomatic or consular services of that Member State in the country of origin of the person concerned or in the country where he is permanently resident.

The Court added that this kind of system may make the grant of permits subject to the condition that the persons concerned must show a genuine intention of taking up employment as a self-employed person without at the same time entering into employment or having recourse to public funds.[89]

2.7 Application of the Europe Agreement in Bulgaria

Due to the late entry into force of the Europe Agreement, Bulgaria's application of the agreement is very modestly represented, for example, by a couple of decisions of the regulatory authority in the field of competition law, the Competition Protection Commission. In the *'168 HOURS' EOOD* v. *the Competition Protection Commission* case,[90] which is discussed in detail in section 2.3 above, the Court referred to the Europe Agreement as forming the legal grounds for the

---

[86] See para. 91 of the judgment.

[87] It is worth mentioning another reference from the Dutch court registered as Case C-58/03 *Y.G. Encheva* v. *Staatssecretaris van Justitie*. It has been withdrawn and consequently removed from the register following the ECJ's judgment in Case C-327/02 *Panayotova* (*OJ* 2005 C 106/21).

[88] ECJ, Case C-327/02 *Lili Georgieva Panayotova, Radostina Markova Kalcheva, Izabella Malgorzata Lis, Lubica Sopova, Izabela Leokadia Topa, Jolanta Monika Rusiecka* v. *Minister voor Vreemdelingenzaken en Integratie* [2004] *ECR* I-110055.

[89] Para. 39 of the judgment.

[90] J-4420/30.07.1999 of the SAC on C-1257/1999.

approximation of Bulgarian law to the law of the European Union. Apart from this important judgment, it may be observed that a majority of the judgments of the Supreme Administrative Court refer to Article 11(1) EA Bulgaria.[91] For example in the *Christov* v. *Varna Regional Customs Directorate* case,[92] the Court held that 'the customs authorities have applied the Europe Agreement … in force for the Republic of Bulgaria on 1 February 1995, which is part of our domestic legislation on the basis of Article 5(4) of the Constitution'. This is one of several judgments that refer to the EA Bulgaria as part of the national legal order of Bulgaria.

In the *British American Tobacco Bulgaria EOOD* v. *Blagoevgrad Regional Court* case,[93] the Court dismissed the appeal against the judgment of the regional court and, by referring to the EA Bulgaria, noted:

> The provision of Article 11(4) of the Europe Agreement imposes on Bulgaria an obligation to abolish quantitative restrictions on imports into Bulgaria of products originating in the Community and measures having equivalent effect. The obligation arising out of the provision of Article 19(2)(6) of the Tobacco and Tobacco Products Act[94] to pay a fee to the Tobacco Fund does not create quantitative restrictions on imports and may not be treated as a measure having equivalent effect.

3. PRE-ACCESSION COOPERATION BEYOND THE EUROPE AGREEMENT

Notwithstanding the Europe Agreement and its numerous additional protocols and sectoral trade-oriented agreements,[95] the treaty relations of the European Union/Community and Bulgaria have been enhanced in various areas. In many ways, these developments are part of a broader framework for closer cooperation between the European Union and its neighbours (not only those from Central and

[91] Art. 11(1) EA Bulgaria provides: 'Customs duties on imports applicable in Bulgaria to products originating in the Community, which are listed in Annex IV, shall be abolished on the date of entry into force of the Agreement.' See the most recent judgments of the Supreme Administrative Court which refer to the EA: J-3650/22.04.2005 of the SAC on C-8105/2004; J-3019/04.04.2005 of the SAC on C-9668/2004; J-10486/15.12.2004 of the SAC on C-10841/2003; J-2980/28.03.2003 of the SAC on C-4722/2002. Source: <http://www.sac.government.bg>.

[92] See J-2076/09.03.2005 of the SAC on C-7166/2004. Source: <http://www.sac.government.bg>.

[93] J-11393/13.12.2002 of the SAC on C-5010/2002.

[94] Закон за тютюна и тютюневите изделия, обн. ДВ бр. 101/30.11.1993 г. [Tobacco and Tobacco Products Act, promulgated in State Gazette No. 101 of 30 November 1993].

[95] See, e.g., Agreement in the form of an Exchange of Letters between the European Community and the Republic of Bulgaria on reciprocal preferential trade concessions for certain wines and spirits, *OJ* 2001 L 94/6.

Eastern Europe).[96] In other words, a lot of similar agreements were concluded with the countries that became Member States in 2004, as well as with candidate or potential candidate countries and the EFTA states. With regard to the first pillar of the European Union, it is worth mentioning the agreement between the European Community and Bulgaria on the conditions for the carriage of goods by road and the promotion of combined transport.[97] It was signed on 26 July 2000 and entered into force almost a year later on 1 May 2001. Following the ECJ's judgments on aviation agreements in 2002, the European Community continues to conclude treaties of this kind with a considerable group of countries.[98] A proposal for a decision on the signature and conclusion of such an agreement with Bulgaria was presented on 22 April 2005.[99] Similarly to other Central and Eastern European countries, Bulgaria has participated in the European Environment Agency as well as the European environment information and observation network in the period preceding its accession.[100]

The above-mentioned cooperation goes beyond the EC framework and also extends to the EU's Common Foreign and Security Policy. Bulgaria not only aligns itself with various CFSP policies and decisions,[101] but also participates in missions under the European Security and Defence Policy (ESDP). In this context, Bulgaria has concluded agreements on its participation in the European Union Police Mission in Bosnia and Herzegovina,[102] EU crisis management

[96] See chapters 4, 5 and 8 in this volume.

[97] Agreement between the European Community and the Republic of Bulgaria establishing certain conditions for the carriage of goods by road and the promotion of combined transport, *OJ* 2001 L 108/6. The Council Decision on its conclusion was annulled by the European Court of Justice in Case C-211/01 *Commission of the European Communities* v. *Council of the European Union* [2003] *ECR* I-8913.

[98] See Communication from the Commission on the consequences of the Court judgments of 5 November 2002 for European air transport policy, COM (2002) 649 final; Communication from the Commission on relations between the Community and third countries in the field of air transport, COM (2003) 94 final.

[99] Proposal for a Council Decision on the signature and provisional application of the Agreement between the European Community and the Republic of Bulgaria on certain aspects of air services; Proposal for a Council Decision on the conclusion of the Agreement between the European Community and the Republic of Bulgaria on certain aspects of air services, COM (2005) 158 final.

[100] Agreement between the European Community and the Republic of Bulgaria concerning the participation of the Republic of Bulgaria in the European Environment Agency and the European environment information and observation network, *OJ* 2001 L 213/66.

[101] It was already in November 1994 that Bulgaria, like other Central and Eastern European countries, was invited to align itself with EU declarations on foreign policy and security related issues. See Mayhew, op. cit. n. 2, at p. 31.

[102] Agreement between the European Union and the Republic of Bulgaria on the participation of the Republic of Bulgaria in the European Union Police Mission (EUPM) in Bosnia and Herzegovina (BiH), *OJ* 2003 L 239/41.

operations[103] and – in connection with the latter – the security procedure for the exchange of classified information.[104]

4. ACCESSION TREATY

4.1 Structure and ratification

As already noted in the introduction, the Accession Treaty signed on 25 April 2005 in Luxembourg envisages the accession of Bulgaria and Romania to the European Union. It is also analysed in chapter 8 of this volume. Since the majority of its provisions apply *mutatis mutandis* to both acceding countries, this analysis is limited to issues relating specifically to Bulgaria. The elaboration on its substantive provisions is preceded by a short introduction dealing with the structure and ratification of the Accession Treaty.

The Accession Treaty was drafted in parallel to the drafting and ratification process of the Treaty establishing a Constitution for Europe,[105] and its structure therefore reflects the possible evolution of the EU treaty framework. In common with previous enlargements, the Accession Treaty *sensu stricto* is fairly short and contains a handful of provisions confirming the accession of Bulgaria and Romania to the European Union, the ratification requirements and the official languages. The conditions of accession are specified in a similarly worded Protocol concerning the conditions and arrangements for accession and an Act on the conditions of accession.[106] Both consist of a main part and numerous annexes. The Protocol will be applicable only when the EU Constitution enters into force. *A contrario*, as long as the EU Constitution is not in force, the Act will form the substantive basis for the enlargement. Following the referenda fiascos in France and the Netherlands, it is almost certain that the entry into force of the Accession Treaty will precede the reform of the EU treaty framework.[107] Therefore, in the remaining parts of this analysis, reference will primarily be made to the Act on the conditions of accession.

---

[103] Agreement between the European Union and the Republic of Bulgaria establishing a framework for the participation of the Republic of Bulgaria in the EU crisis management operations, *OJ* 2005 L 46/50. Within this framework, Bulgaria is participating in the European Union's military operation EUFOR Althea in Bosnia and Herzegovina.

[104] Agreement between the Republic of Bulgaria and the European Union on the security procedure for the exchange of classified information, *OJ* 2005 L 118/53. See also Implementing arrangements for the EU-Bulgaria Security Agreement, Council of the European Union Doc. No. 9608/05.

[105] Treaty establishing a Constitution for Europe, *OJ* 2004 C 310/1.

[106] Hereinafter referred to respectively as Protocol and Act.

[107] See also chapter 3 in this volume.

In order to enter into force, the Accession Treaty requires ratification by all twenty-five EU Member States, as well as at least one of the two acceding countries. As already noted in chapter 3 of this volume, both Bulgaria and Romania have already completed their individual ratification procedures. As a matter of fact, the first country to complete the internal ratification procedure was Bulgaria on 11 May 2005. However, one should remember that the accession of one or both of these states may be delayed if the European Union decides to activate the postponement clause laid down in Article 39 of the Act.[108]

4.2 Institutional provisions

Changes to the institutional structure of the European Union resulting from the accession of Bulgaria and Romania are regulated in the second part of the Act (and the Protocol). They are based on a compromise reached in the framework of the Treaty of Nice in December 2000.[109] During the current term of the European Parliament (2004-2009), Bulgaria will have eighteen seats in the European Parliament following its accession. Elections will be held before 31 December 2007. During the transitional period following accession and prior to these elections, the Bulgarian Parliament will have the right to make the appointments.[110] Following the present term of the European Parliament, the division of seats be rearranged yet again in order to comply with the new threshold of 736 members. As a consequence, the number of seats available to MEPs from Bulgaria will be reduced to seventeen after the 2009 European Parliament elections. From the date of accession, a Bulgarian member of the European Commission will be appointed pursuant to the procedure regulated in Article 45 of the Act.[111] As a fully fledged Member State, Bulgaria will have ten votes in the Council, and the Act provides for the necessary adjustments to the founding treaties. These provisions will apply as long as further decision-making reforms are not introduced or until the EU Constitution enters into force. It should be noted that the Council is equipped with the power to make all the necessary adjustments if the safeguard clause is applied to one of the two acceding countries.[112] The number of judges in the European Court of Justice and the Court of First Instance will be increased to twenty-seven in order to accommodate the Bulgarian and Romanian judges. The Accession Treaty envisages the appointment of new members of the Court of Auditors, the

---

108 Equally Art. 39 of the Protocol.

109 Treaty of Nice amending the Treaty on European Union, the Treaties establishing the European Communities and certain related acts, signed at Nice, 26 February 2001, *OJ* 2001 C 80/1.

110 Art. 24(3) of the Act (equally Art. 21(3) of the Protocol).

111 Equally Art. 45 of the Protocol.

112 Art. 4(2) of the Accession Treaty.

Committee of the Regions and the Economic and Social Committee, as well as other bodies operating within the EU institutional framework.

From the moment of the signature of the Accession Treaty and until the actual accession, the Bulgarian representatives have the right to participate in the work of the European Parliament as observers.[113] More importantly, Bulgaria has observer status in the Council of the European Union and is covered by the information and consultation procedure. The necessary terms and conditions are regulated in a separate agreement annexed to the Accession Treaty.[114] The first months following the signature of the Accession Treaty have proved that the European Parliament was politically and logistically not ready to accommodate the observers and shamelessly postponed their participation in its work.[115] However, a positive decision was finally reached, and on 26 September 2005 the observers from Bulgaria and Romania participated in the work of the European Parliament for the first time.[116]

4.3 Transitional periods

As in the case of previous enlargements, the acceding countries have an obligation to approximate their existing legislation to the *acquis communautaire*. Because no permanent op-outs were available, the accession negotiations concentrated on transitional arrangements. In the case of Bulgaria, these are spelled out mainly in Annex VI to the Act.[117] The transitional periods relating to the free movement of workers were clearly inspired by the 2 + 3 + 2 model employed in the previous Accession Treaty.[118] The other temporal derogations relate to the free movement of services, the free movement of capital, agriculture, transport policy,

---

113 Similar arrangements were made in the previous accessions.

114 Exchange of Letters between the European Union and the Republic of Bulgaria and Romania on an information and consultation procedure for the adoption of certain decision and other measures to be taken during the period preceding accession, *OJ* 2005 L 157/393.

115 See also chapters 3 and 8 in this volume.

116 See L. Kubosova, 'Romanian and Bulgarian observers join the European Parliament', *EUobserver*, 26 September 2005.

117 Equally Annex VI to the Protocol.

118 Treaty between the Kingdom of Belgium, the Kingdom of Denmark, the Federal Republic of Germany, the Hellenic Republic, the Kingdom of Spain, the French Republic, Ireland, the Italian Republic, the Grand Duchy of Luxembourg, the Kingdom of the Netherlands, the Republic of Austria, the Portuguese Republic, the Republic of Finland, the Kingdom of Sweden, the United Kingdom of Great Britain and Northern Ireland (Member States of the European Union) and the Czech Republic, the Republic of Estonia, the Republic of Cyprus, the Republic of Latvia, the Republic of Lithuania, the Republic of Hungary, the Republic of Malta, the Republic of Poland, the Republic of Slovenia, the Slovak Republic, concerning the accession of the Czech Republic, the Republic of Estonia, the Republic of Cyprus, the Republic of Latvia, the Republic of Lithuania, the Republic of Hungary, the Republic of Malta, the Republic of Poland, the Republic of Slovenia and the Slovak Republic to the European Union, *OJ* 2003 L 236/17.

taxation, social policy and employment, energy, telecommunications and information technologies, as well as the environment (air quality, waste management, water quality, industrial pollution and risk management).[119] It is impossible and in a way also pointless to discuss all of them. The rest of this analysis is therefore devoted to the areas of considerable sensitivity in the relations between Bulgaria and the European Union.

4.4 Transitional periods – free movement of workers

The free movement of workers traditionally belongs to the areas of particular interest of the acceding countries. In the perception of the general public, it is the key element that makes EU integration particularly attractive and renders the pre-accession effort worthwhile. As noted above, the Europe Agreements contained rather restrictive provisions in this respect, granting non-discriminatory treatment only to persons admitted legally to the labour markets of the EU Member States. This treatment remained in the hands of the legislators within the EU Member States. It did not come as a surprise that Bulgaria declared its readiness to apply the *acquis* upon accession[120] and did not request transitional periods.[121] It was the European Union that had an interest in imposing transitional arrangements, only gradually allowing Bulgarian nationals access to the labour markets of its Member States. The negotiating position followed the 2 + 3 + 2 model, which was also applied to other countries of Central and Eastern Europe.[122] The relevant provisions of the Accession Treaty meet the European Union's position. It is important to note that the negotiations on chapter 2 were opened in October 2001 and provisionally closed in June 2002. During this period, only fifteen EU Member States were engaged in the negotiations, although the future Accession Treaty was envisaged to be concluded by both the old and the new Member States. This leads to the question to what extent the ten new Member States will restrict access to their labour markets for Bulgarian nationals.

---

[119] For a general overview, see Report on the Results of the Negotiations on the Accession of Bulgaria and Romania to the European Union, European Commission Doc. No. 5859/05.

[120] Details on Bulgarian legislation implementing the free movement of persons *acquis* is available at the official website of the Bulgarian Ministry of Labour and Social Policy, at: <http://www.mlsp.government.bg/en/integration/euro/chapter-2/bg/index.htm>.

[121] Intergovernmental Conference on the Accession of the Republic of Bulgaria to the European Union. Negotiating Position on Chapter 2: 'Freedoms of Movement of Persons', CONF-BG 37/01 and 23/02.

[122] See M. Dougan, 'A Spectre is Haunting Europe… Free Movement of Persons and Eastern Enlargement', in Hillion, op. cit. n. 21, at p. 111; A. Adinolfi, 'Free movement and access to work of citizens of the news Member States: the transitional measures', 42 *CMLRev.* (2005) p. 469. For a more general analysis of the impact of EU citizenship and transitional periods on the new Member States, see N. Reich, 'The Constitutional Relevance of Citizenship and Free Movement in an Enlarged Union', 11 *ELJ* (2005) p. 675.

As a general principle, the restrictions allowed under the Accession Treaty shall not result 'in conditions for access of Bulgarian nationals to the labour markets of the present Member States which are more restrictive than those prevailing on the date of signature of the Accession Treaty.'[123] By way of derogation from Articles 1-6 of Council Regulation 1612/68/EEC,[124] the Member States are allowed to apply domestic law restricting access to their labour markets for an initial period of two years following Bulgaria's accession to the European Union. The existing system will be reviewed after two years.[125] However, the Member States may at that stage declare a desire to continue the application of the transitional periods for another three years. To this end, the Accession Treaty imposes a requirement of notification of the European Commission. In the absence of notification, Articles 1-6 of Council Regulation 1612/68/EEC will become applicable. In the case of serious disturbances on the labour market, or threats thereof, the Member States may continue to apply restrictions for another two years. Again, notification of the Commission is a *conditio sine qua non*.

Under the terms of paragraph 12 of Annex VI to the Act, the Member States may grant Bulgaria's nationals greater access to their labour markets under domestic law. The Accession Treaty allows for the liberalisation of existing restrictions as well as for the possibility of full access to the labour markets. Following the first two years after the accession, the Member States may decide to apply Articles 1-6 of Council Regulation 1612/68/EEC to Bulgarian nationals. For a period of seven years following the accession, they may exceptionally impose restrictions in the case of existing or foreseeable serious disturbances on the labour market (that 'could seriously threaten the standard of living or level of employment in a given region or occupation').[126] To this end, a special procedure was tailored and inserted into the Accession Treaty (para. 1.7 of Annex VI to the Act).[127]

The Accession Treaty allows Bulgaria to impose equivalent restrictions on the nationals of Member States that decide to make use of the transitional periods.

[123] Para. 1.14 of Annex VI to the Act.

[124] Regulation (EEC) No. 1612/68 of the Council of 15 October 1968 on freedom of movement for workers within the Community, *OJ* 1968 L 257/2 (English special edition).

[125] The review will be conducted by the Council on the basis of a report submitted by the European Commission. One further review may be requested by Bulgaria.

[126] Para. 1.7 of Annex VI to the Act.

[127] The procedure may be initiated by any of the existing Member States of the European Union. It shall inform the European Commission and other Member States and supply them with all relevant details. It may request the European Commission to adopt a decision suspending fully or partly the application of Council Regulation 1612/68/EEC. The European Commission shall reach the decision within two weeks. If the suspension decision is adopted, it shall specify the duration and scope of restrictions. Annulment or amendment of the decision may be requested by any Member State within two weeks of the adoption of the decision in question. The Council will have two weeks for reaction and its decision will be taken by a qualified majority.

Moreover, in the case of serious disturbances on the Bulgarian labour market, or serious threats thereof, Bulgaria may apply restrictions to Romanian nationals.[128] In such case, the procedure envisaged in paragraph 1.7 of Annex VI to the Act is applicable.[129]

In order to placate serious concerns on the part of Germany and Austria, special derogations have been allowed in relation to the free movement of selected types of services provided by companies established in Bulgaria.[130] In the case of Germany, the list includes construction services as well as industrial cleaning and the activities of interior decorators. The Austrian list is much longer, running from horticultural service activities to construction and security services. The restrictions can be maintained as long as both countries apply the derogations to Articles 1-6 of Council Regulation 1612/68/EC. Bulgaria is entitled to take equivalent measures, provided that the European Commission is informed.

The Accession Treaty also contains numerous provisions dealing with the status of Bulgarian workers employed in EU Member States prior to the accession. For example,

> Bulgarian workers legally working in a present Member State on the date of accession and admitted to the labour market of that Member State for an uninterrupted period of 12 months or longer will enjoy access to the labour market of that Member State but not to the labour market of other Member States applying national measures.[131]

The Accession Treaty also provides for a special regime applicable to family members of Bulgarian workers.

The main text of the Accession Treaty is supplemented by the Joint Declaration on the free movement of workers, in which the EU Member States promise to make their best endeavours to grant increased access to their labour markets.[132]

---

128 This possibility may be used provided that at least one of the existing Member States imposes restrictions towards Bulgaria.

129 Under the same terms, Romania may impose restrictions towards Bulgarian nationals (see para. 1.11 of Annex VII to the Act).

130 See also Joint declaration by the Federal Republic of Germany and the Republic of Austria on the free movement of workers: Bulgaria and Romania (Annexed to the Final Act).

131 Para 1.2 of Annex VI to the Act.

132 'The European Union stresses the strong elements of differentiation and flexibility in the arrangement for the free movement of workers. Member States shall endeavour to grant increased labour market access to Bulgarian nationals under national law, with a view to speeding up the approximation to the acquis. As a consequence, the employment opportunities in the European Union for Bulgarian nationals should improve substantially upon Bulgaria's accession. Moreover, the EU Member States will make best use of the proposed arrangement to move as quickly as possible to the full application of the acquis in the area of free movement of workers.'

4.5 Transitional periods – free movement of capital

As in the case of some of the ten new Member States, the acquisition of land belonged to the most sensitive areas of the negotiations. From the outset, Bulgaria requested a ten-year transitional period (counting from the day of accession).[133] The rationale for the request was clearly spelled out in Annex I of its negotiating position. The grounds were the following:

1. The land market in the country is in the process of development;
2. The price of land in Bulgaria is several times lower than the price of land in EU Member States;
3. Due to the low income the Bulgarian citizens do not have yet the same possibilities as the citizens of the EU to acquire land;
4. A uniform land cadastre and a property register are not completed yet. Their final completion and the availability of market information are basic prerequisites for further development of the land market;
5. After the completion of land restitution, a process of land consolidation is under way aimed at creation of economically viable farm structures.[134]

Another side of the problem was the Bulgarian Constitution, which at that time contained a prohibition of land ownership by foreigners. This was generally considered to be contrary to EU law.[135] Tanchev noted that 'It is necessary that the subsisting ban on foreigners to acquire land under Article 22 of the Constitution be eliminated.'[136] The potential problem was also diplomatically acknowledged by the European Commission in its opinion on Bulgaria's membership application. It was noted that 'While being compatible with the Europe Agreement, these restrictions hamper the free flow of capital.'[137] Since the amendments to the Bulgarian Constitution are discussed in section 8 of this chapter, it suffices to say at this stage that the necessary revision has already taken place and that the

[133] Intergovernmental Conference on the Accession of the Republic of Bulgaria to the European Union. Negotiating Position on Chapter 4: 'Free Movement of Capital', CONF-BG 35/00.

[134] Ibid., at pp. 4-5.

[135] See, *inter alia*, A. Albi, *EU Enlargement and the Constitutions of Central and Eastern Europe* (Cambridge, Cambridge University Press 2005) p. 109; E. Tanchev, 'National Constitutions and EU Law: Adapting the 1991 Bulgarian Constitution in the Accession to the European Union', 6 *EPL* (2000) p. 229.

[136] E. Tanchev, 'Constitutional amendments due to Bulgarian full EU membership', in A.E. Kellermann, J.W. de Zwaan and J. Czuczai, eds., *EU Enlargement. The Constitutional Impact at EU and National Level* (The Hague, T.M.C. Asser Press 2001) p. 301 at p. 307.

[137] Commission Opinion on Bulgaria's Application for Membership of the European Union, DOC/97/11, at p. 47.

constitutional obstacle has now been removed. The new version of Article 22 of the Constitution of Bulgaria will enter into force at the moment of accession.[138]

The Accession Treaty provides for two transitional periods with regard to the acquisition of secondary residences and the acquisition of agricultural land, forests and forestry land. In the case of the former, Bulgaria may maintain the restrictions for five years from the date of accession. This applies to the acquisition of secondary residencies by nationals of the European Union or EEA-EFTA countries who are non-resident in Bulgaria, as well as legal persons formed in accordance with EU/EEA Member State law. The latter allows the maintenance of the restrictions that apply to nationals of EU/EEA-EFTA countries as well as legal persons established there for seven years following the date of accession. In the period following the signature of the Accession Treaty, these categories of persons cannot be treated in 'a more restrictive way than a national of a third country'.[139] These restrictions do not apply to self-employed farmers who express a wish to establish themselves and reside in Bulgaria. The Accession Treaty provides for the initiation of a review procedure in the third year following the date of accession. In the follow-up, the transitional periods may be shortened by a unanimous decision of the Council of the European Union.

5. DECOMMISSIONING OF THE KOZLODUY NUCLEAR POWER PLANT

The decommissioning of the Kozloduy nuclear power plant has been one of the most difficult issues in Bulgaria's relations with the European Union. The history of the plant goes back to the 1970s, when its construction was closely connected with the energy system of the Soviet Union.[140] The Europe Agreement does not mention the Kozloduy nuclear power plant explicitly. However, it provides a legal basis for cooperation aimed at ensuring a safer use of nuclear energy. According to Article 80 EA Bulgaria, the cooperation in question shall cover, *inter alia*, 'evaluation of the feasibility of backfitting the existing power plant equipped

[138] The new version of Art. 22 of the Constitution of Bulgaria reads '(1) Foreigners and foreign legal persons may acquire property over land under the conditions ensuing from Bulgaria's accession to the European Union, or by virtue of an international treaty that has been ratified, published and entered into force for the Republic of Bulgaria, as well as through inheritance by operation of the law. (2) The law ratifying the international treaty referred to in paragraph 1 shall be adopted by a majority of two-thirds of all members of the Parliament. (3) The land regime shall be established by law.' The translation of the complete text of Bulgarian Constitution is available at the official website of the National Assembly of Bulgaria, at: <http://www.parliament.bg>.

[139] Para. 3.2 of Annex VI to the Act.

[140] Available at: <http://www.kznpp.org/eng/main.php?cont=1>.

with VVER-440 reactors'.[141] In 1999, an understanding envisaging the gradual decommissioning of the Kozloduy power plant was signed between the European Commission and Bulgaria. Its proper implementation has been regularly mentioned on the priority lists of the Accession Partnerships.[142] In line with these commitments, the first two units (1 and 2) were shut down in 2002. It is expected that Units 3 and 4 will be shut down in 2006. The latter obligation is explicitly repeated in Article 30 of the Act. It reads: 'Bulgaria having closed – in line with its commitments – definitively for subsequent decommissioning Unit 1 and Unit 2 of the Kozloduy Nuclear Power Plant before the year 2003, commits to the definitive closure of Unit 3 and Unit 4 of this plant in 2006 and to subsequent decommissioning of these units.' To this end, the European Community provides Bulgaria with financial support.[143] In 2007-2009, the assistance will amount to €210 million in equal annual instalments of €70 million.[144] The decommissioning of this nuclear plant has inspired considerable Euroscepticism and public debate in Bulgaria. For example, it is worth noting that, in May 2002, 72.2 per cent of Bulgarian citizens were of the opinion that the Bulgarian Government should insist on a postponement of the decommissioning. The decommissioning of the Kozloduy power plant will no doubt remain an important issue in EU-Bulgaria bilateral relations for some time to come.

6. FINANCIAL ASSISTANCE TO BULGARIA

The financial assistance of the European Communities dates back to the beginning of the 1990s. It was on 8 May 1990 that the Phare programme was extended to Bulgaria. Since then, Bulgaria has remained a beneficiary of the European Union's financial assistance. At the time of writing, it covers pre-accession

141 On Europe Agreements and energy, see, *inter alia*, M. Hattig, 'Energy', in Ott and Inglis, op. cit. n. 10, at p. 947.

142 See also Communication from the Commission to the Council and the European Parliament on nuclear sector related activities for the applicant countries of Central and Eastern Europe and the New Independent States, COM (1998) 134 final; Communication from the European Commission to the Council and the European Parliament, Commission support to nuclear safety in the Newly Independent States and in Central and Eastern Europe, COM (2000) 493 final.

143 The support of the European Community in particular provides measures in support of decommissioning, environmental upgrading, modernisation of conventional energy production, measures to improve energy efficiency and measures to improve the security of the energy supply. See Art. 30(2) of the Act.

144 Art. 30(2) of the Act. The assistance may be made available via the Kozloduy International Decommissioning Support Fund. It should be noted that the first financial assistance dates back to the early 1990s, when it was provided within the framework of the Phare programme. See also Communication from the Commission to the Council and the European Parliament, Commission support to nuclear safety in the Newly Independent States and Central and Eastern Europe, COM (2000) 493 final.

assistance. However, upon the accession of Bulgaria to the Union, it will be covered by the structural funds under the terms spelled out in the Accession Treaty.[145] Bulgaria has also participated in a number of EC programmes, including MEDIA Plus, Socrates II and many others.[146]

The EC pre-accession instruments have been tailored to assist candidate countries in their pre-accession efforts and are an important element of the enhanced pre-accession strategy.[147] Council Regulation 622/98/EC creates a direct link between implementation of the Europe Agreement and fulfilment of the Copenhagen criteria, on the one hand, and financial assistance, on the other. Article 4 allows for limitations in the case of insufficient fulfilment of the obligations mentioned.[148] For Bulgaria, as previously for the countries that joined the European Union in 2004, this includes Phare, SAPARD and ISPA.

Having been created for a handful of newly independent CEECs, the Phare programme has during the course of the last decade developed into one of the key financial schemes supporting a variety of ambitious objectives in the countries of the region.[149] In general terms, it encompasses support for institution building and the strengthening of the regulatory framework necessary for proper implementation of the *acquis communautaire*. Other priorities include support for the economy and social cohesion, as well as the creation of the institutional and procedural framework necessary for the future effective functioning of the Structural Funds. In 2002-2004, an average of €178 million per annum was allocated to Bulgaria. In 2004, the allocation of funds for particular objectives was as follows:

---

145 See A. Mayhew, 'The Financial and Budgetary Impact of Enlargement and Accession', in Hillion, op. cit. n. 21, at p. 143.

146 Conclusion of the Memorandum of Understanding with Bulgaria on its participation in the Community programmes MEDIA Plus and MEDIA Training, *OJ* 2002 C 190/50; Decision No. 5/2001 of the EU-Bulgaria Association Council of 9 October 2001 adopting the terms and conditions for the participation of Bulgaria in the Youth Community action programme, *OJ* 2002 L 46/33; Decision No. 4/2001 of the EU-Bulgaria Association Council of 9 October 2001 adopting the terms and conditions for the participation of the Republic of Bulgaria in the Culture 2000 programme, *OJ* 2002 L 45/47; Decision No. 3/2001 of the EU-Bulgaria Association Council of 25 July 2001 establishing the financial contribution of Bulgaria for participation in the Socrates II programme in the years 2001 to 2006, *OJ* 2002 L 257/5.

147 This part of the chapter is based on information provided in 2004 Regular Report on Bulgaria's progress towards accession, COM (2004) 657 final.

148 'Where an element that is essential for continuing to grant pre-accession assistance is lacking, in particular when the commitments contained in the Europe Agreement are not respected and/or progress towards fulfilment of the Copenhagen criteria is insufficient, the Council, acting by a qualified majority on a proposal from the Commission, may take appropriate steps with regard to any pre-accession assistance granted to an applicant State.'

149 Commission Regulation (EC) No. 2760/98 of 18 December 1998 concerning the implementation of a programme for cross-border cooperation in the framework of the PHARE programme, *OJ* 1998 L 345/49.

- Political criteria: projects for strengthening the public administration at all levels and the judiciary (€36 million); projects to improve transparency, financial control and the fight against corruption and fraud (€8 million); projects for ethnic minorities, vulnerable groups and civil society (€13 million).
- Economic criteria: projects to promote economic growth and competitiveness and social cohesion (€35 million).
- Meeting the obligations of membership: projects to enhance the administrative and judicial capacity to implement and enforce legislative measures and assume the obligations of EU membership (€42 million); projects to improve the strategic planning and effective utilisation of EU funds and prepare for structural funds (including implementation of EDIS) (€12 million).[150]

Moreover, a total of €36 million is earmarked for cross-border cooperation. This is divided into €20 million for border cooperation with Greece, €8 million for border cooperation with Romania, €3 million for border cooperation with Turkey and Serbia and Montenegro (each) and €2 million for border cooperation with the Former Yugoslav Republic of Macedonia (FYROM).

The other two programmes were created at a much later stage and were tailored to be part of the enhanced pre-accession strategy. They are aimed at assisting agriculture and rural development (SAPARD)[151] and infrastructure projects related to the environment and transport (ISPA).[152] The support provided by these programmes is focused on the Accession Partnership priorities, which are intended to help the candidate countries meet the criteria for membership.[153] For the years 2000-2004, Bulgaria was allocated €57.6 million annually from SAPARD. In the case of ISPA, the sums varied from €93 to €127 million.

7. BULGARIA AND THE EU CONSTITUTION

Like the other acceding and candidate countries at the time, Bulgaria participated in the work of the European Convention.[154] It also took part in the IGC 2003-2004

---

150 Loc. cit. n. 147, at p. 8.

151 Council Regulation (EC) No. 1268/1999 of 21 June 1999 on Community support for pre-accession measures for agriculture and rural development in the applicant countries of central and eastern Europe in the pre-accession period, *OJ* 1999 L 161/87.

152 Council Regulation (EC) No. 1267/1999 of 21 June 1999 establishing an Instrument for Structural Policies for Pre-accession, *OJ* 1999 L 161/73.

153 2002 Regular Report on Bulgaria's progress towards accession, COM (2002) 700 final.

154 For a detailed account of the European Convention, see, *inter alia*, P. Norman, *The Accidental Constitution. The Story of the European Convention* (Brussels, EuroComment 2003).

as an observer and signed the Final Act to the Treaty establishing a Constitution for Europe.[155] The purpose of this section is to take a brief look at Bulgaria's position on the constitutional reform of the European Union.

It is interesting to note that the constitutionalisation of the European Union gained momentum in the political debate from the very outset. Just before the European Convention began its work, the Bulgarian Parliament adopted a resolution on the country's initial position on the debate on the future of the European Union.[156] As noted by Nikolov, 'the Bulgarian Parliament gave its support for the idea of achieving a "single text of a constitutional character" as a final result of this forum'.[157] In addition, the Bulgarian Government had presented its opening position by that time.[158] It argued, for example, for 'the division of the future constitutional treaty in two parts: basic provisions, which should be amendable after the ratification by all Member States, and a second part, consisting of "functional or technical provisions, touching mainly upon common policies", where a "lighter procedure" should be considered for their modification.'[159] The Government supported the insertion of the Charter of Fundamental Rights as a legally binding part of the future Constitution of the European Union. One should also remember the contribution of the Bulgarian members of the European Convention to the constitutional debate.[160]

The current crisis regarding the future of the Constitutional Treaty puts Bulgaria in a very peculiar position. As an outsider to the European Union, it signed the Final Act to the Treaty establishing a Constitution for Europe and is not involved in the ratification procedure. If the EU Constitution enters into force before the Accession Treaty becomes operational, then Bulgaria will become a party to the former on the day of accession. Under the current circumstances, it is

---

155 See, *inter alia*, D. Curtin, A.E. Kellermann and S. Blockmans, eds., *The EU Constitution: The Best Way Forward?* (The Hague, T.M.C. Asser Press 2005).

156 Resolution of the National Assembly of the Republic of Bulgaria on the initial position of the Republic of Bulgaria on the debate on the future of the European Union, text available at: <http://europa.eu.int/constitution/futurum/documents/other/oth270202_en.pdf>.

157 K. Nikolov, 'National Report Bulgaria', in Ch. Frank and D. Pyszna-Nigge, eds., *Positions of 10 Central and Eastern European Countries on EU Institutional Reforms* (Louvain-la-Neuve, Brussels, Université catholique de Louvain 2003) p. 8.

158 Initial position of the Republic of Bulgaria on the debate on the future of the European Union, text available at: <http://europa.eu.int/constitution/futurum/documents/other/oth010202_en.pdf>.

159 Nikolov, loc. cit. n. 159, at p. 8.

160 See, for instance, Intervention by Mrs Nelly Kutzkova, alternate of the Government Representative of Bulgaria, at the fifth plenary session of the European Convention, held on the 6-7 June 2002, text available at: <http://european-convention.eu.int/docs/speeches/937.pdf>; Intervention by Mrs Meglena Kuneva, Representative of the Bulgarian Government, member of the Convention, at the eighth plenary session of the European Convention, held on the 12-13 September 2002, text available at: <http://european-convention.eu.int/docs/speeches/2980.pdf>; Contribution by Mr Daniel Valtchev, member of the Convention – 'Contribution to the Convention Debate on the Functioning of the Institutions', CONV 493/03.

highly probable that it will be the Accession Treaty that will enter into force first. If this is the case, then Bulgaria will join the other Member States in the ratification debate from the moment of its accession.

8. THE CONSTITUTION OF BULGARIA AND MEMBERSHIP OF THE EUROPEAN UNION

Although shortly after the signing of the Accession Treaty, and before the publication of the first monitoring report of the European Commission on the progress of Bulgaria towards accession, there was a prolonged standstill in the parliamentary life in Bulgaria, which questioned the ability of the country to accomplish on time the obligations arising from the Accession Treaty and would probably make it necessary for the whole country to walk an extra mile in order to acquire EU membership, the existence of an awareness among politicians and within academia and civil society of the necessity of amending the Constitution of Bulgaria has never been in doubt. The Europe Agreement and the Commission's White Paper did not impose any direct obligation to change existing provisions of the Constitution that are not in conformity with EU law or to lay down new constitutional norms in various areas.[161] However, this was the case with the Accession Partnerships, which, as already noted, called for the necessary revision.

Since its entry into force on 13 July 1991, the Constitution of Bulgaria[162] underwent two significant amendments. It is interesting to note that constitutional reform belongs to one of the few examples of joint and coordinated steps towards accession to the European Union, in which all political parties have taken part.[163] Both amendments were proposed and passed by one and the same political majority and there is a slight trend towards decreasing support for the amendments.[164]

---

161 Tanchev, loc. cit. n. 135, at pp. 229-241.

162 Конституция на Република България [Constitution of the Republic of Bulgaria], promulgated in State Gazette No. 56 of 13 July 1991.

163 For an overview, see E. Tanchev and J. Peteva, 'Bulgaria', in A.E. Kellermann, et al., eds., *The Impact of EU Accession on the Legal Orders of New EU Member States and (Pre-)Candidate Countries: Hopes and Fears* (The Hague, T.M.C. Asser Press 2006) p. 33.

164 The first amendment was adopted on 24 September 2003 and entered into force on 29 September 2003. The Draft Act to Amend and Supplement the Constitution was supported by 103 members of Parliament. The minutes from the debate on the Draft Act to amend and supplement the Constitution of the Republic of Bulgaria, No. 354-01-76, dated 25 July 2003, indicate that of all 240 members of Parliament, 230 were present at the session and all of them voted for the adoption of the Amendment Act. The second amendment was adopted on 18 February 2005 and entered into force on 28 February 2005. The Draft Act to amend and supplement the Constitution was supported by 84 members of Parliament. The minutes from the debate on the Draft Act to Amend and Supplement the Constitution of the Republic of Bulgaria, No. 454-01-137, dated 8 December 2004, documents that 230 members of Parliament were present at the session, of whom 225 voted for the adoption of the amendment and five against it.

The procedure for amending the Constitution adopted by the members of the Grand National Assembly addressed the apprehension of the 'founding fathers' that passing acts of Parliament to amend the Constitution might be done in a fast and casual manner, which would be perilous for the young democratic traditions of the country. Each amendment of the Constitution starts under the procedure provided for in Chapter IX of the Constitution. The power to adopt the amendment act belongs to the National Assembly, i.e., the Bulgarian Parliament, with the exception of amendments within the powers of the Grand National Assembly. These include amendments affecting the territory of the country, changes in the form of state and form of government, amendments to the provisions of Article 5, paragraphs 2 (direct applicability of the Constitution) and 4 (supremacy over domestic law of international treaties that have been ratified by the Parliament, promulgated in the State Gazette and are in force for Bulgaria), Article 57, paragraphs 1 (irrevocability of fundamental rights) and 3 (limitation of fundamental rights in wartime), and Chapter IX of the Constitution. The Grand National Assembly also has the power to adopt a new Constitution of the Republic of Bulgaria.

The amendments are incorporated in an act of Parliament, which is passed under a procedure more complex than the ordinary legislative procedure. To begin with, the right of legislative initiative is limited to the President and one quarter of all (or eighty) members of Parliament. The draft act is subjected to a debate at a session of National Assembly, which is held no earlier than one month and no later than three months after its submission, thus providing a balance between two factors: having enough time for disseminating the draft act among the MPs and civil society and not allowing the parliamentary debate on the matter to get caught in a backlog. The draft act is passed by Parliament when it has successfully undergone three consecutive readings on three different working days and receives the support of three-quarters of all (or one hundred and eighty) members of Parliament.

8.1 The first amendment

The debate on the first amendment of the Constitution[165] started as part of the judicial reform process in 2001-2002. The draft was presented in Parliament in July 2003 and was finally adopted in September 2003. The amendments to the Bulgarian Constitution introduce changes in three major areas that affect the status of the judiciary:

---

165 Закон за изменение и допълнение на Конституцията на Република България [Act Amending and Supplementing the Constitution of Republic of Bulgaria], promulgated in State Gazette No. 85 of 26 September 2003.

- immunity
- appointment for life
- term of office of administrative managers in the judiciary.

The amendments aim to ensure integrity and unbiased judgments without compromising the independence of the judiciary. Immunity was limited to so-called functional immunity – criminal and civil non-liability for actions performed by members of the Bulgarian judiciary in their official capacity if not qualified as a premeditated offence.

The legislator revised the provisions concerning the appointment for life of the members of the judiciary, extending to five the number of years of service required to achieve this status. Another amendment sets forth that members of the Bulgarian judiciary shall be dismissed when they reach sixty-five years of age. The term of office of administrative managers was previously undetermined and was set at five years after the revision.

8.2 The second amendment

The second amendment of the Bulgarian Constitution[166] brings it into compliance with the provisions of the Treaty establishing the European Community and the Treaty on European Union, as well as the Treaty establishing a Constitution for Europe.[167] A new fundamental principle has been laid down in Article 4(3): 'The Republic of Bulgaria shall participate in the establishment and development of the European Union', thus acknowledging that building up a united Europe is an ongoing task which involves all European states. Although the core of the public debate on the constitutional amendments was Article 22, which governs the regime of land ownership in Bulgaria, the major changes are fourfold. They cover the prohibition of land ownership by foreign persons, the ban on extradition of Bulgarian citizens at the request of the competent authorities of EU Member States, the constitutional guarantees granted to the citizens of the European Union to active and passive voting rights in local elections and elections to the European Parliament, and the parliamentary majority needed to ratify the Accession Treaty.

---

[166] Закон за изменение и допълнение на Конституцията на Република България [Act Amending and Supplementing the Constitution of Republic of Bulgaria], promulgated in State Gazette No. 18 of 25 February 2005.

[167] Доклад на временната комисия за подготовка на изменения в Конституцията на Република България [Report of the *ad hoc* Commission on the Preparation of Amendments to the Bulgarian Constitution on the Draft Act to Amend and Supplement the Constitution of Bulgaria No. 454-01-137].

9. CONCLUSIONS

At the time of writing, the European Union and Bulgaria are taking the final steps to make the forthcoming enlargement a successful reality. The 2005 monitoring reports provide a very thorough analysis of the success stories, as well as of the areas where further efforts are required ahead of accession.[168] From this perspective, it is justified to argue that in 2006 Bulgaria is more a member than a neighbour of the European Union. Following the signature of the Accession Treaty, Bulgaria is covered by the information and consultation procedure and its representatives have observer status in numerous bodies operating within the EU framework (including the Council of the European Union and the European Parliament). At the same time, both parties are struggling with their own internal challenges and problems. The European Union is undoubtedly in the middle of a major constitutional and budgetary crisis. It is still coming to terms with the big bang enlargement and its impact on the European Union and its functioning. On the other side, Bulgaria is implementing the necessary reforms (including long-awaited reform of the judiciary) and proceeding with the approximation of laws. Following the recent parliamentary elections, it has found itself in a political stalemate threatening the pace of its pre-accession efforts. One should not forget the considerable support for EU accession, which, as already argued in the introduction, is often perceived as a panacea for all domestic problems. The extent to which this approach is knowledge-driven and the real grounds for such a positive public perception of the membership are very much open to question.

As envisaged, Bulgaria's path towards EU accession follows the scenarios used for the purposes of the big bang enlargement of 2004. This conclusion is applicable to the pre-accession strategy and the policy tools used to this end, as well as to the Accession Treaty and the transitional periods provided therein. In purely legal terms, it has been based around the Europe Agreement, which was tailored to serve as the framework for association and proved to be a flexible tool, capable of becoming the pre-accession vehicle. Put together with Accession Partnerships, the Europe Agreements have served as a core for the enhanced pre-accession strategy implemented by the European Union in relation to all new Member States from Central and Eastern Europe as well as the remaining acceding countries. An important role was also played by pre-accession financial assistance.

Contrary to public perception in Bulgaria, accession to the European Union will not be a panacea for domestic problems. It is a major policy choice that will require even more intensified efforts when membership turns into an everyday

[168] Communication from the Commission, Comprehensive monitoring report on the state of preparedness for EU membership of Bulgaria and Romania, SEC (2005) 1352 (COM (2005) 534 final).

reality. The forthcoming enlargement will not only be an immense challenge for Bulgaria but also an important test for the European Union. It will force yet another debate about its potential and capacity.

In geographical terms, the accession of Bulgaria and Romania will considerably strengthen the European Union's position in the region. On the one hand, the European Union receives direct access to the Black Sea. On the other, it unlocks EU Member State Greece and strengthens the position of the European Union in the Western Balkans. This undoubtedly necessitates an even more stable, consistent and effective neighbourhood policy. This is where Bulgaria shall find its role in the enlarged European Union. It will have the opportunity to prove that is not only interested in the economic benefits of accession, but that it is also capable of adding value to the further development of the European Union, especially externally. It will be in one of these areas that Bulgaria will be able to use its experience and prove that the newly adopted Article 4(3) of its Constitution is not just a mere declaration of intent but a basis for a long-term commitment.

CHAPTER 8

ROMANIA

Mónika Józon*

Relevant legal documents:

- Treaty between the Kingdom of Belgium, the Czech Republic, the Kingdom of Denmark, the Federal Republic of Germany, the Republic of Estonia, the Hellenic Republic, the Kingdom of Spain, the French Republic, Ireland, the Italian Republic, the Republic of Cyprus, the Republic of Latvia, the Republic of Lithuania, the Grand Duchy of Luxembourg, the Republic of Hungary, the Republic of Malta, the Kingdom of the Netherlands, the Republic of Austria, the Republic of Poland, the Portuguese Republic, the Republic of Slovenia, the Slovak Republic, the Republic of Finland, the Kingdom of Sweden, the United Kingdom of Great Britain and Northern Ireland (Member States of the European Union) and the Republic of Bulgaria and Romania, concerning the accession of the Republic of Bulgaria and Romania to the European Union, *OJ* 2005 L 157/11.
- Additional Protocol to the Europe Agreement establishing an association between the European Communities and their Member States, of the one part, and Romania, of the other part, to take account of the accession of the Czech Republic, the Republic of Estonia, the Republic of Cyprus, the Republic of Latvia, the Republic of Lithuania, the Republic of Hungary, the Republic of Malta, the Republic of Poland, the Republic of Slovenia, and the Slovak Republic to the European Union, *OJ* 2005 L 155/30.
- Agreement between the European Union and Romania establishing a framework for the participation of Romania in the European Union crisis-management operations, *OJ* 2005 L 67/14.
- Agreement between Romania and the European Union on security procedures for the exchange of classified information, *OJ* 2005 L 118/48.
- Agreement between the European Union and Romania on the participation of Romania in the European Union-led forces (EUF) in the Former Yugoslav Republic of Macedonia, *OJ* 2004 L 120/62.
- Agreement between the European Union and Romania on the participation of Romania in the European Union Police Mission (EUPM) in Bosnia and Herzegovina (BiH), *OJ* 2003 L 239/23.

* Sapientia - Hungarian University of Transylvania, Romania.

S. Blockmans and A. Łazowski (eds.), The European Union and Its Neighbours

- Agreement between the European Community and Romania establishing certain conditions for the carriage of goods by road and the promotion of combined transport, *OJ* 2002 L 142/75.
- Agreement between the European Community and Romania concerning the participation of Romania in the European Environment Agency and the European environment information and observation network, *OJ* 2001 L 213/21.
- Agreement in the form of an Exchange of Letters between the European Community and Romania on reciprocal preferential trade concessions for certain wines and spirits, *OJ* L 2001 L 49/14.
- Europe Agreement establishing an association between the European Communities and their Member States, of the one part, and the Romania, of the other part, *OJ* 1994 L 357/2.

1. THE HISTORY OF EC/EU-ROMANIA RELATIONS

1.1 Introductory remarks

Relations between the European Communities/European Union and Romania mirror other political and legal developments in the region in lots of ways.[1] In legal terms, they follow exactly the same pattern used in the relations with the other Central and Eastern European countries.[2] The differences and specificity of the relations with Romania can be easily identified when economic and political factors are taken on board. With its feeble economy, outdated infrastructure and reduced investment capacity, Romania remained at the end of the membership candidates' list. The purpose of this chapter is to analyse the developing relationship between the European Union and Romania, along the rocky road from association to membership.

Romania's relations with the European Communities were almost non-existent in the period preceding the fall of the Iron Curtain.[3] They received a new dimension after the political changes of December 1989, when the democratisation of the country started and the economic reforms were launched.[4] In legal terms, the

[1] A. Mayhew, *Recreating Europe. The European Union's Policy toward Central and Eastern Europe* (Cambridge, Cambridge University Press 1998).

[2] See A. Ott and K. Inglis, eds., *Handbook on European Enlargement. A Commentary on the Enlargement Process* (The Hague, T.M.C. Asser Press 2002).

[3] See, e.g., Agreement between the European Economic Community and the Socialist Republic of Romania on trade in industrial products, *OJ* 1980 L 352/5; Agreement between the European Economic Community and the Socialist Republic of Romania on trade in textile products, *OJ* 1981 L 273/117.

[4] See Mayhew, op. cit. n. 1, at p. 6. For more historico-political background, see, e.g., P. Siani-Davies, *The Romanian Revolution of December 1989* (Ithaca, Cornell University Press 2005); T.

first important step was the trade agreement that entered into force on 1 May 1991.[5] Shortly afterwards, the Europe Agreement was signed.[6] It entered into force on 1 February 1995; however, its trade part became operational on 1 May 1993 on the basis of an interim agreement.[7] The Europe Agreement has not only provided a vital legal framework for cooperation between the parties, but has also influenced the shape of economic and political reforms in Romania during the past fifteen years. Moreover, it has gradually become one of the pre-accession vehicles.[8]

Romania submitted its application for EU membership on 22 June 1995. Following the Commissions' negative assessment, Romania was not invited to join the first group of countries to start accession negotiations in March 1998.[9] The big step forward was a Progress Report published a year later. It explicitly suggested the opening of negotiations with Romania. This was shortly followed by a positive decision of the Helsinki European Council in 1999.[10] All those EU-related developments gave a strong impetus to domestic reforms. Unfortunately, being a late starter in the field of economic and legal reforms, Romania (similarly to Bulgaria) did not manage to catch up with the rest of the candidate countries. It was therefore decided that, both these countries would not be part of the big bang enlargement of 2004.[11] However, it was clear that, once the main hurdles would be overcome, Bulgaria and Romania would become members of the European Union. Following an intensive period of negotiations, the Accession Treaty for Bulgaria and Romania was officially signed on 25 April 2005 in Luxembourg.[12]

Gallagher, *Modern Romania: The End of Communism, the Failure of Democratic Reform, and the Theft of a Nation* (New York, NYU Press 2005).

5 Agreement between the European Economic Community and the European Atomic Energy Community, of the one part, and Romania, of the other part, on Trade and Commercial and Economic Cooperation, *OJ* 1991 L 79/13.

6 Europe Agreement establishing an association between the European Economic Communities and their Member States, of the one part, and Romania, of the other part, *OJ* 1994 L 357/2.

7 Interim Agreement on Trade and Trade-Related Matters between the European Economic Community and the European Coal and Steel Community, of the one part, and Romania, of the other part, *OJ* 1993 L 81/2.

8 See M. Maresceau, 'Pre-accession', in M. Cremona, ed., *The Enlargement of the European Union* (Oxford, Oxford University Press 2003) p. 9; K. Inglis, 'The Pre-accession Strategy and the Accession Partnerships', in Ott and Inglis, op. cit. n. 2, at p. 103; K. Inglis, 'The Europe Agreements Compared in the Light of their Pre-accession Reorientation', 37 *CMLRev.* (2000) p. 1173.

9 See Agenda 2000 – Commission Opinion on Romania's Application for Membership of the European Union, DOC/97/18, Brussels, 15 July 1997.

10 See L. Maurer, 'Negotiations in Progress', in Ott and Inglis, op. cit. n. 2, at p. 113.

11 See European Council Conclusions of the Copenhagen Summit, 12-13 December 2002, in *Bull. EU* 12-2002, point I-1.

12 Treaty between the Kingdom of Belgium, the Czech Republic, the Kingdom of Denmark, the Federal Republic of Germany, the Republic of Estonia, the Hellenic Republic, the Kingdom of Spain, the French Republic, Ireland, the Italian Republic, the Republic of Cyprus, the Republic of Latvia, the Republic of Lithuania, the Grand Duchy of Luxembourg, the Republic of Hungary, the Republic

At the time of writing, its ratification is still underway. As a matter of fact Bulgaria and Romania were the first to complete all the necessary procedures and thereby showed their commitment to European integration.[13] The envisaged date for accession is set for 1 January 2007, subject to fulfilment of all necessary membership requirements. This reinforced conditionality involves ongoing monitoring of the acceding countries' progress towards accession and a disciplinary tool – the postponement clause of Article 39 of the Act of Accession – which, if used, will delay membership until 1 January 2008.[14]

1.2 Challenges of post-Communist Romania

Considerable delays in implementation of necessary reforms have been a result of a multiplicity of internal and external factors that will be briefly discussed in this section.

Romania is a medium-sized country compared to the current Member States of the European Union. It has a territory of 238,391 sq. km and 21.7 million inhabitants.[15] It produces 31.4 per cent of the EU average GDP.[16] Almost half its labour force is concentrated in the agricultural sector (42.3 per cent).[17] Of the remainder, 26.2 per cent of the labour force works in industry and construction and 31.5 per cent in the service sector.[18] More than half (59.2 per cent) of the country's cities and towns have less than 20,000 inhabitants. Most of its towns and cities are dependent on a single industry.[19]

The reasons why reform in Romania was slower and less effective than in the rest of the CEECs are to be found, on the one hand, in the economic and political conditions inherited from fifty years of hard-line Communist dictatorship and, on the other, in the political culture developed after 1990. Political decision makers found it difficult to combine the requirements for setting up a functioning market economy and establishing the rule of law and democracy with the immense social

of Malta, the Kingdom of the Netherlands, the Republic of Austria, the Republic of Poland, the Portuguese Republic, the Republic of Slovenia, the Slovak Republic, the Republic of Finland, the Kingdom of Sweden, the United Kingdom of Great Britain and Northern Ireland (Member States of the European Union) and the Republic of Bulgaria and Romania, concerning the accession of the Republic of Bulgaria and Romania to the European Union, *OJ* 2005 L 157/11.

13 The Romanian Parliament ratified the Accession Treaty on 17 May 2005, the ratification documents were deposited ten days later.

14 See also chapters 3 and 7 in this volume.

15 Source: National Institute of Statistics Bucharest (data from July 2004), available at: <http://europa.eu.int/comm./enlargement/rom/political_profile.htm>.

16 Source: Eurostat, available at: <http://epp.eurostat.cec.eu.int/pls/portal> (22 April 2005).

17 National Development Plan 2004-2006 (data from 2001) p. 2, available at: <http://www.mie.ro/Pdr/Romana/mdp_mie_ro>.

18 Ibid., at p. 2.

19 Ibid., at p. 3.

and political forces that continued to promote the conservation of the economic and institutional structures of a centrally planned economy. In this reform environment, the European Union's technical and financial support programmes played a decisive role during this period in paving the way for the reform strategy. At the same time, however, Romanian authorities failed to support the society in coping with the social costs of those reforms. Economists consider the year 2002 as being the turning point in Romania's development towards economic stabilisation. It was then that privately owned capital had a bigger share in the economy than the public sector. This was the result of the consolidated effect of EU support and the conditionality inherent in the IMF's approach to Romania. The effect of the IMF's conditionality and the 'outsider syndrome' after the European Union signed the Accession Treaty with ten of the candidate countries in 2003[20] was that as of 2004 a considerable number of market regulations and laws aimed at structural reform of the Romanian economy were adopted. This legislative boom focused on those fields of market regulations, which were on standby in Romania's legal reform strategy. Legal measures adopted in 2004 to support the completion of structural reforms have significantly speeded up the accession negotiations, which were technically closed on 14 December 2004, subject to Romania's strong political commitment to improve the implementation and enforcement of the *acquis*, especially in the field of competition policy and cooperation in justice and home affairs.

Eastern enlargement brought Romania closer to the European Union both geographically and economically. As a matter of fact, with the accession of Hungary to the European Union in 2004, Romania became one of its direct neighbours. Two of Romania's neighbouring countries – Ukraine in the north and Serbia and Montenegro in the southeast – also share a border with Hungary and are thus neighbours of the enlarged Union. The remaining neighbours include Moldova (east) and Bulgaria (south). Bulgaria is expected to accede to the European Union together with Romania. This development gives a new dimension to

---

20 Treaty between the Kingdom of Belgium, the Kingdom of Denmark, the Federal Republic of Germany, the Hellenic Republic, the Kingdom of Spain, the French Republic, Ireland, the Italian Republic, the Grand Duchy of Luxembourg, the Kingdom of the Netherlands, the Republic of Austria, the Portuguese Republic, the Republic of Finland, the Kingdom of Sweden, the United Kingdom of Great Britain and Northern Ireland (Member States of the European Union) and the Czech Republic, the Republic of Estonia, the Republic of Cyprus, the Republic of Latvia, the Republic of Lithuania, the Republic of Hungary, the Republic of Malta, the Republic of Poland, the Republic of Slovenia, the Slovak Republic, concerning the accession of the Czech Republic, the Republic of Estonia, the Republic of Cyprus, the Republic of Latvia, the Republic of Lithuania, the Republic of Hungary, the Republic of Malta, the Republic of Poland, the Republic of Slovenia and the Slovak Republic to the European Union, *OJ* 2003 L 236/17. For an academic appraisal, see, *inter alia*, K. Inglis, 'The Union's Fifth Accession Treaty: New Means to Make Enlargement Possible', 41 *CMLRev.* (2004) pp. 937-973, C. Hillion, 'The European Union is Dead. Long Live the European Union… A Commentary on the Treaty of Accession 2003', 29 *ELR* (2004) p. 583.

the accession preparations. Romania's further progress in implementing the European Union's strategy for the 2005-2007 period depends on the country's capacity to build on the advantages of its new geopolitical position. The European Union expects Romania to develop a role as a promoter of regional cooperation in the Western Balkans and Eastern Europe, in line with its reinforced commitment to fulfil the EU membership criteria by January 2007.

2. THE LEGAL RELATIONSHIP BETWEEN THE EUROPEAN UNION AND ROMANIA UNDER THE FRAMEWORK OF THE EUROPE AGREEMENT

2.1 The Europe Agreement – general remarks

Romania's relations with the European Union under the framework of the Europe Agreement started almost at the same time and according to the same patterns as the European Union's relations with the rest of the Central and Eastern European countries (CEECs).[21] The association included a transitional period of ten years, divided into two successive five-year stages.[22] The way that Romania's achievements have evolved within the framework of the agreement are related, on the one hand, to the development of the reform process in Romania and, on the other, to its capacity to benefit from the subsequent development of the Europe Agreement into the pre-accession vehicle.

2.2 Aims of the association

Following the political changes in Central and Eastern Europe, the European Community's main aim with the Europe Agreements was the reassessment of its political relations with these countries and the gradual liberalisation of trade. Although the EA Romania was not tailored to provide a preparatory legal framework for EU membership, it does mention gradual integration into the Community. Article 1 EA Romania, which contains a list of aims of the association, reads as follows:

> The objectives of this association are:
> - to provide an appropriate framework for the political dialogue between the Parties allowing the development of close political relations,

21 See Mayhew, op. cit. n. 1.

22 Art. 7(1) EA Romania.

- to promote the expansion of trade and the harmonious economic relations between the Parties and so to foster the economic development in Romania,
- to provide a basis for economic, social, financial and cultural cooperation,
- to support Romania's efforts to develop its economy and to complete the conversion into a market economy, and consolidate its democracy,
- to set up institutions suitable to make the association effective,
- to provide a framework for Romania's gradual integration into the Community. To this end, Romania shall work towards fulfilling the necessary conditions.

Following the Copenhagen European Council in 1993, both the European Union and its Member States started transforming the Europe Agreements into pivotal elements of the pre-accession strategy. Followed by a series of political instruments and soft laws, defining and refining the requirements of accession, the EA Romania remains the main legal instrument binding both parties, although its legal-political dimension has been somewhat diminished by the increasing weight given to these latter documents.

2.3 General framework of the Europe Agreement

The opening provisions of the EA Romania deal with political dialogue. Article 2 EA Romania envisages the establishment of a 'regular political dialogue' aimed at 'facilitation of Romania's full integration into the community of democratic nations and progressive rapprochement with the Community'. This dialogue shall also 'bring about an increasing convergence of positions on international issues'. In terms of the free movement of goods, Article 8(1) EA Romania provides for the gradual creation of a free trade area 'based on reciprocal and balanced obligations'. Like other Europe Agreements, the EA Romania does not provide for free movement of workers or freedom of establishment. It follows the non-discrimination model without opening labour markets to the nationals of the contracting parties.[23] The other issues covered in the EA Romania include current payments and the movement of capital (Arts. 60-63), competition (Art. 64), approximation of laws (Arts. 69-71), economic cooperation (Arts. 72-98), cultural cooperation (Art. 99) and financial cooperation (Arts. 100-105).

Political and economic criteria are very closely considered in the Europe Agreement and are regarded as constituting a unity. The text of the agreement uses the concept of 'economic approximation', which is meant to drive towards greater political convergence,[24] and provides political instruments for this purpose. Although it is clear from the wording of the agreement that trade liberalisation

---

23 See Arts. 38-55 EA Romania. See E. Guild, 'Workers', in Ott and Inglis, op. cit. n. 2, at p. 427.

24 Art. 2, second tiret, EA Romania.

and legal harmonisation presuppose the approximation of economic policies, the development of the economic reform process shows that this requirement was not understood in the sense of functional compatibility but rather as an obligation related to cross-border issues. The problem at stake was a lack of synchronisation between the legal reforms and various domestic policies. This significantly affected the effectiveness of the implementation and enforcement of the *acquis*. Accession preparations were more of an external policy issue than a complex legal-economic process deeply rooted in domestic micro and macro policies. It cannot be said that the European Union did not stress the economic conditionality of the relationship. However, it is also interesting that the European Union focused more on the establishment of new political instruments instead of building on the legal framework provisions and legal mechanisms of the Europe Agreement.

The reform of public administration is an area where the Europe Agreement provides little guidance. The wording of Article 98 EA Romania is soft, stating that the parties will promote cooperation between their public administrations in order to improve mutual knowledge of the structure and functioning of their respective systems. At this stage of the European Union's relations with the CEECs, the tremendous role of the institutional capacity of a candidate country with regard to implementing the trade liberalisation measures stipulated in the agreement, within the context of the Central and Eastern European institutional culture, has not yet been acknowledged.

2.4 Approximation of laws

A purely literal interpretation of the Europe Agreement's provisions on the approximation of laws may lead to the conclusion that legislative harmonisation has little weight compared to provisions on trade liberalisation. However, when conditions for accession are taken on board, the emerging picture is very different, as the implementation of the *acquis communautaire* is a *conditio sine qua non* for accession. Articles 69 and 70 EA Romania spell out the necessity of legislative approximation in order to achieve the gradual compatibility of Romanian legislation with that of the Community. The wording of Article 69 EA Romania suggests a voluntary undertaking on the part of the associated countries.[25] It has been argued in the literature that this 'best endeavours' clause ought to be reinterpreted from the moment the application for membership was filed.[26] The substantive scope of approximation goes far beyond the list of areas provided

[25] See A. Evans, 'Voluntary Harmonisation in Integration between the European Community and Eastern Europe', 22 *ELR* (1997) p. 201.

[26] A. Łazowski, 'Approximation of Laws', in Ott and Inglis, op. cit. n. 2, at p. 633.

in Article 70 EA Romania and covers the whole *acquis*, including the Schengen *acquis* as well as the remaining third pillar legislation.[27]

Romania's competition policy continues to be one of the most debated areas in the context of the accession preparations. It is interesting to note that Article 64(1) EA Romania contains provisions similar to Articles 81, 82 and 87 TEC. It is supplemented by Article 64(2) EA Romania, which states that 'any practices contrary to this Article shall be assessed on the basis of criteria arising from' relevant provisions of the EC Treaty. Unfortunately, during the past fifteen years, Romania did not succeed in developing the necessary institutional capacity for the successful approximation of its industrial and social policy (which is a precondition for application of EC competition and state aid legislation). Bearing in mind the importance of both areas, Romania's approximation efforts remain under a strict scrutiny. Non-compliance with the membership requirements may lead to the application of the postponement safeguard clause discussed below.[28]

It can be argued that a lack of mutual recognition of technical standards is one of the missing elements in the Europe Agreement. It would have stimulated the associated countries more effectively in respect of legal approximation. This drawback was rectified later by the European Union, in relation to other associated countries, such as Hungary and Slovenia, but not in relation to Romania. It is worth noting that Article 75 EA Romania provides a possibility for the conclusion of additional agreements on mutual recognition; however, this window of opportunity has not been used so far. This is a consequence of the unsatisfactory state of alignment of legislation and implementation and enforcement problems. This situation has significantly limited Romania's chances to benefit fully from trade liberalisation under the framework of the agreement and to better offset the costs of the accession preparations, including legal approximation. It cannot be argued that the agreement did not offer an adequate legal basis for a stricter legislative policy aimed at achieving compatibility in implementation and enforcement even during the early stages of the preparations for integration. During this period, Romania's implementation and enforcement culture could have developed in accordance with the requirements of the *acquis*, even in the absence of additional strategic guidance from the European Union.

---

27 See A. Łazowski, 'Implementation of the Third Pillar Acquis. A Challenge for the Applicant Countries?', in G. de Kerchove and A. Weyembergh, eds., *Sécurité et justice: enjeu de la politique extérieure de l'Union européenne* (Brussels, Éditions de l'Université de Bruxelles 2003) p. 157.

28 See Art. 39(3) of the Act concerning the conditions of accession of the Republic of Bulgaria and Romania and the adjustments to the treaties on which the European Union is founded (hereinafter referred to as the Act) and the identically worded Art. 39(3) of the Protocol concerning the conditions and arrangements for admission of the Republic of Bulgaria and Romania to the European Union (hereinafter referred to as the Protocol).

2.5 Institutional framework of the Europe Agreement

As is the case with the other Europe Agreements, the EA Romania provides for the creation of an institutional framework for association.[29] Shortly after the agreements's entry into force, it became clear that the joint bodies established on the basis of the agreement would play a much broader role, resulting from the transformation of the agreement into a pre-accession vehicle. As a matter of fact, the institutional framework of the EA Romania is fairly standard and comprises an Association Council and an Association Committee, as well as an Association Parliamentary Committee (Arts. 106-114 EA Romania).

The Association Council is composed of members of the Council of the European Union and members of the European Commission, on the EU side, and persons appointed by the Romanian Government, on the other side.[30] It has considerable decision-making powers, including the right to adopt binding decisions. Examples of the latter include Decision No. 1/2005 on the participation of Romania in the Community system for the rapid exchange of information on dangers arising from the use of consumer products (RAPEX system) under Directive 2001/95/EC of the European Parliament and of the Council of 3 December 2001 on general product safety,[31] Decision No. 2/2002 adopting the terms and conditions for Romania's participation in the Community Fiscalis programme,[32] Decision No. 5/2001 establishing the financial contribution of Romania for participation in the Socrates II and Youth programmes in the years 2001 to 2006,[33] Decision No. 2/2001 amending Protocol 4 EA Romania concerning the definition of the concept of 'originating products' and methods of administrative cooperation,[34] and Decision No. 1/98 adopting the terms and conditions for the participation of Romania in the financial instrument of the Community in the field of environment.[35]

Political dialogue, being at the heart of the association, was from the outset meant to take place 'at the highest political level'.[36] Political feedback from the

[29] See A. Evans, 'Institutions', in Ott and Inglis, op. cit. n. 2, at p. 1043.

[30] For an overview of procedural rules, see Decision No. 1/95 of the Association Council between the European Communities and their Member States, of the one part, and the Republic of Romania, of the other part of 10 April 1995 adopting its rules of procedure, *OJ* 1995 L 171/41; Decision No. 2/2005 amending, through the setting up of a Joint Consultative Committee between the Committee of the Regions and the Romanian Liaison Committee for Cooperation with the Committee of the Regions, Decision No. 1/95 adopting the rules of procedure of the Association Council, *OJ* 2005 L 184/55.

[31] *OJ* 2005 L 173/12.

[32] *OJ* 2002 L 280/84.

[33] *OJ* 2001 L 217/9.

[34] *OJ* 2001 L 48/27.

[35] *OJ* 1999 L 35/3.

[36] Art. 3(1) EA Romania.

side of the European Union has been considerable, especially in the European parliamentary group in charge of monitoring Romania's progress. This group has taken a firm position on several sensitive issues during the past ten years. The best-known of these reports are those relating to the conditions of children in orphanages in Romania, the protection of the rights of the child and the living conditions of the Roma population.[37] It appears that parliamentary cooperation was and continues to be the most critical and effective example of cooperation in the European Union's relationship with Romania.

3. TOWARDS EU MEMBERSHIP

3.1 The accession criteria – a critical analysis

The accession criteria defined by the Copenhagen Council have introduced a new approach in the European Union's strategy towards the associated countries. The Copenhagen criteria are a continuation of the political requirements stated in the Europe Agreements, describing the expectations in greater detail and also reaffirming the importance of economic conditionality in the accession preparations.[38]

The accession criteria for the first time stressed the proper synchronisation of legal and institutional measures with economic policies. A very clear message is sent to the candidate countries by two of these criteria, namely the importance of creating a functioning market economy and the need for the candidate country to resist the competitive pressure coming from the internal market following its accession. This way, the European Union reminds the candidates once again that the legislative approximation indeed requires the approximation of sectoral policies and a closer consideration of the micro and macro effects of the accession preparations.

Human rights protection, effective local autonomy and regional policy are the three basic fields that have strong transnational dimensions for the CEECs (current and future EU members). These need to be taken into account when the fulfilment of political criteria and the capacity of the candidate to take on the obligations of membership are assessed by the European Union. Furthermore, it is

---

[37] See European Parliament resolution on Romania's progress towards accession, COM (2003) 667-C5-0534/2003-2003/2203(INI); Report on the extent of Romania's readiness for accession to the European Union (2205/2005(INI).

[38] See, *inter alia*, Ch. Hillion, 'The Copenhagen Criteria and their Progeny', in C. Hillion, ed., *EU Enlargement. A Legal Approach* (Oxford, Hart Publishing 2004) p. 1; K. Smith, 'The Evolution and Application of EU Membership Conditionality', in Cremona, op. cit. n. 8, at p. 105; F. Hoffmeister, 'Changing Requirements for Membership', in Ott and Inglis, op. cit. n. 2, at p. 90; O. Mocanu, 'Some Views on the EU's Conditionality and Pre-accession Policies of the Central and Eastern European Countries', 4 *Romanian Journal of European Affairs* (2004) p. 57.

important to consider that protection of economic rights, effective local public administration, the rule of law, the independence of the judiciary and the transparency of administrative procedures are not purely political issues. In economic terms, they can be seen as market entry barriers and may hinder competition. In the case of Romania, their interaction was hardly considered in the most recent regular reports. This is a result of the European Union's general approach when assessing the accession criteria. In fact, the European Union's expectations under the accession criteria were detailed in the Commission's regular reports, from which the candidate countries could deduce the economic legal and political measures that they were supposed to implement.[39]

Although, these reports have worked as central instruments for framing national strategies, and their effectiveness cannot be contested, certain weaknesses do manifest themselves when considering the achievements of the candidates within the context of their domestic conditionality. One serious weakness of the Commission's approach is that the regular reports take a piecemeal approach to the specific criterion and do not assess the candidates' achievements in the interaction of the criteria. A second one is that these reports compare the achievements of the individual candidate country to the *acquis* and to best practice in the EU Member States, whereas the integration and assimilative capacity of these candidate countries also depend on a series of fundamental conditions that do not exist at all in the well-developed market economies and democracies of the Western European countries or manifest themselves differently. A third problem with the regular reports is that far more emphasis was placed on the political criteria than on the economic ones. In fact, the capacity of the candidate countries was assessed on the basis of their political institutional capacity rather than on economic criteria.

The 2004 Report on Romania marks a turning point in this regard, considering the achievements of the 2003-2004 period as part of a longer reform process and in the context of their interaction. The Commission's 2005 Comprehensive Monitoring Report confirms this.[40] This is the reason why, despite the non-satisfactory implementation of the *acquis*, Romania was deemed to have fulfilled the political and economic criteria of accession. It was noted that the reforms are still characterised by ineffective legislation, weak institutional capacity, a judiciary whose independence is sometimes questionable and weak *de facto* local autonomy. At first sight, it may be considered that there are contradictions in those conclusions and findings of the regular reports, and even within the same report.

39 2002 Regular Report on Romania's Progress towards Accession, SEC (2002) 1409; 2003 Regular Report on Romania's progress towards accession, pp. 33-35, available at: <http://europa.eu.int/comm/enlargement/report_2003>; 2004 Regular Report on Romania's progress towards accession, SEC (2004) 1200.

40 COM (2005) 534 final, Brussels, 25 October 2005, SEC (2005) 1354.

In reality, this is not the case when we consider that the *acquis* is indeed in place in terms of legislation and the institutional framework, so the achievements of the candidate country receive high grades. The real problem is that these rules are applied in interaction with the rest of the factors of the business and political environment of transnational market creation, for which there is no *acquis* or even no EC concern at all. The political, legal and institutional culture in the CEECs is different from the rest of Europe, and such differences come to surface when the effectiveness of legislative reform is assessed for purposes of integration.

The significance of this different approach by the European Commission is that it is the capacity to undertake the obligations of membership that matters and not the capacity to fulfil the accession criteria. There is a significant difference between the two, although at the level of integration strategy they are regarded as being identical, since they are based on the requirements expected from the new members upon accession. In some respects, such as the political conditionality, the accession criteria went further than the obligations of membership framed in the EC Treaty, whereas the assessment of the economic performance of the candidates was based on much lighter criteria than what is actually required by membership. Furthermore, the Copenhagen criteria were set up on the basis of the *acquis communautaire* and little thought was given to the specific economic, political and social conditions of the candidates.

It was not closely considered from the EU standpoint to what extent the transposition of the *acquis* into the legal system of the candidates might bring their domestic political and economic situation into functional compatibility with the requirements framed in the accession criteria. The assessment of achievements was considered accordingly. It was left to the candidates to identify and put into practice those laws and policies that were necessary to lay the foundations for and back up the regulatory and policy reforms promoted by the accession preparations. Therefore, the regular reports' findings regarding the fulfilment of the accession criteria are often satisfactory when compared to the *acquis communautaire*, but may not guarantee the same effects in the Central and Eastern European environment as they would in the old Member States. This is why the performance of Romania with regard to the effective implementation of the *acquis* still needs to be improved and why it is required to achieve a higher efficiency in meeting the economic and political criteria of accession. The technical assistance projects, which made financial assistance conditional upon legal and institutional reform, only played a limited role in promoting performance-oriented domestic strategies. Romania could not efficiently convert EU conditionality into domestic policies, although the preparations for accession could have been used efficiently to reduce domestic political market failure in the desperately needed reforms. Today, despite the high degree of legal approximation and implementation of the *acquis communautaire*, functional compatibility is poor due to the weak assimilative capacity of the economy and the non-approximation of sectoral policies, as will be seen later on in this chapter. The transposition of EU law has cured a series of market failures, but has not been sufficient to serve as a substitute for the general legal and economic reforms that are meant to ensure a level playing field in the domestic market, which in turn is necessary for the creation of the right conditions for a transnational market.

3.2 The White Paper on the preparations of the associated countries to join the internal market

The 1995 White Paper on the preparations of the candidate countries of Central and Eastern Europe for integration into the internal market of the Union raised the expectations of the associated countries by providing guidelines for their integration into the internal market, but without any bilateral consultation with the countries concerned.[41] It recommended a two-stage approach for the implementation of the internal market *acquis* to these countries, leaving them free to set the priorities of this complex economic, institutional and legal process in accordance with domestic conditions.

Romania started the legislative approximation enthusiastically, following the recommendations of the White Paper. However, it did so without a significant political commitment towards the approximation of its sectoral policies. The latter was necessary in order to create the indispensable economic environment facilitating the full implementation of EU law. On the basis of these recommendations, Romania set up the first national plan that has been updated on an annual basis.[42]

With regard to the relationship between the speed of legislative and economic reform in Romania, one could say that the legal reform could not achieve its aims due to conflicting policies. The Structured Dialogue,[43] which established a multilateral framework for cooperation between Romania and the EU institutions in the field of all common policies, was intended by the European Union as a new stage in the development of institutional cooperation, but the effectiveness of this type of cooperation was low and it was instead regarded as a monologue.[44] One of the characteristics of this period was therefore a high level of inefficiency in the implementation and enforcement of legislation, and Romania lost track of the rest of the Central and Eastern European countries in pursuing systemic economic

41 COM (1995) 163 final.

42 The first National Plan on Romania's Integration into the European Union was adopted in June 1999, available at: <http://inforeuropa.ro>.

43 Communication from the Commission to the Council, Follow up to Commission Communication on 'The Europe Agreements and Beyond: A Strategy to Prepare the Countries of Central and Eastern Europe for Accession', COM (1994) 361.

44 Agenda 2000 states that the 'the present structured dialogue no longer appears appropriate'. Agenda 2000, loc. cit. n. 9, at p. 62.

reform under the umbrella of the Europe Agreement. However, it cannot be contested that, despite these phenomena, the implementation of the agreement created a framework for economic and political transition in Romania.

3.3 Accession Partnership

In 1998, the European Union redefined its approach regarding the two countries left out of the first wave of enlargement and invited Romania and Bulgaria to start accession negotiations. The European Union also established the Accession Partnership, a new instrument to assist the candidates even better in their further preparations for accession.[45]

The Accession Partnership guides Romania's efforts to meet its commitments under the Europe Agreement. On its basis, Romania adopted a national plan for the adoption of the *acquis* and a national strategy of short-term economic development.[46] As the accession negotiations have progressed, almost every second year saw the adoption of an Accession Partnership setting the priorities for the coming year.[47] The European Union continues to monitor and score the implementation of the agreement, on the basis of the evolving goals of the partnership. The Accession Partnership set out the principles, conditions and objectives that specify the adjustments required and the financial instruments provided by the European Union. As a result, the patterns of the reform measures were more suited to the specific conditions of Romania and less room was given to the decision makers in terms of choosing the timing and form of the measures required to achieve the targets set by the European Commission. In parallel with the gradual liberalisation of trade within the framework of the agreement and the legal approximation achieved, the capacity to implement the timetable of the Accession Partnership was considered by the European Union as an indicator of the country's readiness for accession. However, Romania continued to have difficulties in meeting these deadlines.[48]

---

45 See K. Inglis, 'The Pre-accession Strategy and the Accession Partnerships', in Ott and Inglis, op. cit. n. 2, at pp. 106-111.

46 National Strategy for the Adoption of the *Acquis Communautaire*, submitted to the European Commission on 14 June 1999, available at: <http://www.infoeuropa.ro>; National Strategy of short-term economic development of Romania, available at: <http://www.cdep.ro/pls>.

47 The most recent one is Council Decision 2003/397/EC of 19 May 2003 on the principles, priorities, intermediate objectives and conditions contained in the Accession Partnership with Romania, *OJ* 2003 L 145/21.

48 On the sanctions and the monitoring mechanism of Art. 4 of Council Regulation (EC) No. 622/98 on assistance to the applicant States in the framework of the pre-accession strategy, and in particular on the establishment of Accession Partnerships, *OJ* 1998 L 85/1, see chapter 3 in this volume.

3.4 Roadmap for Romania and Bulgaria

Within the framework of the support for Romania and Bulgaria to join the European Union by 2007, the European Union adopted the Roadmap for Bulgaria and Romania, aimed at assisting the two countries to meet the accession criteria, at the Copenhagen European Council in December 2002.[49] The Roadmap indicates the tasks to be completed and the necessary financial support. The Roadmap for Romania concentrates in particular on the administrative and judicial capacity required in order to implement the *acquis*, as well as on economic reform. This document covers the period up to the accession. Priorities set in the field of economic reform reflect the fact that the European Union considers the piecemeal achievements of the national strategy as satisfactory. However, achievements in some areas are regarded as less satisfactory: reduction of state aid, rate of inflation, energy costs, tax reform, bankruptcy procedures, budgetary reform, enforcement of property rights, transactions and prices for agricultural land, public enterprise reform, completion of privatisation in the banking sector and public investment in infrastructure. The effectiveness of these instruments can be assessed only within the context of the complex interaction of Romania's political development and international economic conditions. Since 2002, however, significant changes have occurred in the speed of legislative approximation, and the economic indicators of Romania have improved.[50]

On 6 October 2004, in its Strategy Paper on progress in the enlargement process,[51] the European Commission reiterated its objective to finalise the negotiations with Romania in 2004 and sign the Accession Treaty by 2005. From the Strategy Paper, it appears that the European Union has become more prudent in its evaluation of the chances of aligning economic discrepancies upon accession. When compared to its previous regular reports, which focused mostly on legislative activity and institutional capacity, the 2004 Strategy Paper redirects the approach of the European Union towards a more performance-oriented assessment.

4. THE ACCESSION TREATY OF 2005

4.1 Introduction

The conclusions of the European Commission's regular reports, especially that of 2004, as well as the conclusions of the European Council in December 2004,

[49] Communication from the Commission to the Council and the European Parliament, Roadmaps for Bulgaria and Romania, COM (2002) 624 final, Brussels, 13 November 2002.

[50] The economic growth rate was 5 per cent in 2002, 5.2 per cent in 2003 and 8.3 per cent in 2004. Source: <http://europa.eu.int/comm/enlargement/romania/economical_profile.htm>.

[51] COM (2004) 657 final.

suggested that the Treaty to be concluded with Romania and Bulgaria could have a different approach than that underpinning the 2004 enlargement, with a series of highly demanding legal obligations with clear preventive and corrective sanctions. The reason behind these expectations was that the performances of the two candidates, especially that of Romania, differed significantly from the achievements of the rest of the CEECs. These differences related not only to the time frame and speed of the implementation of the reform measures, which would justify longer periods of transitional arrangements, but also to the domestic problems, which might require a different strategy in order to guarantee the country's alignment with the membership obligations. Surprisingly, apart from the postponement clause, the Accession Treaty does not significantly depart from its approach towards the ten new Member States in 2003. This is because, in spite of differences between the two groups of countries, their performance was assessed according to the same criteria. These related not so much to their economic and legal capacity, but primarily to their political commitment to continue the fulfilment of the obligations undertaken during the accession negotiations. In fact, none of the CEECs had fully implemented the *acquis* at the time of accession and all of them still have to undertake significant measures for the effective transposition, implementation and enforcement of the *acquis*.

The economics of the transitional arrangements of the Accession Treaties needs to be considered at the level of the areas concerned and those directly affected by the further integration capacity of certain new Member States. The entire range of arrangements may be regarded as a distinct instrument of integration, given the scale of the enlarged internal market. It is therefore too early to speculate about the effect of the transitional measures handed to a specific Member State in isolation from the effect of these measures on the whole area.

4.2 Safeguard clauses

The Accession Treaty contains a number of safeguard clauses that may be applicable during a three-year period following accession. All these clauses have been discussed in detail in chapters 3 and 7 of this volume, hence there is no need for further elaboration here. However, it is worth taking a closer look at the postponement clause, which in part relates only to Romania.

Notwithstanding the general clause of Article 39(1) of the Act (and the Protocol), the Council of the European Union may postpone the accession of Romania in the following two situations. Firstly, accession may be postponed if there are 'serious shortcomings' in the fulfilment of the commitments specified in Annex IX, part I of the Act. These commitments include, *inter alia:*

- implementation of the Schengen Action Plan,
- improvement of border control and facilities as well as implementation of measures aimed at combating illegal immigration,

- development and implementation of the Action Plan and Strategy for the Reform of the Judiciary,
- further fight against corruption, including, *inter alia*, enforcement of the anticorruption legislation and strengthening of the National Anti-Corruption Prosecutors' Office,
- development and implementation of the multi-annual anti-crime strategy.

Secondly, accession may be postponed if Romania fails to meet the obligations related to proper implementation of state aid legislation. Detailed commitments are specified in Annex IX, part II of the Act. The list includes ensuring effective control by the Competition Council of state aid, strengthening the enforcement of the legislation, submission of the revised steel restructuring plan and further strengthening of the Competition Council.

The decision on the postponement of accession on the basis of this clause may be adopted by the Council of the European Union by a qualified majority on the initiative of the European Commission. This arrangement is different to the general postponement clause that requires unanimity in the Council.

The Council is expected to decide on the entry date for Romania and Bulgaria in the second half of 2006.[52]

4.3 Transitional measures

4.3.1 *General overview*

The transitional measures relating to Romania are listed in Annex VII to the Act.[53] The rationale and model for transitional arrangements follows the pattern known from the previous Accession Treaty.[54] In the case of Romania, transitional arrangements have been negotiated in the following areas: free movement of persons, freedom to provide services, free movement of capital, competition policy, agriculture, transport policy, taxation, energy and environment. A complete survey of all the derogations would exceed the limits of this chapter. However, certain aspects having specific relevance from the point of view of the EU Member States and Romania's integration capacity need to be considered.

Competition law and JHA are the two sectors where Romania still has serious shortcomings in fulfilling the requirements of the accession conditionality. These sectors were therefore debated extensively before the closure of the accession

---

52 As stated by the Council of the European Union in its Presidency Conclusions of 16 June 2006, Doc. 10633/06, CONCL 2, para. 52.

53 And in Annex VII to the Protocol.

54 See K. Inglis, 'The Accession Treaty and its Transitional Arrangements: A Twilight Zone for the New Members of the Union', in Hillion, op. cit. n. 38, at p. 77.

negotiations at the end of 2004 and led to the adoption of the above-mentioned Annex IX. Free movement of persons has been one of the most sensitive issues in relation to enlargement. The case of Romania is a very special one, due to the fears that have accumulated during the past ten to fifteen years because of the high number of Romanian immigrants and illegal workers entering EU Member States. The legal and financial framework of Romania's participation in the CAP is another sensitive issue for Member States due not only to the low development and poor infrastructure of the sector but also to the fact that a relatively high proportion of the Romanian labour force works in this sector.[55]

4.3.2 *Free movement of persons*

Transitional arrangements on the free movement of persons are based on the model already used in the previous Accession Treaty.[56] Derogations relate primarily to Article 39 TEC and Articles 1-6 of Council Regulation 1612/68/EEC[57] for two years following accession.[58] Thus, national laws and bilateral agreements regulate the access of Romanian nationals to the labour market of the Member States. The restriction may be prolonged for another three years. The Treaty leaves open another possibility for the Member States in case of serious disturbances of their labour markets, allowing them to apply such national measures or bilateral agreements for another two years. A serious disturbance is defined as a situation in which the labour inflow could seriously threaten the standards of living or level of employment in a given region or occupation. Concerning the rights of family members of workers, the Treaty provides that for the period of the transitional measures, the provisions of Directive 2004/38/EC[59] shall apply in Romania with regard to nationals of the Member States and in the Member States with regard to the nationals of Romania, subject to a stay for a period of less then twelve months. Directive 2004/38/EC relates to spouses and descendents of workers younger than twenty-one years of age. However, the Member States may apply more favourable national or bilateral measures if they wish to. Romania may also maintain in force equivalent measures with regard to the nationals of the Member State concerned. The Treaty does not preclude the right of any Member

[55] See *supra* section 1.2.

[56] See M. Dougan, 'A Spectre is Haunting Europe… Free Movement of Persons and the Eastern Enlargement', in Hillion, op. cit. n. 38, at p. 111; A. Adinolfi, 'Free Movement and Access to Work of Citizens of the New Member States: The Transitional Measures', 42 *CMLRev.* (2005) p. 469.

[57] Regulation (EEC) No. 1612/68 of the Council of 15 October 1968 on freedom of movement for workers within the Community, *OJ* 1968 L 257/2 (English special edition).

[58] See Annex VII, part 1, of the Act.

[59] Directive 2004/38/EC of the European Parliament and of the Council of 29 April 2004 on the right of citizens of the Union and their family members to move and reside freely within the territory of the Member States, *OJ* 2004 L 158/77.

States to grant full freedom to Romania at an earlier time. Germany and Austria set specific sector-related limitations for Romania. In Germany, the construction sector and related branches, industrial cleaning and the interior decorators market are considered sensitive for the inflow of labour, while in Austria horticultural activity, the cutting, shaping and finishing of stone, the manufacture of metal, construction, security activities, industrial cleaning, home nursing, social work and activities without accommodation are protected. Romania may also take equivalent measures in relation to these countries after notification of the proposed measures to the European Commission.

4.3.3 *Competition policy*

Transitional measures in the field of competition policy predominantly concern fiscal state aid and the restructuring of the Romanian steel industry.[60] Accordingly, Romania may continue the corporate tax exemptions for deprived areas, according to the following criteria: for three listed deprived areas up to 31 December 2008, for twenty-two listed areas up to 31 December 2009 and for three listed areas up to 31 December 2010. These areas are located in the western part of the country, where the mining industry prevails. Romania is allowed to grant tax exemptions until 31 December 2011, provided that it meets the strict conditions spelled out in the Act. The Accession Treaty also deals extensively with the restructuring of the Romanian steel industry.

4.3.4 *Free movement of services*

The transitional periods relating to the free movement of services[61] deal only with the application of European Parliament and Council Directive 97/9/EC on investor-compensation schemes.[62] The minimum level of investor compensation provided for under Article 4(1) of Directive 97/9/EC shall not apply to Romania until 31 December 2011. It is scheduled as a gradual approximation to the *acquis*, starting from €4,500 by January 2007, €9,000 by 2009 and €15,000 for the period of 1 January 2011 until 31 December 2011. During this period, the Member States will have the right to prevent a branch of a Romanian investment firm established on their territory from operating unless that branch has joined an officially recognised investor compensation scheme on their territory in order to cover the difference between the Romanian level of compensation and the minimum level referred to in Directive 97/9/EC.

---

60 See Annex VII, part 4, of the Act and Appendix A to Annex VII of the Act.

61 See Annex VII, part 2, of the Act.

62 Directive 97/9/EC of the European Parliament and of the Council of 3 March 1997 on investor-compensation schemes, *OJ* 1997 L 84/22.

4.3.5 *Free movement of capital*

For a period of five years from the date of accession, Romania may maintain the restrictions in its domestic legislation on the acquisition of ownership of land for secondary residence by nationals of EU Member States who are non-resident in Romania or by companies registered in accordance with the laws of a Member State that are neither established nor have a branch or representative agency in Romania. However, companies registered in Romania, regardless of their ownership, benefit from the same treatment as domestic companies. This restriction does not apply to the nationals of EU Member States who are legally resident in Romania, who are treated as Romanian nationals. This restriction thus does not constitute a significant barrier for EU based companies to enter the Romanian market, although it does not allow for full free movement of capital.

With regard to the acquisition of agricultural land, forest and forestry by foreigners, the restrictions in force in Romania may be maintained for seven years in the case of EU nationals and companies established in Romania, except for self-employed farmers who wish to establish themselves and reside in Romania. The Treaty leaves open the possibility to revise these arrangements three years after the date of accession.

4.3.6 *Agriculture*

Investment support for agricultural holdings has been set at a maximum of 50 per cent, and in less favourable areas at 60 per cent, of the relevant rural development regulation, fixed as percentage of the volume of eligible investment.[63] For young farmers, this percentage may reach 55 per cent or 65 per cent, respectively. This support is aimed to improve the pricing and marketing of agricultural products, subject to the applicants having been granted a transitional period after accession to meet minimum standards on environmental protection and food hygiene. For the 2007-2013 programming period in areas covered by Objective 1, the contribution of the Community may amount to either 85 per cent of agro-environmental and animal welfare measures and 80 per cent of other measures, or the percentages established in the regulations concerning rural development, whichever is higher.

As regards the implementation of agricultural legislation, derogations will apply in the case of Romania for the common organisation of the market in wine.[64] By derogation from Article 19(1) to (3) of Council Regulation 1493/1999/EC, a

---

63 Annex VIII of the Act

64 Council Regulation (EC) No. 1493/1999 of 17 May 1999 on the common organisation of the market in wine, *OJ* 1999 L 179/1.

transitional period on replanting rights was granted to Romania up to 31 December 2014.[65] However, the restructuring and conversion of these vineyards will not be eligible for support under this regulation (although national state aid may be given for this purpose). Temporary derogations for sanitary and veterinary measures are provided for a period of three years, when products not complying with the *acquis* may still be commercialised on the domestic market. These derogations relate to the structural requirements of European Parliament and Council Regulation (EC) No. 852/2004 on the hygiene of foodstuffs.[66] The products benefiting from derogation, however, must bear different health and identifications marks. Derogations have also been allowed from the provisions of Council Directive 91/414/ECC concerning the placing of plant protection products on the market.[67]

4.4 Institutional framework for the accession

The institutional arrangements relating to Bulgaria and Romania have been thoroughly analysed in chapter 7 of this volume. The following analysis is therefore devoted to a limited number of issues relating specifically to Romania. Following accession, the country will have fourteen votes in the Council (Art. 10 of the Act). The number of representatives in the European Parliament will be thirty-three. Moreover, it will have fifteen representatives on the Economic and Social Committee (Art. 12 of the Act) and fifteen on the Committee of the Regions (Art. 13 of the Act). As already mentioned in chapters 3 and 7 of this volume, Romania is covered by an information and consultation procedure.[68] Moreover, its observers are meant to participate in the work of the European Parliament in the period preceding accession. The latter proved to be fairly difficult and their participation was delayed until 26 September 2005 for political reasons.[69]

4.5 Conclusions

The transitional measures discussed briefly in the preceding paragraphs have their own sectoral consequences in Romania at micro and macro level, as well as on

65 Annex VII, part 5, of the Act.

66 Regulation (EC) No. 852/2004 of the European Parliament and of the Council of 29 April 2004 on the hygiene of foodstuffs, *OJ* 2004 L 139/1.

67 Council Directive 91/414/EEC of 15 July 1991 concerning the placing of plant protection products on the market, *OJ* 1991 L 230/1 (as amended).

68 Exchange of Letters between the European Union and the Republic of Bulgaria and Romania on an information and consultation procedure for the adoption of certain decisions and other measures to be taken during the period preceding the accession, *OJ* 2005 L 157/393.

69 See L. Kubosova, 'Romanian and Bulgarian observers join European Parliament', *EUObserver*, 26 September 2005.

the internal market, but their real economic and social effects at both levels still need to be assessed, especially in the context of their interplay with the transitional arrangements granted to the rest of the Central and Eastern European countries. These effects will also shape the costs of membership in the period when the *acquis* will fully apply for these countries. Thus, the long-term implications of the Accession Treaty require a consideration of the whole Central and Eastern European market.

We cannot say that there is more asymmetry in the Accession Treaty with Romania than in the case of the ten new Member States which acceded to the European Union in May 2004, when considering the nature and length of the transitional measures, as well as the commitments and obligations undertaken by Romania, on the one hand, and the rights earned by the actual date of accession, on the other. This does not mean that we ignore the fact that, in general, the rights and obligations of the Accession Treaties within the framework of eastern enlargement are indeed very asymmetrical compared to the limitations imposed by the rest of the Member States on the free movement of persons. The four basic freedoms may therefore not manifest themselves in all their complexity in the new Member States, and this gives rise to increasing asymmetry between the obligations of the new Member States and the status of the old ones. One should also note that none of the Central and Eastern European Member States have obtained any permanent opt-outs comparable to those of the United Kingdom and Denmark in relation to the Schengen *acquis* and economic and monetary union. The Accession Treaty states that Romania will be member of EMU from the date of its accession, but subject to the derogations provided for in Article 122 TEC.[70] However, the text of the Accession Treaty does not establish any deadlines concerning the fulfilment of conditions in this field. Concerning the Schengen *acquis*, the Treaty contains a list of the provisions to be implemented by the date of accession, but also stresses that Romania will not be part of the Schengen zone at the time of its accession.[71]

When all the transitional periods are taken into account, the question arises whether the internal market can be completed in the enlarged Union. Central and Eastern European Member States have adhered to stricter criteria than the rest of the Member States during the pre-accession period, with high economic and social costs, and following accession will not fully benefit from the currently applicable redistribution system of the Common Agriculture Policy. This reality justifies the argument that the last two Accession Treaties have created the legal and institutional conditions for a two-tier Europe, where the principle of equality does not apply in the European Union based on the principle of non-discrimination.

---

70 Art. 5 of the Act (*mutatis mutandis* Art. 5 of the Protocol).
71 Art. 4 of the Act (*mutatis mutandis* Art. 4 of the Protocol).

This is definitely a regression compared to the achievements of the post-Amsterdam process, and also calls into question whether the commonly cited principle of proportionality fully applies in the context of the transitional mechanisms of these Accession Treaties, if we search for a balance between the economic and political legitimacy of certain measures in the general European context. The most obvious example remains the limitations on the free movement of workers, an area dominated by a considerable number of economic arguments against such limitations. They include, *inter alia*, shortage of qualified labour in the short term at EU level and the much lower mobility of labour in Central and Eastern Europe than in Western European countries. Thus, the outcome of the Accession Treaties on free movement of persons from the new Member States is the result of the transposition of domestic social policy concerns and frustrations of the old Member States to EU level rather than of economic impact assessment studies based on macro and micro economic arguments.[72]

However, the real threat for the old Member States and the functioning of economic integration in the enlarged Union is not the free movement of persons and services from the new Member States, nor the social policy consequences of the enlargement, but the scale effects of the diversity in market conditions and legal and institutional culture brought into the European Union by the new entrants. This, however, should be a common undertaking of the Member States which should comprise, besides derogations and new common measures, mechanisms that take account of the specific conditions not only of these markets but also of these societies. Otherwise, the already fragile democratic legitimacy of the European Union will be endangered and questioned from both sides – West and East. Dissatisfaction may arise in the business communities of the older Member States if the harmonised rules transposed in the CEECs do not assure the same conditions as in the well-established market economies. On the other hand, the differentiated treatment of the citizens of the CEECs may drive them towards euroscepticism, especially in the first years following accession, when the micro economic costs of membership are extremely high for all these countries. As already argued, it seems that political fears rather than economic realities determined the approach of the Accession Treaties in respect of the free movement of persons and the CAP. It will be difficult to implement the basic principle of non-discrimination in an enlarged internal market when differentiated treatment applies by virtue of the Accession Treaty.

Another important and interesting factor in the case of Romania is formed by the monitoring and transitional arrangements for the 2005-2007 period and in the

---

72 See Communication from the Commission to the Council, the European Parliament, the European Economic and Social Committee and the Committee of the Regions – Report on the Functioning of the Transitional Arrangements set out in the 2003 Accession Treaty (period 1 May 2004-30 April 2006), COM (2006) 48 final.

years following accession. There is an asymmetry between the findings of the regular reports of the European Commission on the fulfilment of the political criteria of accession, especially those related to human rights protection, including economic rights, and the Accession Treaty. The Accession Treaty devotes little or no attention to the political conditionality of Romania's accession, apart from continued monitoring to ensure the functioning of the separation of powers, the independence of the judiciary and the protection of human rights. We should not neglect that economic integration is more closely related to political integration in Central and Eastern Europe, where the economy is a highly politicised issue, than it is in the western part of the European Union. Enlargement somehow brings us back to the original idea of European unity, that of assuring peace, democracy and security. The process of the accession negotiations and the approach of the Accession Treaties, both built on political instruments, demonstrate that the European decision makers have recognised this reality, but it is still an open question within Central and Eastern European political culture whether as a result of the accession of these countries to the European Union, a stronger shift from the level of political instruments onto to the legal ones will or may work as effective incentives for the new Member States.

The wording of the Accession Treaty as regards monitoring and sanctions shows that the European Union does not yet have clear solutions and is still in search of them. It only leaves room for 'Community corrective actions', which can be interpreted both as a high level of flexibility and adaptability in solutions for situations that may appear in relation to the integration capacity of the new Member States, but also as a legislative concept that lacks the effectiveness of clear legal measures. Political expectations and commitments will thus continue to frame the development of market regulations in the enlarged Union in the coming years.

5. FINANCIAL ASSISTANCE TO ROMANIA

The pre-accession financial assistance granted by the European Union to Romania has been substantial and is still increasing. During the period from 1990 to 2004, the total amount allocated to Romania under the three main assistance programmes (Phare, SAPARD and ISPA) was €4.8 billion. The total volume of pre-accession assistance available to Romania in 2004 amounted to more than €900 million, approximately 1.5 per cent of Romanian GDP.[73] Romania's absorption

[73] During the 1992-1999 period, EU assistance amounted to €1.2 billion. The Berlin European Council of 24-25 March 1999 decided to double the financial aid to achieve the objectives laid down in the pre-accession strategy. During the 2000-2003 period, Romania received approximately €660

capacity of funds in terms of commitments has been stable at 97 per cent since the year 2000. This means that Romania will be able to benefit almost fully from EU funds after accession.[74]

Phare remains the main instrument of EU assistance in the pre-accession phase and focuses on institution building and investment support. It also finances measures in the fields of cross-border cooperation and nuclear safety. During the 2000-2003 period, Romania benefited from more than €1 billion in Phare funding allocated through cross-border cooperation programmes with Hungary and Bulgaria (e.g., strengthening border management and control),[75] specific programmes such as in the field of nuclear safety,[76] and the National Programme on the fulfilment of the political and economic Copenhagen criteria.[77] The 2004 Phare Programme for Romania consisted of an allocation of €405.3 million for the National Programme. The allocations for 2005 and 2006 are €435 million and €481 million respectively.

In November 2000, the Commission approved the Romanian SAPARD programme to support sustainable and rural development.[78] The annual SAPARD allocation for 2005 and 2006 amounts to €175.2 million, up from €158.7 million in 2004.[79] ISPA funding focuses both on the improvement of transport infrastructure (modernisation of roads, upgrading of railway networks, etc.) as well as on the rehabilitation of the environment (management of waste, sewage systems, wastewater treatment, etc.).[80] During the 2000-2002 period, Romania benefited from ISPA funding amounting to roughly €200 million per year. In 2003, a total

million per year through the three pre-accession programmes. Following the Commission's proposal to considerably increase the assistance for the candidate countries in order to support them in taking the remaining steps necessary to meet the membership criteria, Romania will receive supplementary funds representing an increase of up to 40 per cent in 2006 (around €2.8 billion). Source: Mission of Romania to the EU: <http://ue.mae.ro>.

74 See <http://www.europa.eu.int/comm/enlargement/romania/eu_relations.htm>.

75 The 2004 Phare Programme for Romania allocated €28 million for cross-border cooperation. For the 2004-2006 period, in the framework of the Wider Europe initiative, Phare finances the neighbourhood programmes of Romania with Moldova, Serbia and Montenegro and Ukraine. See <http://ue.mae.ro>.

76 See Phare 2004 Standard Project Fiche 'Consolidation of the energy sector', CRIS Number: PHARE 2004/016-772.03.10.

77 For the 2004-2006 period, the National Programme includes a multi-annual component consisting of key sector reform programmes such as public administration, public finance, justice (e.g., assistance to enhance the independence, professionalism and management capacity of the judiciary), minorities (e.g., conditions of the Roma) and economic and social cohesion. Sector programmes are based on sector strategies, with annual project fiches and an annual component covering various specific needs related to the implementation of the *acquis*. For an overview, see <http://www.europa.eu.int/comm/enlargement/romania/eu_relations.htm>.

78 Council Regulation (EC) No. 1268/99, *OJ* 1999 L 161/87, as last amended by Commission Regulation (EC) No. 2278/2004, *OJ* 2004 L 396/36.

79 See <http://www.sapard.ro>.

80 Council Regulation (EC) No. 1267/1999, *OJ* 1999 L 161/73, as last amended by Council Regulation (EC) No. 2257/2004 to take account of Croatia's candidate status, *OJ* 2004 L 389/1.

commitment of €272.3 million was approved. The overall allocation for 2004 was €316 million.

The European Commission and the European Investment Bank (EIB) have declared their readiness to help Romania cope with the consequences of the catastrophic floods which also hit the region in the summer of 2005. At the time of writing, the Commission was dealing with applications from Romania and Bulgaria for financial assistance under the EU Solidarity Fund.[81] The EIB has provided an emergency loan of up to €600 million to finance the necessary measures to repair and upgrade the damaged road and rail infrastructure of Romania.[82]

6. REGIONAL CROSS-BORDER COOPERATION

6.1 **Introduction**

The programmes and projects launched by the European Union in 2003 in the field of cross-border cooperation will speed up reforms in the fields of culture, education, development of civil society and cooperation among non-profit organisations. These programmes will also influence political culture in the region, including at central level. An analysis of the contents of cross-border cooperation programmes in which Romania also participates, and the geographical location of local communities involved in the projects, affirms that the European Union takes into consideration existing cultural, historical and social determinants of cooperation on both sides of the EU border. However, the fact that these programmes so far have no legal components means that the success of these projects is strongly dependent on legal developments under the pre-accession strategy. These programmes complement the general legal reforms, but their effect will be reduced in the absence of further measures related to the reform of local public administration, regional development and the creation of a transparent regulatory environment for the promotion of transnational trade. Hopefully, strong economic and cultural cooperation along the borders will influence sufficiently central policy considerations related to regional development and local economic autonomy and be able to reduce existing gaps between the centre and periphery.

The security of national borders and border control concerns are also relevant in the context of the European Neighbourhood Policy and the implementation of the Schengen *acquis* on the European Union's eastern borders.[83] The current

---

81 See EC Press Release No. IP/05/1071 of 26 August 2005.

82 See EIB Press Release No. BEI/05/84 of 27 September 2005.

83 Communication from the Commission to the Council and the European Parliament, Wider Europe – Neighbourhood: A New Framework for Relations with our Eastern and Southern Neighbours, COM (2003) 104 final; Communication from the Commission, Strategy Paper: European Neighbourhood Policy, COM (2004) 373 final. See also chapters 1 and 2 in this volume.

security concerns of the CEECs can only be adequately understood by reviewing the impact of the European Union's pre-accession policy on these issues. The European Union supported the conclusion of bilateral treaties on good neighbourliness among the CEECs during the pre-accession period and, once these were in place, border security and cross-border cooperation related to ethnic groups were regarded as legally settled. Today, however, the European Union is left without a solution for the effects of the implementation of the Schengen Agreement on the eastern border of the enlarged Union, on the neighbouring countries of the new Member States and especially on their ethnic nationals living outside the Union. On both sides of the eastern borders of the enlarged Union, the question is whether the Schengen border will act as a new curtain, despite existing efforts under the umbrella of European Neighbourhood Policy. The central question continues to be whether regional cooperation in the border regions of those concerned will sufficiently influence country-wide developments. However, the performance of these countries under the framework of these programmes will help the EU institutions to better understand the historical, cultural and social factors of these regions and how these factors influence country-wide legal and political culture related to European integration. Once the European Union recognises the transnational nature of this conditionality, the active role of the neighbours in these projects may develop their capacity to promote such values at Community level as well.

Therefore, paying close attention to the developments under the framework of the European Neighbourhood Policy and cross-border cooperation is in the common interest of both sides of the border of the European Union. Hopefully, cross-border cooperation will sufficiently influence the private sector and non-profit organisations to develop a nationwide capacity and take part in European policy-making processes during the time left before Romania's actual accession. In Romania, the role of the private and non-profit sectors in actively influencing sectoral policy making and market regulation is not sufficiently developed compared to the situation in the other EU Member States. Last but not least, cross-border cooperation and the implementation of the European Neighbourhood Policy also depend on the consolidated effect of the conditionality imposed by the technical and financial support delivered by other international organisations. The overlapping support and requirements of the European Union and other international organisations have strengthened the commitment of Romania to make progress in the implementation of economic and political measures. In certain cases, the synergy among these projects has significantly consolidated the progress made during the accession preparations, whereas in other cases the lack of coordination weakens and reduces the effectiveness of the assistance. The cooperation of other international institutions, such as the World Bank, and the European Union in the same technical assistance programmes and projects is more welcome than the operation of separate projects by each institution. However, although the measures targeted by the participating institutions converge in terms of the economic, legal or institutional outcome they seek to achieve, in practice each institution tries to use the best model available based on what are sometimes conflicting approaches. The reform process in Romania therefore also needs to be assessed from this point of view, although the central and strongest reform incentive remains membership conditionality.

6.2 Programmes

Administrative reform and the development of an effective regional policy in Romania do not belong to the areas of smooth reform. Romania's efforts to develop the legal framework in support of regional development started early in the 1990s, but have so far not made significant progress. The centralised management of regional development policies has created an increased discrepancy between the centre and periphery, which continues to cause serious regional disparities. Economic development is highly concentrated around the capital city of Bucharest. The rest of the national infrastructure is underdeveloped and cannot act as an investment-facilitating factor.

The managing authorities in Romania are at very different stages of preparation. Intermediary bodies to manage structural funds were only designated by a law issued in June 2004.[84] The transfer of responsibilities to local authorities is not effective, because it is not backed by an adequate transfer of resources.[85] The ability to raise local revenue is limited, and legislation governing financial transfers lacks objective criteria, maintaining a strong controlling function at county level at the expense of local councils.[86] Co-financing capacity at local level is a serious problem, as the debt limitation provision in the local public administration law is a serious constraint to their capacity to finance pre-accession funds. For the reduction of regional disparities, it is important for Romania to reconsider its current policy on local public finances, which does not allow regions to keep most of the income generated locally for local purposes, as the centralised redistribution of local income is still strong. A framework law on decentralisation was adopted in July 2004, reaffirming the concept of deconcentration and the role of centrally appointed government representatives at local level.[87] However, this law only lays down the principle of deconcentration, which needs to be complemented by a

[84] Law No. 315 of 28 June 2004 on regional development in Romania, *Official Journal of Romania* No. 557 of 29 June 2004.

[85] 2004 Regular Report, loc. cit. n. 39, at p. 17.

[86] Emergency Ordinance No. 45 of 5 July 2003 on local public finances, amended by Emergency Ordinance No. 9 of 24 February 2004, *Official Journal of Romania* No. 174 of 28 February 2004.

[87] Law No. 339 of July 2004, *Official Journal of Romania* No. 668 of 26 July 2004.

series of implementing laws. It is promising that this law allows the local public authorities to try, in the form of pilot programmes, to organise centres for the decentralised management of certain public services for a limited period of time.

We cannot yet regard Romanian legislation on local public administration as promoting local economic and financial autonomy sufficiently to strengthen the capacity of local communities to fully benefit from the European Union's Structural Funds, although significant measures have been adopted in this regard in recent years. This reality will also seriously affect Romania's capacity to perform within the framework of INTERREG programmes.

In the 2007-2013 period, the INTERREG programme will cover the five borders of Romania (with Bulgaria, Serbia and Montenegro, Ukraine, Moldova and Hungary), which will involve nineteen of its forty-one counties. Phare CBC projects with Bulgaria and Hungary have been in place for the past five to six years. The Ministry of European Integration is the body responsible for the implementation of INTERREG. In the case of Hungarian-Romanian relations, cross-border cooperation is financed from both Phare CBC (on the territory of Romania) and INTERREG III A (on the territory of Hungary). For the first time, a multi-annual programme (2004-2006) based on EU regulations will take place with Serbia. In addition, there is a three-county cross-border programme for Hungary, Romania and Serbia and Montenegro, involving three Euroregions (DKMT, Bihor-Hajdu-Bihar and Carpatica). In September 2004, a further bilateral programme was launched between Romania and Serbia and Montenegro, the Common Fund for Small Projects, within the context of Phare CBC.

Romania participates in nine Euroregions: Carpatica (Romania, Hungary, Poland, Ukraine and Slovenia), Danube-Kris-Mures-Tisza (DKMT) (Romania, Hungary and Vojvodina) Giurgiu-Russe (Romania and Bulgaria), South Danube (Romania and Bulgaria) Danubius (Romania and Bulgaria) Lower Danube (Romania, Ukraine and Republic of Moldova) Upper Prut (Romania, Republic of Moldova and Ukraine) and Siret-Prut-Nistru (Romania and Republic of Moldova).[88] In 1997, Romania joined the Carpathian Euroregion. The other members of the Carpathian Euroregion are Hungary, Poland, Ukraine and Slovenia. The project covers seven Romanian counties, targeting cooperation projects in the field of transport and infrastructure development and developing cooperation in the fields of tourism, culture and science.

The effectiveness of the European Union's support programmes on cross-border cooperation is strongly influenced by the creation of administrative structures for regional development and effective local public administration in the countries concerned. Cooperation today is weakened by the diverging competences of the local authorities on the other side of the border. In 1998, Romania

88 See <http://www.mae.ro> (website of the Romanian Ministry of Foreign Affairs).

established the development regions with the aim of creating such regional capacity.[89] Eight development regions were established, corresponding to NUTS II. However, the criteria for setting up such regions do not correspond fully to the European standards, since these regions lack legal personality and are not considered administrative territorial units by law. Therefore, the only possibility for cooperation is to set up so-called associations of local authorities at national and local level. The Romanian administrative system is decentralised, similar to the French approach to local public administration but with less local autonomy. In spite of the fact that in its regular reports the European Commission continues to criticise Romania's lack of progress in pursuing an effective institutional reform of local public administration in order to develop the necessary capacity to implement a European regional policy, this issue receives little attention in the Romanian national development strategies. An effective financial control mechanism for EU funds and EC financial interests is still not fully in place, and Romania's institutional capacity needs further strengthening. The decentralisation of preventive financial control from the Ministry of Public Finance to the income and spending centres has just started. However, if the reform process is not accelerated during the 2004-2006 period, it will be very difficult for Romanians to benefit from the European Structural Funds.

6.3 Impact of enlargement

For a country like Romania, which lies on the border between two of the main cultural regions of Europe, between Central and Eastern Europe and the Western Balkans, the enlargement of the European Union and the country's expected membership open a series of opportunities that complement and support the domestic economic, social and political reform processes. The benefits of the latest enlargement round can be summarised as follows:

(a) Cross-border cooperation contributes to a reduction in regional disparities in the post-accession phase for the new Member State. Well-developed regions in neighbouring countries are cooperating areas in the new Member State which are less developed, but which, compared to the rest of the participating regions outside the European Union's borders, are more developed.

(b) Cross-border cooperation may also reduce regional disparities in neighbouring countries, and this is especially true in the case of Romania.

---

[89] Law No. 151 of 15 July 1998 on regional development, *Official Journal of Romania* No. 265 of 16 July 1998, see also the new law on regional development: Law No. 315 of 28 June 2004, *Official Journal of Romania* No. 557 of 29 June 2004.

(c) Cross-border cooperation may diminish existing ethnic tensions through the development of closer cultural, scientific and economic relations on both sides of the border and may also positively influence central government policy towards minorities. There is no *acquis* on collective minority rights, but this should be considered at European level in the future.
(d) Cross-border cooperation in the framework of European Neighbourhood Policy may contribute to the solution of bilateral border security concerns that cannot be effectively handled on a bilateral basis. The most recent example is the dispute between Ukraine and Romania on the delimitation of the continental shelf in the Black Sea.
(e) The trade creation effects of cross-border cooperation may offset the post-accession costs of the new Member States. This effect is also strengthened by the benefits of trade liberalisation within the framework of the Europe Agreement with Romania.
(f) The costs and benefits of the latest enlargement round will not come to the surface before 2007, due to the transitional arrangements in force until that date, which may overlap with the date of accession of Romania and Bulgaria to the European Union.

By the time of the next round of EU enlargement, the scale effect of transnational market creation will increase for both old and new members, offset enlargement costs and assist the countries that recently acceded to the European Union in 2004 to develop from peripheries into central synergy points of the Central and Eastern European part of the internal market.

7. THE CFSP, BORDER CONTROL AND THE IMPLEMENTATION OF THE SCHENGEN *ACQUIS*

Border security and control in the area of Central and Eastern Europe and the Western Balkans does need to be considered in the light of both the European Union's approach to the Common Foreign and Security Policy (CFSP) and the external policy traditions of the candidates and the new Member States. The effectiveness of the European Union's approach should be assessed accordingly. Romania continues to align itself with the CFSP and, by the same token, is involved in European efforts aimed at strengthening stability in South-Eastern Europe.[90] In purely legal terms, it is worth noting that Romania has concluded a

[90] See D. Călic, 'Romania and the EU Common Foreign and Security Policy', 3 *Romanian Journal of European Affairs* (2003) p. 68.

number of agreements with the European Union and has participated in some of its ESDP missions.[91]

At regional level, Romania takes part in the Stability Pact and chaired the South-East European Cooperation Process in 2004-2005. Romania's role in pursuing regional cooperation in the Black Sea region has further potential to develop thanks to the country's geopolitical position. In this regard, Romania's involvement in the Organisation of the Black Sea Economic Cooperation, the GUUAM Group and the Danube Cooperation Process gain special importance.[92]

Since 1 January 2002, Romanian citizens may travel visa-free to the Schengen area.[93] A stay of up to ninety days is allowed without a visa or residence requirement. The Romanian border police continues to make progress in modernising its structures and working practices. The demilitarisation of border control is in progress. The Schengen Action Plan issued in July 2004 envisages a two-step implementation mechanism for the Schengen *acquis*.[94]

Romania is expected by the European Union to prevent illegal immigration of third-country nationals transiting Romania, especially from Moldova and other countries of the former Soviet Union, and to take effective border control measures with its eastern neighbours. However, cooperation with neighbouring states to enhance border security remains weak, both in relation to the Republic of Moldova and Ukraine. Romania has not introduced a visa regime with the Republic of Moldova, although the latter is on the negative list of Schengen countries.[95] The reason for this is the high number of ethnic Romanians in the Republic of Moldova, for whom the visa requirement would act as a new iron curtain. Also interesting, from a legal point of view, are Romania's real concerns and economic and political efforts to support Romanian minorities living outside its borders and the fact that it regards similar efforts by its neighbours relating to the national minorities within its own territory as a highly sensitive political issue, without

91 Agreement between Romania and the European Union on security procedures for the exchange of classified information, *OJ* 2005 L 118/48; Agreement between the European Union and Romania establishing a framework for the participation of Romania in the European Union crisis-management operations, *OJ* 2005 L 67/14; Agreement between the European Union and Romania on the participation of Romania in the European Union-led forces (EUF) in the Former Yugoslav Republic of Macedonia, *OJ* 2004 L 120/62; Agreement between the European Union and Romania on the participation of Romania in the European Union Police Mission (EUPM) in Bosnia and Herzegovina (BiH), *OJ* 2003 L 239/23.

92 See <http://www.mae.ro>.

93 Council Regulation (EC) No. 2414/2001, amending Regulation (EC) No. 539/2001 listing the third countries whose nationals must be in possession of visas when crossing the external borders of Member States and those whose nationals are exempt from that requirement, *OJ* 2001 L 327/1.

94 Government Decision No. 2365 of 21 December 2004, *Official Journal of Romania* No. 129 of 10 February 2005.

95 See Council Regulation (EC) No. 539/2001 listing the third countries whose nationals must be in possession of visas when crossing the external borders and those whose nationals are exempt from that requirement, *OJ* 2001 L 81/1.

treating the problem according to the same approach it applies towards Romanian minorities abroad.

In 2003, Romania signed a cooperation agreement with Europol.[96] In order to manage illegal immigration from Romania to the European Union effectively, readmission agreements are in place with several countries. In 2004, Romania brought its legislation on asylum into line with the Geneva Convention on Refugees.[97] The number of asylum applicants in Romania is low, but Romania continues to serve as transit country for illegal immigrants to Western Europe. However, the effectiveness of a border security policy involving Romania will depend on the capacity of the new Member States to build a common platform *vis-à-vis* the third countries. This is especially true in the case of Poland, Hungary and the Czech Republic *vis-à-vis* their eastern neighbours. Stability on the borders of the European Union cannot be treated on a piecemeal basis. An integrated strategy therefore needs to be developed by the European Union and the outsiders.

8. CONCLUDING REMARKS

The development of the European Union's policy on Romania in the context of eastern enlargement is the result of an uneven combination of external and domestic legal and political factors that have irreversibly shaped the reforms in Romania. From a purely legal point of view, it is difficult to qualify the character of this relationship other than as that generally applied by the European Union in relation to its eastern neighbours with candidate status. EU enlargement, like EU integration, is an interdisciplinary undertaking where law, politics and economics meet and where the effects of a certain type of pre-accession instrument cannot be assessed in isolation. The effectiveness of the assessment criteria applied by the European Union for ranking Romania's achievements in the pre-accession phase are those applied in relation to all the candidate countries. These can be generally criticised for not being sufficiently suited to effectively evaluating the effects of transposition of the *acquis* into the specific market conditions and legal and institutional culture of the candidates. This issue, however, cannot be approached merely from the viewpoint of the candidate countries. Hence, the only yardstick available to the European Union was the best practice at European level and in the Member States, regardless of the different conditions in the CEECs that did not always justify such comparisons. Enlargement is thus costly for both the former and the new Member States.

---

[96] Law No. 197 of 25 May 2004, *Official Journal of Romania* No. 498 of 2 June 2004.

[97] Government Ordinance No. 43 regarding the status of refugees in Romania, *Official Journal of Romania* No. 31 of 29 January 2004.

The central question of the enlargement remains whether the legislative approximation process can create the same market mechanisms and the same level playing field as in the well-developed market economies of the Western European Member States. Not only Romania, but also the rest of the new Member States, still have to perform a series of obligations before achieving a functional compatibility with the requirements of the internal market. Compared to the rest of the CEECs, Romania's case differs on the basis of the late and not yet completed structural reform of its industry and its weak capacity to successfully convert the external conditionality of the membership preparations into micro and macro economic goals at the domestic level. The over-politicisation of integration has affected not only the strength of the economic reform process but also Romania's institutional capacity to implement the legal reforms required by the accession criteria. It depends mostly on the candidate country's ability to offset the costs against the benefits of trade liberalisation, which strongly depends on the competitive capacity developed within the process of pre-accession. In this regard, Romania is far behind the rest of the new Member States, because its strategy did not focus enough on the preparation of the private sector for EU accession.

The 2004 enlargement of the European Union has significantly accelerated the efforts of Romania towards fulfilling the accession criteria. During 2004, legal reform took place at an almost unprecedented pace, and Romania enacted laws which had been postponed for years.[98] This is a clear commitment from Romania

---

98 Acceleration of the reform of local public administration: Framework Law No. 339/2004 on decentralization, *Official Journal of Romania* No. 668 of 26 July 2004; Law No. 441 for the amendment of the law on local public administration No. 215/2004, *Official Journal of Romania* No. 396 of 4 May 2004; Law No. 315 of 28 June 2004 on regional development in Romania, *Official Journal of Romania* No. 557 of 29 June 2004.

Human rights protection: Law No. 273/2004 of the legal regime of child adoption, *Official Journal of Romania* No. 557 of 23 June 2004; Law No. 272 on the protection and promotion of children's rights, *Official Journal of Romania* No. 557 of 23 June 2004.

Rule of law and democracy: Law No. 365 on the ratification of the UN Convention against corruption, *Official Journal of Romania* No. 903 of 5 October 2004; Law No. 7 on the Code of Conduct for public servants, *Official Journal of Romania* No. 157 of 23 February 2004.

Acceleration of privatization: Government Decision No. 27/2004, *Official Journal of Romania* No. 88 of 31 January 2004; Ordinance No. 36/2004, *Official Journal of Romania* No. 90 of 31 January 2004; Law No. 36/2004 for the promotion of restructuring, reorganization and privatization of commercial companies, national companies and state-owned commercial companies, *Official Journal of Romania* No. 269 of 6 March 2004; Law No. 191/2004 on the acceleration of privatization, *Official Journal of Romania* No. 470 of 26 May 2004; Emergency Ordinance No. 134 on measures concerning the privatization of the SIDEX company, *Official Journal of Romania* No. 1234 of 21 December 2004.

Restructuring of the mining and metallurgical sectors: Government Decision No. 615 on the approval of the mining strategy for the period of 2004-2010, *Official Journal of Romania* No. 411 of 7 May 2004; Government Decision No. 655 on the approval of the strategy on restructuring the metallurgical industry for the period of 2004-2010, *Official Journal of Romania* No. 425 of 12 May 2004.

not only in the direction of complying with the accession criteria but also with regard to strengthening its integration and assimilative capacity in order to undertake the obligations of membership by 2007. The European Union's reassurance of its openness towards the accession of Romania by January 2007, but with a series of safeguard clauses in case of the regression or stagnation of the reforms, may be regarded as a more performance-oriented approach towards Romania's achievements than in previous years.

The strategic decision of the European Union to stage a second round of eastern enlargement so shortly after the accession of the ten new Member States is a very welcome development, since without such a clear timing and conditioning of Romania's membership the 'outsider syndrome' would have significantly slowed down the domestic reforms, and the legitimacy of continuing reform measures, with a high social cost, would have been extremely difficult to sustain in the face of political and social pressure groups.

However, the specificity of Romania's case in the EU enlargement context should not be overestimated, as the country is only one pillar of the diversity brought into the European Union by the new Member States, and the effects of its membership will be mostly framed by the European solutions that need to be developed to handle the scale effects of diversity by means of new policies and new instruments. Last but not least, such a European strategy needs to acknowledge that diversity in unity is characteristic of Central and Eastern Europe even more so in the rest of the European Union.

CHAPTER 9

TURKEY (INCLUDING NORTHERN CYPRUS)

Edgar Lenski*

Relevant legal documents:

Turkey

- Agreement of 12 September 1963 establishing an Association between the European Economic Community and Turkey, *JO* 3687/64; English version, *OJ* 1977 L 361/29.
- Additional Protocol and Financial Protocol signed on 23 November 1970, annexed to the Agreement establishing an Association between the European Economic Community and Turkey and on measures taken for their entry into force, *JO* 1972 L 293/68; English version, *OJ* 1977 L 361/60.
- Additional Protocol to the Agreement establishing an Association between the European Economic Community and Turkey following the enlargement of the European Union, *OJ* 2005 L 254/58.
- Decision No. 2/76 of the EEC-Turkey Association Council (Free Movement of Workers).[1]
- Decision No. 1/80 of the EEC-Turkey Association Council of 19 September 1980 on the development of the Association (Free Movement of Workers).[2]
- Decision No. 3/80 of the EEC-Turkey Association Council on the application of social security schemes of the member states of the European Communities to Turkish workers and members of their families, *OJ* 1983 C 110/60.
- Decision No. 1/95 of the EC-Turkey Association Council of 22 December 1995 on implementing the final phase of the Customs Union, *OJ* 1996 L 35/1.
- Council Decision 2006/35/EC of 23 January 2006 on the principles, priorities and conditions contained in the Accession Partnership with Turkey, *OJ* 2006 L 22/34.

* Lecturer, Humboldt-University Berlin. This chapter is partly based on my article: 'Turkey and the EU: On the Road to Nowhere?', 63 *ZaöRV* (2003) pp. 77-102, available at: <http://www.whi-berlin.de/turkey.htm>.

1 A German version was published in EC Council, *Assoziation zwischen der EWG und der Türkei, Sammlung von Rechtsakten*, Vol. 1 (Luxembourg, Eur-OP 1979) p. 24.

2 EC Council, *EEC-Turkey Association Agreement and Protocols and other basic texts* (Luxembourg, Eur-OP 1992) p. 327.

S. Blockmans and A. Łazowski (eds.), The European Union and Its Neighbours

Northern Cyprus

- Act concerning the conditions of accession of the Czech Republic, the Republic of Estonia, the Republic of Cyprus, the Republic of Latvia, the Republic of Lithuania, the Republic of Hungary, the Republic of Malta, the Republic of Poland, the Republic of Slovenia and the Slovak Republic and the adjustments to the Treaties on which the European Union is founded – Protocol No. 10 on Cyprus, *OJ* 2003 L 236/955.
- Council Regulation (EC) No. 866/2004 of 29 April 2004 on a regime under Article 2 of Protocol No. 10 to the Act of Accession, *OJ* 2004 L 161/128.
- Council Decision 2004/511/EC of 10 June 2004 concerning the representation of the people of Cyprus in the European Parliament in case of a settlement of the Cyprus problem, *OJ* 2004 L 211/22.
- Council Regulation (EC) No. 389/2006 of 27 February 2006 establishing an instrument of financial support for encouraging the economic development of the Turkish Cypriot community and amending Council Regulation (EC) No. 2667/2000 on the European Agency for Reconstruction, *OJ* 2006 L 65/5.

Turkey's relationship with the European Union started more than forty years ago. Over the years, the two partners have faced a number of setbacks and improvements. Nevertheless, the time of being neighbours is coming to an end. Accession negotiations with Turkey started in October 2005. The European Union's relationship with Northern Cyprus is even more complicated. In 2004, the Republic of Cyprus joined the Union without prior reunification, meaning that the 'Cyprus question' was not solved. The Turkish Republic of Northern Cyprus therefore remains an outsider. After the accession of the Central and Eastern European countries (CEECs), the Republic of Cyprus and Malta on 1 May 2004, the European Union's future relations with Turkey came into the focus of the enlargement debate. However, the likelihood of resolving the 'Cyprus question' has decreased considerably. Further steps by the European Union with regard to Northern Cyprus thus remain on a rather technical level.

1. THE HISTORY OF EU RELATIONS WITH TURKEY AND NORTHERN CYPRUS

In 1963, the then European Economic Community and the Republic of Turkey concluded an association agreement. The primary objective of the so-called Ankara Agreement was 'to promote the continuous and balanced strengthening of trade and economic relations'[3] between Turkey and the Community by establishing a

[3] Art. 2(1) AA Turkey.

customs union.[4] Yet, the preamble and Article 28 of the Agreement stated another objective, namely to facilitate the accession of Turkey to the EEC 'at a later date'.[5] At the 1999 Helsinki European Council, Turkey obtained the status of a candidate country and has since then continuously proceeded towards accession (negotiations).[6]

In contrast, Northern Cyprus appears to be excluded from this path for the time being, after Greek Cypriots rejected reunification in the referendum of 24 April 2004.

1.1 Development of the European Union's association with Turkey

The relationship between the then European Economic Community and Turkey began in 1959, when the Turkish Government asked the EEC to enter into negotiations with it about an association agreement.[7] Before Turkey's rapprochement to European integration, it had already become a member of the OECD in 1948, joined the Council of Europe in 1949 and acceded to NATO in 1952.[8] After negotiations lasting almost four years, the Association Agreement between the EEC and Turkey was signed on 12 September 1963 in Ankara and entered into force on 1 December 1964. At the time of its conclusion, political reasons (namely concerning security policy) prevailed over economic reasons, which were considered to be of rather minor importance.[9]

According to Article 2(3) AA Turkey, the association was to be divided into a preparatory stage, a transitional stage and a final stage.

The preparatory stage was established in order to allow Turkey to strengthen its economy with aid from the Community. The purpose of this was to enable it to sustain the transitional and the final stage.[10] The Agreement provides for a period of five years for this first stage. On Turkey's initiative, negotiations to enter into the transitional stage began in 1968. These negotiations ended with the signing of the Additional Protocol on 23 November 1970 and its entry into force on 1 January 1973. This instrument lays down the preparatory work for the establishment

4 Art. 2(2) AA Turkey.

5 Fourth recital of the preamble and Art. 28 of the Association Agreement. The French version states 'qu['il] facilitera ultérieurement l'adhésion de la Turquie à la Communauté' instead of 'at a later date'.

6 See Bull. *EU* 12-1999, point I.1.

7 Initially, Turkey even wanted to start accession negotiations with the EEC immediately.

8 On the history of and political developments in Turkey in general, see *The Europa World Yearbook*, 37th edn. (London, Europa Publisher 1996) pp. 3172-3178.

9 K. Ertekin, *Der türkische Beitritt zur Europäischen Gemeinschaft* (Frankfurt, Peter Lang 1989) p. 23. This perception seems not to have changed substantially since then. See J. Solana, 'Europe's Path for Turkey', *International Herald Tribune* (7 December 2002).

10 Art. 3(1) AA Turkey.

of the customs union and the alignment of the economic policies of the two partners based on mutual and balanced obligations.[11] In addition, the free movement rights were set out as guidelines for the transitional stage.[12]

The transitional stage was planned to last twelve years. However, this ambitious aim was not achieved due to several complications in the development of Turkish politics. During the 1970s, Turkey faced an almost permanent political and economic crisis.[13] Another problem was – and to a certain extent still is – the presence of Turkish troops in Northern Cyprus since 1974.[14] Between 1976 and 1980, the association practically stood still.[15] The Association Council – the body established by the Agreement – held no meetings and no further steps were taken to deepen the relationship.

After relations improved briefly in 1980,[16] a military coup under General Evren led to a further setback in the development of the association. Despite the pro-European attitude of the junta,[17] the Community adopted a waiting position and in fact suspended the implementation of the association from the autumn of 1981 onwards,[18] following various resolutions of the European Parliament on massive violations of human rights and the lack of redemocratisation in Turkey.[19] Due to this development, the schedule for the transition to the final stage of the association was not adhered to: the customs union was not established and the free movement of workers was not introduced. The period fixed by Article 36 of the Additional Protocol, which provided for the progressive safeguarding of the free movement of workers until 1 December 1986 (twenty-two years after the entry into force of the Association Agreement), expired without any measures being taken.[20]

It was only in 1986, after improvements in the Turkish political system, that the association was revived with a meeting of the Association Council on 16 September 1986. Nevertheless, very little was achieved in the time following this

---

11 Art. 2 et seq. of the Additional Protocol, Art. 4(1) AA Turkey.

12 Art. 36 et seq. of the Additional Protocol, Art. 12 et seq. AA Turkey.

13 For a more detailed description, see M. Bozkurt, *Die Beziehungen der Türkei zur Europäischen Union* (Frankfurt, Peter Lang 1995) pp. 42-59.

14 See *infra* section 1.2.

15 E. Esen, *Die Beziehungen zwischen der Türkei und der EG unter besonderer Berücksichtigung der innertürkischen Auseinandersetzungen um die Assoziation 1973-1980* (Bonn, Centaurus 1990) p. 223 et seq.

16 See Decision No. 1/80 of the Association Council.

17 European Commission, *XVth General Report* (1981) p. 263 et seq. See also the decision of the Turkish National Security Council (the *de facto* government) of 25 March 1981 on preparing Turkey internally for accession to the Community, in Bozkurt, op. cit. n. 13, at p. 60.

18 *Bull. EC* 12-1981, point 2.2.45. Decision No. 1/83 of the Association Council, *OJ* 1983 L 112/2, dealt only with administrative matters, namely the introduction of the ECU).

19 See, for example, *OJ* 1980 C 265/55 and *OJ* 1981 C 101/110. On the European Parliament's concerns about Turkey, see, *inter alia*, the Balfe Report on the human rights situation in Turkey, *OJ* 1985 C 343/60.

20 On the resulting problems, see *infra* section 2.2.2.

meeting, mostly because of the Community's opposition to further measures in the field of the Financial Protocol and the free movement of workers. Turkey therefore decided to improve its position in general and applied for membership of the Community on 14 April 1987.[21] The application was forwarded to the Commission by the Council on 17 April 1987 and was considered by the Commission until 18 December 1989. The Commission recommended not to enter into negotiations with Turkey. It put forward the constitutional situation of the EEC at the time, as well as economic, democratic and human rights reasons, as grounds on which the application should be rejected.[22] Instead, the Commission proposed to enter into negotiations about a customs union. The Council accepted this recommendation on 3 February 1990[23] and thereby rejected the Turkish application for the time being.

In spite of this setback, the Community and Turkey continued to negotiate with a view to entering the final stage of the association. In the early 1990s, Turkey showed that it was making further efforts to enter into a customs union with the European Community by implementing measures towards this end. Decision No. 1/95 of the EC-Turkey Association Council[24] was a result of this development. By means of this decision, the customs union, as provided for in Article 5 of the Ankara Agreement, was established gradually from the entry into force of the decision on 31 December 1995. The customs union forms the basis of the final stage of the association.

Turkey's will to accede to the European Union remains unchanged. Virtually all Turkish governments have put this on their political agenda. In 1996 and 1997, Turkey even threatened to veto the envisaged accession of the CEECs to NATO if it was not accepted as a candidate for EU membership. This attempt was harshly rejected by the European Union.[25] In 1997, the Luxembourg European Council decided not to invite Turkey to the enlargement negotiations with the CEECs.[26] This led to a suspension of the political dialogue with the European Union by the Turkish Government[27] and to a systematic blockade of all EU attempts towards reconciliation.[28] Only after the Commission proposed strategies to involve Turkey

---

21 *Bull. EC* 4-1987, points 1.3.1 and 1.3.2.

22 SEC (1989) 2290 final/2 of 20 December 1989.

23 *Bull. EC* 1/2-1990, p. 77 et seq.; European Commission, *XXIVth General Report* (1990) p. 285.

24 *OJ* 1996 L 35/1.

25 See T. Buerkle, 'EU Confirms Turkey's Right to Join, but Not Now', *International Herald Tribune* (17 March 1997) p. 5.

26 See *Bull. EU* 12-1997, point I.2.

27 See 'Türkei kündigt aus Enttäuschung Ende des Dialogs mit der EU an', *Der Tagesspiegel* (15 December 1997) p. 1.

28 See P. de Graaf, 'EU wil relatie met Turkije verbeteren' [EU wants to improve relationship with Turkey], *De Volkskrant* (5 March 1998) p. 4; T. Gack, 'Die Türkei kommt aus dem Schmollwinkel nicht heraus', *Der Tagesspiegel* (12 March 1998) p. 6.

in the enlargement process, and after the first steps to that end were taken by the Cardiff European Council of 15 and 16 June 1998,[29] did Turkey put an end to its self-imposed isolation and re-engage in a dialogue with the European Union.

The 1999 Helsinki European Council finally accorded Turkey the status of an EU candidate country.[30] This led the 2002 Copenhagen European Council to envisage accession negotiations in 2005 if Turkey fulfilled the Copenhagen political criteria.[31] After the Commission recommended accession negotiations with Turkey in October 2004,[32] the European Council of December 2004 decided to start negotiations on 3 October 2005.[33] As scheduled, the membership talks officially started in the night of 3 October 2005.[34] Consequently, Turkey's time as a neighbour is coming to an end. However, the accession negotiations might last at least ten to fifteen years.

1.2 The European Union's relationship with Northern Cyprus

The European Union's relationship with the northern part of Cyprus is even more complicated but also very brief. In 1974, Turkish troops occupied the northern part of the island. Turkey explained this intervention by referring to the *coup d'état* in Cyprus, which was carried out by the Cypriot National Guard and backed by the junta in Athens. Although the Turkish military action was condemned by the UN Security Council,[35] Turkish troops remained in northern Cyprus. In 1983, the Turkish Cypriots proclaimed the Turkish Republic of Northern Cyprus (hereinafter, 'TRNC'), an entity that is not internationally recognised – except by Turkey. The European Union has no official diplomatic contacts with the TRNC since only the Greek-Cypriot Government of the Republic of Cyprus is accepted as the official representative of the island.[36] However, informal relations did evolve, especially during the accession negotiations with the Republic of

---

[29] European Commission, Communication of 4 November 1998, COM (1998) 124 final. See 'Türkei nimmt Beziehungen zur EU wieder auf', *Der Tagesspiegel* (6 November 1998) p. 2; and *Bull. EU* 6-1998, point I.21.68.

[30] See *Bull. EU* 12-1999, point I.12.

[31] See *Bull. EU* 12-2002, point I.6.19.

[32] European Commission, Recommendation on Turkey's progress towards accession, COM (2004) 656 final, p. 9 et seq.

[33] See *Bull. EU* 12-2004, point I.7.22. The European Council made the opening of negotiations subject to the political condition that Turkey enact amendments to six statutes relating mainly to the judiciary and judicial rights. Moreover, Turkey had to recognise the Republic of Cyprus by signing the Adaptation Protocol to the Ankara Agreement, see *infra* sections 4 and 4.1.2.1.

[34] See *Bull. EU* 10-2005, point 1.5.3.

[35] Notably UN Security Council resolution 353 (1974) of 20 July 1974.

[36] For a critical view on this policy, see P. Pernthaler, 'Some critical aspects regarding the UN Secretary General's proposal for a comprehensive settlement of the Cyprus problem', 1 *Yeditepe Üniversitesi Hukuk Fakültesi Dergisi* [Yeditepe University Law Journal] (2004) p. 119 et seq.

Cyprus, despite the fact that there were no Turkish representatives on the Cypriot delegation.[37] The European Union strongly backed the so-called Annan Plan for the reunification of Cyprus and deeply regretted the Greek-Cypriot *'οχι'* (no) in the referendum of 24 April 2004.

From a legal point of view, the northern part of Cyprus acceded to the Union as part of the Republic of Cyprus. Application of the *acquis*, however, is suspended for those areas in which the Government of the Republic of Cyprus does not have effective control, that is to say, Northern Cyprus.[38]

2. THE LEGAL RELATIONSHIP WITH TURKEY: THE ASSOCIATION AGREEMENT

As already mentioned, the Ankara Agreement was supplemented by the 1970 Additional Protocol, various Financial Protocols and several decisions of the Association Council. This collection of instruments forms the 'law of association'.[39]

2.1 **Institutional issues**

The Ankara Agreement provides only for an Association Council, although a number of special bodies have been set up over the last forty years.

The Association Council has the task to 'ensure the implementation and the progressive development of the Association.'[40] It consists of government officials from the Member States and members of the Council and the Commission, on the one hand, and members of the Turkish Government, on the other. Its decision-making powers are exercised by unanimous voting with each of the two sides having one vote.[41] The office of President of the Council is held alternately by a representative of the European Union and a representative of Turkey.[42] The Agreement provides for the power to adopt decisions[43] and make recommendations.

---

37 F. Hoffmeister, 'The role of the EU in the Cyprus conflict', in Th. Giegerich, ed., *The EU Accession of Cyprus – Key to the Political and Legal Solution of an 'Insoluble' Ethnic Conflict?* (Baden-Baden, Nomos 2006) s. II.3.a. For a critical analysis of the European Union's policy towards the Cyprus conflict, see N. Tocci, 'EU Intervention in Ethno-political Conflicts: The Cases of Cyprus and Serbia-Montenegro', 9 *EFA Rev.* (2004) p. 551 et seq.

38 Art. 1 of Protocol No. 10 to the Act of Accession of 16 April 2003, *OJ* 2003 L 236/955.

39 On the legal framework of the customs union, see S. Peers, 'Living in Sin: Legal Integration under the EC-Turkey Customs Union', 7 *EJIL* (1996) p. 411 et seq.

40 Art. 6 AA Turkey.

41 Art. 23 AA Turkey.

42 Art. 24 AA Turkey.

43 Here 'decision' is used in the meaning of the German 'Beschluss'. On the terminology and typology of Community measures, see A. von Bogdandy, et al., 'Handlungsformen im Unionsrecht – Empirische Analysen und dogmatische Strukturen in einem vermeintlichen Dschungel', 62 *ZaöRV*

Article 22(3) AA Turkey stipulates a residual competence comparable to Article 308 TEC.[44]

The Association Committee, which was set up by Association Council Decision No. 3/64,[45] assists the Association Council in order to assure continuity and cooperation within the association.

The Ankara Agreement confers on the Association Council the duty to promote the necessary cooperation and contacts between the European Parliament and the Turkish Parliament. This was implemented by Decision No. 1/65,[46] which established the Parliamentary Committee. This body now consists of twenty-five members of the European Parliament and the same number of members of the Turkish Grand National Assembly. It can make recommendations to the Association Council, but has no legislative role within the association.

The Customs Cooperation Committee, which was set up by Decision No. 2/69,[47] and the Customs Union Joint Committee, which was established by Article 52 of Decision No. 1/95, facilitate the exchange of views and mutual information in the context of the customs union. Article 56 of Decision No. 1/95 provides that Turkey is to be informed of the adoption of new Community legislation in all areas of the *acquis* that have any relevance for the customs union. Obviously, Turkey has no veto in this area.

Within the framework of the Accession Partnership, eight sub-committees of the Association Council have been set up in order to prepare Turkey for the adoption of the *acquis communautaire*.[48]

Apart from this institutional cooperation under the association regime, Turkey takes part in the activities of the European Environment Agency[49] and can also take part in virtually all other Community programmes.[50]

(2002) p. 77 et seq.; J. Bast, 'On the Grammar of EU Law: Legal Instruments', *Jean Monnet Working Paper* 9/03 (2003) p. 23 et seq.; and A. von Bogdandy and J. Bast, '*La loi européenne*: Promise and Pretence', in D. Curtin, A.E. Kellermann and S. Blockmans, eds., *The EU Constitution: the best way forward?* (The Hague, T.M.C. Asser Press 2005) p. 171 et seq.

44 See Art. I-18 TCE.

45 EC Council, op. cit. n. 2, at p. 322 (French version only).

46 EC Council, op. cit. n. 2, at p. 323 (French version only).

47 Decision No. 2/69 of the Association Council, in EC Council, op. cit. n. 2, at p. 325 (French version only).

48 Decision No. 3/2000 of the Association Council, *OJ* 2000 L 138/28. The sub-committees deal with: agriculture and fisheries; internal market and competition; trade, industry and ECSC products; economics and monetary issues, capital movements and statistics; innovation; transport, environment and energy (including TENs); regional development, employment and social policy; and customs, taxation, drug trafficking and money laundering.

49 Agreement between the European Community and the Republic of Turkey concerning the participation of the Republic of Turkey in the European Environment Agency and the European environment information and observation network, *OJ* 2001 L 213/111.

50 Framework Agreement between the European Community and the Republic of Turkey on the general principles for the participation of the Republic of Turkey in Community programmes, *OJ* 2002 L 61/27.

The Ankara Agreement provides for dispute settlement by the Association Council,[51] which can either settle the dispute itself by adopting a decision or submit it to the Court of Justice of the European Communities (ECJ) or to any other court or tribunal. If dispute settlement is not possible under these rules, the Association Council itself has to determine the rules for arbitration or any other procedure.[52] Perhaps because no such procedure has ever been initiated, the ECJ considers itself competent to decide on matters of association law. In *Demirel*,[53] it held that association agreements are an act of the institutions within the meaning of Article 234(1)(b) TEC and that it therefore has jurisdiction over these matters. In *Sevince*, the ECJ extended this case law to decisions of the Association Council.[54]

2.2 Substantive provisions

The substantive provisions of the Ankara Agreement are more or less shaped according to the model of the original EEC Treaty: the four freedoms, competition, approximation of laws and financial assistance.

2.2.1 *Free movement of goods*

In the field of free movement of goods, the Association Agreement only sets out basic guidelines that are to be followed by implementing the customs union. Article 10 of the Ankara Agreement simply mentions the prohibition of any customs duties, quantitative restrictions as well as measures having equivalent effect between Turkey and the European Community. The Additional Protocol provides for a progressive abolition of customs duties and prohibits the introduction of new ones.[55] Decision No. 1/95 finalised this development by prohibiting all customs duties on imports and exports, as well as charges having equivalent effect, and all quantitative restrictions on imports and exports, as well as measures having equivalent effect.[56] Article 7, modelled on Article 30 TEC, allows for exceptions on the grounds of public morality, public policy and so forth (cf., Art. 29 of the Additional Protocol). Furthermore, Turkey is obliged to incorporate Community instruments dealing with the removal of technical barriers to trade into its legal order.[57] With regard to

---

51 Art. 25 AA Turkey.

52 Decision No. 1/95 provides for some additional forms of arbitration. See Peers, loc. cit. n. 39, at p. 411 et seq.

53 ECJ, Case 12/86 *Demirel* v. *Stadt Schwäbisch Gmünd* [1987] *ECR* 3719.

54 ECJ, Case C-192/89 *S.Z. Sevince* v. *Staatssecretaris van Justitie* [1990] *ECR* I-3461.

55 Art. 7 et seq. of the Additional Protocol.

56 Art. 4 et seq. of Decision No. 1/95.

57 Art. 8 of Decision No. 1/95.

commercial policy, Turkey has to adopt legislation that is substantially similar to the Community instruments in the areas of import and export rules, anti-dumping measures and, notably, trade in textiles.[58] Article 13 of Decision No. 1/95 complements Article 17 of the Additional Protocol by requiring Turkey to align its customs tariff to the European Union's common customs tariff. Although these obligations have been in force for ten years, Turkey still shows fundamental shortcomings in complying with these provisions as well as with various other rules of the *acquis* on the free movement of goods.[59]

In the field of agricultural products, one of the main sectors of Turkey's exports,[60] the Additional Protocol and Decision No. 1/95 recognise the existence of difficulties and hence only provide for an adjustment of Turkish agricultural policy to that of the Community in order to achieve free movement in this field as well.[61] Decision No. 1/98 contains a detailed trade regime for agricultural products.[62]

2.2.2 *Free movement of workers*

The hotly debated issue of free movement of workers[63] can already be found, although in a vague formulation, in Article 12 of the Ankara Agreement. It identifies Articles 48, 49 and 50 TEEC (Arts. 39, 40 and 41 TEC) as a guideline for the association and was further developed in the Additional Protocol and in Decisions Nos. 2/76, 1/80 and 3/80 of the Association Council. According to the Additional Protocol, free movement was to be secured within the period between the end of the twelfth and the end of the twenty-second year after the entry into force of the

---

58 Art. 12 of Decision No. 1/95. See E. Örücü, 'Turkey Facing the European Union – Old and New Harmonies', 25 *ELR* (2000) p. 526 et seq.

59 European Commission, Turkey: 2005 Progress Report, COM (2005) 561 final, 9 November 2005, p. 55 et seq.

60 See *The Europa World Yearbook*, op. cit. n. 8, at p. 3184.

61 Art. 32 et seq. of the Additional Protocol; Art. 24 et seq. of Decision No. 1/95. Decision No. 1/97 of the Association Council, *OJ* 1997 L 127/22, elaborates on this. See also European Commission, Working Document on 'Issues arising from Turkey's membership perspective', SEC (2004) 1202, p. 30 et seq.

62 Decision No. 1/98 of the EC-Turkey Association Council of 25 February 1998 on the trade regime for agricultural products, *OJ* 1998 L 86/1.

63 See W. Quaisser and A. Reppegather, 'EU-Beitrittsreife der Türkei und Kosequenzen einer EU-Mitgliedschaft', Osteuropa Institut München Working Paper No. 252 (January 2004) p. 73 et seq.; R. Yagli, 'Die Rechtsstellung der türkischen Arbeitnehmer in der EU', 3 *ZEuS* (2000) p. 507; C. Vedder, 'Rechtswirkungen von Assoziationsratsbeschlüssen – Die Kus-Entscheidung des EuGH', 29 *EuR* (1994) p. 202; C. Denys, 'Besluit 1/80: ook Turkse onderdanen mogen werk zoeken' [Decision 1/80: Turkish citizens may also seek employment], *NTER* (1997) p. 65 at p. 68; P. Kapteyn and P. VerLoren van Themaat, *Inleiding tot het recht van de Europese Gemeenschappen* [Introduction to the Law of the European Communities], 5th edn. (Deventer, Kluwer 1995) p. 809. See also H. Schmidt, 'Sind die Türken Europäer?', *Die Zeit* 50/2002, p. 1.

Ankara Agreement, that is to say, until 1 December 1986.[64] However, this was accompanied by a reservation concerning the adoption of the necessary rules by the Association Council.

Due to political problems and opposition to the free movement of Turkish workers within the Community,[65] the Association Council achieved only minor improvements. Decision No. 2/76 provided for the progressive establishment of the free movement of workers within ten years (from 1 December 1976 until 1 December 1986, pursuant to Art. 36 of the Additional Protocol). Decision No. 1/80[66] recorded this development and Decision No. 3/80[67] introduced social security measures for Turkish workers in the European Union. No further measures towards the free movement of workers were adopted by the Council of Association, as the association was in fact suspended after the military coup in 1980.

It was the European Court of Justice that continued to develop the right of free movement of Turkish workers in several decisions. In the *Demirel* judgment,[68] the Court considered Article 12 of the Ankara Agreement and Article 36 of the Additional Protocol not to be sufficiently precise to confer rights upon individuals after the expiry of the period provided for in the Additional Protocol (1 December 1986).[69] However, faced with the issue whether Decisions Nos. 2/76 and 1/80, in particular their Articles 2 and 7 and Articles 6 and 13 respectively, were directly effective, the Court held in *Sevince*[70] that individuals could rely on these measures[71] although the Decisions had not been published[72] and contained clauses stating that the Member States had to implement these provisions in their national legislation.[73] In a number of subsequent decisions, the ECJ developed a solid case law on the right of free movement.[74]

---

64 Art. 36 of the Additional Protocol.

65 Notably, the Federal Republic of Germany did not want to improve the position of Turkish workers and opposed further measures vigorously, see Bozkurt, op. cit. n. 13, at pp. 45 and 91 et seq.; Kapteyn and VerLoren van Themaat, op. cit. n. 63, at p. 809, n. 190.

66 EC Council, op. cit. n. 2, at p. 327.

67 *OJ* 1983 C 110/60.

68 ECJ, Case 12/86 *Demirel* v. *Stadt Schwäbisch Gmünd* [1987] *ECR* 3719.

69 However, this judgment was not unequivocally accepted in legal doctrine, see C. Rumpf, 'Freizügigkeit der Arbeitnehmer und Assoziation EG-Türkei', *RIW* (1993) p. 214 at p. 217 et seq., considering Art. 36 TEEC in conjunction with Art. 48 TEEC (Art. 39 TEC) to be sufficiently clear.

70 ECJ, Case C-192/89 *S.Z. Sevince* v. *Staatssecretaris van Justitie* [1990] *ECR* I-3461.

71 Ibid., at para. 22.

72 Ibid., at para. 24.

73 Art. 12 of Decision No. 2/76 and Art. 29 of Decision No. 1/80.

74 On Decision No. 1/80 of the Association Council, see ECJ, Case 237/91 *Kazim Kus* [1992] *ECR* I-6781; ECJ, Case C-434/93 *Bozkurt* [1995] *ECR* I-1465; ECJ, Case C-171/95 *Recep Tetik* [1997] *ECR* I-329; ECJ, Case C-98/96 *Kasim Ertanir* [1997] *ECR* I-5179; ECJ, Case C-1/97 *Mehmet Birden* [1998] I-7747; ECJ, Case C-95/98 *Safet Eyüp* [2000] *ECR* I-4747; ECJ, Case C-285/95 *Suat Kol* [1997] *ECR* I-3069; ECJ, Case C-340/97 *Ömer Nazli et al.* [2000] *ECR* I-957; ECJ, Case 329/97 *Sezgin Ergat* [2000] *ECR* I-1487; ECJ, Case C-65/98 *Safet Eyüp* [2000] *ECR* I-4747; ECJ, Case

Today, the free movement of Turkish workers who live and work within the European Union has been realised to a considerable extent. However, access to the EU labour markets for Turkish nationals living outside the European Union is still widely barred.[75] On the other hand, it must not be overlooked that Turkey has not opened its labour market to Europeans either and that it restricts the conditions of employment in a significant manner.[76]

2.2.3 *Freedom of establishment and freedom to provide services*

In a similar manner to Article 12, Articles 13 and 14 of the Association Agreement identify the provisions of the EC Treaty on freedom of establishment and freedom to provide services as guidelines for the association. The Additional Protocol does not elaborate on this, but provides for a 'stand-still clause' with regard to these freedoms and confers the power to determine a timetable for and the actual shaping of these freedoms on the Association Council.[77] Although Turkey and the European Union are currently negotiating this issue,[78] the Association Council has not yet adopted any measures. At the moment, neither Turkish nationals nor Union citizens can rely on association law when they want to provide services or establish themselves, respectively, in the European Union or Turkey.[79]

2.2.4 *Competition law*

The Ankara Agreement already contained a vague clause on competition law.[80] Further clarification was achieved in Article 43 of the Additional Protocol, according to which the Association Council is charged with the task of adopting

---

188/00 *Bülent Kurz* [2001] *ECR* I-10961; ECJ, Case C-171/00 *Wählergruppe 'Gemeinsam Zajedno/Birlikte Alternative und Grüne GewerkschafterInnen/UG'* [2003] *ECR* I-2301; ECJ, Joined Cases C-317/01 and C-369/01 *Eran Abatay et al.* and *Nadi Sahin* [2003] *ECR* I-12301; ECJ, Case C-275/02 *Engin Ayaz* [2004] *ECR* I-8765; ECJ, Case C-467/02 *Inan Cetinkaya* [2004] *ECR* I-10895. On Decision No. 3/80 of the Association Council, see ECJ, Case C-277/94 *Taflan-Met et al.* [1996] *ECR* I-4085; ECJ, Joined Cases C-102/98 and C-211/98 *Ibrahim Kocak* and *Ramazan Örs* [2000] *ECR* I-1287; ECJ, Case 373/02 *Sakir Öztürk* [2004] *ECR* I-3605.

[75] For the situation for workers from the CEECs before the enlargement of 1 May 2004, on the other hand, see ECJ, Case C-257/99 *Barkoci and Malik* [2001] *ECR* I-655; D. Thym, 'Zur Ausweitung der Niederlassungsfreiheit auf die EU-Beitrittskandidaten', *NVwZ* (2002) p. 311.

[76] European Commission, op. cit. n. 59, at p. 59.

[77] Art. 41 of the Additional Protocol. In Case C-37/98 *Abdulnasir Savas* [2000] *ECR* I-2927, the ECJ considered this provision to be directly effective.

[78] See Decision No. 2/2000 of the EC-Turkey Association Council of 11 April 2000 on the opening of negotiations aimed at the liberalisation of services and the mutual opening of procurement markets between the Community and Turkey, *OJ* 2000 L 138/27.

[79] European Commission, op. cit. n. 59, at p. 60.

[80] Art. 16 AA Turkey reads: '[T]he principles laid down in the provisions on competition … of the Treaty establishing the Community must be made applicable in [the] relations within the Association.'

measures for the application of Articles 81, 82, 86 and 87 TEC. This obligation was implemented by Articles 32, 33 and 34 of Decision No. 1/95 (which are virtually identical to Articles 81, 82, 87 TEC). Article 35 of Decision No. 1/95 provides that the assessment of practices contrary to the aforementioned articles shall be made on the basis of the criteria established in Community law. However, Article 37 of Decision No. 1/95 provides for another implementing measure by the Association Council in order to lay down the exact rules for the application of Article 34 (state aids). Until the adoption of this measure, Articles 32 and 33 are none the less applicable in accordance with Article 37(2)(a). Similarly, Article 37(2)(b) renders Article 34 applicable, albeit under the provisions of the then GATT Subsidies Code.[81]

2.2.5 *Approximation of legislation*

Chapter IV of Decision No. 1/95 sets out the fields in which Turkey has to approximate its laws to those of the Community. This concerns, in particular, intellectual property law,[82] competition law,[83] trade defence instruments[84] and taxation.[85] However, Turkey's legislation only improved slightly in most of these policy fields[86] and even worsened in one case.[87] Further harmonisation is required to facilitate the possible accession of Turkey to the European Union. All chapters of the *acquis* have to be incorporated into Turkish law. The aforementioned subcommittees of the Association Council partly deal with these questions already.[88]

2.2.6 *Financial assistance*

From the beginning of the association, Turkey has received financial assistance in the form of aid, loans and investment schemes from the Community, especially under the Financial Protocols.[89] At present, Turkey fully participates in the pre-

---

81 See Peers, loc. cit. n. 39, at p. 417 et seq.; Örücü, loc. cit. n. 58, at p. 526. Under the WTO rules. the GATT Subsidies Code is replaced by the Agreement on Subsidies and Countervailing Measures of 15 April 1994, *OJ* 1994 L 336/156.

82 Art. 31 of Decision No. 1/95.

83 Arts. 39-43 of Decision No. 1/95.

84 Art. 44 et seq. of Decision No. 1/95.

85 Arts. 49-51 of Decision No. 1/95.

86 European Commission, op. cit. n. 59, at p. 66 et seq. (intellectual property) and p. 68 et seq. (competition policy).

87 Ibid., at p. 63 et seq. (public procurement).

88 On the subcommittees, see *supra* n. 48. On Turkey's alignment with the various chapters of the *acquis*, see *infra* section 4.1.2.4.

89 First Financial Protocol, *JO* 1964 3705/64; Second Financial Protocol, *JO* 1977 L 361/118; Third Financial Protocol, *OJ* 1979 L 67/1.

accession strategy[90] and receives aid from various Community funds. Since 2000, an average annual sum of almost €180 million has been provided to Turkey. The Commission expected to double this sum in 2006. Financial assistance for the priorities identified in the recently adopted Accession Partnership will be made available through annual financing decisions taken by the Commission, following the procedure set out in Article 8 of Council Regulation (EC) No. 2500/2001 of 17 December 2001 concerning pre-accession financial assistance for Turkey (for the 2006 programme) and in the Regulation for the Instrument for Pre-accession Assistance (IPA), once this has been adopted (for the 2007 to 2013 programmes). The financing decisions will be followed by a financing agreement signed with Turkey.[91]

2.2.7 *Common Foreign and Security Policy and Justice and Home Affairs*

Although not covered by association law in a strict sense, this section takes a very brief look at Turkey's involvement in second and third pillar issues.

To a large extent, Turkey aligns itself with CFSP statements.[92] A certain reluctance is perceivable, especially regarding human rights and national security concerns. However, Turkey endeavours to play a stabilising role in the Middle East region[93] and is taking part in the EUFOR-ALTHEA mission in Bosnia-Herzegovina – as it did in SFOR – as a troop-contributing nation. In addition, Turkey was involved in the EU police mission in Macedonia (EUPOL Proxima).[94]

Turkey's path towards harmonisation in the area of Justice and Home Affairs seems to be thornier. The Commission has identified various fields where progress is needed, for example reform of the judiciary, the fight against corruption and cooperation with the European Union on illegal migration and the fight against human trafficking, as well as some aspects of the 1951 Geneva Convention on Refugees.[95]

---

90 Regulation (EC) No. 390/2001, *OJ* 2001 L 58/1; Regulation (EC) No. 2500/2001, *OJ* 2001 L 342/1, as last amended by Regulation (EC) No. 2112/2005, *OJ* 2005 L 344/23; EU-Turkey Framework Agreement of 26 February 2002, *OJ* 2002 L 61/29.

91 European Commission, Proposal for a Council Regulation establishing an Instrument for Pre-Accession Assistance (IPA), COM (2004) 627 final, 29 September 2004.

92 For a detailed overview, see H. Kramer, 'Die Gemeinsame Außen- und Sicherheitspolitik der Europäischen Union und die Türkei', 27 *Integration* (2004) p. 44 et seq.

93 European Commission, op. cit. n. 59, at p. 128 et seq.

94 Agreement between the European Union and the Republic of Turkey on the participation of the Republic of Turkey in the European Union Police Mission (EUPOL Proxima) in the former Yugoslav Republic of Macedonia, *OJ* 2004 L 354/89.

95 European Commission, op. cit. n. 59, at p. 110 et seq.

2.3 Conclusion

The law of the association, in particular the customs union, has led to a situation in which almost no customs duties 'protect' Turkey's economy from its EU competitors. Turkey therefore has to cope with increasing competition that is already preparing it for accession to the European Union.[96] It already had to adopt a considerable amount of economic Community legislation under the association regime, but a lot of legislative work remains to be done. Decision No. 1/95 established procedures for informing and consulting Turkey on new EU decision making, but Turkey has no formal right of involvement in the legislative process. The firm (and only possible) attitude of the European Union regarding the *acquis* is that of 'take it or leave it'. Finally, it should not be overlooked that the substantive provisions of the Association Agreement and the subsequent measures are only truly effective for Turkish citizens in the European Union and not vice versa. European Union citizens still face substantial obstacles when doing business in Turkey.[97] Despite these difficulties, Turkey has already achieved a substantial level of legal harmonisation with the EU system.

3. THE RELATIONSHIP WITH THE NORTHERN PART OF CYPRUS

Formal legal relations with the northern part of Cyprus do not exist, since the TRNC is recognised neither by the European Union nor by its Member States.[98] After the failure of the reunification referendum in April 2004, some adjustments to the Accession Treaty and new secondary legislation were necessary, as the application of the *acquis* is suspended for the northern part of Cyprus. However, these provisions are of a rather technical nature. The Republic of Cyprus, one of the ten new Member States, is the sole representative of Cyprus. While the European Union supports efforts towards the reunification of Cyprus, no substantive rules on direct trade between the Member States and the northern part of the island have so far been adopted. The current deadlock in the Council on a proposed regulation in this regard[99] is caused to a certain extent by the Republic of Cyprus, which considers the chosen legal basis (Art. 133 TEC) to be inappropriate.[100] A regulation on

---

[96] See Ç. Akkaya, et al., *Länderbericht Türkei* (Darmstadt, Wissenschaftliche Buchgesellschaft 1998) p. 96 et seq.

[97] European Commission, op. cit. n. 59, at p. 134 et seq.

[98] On the problems arising as a result – already and especially under the association regime with Cyprus – see S. Talmon, 'The Cyprus Question before the European Court of Justice', 12 *EJIL* (2001) p. 727 et seq.

[99] Proposal for a Council Regulation on special conditions for trade with those areas of the Republic of Cyprus in which the Government of the Republic of Cyprus does not exercise effective control, COM (2004) 466 final.

[100] Hoffmeister, loc. cit. n. 37, at section IV.

financial assistance to the Turkish Cypriot community has recently been adopted.[101] Under this regulation (based on Art. 308 TEC) €139 million is to be spent on various activities aimed at the reunification of Cyprus.[102]

4. ACCESSION OF TURKEY TO THE EUROPEAN UNION

The following section deals with the issue of Turkey's accession to the European Union and focuses on some core questions.[103] Since the 1999 Helsinki European Council, and in particular since 2002, Turkey has adopted an impressive amount of internal legal reforms.[104] However, much remains to be done.

4.1 The criteria for accession

Article 49 TEU sets out the legal basis for accession.[105] In addition, the 1999 Helsinki European Council decided also to apply the criteria established by the 1993 Copenhagen European Council[106] to Turkey.[107] In the case of Turkey, almost

---

101 Council Regulation (EC) No. 389/2006 establishing an instrument of financial support for encouraging the economic development of the Turkish Cypriot community and amending Council Regulation (EC) No. 2667/2000 on the European Agency for Reconstruction, *OJ* 2006 L 65/5.

102 See Council Conclusions of 27 February 2006, in Press Release No. 6343/06 (Presse 45).

103 An in-depth analysis from a political point of view is carried out by the European Commission in its regular reports. See, for example, European Commission, op. cit. n. 59.

104 See the (revised) Turkish National Programme for the Adoption of the Acquis, available at: <http://ec.europa.eu/comm/enlargement/turkey/npaa_2003.htm> (last visited 30 July 2006). On recent amendments to the Turkish legal system, see European Commission, op. cit. n. 59, *passim*; Council of Europe Parliamentary Assembly Report by M. Delvaux-Stehres and L. Van den Brande, 'Honouring of obligations and commitments by Turkey', Doc. No. 10111 (17 March 2004), available at: <http://assembly.coe.int/documents/WorkingDocs/doc04/Edoc10111.htm> (last visited 30 July 2006); H. Kramer, 'Ein wichtiger Schritt in Richtung EU', *SWP Aktuell* 29/02 (2002) p. 1 et seq.; P. Tanlak, 'Turkey EU Relations in the Post Helsinki Phase and the EU Harmonisation Laws Adopted by the Turkish Grand National Assembly in August 2002', *SEI Working Paper* No. 55 (Brighton 2002) pp. 8-12.

105 In the current Constitutional Treaty, Art. I-58, in conjunction with Arts. I-1(2) and I-2, contains the relevant law. Former Art. O TEU, which had the same wording as Art. 237 TEEC, only required that the state was European.

106 *Bull. EU* 6-1993, point I.13.

107 *Bull. EU* 12-1999, point I.12. On the European Union as a subject of international law acts through the European Council as its organ, see J.C. Wichard, in C. Callies and M. Ruffert, eds., *EUV/EGV-Kommentar*, 2nd edn. (Neuwied, Luchterhand 2002) Art. 1 EG para. 13. See also the opposite views on the legal personality of the European Union described by Wichard, ibid., at para. 5 et seq. Even if one follows these opposite views, the acts of the European Council must be seen as joint acts of the Member States. The extent to which states and an organisation like the EU are bound by their unilateral acts is currently still under discussion. See the debate in the ILC, 'Report on the work of its 53rd Session 2000', *General Assembly Official Records, 54th Session Supplement No. 10*, Doc. A/54/10, p. 176 et seq.; ILC, 'Report on the work of its 53rd Session 2001', *General Assembly Official Records, 55th Session Supplement No. 10*, Doc. A/55/10, p. 522 et seq.; ILC, 'Report on the

all of these requirements (democracy, respect for human rights and the rights of minorities, the rule of law, stable political institutions, a functioning market economy, the ability and will of the candidate to take on the obligations arising from membership, adherence to the aims of political, economic and monetary union and the ability of the European Union to absorb new members) prove difficult. One specific issue was and remains that of Cyprus.

It is generally accepted that the Council enjoys a discretionary power in the field of accession and consequently is not legally obliged to accept the application of a candidate even if it fulfils all the criteria.[108] Moreover, the Ankara Agreement only obliges the European Union to *facilitate* the accession of Turkey to the Union at a later date.[109] It does not create a legal obligation for the European Union to allow accession without conditions. Ahead of the Council's decision to start negotiations, the Commission, in its capacity as the major player in the accession process,[110] proposed a Negotiation Framework. This Framework was adopted by the Council in October 2005 and is based on three pillars.[111] The first pillar is designed to support the reform process in Turkey. The Commission will continue to deliver regular reports on the basis of a revised Accession Partnership for Turkey.[112] The second pillar will design the actual framework for the negotiations. Finally, the third pillar will comprise measures aimed at strengthening the

---

work of its 54th Session 2002', *General Assembly Official Records, 56th Session Supplement No. 10*, Doc. A/56/10, p. 193 et seq. As a basic rule, subjects of international law have to abide by their commitments, at least as long as they do not expressly revoke their statements. See ICJ, *Nuclear Tests Case*, ICJ Rep. 1974, p. 253 at p. 269 et seq. See also C. Tomuschat, 'International Law: Ensuring the Survival of Mankind on the Eve of a New Century – General Course on Public International Law', *RdC* 281 (1999) (The Hague, The Hague Academy 2001) p. 344 et seq. with further references.

108 W. Müller, in H. Smit and P. Herzog, eds., *The Law of the European Community*, Vol. 6 (New York, Matthew Bender 1996) Art. 237, p. 372. See also ECJ, Case 93/78 *Lothar Matheus* v. *Doego Fruchtimport und Tiefkühlkost eG* [1978] *ECR* 2203 para. 7. *Contra* J. Zeh, *Recht auf Beitritt* (Baden-Baden, Nomos 2002) *passim*. The wording of the accession articles in the European Constitution might support this view – at least to the extent that a political claim can be derived from the fact that the criteria are fulfilled. See Independent Commission on Turkey, *Turkey in Europe: More than a promise?* (Brussels, British Council 2004) p. 9.

109 Naturally, Turkey and the then EEC agreed on a possible accession. This, however, is not possible any more since the Maastricht Treaty repealed Art. 237 TEEC and replaced it with Art. O TEU (now Art. 49 TEU). At the time of a possible accession, a provision similar to Art. I-58 TCE will probably be in force already. These amendments do not change the nature of the obligation. Today, accession to the European Community can be achieved only by acceding to the European Union. See U. Everling, 'Reflections on the Structure of the European Union', 29 *CMLRev.* (1992) p. 1063.

110 See F. Hoffmeister, 'Changing Requirements for Membership', in A. Ott and K. Inglis, eds., *Handbook on European Enlargement* (The Hague, T.M.C. Asser Press 2002) p. 99 et seq.

111 The Framework is available at: <http://ec.europa.eu/comm/enlargement/turkey/pdf/st20002_en05_TR_framedoc.pdf>.

112 Council Decision 2006/35/EC of 23 January 2006 on the principles, priorities and conditions contained in the Accession Partnership with Turkey, *OJ* 2006 L 22/34.

political and cultural dialogue through civil society in Turkey and the European Union.

4.1.1 *European state*

The criterion according to which the candidate must be European is not very clear-cut, and this was probably intentional. The Commission gave a vague definition of this concept in 1992, saying that 'it combines geographical, historical and cultural elements.'[113] On the occasion of the conclusion of the Ankara Agreement, the then President of the Commission, Walter Hallstein, stated that 'Turkey is a part of Europe.'[114] The 1987 application of Turkey was not (initially) rejected on the grounds that Turkey was not European (as in the case of Morocco[115]) but for several other reasons.

From a geographical point of view, Turkey belongs – at least partly – to Europe. Thrace, consisting of the western-most provinces of Turkey, is undoubtedly on the European continent. If one defines 'Europe' as the western 'peninsula' of the Eurasian continent, the Bosphorus does not necessarily constitute Europe's eastern border.[116] The other elements – history and culture – are subject to debate.[117] Whatever culture is exactly, Turkey's culture is based on the Islamic faith and is influenced by Christian, Jewish and classical thought.[118] However, it must not be forgotten that an Islamic culture can simultaneously be a European one (e.g., Bosnia-Herzegovina and Albania). Turkey's culture cannot be described as Asian or Islamist.[119] There has been a continuous exchange between different cultures in South-Eastern Europe. The Balkans have embraced much of the Ottoman culture over the course of centuries.[120] The south-eastern

---

113 European Commission, Europe and the Challenge of Enlargement, Supplement 3/92 – *Bull. EC* 3-1992, point 7. See F.C. Mayer and J. Palmowski, 'European Identities and the EU', 42 *JCMS* (2004) p. 573 at p. 579 et seq.

114 W. Hallstein, Speech in Ankara on 12 September 1963 ('La Turquie fait partie de l'Europe'), German translation in T. Oppermann, ed., *Walter Hallstein – Europäische Reden* (Stuttgart, DVA 1979) p. 439 et seq.

115 The application of Morocco of 8 July 1987 was rejected on the grounds that it was apparently not a European state, see *Bull. EC* 9-1987, point 2.2.19.

116 See C. Dorau, 'Die Öffnung der Europäischen Union für europäische Staaten', 34 *EuR* (1999) p. 736 at pp. 738-739.

117 See Hoffmeister, loc. cit. n. 110, at p. 92.

118 Akkaya, et al., op. cit. n. 96, at p. 164 et seq.; Y.S. Tezel, 'Gefangen zwischen Demokratie und Autoritarismus', 11 *Internationale Politik* (2001) p. 1 et seq.; Örücü, loc. cit. n. 58, at p. 523, quoting former Turkish Prime Minister B. Ecevit; E.J. Zürcher, 'Turk is niet minder Europees dan Siciliaan' [Turks are no less European than Sicilians], *De Volkskrant*, 21 April 1997, p. 7.

119 For a contrary view reducing Europe to Christian culture, see L. Siedentop, *Democracy in Europe* (London, Penguin 2000) p. 189 et seq.

120 On the general interrelations of Christianity and Islam regarding Turkey, see G. Luciani, 'Die Türkei und der Islam', 3 *Internationale Politik* (2002) p. 27 et seq.

part of Anatolia is undoubtedly underdeveloped and very different from urban sites in Western Europe. However, the Turkish political elite and a majority of Turkey's population are constantly orientated towards the West and modernisation as well as secularism.[121]

The political debate on the issue whether Turkey 'fits' into the European Union often focuses on the criterion of whether or not it is a 'European state'. Public opinion in Europe is split on this topic. For example, while the President of the European Convention, Valéry Giscard d'Estaing, and with him a number of national conservative parties heavily oppose Turkish membership of the European Union,[122] a large number of political and economic players are strong proponents of Turkey's accession.[123] However, one should bear in mind that in principle this issue was already decided in 1963. The Ankara Agreement qualifies Turkey as a European state.

4.1.2 *Respect for the principles of the Union*

Respect for the basic principles of the European Union, as identified by Article 6(1) TEU and the Copenhagen criteria, is an indispensable prerequisite for any accession candidate. Although these principles are subject to political assessment, they are of a legal nature and therefore subject to legal scrutiny.

4.1.2.1 Human rights, minority rights and the principle of liberty

The requirement of respect for human rights and fundamental freedoms still seems to constitute a major problem in relation to the possible accession of Turkey.[124]

---

121 See G. Goltz and H. Kramer, 'Politischer Erdrutsch bei den Wahlen in der Türkei', *SWP Aktuell* 48/02 (2002) p. 1 et seq.; D. Akagül, 'Le cinquième élargissement de l'Union européenne et la question de la candidature turc', *RMCU* (1988) p. 359 at p. 360. See further W. Schönbohm, 'Auf dem Weg nach Europa', 11 *Internationale Politik* (2001) p. 18. Naturally, a simple orientation towards Europe cannot lead to a qualification as European. Still, it shows a certain tendency. This has not been undermined by the idea of military leaders to focus on a separate Eurasian perspective for Turkey that has been raised from time to time, see I.D. Dagi, 'Competing Strategies for Turkey: Eurasianism or Europeanism?', *Central Asia-Caucasus Analyst*, 8 March 2002, available at: <http://www.cacianalyst.org/view_article.php?articleid=1189> (last visited 3 July 2006).

122 V. Giscard d'Estaing, 'Pour ou contre l'adhésion de la Turquie à l'Union européenne', *Le Monde*, 9 November 2002; ibid., 'Zurück zur Vernunft', *Frankfurter Allgemeine Zeitung*, 26 November 2004, p. 10. See also 'Turkey and the EU – The impossibility of saying no', *The Economist*, 18 September 2004.

123 See J. Solana, loc. cit. n. 9. See also 'Why Europe must say yes to Turkey', *The Economist*, 18 September 2004. Moreover, 53 per cent of Europeans are in favour of future enlargements (including Turkey) according to the European Commission's poll in *Eurobarometer No. 62* (Autumn 2004) p. 19.

124 For a more detailed description of the human rights situation see, for example, European Commission, op. cit. n. 59, at pp. 18, 103 et seq.; Amnesty International, 'Amnesty International

According to the wording of Article 2 of the Turkish Constitution, the Turkish state is based on human rights. In fact, the human rights situation has improved only in recent years.[125] The relevant constitutional provisions on human rights were amended in October 2001.[126] A number of implementing laws have been enacted since. Since May 2004, moreover, international human rights instruments prevail over internal legislation.[127] However, the most apparent problem is still that of torture in Turkish prisons. The European Committee for the Prevention of Torture (CPT)[128] reports annually on torture in Turkish police custody and has twice even published a public statement[129] – a truly extraordinary step. Since 2002, the CPT reports are more optimistic. In general, the situation has improved. It appears that grave forms of torture are no longer applied systematically, but the implementation of anti-torture legislation is still a weak point. The situation conforms neither with the standards of the Council of Europe[130] nor with those of the European Union.[131] Even compared to other accession candidates like Bulgaria[132] or Romania,[133] which carry a legacy of forty years of dictatorial rule, the situation in Turkey is deplorable. The CPT reports reveal horrifying practices in Turkish prisons. Moreover, investigations into various 'disappearances' of opposition

---

Report 2006 – Turkey', available at: <http://web.amnesty.org/report2006/tur_summarry_eng> (last visited 30 July 2006); N. Güney, 'Das *Antiterrorgesetz*-Urteil des türkischen Verfassungsgerichts vom 6. Januar 1999 – Zugleich ein Beitrag zu den Grenzen der Beschränkbarkeit von Grundrechten nach der türkischen Verfassung', 62 *ZaöRV* (2002) p. 473, coming to a more optimistic conclusion based on the case law of the Turkish Constitutional Court.

125 For an analysis of the (very poor) state of play in the early 1990s, see W. van Genugten, 'Turkije en de mensenrechten' [Turkey and human rights], 68 *NJ* (1993) p. 720 et seq.

126 Act No. 4709 of 3 October 2001, *Turkish Official Journal* of 17 October 2001, No. 24556.

127 For a brief analysis, see K. Başlar and E. İshakoğlu, 'Turkey', in A.E. Kellermann, et al., *Impact of EU Accession on the Legal Orders of New Member States and (Pre-)Candidate Countries – Hopes and Fears* (The Hague, T.M.C. Asser Press 2006) p. 195.

128 Established according to Art. 1 of the European Convention on the Prevention of Torture and Inhuman or Degrading Treatment of 26 November 1987, ETS No. 126, entry into force on 1 February 1989.

129 CPT, Public Statement on Turkey, 15 December 1992, 14 *HRLJ* (1993) p. 49 et seq.; CPT, Public Statement on Turkey, 6 December 1996, 18 *HRLJ* (1997) p. 294 et seq.; CPT, Reports on Turkey, available at: <http://www.cpt.coe.int/en/states/tur.htm> (last visited 4 July 2006). On the problem of torture in Turkey, see R. Alleweldt, 'Auf dem Weg zu wirksamer Folterprävention in der Türkei?', 27 *EuGRZ* (2000) p. 193 et seq.

130 CPT, The CPT Standards 2004 (revised version), available at: <http://www.cpt.coe.int/en/documents/eng-standards-scr.pdf> (last visited 4 July 2006).

131 See Gerechtshof te 's-Gravenhage [Hague Court of Appeal], Case 04/1595/KG *The Netherlands* v. *N. Kesbir*, 20 January 2005, available at: <http://www.rechtspraak.nl> (last visited 4 July 2006). See also European Commission, op. cit. n. 59, at pp. 18, 103 et seq., which – although more optimistic – lists an impressive number of human rights problems.

132 See CPT, Reports on Bulgaria, available at: <http://www.cpt.coe.int/en/states/bgr.htm> (last visited 4 July 2006).

133 See CPT, Reports on Romania, available at: <http://www.cpt.coe.int/en/states/rom.htm> (last visited 4 July 2006).

leaders and intellectuals, extra-judicial executions, the oppression of trade unions and the media and so forth are not yet pursued thoroughly.[134] A whole range of fundamental human rights, especially women's rights, were and continue to be violated,[135] particularly in Kurdistan. Even now, a considerable number of journalists and writers are held in custody for their writings.[136] Even members of the Turkish Grand National Assembly are sentenced for their political actions.[137] Despite various improvements,[138] much therefore remains to be done. A positive development is the abolition of the death penalty.[139]

Although Turkey already acceded to the Council of Europe in 1954, it recognised the individual complaint procedure (former Art. 25 ECHR) only in 1987 and the compulsory jurisdiction of the European Court of Human Rights (former Art. 46 ECHR) in 1990. However, the individual complaint procedure, which forms the main possibility for citizens to seek protection, is becoming more and more effective. In 1991, only ninety complaints were lodged against Turkey (cf., the Netherlands with a quarter of the population and 165 applications[140]). In 2005, the European Court of Human Rights registered 1,812 new applications regarding Turkey.[141] The number of applications is alarming and encouraging at the same time. Although an enormous number of Turkish citizens feel that their human rights are infringed by government authorities, they do make use of the complaint procedure and therefore induce Turkey to ameliorate its human rights record.

---

134 See Reporters sans frontières, 'Turkey still far from European standards of press freedom', 16 December 2004, available at: <http://www.rsf.org/article.php3?id_article=12096> (last visited 4 July 2006); T. Sommer, 'Gesucht: ein moderner Atatürk', *Die Zeit*, 6 June 1997, p. 7; H. Müller, 'De waarheid van de Turkse media' [The truth of the Turkish media], *De Volkskrant*, 7 June 1997, p. 51.

135 See Amnesty International, op. cit. n. 124, and the following judgments of the European Court of Human Rights: *Akdivar and others* v. *Turkey*, judgment of 16 September 1996, Rep. 1996-IV, p. 1192 et seq.; *Zana* v. *Turkey*, judgment of 25 November 1997, Rep. 1997-II, p. 2534 et seq.; *Mentes and others* v. *Turkey*, judgment of 28 November 1997, Rep. 1997-VIII, p. 2690 et seq.; *Kurt* v. *Turkey*, judgment of 25 May 1998, Rep. 1998-III, p. 1153 et seq.

136 Sommer, loc. cit. n. 134, at p. 7, mentioning Turkey as the state with the highest number of journalists and writers held in prison of all. Charges brought against the author O. Pamuk for mentioning the massacres of Armenians were dropped only after EU pressure, cf., S. Hacaoğlu, 'Turkish Court drops charges against novelist', *The Independent*, 23 January 2006, p. 4.

137 European Court of Human Rights, *Sakik and others* v. *Turkey*, judgment of 26 November 1997, Rep. 1997-VII, p. 2609 et seq.

138 Human Rights Watch, 'Turkey – A Crossroads for Human Rights' (15 December 2004), available at: <http://hrw.org/doc?t=europe&c=turkey> (last visited 4 July 2006); Reporters sans frontières, '2004 Annual Report – Turkey', available at: <http://www.rsf.org/article.php3?id_article=10265> (last visited 4 July 2006).

139 European Commission, op. cit. n. 59. See Güney, loc. cit. n. 124, at p. 468 et seq. It should be noted, however, that this penalty has already not been enforced any for several years.

140 European Commission of Human Rights, *Survey of Activities and Statistics 1991* (Strasbourg 1992) p. 23.

141 European Commission, op. cit. n. 59, p. 19.

However, Turkey's willingness to execute judgments of the ECHR has improved only slightly.[142]

The situation of minorities and freedom of religion is also in a fairly poor state. The 1923 Lausanne Agreement[143] granted certain rights to (some) non-Islamic minorities (Greeks, Armenians and Jews), but the major problem is still that of the Kurdish minority. After recent changes in Turkish law,[144] legal discrimination against the Kurds has been partly abolished. Too often, however, judicial and administrative practice remains highly discriminatory.[145] Discrimination against other minorities[146] and non-Muslim communities in Turkey exists in fact and in law, for example in relation to cultural life.[147] In general, problems regarding respect for minority rights will remain, as these rights are still largely regarded as violating the constitutional principle of the indivisible unity of the Turkish nation[148] (Art. 3 of the Turkish Constitution).[149]

Moreover, Turkey's position in the ongoing dispute about Northern Cyprus, though moderate compared to the past, is another complicated aspect within the accession process. Since the Ankara Agreement contained a clause on its territorial scope in which the application of the agreement was confined to the then Member States and Turkey, each enlargement had to be accompanied by a subsequent amendment of the Ankara Agreement. In December 2004, Turkey promised to recognise the Republic of Cyprus and ratify the Adaptation Protocol to the Ankara Agreement before the start of the accession negotiations. The Conclusions of the Presidency of the European Council of December 2004 did not expressly make the recognition of Cyprus by Turkey a precondition for the opening of

142 See Council of Ministers of the Council of Europe, Interim Resolution IntResDH (2004) 38, but see also Interim Resolutions IntResDH (2004) 31 and IntResDH (2002) 98, available at: <http://wcd.coe.int/ViewDoc.jsp?id=138187> and <http://wcd.coe.int/ViewDoc.jsp?id=294871> (last visited 30 July 2006) and Parliamentary Assembly of the Council of Europe, Resolution 1268 (2002), 23 *HRLJ* (2002) p. 110. However, recent amendments provide for the revision of judgments if the ECHR finds them to be in violation of European human rights law. See Arts. 445 and 448 of the Code of Civil Procedure and Arts. 327 and 335 of the Code of Criminal Procedure, as amended by Act of 3 August 2002. See Kramer, loc. cit. n. 104, at p. 5 et seq.; Tanlak, loc. cit. n. 104, at p. 10 et seq.

143 Peace Treaty between the Allies and Turkey of 24 July 1923, 18 *LNTS* 12.

144 See Kramer, loc. cit. n. 104, at p. 3.

145 European Commission, op. cit. n. 59, at p. 36.

146 There is, for example, a Roma community, and Alevi muslims are sometimes also regarded as a minority. See Akkaya, et al., op. cit. n. 96, at p. 185 et seq.; European Commission, op. cit. n. 59, at p. 35 et seq.

147 H. Kramer, 'Die Türkei und die Kopenhagener Kriterien', *SWP-Studie* 39/02 (Berlin 2002) p. 35.

148 Turkish Constitutional Court, judgment of 30 June 1994, quoted in C. Rumpf, *Das türkische Verfassungssystem* (Wiesbaden, Harrassowitz 1996) p. 254.

149 It should be noted, however, that France also has a constitutional provision that establishes indivisibility of the nation as a fundamental principle, see Art. 1 of the French Constitution of 4 October 1958, available at: <http://www.assemblee-nationale.fr/english/8ab.asp> (last visited 10 July 2006).

accession talks.[150] In October 2005, the European Union – pressed for time – decided to open accession negotiations after Ankara had accepted the Adaptation Protocol.[151] But Turkey still claims that this does not constitute a recognition of Cyprus, and it still opposes the application of EU-Turkey association law to Cyprus. EU enlargement commissioner Olli Rehn has recently urged Turkey to implement the protocol and open its ports and airspace to Greek-Cypriot ships and planes if it wants to proceed smoothly with membership talks.[152]

4.1.2.2 Stable democracy and the rule of law

Even within the European Union, democratic systems vary considerably. Democracy is not easy to define.[153] Described in a general way, it requires that all government authority emanates from the citizens and that they (can) participate in government.[154] In order to satisfy the condition of being a 'stable democracy', a candidate country must also respect the European Union's standards of factual and institutional safeguards for democracy.

The wording of the Turkish Constitution satisfies the requirements of this test.[155] It vests legislative power in the unicameral Turkish Grand National Assembly,[156] which is elected by universal suffrage. General elections are held every

---

150 From a legal point of view, recognition is not crucial since it is merely of a declaratory nature, see I. Brownlie, *Public International Law*, 6th edn. (Oxford, OUP 2003) p. 86 et seq. Politically and economically, however, it is an imperative.

151 Additional Protocol to the Agreement establishing an Association between the European Economic Community and Turkey following the enlargement of the European Union, *OJ* 2005 L 254/58.

152 L. Kubosova, 'EU urges Turkey to keep its word on Cyprus', *EUObserver.com*, 10 March 2006. Apart from these current problems arising from the Cyprus conflict, Turkey's position regarding the 1915-1916 massacres of Armenians likewise causes astonishment. It must be admitted that some Armenian interest groups tackle the problem very aggressively. Nevertheless, Turkey's refusal to discuss the issue is telling. See the publications of the Turkish Parliament on the genocide inflicted upon Turks by Armenians, available at: <http://www.tbmm.gov.tr/yayinlar/yayin3/atrocity.htm> (last visited 30 July 2006).

153 See, for example, the overview and analysis by D. Held, *Models of Democracy* (Cambridge, Polity Press 1996).

154 See Abraham Lincoln's Gettysburg Address of 19 November 1863, available at: <http://www.loc.gov/exhibits/gadd/gatr1.html> (last visited 30 July 2006): 'Government of the people by the people for the people.'

155 Art. 2 of the Constitution already shows Turkey's general commitment to democracy: 'The Republic of Turkey is a democratic, secular and social State governed by the rule of law; bearing in mind the concepts of public peace, national solidarity and justice; respecting human rights; loyal to the nationalism of Atatürk, and based on the fundamental tenets set forth in the Preamble.' Turkish Constitution of 18 October 1982 (translation by the Turkish Foreign Ministry), as amended on 7 May 2004 by Act No. 5170, available at: <http://www.tbmm.gov.tr/english/constitution.htm> (last visited 30 July 2006).

156 Art. 7 of the Turkish Constitution.

five years[157] on the basis of proportional representation, on the basis of lists drawn up by political parties. Turkey has a multiparty political system. Parliament elects the President, who holds executive power, for a period of seven years. The President is empowered to appoint a Prime Minister and senior members of the judiciary,[158] which comprises judicial, administrative and military courts, as well as a Constitutional Court. In addition, there is the National Security Council, which (officially) serves as an advisory body.

However, certain doubts remain. In order to receive a seat in the Turkish Grand National Assembly, a party has to receive 10 per cent of the votes cast. This is the highest threshold for entry into parliament in Europe.[159] The outcome of the last general elections in November 2002 led to a situation in which 34.2 per cent of the votes resulted in 66 per cent of the seats in the Grand National Assembly.[160] In total, 45.4 per cent of the votes cast did not count towards seats in Parliament at all, although 36.5 per cent were cast for parties which each received more than 5 per cent of the votes.[161]

Moreover, the role of the National Security Council (NSC) gives rise to doubts regarding the institutional framework of democracy in Turkey. The NSC is composed of the five highest-ranking military commanders, on the one hand, and (at least) seven civilians, namely the President, the Prime Minister, the Vice Prime Ministers (currently three) and the Ministers for Home Affairs, Foreign Affairs, Justice and Defence, on the other.[162] The NSC was established as an advisory body but in fact still has a very influential role in the field of security policy and beyond in practically all areas of Turkish politics.[163] The 2001 Turkish national programme preparing for accession therefore already envisaged a review of the relevant provisions on the role of the NSC.[164] Some improvements were enacted in recent years. Since the 2001 constitutional amendments, the NSC

---

157 Art. 77 of the Turkish Constitution.

158 Art. 104 of the Turkish Constitution.

159 In Poland, party alliances must receive 8 per cent of the vote to enter the *Sejm*, the Polish Lower House, while individual parties require 5 per cent. Georgia introduced a threshold of 7 per cent for entry into its Parliament. To enter the Parliament of Azerbaijan 6 per cent is needed. A requirement of 4 or 5 per cent is widely applied in Europe. See also W. Ismayr, 'Die politischen System der EU-Beitrittsländer im Vergleich', 5-6 *APuZ* (2004) p. 10 et seq.; Parliamentary Assembly of the Council of Europe, Resolution 1380 (2004) of 22 June 2004, para. 6.

160 See Goltz and Kramer, loc. cit. n. 121, at p. 1 et seq.

161 Ibid.

162 Art. 118 of the Turkish Constitution.

163 European Commission, op. cit. n. 59, at p. 14; Kramer, loc. cit. n. 147, at p. 20 et seq. On the situation before the 2003 legislative changes, see the chapter on national security policy in the Ministry of Defence's White Paper 2000, available at: <http://www.msb.gov.tr/Birimler/GnPPD/pdf/p3.pdf> (last visited 30 July 2006).

164 Turkish National Programme for the Adoption of the Acquis (adopted in March 2001), available at: <http://europa.eu.int/comm/enlargement/turkey/pdf/npaa_full.pdf> (last visited 4 July 2006) p. 27.

comprises a majority of civilian members and, since August 2004, even its Secretary General – a powerful position – is a civilian. The NSC's direct influence on education and media policy was curtailed by the 2004 reforms. However, the NSC is politically still dominated by its military members[165] and therefore a potential source of unaccountable political decisions. Although the reforms go very far – at least in terms of Turkish politics – the shape and role of the NSC still conflicts with European standards. At the moment, no major conflicts regarding European integration exist between the Erdoğan Government and the military. However, given the paramount position that the NSC and – in particular – its military members used to have in Turkish politics, it is unclear whether this 'peace' will last. The recognition of the Republic of Cyprus might become a critical test of this relationship.

Regarding the stability of Turkish democracy, fears of a military coup under the guise of safeguarding secularism remain, but this is no longer an imminent danger.[166] Another critical issue is the case law of the Turkish Constitutional Court prohibiting certain political parties (Art. 69 of the Turkish Constitution). Among others, the Welfare Party of former Prime Minister Erbakan was dissolved.[167] Corruption and political instability at governmental level determined the political scene in Turkey for decades.[168] Despite major improvements, the democratic standards in Turkey therefore still have to improve.

The rule of law should also be secured more thoroughly. Article 2 of the Turkish Constitution prominently states the country's commitment to the rule of law. In general terms, the rule of law comprises the components of freedom, legal certainty and material justice, as well as the principle that all public authorities are bound by law.[169] The rule of law is therefore intrinsically linked, first of all, to respect for fundamental rights and a democratic political system. As mentioned

---

165 European Commission, op. cit. n. 59, at p. 14.

166 See Kramer, loc. cit. 147, at p. 21.

167 See ECHR, *Refah Partisi and others* v. *Turkey*, judgments of 31 July 2001 (Chamber) and 3 February 2003 (Grand Chamber), available at: <http://hudoc.echr.coe.int> (last visited 4 July 2006), in particular the joint dissenting opinion of Judges Fuhrmann, Loucaides and Bratza and the separate opinions of Judges Ress and Kovler; ECHR, *Socialist Party of Turkey (STP) and Others* v. *Turkey*, judgment of 12 November 2003; ECHR, *Yazar, Karataş, Aksoy and the People's Labour Party (HEP)* v. *Turkey*, judgment of 9 April 2002. See also 'Hof Turkije verbiedt Welzijnspartij' [Turkish Court of Appeal bans Welfare Party], *De Volkskrant*, 17 January 1998, p. 1.

168 T. Seibert, 'Filz zwischen Staat und Mafia in der Türkei', *Der Tagesspiegel*, 21 January 1998, p. 6; see also Kramer, loc. cit. n. 147, at p. 20 et seq.

169 The concept of the rule of law differs considerably between legal systems. On German constitutional law, see Bundesverfassungsgericht, *BVerfGE* 7, pp. 92-93. A. Dicey, *Introduction to the Study of the Law of the Constitution* (London, MacMillan 1881, reprint 1961) p. 200 et seq. (and with him most of the English legal tradition) defines the rule of law as 'the absolute supremacy or predominance of regular law as opposed to the influence of arbitrary power, […] equality before the law [and formal or procedural justice].'

above, the fulfilment of these criteria is partly questionable. Until now, the situation has only improved slightly, despite constitutional changes in 1995 and especially since 2001.[170] A number of changes have been made to acts of parliament, but administrative and judicial implementation and interpretation still have to follow.[171] In addition, the rule of law encompasses the principle of separation of powers, the need for a legal basis for all state action that interferes with the fundamental rights and freedoms of citizens as well as effective remedies before impartial judges. The separation of powers is guaranteed by Article 7 et seq. of the Turkish Constitution. However, the position of the National Security Council remains a potential danger despite recent constitutional amendments.[172] In fact, the 'recommendations' issued by the National Security Council still have a considerable political impact.[173]

The right to an impartial judge is not entirely secured either. Following judgments of the European Court of Human Rights[174] and pressure from the European Union, the State Security Courts were finally abolished by means of an amendment of the Constitution in 2004.[175] As regards Article 6(1) ECHR, however, a considerable share of Turkish criminal proceedings, especially those before Military Courts (Art. 145 of the Turkish Constitution), still does not fully live up to European human rights standards.[176] Moreover, the impartiality of judges is undermined by the constant danger of being disciplined (i.e., sent to another court, especially in the south-east of the country). This is done by means of a

---

170 M. Charriot, 'La Turquie: un difficile partenaire pour l'Union Européenne', *RMCU* (1995) p. 432 et seq.; see Kramer, loc. cit. n. 147, at p. 23 et seq.; *contra* Tanlak, loc. cit. n. 104, at p. 14, who believes that Turkey is already in accordance with the Copenhagen criteria.

171 E. Örücü, 'The Turkish Constitution Revamped?', 8 *EPL* (2002) p. 217. See H.-H. Kühne, 'Der Rechtsstaat und seine Implementierung in der modernen Türkei am Beispiel des Bankgesetzes', 16 *EuZW* (2005) p. 75 et seq., who questions the conformity of the newly introduced Bank Act with rule of law standards.

172 Art. 118(3) of the Turkish Constitutions reads: 'The National Security Council shall submit to the Council of Ministers its views on the advisory decisions that are taken and ensuring necessary coordination with regard to the formulation, establishment, and implementation of the national security policy of the State. The Council of Ministers shall evaluate decisions of the National Security Council concerning the measures that it deems necessary for the preservation of the existence and independence of the State, the integrity and indivisibility of the country and the peace and security of society.'

173 See Kramer, loc. cit. n. 147, at p. 21; S. Kardas, 'Human Rights and Democracy Promotion: the Case of Turkey-EU Relations', 1 *Alternatives: Turkish Journal of International Relations* (2002) p. 144. On the general perception of the Army as a guarantor of political stability, see Schönbohm, loc. cit. n. 121, at p. 17 et seq.

174 ECHR, *Incal* v. *Turkey*, judgment of 9 June 1998, available at: <http://hudoc.echr.coe.int> (last visited 4 July 2006).

175 Act No. 5170 of 7 May 2004, *Turkish Official Journal* of 22 May 2004, No. 25469.

176 Amnesty International, op. cit. n. 124. See R. Kolb, 'The Jurisprudence of the European Court of Human Rights on Detention and Fair Trial in Criminal Matters, Addenda 1999-2000', 22 *HRLJ* (2001) pp. 351, 356 and 361; Kramer, loc. cit. n. 147, at p. 25.

decision of the Supreme Council of Judges and Public Prosecutors, which is presided over by the Minister of Justice and against which no appeal is available (Art. 159 of the Turkish Constitution). This mechanism has a considerable influence on the administration of justice.

4.1.2.3 A functioning market economy

The issue of a functioning market economy could be another obstacle to accession. Although Turkey has made considerable efforts to establish a more stable economy,[177] there is still a gap between the European Union and Turkey. The Turkish economy is on a level equivalent to that of Bulgaria or Romania.[178] In order to be able to cope with competition in the common market, Turkey will have to undergo further substantial reforms. However, an in-depth examination of this issue should be left to economic analysis.

4.1.2.4 Ability and will to accept the duties arising from membership

The criterion concerning the 'ability and will to accept the duties arising from membership' comprises adherence to the aims of political, economic and monetary union as well as the acceptance of the *acquis communautaire*. The assessment of these criteria is of a political nature. In substance, however, the implementation of the *acquis* deals with the entire legal corpus of EU law. Turkey has made substantial progress in many fields of Community law. In general, however, this progress can only serve as a basis for future efforts. In virtually all areas of the *acquis*, numerous laws and regulations still have to be enacted or amended.[179] Turkey's progress is hampered by the fact that newly enacted laws sometimes even move away from the *acquis*. Moreover, much remains to be done on the administrative level and with regard to implementation in general. Finally, not only should the discrimination against Cyprus be ended but equal treatment of Turkish and EU citizens, goods and services should also be achieved in general.

---

[177] European Commission, op. cit. n. 59, at p. 43 et seq. See Quaisser and Reppegather, op. cit. 63, at p. 10 et seq. On developments since the mid-1990s, see Akagül, loc. cit. n. 121, at p. 363 et seq.; B. Yilmaz, 'Wirtschaftskrise in der Türkei', 1 *Internationale Politik* (1998) p. 35; F. Şen, 'Die Türkei zu Beginn der EU-Beitrittspartnerschaft', 13-14 *APuZ* (2001) p. 31 et seq. On the situation in 1989, see J. van Ginderachter, 'L'élargissement de la Communauté: le cas de la Turquie', *RMC* (1989) p. 587 et seq.; J. Bourrinet, 'La CEE confrontée à la demande d'adhésion de la Turquie', *RMC* (1989) p. 78 et seq.

[178] See K. Hughes, 'Turkey and the European Union: Just Another Enlargement?' Friends of Europe Working Paper (June 2004) p. 8 et seq.; Eurostat, Structural indicators of candidate countries in 2000, available at: <http://europa.eu.int/comm/enlargement/turkey/pdf/indicators.pdf> (last visited 4 July 2006).

[179] European Commission, op. cit. n. 59, at p. 134 et seq.

However, one major aspect of the ability to accept the *acquis* cannot be fulfilled as long as the transfer of sovereign rights to any international or supranational institution is constitutionally impossible.[180] The preamble of the Turkish Constitution clearly states that 'sovereignty is vested fully and unconditionally in the Turkish nation.'[181] Consequently, Article 6 of the Turkish Constitution only allows for the exercise of sovereign rights by the organs of the state. The delegation of sovereign rights is explicitly forbidden.[182] Articles 7-9 of the Turkish Constitution elaborate on this in relation to legislative, executive and judicial power. An amendment of these provisions is indispensable for accession to the Union.[183]

Apart from this constitutional obstacle, the will to integrate Turkey into a supranational union, which entails a considerable loss of power at national level, still seems to require an enormous change in Turkish political thinking.[184] Although the Turkish political and economic elite strongly supports accession to the European Union, the general attitude towards European integration within these circles is not very integrationist. It seems that the implications of EU membership on the entire national constitutional system[185] have not yet been internalised.[186] The European Union has become a sophisticated political entity with a legal system that is not just limited to economic issues. Although the European Union is not a state, it exercises many of the traditional functions of a state. Since this complex system requires a strong political will to integrate, the (future) largest

---

[180] Başlar and İshakoğlu, loc. cit. n. 127, at pp. 200-201. See also M. Soysal, 'Introduction to the Constitutional Problems of the Accession of Turkey', in A.E. Kellermann, et al., eds., *EU Enlargement: The Constitutional Impact at EU and National Level* (The Hague, T.M.C. Asser Press 2001) p. 259 et seq. See also the remarks by Örücü, loc. cit. n. 58, at p. 218.

[181] Third recital of the Preamble of the Turkish Constitution: '[The Constitution embodies…] the understanding of the absolute supremacy of the will of the nation and of the fact that sovereignty is vested fully and unconditionally in the Turkish nation and that no individual or body empowered to exercise this sovereignty in the name of the nation shall deviate from liberal democracy and the legal system instituted according to its requirements.'

[182] Art. 6 of the Turkish Constitution: '(1) Sovereignty is vested fully and unconditionally in the Nation. (2) The Turkish Nation shall exercise its sovereignty through the authorised organs as prescribed by the principles laid down in the Constitution. (3) The right to exercise sovereignty shall not be delegated to any individual, group or class. No person or agency shall exercise any state authority which does not emanate from the Constitution.'

[183] Başlar and İshakoğlu, loc. cit. n. 127, at p. 201; Soysal, loc. cit. n. 180, at p. 261.

[184] See A. Savaş Akat, 'Türkei spielt europäische Karte aus', *Süddeutsche Zeitung* (14 January 2003) p. 2; Şen, loc. cit. n. 177, at p. 29; Örücü, loc. cit. n. 58, at p. 535.

[185] On these implications, see I. Pernice, 'Multilevel Constitutionalism in the European Union', 27 *ELR* (2002) p. 511 et seq.

[186] See M. Yilmaz (former Turkish Prime Minister), 'Die Türkei und die Europäische Union', speech within the *Forum Constitutionis Europae*, available at: <http://www.whi-berlin.de/yilmaz.htm> (last visited 4 July 2006), who seems to perceive the European Union mainly as a coordination of foreign policies.

Member State, in particular, has a duty to keep the European Union on the path of political integration. National interests are to be incorporated into the pursuit of the common welfare. The European Union should not attach little value to its achievements and it should beware of becoming a mere 'customs union *plus*'.

4.1.2.5 Ability of the Union to absorb new members

The assessment whether the Union is able to absorb Turkey as a new Member State is basically of a political and economic nature. This especially holds true for the proposed costs of accession. A detailed analysis of the implications on the Common Agricultural Policy, the regional and structural policy and the EU budget cannot be made here.[187] Calculations on the financial impact of transfer payments vary from €10 billion to more than €30 billion per year.[188] However, some legal caveats regarding European constitutional law can be addressed.

The Union declared itself ready for the accession of new Member States by concluding the Nice Treaty.[189] In fact, this goal was only partially reached.[190] The Convention on the Future of Europe[191] again tried to establish a solid basis for the future European Union. At that time the 2004 enlargement took place. A widely accepted aim of the entire constitutional process was and remains to preserve the supranational, integrationist character of the Union. This aim will be the basis for a future European Union based on a European Constitution. Naturally, a European Union composed of twenty-five states is already very different from the initial Community of six. However, the accession of Turkey will confront the EU framework with even greater institutional challenges.

Just the size of Turkey will be a problem for the European constitutional system. At present, Turkey has a population of almost 70 million citizens, which will rise to almost 80 million shortly after 2010 and consolidate at close to 100 million by 2035.[192] Following the 2004 enlargement, the European Union has approximately 450 million inhabitants, and it will have some 480 million citizens after the accession of the twenty-seventh Member State. Turkey will become the largest

187 On these issues, see, for example, European Commission, op. cit. n. 59; Quaisser and Reppegather, op. cit. n. 63, at p. 55 et seq.; W. Quaisser and S. Wood, 'EU Member Turkey?', 25 *Forost Arbeitspapier* (October 2004) p. 44 et seq.

188 See Quaisser and Wood, op. cit. n. 187, at p. 46 et seq.

189 Nice Intergovernmental Conference, Declaration No. 23, para. 2, *OJ* 2001 C 80/85.

190 See the critique by P. Pescatore, 'Nice – Aftermath', 38 *CMLRev.* (2001) p. 265 et seq.

191 The official homepage of the Convention can be found at: <http://european-convention.eu.int>. Turkey took part in the Convention like the other candidate countries. The Turkish Government was subsequently represented by M. Yilmaz, Y. Yakiş and A. Gül. Z. Akcam and K. Derviş represented the Turkish Grand National Assembly. Until December 2002, this task was performed by A. Tekin and A. Yilmaz.

192 See *Turkey's Window of Opportunity* (Istanbul, TÜSIAD 1999) p. 34.

Member State at the time of its accession or shortly afterwards, as well as one of the poorest. On the other hand, Turkey will become the most influential Member State in the European Union simply because of its size, that is to say, the number of Turkish MEPs and Turkey's weight in the Council will be the greatest of all Member States. As regards the European Parliament, this is not likely to create extensive problems, since Turkish MEPs will probably integrate into the existing European political structures with relative ease, much like a Turkish Commissioner would also do within the Commission. To be precise, the problem lies in the Council. Since the Council is much more likely to be influenced by national interests than the European Parliament, Turkey could block decision making in the European Union more easily than any other Member State, even if it could not veto legislation on its own.[193] Moreover, disparities between the members of the Council might rise if Turkey does not take huge steps forward on the political and economic plane.

4.2 Conclusion

To sum up, Turkey still has to undergo enormous changes before accession, but the European Union also faces challenges. The European Neighbourhood Policy and the Common Foreign and Security Policy will have to deal with new neighbours like Georgia, Armenia, Syria, Iran and Iraq. Above all, however, the entire political balance in the European Union, which was more or less achieved in Nice and has now been reshaped by the European Constitution, might be altered considerably again. The accession of Turkey is mostly discussed in terms of religion or culture, whereas the debate on the institutional implications is not conducted as intensely.[194] If the ambitious goal of political integration is not supported by Turkey, the degeneration of the European Union into an expanded customs union is almost certain. Although closer cooperation between those Member States that are willing to proceed on the path of political integration is a possible way out,[195] it is not desirable to aim for this from the beginning. The EU institutions should therefore take a close look at the conditions for accession.

---

193 This is underlined, in particular, by the weighting of votes according to the size of the population, as provided for in Art. I-25 TCE. Art. 205(4) TEC already requires the concurring votes of Member States representing at least 62 per cent of the EU population. This is overlooked by G. Avci, 'Putting the Turkish EU Candidacy into Context', 7 *EFA Rev.* (2002) p. 104.

194 But see Giscard d'Estaing (2004), loc. cit. n. 122.

195 See only the 'centre of gravitation' proposed by J. Fischer, 'From Confederacy to Federation: Thoughts on the Finality of European Integration', speech within the *Forum Constitutionis Europae*, available at: <http://www.whi-berlin.de/fischerengl.htm> (last visited 4 July 2006).

5. OUTLOOK

To a certain extent, the 2004 enlargement paved the way for Turkish membership despite the unresolved Cyprus problem. However, the new negotiation strategy adopted by the Council will result in a very different approach to accession talks. This time around, the European Union will look much deeper into the actual implementation of the *acquis*. It should therefore be welcomed that the Commission has proposed strong support for the reform process in Turkey and fostered a political and cultural dialogue between the current Member States and Turkey.[196]

However, some problems are not likely to be solved during the accession talks. This has led the Commission to propose long transition periods or even – in the case of the free movement of workers – permanent safeguard clauses. Although this approach seems to be reasonable from the point of view of some Member States, it is questionable as a permanent solution for a constitutional system like that of the European Union.[197] Another argument put forward in favour of Turkey's membership is that the integration of Turkey into the EU system could secure stability and peace in the region.[198] It is doubtful that Turkey will be capable of bringing stability to its neighbouring countries or building a bridge to the Arab world, especially since the rule of the Ottoman Empire over large parts of the region has not been forgotten by these countries. The predominant attitude of Turkey's neighbours towards Turkish ambitions in the region is rather reluctant.[199]

Turkey's path towards accession will be a long and winding road.[200] Negotiations with the CEECs took four and a half years; talks with Turkey will undoubtedly last much longer.

---

196 European Commission, op. cit. n. 32, at p. 2 et seq.

197 See U. Becker, 'EU-Enlargements and Limits to Amendments of the EC Treaty', 15 *Jean Monnet Working Paper* (2001), available at: <http://www.jeanmonnetprogram.org> (last visited 4 July 2006) p. 11 et seq.; A. Bodnar, 'Transitional Periods for Employment – "Second Class" EU Citizenship?', in O. Zetterquist, ed., *Law and Modernity* (Cracow, Polpress 2004) p. 138 et seq.; C. Hillion, 'The European Union is dead. Long live the European Union…', 29 *ELR* (2004) p. 583 at p. 593 et seq. For a more optimistic view, see D. Thym, *Ungleichzeitigkeit im Europäischen Verfassungsrecht* (Baden-Baden, Nomos 2002) p. 341 et seq.

198 G. Verheugen, 'For a more Inclusive Union', *Private View – Quarterly Int'l Review of the Turkish Industrialists' and Businessmen's Association* (Spring 2000) p. 45, also available at: <http://www.tusiad.org/yayin/private/spring00/union.pdf> (last visited 4 July 2006); Independent Commission on Turkey, op. cit. 108, at p. 17 et seq. For a more balanced view, see H. Kramer, 'EU-kompatibel oder nicht?', *SWP-Studie* 34/2003 (Berlin 2003) p. 20 et seq./28 et seq.

199 See G. Höhler, 'Ankaras Verhältnis zu den Nachbarn – eine Geschichte von Konflikten', *Handelsblatt*, 13 December 2004, p. 6.

200 Not only do the Member States' Parliaments have a veto on each Act of Accession, but referenda will also be held in some Member States on the possible accession of Turkey and before any of the changes of the European Constitution can enter into force. Moreover, the European Parliament will have a close look at the situation in Turkey, as it did throughout recent decades. See, for example, the Eurlings Report on the 2004 Regular Report on Turkey, adopted by the European Parliament on 15 December 2004, Doc. No. A6-0063/2004.

CHAPTER 10

WESTERN BALKANS (ALBANIA, BOSNIA-HERZEGOVINA, CROATIA, MACEDONIA AND SERBIA AND MONTENEGRO, INCLUDING KOSOVO)*

Steven Blockmans**

Relevant legal documents:
- Stabilisation and Association Agreement between the European Communities and their Member States, of the one part, and the Republic of Croatia, of the other part, *OJ* 2005 L 26/3, and Protocol to the Stabilisation and Association Agreement between the European Communities and their Member States, of the one part, and the Republic of Croatia, of the other part, to take account of the accession of the Czech Republic, the Republic of Estonia, the Republic of Cyprus, the Republic of Hungary, the Republic of Latvia, the Republic of Lithuania, the Republic of Malta, the Republic of Poland, the Republic of Slovenia and the Slovak Republic to the European Union, *OJ* 2005 L 26/222.
- Stabilisation and Association Agreement between the European Communities and their Member States, of the one part, and the former Yugoslav Republic of Macedonia, of the other part, *OJ* 2004 L 84/13, and Protocol to the Stabilisation and Association Agreement between the European Communities and their Member States, of the one part, and the former Yugoslav Republic of Macedonia, of the other part, to take account of the accession of the Czech Republic, the Republic of Estonia, the Republic of Cyprus, the Republic of Latvia, the Republic of Lithuania, the Republic of Hungary, the Republic of Malta, the Republic of Poland, the Republic of Slovenia and the Slovak Republic to the European Union, *OJ* 2004 L 388/3.
- Council Regulation (EC) No. 533/2004 on the establishment of European partnerships in the framework of the Stabilisation and Association Process, *OJ* 2004 L 86/1.

* The term 'Macedonia' is used in this chapter as an informal name for the former Yugoslav Republic of Macedonia. Greece believes that the name Macedonia should properly be applied to its own northern region with origins dating from the time of Alexander the Great. Similarly, the name 'Kosovo' is used in this chapter in spite of the Albanian and Serb appellations for the region, respectively 'Kosova' and 'Kosovo-Metohija'. Croatia, which received candidate country status in 2004, remains part of the stabilisation and association process and will continue to be eligible for CARDS regional funds. In spite of the special attention devoted to it in the next chapter, Croatia is referred to in this chapter to stress the importance of the European Union's approach towards the region as a whole.

** Researcher in European Union Law, T.M.C. Asser Institute, The Hague.

S. Blockmans and A. Łazowski (eds.), The European Union and Its Neighbours

- Council Regulation (EC) No. 1946/2005 amending Regulation (EC) No. 2007/2000 introducing exceptional trade measures for countries and territories participating in or linked to the European Union's Stabilisation and Association Process, *OJ* 2005 L 312/1.
- Council Regulation (EC) No. 2666/2000 on assistance for Albania, Bosnia and Herzegovina, Croatia, the Federal Republic of Yugoslavia and the Former Yugoslav Republic of Macedonia, repealing Regulation (EC) No. 1628/96 and amending Regulations (EEC) No. 3906/89 and (EEC) No. 1360/90 and Decisions 97/256/EC and 1999/311/EC, *OJ* 2000 L 306/1 (as amended).
- Council Regulation (EC) No. 2068/2004 amending Council Regulation (EC) No. 2667/2000 on the European Agency for Reconstruction, *OJ* 2004 L 358/2.
- Council Joint Action 2005/826/CFSP on the establishment of an EU Police Advisory Team (EUPAT) in the Former Yugoslav Republic of Macedonia (FYROM), *OJ* 2005 L 307/61.
- Council Joint Action 2005/824/CFSP on the European Union Police Mission, *OJ* 2005 L 307/55.
- Agreement between the European Union and Bosnia and Herzegovina (BiH) on the activities of the European Union Police Mission (EUPM) in BiH, *OJ* 2002 L 293/2.
- Council Joint Action 2004/570/CFSP on the European Union military operation in Bosnia and Herzegovina, *OJ* 2004 L 252/10.

1. THE EUROPEAN UNION'S ROUGHEST NEIGHBOURHOOD

The decomposition of the former Socialist Federal Republic of Yugoslavia (SFRY or Yugoslavia) has been one of the most tragic events in Europe since the end of the Second World War. After almost fifty years of peace, the spectres of war and dissolution reared their ugly heads in South-Eastern Europe, exactly at a time when twelve Western European countries redefined their organised cooperation with the establishment of the European Union, characterised by prosperity, democracy and 'ever-closer integration'.

From the very beginning of the Yugoslav crisis, after the outbreak of war in Slovenia and Croatia in 1991, the European Communities and later the European Union were at the forefront of international efforts to stop the escalation of the armed conflict. But even if some heralded that 'the hour of Europe ha[d] dawned',[1] the Yugoslav crisis arrived at the wrong moment for the European Communities. While the European Community had developed itself into a powerful trading bloc, foreign affairs, let alone international security issues, still largely remained outside the ambit of its competences. Although Article 30 of the Single European Act had established the first legal basis for cooperation in the foreign policy field, the legal foundations for a more comprehensive Common Foreign and Security Policy (CFSP) were still being negotiated in the framework of the

[1] Declaration of J. Poos, Luxembourg's Foreign Minister, to the international press, 29 June 1991.

pre-Maastricht Intergovernmental Conference. After Maastricht and throughout the rest of the 1990s, the European Union remained what it was once famously compared to by Belgian Minister of State Mark Eyskens: 'an economic giant, political mouse and military worm'.[2] The instruments through which the European Union could wield real influence were therefore economic and only to a much lesser extent diplomatic and political, but by no means military in nature. The lack of a comprehensive set of instruments to address the violent conflicts in the former Yugoslavia may well explain why the autonomous efforts of the European Union were sometimes partially successful, but generally failed miserably to attain their objectives.[3]

Then again, the disintegrative violence that seems so characteristic of the Balkans – often referred to as 'Balkanisation' or 'Balkanism'[4] – is hard to contain in either time or space. Up to the present, no single international or European organisation has been capable of preventing or solving a conflict in the Balkans by itself. So far, this has only been achieved through cooperation between several functionally specialised organisations. Sadly, however, cooperation between the European security organisations has not prevented the outbreak of two of Europe's gravest conflicts since the end of World War II, namely in Bosnia and Kosovo. Neither has NATO's single-handed armed intervention in Kosovo eliminated any of the fundamental socio-economic and political threats to the stability of South-Eastern Europe. While it did bring a temporary conclusion to the ten-year ethnic-territorial decomposition of Yugoslavia, it unfortunately also gave rise to new security threats for certain countries as well as for the region as a whole. Ethnically motivated violence in Kosovo (March 2004 and August 2005) and Macedonia (November 2004) suggest a growing consensus that the whole region's recomposition should not be excluded and that any stable, long-term settlement in the Western Balkans will not be possible until all ethnic-territorial disputes are resolved. At the EU-Western Balkans Summit in Thessaloniki on 21 June 2003, it was agreed that the European Union and the United States would back future direct talks between Serbia and Kosovo that might eventually lead to an agreement on how the two could peacefully separate from each other, with internationally recognised borders.[5] However, such negotiations could also open

---

[2] M. Eyskens, *Bron en horizon. Het avondland uit de impasse* (Leuven, Lannoo 1985) p. 316.

[3] For an analysis of the impact of the European Community/Union on the conflicts in ex-Yugoslavia from 1991 to 1995, see R. Ginsberg, *The European Union in International Politics – Baptism by Fire* (Lanham, Rowman & Littlefield Publishers Inc. 2001) pp. 57-104.

[4] For a critique of the use of these generic terms, see J. Stilhoff Sörensen, 'Balkanism and the New Radical Interventionism: A Structural Critique', 9 *International Peacekeeping* (2002) pp. 1-22. For a more nuanced analysis, see I. Kadare, 'The Balkans: Truths and Untruths', in D. Triantaphyllou, ed., 'The Southern Balkans: Perspectives from the Region', 46 *Chaillot Papers* (2001) pp. 5-16.

[5] See *Bull. EU* 6-2003, point 1.6.70, reaffirmed in the GAERC Conclusions of 21 July 2003, Press Release No. 11439/03 (Presse 209). Following Ambassador Kai Eide's Comprehensive Review

one or more of Pandora's many Balkan boxes, since Albanian nationalists might use the chance of an independent Kosovo to create a greater Albania, as might the ethnic Albanians in neighbouring Macedonia. The fact that the final status talks on Kosovo could unravel the tenuous state union forged between Serbia and Montenegro by the European Union is perhaps of a lesser concern, for both parties seem to be in favour of dismantling the union. Hence, the critical mass for security stabilisation in the Balkans lies at the junction of Serbian-Albanian interests.[6]

The determinants of security stabilisation in the Balkans are not just political. An integrated approach towards reconstruction is key to the efforts geared at stabilising the region. A strategy for lasting peace has to aim at the creation of an opposite logic to that of war. This implies the establishment of autonomous communities and the creation of new or reformed administrative, legislative and judicial structures which guarantee the rule of law instead of the 'law of the ruler'. But there is more than that. The establishment of effective democratic structures has to go hand in hand with macroeconomic stabilisation and liberalisation. Finally, a good approach will adapt to local and regional differences. This is the consequence of disintegration and fragmentation. Hence, what is needed is a flexible, multi-layered approach that recognises these specificities and provides a form of assistance which is designed to encourage political, economic, and social integration in the Balkans and in Europe, a process that would render states and borders relatively unimportant.[7]

The recent establishment of a real and credible CFSP towards the Western Balkans[8] and the launch of the first-ever EU missions in the framework of the

---

of the situation in Kosovo, the UN Security Council on 24 October 2005 endorsed final status talks (UN Doc. S/PRST/2005/51). On 10 November 2005, the Security Council endorsed the Secretary-General's intention to appoint Martti Ahtisaari, former President of Finland, as his Special Envoy to lead the political process and established the guiding principles for the process as agreed to by the Contact Group (UN Doc. S/2005/709). On 7 November, the Council of the European Union endorsed the appointment of Stefan Lehne as EU representative to support the UN Status Envoy in the implementation of his mandate. See Council Conclusions of 7 November 2005 in Press Release No. 13622/05 (Presse 274). Ahtisaari started the final status talks on 21 November 2005 with a fact-finding mission to Priština. The process is expected to last for several months.

[6] See M. Hadzić, 'Kosovo and the Security Stabilization of South-East Europe', 7 *International Peacekeeping* (2000) pp. 83-94; D. Triantaphyllou, ed., 'What Status for Kosovo?', 50 *Chaillot Papers* (2001); P. Jureković, ed., *Building Stability in Weak States: The Western Balkans* (Vienna, National Defence Academy 2002).

[7] M. Kaldor, V. Bojicić and I. Vejvoda, 'Reconstruction in the Balkans: A Challenge for Europe?', 2 *EFA Rev.* (1997) pp. 329-350 at pp. 344-346.

[8] Since the entry into force of the Treaty of Amsterdam, Member States have actively used the *diplomatic* structures with which they had endowed 'their' CFSP. Much to his credit, Javier Solana, Secretary General /High Representative for the CFSP (SG/HR), supported by his staff at the Council, has made the most of the cautious wording of his tasks in Art. 26 TEU. The SG/HR, with the support of NATO, the United States and the OSCE, brokered a peace deal between the government and the

European Security and Defence Policy (ESDP)[9] are helpful to restore order in the Balkans. Maintaining the 'negative peace' (absence of hostilities) is a necessary condition for establishing and maintaining a 'positive peace' in Bosnia, Kosovo and Macedonia. However, it does not, on its own, deal with the underlying causes and conditions of the symptoms of violent conflict in the whole of the Western Balkan region. In order to fill the relative 'Hobbesian void' in South-Eastern Europe with conflict controlling and resolving mechanisms and to create a belt of security, stability and prosperity stretching from Albania in the west to Turkey in the east, thereby unlocking the geographically-isolated EU Member State of Greece, the European Union has for some years now engaged in longer-term conflict prevention, for which it is far better equipped.[10] It has committed itself to a stabilisation process that capitalises on the European Union's greatest asset, namely the promise of association and future membership.

The adoption on 29 April 1997 by the General Affairs Council of a regional approach towards the Western Balkans represented the first step of the European Union towards the formulation of its own strategy designed to favour a progressive process of stabilisation and association with regard to Albania, Bosnia-Herzegovina (BiH or Bosnia), Croatia, Serbia and Montenegro (SaM, including Kosovo as defined by UN Security Council resolution 1244) and the Former Yugoslav Republic of Macedonia (FYROM or Macedonia).[11] Over the years, this strategy has been defined, refined and redefined. Because it has always revolved around the application of the conditionality principle – which in one way or

---

Albanian separatists in Macedonia (the Ohrid Framework Agreement of 13 August 2001, available at: <http://faq.macedonia.org/politics/framework_agreement.pdf>) and has forced a Constitutional Charter and Implementing Law upon Serbia and Montenegro. (The Constitutional Charter was adopted and proclaimed by the Parliament of SaM on 6 February 2003. It is underpinned by the Belgrade Agreement of 14 March 2002, reproduced in *CEPS Europa South-East Monitor*, Issue 31, January/February 2002).

[9] The ESDP was – somewhat prematurely – declared operational at the European Council of Laeken on 14-15 December 2001. See *Bull. EU* 12-2001, points I.5.6 and I.28. Despite recognised shortfalls in the Union's operational capability across the full range of Art. 17 TEU tasks, the European Union has been eager to show its 'Petersberg' potential in the Western Balkans through the deployment of its first-ever military operation (Concordia) and the civilian follow-up missions (Proxima and EUPAT) in Macedonia, and the EU Police Mission and the military operation EUFOR-Althea in Bosnia-Herzegovina. Especially the latter underlines the Union's pledge to promote stability and security in the region and is a practical example of the strategic partnership in crisis management with NATO. More information on ESDP operations is available at: <http://www.consilium.eu.int>. See also my contribution 'EU Conflict Prevention in the Western Balkans', in V. Kronenberger and J. Wouters, eds., *The European Union and Conflict Prevention: Policy and Legal Aspects* (The Hague, T.M.C. Asser Press 2004) pp. 293-321.

[10] The distinction between short- and long-term conflict prevention has an operational assumption. See European Commission, *Conflict Prevention*, COM (2001) 211 final, Brussels, 11 April 2001.

[11] Council conclusions on the principle of conditionality governing the development of the European Union's relations with certain countries of South East Europe, *Bull. EU* 4-1997, point 2.2.1.

another has always been part of EC/EU policies directed towards third countries and which since 1993 has been firmly embedded in the enlargement framework – EU-Western Balkan relations have had their fair share in the gradual development of EU conditionality.

This chapter focuses on the application of the conditionality principle as the cornerstone of relations between the European Union and the Western Balkans. It builds upon earlier legal and political studies on the evolving nature of EU conditionality[12] and examines its integration in the main policy instruments that define the relationship between the European Union and the five countries of the Western Balkans (section 2). Particular attention is devoted to the Stabilisation and Association Agreements, the most prestigious legal instruments of these policies (section 3), as well as to the recently adopted European Partnerships (section 4). The chapter explores whether these new instruments based on the experience of previous enlargements introduce new elements of conditionality and whether they can bolster the Union's Stabilisation and Association Process to integrate each of the Western Balkan countries into the European Union. It touches upon the level of commitment, on the part of both the European Union and the countries of the Western Balkans, as the main variable determining the success of conditionality and recommends the use of positive conditionality in the form of medium- and long-term benefits attached to the fulfilment of the different criteria (sections 5 and 6).

2. MAIN POLICY INSTRUMENTS

2.1 **Regional approach**

At the end of 1995, a controversial peace agreement reached after heavy American arm-twisting on the Patterson-Wright air force base in Dayton (Ohio) and signed in Paris ended the war in Bosnia and therefore also the need for sanctions.[13] At first, as a consequence of the European Union's subsidiary role in the US-led efforts to end the Bosnian war and bring 'positive peace' to the region, the Union's objectives were embedded in the international community's initiative to adopt a comprehensive and encompassing approach to deal with the plethora of

---

12 See chapter 3 in this volume and the literature referred to therein.

13 The present structure of Bosnia-Herzegovina was established under the General Framework Agreement for Peace, initialled in Dayton on 21 November 1995, signed in Paris on 14 December 1995, consolidated in Rome on 18 February 1996 and published in 35 *ILM* (1996) p. 75. For a brilliant account of the negotiations leading up to Dayton, see R. Holbrooke, *To End a War* (New York, Random House 1998). For an analysis of the problems concerning the implementation of the agreement, see S. Bose, *Bosnia after Dayton – Nationalist Partition and International Intervention* (London, Hurst & Company 2002).

issues in South-Eastern Europe. At the Royaumont summit of 13 December 1995, which brought together the Ministers of Foreign Affairs of the EU Member States, representatives of four of the former Yugoslav republics (BiH, Croatia, FRY and FYROM), representatives of neighbouring countries in the region, delegations from the United States and Russia, as well as representatives of NATO, the OSCE and the Council of Europe to formalise the Dayton Agreement, the international community unveiled the process for stability and good neighbourliness in South-Eastern Europe.[14] The so-called Royaumont process was geared towards supporting the implementation of the Dayton and Paris Agreements and to encourage democratisation through regional projects in fields like human rights, culture and civil society.[15]

As a complement to the Royaumont process, the European Union launched its own regional approach, designed for those countries that – at the time – did not qualify for the conclusion of Association Agreements.[16] As the Council had already signed Europe Agreements with Romania and Bulgaria,[17] and as it had just adopted negotiating directives for a Europe Agreement with Slovenia,[18] Albania remained the only country outside the borders of ex-Yugoslavia that could be integrated into the regional approach. Within the framework of the regional approach, the European Union offered financial assistance and unilateral trade preferences, subject to the Western Balkan countries' commitment to restore economic cooperation with each other. Since, with the exception of Albania, which had concluded a Trade, Commercial and Economic Cooperation Agreement with the European Community,[19] none of the countries involved had any significant contractual relations with the European Union, it was hoped that the prospect of a comprehensive cooperation agreement, enabling them to gain improved access to the internal market for a large number of their products, would serve as an incentive for economic reforms and the development of good neighbourly relations.[20]

---

14 See Council Conclusions and Declaration on former Yugoslavia, *Bull. EU* 1/2-1996, point 1.4.108.

15 See H.-G. Ehrhart, 'Prevention and Regional Security: The Royaumont Process and the Stabilization of South-Eastern Europe', 4 *OSCE Yearbook* (1998) pp. 327-346.

16 See Council Conclusions and Declaration on former Yugoslavia, *Bull. EU* 1/2-1996, point 1.4.108.

17 The EAs with Romania and Bulgaria were signed on 8 March 1993 and published in *OJ* 1994 L 357/2 and *OJ* 1994 L 358/3 respectively.

18 Negotiations on the EA with Slovenia started in March 1995. The agreement was signed on 10 June 1996, see *OJ* 1996 L 51/3.

19 *OJ* 1992 L 343/1. This agreement is still in force but will be replaced by a Stabilisation and Association Agreement. See *infra* section 3.2.2.

20 See F.-L. Altmann, 'Die Balkanpolitik der EU – Regionalansatz und Prinzip der Konditionalität', 47 *Südosteuropa* (1998) pp. 503-515 at p. 504. See also O. Kovać, 'Regional Approach of the European Union to Cooperation among Countries of the Former Yugoslavia', 47 *Review of International Affairs* (1996) pp. 1-5.

Apart from strong commitments to regional cooperation and the free market ideal, political conditionality, too, was at the heart of the European Union's regional approach. The Council made it clear that any consideration of establishing contractual relations would 'depend on the willingness of the countries concerned to work towards consolidating peace and to respect human rights, the rights of minorities, and democratic principles.'[21] In addition, the Union's offers were coupled to a clear expectation that all republics that had emerged from the violent implosion of the Socialist Federal Republic of Yugoslavia would fully comply with their commitments under the Dayton and Paris Agreements (in particular those regarding the return of internally displaced persons and refugees to their place of origin and cooperation with the International Criminal Tribunal for the Former Yugoslavia (ICTY) in The Hague). The Council warned that, in case of non-compliance by any of the parties, it would consider taking 'specific measures' in response.[22]

The new strategy was soon put into legal practice. In July 1996, the Council adopted Regulation (EC) No. 1628/96 on reconstruction in Bosnia, Croatia, Macedonia and the FRY (the so-called 'OBNOVA' Regulation), which in Article 2 explicitly identified the respect for democratic principles, the rule of law and human rights and fundamental freedoms as 'essential elements' for the application of the entire programme.[23] The OBNOVA conditionality clause went one step further than comparable human rights and democracy clauses in earlier trade, cooperation and Association Agreements concluded by the Community with third states[24] by stating that the 'specific conditions' defined by the Council for the former Yugoslav republics were also to be regarded as essential elements of the regulation and, hence, their fulfilment as a precondition for the granting of Community aid. The specific conditions mentioned in the regulation referred to the Council Conclusions of 26 February 1996 and the simultaneously adopted Declaration on former Yugoslavia.[25]

---

[21] Council Conclusions and Declaration on former Yugoslavia, *Bull. EU* 1/2-1996, point 1.4.108.

[22] Ibid. See also European Commission, Common Principles for Future Contractual Relations with Certain Countries in South-Eastern Europe, COM (1996) 476 final, Brussels, 2 October 1996.

[23] *OJ* 1996 L 204/1. 'Obnova' means 'reconstruction' in the language formerly known as Serbo-Croat. The Regulation was repealed in December 2000 and replaced by a new funding instrument, the so-called 'CARDS' Regulation. See *infra* section 3.4.

[24] See, generally, F. Hoffmeister, *Menschenrechts- und Demokratieklauseln in den vertraglichen Außenbeziehungen der Europäischen Gemeinschaft* (Berlin, Springer 1998) pp. 117-175; E. Riedel and M. Will, 'Human Rights Clauses in External Agreements of the European Communities', in P. Alston, ed., *The European Union and Human Rights* (Oxford, OUP 1999) pp. 723-754; M. Bulterman, *Human Rights in the Treaty Relations of the European Community* (Antwerp, Intersentia 2001).

[25] Council Conclusions and Declaration on former Yugoslavia, *Bull. EU* 1/2-1996, point 1.4.108.

The criteria entailed in these documents were, however, formulated in broad terms and thus fairly fuzzy. This problem was addressed by the Council on 29 April 1997 with the adoption of specific guidelines in the form of 'Conclusions on the principle of conditionality governing the development of the European Union's relations with certain countries of south-east Europe'.[26] For the first time, these guidelines distinguished conditions that apply to all countries of the region from conditions that apply to individual countries only. They also established a graduated approach, within which trade preferences, financial assistance and the establishment of contractual relations are subject to different degrees of conditionality. This was thought to solve a principle dilemma of the European Union's Western Balkans policy, manifested in its desire to differentiate more effectively between the countries concerned in terms of their political and economic development, while at the same time continuing to apply a coherent strategy towards the region as a whole. Hence, while the Council reaffirmed that all offers continued to be available to all countries of the region and that the European Union's strategy was meant as an incentive, not an obstacle, to the countries to meet the relevant criteria, the refined approach towards conditionality followed the basic principle that the closer a country wants to move towards the European Union, the more conditions it has to fulfil. The guidelines of 29 April 1997 clearly reflected a combination of both positive and negative conditionality. Progressive compliance with the conditions established by the Council was rewarded with intensified bilateral cooperation, including the establishment of contractual relations. However, in case of serious and repeated non-compliance with the conditions underpinning the respective level of cooperation, trade preferences could be withdrawn, Community assistance frozen and, where applicable, an agreement suspended.[27]

Thus, the contours of a distinctive model of EU conditionality towards the Western Balkans became clear. EU conditionality for the Western Balkans was based on the 1993 Copenhagen criteria, the defining component of the Union's relations with the Central and Eastern European Countries (CEECs),[28] but extra elements were added to reflect the special needs to stabilise the region.[29] The

---

26 *Bull. EU* 4-1997, point 2.2.1.

27 For a detailed account of these measures and their legal bases, see C. Pippan, 'The Rocky Road to Europe: The EU's Stabilisation and Association Process for the Western Balkans and the Principle of Conditionality', 9 *EFA Rev.* (2004) pp. 219-245 at pp. 229-238.

28 *Bull. EU* 6-1993, point 13. See C. Hillion, 'The Copenhagen Criteria and their Progeny', in C. Hillion, ed., *EU Enlargement: A Legal Approach* (Oxford, Hart Publishing 2004) pp. 1-22.

29 Council Conclusions of 29 April 1997, sections on 'Phare' and 'Contractual Relations'. Annex I enumerates the key elements which the European Union deemed essential in any interpretation of democratic principles, human rights, minority rights and principles of market economy. With this demonstrative list of standards, the European Union has helped to clarify the normative content of the conditionality principle that it applies towards the Western Balkans.

European Union's regional approach represented an ambitious attempt to deal with the Western Balkans on a regional basis, recognising that all political units and conflicts in the region are interconnected components of a larger whole: to deal effectively with any one unit or conflict means that, ultimately, the others have to be dealt with as well, if not simultaneously then certainly in sequence. Although the aim of the regional approach was never to put the Yugoslav jigsaw back together, betting on the results of such an approach for the Western Balkans was extremely risky at the time of its adoption. For no sooner had each break-away republic become independent – in essence given *itself* a new identity – than it needed to integrate again on a regional basis and eventually become member of a new larger entity. While the European Union's efforts looked good on paper, in reality regional cooperation and bilateral relations barely progressed in the post-1997 period and negative conditionality prevailed in the form of limited contractual relations and exclusions from Association Agreements. In the period from 28 February 1998 to 5 November 2001, the European Union even adopted a whole new range of sanctions against the Federal Republic of Yugoslavia because of its role in Kosovo.[30]

2.2 Stability Pact for South-Eastern Europe

The Kosovo crisis of 1999 showed the shortcomings of the Royaumont process in addressing the complex and volatile situation in the Western Balkans and triggered a response by the international community. On 17 May 1999, amid ongoing NATO air strikes against Serbia, the EU Ministers of Foreign Affairs, following an initiative by the German Presidency, launched the Stability Pact for South-Eastern Europe.[31] What marked a fundamental shift in the European Union's strategy towards the Western Balkans was the Council's self-declared willingness to draw the countries of the region closer to the perspective of full integration into EU structures, through a new kind of contractual relationship, 'with a perspective of EU membership on the basis of the Treaty of Amsterdam once the Copenhagen criteria have been met.'[32] This explicit offer of future EU membership for the five countries of the Western Balkans was firmly endorsed by the European Council at its summit in Santa Maria da Feira on 19-20 June 2000.[33] Against the backdrop of yet another violent crisis in the Western Balkans, the political leaders of the

[30] For an overview of the legal and political aspects of these sanctions, see my contribution 'The European Union's Troubled Relations with the Federal Republic of Yugoslavia (1991-2001)', in J. de Zwaan et al., eds., *The European Union: An Ongoing Process of Integration – Liber Amicorum Alfred E. Kellermann* (The Hague, T.M.C. Asser Press 2004) pp. 337-356.

[31] Common Position 1999/345/CFSP, *OJ* 1999 L 133/1.

[32] Ibid., preamble, para. 7.

[33] *Bull. EU* 6-2000, point I.49.67.

European Union reached the conclusion that a policy aimed at economic reconstruction, political reform and regional cooperation was, as such, not enough to bring lasting peace and stability to the region. Only the additional prospect of full EU membership brings about the reforms necessary to achieve 'positive peace'.[34] Hence, the European Union brought its Western Balkans policy in line with the logic behind its decision to fully open its doors to the CEECs in the early 1990s.

Although initiated by the Union within the framework of its CFSP, the Stability Pact is not an EU instrument. While the Union plays a leading role in it, the Pact was endorsed at an international meeting held on the fringes of the European Council summit in Cologne on 10 June 1999[35] – the day that NATO's seventy-eight-day bombing campaign against Serbia ended – where its further development and implementation was vested in the OSCE. A Special Coordinator, appointed by the European Union in consultation with the OSCE, chairs the South-Eastern Europe Regional Table, the most important political forum of the Pact.[36] The Regional Table is responsible for the coordination of the activities of more than forty participating and facilitating states, international organisations and regional initiatives, which contribute in varying degrees to the so-called Working Tables on (1) Democratisation and Human Rights; (2) Economic Reconstruction, Cooperation and Development; and (3) Security Issues. Hence, the Stability Pact serves as a platform for international cooperation and is geared towards supporting the implementation of the Dayton and Paris Agreements, facilitating political stability and economic prosperity, improving coordination and, as a result of this, increasing the efficiency of the instruments of all of the actors in the region.[37]

Pippan has argued that, in respect of the South-East European countries' *rapprochement* to the European Union, 'the Council's unilateral "Common Position" on the Union's launching of the Pact was, at the time of its adoption, probably of more importance than the Pact itself.'[38] Indeed, not only has the Stability Pact created expectations that, in view of the available resources, it cannot hope to meet, but it also remains one of the most enigmatic political inventions for South-Eastern

---

[34] See T. King, 'The European Community and Human Rights in Eastern Europe', 23 *LIEI* (1996) pp. 93-125 at p. 123; P. Pantev, 'Security Risks and Instabilities in Southeastern Europe', in W. van Meurs, ed., *Beyond EU Enlargement, Volume 2: The Agenda of Stabilisation for Southeastern Europe* (Gütersloh, Bertelsmann Foundation Publishers 2001) pp. 118-138.

[35] See also *Bull. EU* 6-1999, point I.26.71. For the final text of the Stability Pact of 10 June 1999, see <http://www.stabilitypact.org>.

[36] The post is currently held by Erhard Busek, who was appointed in December 2001. His mandate was renewed until 31 December 2006 by Council Decision 2005/912/EC, *OJ* 2005 L 331/32.

[37] See, *inter alia*, H.-J. Axt, 'Der Stabilitätspakt für Südosteuropa: Politischer Aktionismus oder langfristig tragfähiges Konzept?', 48 *Südosteuropa* (1999) pp. 401-416; L. Friis and A. Murphy, '"Turbo-charged negotiations": The EU and the Stability Pact for South Eastern Europe', 7 *Journal of European Public Policy* (2000) pp. 767-786.

[38] See Pippan, loc. cit. n. 27, at p. 227.

Europe of the last century.[39] Since the declaration of the European Council at Santa Maria da Feira, the accession of Albania, Bosnia-Herzegovina, Croatia, Macedonia and Serbia and Montenegro to the European Union is no longer a matter of *if*, but of *when* and *how*. As to the *how*, it is reassuring to note that, by referring to both Article 49 TEU and the Copenhagen criteria in Common Position 1999/345/CFSP, the Council has emphasised that the political and economic criteria formulated by the European Council in June 1993 for the enlargement of the Union remain fully valid. In light of these criteria, it is evident that the full integration of the countries of the Western Balkans into EU structures requires a long-term commitment on both sides. The European Union, for its part, has responded to this challenge by transforming its regional approach into a more sophisticated policy framework: the Stabilisation and Association Process.

2.3 Stabilisation and Association Process

Initiated by the Commission in 1999,[40] the Stabilisation and Association Process (SAP) specifically aims to assist each of the five countries of the Western Balkan countries in meeting the relevant EU criteria and to be *ultimately* accepted as official candidates for membership. The one incentive the SAP shrank from providing, however, was an explicit *promise* of membership. At the 2000 Santa Maria da Feira European Council, the European Union stated that the SAP countries are 'potential candidates', which undisputedly represents a promotion compared to the regional approach but not a breakthrough that goes all the way.[41]

The SAP was built upon the Union's regional approach and consists of modified and new offers to the Western Balkan countries, including enhanced trade liberalisation, improved financial and economic assistance, a regular political dialogue, cooperation in justice and home affairs and, in particular, a new, tailor-made category of contractual relations: the Stabilisation and Association Agreements. The instruments covered by the SAP are open to all countries of the region on equal terms. Their actual availability, however, continues to depend on each country's compliance with the general and country-specific conditions set out by

---

[39] See W. van Meurs, 'The Stability Pact Beyond EU Enlargement', in D. Lopandić, ed., *Regional Cooperation in South Eastern Europe – Conference Proceedings* (Belgrade, European Movement in Serbia 2002) pp. 39-45. For an exploratory assessment of the effectiveness of the Stability Pact to serve as a conflict prevention/management regime, see D. Sandole, 'The Balkans Stability Pact as a Regional Conflict Management and Prevention "Space": An Evaluation', in P. Jureković, ed., *The Stability Pact for South East Europe – Dawn of an Era of Regional Co-operation* (Vienna, National Defence Academy 2002) pp. 20-36.

[40] See COM (1999) 235 final, Brussels, 26 May 1999.

[41] *Bull. EU* 6-2000, point I.49.67. For a critical view on this 'promise of a perspective of membership', see O. Anastasakis and D. Bechev, *EU Conditionality in South East Europe: Bringing Commitment to the Process* (Oxford, SEESP 2003).

the European Union. Hence, conditionality remains the glue of the SAP. Although anchored in a common set of political and economic conditions, the approach of the SAP is flexible enough to allow each country to move ahead at its own pace. An annual review mechanism assesses each country's performance in meeting the conditions. The recommendations contained in the Commission's ('progress') reports, as well as the Council's annual assessment, are intended to help the SAP countries focus their attention for the year ahead on specific priority areas. Thus, the process places an emphasis on *differentiation* according to the specific needs and situations of each country, as well as on improvements in the relations within the entire region.

The 21 November 2000 Zagreb Summit of heads of state and government of EU Member States and SAP countries set the seal on the process by gaining the region's agreement to the applicable set of objectives and conditions.[42] At the 21 June 2003 EU-Western Balkans Summit in Thessaloniki, it was acknowledged that the SAP will remain the framework for the European course of the Western Balkan countries, 'all the way to their future accession'.[43] Indeed, the SAP and the prospects it offers serve as the anchor for reform in the Western Balkans, in the same way the accession process has done in Central and Eastern Europe. In the light of the latter, the European Council endorsed 'The Thessaloniki Agenda for the Western Balkans: Moving Towards European Integration' to further strengthen and enhance the political visibility of the SAP, *inter alia*, by launching the high-level multilateral EU-Western Balkans Forum, 'European Partnerships', as well as the decisions for enhanced cooperation in the areas of political dialogue and the Common Foreign and Security Policy, parliamentary cooperation, support for institution-building and the opening of Community programmes.[44]

3. STABILISATION AND ASSOCIATION AGREEMENTS

3.1 **Legal basis**

Article 310 TEC, on the basis of which the European Economic Area was established and the Europe Agreements (EAs) with the countries from Central and Eastern Europe were concluded, has provided the legal basis for the Stabilisation and Association Agreements (SAAs) that the European Union is offering to

---

[42] *Bull. EU* 11-2000, point I.6.57.

[43] For the full text of the declaration of the EU-Western Balkans Summit at Thessaloniki, see *Bull. EU* 6-2003, point 1.6.70.

[44] For the text of the Thessaloniki Agenda, see Annex A to Council Conclusions of 16 June 2003, Press Release No. 10369/03 (Presse 166).

countries in the Western Balkans. Content-wise, the SAAs are also based on the existing EAs, even if they include new elements reflecting the specific situation of the Western Balkan countries. This was to be expected given the short period of time that the Commission had to develop the SAAs. In crisis situations – here even in a literal sense – the European Union traditionally acts conservatively and instinctively falls back on an existing policy approach (so-called 'path dependency behaviour').[45] Nonetheless, the Commission was keen to differentiate between this 'new type of contract' and the EAs. It argued that the conclusion of SAAs would provide an appropriate alternative to the EAs, which are regarded as leading to EU membership, and the Partnership and Cooperation Agreements (PCAs), which have been concluded with almost all the successor states of the Soviet Union and have far less ambitious goals.[46] As Phinnemore explains, the reasons for this were essentially two-fold. First, the challenges in the Western Balkans went beyond those concerning economic and political transition, which had been posed by the CEECs over the last decade. Therefore, a new and dedicated type of relationship responding to the particular needs of the Western Balkans was deemed necessary. Second, by spring 1999, the European Union was making headway towards realising its most ambitious enlargement to date. The prospect of up to twelve new entrants over the next few years was unprecedented. Added to this was the question of admitting Turkey into the accession process. Faced with such an overwhelming enlargement agenda, there was little enthusiasm for widening it further by offering EAs to the countries of the Western Balkans, thereby raising expectations of pre-accession aid and encouraging membership applications. Mindful of this and anxious about causing concern among the candidate countries about their position in the enlargement process, the European Union had to avoid any formulation that might raise objections and potentially undermine reform efforts in those countries. This was recognised in the title of the SAAs: their purpose was not just association but, in the short term at least, stabilisation.[47]

---

45 See J. Peterson, 'The European Union as a Global Actor', in J. Peterson and H. Sjursen, *A Common Foreign Policy for Europe?* (London, Routledge 1998) pp. 3-17.

46 See COM (1999) 235 final, Brussels, 26 May 1999. On EAs, see, *inter alia*, M. Maresceau, ed., *Enlarging the European Union: Relations Between the EU and Central and Eastern Europe* (London, Longman 1997); A. Mayhew, *Recreating Europe: The European Union's Policy towards Central and Eastern Europe* (Cambridge, CUP 1998). On PCAs, see, e.g., C. Hillion, 'The Evolving System of European Union External Relations as Evidenced in the EU Partnerships with Russia and Ukraine', PhD thesis, Leiden University, 22 February 2005.

47 Analysis of the two existing SAAs shows considerable similarities with the earlier EAs. See D. Phinnemore, 'Stabilisation and Association Agreements: Europe Agreements for the Western Balkans?', 8 *EFA Rev.* (2003) pp. 77-103 at pp. 79-81.

3.2 Procedure

In the procedure for the conclusion of an SAA, the application of conditionality has to be seen as a graduated process, as the start of SAA negotiations requires a lower level of compliance than the conclusion of the agreement. Before negotiations for the conclusion of an SAA can start, a certain level of progress must be made. The Commission observes and evaluates the situation in the country, in particular the fulfilment of the relevant conditions set out in the Council Conclusions of 29 April 1997, such as the presence of functioning democratic structures, respect for human rights, fundamental freedoms and the rule of law, as well as cooperation with neighbouring countries. In doing so, the Commission is guided by reports of international organisations, committees or institutions that are active in the region, such as NATO, the OSCE and the Council of Europe. The results are published in annual country reports, in which the Commission reviews compliance with the European Union's political and economic criteria by each of the countries concerned.[48] Once the Commission judges that a country has made sufficient progress in its domestic reform process, it begins, with the approval of the Council, to carry out a study on the feasibility of the opening of negotiations for an SAA. Following the completion of this so-called 'feasibility study' and a positive assessment by the Council that a Western Balkan country has indeed made sufficient progress in meeting the SAP conditions and that it has the capacity to negotiate and implement the far-reaching political and economic obligations under an SAA, the Commission establishes a formal proposal for negotiating directives for an SAA. If accepted by the Council, the negotiations are conducted by the Commission in consultation with a special committee created by the Council for that purpose. SAAs, like EAs, are mixed agreements. Hence, to enter into force they require the approval of the Council (by way of a Council decision),[49] the assent of the European Parliament (Arts. 300(3) and 310 TEC) as well

48 The individual country reports are annexed to the Commission's annual reports on the SAP. For the European Commission's three SAP reports, see COM (2002) 163 final, Brussels, 4 April 2002; COM (2003) 139 final, Brussels, 26 March 2003; and COM (2004) 202 final, Brussels, 30 March 2004. In a speech to the EU-Western Balkan Forum on his first day in office as Commissioner for Enlargement, Olli Rehn announced that the Commission's annual report on the SAP would be moved to the autumn to make the SAP report coincide with the regular reports on the candidate countries. See SPEECH/04/487, Brussels, 22 November 2004. Indeed, the Commission's '2005 enlargement strategy paper' combines general reports on the progress made by Turkey and the Western Balkans. See COM (2005) 561 final, Brussels, 9 November 2005. This facilitates a more consistent and systematic approach to assess and advise both candidate and 'potential' candidate countries on their track towards EU integration. On the use of the concept 'potential' candidate countries, see *infra* section 5.

49 With the transfer of responsibility for relations with the Western Balkans from DG External Relations to DG Enlargement in November 2004, SAAs are now signed by a ministerial representative of the country holding the Presidency of the Council, the EU Commissioner for Enlargement and a ministerial representative of the Western Balkan country concerned.

as ratification by all EU Member States and the non-Member State concerned. In anticipation of the full ratification of an SAA, the trade provisions may enter into force via interim agreements. Political dialogue can already be established as well.

3.2.1 *Macedonia and Croatia*

At the time of writing, SAAs had been signed with Macedonia (on 9 April 2001)[50] and with Croatia (on 29 October 2001).[51] Ratification in both Macedonia and Croatia followed shortly after the respective agreements were signed (on 12 April 2001 and 5 December 2001 respectively). The European Parliament was also quick to give its assent to the agreements (on 3 May 2001 and 12 December 2001 respectively). In anticipation of the full ratification of both SAAs, the trade provisions already entered into force via interim agreements.[52] After ratification by the then still fifteen Member States of the European Union, the SAA FYROM entered into force on 1 April 2004.[53] While a majority of the Member States also ratified the SAA Croatia within the usual time frames, the Netherlands, the United Kingdom and Italy for a long time withheld (notification of) ratification of the agreement because of their negative perception of Croatia's willingness to cooperate with the ICTY.[54] Like mixed agreements, SAAs are open to national

---

[50] See COM (2001) 90 final, Brussels, 19 February 2001.

[51] See COM (2001) 371 final, Brussels, 9 July 2001.

[52] The interim agreements entered into force on 1 June 2001 and 1 March 2002. See Interim Agreement on trade and trade-related matters between the European Community, of the one part, and the former Yugoslav Republic of Macedonia, of the other part, *OJ* 2001 L 124/2; Interim Agreement on trade and trade-related matters between the European Community, of the one part, and the Republic of Croatia, of the other part, *OJ* 2001 L 330/3.

[53] The SAA FYROM thereby replaced the Cooperation Agreement between the European Community and Macedonia which had been in force since 1 January 1998, see *OJ* 1997 L 348/2. For the text of the SAA FYROM, see *OJ* 2004 L 84/13. On 21 February 2005, the Council and the Commission adopted Decision 2005/192/EC, *OJ* 2005 L 63/21, on the conclusion of the Protocol to the SAA FYROM to take account of the accession to the European Union of the ten new Member States. For the text of the Protocol, see *OJ* 2004 L 388/3. With the entry into force of an SAA, a new set of joint bodies was established at ministerial level (Stabilisation and Association Council), at senior official level (Stabilisation and Association Committee) and at the technical level (subcommittees). Following the entry into force of the SAA FYROM, the first meeting of the Stabilisation and Association Committee took place on 3 June 2004 in Skopje. The Committee is to ensure continuity of the association relationship between Macedonia and the European Union and the proper functioning of the SAA. It decided to set up seven sub-committees (on trade, industry, customs and taxation; agriculture and fisheries; internal market and competition; economic and financial issues; justice and home affairs; human resources, research, technological development and social policy; and transport, environment, energy and regional development) covering all areas of cooperation under the SAA.

[54] See also chapter 11 in this volume. These countries referred to Croatia's apparent inability to arrest the indicted general Ante Gotovina and hand him over to the ICTY in The Hague. Gotovina, the tribunal's third most wanted fugitive, disappeared the day before the ICTY made his indictment

interpretation, but this raises the question whether individual Member States should maintain the power to impose, unilaterally and at such a late stage, political conditionality on SAA candidates. Such action undermines the authority of the Commission to evaluate the fulfilment of the key conditions for association and blocks the Union's efforts to build a common policy to engage candidate associates. In the second half of 2004, an Enlargement Protocol to the SAA Croatia had to be negotiated in order to take account of the accession of ten new Member States to the European Union on 1 May 2004. On 21 December 2004, the Protocol was signed.[55] Via the Enlargement Protocol, the new Member States became party to the SAA.[56] The SAA Croatia entered into force on 1 February 2005.[57]

3.2.2 *Albania*

On the basis of a positive evaluation of the political stability and progress on reforms, negotiations on an SAA with Albania were opened by the Commission on 31 January 2003. But talks soon stalled. This was largely due to the Commission's firm opinion that Albania was not demonstrating a great determination to fight organised crime, all types of 'trafficking', money laundering and corruption.[58] The general elections of 3 July 2005 were widely seen as an important test of the country's democratic credentials and a condition for reviving the SAA talks. The Commission, in its Progress Report of 9 November 2005, paved the way for the conclusion of the SAA negotiations.[59] By considering that the political situation in the country had improved, it seems that the Commission gave precedence to political expediency over concerns about the killing of three individuals in electoral violence, the OSCE's statement that the election complied 'only partially' with democratic norms, and a political comeback that is unprecedented

public, in July 2001, and was finally arrested on 7 December 2005 in a hotel in the resort of Playa de las Americas in Tenerife and subsequently transferred to The Hague. He is indicted for ordering the killing of more than 100 ethnic Serbs and expelling 150,000 more during and after Zagreb's final offensive in August 1995 to recapture Croatian lands seized by Serb forces. The pressure on Croatia to find and arrest Gotovina has provoked negative feelings towards the European Union, as many Croatians perceive him as a war hero rather than a war criminal.

55 Council Decision 2005/205/EC, *OJ* 2005 L 68/30.

56 For the text of the Protocol, see *OJ* 2005 L 26/222.

57 For the text of the SAA Croatia, see *OJ* 2005 L 26/3.

58 See the Commission's Third Annual SAP Report, COM (2004) 202 final, Brussels, 30 March 2004.

59 See COM (2005) 561, Brussels, 9 November 2005, SEC (2005) 1421. In a similar vein, see Council Decision 2005/809/EC concerning the conclusion of the Agreement between the European Community and the Republic of Albania on the readmission of persons residing without authorisation, *OJ* 2005 L 304/14.

even in the revolving-door world of Balkan politics. Sali Berisha – a former President (and personal physician to Albania's late Stalinist leader Enver Hoxha) who was forced out of office in 1997 when fraudulent pyramid savings schemes sparked civil unrest – and his newly installed Democratic Party government must have somehow convinced the Commission of the sincerity of their pledge to step up reforms and to fight organised crime and corruption, as well as solving property issues and improving the work of the customs administration. European Commission President Barroso himself announced the conclusion of the SAA negotiations on 18 February 2006.[60]

3.2.3 *Bosnia-Herzegovina*

The substantial completion of the so-called 'Road Map' for Bosnia-Herzegovina and the establishment of the first elected government for a four-year term were rewarded by the Commission with the launching of a feasibility study in June 2003.[61] The study was adopted on 18 November 2003.[62] Nevertheless, in its Third Annual Report on the SAP, the Commission identified sixteen new priorities on which it demanded further political and economic reform and progress in 2004 to make the country a self-sustaining state based on the rule of law before negotiations on the SAA would be considered. In particular, cooperation with the ICTY was declared less than satisfactory. In the Federation of BiH, serious inadequacies were noted on the part of the Bosnian Croats. The Republika Srpska was dismissed for its failure to locate or arrest even a single indicted fugitive. After a wave of extraditions of both Bosnian Serb and Muslim indictees to the ICTY in the first three months of 2005, the European Commissioner for Enlargement announced that Bosnia-Herzegovina could start negotiations on an SAA by the end of 2005 if cooperation with the ICTY would continue and would lead to 'full cooperation'.[63] Despite the fact that the two most wanted Bosnian Serb indictees, Radovan Karadzić and Ratko Mladić were still at large – reportedly thanks to well-organised systems of support,[64] the Commission nonetheless recommended

---

60 José Manuel Barroso, 'Building for the future: Making a success of the Stabilization and Association Agreement', Parliament of Albania, Tirana, 18 February 2006, SPEECH/06/103.

61 The Road Map was presented by the Commission in March 2000 and set out eighteen essential steps to be undertaken by BiH before any further advance of the country within the SAP would be considered by the European Union. The Road Map is available at: <http://www.esiweb.org/bridges/bosnia/EURoadMap.pdf>.

62 COM (2003) 692 final, Brussels, 18 November 2003.

63 See E. Vucheva, 'Bosnia and Herzegovina a step further on the EU path', *EUObserver.com*, 21 March 2005.

64 Interestingly, the outspoken Minister of Foreign Affairs of SaM, Vuk Drasković, claimed that Mladić was hiding with the help of Serbian security forces. See, E. Jansson, 'Serbian authorities "know where Mladić is hiding"', *Financial Times*, 5 April 2005.

the opening of negotiations on an SAA with Bosnia and Herzegovina and presented draft negotiating directives for adoption by the Council.[65] SAA negotiations were officially opened on 25 November 2005, in the same week that the world celebrated the tenth anniversary of the Dayton/Paris Peace Accords.

3.2.4 *Serbia and Montenegro*

Internal disputes surrounding the endorsement of the Internal Market and Trade Action Plan by the State Assembly of Serbia and Montenegro led the Commission to stall the feasibility study for an SAA with this country. It took a full endorsement of the European Union's so-called 'twin-track' approach by the political leaders of both Serbia and Montenegro to re-launch the feasibility study in October 2004. The twin-track approach to SAA negotiations means that the European Union deals with the two republics on policies that they conduct separately, notably trade, economic and sectoral policies, while it continues to work with the state union where it is the competent authority, for example in the field of international political obligations and human rights; that is, as long as the state union continues to exist. Montenegro is set to hold a referendum on independence on 21 May 2006, which it is entitled to do under the terms of the Belgrade Agreement. The European Union is ready to accept any result in the Montenegro referendum – be it independence or federation with Serbia – as long as the vote is 'legitimate', i.e., if it passes a 50 percent threshold for participation and 55 percent for approval for any result.[66] A pro-independence vote will require the European Union to completely disentangle the SAA talks with the two republics. In principle, this should not be a problem, as the 'twin-track' approach has become a standard working method for the Commission. As two independent countries, however, Serbia and Montenegro will then be in slightly different positions in terms of establishing closer links with the European Union: not only in terms of cooperation with the ICTY, but also because the republics have quite different economies. While the Serbian economy is based on production, industry, agriculture and its internal market needs some protection, Montenegro's economy is quite open and based mainly on services. Logically speaking, Montenegro should therefore be in a better position than Serbia to make fast progress in its SAA negotiations with the EU.

---

65 Communication from the Commission to the Council on the progress achieved by Bosnia and Herzegovina in implementing the priorities identified in the 'Feasibility Study on the preparedness of Bosnia and Herzegovina to negotiate a Stabilisation and Association Agreement with the European Union (COM (2003) 692 final)', COM (2005) 529 final, Brussels, 21 October 2005.

66 See Council Conclusions of 27 February 2006 in Press Release No. 6344/06 (Presse 46).

As far as cooperation with the ICTY is concerned, SaM was under enormous pressure from the European Union's Secretary General/High Representative (SG/HR) and the Commission to extradite alleged war criminals in order to finalise the feasibility report on 12 April 2005. As a result, the authorities made serious headway in their cooperation with the ICTY by arresting, in the first three months of 2005, half a dozen suspects that were believed to be hiding in Serbia. In response, the General Affairs Council gave the Commission the mandate to conduct negotiations on an SAA with Serbia and Montenegro.[67] Their opening by European Commissioner Olli Rehn in Belgrade on 10 October 2005 marked the fifth anniversary of the democratic uprising that removed Slobodan Milošević from the Presidential *peluche*. On that occasion, Rehn warned that the conclusion of the SAA negotiations was only possible if Karadzić and Mladić were handed over to The Hague tribunal in the meantime.[68] However, after the ICTY's Chief Prosecutor told the BBC in February 2006 that General Mladić was within 'immediate reach' of the Belgrade authorities, a statement which provoked a flurry of media reports which first claimed and later denied that Mladić had been captured, the European Union hardened its tone.[69] It suspended the SAA talks after twice having given Serbia and Montenegro a one-month deadline to send Mladić to The Hague or face disruption of the SAA talks.[70] As SaM was unable to meet the deadline, the Union cancelled the political round of SAA talks with Serbia and Montenegro. Full cooperation of SaM with the ICTY will remain the single most important issue upon which the progress (or disruption) of the SAA negotiations hinges.

3.2.5 *Kosovo*

The European perspective of the Western Balkans, as stated in the Zagreb Declaration of November 2000, is also open to Kosovo.[71] However, pending a final

[67] See Council Conclusions of 3 October 2005 in Press Release No. 12515/1/05 REV 1 (Presse 242).

[68] European Commission, 'Serbia and Montenegro Open Association Talks with EU', in *Enlargement Newsletter*, 28 October 2005.

[69] See E. Krasniqi, 'EU ministers back Balkans war crimes ultimatum', *EUObserver.com*, 27 February 2006; and Council Conclusions of 27 February 2006, in Press Release No. 6344/06 (Presse 46).

[70] The controversies over the death and burial of former President Slobodan Milošević on 11 March 2006 complicated Belgrade's efforts to transfer the war-time general to The Hague, while at the same time, the authorities had come under increased pressure from the ICTY and the EU to capture Mladić. This was recognised by the European Union; hence the one-month extension of the initial deadline of one month.

[71] *Bull. EU* 11-2000, point I.6.57. On 20 April 2005, the European Commission adopted a Communication entitled 'A European Future for Kosovo,' which reinforces the Commission's commitment to Kosovo. See COM(2005) 156 final, Brussels, 20 April 2005.

settlement of its status,[72] UN-administered Kosovo (as defined by UNSC Res. 1244 (1999)) was not able to commence with the SAP. To ensure that UNMIK and the PISG would follow EU-compatible practices in the political, economic and sectoral reform process, UNMIK and the European Commission agreed that an instrument was needed to monitor and drive the process. It was deemed profitable for Kosovo to follow the methodology and substance of the SAP and thus avoid isolation from the path of EU-compatible transition and development of the rest of the region.[73] To that end, on 6 November 2002, the Commission commenced the so-called 'Stabilisation and Association Process Tracking Mechanism' (STM).[74] The STM is a regular forum of the European Commission, UNMIK and Kosovo's PISG, which is intended to help the authorities in Kosovo to prepare for reinforced policy-making relations within the framework of the European Union's Stabilisation and Association Process.[75] It tracks the progress made in the implementation of the European Partnership[76] and provides policy advice on the building of EU-compatible institutional, legislative, economic and social frameworks. As such, Kosovo benefits from all the elements of the SAP, with the notable exception of the possibility of contractual relations with the European Union. However, depending on the outcome of status talks, Kosovo may in due course engage in contractual relations with the Union as appropriate.

At the moment of writing, the European Union's main focus is on improving capacity building through regular cooperation and joint initiatives with a number of line ministries, particularly the Ministry of Finance and Economy and the Ministry of Trade and Industry. Together with these ministries, the EU pillar in UNMIK has led free-trade negotiations and facilitated Kosovo's involvement in a number of regional and wider European initiatives, such as the Energy Community Treaty,[77] the South-East European Transport Observatory, the European Common Aviation Area and the European Charter for Small Enterprises.[78]

---

72 The resignation of Ramush Haradinaj as Kosovo's Prime Minister on 9 March 2005 and his surrender to the ICTY created a possibility for *rapprochement* between Priština and Belgrade to engage in final status talks, which started on 21 November 2005. This is not to say that the negotiations will be easy. The process is expected to take at least a few months.

73 The EU was also eager to apply the same standards in the whole region.

74 EU Ministers endorsed the launch of technical talks at the Thessaloniki Summit on 21 June 2003, *Bull. EU* 6-2003, point 1.6.70.

75 In fact, STM meetings are the main channel for dialogue between the Commission and Kosovo. To date eight STM meetings took place. The 6th STM meeting, which was held on 16 February 2005 in Priština, was the first meeting with the newly elected government.

76 The STM and the Annual Progress Report are the main instruments of the European Commission for monitoring Kosovo's progress in the SAP. On the European Partnership, see *infra* section 4.

77 See *infra* n. 86.

78 See Council Decision No. 2006/56/EC of 30 January 2006 on the principles, priorities and conditions contained in the European Partnership with Serbia and Montenegro including Kosovo as defined by the United Nations Security Council Resolution 1244 of 10 June 1999 and repealing Decision 2004/520/EC, *OJ* 2006 L 35/32.

3.3 General principles

3.3.1 *Essential elements*

Both existing SAAs set out various principles to which the parties are committed.[79] The preamble and Article 1(2) of both agreements describe the objectives of the new associations: the establishment of an appropriate framework for political dialogue between the associate and the European Union, the approximation of the associate's legislation to that of the European Union, the development of a climate conducive to increased trade and investment, the transition of the associate's economy into a market economy, EC support for reform and regional cooperation in all fields covered by the SAA. To these ends, both SAAs confirm in almost identical provisions that the conclusion and implementation of the agreements fall within the framework of the conclusions of the Council of the European Union of 29 April 1997 and are based on individual merits of the respective SAP partner (Art. 3). The conditionality clause used in Article 2 of the SAAs includes such 'essential elements' as the

> [r]espect for the democratic principles and human rights as proclaimed in the Universal Declaration of Human Rights and as defined in the Helsinki Final Act and the Charter of Paris for a New Europe, respect for international law principles and the rule of law as well as the principles of market economy as reflected in the Document of the CSCE Bonn Conference on Economic Cooperation…

Unlike the EAs, 'respect for international law principles and the rule of law' are also mentioned among the general principles of the SAAs. In the case of Croatia, a commitment to the right of return for all refugees and to compliance with the 1995 Dayton/Paris and Erdut Agreements is also reaffirmed (in the preamble).

By qualifying the criteria mentioned in Article 2 as 'essential elements' of the contractual relationship, both SAAs borrow the language of the 1969 Vienna Convention on the Law of Treaties. Article 60(3) of the Convention allows for the unilateral suspension or termination of international agreements by one of the parties in cases of 'material breach' of a treaty, caused, for instance, by '(b) the violation of a provision essential to the accomplishment of the object or purpose of the treaty'. In line with the European Community's international treaty practice, the essential elements clause of Article 2 is complemented by a standard

---

[79] For an analysis of the SAAs with Macedonia and Croatia, prior to their publication in the *Official Journal of the European Union*, see J. Marko and J. Wilhelm, 'Stabilisation and Association Agreements', in A. Ott and K. Inglis, eds., *Handbook on European Enlargement – A Commentary on the Enlargement Process* (The Hague, T.M.C. Asser Press 2002) pp. 165-174; Phinnemore, loc. cit. n. 47.

non-compliance clause. This so-called 'Bulgarian clause' enables either party to take 'appropriate measures', that is to say, measures taken in accordance with international law (principle of proportionality, etc.), if it considers that the other party has failed to fulfil an obligation under the SAA.[80] The party considering such measures must, 'except in cases of special urgency, first supply the Stabilisation and Association Council (SAC) with all relevant information required for a thorough examination of the situation with a view to finding a solution acceptable to both parties.' A joint declaration annexed to the final act of each SAA clarifies that the notion 'cases of special urgency' should be interpreted to mean 'cases of material breach of the Agreement by one of the two Parties'. A material breach of the SAA is considered to consists of 'repudiation of the Agreement not sanctioned by the general rules of international law [and] violation of the essential elements of the Agreement as set out in Article 2.' As a result, any infringement of democratic principles, human rights and fundamental freedoms, international law principles (e.g., full and unequivocal cooperation with the ICTY), the rule of law and principles of market economy constitutes, at least in principle, a case of special urgency, entitling the sanctioning party to take appropriate measures, without the need for prior consultations in the SAC. It would seem that the immediate adoption of such measures, without a prior attempt to find an adequate solution in the SAC, is reserved for gross, widespread and persistent violations of one or more of the requirements enshrined in the essential elements clause.

Pippan has rightly pointed out that, with their references to the rights and freedoms contained in the 1948 Universal Declaration of Human Rights, the 1975 Helsinki Final Act and the 1990 Charter of Paris for a New Europe, as well as the political and economic principles enshrined in the Document of the CSCE Bonn Conference on Economic Cooperation, the essential elements clauses in the SAAs with Macedonia and Croatia set a considerably high standard. From the time of entry into force of the SAAs, the parties to these bilateral relationships are contractually bound, for example, to undertake 'to build, consolidate and strengthen democracy as the only system of government'.[81] This requires, *inter alia*, a representative and pluralistic government that is 'based on the will of the people, expressed regularly through free and fair elections', and ensures 'accountability to the electorate' as well as 'justice administered impartially'.[82] Under the SAAs, the creation of – or the return to – a non-democratic form of government by one of

80 See Art. 118(2) SAA FYROM and Art. 120(2) SAA Croatia. If a party takes a measure in a case of special urgency pursuant to these articles, the other party may avail itself of a dispute settlement procedure. For an explanation on the emergence and importance of the 'Bulgarian clause', see Bulterman, op. cit. n. 24, at pp. 204-205.

81 Charter of Paris for a New Europe, section on Human Rights, Democracy and the Rule of Law, para. 1.

82 Ibid., paras. 3 and 4.

the treaty partners is therefore illegal. This is not only an important regional contribution to a general trend in contemporary international law that increasingly outlaws military or one-party civil regimes and endorses pluralistic, democratic governance as the only legitimate expression of the peoples' right to (internal) self-determination. It is also a remarkable normative advancement given the fact that the Universal Declaration of Human Rights, as well as the Helsinki Final Act and the Charter of Paris, are, as such, legally non-binding instruments.[83]

3.3.2 *Regional cooperation*

Whereas regional cooperation was encouraged among the countries that signed Europe Agreements with the European Union, it was never made a distinct feature of their associations. In the case of the SAAs, it is viewed as key to the stabilisation of South-Eastern Europe and made an explicit condition before the countries of the Western Balkans can join the European Union (Art. 3). However difficult it is to enforce this additional conditionality, the importance attached to it has been underlined by the Commission, which noted – in bold – in its First Annual Report on the SAP: 'Integration with the EU is only possible if future members can demonstrate that they are willing and able to interact with their neighbours as EU Member States do.'[84] In Article 4, Macedonia and Croatia commit themselves to 'continue and foster cooperation and good neighbourly relations with the other countries of the region'. The SAAs explicitly refer to such relations covering the movement of persons, goods, capital and services, as well as the development of projects of common interest. In the SAA with Croatia, specific examples are given: refugee return and combating organised crime, corruption, money laundering, illegal migration and trafficking. To achieve regional cooperation on these issues, the SAA countries are expected to conclude conventions between each other within two years after entry into force of the second SAA (Art. 12), that is to say, before 1 February 2007.[85]

SAA signatories are also obliged to engage in regional cooperation with the other countries covered by the SAP (Art. 13).[86] The political dialogue, held within

---

[83] See Pippan, loc. cit. n. 27, at pp. 237-238.

[84] See COM (2002) 163 final, Brussels, 4 April 2002, at p. 11.

[85] So far, Croatia has signed at least one such bilateral agreement with Macedonia. See chapter 12 in this volume. In practice, this requirement does not pose any problems, as states in the region are again cooperating in various fields.

[86] Croatia, for example, has established free trade agreements with BiH and SaM. See chapter 12 in this volume. The signing on 25 October 2005 of the Energy Community Treaty, the first-ever multilateral treaty in South-Eastern Europe, between the European Union and Croatia, BiH, Serbia, Montenegro, Macedonia, Albania, Romania, Bulgaria and UNMIK on behalf of Kosovo can also be regarded as a fulfilment of the Art. 13 obligation. See Commission Press Release No. IP/05/1346 of 25 October 2005 and Council Decision 2005/905/EC on the signing by the European Community of the Energy Community Treaty, *OJ* 2005 L 329/30.

a multilateral framework (Arts. 7 and 8), shall also contribute to the development of regional cooperation and good neighbourly relations. It seems that these provisions are codifying a proliferation process that was already underway in South-Eastern Europe. Among those initiatives for multilateral cooperation in the region worth mentioning are the Central European Initiative (CEI), the Black Sea Economic Cooperation (BSEC), the Central European Free Trade Agreement (CEFTA), the South East Europe Cooperation Process (SEECP), the Southeast European Cooperation Initiative (SECI) and the Adriatic-Ionian Initiative (AII).[87] The biggest achievement of these initiatives is without doubt the sustainable political dialogue between the countries involved in these frameworks. But with partly overlapping memberships and agendas indicating lack of complementarities, competitiveness is growing among them. Many regional initiatives have been criticised because of the modesty of their objectives and the limited concrete results they have yielded. Moreover, most of them are only addressing the immediate post-conflict situation, and all but the SEECP have been created as a consequence of external incentives by resuscitating and broadening existing initiatives. It seems that, in the search for the most appropriate regional initiative, valuable resources are being wasted.[88]

3.3.3 *Approximation of legislation*

The approximation of the associate's legislation to that of the European Union is another important aspect of the SAAs as far as the perspective of future integration is concerned. The existing SAAs define the rules of the internal market as *priorities* for legislative approximation by Macedonia and Croatia.[89] The SAA Croatia declares that this legislative approximation process shall be fully implemented within six years after the entry into force of the agreement (Arts. 5 and 69), that is to say, before 1 February 2011. In the case of Macedonia, the approximation shall take place within a time frame of ten years, divided into two successive stages (Arts. 5 and 68). In the first phase of implementation of this SAA (until 9 April 2009), the approximation shall cover fundamental elements of the internal market *acquis* and other trade-related areas. This includes competition law, intellectual property law, standards and certification law, public procurement law and data protection law. During the second phase (until 9 April 2014), the remaining elements of the *acquis* shall be covered. The reasoning behind the

87 For an overview and analysis of these initiatives, see D. Lopandić, *Regional Initiatives in South Eastern Europe* (Belgrade, European Movement in Serbia 2001).

88 See J. Minić, 'Summary and Recommendations of the Conference', in Lopandić, op. cit. n. 39, at pp. 9-17.

89 This is clearly an advancement compared to the one-size-fits-all approach prescribed in the EAs. See A. Łazowski, 'Approximation of Laws', in Ott and Inglis, op. cit. n. 79, at pp. 631-639.

shorter time frame and the absence of stages in the SAA with Croatia reflects the belief among the EU Member States that Croatia is in a better position, both economically and politically, to meet its obligations under the SAA. The focus on internal market law carries the risk of an unbalanced situation in the approximation process, leaving behind other essential areas such as social or environmental policy. Yet, it is a critical component within the SAA, essentially extending the European Union's own philosophy to the Western Balkans that the adoption of the hard core of economic standards based on a free market economy is a route to national as well as regional peace, stability and growth and that such integration serves the mutual interests of all countries concerned. Full implementation of the SAAs will help the countries of the Western Balkans in their preparations for EU membership. They are assisted in this task by the Commission with technical advice and financial assistance.

3.4 Financial and technical assistance

As an overarching, multi-country strategy, the SAP not only pledges political but also financial and technical support by the European Union to the five countries of the Western Balkans. The Community Assistance for Reconstruction, Development and Stabilisation (CARDS) programme is the Community's funding instrument dedicated to the region of South-Eastern Europe and supports the actions undertaken within the SAP and under the SAAs.[90] It replaced the OBNOVA and Phare[91] programmes and established a single legal framework for EU assistance to the countries of the region.[92] In addition, a special European Agency for Reconstruction (EAR) was entrusted with the local administration of EC assistance to Kosovo, Macedonia and Serbia and Montenegro.[93] Under the

---

[90] Council Regulation (EC) No. 2666/2000, *OJ* 2000 L 306/1. See also European Commission, CARDS Assistance Programme to the Western Balkans: Regional Strategy Paper 2002-2006, Brussels, 22 October 2001.

[91] Albania, Bosnia-Herzegovina and Macedonia were previously recipients of Phare assistance. Upon receiving candidate status (see *infra* section 5), Croatia was included as a beneficiary of Phare, ISPA and SAPARD. See Council Regulation (EC) No. 2257/2004 amending Regulations (EEC) No. 3906/89, (EC) No. 1267/1999, (EC) No. 1268/1999 and (EC) No. 2666/2000, to take account of Croatia's candidate status, *OJ* 2004 L 389/1. See also the Framework Agreement between the European Community and the Republic of Croatia on the general principles for the participation of the Republic of Croatia in Community programmes, *OJ* 2005 L 192/16. At the time of writing, similar decisions concerning Macedonia, which received candidate country status in December 2005, had not been taken.

[92] In 2005-2006, CARDS financial assistance will cover the 'potential' candidate countries of the Western Balkans (Albania, BiH, SaM (including Kosovo under UN administration)) and candidate country Macedonia (until decided otherwise). Croatia will continue to be eligible for CARDS regional funds. See, again, Council Regulation (EC) No. 2257/2004.

[93] Council Regulation (EC) No. 2068/2004 amending Regulation (EC) No. 2667/2000 on the European Agency for Reconstruction, *OJ* 2004 L 358/2. The EAR has its headquarters in Thessaloniki

unified procedures of CARDS, which became fully operational in 2002, the Commission draws up multi-annual country strategies, as well as a regional strategy, in collaboration with the Western Balkan countries, EU Member States, other donors and, insofar as possible, representatives of civil society. These strategy papers form the basis for annual programmes for each of the five countries concerned.[94] Under the CARDS programme for the 2000-2006 period, a budget of €4.65 billion has been agreed.[95] To achieve its objective of facilitating the SAP, CARDS assistance finances investment, institution building and other programmes in four major areas: (i) reconstruction, democratic stabilisation, reconciliation and the return of refugees; (ii) institutional and legislative development, including approximation of domestic legislation to EU norms to underpin democracy and the rule of law, human rights, civil society and the media, as well as the operation of a free market economy; (iii) sustainable economic and social development, including structural reform; and (iv) the promotion of closer relations and regional cooperation among SAP countries and between them, the European Union (including the new Member States) and the candidate countries (Bulgaria, Romania and Turkey).

The Regional Strategy Paper (RSP) was adopted by the Commission in October 2001 and provides a strategic framework for programming the regional envelope of the CARDS programme during the 2002-2006 period.[96] Some 10 per cent of the available CARDS budget will be directed towards raising the levels of regional cooperation between the countries of the Western Balkans. As mentioned earlier, addressing this issue is a key goal within the SAP. The RSP has earmarked funds for support in four priority areas: (i) integrated border management to help tackle cross-border crime, facilitate trade across borders and stabilise the border regions themselves; (ii) institutional capacity building to help raise awareness of EU policy and laws that the region should increasingly be moving towards; (iii) democratic stabilisation to help cement advances on democracy and boost the involvement of civil society in the region's development; and (iv) integration of the region's transport, energy and environmental infrastructure into the wider European networks. These areas were selected because of their contribution to regional cooperation or because the support could be best delivered at the regional level. The Multi-Annual Indicative Programme (MIP) attached to the

---

and runs operational centres in Belgrade, Priština, Podgorica and Skopje. It is accountable to both the Council and the European Parliament and is overseen by a governing board composed of the Commission and representatives from EU Member States.

94 The 2002-2006 Strategy Papers and the most recent annual programmes can be retrieved from <http://www.europa.eu.int/comm/external_relations/see/docs/index.htm>.

95 Annex B to the First Annual Report of the SAP, COM (2002) 163 final, Brussels, 4 April 2002, at p. 23.

96 European Commission, CARDS Regional Strategy Paper, Brussels, 22 October 2001, IP/01/1464.

RSP provides strategic guidance for implementing the CARDS regional assistance. The amount of the CARDS regional financial allocation for 2005-2006 is €85 million.[97]

Table 1: CARDS Programme Allocation for 2000-2006 (million €)

	2000	2001	2002	2003	2004	2005	2006	TOTAL
Albania	33.4	37.5	44.9	46.5	63.5	44.2	45.5	315.5
Bosnia-Herzegovina	90.3	105.2	71.9	63.0	72.0	49.4	51.0	502.8
Croatia (transfer to pre-accession from 2005)	16.8	60.0	59.0	62.0	81.0	-	-	278.8
The former Yugoslav Republic of Macedonia	13.0	56.2	41.5	43.5	59.0	45.0	40.0	298.2
Serbia and Montenegro[a]	650.5	385.5	351.6	324.3	307.9	282.5	245.5	2547.8
Interim Civilian Administrations	10.0	24.5	33.0	32.0	35.0	36.0	35.0	205.5
Regional	20.2	20.0	43.5	31.5	23.0	47.9	42.0	228.1
Other[b]	141.5	118.0	11.0	17.0	22.5	19.7	19.8	349.5
Macro-Financial Assistance (grants)[c]	70.0	120.0	100.0	15.0	16.0	33.0	50.0	404.0
TOTAL	1045.7	926.9	756.4	634.8	679.9	557.7	528.8	5130.2
Croatia, pre-accession 2005-6						105	140	245
TOTAL, including Croatia 2005-6						662.7	668.8	5375.2

Note 1: Figures for the year 2006 are purely indicative and correspond to the multi-annual indicative programming (MIP).
Note 2: Figures include assistance from Phare and Obnova where relevant in 2000, and from CARDS 2001 and onwards.
Note 3: 2005 budget implementation: Re-use of recoveries from 2004/5, i.e., above budget allocation 2005: 6m for fYRoM, 7.5m for regional programme.
(a) Includes the Republic of Serbia, the Republic of Montenegro and the province Kosovo, which is currently under UN administration. Amounts for Serbia in 2002-03 include assistance from Regional Programme for Integrated Border Management destined for the whole of FRY/Serbia and Montenegro. In 2004, 8 Mio. € for that purpose is shown under the regional programme.
(b) Until 2001 (incl.): Humanitarian aid, Specific Measures, Rapid Intervention Operations, EIDHR and CFSP From 2001 (incl.): Administrative costs and the Western Balkans' contribution to the European Training Foundation.
(c) For 2000-2002: disbursements and not commitments.

Source: <http://europa.eu.int/comm/enlargement/financial_assistance.htm>

[97] Priority areas where regional CARDS assistance will be focused in 2005-2006 are: institution building (€16-18 million), justice and home affairs (€5-6 million), cross-border cooperation (€33-39 million), private sector development (€2.5-3.5 million) and infrastructure development (€21-26 million).

The country strategy papers (CSPs) provide the strategic framework in which EC assistance will be provided to each country in the 2000-2006 period. Each CSP sets out cooperation objectives, policy responses and priority fields of cooperation based on a thorough assessment of the partner country's policy agenda and political and socio-economic situation. The MIP attached to each CSP sets out the EU response in more detail, highlighting programme objectives, expected results and conditionality in the priority fields of cooperation. Malfunctioning governance, combined with organised crime, corruption and smuggling, constitutes the most serious obstacle to a rapid improvement of the situation in most of the Western Balkan countries.[98] Within this context, and taking into account the objectives of the SAP, it is notable that the EU response to the partner countries under the CARDS programme focuses on the sustainable return of refugees and displaced persons, the full integration of ethnic minorities into society, democratic stabilisation, administrative capacity building, an effective and accountable legal system, economic and social development, environment and natural resources and justice and home affairs.[99]

The main beneficiaries of CARDS assistance are the central governmental institutions, but regional and local bodies, social partners, cooperatives, associations and NGOs are also eligible to apply.[100] In the past, the latter's rights have proved to be of particular importance, as they create the possibility of a direct, 'decentralised' form of cooperation that can be maintained even if the state's central government falls short of complying with the conditions set out by the European Union in Article 5 of Council Regulation (EC) No. 2666/2000 on CARDS:

1. Respect for the principles of democracy and the rule of law and for human and minority rights and fundamental freedoms is an essential element for the application of this Regulation and a precondition for Community assistance. If these principles are not respected, the Council, acting by qualified majority on a proposal from the Commission, may take the appropriate measures.
2. Community assistance shall also be subject to the conditions defined by the Council in its Conclusions of 29 April 1997, in particular as regards the recipients' undertaking to carry out democratic, economic and institutional reforms.

---

98 Bosnia-Herzegovina faces even greater challenges over the medium term, notably strengthening the State of BiH and reinforcing the administration. The CSPs for SaM and Macedonia set out an approach that is designed to require the least modification possible, whatever the outcome of the final status talks on Kosovo.

99 For 'facts and figures' on assistance to each of the five Western Balkan countries, see the RSP, CSPs, and MIPs, available at: <http://www.europa.eu.int/comm/external_relations>. See also the joint initiative of the European Commission and the World Bank for the economic reconstruction and development in South-Eastern Europe, at: <http://www.seerecon.org>.

100 Art. 1(2) of Council Regulation (EC) No. 2666/2000.

This provision reflects one of the most comprehensive conditionality clauses ever embodied in a Community legal instrument regulating external assistance.[101] Apart from giving expression, in its first paragraph, to the importance of the 'political' part of the 1993 Copenhagen criteria as a precondition for Community assistance, it also explicitly incorporates the entire set of political and economic conditions entailed in the April 1997 Council Conclusions on conditionality as additional conditions for EU financial support to the countries of the Western Balkans. Moreover, the CARDS Regulation does not only rely on punitive measures in order to promote the exceptionally broad range of political and economic standards applied by the European Union towards the countries concerned. It also provides for the application of positive measures, namely the financing of projects and programmes aimed at supporting 'the creation of an institutional and legislative framework to underpin democracy, the rule of law, and human and minority rights, reconciliation and the consolidation of civil society'.[102]

3.5 Trade preferences

In addition to the significant amounts of European aid that the countries of the Western Balkans receive, all five benefit from generous trade preferences. In March 2000, the Lisbon European Council decided that future Association Agreements with the Western Balkans should be preceded by a regime of asymmetrical trade liberalisation.[103] The decision to improve access for exporters from the Western Balkans to the single market creates a win-win situation, as it meets a paramount interest of the countries of the region (the European Union is by far their most important trading partner) and involves as good as no economic risks but plenty of benefits for the European Union.[104] As part of the SAP, the Council of Ministers implemented the decision taken by the European Council at Lisbon by adopting Council Regulation (EC) No. 2007/2000, which provided for duty and quota free access to the EU market for nearly all industrial products and most agricultural products from the Western Balkan countries.[105] Preferential quotas

---

[101] See Pippan, loc. cit. n. 27, at p. 232.

[102] Art. 2(2)(b) of Council Regulation (EC) No. 2666/2000. Between 1998 and 2002, Community assistance devoted to the field of 'democratic stabilisation' (including aid to refugees) represented 20 per cent of the total assistance allocated to the Western Balkans. See COM (2003) 139 final, Brussels, 26 March 2003, at p. 23.

[103] See Council Conclusions, *Bull. EU* 3-2000, point I.21.47.

[104] The general level of imports from the Western Balkan countries is less than 1 per cent of all Community imports, whereas 70 per cent of all Croatian exports, for example, currently go to the European market.

[105] *OJ* 2000 L 240/1. The period of validity of Regulation (EC) No. 2007/2000 was prolonged for a further period, from 1 January 2006 to 31 December 2010 by Council Regulation (EC) No. 1946/2005 of 14 November 2005, *OJ* 2005 L 312/1.

were retained, however, for baby-beef, fisheries and wine products. While the Regulation was initially limited to Albania, Bosnia-Herzegovina, Croatia and certain 'territories' linked to the SAP (Kosovo and Montenegro),[106] its application was soon extended to Macedonia and, after the political uproar that led to the fall of the Milošević regime, to the whole territory of Serbia and Montenegro.[107] Council Regulation (EC) No. 2563/2000 improved the existing autonomous trade preferences and provided for an autonomous trade liberalisation of 95 per cent of all of the five countries' exports to the European Union, meaning that imports of such products into the Union should be admitted without quantitative restrictions or measures having equivalent effect. These arrangements are even more generous than those enjoyed by the ten new Member States before they joined the Union. The Enlargement Protocols to the SAAs with Macedonia and Croatia did not change this regime; they simply adapted the trade provisions of the SAAs to increase the volume of tariff quotas in order to take into account traditional trade between Macedonia and Croatia on the one hand, and the new Member States, on the other. The quotas for fisheries and wine products from Macedonia and Croatia have thus been increased, thereby providing new export opportunities for the SAA countries.

The preamble to Council Regulation (EC) No. 2007/2000 on exceptional trade preferences refers to the political conditions enshrined in the Council Conclusions of 29 April 1997. The granting of autonomous trade preferences is linked to respect for fundamental principles of democracy and human rights, but political conditionality is not repeated in the operative part of the Regulation. Article 2 of the Regulation links the granting of improved autonomous trade preferences in favour of countries participating in the SAP to their readiness to engage in effective economic reforms and in regional cooperation, in particular through the establishment of free trade areas in line with Article XXIV of the 1994 GATT and other relevant WTO provisions. In addition, entitlement to benefit from autonomous trade preferences is conditional on the beneficiaries' involvement in effective administrative cooperation with the Community in order to prevent any risk of fraud. According to the same Article 2, the Council may, in the event of non-compliance by one of the beneficiary countries, take 'appropriate measures' – thus including the suspension or withdrawal of exceptional trade preferences – by a qualified majority vote, on the basis of a Commission proposal. From a legal

---

[106] In the case of Kosovo and Montenegro, limited trade preferences were granted for certain products that were not produced in other parts of the FRY, which, as such, remained excluded from EC trade preferences until November 2000.

[107] Council Regulation (EC) No. 2563/2000, *OJ* 2000 L 295/1. Council Regulation (EC) No. 2007/2000 was amended by Council Regulation (EC) No. 1946/2005, *OJ* 2005 L 312/1 to take account of the fact that the Republic of Montenegro, the Republic of Serbia and Kosovo each constitute separate customs territories.

standpoint, exceptional trade preferences, which, by definition, go beyond the Community's general obligations stemming from its WTO membership, do not reflect a legally binding commitment on the side of the European Community *vis-à-vis* beneficiary countries, provided that such preferences are not governed by bilateral agreements.[108] Therefore, any subsequent decision to suspend or withdraw these preferences in a specific situation remains at the discretion of the competent EU institutions. As indicated in the preamble to Council Regulation (EC) No. 2007/2000, such a decision will be based on all requirements set out by the Council in respect of the granting of autonomous trade preferences in its 29 April 1997 Conclusions, including respect for the fundamental principles of democracy and human rights. Hence, political conditionality is introduced via the back door.[109]

4. EUROPEAN PARTNERSHIPS: CONDITIONS AND CONSEQUENCES

At the Thessaloniki Summit in June 2003, it was determined that the SAP should be bolstered by new methods based on the experience of previous enlargements of the European Union. The chief one of these is the introduction of so-called 'European Partnerships'.[110] On 30 March 2004, the Council of Ministers approved the first-ever European Partnerships with Bosnia-Herzegovina, Macedonia, Albania and Serbia and Montenegro.[111] The first European Partnership with Croatia was published at the same time as the Commission's positive *avis* on Croatia's application for membership.[112]

Modelled on the Accession Partnerships developed to prepare past aspirants for EU membership, the European Partnerships were heralded as a milestone in the relations between the European Union and the Western Balkan countries, but the difference in the qualifying adjective suggests otherwise: the emphasis is on 'partnership' rather than 'accession'. This impression is reinforced when one

---

[108] See B. Brandtner and A. Rosas, 'Trade Preferences and Human Rights', in Alston, op. cit. n. 24, pp. 699-722 at p. 706.

[109] See Pippan, loc. cit. n. 27, at p. 231.

[110] See *Bull. EU* 6-2003, point 1.6.70.

[111] Council Decisions 2004/515/EC, 2004/518/EC, 2004/519/C, and 2004/520/EC, *OJ* 2004 L 221/10, L 222/20, L 223/20 and L 227/21 respectively. These acts were repealed and replaced by Council Decisions 2006/55/EC, 2006/57/EC, 2006/54/EC and 2006/56/EC, *OJ* 2006 L 35/19, 57, 1 and 32 respectively.

[112] See Council Decision 2004/648/EC on the principles, priorities and conditions contained in the European Partnership with Croatia, *OJ* 2004 L 297/19, repealed and replaced by Council Decision 2006/145/EC on the principles, priorities, and conditions contained in the *Accession* Partnership with Croatia, *OJ* 2006 L 55/30 [emphasis added] so as to reflect the new status of Croatia as a candidate for EU accession.

considers that, while the partnerships for the Western Balkan countries were first announced as 'European integration partnerships' in the Commission's proposal from 2003,[113] they were tellingly re-dubbed as 'European Partnerships' in Council Regulation (EC) No. 533/2004 of 22 March 2004, the basic legal act by which they were established.[114] The Accession Partnerships for the CEECs were endorsed by the European Council of Luxembourg in December 1997 as a key element to strengthen the pre-accession strategy for the candidate countries. They set out the priorities for each country as they were preparing themselves to become members of the European Union. The first accession strategies were decided in March 1998 for the ten CEECs, in 2000 for Cyprus and Malta and in 2003 for Turkey. They highlighted the main instruments and financial resources available, which had to be maximised to target the objectives effectively. Each candidate country was supposed to establish a national programme for the adoption of the *acquis* (NPAA), setting out in detail the way in which the priorities would be realised. The Commission assessed each country's progress annually in its regular reports.

While the European Partnerships are of considerable similitude when compared to Accession Partnerships, their legal basis is nevertheless different. Council Regulation (EC) No. 533/2004 of 22 March 2004 on the establishment of the European Partnerships[115] is based on Article 181a(2) TEC rather than Article 308 TEC (ex Art. 235 TEC), which was the legal basis for Regulation (EC) No. 622/98 on the establishment of Accession Partnerships.[116] It would seem that Article 181a(2) was used for the adoption of European Partnerships because it is the only provision which is capable of referring both to Association Agreements and agreements still 'to be concluded with the states which are candidates for accession to the Union.' As such, this provision could appropriately serve as a legal basis for the adoption of European Partnerships with SAP countries which either have already signed an SAA (Macedonia, Croatia and Albania) or will do so in the future (BiH and SaM). But this conclusion hinges on the assumption that the interpretation of 'candidates' in Article 181a(2) equals 'potential candidates'. Unfortunately for the SAP countries, this liberal interpretation does not constitute a Freudian slip on the part of the EU institutions, in the sense that, with the adoption of Council Regulation (EC) No. 533/2004, all Western Balkan states have indirectly been promoted to the level of candidate states. European Partnerships

[113] European Commission, The Western Balkans and European Integration, COM (2003) 285 final, Brussels, 21 May 2003.

[114] *OJ* 2004 L 86/1. The Council rephrased the policy instrument as early as 16 June 2003. See Thessaloniki Agenda, in Annex A to Council Conclusions of 16 June 2003, Press Release No. 10369/03 (Presse 166).

[115] *OJ* 2004 L 86/1.

[116] *OJ* 1998 L 85/1.

do not endow their addressees with candidate country status and cannot be thought of as pre-accession instruments in the same way as the Accession Partnerships, because they are used to programme the work of a range of states even *prior to* the existence of contractual relations with the European Union. The Accession Partnerships, on the other hand, were proposed to candidate countries that were recognised as such and already signatories to a European Agreement.[117]

On paper, the European Partnerships and the Accession Partnerships seem to offer the same framework, the same organisation and the same means of assessment. They are both structurally divided into short- and medium-term priorities. Based on the Commission's Annual SAP Report, the European Partnerships are tailored to each Western Balkan country's specific needs, setting out priorities for the short term (one to two years) and the medium term (three to four years). The partnerships are intended to help governments concentrate reform efforts and available resources where they are most needed. The competent authorities are expected to respond with a detailed plan for the implementation of their European Partnership priorities, setting out the concrete measures to be taken and a timetable and demonstrating what human and financial resources will be devoted to the tasks involved (a sort of NPAA).[118] The priorities identified in the European Partnerships will also influence the allocation of the financial assistance from the European Union. Thus, clearly, European Partnerships cannot be regarded as contractual relationships. They are EU policy tools to encourage reforms and serve as checklists against which to measure progress.[119] Furthermore, they provide guidance for Community and Member State financial assistance. They reflect the particular stages of development of each country and, to that end, each contains a conditionality clause: according to common recital 5 of the preamble to the European Partnerships, non-compliance with the 1993 Copenhagen political

---

[117] See also chapter 3 in this volume.

[118] A first discussion on a national plan for the implementation of the priorities set out as part of the European Partnership with Macedonia took place in Skopje on 3 July 2004 within the then newly established Stabilisation and Association Committee.

[119] Due to the unsettled status of Kosovo, the Commission proposed a separate list of priorities and recommendations, based on the 'Standards for Kosovo' (presented by the UN Special Representative of the Secretary General and representatives of the PISG in December 2003 and endorsed by the Security Council). While the European Union continued to underline that final status talks could not be delayed indefinitely, it would appear that the European Partnership with SaM strengthened the existing 'standards before status' policy of the international community – even when this policy has already been declared dead in the region. At the same time, however, by treating Kosovo's priorities separately, the European Partnership gave tacit support to a decentralisation process, something Serbia vehemently opposes. This situation was not remedied in the new European Partnership with SaM, including Kosovo, even though it was already clear at the moment of its adoption that final status talks would commence. This shows the EU Member States' firm belief that, by gradually merging the standards for Kosovo into the European Partnership, the European Commission is creating a framework for credibly monitoring and accompanying Kosovo's development towards a stable and multi-ethnic society in the European mainstream.

criteria and a lack of progress in meeting the specific priorities of the European Partnerships themselves could lead the Council to unilaterally suspend Community assistance under the SAP.[120] Community assistance is also subject to the conditions defined by the Council in its Conclusions of 29 April 1997 and 21-22 June 1999, in particular as regards the recipients' undertaking to carry out democratic, economic and institutional reforms.

In short, the added value of the European Partnerships lies primarily in the fact that their adoption represents a new step towards further integration with the European Union, as the SAP is increasingly being modelled on the pre-accession process of the CEECs: these policy instruments finally provide each of the five countries with a timetable and a road map towards EU membership. The partnerships are necessary to measure progress and build motivation to persist with the painful reforms that are necessary to attract private domestic and direct foreign investment, help stimulate economic growth and overcome high unemployment. The timeframe for their implementation will of course depend on the pace of political and economic reform in each country (the 'ownership' principle), but in view of the many unresolved issues, it seems reasonable to expect that at least another four to ten years will be necessary to complete the integration process.

5. FROM 'POTENTIAL' TO FULL MEMBERSHIP

In contrast to the preambular reference to accession in the Europe Agreements, the preambles of the SAAs recall not simply the European Union's readiness to integrate Macedonia and Croatia 'to the fullest possible extent … into the political and economic mainstream of Europe', but also the status of the two associates as 'potential' candidates for EU membership. The membership perspective is set out in the final recital of the preamble to the two existing SAAs:

> [The contracting parties recall] the European Union's readiness to integrate to the fullest possible extent the [associate] into the political and economic mainstream of Europe and its status as a potential candidate for EU membership on the basis of the Treaty on European Union and fulfilment of the criteria defined by the European Council in June 1993, subject to successful implementation of this Agreement, notably regarding regional cooperation.

From the wording of the recital as well as the *travaux préparatoires*, it becomes clear that, for reasons already explained, the inclusion of the membership perspective came against a background of reticence towards any firm commitment to

120 The conditionality clause invokes Article 5 of the CARDS Regulation.

admit the SAA countries into the European Union at a future date.[121] This is apparent in the Commission's May 1999 Communication on the SAP, which made no explicit mention of the word 'membership' at all, but instead referred to the SAAs 'draw[ing] the [Western Balkan] region closer to the perspective of full integration into EU structures.'[122] One month later, the Cologne European Council agreed to a similar wording but acknowledged that this would be done 'with a prospect of European Union membership on the basis of the Amsterdam Treaty and fulfilment of the criteria defined at the Copenhagen European Council in June 1993.'[123] In the course of drawing up the SAAs, the European Union watered down the strength of the commitment.[124] The current wording of the recital follows declarations that were made at the June 2000 Feira European Council and at the Zagreb summit of EU leaders and their counterparts from South-Eastern Europe in November 2000 to the effect that the Western Balkan countries are 'potential candidates' for EU membership.[125] Although this notion has no official definition and does not confer on the holder a legally enforceable right to membership, politically speaking, the term 'potential candidate' recognises the Union's willingness to see the membership ambitions of the status holder realised in the future. In the words of Friis and Murphy:

> This promise, however vague and conditional, cannot be withdrawn... [I]t will force the Union to increase its level of engagement with the region and to advance the on-going enlargement process... [The] genie is now out of the bottle.[126]

However half-hearted the Member States' commitment to enlarge 'their' Union with the countries of South-Eastern Europe may at first have seemed, its repeated confirmation[127] has provided the 'able and willing' governments of the Western Balkan countries with a justification for difficult political and economic reforms and a means to rally support for tough decisions at home.[128] Croatia's bid for

---

[121] See *supra* section 2.1. See also R. Biermann, 'Die Europäische Perspektive für den westlichen Balkan', 51 *Osteuropa* (2001) pp. 922-937 at pp. 926-927.

[122] COM (1999) 235 final, Brussels, 26 May 1999, at p. 4.

[123] *Bull. EU* 6-1999, point I.26.72.

[124] See R. Biermann, 'The Stability Pact for South Eastern Europe: Potential, Problems and Perspectives', C56 *ZEI Discussion Papers* (1999) at pp. 15-19.

[125] *Bull. EU* 6-2000, point I.49.67; *Bull. EU* 11-2000, point I.6.57.

[126] L. Friis and A. Murphy, 'Enlargement of the European Union: Impacts on the EU, the Candidates and the "Next Neighbours"', 14 *ECSA Rev.* (2001).

[127] Most vocally at Zagreb in 2000 and Thessaloniki in 2003, *Bull. EU* 11-2000, point I.6.57 and *Bull. EU* 6-2003, point I.17 respectively.

[128] Others have criticised the European Union's unwillingness to make a full commitment to integrate the countries concerned and have pointed out that an integration strategy that revolves around the promise of the perspective of membership does not necessarily trigger the reforms most needed in instable societies. See, e.g., Anastasakis and Bechev, op. cit. n. 41; D. Triantaphyllou, 'The

membership on 20 February 2003,[129] Macedonia's application for accession on 22 March 2004,[130] the eagerness of Prime Minister Terzić to guide Bosnia-Herzegovina into the European Union and the increasingly louder calls in Podgorica for a peaceful separation of Serbia and Montenegro to speed up the process of European integration all attest to the fact that the only worthwhile 'carrot' the European Union can offer the Western Balkan countries in exchange for a concerted effort to create lasting peace and stability in the region is the prospect of membership.

On 17-18 June 2004, the European Council finally crossed the Rubicon when it decided to follow up on the Commission's positive *avis* on Croatia's application for membership and grant the country candidate status, thereby opening it up to increased financial and technical assistance.[131] The European Council, at its 16-17 December 2004 summit in Brussels, requested the Council of Ministers to agree on a negotiating framework with a view to opening accession negotiations with Croatia on 17 March 2005, thereby rewarding Croatia's ongoing preparations for membership with a firm date for starting accession talks.[132] The opportunity, however, was subject to an equally firm condition: full and unequivocal cooperation with the ICTY. Croatia was thus given exactly three months to 'smoke Gotovina out of his hole' and hand him over to the ICTY in The Hague. Despite strong eleventh-hour lobbying by Croatia to prevent the consequences of its failure to arrest and extradite Gotovina, 'the absence of a common agreement' among the twenty-five EU Member States on the issue of full cooperation with the ICTY led the Council to take the unprecedented decision to postpone the start of membership talks.[133] The Council was careful, however, to underline that accession negotiations with Croatia could open as soon as there was proof that Croatia was fully cooperating with the Tribunal. To prove its point, but without offering an early resolution of the stand-off, the Council adopted the negotiating mandate for the Commission[134] and created a special task force to

Balkans between Stabilization and Integration', in J. Blatt et al., 'Partners and Neighbours: A CFSP for a Wider Europe', 64 *Chaillot Papers* (2003) pp. 60-76.

129 See Doc. 6991/03 ELARG 19 COWEB 28.

130 See Council Conclusions of 17 May 2004, Press Release No. 9210/04 (Presse 149).

131 For the *avis*, see COM (2004) 257 final, Brussels, 20 April 2004; for the decision by the European Council, see *Bull. EU* 6-2004, point I.7.31. See further *supra* nn. 91 and 92.

132 See *Bull. EU* 12-2004, point I.6.16. The European Council agreed on a general new framework for future accession negotiations, to be created 'according to own merits and specific situations and characteristics of each candidate state' and under which long transition periods, derogations, specific arrangements or permanent safeguard clauses (defined as 'clauses which are permanently available as a basis for safeguard measures') can be imposed in areas such as freedom of movement of persons, structural policies or agriculture. See *Bull. EU* 12-2004, point I.8.23.

133 Council Conclusions of 16 March 2005, Press Release No. 6969/05 (Presse 44), reproduced in *Bull. EU* 3-2005, point 1.5.1.

134 Ibid.

monitor Zagreb's cooperation with the ICTY.[135] Just hours ahead of the crucial 'enlargement' meeting of the Council of Ministers on 3 October 2005 in Luxembourg, the task force gave its positive opinion after it was informed by the Chief Prosecutor of the ICTY that, despite the fact that Gotovina remained at large, Croatia was 'fully cooperating' with the Tribunal.[136] Noting the clear commitment by the Croatian Prime Minister that full cooperation would be maintained until the last remaining indictee was in The Hague, and as long as required by the ICTY, the Council concluded that Croatia had fulfilled the outstanding condition for the start of accession negotiations.[137] The accession negotiations were launched immediately after the meeting, i.e., in the early hours of 4 October 2005.

When the Council requested the Commission to give its *avis* on Macedonia's application for accession on 1 October 2004, the Commission handed over to the Macedonian authorities a *questionnaire* with over 2,500 questions on the political, economic and administrative situation in the country. The answers, which were handed over to the Commission on 14 February 2005, formed the basis for the *avis* on the starting of accession negotiations. In the preparation of its opinion, the Commission also used feedback from its delegation in Skopje, from the international organisations active in the country, and statistical and economic

---

135 See L. Kubosova, 'EU to send monitoring team to Croatia', *EUObserver.com*, 23 March 2005. Chaired, at first, by the Minister of Foreign Affairs of Luxembourg, the task force brought together representatives of the Commission, the SG/HR and the next two EU presidencies – the United Kingdom and Austria (which held diametrically opposed views during the Council debate of 16 March 2005).

136 Carla del Ponte was heavily criticised by her own staff for the sudden U-turn in the approach taken towards Croatia. She was reported as having said at a press conference in Luxembourg, that '[f]or a few weeks now, Croatia has been cooperating fully with us and is doing everything it can to locate and arrest Ante Gotovina.' This statement stood in sharp contrast to what the Chief Prosecutor said after a one-and-a-half-hour meeting with Prime Minister Ivo Sanader and President Stipe Mesić in Zagreb on 30 September 2005: 'You cannot imagine how disappointed I am. [The] prime minister has promised me full cooperation but we still have the same problem. Gotovina is still at large.' It is thought that del Ponte succumbed to heavy political pressure. The Chief Prosecutor herself denied such allegations. See 'Carla del Ponte bescheinigt Zagreb überraschend "uneingeschränkte Zusammenarbeit" bei der Kriegsverbrecher-Suche', *Süddeutsche Zeitung*, 4 October 2005. Whatever there may be of this, del Ponte's announcement on 3 October greatly facilitated an agreement by Austria – a strong ally of Croatia – on the opening of accession talks with Turkey, which Vienna had blocked until the last minute. See also chapter 9 in this volume. Gotovina was eventually arrested on 7 December 2005. See *supra* n. 54.

137 See Council Conclusions of 3 October 2005 in Press Release No. 12514/1/05 REV 1 (Presse 241). The Council confirmed that sustaining full cooperation with the ICTY would remain a requirement for progress throughout the accession process. It invited the Commission to continue to monitor this closely, on the basis of regular reports from the ICTY, and report back to the Council if full cooperation was not maintained. The Council noted that an assessment of cooperation with the ICTY would form part of the Commission's reports to the Council on Croatia's fulfilment of the political criteria. The Council agreed that less than full cooperation with the ICTY at any stage would affect the overall progress of the negotiations and could be a ground for triggering the mechanism in paragraph 12 of the negotiating framework.

information from sources such as the OECD and the IMF. On 9 November 2005, the Commission published its *avis*.[138] Despite this positive stance towards the opening of accession negotiations with Macedonia, the granting of candidate country status was thrown into doubt when France threatened the other Member States to put all enlargement issues aside if the Council could not agree on its 2007-2013 budget, the first budget to include the ten new Member States.[139] After two days of nervous negotiations, the European Council reached an agreement on the financial perspectives, thereby averting the threat of deep political rifts within the European Union as well as delays over further enlargement. Macedonia was granted EU candidate country status in the early hours of 17 December 2005.

The European Council spoke highly of Macedonia's 'significant progress' in securing minority rights, implementing the SAA and fulfilling the political and economic criteria for EU membership, but made it clear that Skopje's new status did not automatically mean the opening of accession negotiations, referring to the Union's own 'absorption capacity' as one of the 'specific benchmarks' for taking 'further steps'.[140] Thus, the country's entry has been linked to a future debate among the EU-25 on the Union's future and its ability to absorb more newcomers.[141] Accordingly, it may take months, years even, before Skopje opens membership talks.

6. CONCLUDING REMARKS

The adoption of European Partnerships, the entry into force of two SAAs and the decision to grant candidate country status to Croatia and Macedonia do not allow for the conclusion that any of the countries of the Western Balkans are likely to join the European Union as a full member any time soon. But these developments underline the Union's strategic objective towards the Western Balkans: the further expansion of the European Union south-eastwards. This strategic reorientation has prompted the European Union to vigorously reinforce a guiding principle that has characterised its relations with third countries in general: the principle of conditionality. At the same time, the *tangible* prospect of EU membership is the key instrument for transformation of the Western Balkans. It finally gives the governments that were still in doubt whether or not to take the European Union's 'perspective of membership' offer seriously a strong incentive and clear

---

138 COM (2005) 562, Brussels, 9 November 2005.

139 See A. Rettman, 'Macedonia should not be held hostage, Denmark says', *EUObserver.com*, 15 December 2005.

140 Presidency Conclusions of Brussels European Council of 15-16 December 2005, Press Release No. 15914/05, CONCL 3, 17 December 2005.

141 On the absorption capacity of the Union, see chapter 3 in this volume.

message to convince their electorates of the advantages of ethnic reconciliation and the tightening of belts to reform their countries' political and economic structures. But it is important that the Union does not give the impression that membership is too distant, as this might lead to rapid domestic deterioration. Pressure is required. Today, probably more than ever, the balanced application of the conditionality principle is key to ever-closer relations between the European Union and the Western Balkans. It has rightly been noted by Van Meurs that the structural tension between a regional approach and bilateral conditionality may endanger the coherence of international action towards a region still known to many as a powder keg, as the best pupils of the class will 'leave' the region by acquiring a different contractual status in their relations with the Union, thereby increasing rather than reducing the disparities within the region.[142] While official EU documents have always shunned a prioritisation between the Stability Pact and the SAP, it is clear that, in practice, the SAAs (as part of the SAP) are seen, both by the countries in the region and the international community, as the most important instruments to achieve lasting peace and stability in the Western Balkans, because they offer the prospect of EU accession. Thus, priority is given to bilateralism where appropriate and to regionalism where possible.

With these principles firmly and explicitly built into all phases of the (pre-) accession process, the countries of the Western Balkans have a clearly marked path and timetable to follow, aware of the consequences of not abiding by the (mutually agreed) conditions: postponement or cancellation of political negotiations and/or suspension or termination of contractual relations. By granting Croatia and Macedonia candidate country status, the European Union has reinforced its commitment. It is to be hoped that it is equally serious about integrating the other Western Balkan countries, because transcending the 'potential members' mindset and addressing the issue of SAP *finalité* for all Western Balkan countries would undoubtedly empower the European Union and render the SAP a much more credible framework. The first test was Croatia's bid to open accession negotiations. In many ways Croatia stands out as a model for the rest of the region. The way in which the Croatian application was handled would thus have important consequences for the other countries of the Western Balkans. For the Croatian case to serve as a positive example, the rest of the SAP countries had to be persuaded that the European Union is serious about settling the legacy of the Yugoslav wars of the 1990s and does not apply a double standard. Seen in this light, the European Union was right to play hard-ball with Croatia and enforce its conditionality principle by not opening accession talks when Croatia failed to show full cooperation with the ICTY. On the basis of this precedent, Serbia and Montenegro could have known that, by failing to transfer Mladić to The Hague, it would force the Union to suspend SAA talks.

142 Van Meurs, loc. cit. n. 39, at p. 41.

Now that Croatia has been set firmly on the reform track, Macedonian success in this process will mean even more for confidence building in the region, for the Macedonian model could be used as a source of inspiration to reconcile Serb-Albanian interests in Kosovo and bring lasting peace and stability across the whole region. For this greater good, it is to be hoped that Macedonia will not be held hostage by a Union which is currently unable to break the deadlock over its institutional reform.

CHAPTER 11

CROATIA

Siniša Rodin*

Relevant documents:

- Stabilisation and Association Agreement between the European Communities and their Member States, of the one part, and the Republic of Croatia, of the other part, *OJ* 2005 L 26/3.
- Protocol to the Stabilisation and Association Agreement between the European Communities and their Member States, of the one part, and the Republic of Croatia, of the other part, to take account of the accession of the Czech Republic, the Republic of Estonia, the Republic of Cyprus, the Republic of Hungary, the Republic of Latvia, the Republic of Lithuania, the Republic of Malta, the Republic of Poland, the Republic of Slovenia and the Slovak Republic to the European Union, *OJ* 2005 L 26/222.
- Council Decision 2006/145/EC on the principles, priorities, and conditions contained in the accession partnership with Croatia, *OJ* 2006 L 55/30.
- Framework Agreement between the European Community and the Republic of Croatia on the general principles for the participation of the Republic of Croatia in Community programmes, *OJ* 2005 L 192/16.
- Council Regulation (EC) No. 2257/2004 amending Regulations (EEC) No. 3906/89, (EC) No. 1267/1999, (EC) No. 1268/1999 and (EC) No. 2666/2000, to take into account of Croatia's candidate status, *OJ* 2004 L 389/1.
- Communication from the Commission, Opinion on Croatia's Application for Membership of the European Union, COM (2004) 257 final, 20 April 2004, Brussels.
- Decision No. 1/2002 of the Interim Committee between the European Community, of the one part, and the Republic of Croatia, of the other part, of 19 April 2002 concerning the adoption of its rules of procedure, *OJ* 2002 C 227/2.
- Interim Agreement on trade and trade-related matters between the European Community, of the one part, and the Republic of Croatia, of the other part, *OJ* 2001 L 26/3.
- Zakon o potvrđivanju Sporazuma o stabilizaciji i pridruživanju između Republike Hrvatske i Europskih zajednica i njihovih država članica (Law on the Ratification of the Stabilisation and Association Agreement between the European Communities and their Member States, of the one part, and the Republic of Croatia, of the other part, *Narodne novine - Međunarodni ugovori* [Official Gazette - International Treaties] No. 14/2001 of 27 December 2001.

* Jean Monnet Professor of EU Law, Faculty of Law, Zagreb University.

S. Blockmans and A. Łazowski (eds.), The European Union and Its Neighbours

1. RELATIONS BETWEEN THE EUROPEAN COMMUNITY/UNION AND CROATIA: FROM ISOLATION TO CANDIDACY

On 25 June 1991, the Croatian Parliament, implementing a constitutional provision of what was then Article 140 of the Constitution (enabling withdrawal from the Socialist Federal Republic of Yugoslavia) and following the referendum on sovereignty and independence held on 19 May 1991, adopted the Constitutional Decision on Sovereignty and Independence and the Declaration on the Sovereign and Independent Republic of Croatia.[1] Two days later, the Serbian dominated 'federal' army (JNA) started its military intervention in Slovenia, which subsequently spread to Croatia and other post-Yugoslav states.[2] The European Communities extended diplomatic recognition to Croatia on 15 January 1992.[3] Unlike Slovenia and other post-Communist countries of Central and Eastern Europe, which started to develop contractual relations with the European Union and ultimately became members on 1 May 2004, relations between the European Union and Croatia were characterised by a long period of stagnation and exclusion from the mainstream integration process. In this period, the relationship between the European Union and Croatia was burdened with the realities of a war of independence and attempts by the country to regain control over its Serb-held territory. While Croatia engaged in legal and structural reforms on its own,[4] their scope and outcome was limited, as they were pursued in the absence of contractual relations with the European Union. Instead, the Community extended its general system of preferences to Croatia on similar terms to those granted to the former SFR Yugoslavia.[5] At that time, in the absence of a more developed relationship,

---

[1] Deklaracija o proglašenju suverene i samostalne Republike Hrvatske [Declaration on Sovereignty and Independence of the Republic of Croatia], *Narodne novine* [Official Gazette] No. 31/1991 of 25 June 1991. See also S. Sokol and B. Smerdel, *Ustavno pravo* (Zagreb, Informator 1998).

[2] For an historical and political account of the dissolution of Yugoslavia and the war in Bosnia, see L. Silber and D. Little, *The Death of Yugoslavia*, 2nd edn. (London, Penguin 1996); and M. Glenny, *The Fall of Yugoslavia*, 3rd edn. (London, Penguin 1996).

[3] On 17 December 1991, the Council of Ministers adopted the Declaration on the Guidelines on the Recognition of New States in Eastern Europe and the Soviet Union and the Declaration on Yugoslavia, see *Bull. EC* 12-1991, points 1.4.5. and 1.4.6, which formed the mandate of the so-called Badinter Arbitration Commission. In Opinion No. 5 delivered on 11 January 1992, the Badinter Commission stated that Croatia was not fully in compliance with the provisions proposed by the EC concerning the special status of minorities, but that it otherwise 'meets the necessary conditions for its recognition.' For the text of the opinion, see 31 *ILM* (1992) p. 1488. For background information on the creation, work and impact of the Badinter Commission, see S. Terrett, *The Dissolution of Yugoslavia and the Badinter Arbitration Commission: A Contextual study of Peace-making Efforts in the Post-Cold War World* (Aldershot, Ashgate 2000).

[4] See Government of the Republic of Croatia, Office for European Integration, Action Plan for European Integration (September 1999). This 564-page volume attempted to replicate the screening process without the assistance of the EC.

[5] Council Regulation (EEC) No. 3567/91 of 2 December 1991 concerning the arrangements applicable to the import of products originating in the Republics of Bosnia-Herzegovenia, Croatia,

the European Union used these trade preferences as a mechanism of influence linked to respect for fundamental principles of democracy and human rights and readiness to allow the development of economic relations with other countries in the region.[6] Subsequent extensions of exceptional trade measures to countries in the region, including Croatia, were based on the conclusions of the Lisbon European Council of 23 and 24 of March 2000, which concluded that the establishment of free trade areas between the countries in the region 'should be preceded by asymmetrical trade liberalisation.'[7] The Feira Council noted the democratic progress and proceeded with asymmetric trade liberalisation.[8] Accordingly a large segment of imports from Croatia and other ex-Yugoslav countries to the European Union was liberalised while Croatia and other beneficiary states were allowed to keep their customs protection. This mechanism, which was subsequently integrated into the contractual relations with the European Communities is widely understood as an instrument that allows more advanced states in the region to get closer to EU trade standards while allowing them to develop or maintain patterns of trade among themselves.

In the early 1990s, the relationship with the European Community/Union was burdened by the arms embargo imposed on Yugoslavia by the Member States on 5 July 1991 and renewed in subsequent years.[9] Non-discriminatory at first sight, the arms embargo in effect left Croatia to the mercy of the JNA and Serb irregulars. The arms embargo was not lifted in respect of Croatia until 20 November 2000.[10] In Croatia, the arms embargo was widely understood as a policy choice by

Macedonia and Slovenia, *OJ* 1991 L 342/1. The granting of GSP aid is subject to conditionality. See chapter 10 in this volume and my contribution in N. Horn, J.S. Baur and K. Stern, eds., *Zukunftsprobleme der Europäischen Union – Erweiterung nach Osten oder Vertiefung, oder Beides – Die kroatische Perspektive*, Schriften des Rechtzentrums für Europäische und Internationale Zusammenarbeit (R.I.Z.) (Berlin and New York, Walter de Gruyter 1997) pp. 125-138.

[6] *Bull. EU* 4-1997, point 2.2.1.

[7] 13 *CEPS Europa South-East Monitor* (July 2000) p. 4.

[8] Council Regulation (EC) No. 2007/2000 of 18 September 2000 introducing exceptional trade measures for countries and territories participating in or linked to the SAP, *OJ* 2000 L 240/1. See also Explanatory Memorandum, 13 *CEPS Europa South-East Monitor* (July 2000) p. 3 et seq.; and see chapter 10 in this volume.

[9] See, e.g., Council Common Position 96/184/CFSP concerning arms exports to the former Yugoslavia, *OJ* 1996 L 58/1 (as amended): 'The Council of the European Union therefore decides that: (i) during the period of the deployment of IFOR and UNTAES, as well as other operations including IPTF, the EU embargo on arms, munitions and military equipment will be maintained towards Bosnia and Herzegovina, Croatia and the Federal Republic of Yugoslavia'. At first, the Community's arms embargo fell within the Member States' scope of competence. This changed with the Treaty of Maastricht. See S. Blockmans, 'The European Union's Troubled Relations with the Federal Republic of Yugoslavia (1991-2001)', in J. de Zwaan, et al., eds., *The European Union: An Ongoing Process of Integration – Liber Amicorum Alfred E. Kellermann* (The Hague, T.M.C. Asser Press 2004) pp. 337-356 at p. 341.

[10] Council Common Position 2000/722/CFSP amending Common Position 96/184/CFSP concerning arms exports to the former Yugoslavia, *OJ* 2000 L 292/1.

the European Union to 'let might make right'. Negative attitudes towards the European Union generated in the early 1990s are still relevant on the political scene in Croatia.

The first major shift in the Union's policy concerning Croatia was designed by the Commission in 1996,[11] when conditionality or, as it is sometimes called, the *regional* approach governing the development of the European Union's relations with 'certain countries of south-east Europe', Croatia included, was framed. On 29 April 1997, following the Commission's report, the EU General Affairs Council adopted a regional approach introducing political and economic conditionality for the development of relations with countries in the region.[12] This approach was further developed in June 1999, following the Commission's proposal of 26 May for the creation of a Stabilisation and Association Process (SAP) for the countries of South-Eastern Europe,[13] Croatia included.[14] The main conditions to be complied with by those countries were specified as compliance with democratic principles, human rights and rule of law, respect for and protection of minorities, market economy reforms, regional cooperation and compliance with obligations under international peace agreements (Dayton/Paris[15] and Erdut[16]). Compliance with the above-mentioned criteria may qualify the countries concerned for:

- a Stabilisation and Association Agreement (SAA);
- autonomous trade measures and other economic and commercial relations;
- economic and financial assistance;
- aid for democratisation and civil society;

[11] Report from the Commission to the Council and the European Parliament, Common principles for future contractual relations with certain countries in South-Eastern Europe, COM (1996) 476 final of 2 October 1996; see also Commission Staff Working Paper on the EU Stabilisation and Association Process for countries of South-Eastern Europe, SEC (2000) 168.

[12] Council conclusions on the principle of conditionality governing the development of the European Union's relations with certain countries of south-east Europe, *Bull. EU* 4-1997, point 2.2.1.

[13] Conclusions of the General Affairs Council of 21 June 1999, based on the Commission Communication to the Council and the European Parliament on the Stabilisation and Association Process for countries of South-Eastern Europe, COM (1999) 235 of 26 May 1999. See also COM (1996) 476 and *Bull. EU* 10-1996, point 1.4.65.

[14] Council conclusions on the development of a comprehensive policy based on the Commission communication on the Stabilisation and Association Process for countries of south-eastern Europe, *Bull. EU* 6-1999, point 1.3.91.

[15] The General Framework Agreement for Peace, initialled in Dayton on 21 November 1995, signed in Paris on 14 December 1995 and consolidated in Rome on 18 February 1996, is published in 35 *ILM* (1996) p. 75.

[16] The Basic Agreement on the Region of Eastern Slavonia, Baranja and Western Sirmium, signed in Erdut and Zagreb (Croatia) on 12 November 1995 is published in US Institute of Peace, *The United States and Croatia: a documentary history, 1992-1997* (Vienna, USIA Regional Program Office 1997) pp. 270-271, also available at: <http://www.usip.org/library/pa/croatia/croatia_erdut_11 121995.html>.

- humanitarian aid for refugees, returnees and others;
- cooperation on justice and home affairs;
- development of political dialogue.

The creation of the SAP indicated that the European Union's relations with Croatia were formally taking a path different from the one offered to the countries that joined the European Union in May 2004. The perspective of EU membership was blurred, and relations with the European Union were tied to closer cooperation with other countries in the region.

Following a series of ups and downs prompted partly by the political landscape in Croatia, which was characterised by an authoritarian right-wing government and partly by turbulent post-conflict developments in the region, a new stage in the relations between the European Union and Croatia commenced following the general elections held in January 2000 and the political shift introduced by the new centre-left parliamentary majority, allied in a six-party coalition led by Social Democrats. Soon after the elections, the presidential system was dismantled by constitutional amendment and replaced by parliamentary government.[17]

On 24 May 2000, as a consequence of the changed political environment in Croatia, the Commission adopted a positive feasibility study for opening the negotiations for conclusion of a Stabilisation and Association Agreement with Croatia.[18] The feasibility report was introduced as part of the SAP for the countries of South-Eastern Europe in 1999 as an additional test of compliance with democratic criteria. According to the study, the parameters of the future SAA were to include: formalisation and enhancement of political dialogue, improvement and consolidation of regional cooperation, liberalisation of the trade regime in industrial goods, agriculture and fisheries, services and the right of establishment, current payments and movement of capital, approximation of legislation in the areas of technical standards and certification, competition and state aids, public procurement, intellectual, industrial and commercial property, telecommunications and the information society, consumer protection, labour law and equal opportunities for men and women, cooperation in the area of justice and home affairs, as well as economic and financial cooperation in numerous areas.[19] On 24 May 2000, the European Commission subsequently adopted a feasibility study and proposed to the Council on the opening of negotiations on the conclusion of

---

[17] Promjena Ustava Republike Hrvatske [Amendment of the Constitution of the Republic of Croatia], *Narodne novine* No. 113/2000.

[18] Report from the Commission on the feasibility of negotiating a Stabilisation and Association Agreement with the Republic of Croatia, COM (2000) 311 final of 24 May 2000.

[19] Such as statistics, industry, customs and taxation, education and training, environment, etc. These areas were indeed incorporated into the SAA.

an SAA between the European Communities and its Member States, of the one part, and Croatia, of the other.[20] The negotiations on the SAA opened on 24 November 2000 at the EU-Balkans summit in Zagreb. The occasion was used to mark the end of negotiations between the European Union and FYR Macedonia.[21] Croatia completed the negotiations during the Swedish Presidency (i.e., by 1 July 2001) and the agreement – the second of its kind – was signed on 29 October 2001.[22]

The term 'Stabilisation and Association Agreement' was coined by the Feira European Council in accordance with the name of the process and was designed to be its main individualised legal instrument, possibly leading to a closer relationship with the European Union.[23] Its nature is clearly stated in a later document,[24] which describes it as a '... fundamental element of a multi-faceted EU strategy designed to favour a progressive process of integration of the countries of the Western Balkans into the EU.' In Feira, the European Council for the first time mentioned the possibility of EU membership for the countries concerned, baptising them *potential candidates* for membership.[25] In that way, the SAP was clearly differentiated from enlargement and was tucked away under the external relations competence of the European Communities, while at the same time leaving the door open for possible candidacy. Since Feira, potential candidate status has been mentioned in many subsequent documents and has become part of the standard preambular wording of the SAAs.[26]

---

[20] Report from the Commission on the feasibility of negotiating a Stabilisation and Association Agreement with the Republic of Croatia, COM (2000) 311 final, Brussels, 24 May 2000.

[21] For the final declaration of the Zagreb Summit, see 9 *Euroscope* (2000) pp. 51-52.

[22] COM (2001) 371 final, Brussels, 9 July 2001. On the same day, Macedonia and the European Union also signed an Interim Agreement allowing the parties to put into force the trade and trade-related aspects of the SAA as of 1 June 2001 without having to wait for the ratification of the SAA by the EU Member States. On the occasion of the signing of the SAA, Swedish Foreign Minister Anna Lindh said: 'This is an historic day for FYROM and for the European Union. It signifies a major step towards the gradual integration of FYROM into the European Union.' Source: <http://www.eu2001.se/eu2001/news/news_read.asp?iInformationID=13885>.

[23] Presidency Conclusions, 19-20 June 2000, *Bull. EU* 6-2000, point I.49.67: 'The European Council confirms that its objective remains the fullest possible integration of the countries of the region into the political and economic mainstream of Europe through the Stabilisation and Association Process, political dialogue, liberalisation of trade and cooperation in Justice and Home Affairs.'

[24] 'On the road to Europe: First Stabilisation and Association Agreement to be signed on 9 April 2001 with the former Yugoslav Republic of Macedonia', MEMO/01/127 – Brussels, 6 April 2001.

[25] See chapter 10 in this volume.

[26] See, e.g., preamble to the SAA Croatia: 'Recalling the European Union's readiness to integrate to the fullest possible extent Croatia into the political and economic mainstream of Europe and its status as a potential candidate for EU membership on the basis of the Treaty on European Union and fulfilment of the criteria defined by the European Council in June 1993, subject to the successful implementation of this Agreement, notably regarding regional cooperation.'

The SAA was framed as a new form of bilateral agreement between the European Union and third countries that were not automatically recognised as candidates for EU membership, namely Albania, Bosnia-Herzegovina, Croatia, Macedonia and the Federal Republic of Yugoslavia. Designed as a mixed agreement, in order to become effective, the SAA had to be ratified by the Croatian Parliament (*Sabor*), the European Parliament and by the Member States of the European Union according to their constitutionally provided procedures. The *Sabor* ratified the agreement on 5 December 2001,[27] the European Parliament on 12 December 2001,[28] while the last ratification by one of original fifteen Member States came from Italy in October 2004.[29] In the meantime, on 28 January 2002, pending the entry in force of the SAA, the Council of Ministers adopted the Interim Agreement giving effect to the trade-related provisions of the SAA.[30] Croatia ratified the Interim Agreement on 5 December 2001.[31]

Croatia presented its application for membership of the European Union on 21 February 2003, and the procedure was initiated by the Council of Ministers on 14 April 2003. The strongest statement opening the path to EU membership for all countries in the region came from the EU-Western Balkans Summit in Thessaloniki on 21 June 2003. The Thessaloniki Council, the venue for the signing of the Accession Treaty with the ten CEECs, was used as a backdrop for opening the door of the European Union to the countries of South-Eastern Europe. As stated in the Declaration of the Summit,

---

27 See Zakon o potvrđivanju Sporazuma o stabilizaciji i pridruživanju između Republike Hrvatske i Europskih zajednica i njihovih država članica [Law on Ratification of the Stabilisation and Association Agreement Between the Republic of Croatia and the European Communities and its Member States], *Narodne novine - Međunarodni ugovori* [Official Gazette - International Treaties] No. 14/2001 of 27 December 2001.

28 European Parliament legislative resolution on the proposal for a Council and Commission decision on the conclusion of the Stabilisation and Association Agreement between the European Communities and their Member States, of the one part, and the Republic of Croatia, of the other part (11172/2001-COM(2001)371 – C5-0565/2001 – 2001/0149 (AVC)). The final decision of the Council and the Commission on the conclusion of the SAA was adopted on 13 December 2004: Council and Commission Decision 2005/40/EC, Euratom of 13 December 2004 concerning the conclusion of the Stabilisation and Association Agreement between the European Communities and their Member States, of the one part, and the Republic of Croatia, of the other part, *OJ* 2005 L 26/1.

29 Austria ratified the SAA on 21 February 2002, Ireland on 17 April 2002, Denmark on 30 April 2002, Germany on 12 July 2002, the Netherlands on 10 September 2002 (but it withheld notification until 30 April 2004), Spain on 19 September 2002, Sweden on 19 February 2003, France on 4 March 2003, Luxembourg on 3 June 2003, Greece on 5 June 2003, Portugal on 1 July 2003, Belgium on 11 December 2003, Finland on 19 December 2003, United Kingdom on 3 September 2004 and Italy on 8 October 2004.

30 Council Decision 2002/107/EC on the conclusion of an Interim Agreement on trade and trade-related matters between the European Community, of the one part, and the Republic of Croatia, of the other part, *OJ* 2002 L 40/9. For the text of the Interim Agreement, see *OJ* 2001 L 330/3.

31 *Narodne novine - Međunarodni ugovori* No. 15/2001. The Agreement entered into force on 1 March 2002, subject to a notice of the Ministry of Foreign Affairs of 5 February 2002, *Narodne novine - Međunarodni ugovori* No. 3/2002 of 22 February 2002.

> The EU reiterates its unequivocal support to the European perspective of the Western Balkan countries. The future of the Balkans is within the European Union. The ongoing enlargement and the signing of the Treaty of Athens in April 2003 inspire and encourage the countries of the Western Balkans to follow the same successful path. Preparation for integration into European structures and ultimate membership into the European Union, through adoption of European standards, is now the big challenge ahead. The Croatian application for EU membership is currently under examination by the Commission. The speed of movement ahead lies in the hands of the countries of the region.[32]

While the Thessaloniki Council declared Croatia's path towards membership open, several obstacles had to be overcome. For instance, Croatia's application for membership was clouded by the reluctance of the United Kingdom and the Netherlands to ratify the SAA, due to their doubts concerning the full cooperation of Croatia with the ICTY. On 1 May 2004, ten new states joined the European Union and the SAA had not entered in force. When ratification by the fifteen Member States was completed on 8 October 2004, the new Member States still had to accede to the agreement, either by ratification, or in the manner envisaged by Article 6 of the Act of Accession, that is, by conclusion of a protocol to the SAA between the Council, acting unanimously on behalf of the Member States, and Croatia.[33] The so-called Enlargement Protocol was signed by the Commission and Croatia on 21 December 2004 and was submitted to the Council for adoption. It entered into force at the same time as the SAA itself, namely on 1 February 2005.[34]

Another obstacle concerned the dilemma whether a positive opinion of the Commission and the commencement of membership negotiations could be achieved in the face of the doubts that had held up the ratification of the SAA. Although the two are not directly related, the political intention behind them was the same: using a national voice in different stages of *rapprochement* in order to achieve foreign policy goals – in the case of Croatia, full cooperation with the ICTY. On 20 April 2004, regardless of the described political stance, the European Commission adopted an opinion recommending to the Council of Ministers to extend candidate country status to Croatia and commence membership negotiations.[35] Two months later, on 17-18 June 2004, the European Council declared

---

[32] Thessaloniki, 21 June 2003, 10229/03 (Presse 163).

[33] Act concerning the conditions of accession of the Czech Republic, the Republic of Estonia, the Republic of Cyprus, the Republic of Latvia, the Republic of Lithuania, the Republic of Hungary, the Republic of Malta, the Republic of Poland, the Republic of Slovenia and the Slovak Republic and the adjustments to the Treaties on which the European Union is founded, *OJ* 2003 L 236/33.

[34] Council Decision 2005/205/EC concerning the conclusion of the Enlargement Protocol to the SAA Croatia, *OJ* 2005 L 68/30. For text of the Protocol, see *OJ* 2005 L 26/222.

[35] Communication from the Commission, Opinion on Croatia's Application for Membership of the European Union, Brussels, 20 April 2004, COM (2004) 257 final.

Croatia a candidate country for membership of the European Union.[36] In the same suit, and based on Council Regulation (EC) No. 533/2004 of 22 March 2004 on the establishment of European Partnerships in the framework of the SAP,[37] the Council of Ministers adopted the first European Partnership for Croatia on 13 September 2004.[38]

Finally, driven by the mandate to devise a pre-accession strategy for Croatia and to closely define the priorities and the framework for the membership negotiations, the European Commission adopted the pre-accession strategy on 6 October 2004, extending pre-accession financial instruments to Croatia.[39] In designing the negotiation framework, the Commission reiterated the conditionality approach, this time underpinned with a suspension clause according to which accession can be suspended '... in the case of a serious and persistent breach of the principles of liberty, democracy, respect for human rights and fundamental freedoms and the rule of law on which the Union is founded.'[40] Finally, the Brussels European Council of 17-18 December 2004 invited the Commission to present to the Council a proposal for a framework for negotiations with Croatia, taking full account of the experience of the fifth enlargement. It requested the Council to agree on that framework with a view to opening the accession negotiations on 17 March 2005, provided that Croatia cooperated fully with the ICTY.[41] As apparent from political statements, the last outstanding issue of full cooperation with the Tribunal was the apprehension and surrender of one remaining indictee.[42] On 16 March 2005, the Ministers were not unanimous that

---

36 Presidency Conclusions, 17-18 June 2004, *Bull. EU* 6-2004, point I.7.31: 'The European Council welcomes the Commission Opinion on Croatia's application for EU membership and the recommendation that accession negotiation should be opened. The European Council considered the application on the basis of the Opinion and noted that Croatia meets the political criteria set by the Copenhagen European Council in 1993 and the Stabilisation and Association Process conditionalities established by the Council in 1997. It decided that Croatia is a candidate country for membership and that the accession process should be launched.'

37 *OJ* 2004 L 86/1. The basic Regulation indicated that the partnerships '... will identify priorities for action in order to support efforts to move closer to the European Union while serving as a checklist against which to measure progress. They will be adapted to the countries' specific needs and respective stages of preparation, and to the specificities of the Stabilisation and Association Process, including regional cooperation.'

38 Council Decision 2004/648/EC on the principles, priorities and conditions contained in the European Partnership with Croatia, *OJ* 2004 L 297/19, repealed and replaced by Council Decision 2006/145/EC on the principles, priorities, and conditions contained in the *accession* partnership with Croatia, *OJ* 2006 L 55/30 [emphasis added], so as to reflect the new status of Croatia as a candidate for EU accession.

39 Communication from the Commission to the Council and to the European Parliament, Strategy Paper of the European Commission on progress in the enlargement process, SEC (2004) 1199, 1200, Brussels, 6 October 2004, COM (2004) 657 final, *OJ* 2004 C 117/11.

40 Ibid., pt. 3.2.

41 See *Bull. EU* 12-2004, point I.6.16.

42 See, e.g., 'EU and NATO tell Croatia "Gotovina is final issue"', 13 *New Europe*, No. 615, 6-12 March 2005, p. 9.

there was full cooperation with the Tribunal and the negotiations were postponed. However, the Council adopted the negotiating framework and cleared the way for the commencement of negotiations as soon as it would be satisfied that Croatia had met the remaining requirement.[43] The Ministers agreed to appoint a 'task force' comprising a representative from the EU presidency, a delegate from the European Commission and representatives from the United Kingdom and Austria, to evaluate Croatia's cooperation with the ICTY as a condition for starting EU accession negotiations. On 3 October 2005, the task force adopted a positive opinion following a positive report from the ICTY's Chief Prosecutor who was satisfied that Croatia was fully cooperating with the Tribunal. Subsequently, on the same day, the General Affairs and External Relations Council concluded that negotiations should be opened.[44] The negotiations were opened in the early morning hours of 4 October 2005. The formal start of the accession negotiations was followed by the opening of the so-called 'screening process' by the Commission on 20 October 2005. Former Croatian army general Ante Gotovina was eventually arrested in Spain on 7 December 2005 and was subsequently transferred to the ICTY in The Hague.

2. SAA CROATIA – THE MAIN LEGAL INSTRUMENT

As can be easily noted, the SAA Croatia bears significant similarities to the Europe Agreements – the Association Agreements that were concluded with the CEECs that joined the European Union in May 2004.[45] This primarily refers to their structure, institutional framework, free movement provisions, approximation of laws and cooperation policies. On the other hand, differences can be detected in respect of the aims of association, political dialogue and conditionality requirements. Nevertheless, bearing in mind that both generations of the agreement are sensitive to the wider political context, their object and purpose are susceptible to change. In fact, the perspective of EU membership for the signatories of the Europe Agreements emerged only later, as a result of the Copenhagen European Council in 1993,[46] and for countries of South-Eastern Europe after the Feira European Council in 2000.[47]

---

43 Council Conclusions of 16 March 2005, Press Release No. 6969/05 (Presse 44). The Council referred to the importance of full cooperation with the ICTY as an essential requirement for closer relations with the European Union.

44 Council Conclusions of 3 October 2005, Press Release No. 12514(05) (Presse 241). The Council reiterated that 'sustaining full cooperation with the ICTY would remain a requirement for progress throughout the accession process' and invited the Commission to closely monitor it.

45 See, e.g., D. Phinnemore, 'Stabilisation and Association Agreements: Europe Agreements for the Western Balkans?', 8 *EFA Rev.* (2003) p. 77 at p. 80.

46 M. Maresceau, 'A Legal Analysis of the Community's Association Agreements with Central and Eastern European Countries: General Framework, Accession Objectives and Trade Liberalization',

2.1 Preamble and political context

The preamble of the SAA Croatia takes the above-mentioned contextual sensitivity into account, thereby expressing the dynamic nature of the SAP. The Union reiterates its 'readiness to integrate to the fullest possible extent Croatia into the political and economic mainstream of Europe and its status as a potential candidate for EU membership.'[48] However, potential membership depends on acceptance of values specified by Article 6 TEU, fulfilment of the criteria defined by the Copenhagen European Council in 1993, as supplemented by the Madrid European Council in December 1995,[49] and the successful implementation of the agreement, notably in the area of regional cooperation. So far, the preamble does not add anything new to the Presidency Conclusions adopted in Feira. When read together with other relevant provisions, the preamble designates the SAA as an acceleration lane taking Croatia closer to the European Union, where EU membership is not explicitly mentioned but has to be drawn out of the political context. The described vagueness of terms generated fears that the agreement with Croatia was framed in a way that was substantially different to the Europe Agreements, with the consequence that Croatia would be left outside the European Union for a longer period of time. This fear was fuelled by the exclusion of Croatia from key political events and documents. For example, while the Nice IGC paved the way for the Eastern enlargement of the European Union, and even allocated seats in Community institutions to prospective members, Croatia, being absent not just from the negotiating table but also from the minds of European leaders, was not included in the allocation.[50] While this is not unusual, comparatively speaking, and can be solved by adding a protocol to the eventual accession treaty, the psychological consequences of such an exclusion are obvious.

On the other hand, explicit provisions in Association Agreements referring to EU membership are more the exception than the rule. In fact, early drafts of Europe Agreements[51] did not employ provisions directly referring to accession to

---

in S.V. Konstadinidis, ed., *The Legal Regulation of the European Community's External Relations after the Completion of the Internal Market* (Dartmouth 1996) pp. 125-129; see also Phinnemore, loc. cit. n. 45, at p. 79.

47 See n. 23 *supra*.

48 Stabilisation and Association Agreement between the European Communities and their Member States, of the one part, and the Republic of Croatia, of the other part, *OJ* 2005 L 26/3.

49 In Madrid, it was added that the candidate country must have created the conditions for its integration through the adjustment of its administrative structures. EU law transposed into national legislation has to be implemented effectively through appropriate administrative and judicial structures. See Madrid European Council, 15 and 16 December 1995, Presidency Conclusions, pt. III.A.

50 See Protocol on the Enlargement of the European Union attached to the Treaty on European Union and of the Treaty Establishing the European Community (consolidated version), *OJ* 2002 C 325/01.

51 The Europe Agreements were concluded between the European Communities and their Member States, on the one hand, and each of the following countries of Central and Eastern Europe, on

the European Union. Those provisions were negotiated under pressure of some states and even then are phrased in relatively vague terms.[52] Moreover, not even an explicit reference to the future membership of the European Union in the Europe Agreements would amount to a guarantee of membership.[53] The main difference in this respect between the SAAs and the Europe Agreements seems to lie in an enhanced degree of conditionality, corresponding to the needs of democratic and economic reforms that have to be implemented before political commitment to membership is made by the European Union. This leads to the conclusion that the commitment of EU membership does not seem to be an inherent part of the SAAs in terms of their legal characteristics, such as legal basis, structure or teleology,[54] but that it is contingent on political developments and instruments, such as Presidency Conclusions, accession partnerships, pre-accession strategies, and so forth. Second, the legal basis for the signing of the SAAs, which – just like the Europe Agreements – are negotiated on the legal basis of the provisions of Article 300 TEC and concluded on the legal basis of Article 310 TEC, is a necessary but not sufficient condition for further progress towards EU membership. In short, progress towards membership depends primarily on political assessment and not on contractual commitments.

---

the other: Bulgaria, the Czech Republic, Estonia, Hungary, Latvia, Lithuania, Poland, Romania, the Slovak Republic and Slovenia.

52 Maresceau, loc. cit. n. 46. The Opinion of AG Mayras in *Haegeman* is also worth noting: 'But Article 238 does not define the association and does not particularise in any way the possible contents of an Association Agreement. It follows that such a type of agreement may lead to the establishment of a very close institutional cooperation between the Community and the associated country without going as far as the unconditional accession of that country.' ECJ, Case 96/71 *Haegeman* v. *Belgium* [1972] *ECR* 1005, at 1023.

53 As noted by Smit and Herzog, 'association signifies close and continuous cooperation with the Community. [A]n interest only in financial or trade arrangements, let alone mere consultation agreements is not enough. Agreements seeking this involve only exchanges of reciprocal advantages, while association implies common goals and institutional framework.' H. Smit and P. Herzog, *The Law of the European Economic Community: A Commentary on the EEC Treaty*, Vol. G 6 (New York, Bender 1976-1995). Frank S. Benyon, 'Community Association Agreements: From the Sixties to the Nineties', in S.V. Konstadinidis, ed., *The Legal Regulation of the European Community's External Relations After the Completion of the Internal Market* (Aldershot, Dartmouth 1996) pp. 51-52.

54 As far as the inherent elements of Europe Agreements are concerned, Macleod, Hendry and Hyett have outlined the following key elements: close relationship between the parties, extending to a participation of the associated country in certain of the objectives of the EC treaty; the content of association which goes beyond merely commercial matters and covers a number of fields of Community activity; the institutions created, which are highly developed and include organs endowed with decision-making power; and the permanent nature of links and indefinite or extended periods of application. Most of these elements can indeed be found in the text of the SAAs concluded so far. None of them, however, provide a firm guarantee of membership, either by themselves or taken together. I. Macleod, I.D. Hendry and S. Hyett, *The External Relations of the European Communities* (Oxford, Oxford University Press 1996) p. 370 et seq.

2.2 Aims

The aims of the association are recited in Article 1 of the SAA. They are:

- to provide an appropriate framework for political dialogue, allowing the development of close political relations between the parties;
- to support the efforts of Croatia to develop its economic and international cooperation, also through the approximation of its legislation to that of the Community;
- to support the efforts of Croatia to complete the transition to a market economy, to promote harmonious economic relations and gradually develop a free trade area between the Community and Croatia; and
- to foster regional cooperation in all the fields covered by the agreement.

When compared with the aims of the Europe Agreements, for example the EA Slovenia, the SAA Croatia differs to a certain extent. The most obvious difference noted by commentators is the absence in the SAA Croatia of the aim to '... provide an appropriate framework for gradual integration into the European Union', which is included in the Europe Agreements. This led Phinnemore to speculate about the 'lesser status' of the SAAs compared to the Europe Agreements.[55] While such an explanation precisely addresses Croatia's fears, the missing aim is built into provisions on political dialogue that explicitly refer to 'Croatia's full integration into the community of democratic nations and gradual rapprochement with the European Union'.[56] In other words, the perspective of joining the European Union, subject to compliance with the criteria described in section 1 *supra*, brings the SAA close to the Europe Agreements. A diligent interpretation of its provisions must not underestimate the combined weight of the preamble, the aims and provisions on political dialogue and their role in shifting the aims of the agreement towards potential and eventually actual membership. However, every stage in the process towards membership has to be triggered by a political decision and an assessment of compliance by the Commission.

2.3 Institutional framework

The institutional framework established by the SAAs is very similar to that applied in the earlier instance of the Association Agreements. The institutions concerned are highly developed and include organs endowed with decision-making power.[57]

---

[55] See, e.g., Phinnemore, loc. cit. n. 45, at p. 84.
[56] Art. 7 SAA Croatia.
[57] See Macleod, Hendry and Hyett, op. cit. n. 54.

In line with the well-established practice of other Association Agreements, which was also followed in the case of the Europe Agreements, the SAAs establish an association council, this time under the name of Stabilisation and Association Council (SAC). The SAC has the power to make decisions within the scope of the SAA that are binding on the parties, which shall take the necessary measures to implement the decisions taken.[58] The SAC can delegate any of its powers to a Stabilisation and Association Committee (hereinafter, the Committee), a permanent body responsible for the preparation of the meetings of the SAC that can comprise members of the European Commission. However, the legal effects of the above-mentioned decisions, whether taken by the SAC or the Committee, may be different in the Community and in Croatia. This issue requires additional clarification and will be discussed below in section 2.4.

Pending the entry into force of the SAA Croatia, an Interim Committee was established under the Interim Agreement.[59] Its powers correspond to those of the SAC, but within the scope of the Interim Agreement. The Interim Committee meets regularly and its decisions, when adopted, are published in the Croatian Official Gazette.[60] Following the entry into force of the SAA, the first meeting of the Stabilisation and Association Council was held in Brussels on 14 July 2005.

Another institution created under the SAAs is the Stabilisation and Association Parliamentary Committee, which comprises members of the European Parliament and parliamentarians from the relevant SAP country and serves as a forum for the exchange of views.[61]

Despite some differences in the institutional setting that have been noted by other authors, such as different arbitration procedures and different modes of participation of the Community in the rotating presidency of the SAC,[62] the institutional provisions do not differ significantly from those employed in earlier Association Agreements. However, it should not be forgotten that activities taking place outside the framework of the SAA are by no means less important than those taking place under the SAA. This issue will be addressed in section 4.

2.4 Substantive provisions: free movement and competition

Similarly to the earlier generations of Association Agreements, the SAA Croatia mirrors the free movement and competition law provisions of the EC Treaty,

58 Art. 112 SAA Croatia.

59 Art. 38 of the Interim Agreement on trade and trade-related matters between the European Community, of the one part, and the Republic of Croatia, of the other part, *OJ* 2001 L 330/3.

60 The only one that was published in *Narodne novine* is Decision No. 1/2002 of the Interim Committee between the European Community, of the one part, and the Republic of Croatia, of the other part, of 19 April 2002 concerning the adoption of its Rules of Procedure, *Narodne novine - Međunarodni ugovori* No. 8/2003.

61 Art. 116 SAA Croatia.

62 Phinnemore, loc. cit. n. 45, at p. 95.

albeit in an asymmetric way. While a full elaboration of these provisions would merit a separate study, a few remarks on the free movement of goods and competition deserve attention here.

As far as the free movement of goods is concerned, a free trade area is to be established within six years of the entry into force of the agreement, starting from the date of application of the Interim Agreement, that is, 1 March 2002. Subject to Article 18 SAA Croatia, all customs duties on imports from the European Union to Croatia shall be progressively abolished by 1 January 2007. In addition, pursuant to the standstill clause in Article 33, all customs duties and charges having equivalent effect must not be increased or introduced after the SAA Croatia has entered into force.

Competition is addressed in Article 70 SAA Croatia, which specifies that any practices contrary to this article '… shall be assessed on the basis of criteria arising from the application of the competition rules applicable in the Community, in particular from Articles 81, 82, 86 and 87 of the Treaty establishing the European Community and interpretative instruments adopted by the Community institutions.' This in fact creates an obligation to apply the Community competition *acquis* from the date that the Interim Agreement enters into force.

No less importantly, Article 69 provides for Croatia's commitment to '… ensure that its existing laws and future legislation will be gradually made compatible with the Community *acquis*.' This provision, read in conjunction with the Article 120,[63] which mirrors the duty to cooperate specified by Article 10 TEC, arguably introduces not only an obligation to harmonise but also an obligation for Croatian courts to interpret existing Croatian law in accordance with Community law.

The provisions on the free movement of goods and competition are capable of having direct effect in the Community legal order. Their possible effects in Croatia will be explained in detail below.

2.5 Interpretation of the SAA Croatia

The SAA between the European Communities and its Member States, of the one part, and Croatia, of the other, is the key legal instrument regulating Croatia's path of integration and the harmonisation of its legal system with the *acquis communautaire*. Certainly, the application of the agreement will largely depend on its interpretation. Although it may sound premature to speculate about possible interpretative approaches, the European Court of Justice has on many occasions

63 Art. 120 SAA Croatia: 'The Parties shall take any general or specific measures required to fulfil their obligations under this Agreement. They shall see to it that the objectives set out in this Agreement are attained.'

interpreted Association Agreements of earlier generations.[64] Positions taken by the ECJ are also of great relevance for the definition and application of SAAs. However, it should be stressed that this chapter focuses on EU policies and that the position and understanding of the SAA Croatia in the European Union may differ from its position and understanding in Croatia. For example, the Union will be concerned exclusively with the *bona fide* performance of the agreement and not with the instruments for its implementation in national law.[65]

The consequences of the ECJ's case law concerning the direct application of Europe Agreements[66] for the interpretation of SAAs appear to be as follows:

- they can be expected to have direct effect in the Community legal order under the *Pabst* doctrine, building on the *Van Gend en Loos* case, according to which a provision of an international agreement in order to be directly effective in the Community legal order has to contain '... a clear and precise obligation which is not subject, in its implementation or effects, to the adoption of any subsequent measure';[67]
- the same should hold for secondary association law under the *Sevince* doctrine, according to which the direct effect of secondary association law (i.e., decisions of an association council) cannot be excluded;[68] and
- interpretation will largely depend on the 'purpose and nature' of the agreement (*Kondova*, *Gloszczuk*), and the so-called provisions of Association Agreements mirroring the founding treaties need not be interpreted in the same way as the founding treaties themselves.[69]

---

64 An Association Agreement may be subject to interpretation either by the ECJ or by the courts of a contracting party (an associated state). The ECJ can interpret it either in the process of its making, under Art. 300(6) TEC, or *ex post*, following its entry into force, if a case concerning its application is brought before the Court in the preliminary ruling procedure.

65 Cf., M. Cremona, 'External Relations and External Competence', in Paul P. Craig and G. de Búrca, *The Evolution of EU Law* (Oxford, Oxford University Press 1999) p. 143.

66 See chapter 2 in this volume.

67 ECJ, Case 17/81 *Pabst & Richarz* [1982] *ECR* 1331.

68 ECJ, Case C-192/89 *Sevince* [1990] *ECR* I-3461. At the first sight, the wording of the relevant SAA articles does not seem to be intended to produce direct effects: 'The decisions taken shall be binding on the Parties, which shall take the measures necessary to implement the decisions taken.' However, as witnessed in the *Sevince* case, this did not prevent the ECJ from recognising the direct effect of secondary association law. In addition, since the legal form of SAC decisions is similar to directives under Article 249 TEC, their possible direct effect in the case of non-implementation cannot be excluded. There is, of course, no explicit obligation to draw any parallels from the ECJ's case law related to vertical direct effect of directives.

69 See ECJ, Case C-235/99 *Secretary of State for the Home Department, ex parte: Eleanora Ivanova Kondova* [2001] *ECR* I-06427; ECJ, Case C-63/99 *Secretary of State for the Home Department, ex parte: Wieslaw Gloszczuk et Elzbieta Gloszczuk* [2001] *ECR* I-06369. For a confirmation of the direct effect of the provisions of association treaties, see also ECJ, Case C-268/99 *Aldona Malgorzata Jany and Others* v. *Staatssecretaris van Justitie* [2001] *ECR* I-08615. See also ECJ, Case

The last consequence seems to be of crucial importance for the interpretation of SAAs. Specifically, the question is whether SAAs can be interpreted in the same way as the earlier generation of Europe Agreements or whether they have to be judged on their own purpose and nature. There is no ECJ case law on the point. However, the aims of an Association Agreement are, as a matter of practice, explicitly specified in the text. They reflect a number of political considerations that are expressed in various official documents, such as Council conclusions and other similar documents. As pointed out earlier, the Presidency Conclusions adopted at Feira[70] were echoed in the preamble of the SAA Croatia and further confirmed by the Presidency Conclusions of the Nice European Council[71] and, more recently, the Thessaloniki Council.[72] In all those documents, the purpose of the association relationship and, accordingly, the perspective of EU membership is phrased in a different way than in the earlier generation of agreements, and this can be of consequence for their interpretation.

Regardless of the developments described above, the understanding of the SAA and secondary association law in Croatia differs from its understanding in the European Union, especially in the case of the ECJ. The question whether regulatory powers have to be transferred to the SAC already arose during the ratification process of the SAA. Due to the political balance in the Croatian Parliament, the agreement was ratified by a majority of all representatives but fell short of the two-thirds majority that is required for the transfer of powers.[73] In response to the claim by the right-wing parties that the SAA would strip Croatia of its national sovereignty, the Croatian Prime Minister and Minister for European Integration classified the SAA as an ordinary international treaty and did not push for the two-thirds majority ratification that would have been required by the Constitution in the case of the transfer of regulatory powers to supranational bodies.[74]

C-257/99 *Secretary of State for the Home Department, ex parte: Julius Barkoci et Marcel Malik* [2001] *ECR* I-06557, para. 39.

70 See n. 23 *supra*.

71 Presidency Conclusions, 7-9 December 2000, *Bull. EU* 12-2000, point I.36.60: '... the EU will continue to support the Western Balkans' efforts in their progress towards democracy, the rule of law, reconciliation and cooperation based on respect for existing borders and other international obligations which will contribute to the rapprochement of each of these countries with the Union and form a whole.' The Presidency further concluded that all countries of the Western Balkans have '... a clear prospect of accession, indissolubly linked to progress in regional cooperation, in accordance with the conclusions of Cologne and Feira.'

72 Presidency Conclusions, 19-20 June 2003, *Bull. EU* 6-2003, point I.17.40: 'The European Council, recalling its conclusions in Copenhagen (December 2002) and Brussels (March 2003), reiterates its determination to fully and effectively support the European perspective of the Western Balkan countries, which will become an integral part of the EU, once they meet the established criteria.'

73 Izvješća Hrvatskog Sabora [Reports of the Croatian Parliament], No. 315, 20 December 2001.

74 See, e.g., the speech by Minister Neven Mimica in the Croatian Parliament on 24 October 2001, in which he stated that no constitutional regulatory authority would be transferred to the Stabilisation and Association Council. Source <http://www.mei.hr>.

This method of ratification gave rise to questions as to whether decisions of the SAC could be directly applicable in the absence of implementing legislation. In order to address this issue, the Croatian Parliament adopted the Law Implementing the SAA, apparently in pursuance of the position that the SAC may not, without further implementing measures, exercise constitutional regulatory powers.[75] Article 6 of this Law applies a radical dualist approach according to which decisions of the Association Council are subject to parliamentary ratification. This is a clear departure from the constitutional mandate of monism stipulated under Article 140 of the Constitution, which renders ratified international treaties part of national law. For this reason, the compatibility of the Law and the Constitution is questionable. So far, no practice of application of the SAA has been reported by the Croatian courts. Due to their extremely formalist attitude, however, Croatian judges are inclined to look into the most precise regulation available.[76] Instances of regulatory infringement of the SAA have already occurred, but have not been brought before Croatian courts.[77]

3. CONDITIONALITY

In broad and plain terms, the conditionality approach can be described as a 'carrot and stick' mechanism that can be used by the European Union to influence the policies of associated states and control the speed of rapprochement.[78] Not surprisingly, conditionality requirements are often understood not as incentives for faster integration but as limitations upon national sovereignty in candidate countries. In Croatia, for instance, the signature of the SAA was criticised by the right-wing opposition as a limitation of state sovereignty.[79] In the context of the SAP, the European Union has thus far adopted at least two distinctive conditionality requirements: human rights conditionality, which is nowadays considered an

---

[75] Zakon o provedbi sporazuma o stabilizaciji i pridruživanju [Law on Implementation of the Stabilisation and Association Agreement], *Narodne novine - Međunarodni ugovori* No. 15/2001.

[76] See T. Ćapeta, D. Mihelin and S. Rodin, 'National Report on Croatia', in A.E. Kellermann, J. Czuczai, S. Blockmans, A. Albi and W.Th. Douma, eds., *Impact of EU Accession on the Legal Orders of New Member States and (Pre-)Candidate Countries: Hopes and Fears* (The Hague, T.M.C. Asser Press 2006) p. 69.

[77] See Naredba o visini naknade za upis broda, jahte i brodice u upisnik brodova, odnosno jahti i očevidnik brodica [Order on Registration Fees for Yachts and Boats with the Register of Boats or Yachts and with the Register of Boats], *Narodne novine* No. 2/2005. This ministerial order imposes a discriminatory charge on the registration of Croatian-made and imported boats.

[78] On the difficulties of defining the concept of conditionality, see chapter 3 in this volume.

[79] In Estonia, the constitutional definition of sovereignty seemed to be inappropriate for the purpose of EU membership. See, e.g., A. Albi, 'Europe Agreements in the Light of Sovereignty and Legitimacy: The Case of Estonia', in A.E. Kellermann et al., eds., *EU Enlargement: The Constitutional Impact at EU and National Level* (The Hague, T.M.C. Asser Press 2001) p. 195 et seq.

essential element of all Association Agreements,[80] and the conditionality of regional cooperation. The European Union's conditionality policy towards the Western Balkans has been supplemented by other benchmarks that reach beyond the 1993 Copenhagen criteria[81] and the 1995 Madrid criteria.[82] Those include benchmarks for the commencement and conclusion of SAAs that were elaborated in 1997 by the Luxembourg European Council.[83] In the SAA Croatia, conditionality is extended to yet other areas, such as cooperation with the ICTY and the development of good neighbourly relations. The latter two will not be discussed further in this chapter.[84]

The 1997 Luxembourg criteria for the *commencement* of negotiations on SAAs are: respect for the rule of law and the principle of democracy; compliance with human and minority rights, including freedom of the media; free and fair elections; full implementation results; absence of discriminatory treatment; implementing first steps of economic reform, including privatisation and abolition of price controls; proven readiness for good neighbourly relations; compliance with obligations undertaken under the Dayton Agreement; cooperation with the ICTY; and the return of refugees. At the same time, the conditions for *concluding* negotiations are: substantial progress in the achievement of objectives and conditions for opening negotiations; substantial results in field of political and economic reforms (stable economic environment, price liberalisation, regulatory framework, competitive banking sector, etc.); proven regional cooperation; and good neighbourly relations. Compliance with those criteria is technically monitored by the Commission. In fact, what we have witnessed up to this day is not an enhancement of membership criteria, which continue to be set by the EU Treaty, but a gradual introduction of a complex benchmarking method as a means of measuring the progress of the countries concerned.

---

80 See, generally, M. Nowak, 'Human Rights "Conditionality" in Relation to Entry to, and Full Participation in, the EU', in P. Alston, ed., *The European Union and Human Rights* (Oxford, OUP 1999) p. 687 et seq.; and M. Bulterman, *Human Rights in the Treaty Relations of the European Community* (Antwerp, Intersentia 2001).

81 *Bull. EU* 6-1993, point 13.

82 As decided by the Madrid European Council in December 1995, '…the candidate country must have created the conditions for its integration through the adjustment of its administrative structures'. See Madrid European Council, 15 and 16 December 1995, Presidency Conclusions, pt. III.A.

83 European Council Conclusions – Luxembourg, 29 April 1997, Guidelines on the Principle of Conditionality Governing the Development of the European Union's Relations with Certain Countries of South-East Europe, *Bull. EU* 4-1997, point 2.2.1.

84 See chapter 10 in this volume and C. Pippan, 'The Rocky Road to Europe: The EU's Stabilisation and Association Process for the Western Balkans and the Principle of Conditionality', 9 *EFA Rev.* (2004) pp. 219-245.

3.1 Human rights conditionality

Human rights conditionality is anchored in Article 6 TEU, according to which the Union is founded on the principles of liberty, democracy, respect for human rights and fundamental freedoms and the rule of law, principles which are common to the Member States. Respect for these principles is an absolute requirement for membership according to Article 49 TEU. The position that the legal basis for human rights conditionality is not necessarily Article 310 TEC has been confirmed by the ECJ:

> The mere fact that Article 1(1) of the Agreement provides that respect for human rights and democratic principles 'constitutes an essential element' of the Agreement does not justify the conclusion that that provision goes beyond the objective stated in Article 130u(2) of the Treaty. The very wording of the latter provision demonstrates the importance to be attached to respect for human rights and democratic principles, so that, amongst other things, development cooperation policy must be adapted to the requirement of respect for those rights and principles.[85]

Early Europe Agreements, such as the one with Hungary, did not provide for human rights conditionality *expressis verbis*. Later on, conditionality provisions were gradually included in all Association Agreements, regardless of their generation. For example, Article 6 EA Romania introduced human rights conditionality in the form of an 'essential element clause'.[86] The same practice was applied in the case of the SAA Croatia, where respect for human rights was made one of the essential elements of the agreement[87] and a legal basis for suspension of its application.[88]

---

[85] ECJ, Case C-268/94 *Portugal* v. *Council* [1996] *ECR* I-6177, para. 24. See also E. Shaver Duquette, 'Human Rights in the European Union: Internal Versus External Objectives', 34 *Cornell Int'l L.J.* 363 (2001).

[86] *OJ* 1994 L 357/2: 'Respect for the democratic principles and human rights established by the Helsinki Final Act and the Charter of Paris for a New Europe, as well as the principles of market economy, inspire the domestic and external policies of the Parties and constitute essential elements of the present association.' See also Art. 2 EA Latvia, *OJ* 1998 L 26/3. For a broader discussion of the so-called human rights clauses, see F. Hoffmeister, *Menschenrechts- und Demokratieklauseln in den vertraglichen Außenbeziehungen der Europäischen Gemeinschaft* (Berlin, Springer 1998) pp. 117-175; and E. Riedel and M. Will, 'Human Rights Clauses in External Agreements of the European Communities', in Alston, op. cit. n. 80, pp. 723-754.

[87] See Art. 2 SAA Croatia: 'Respect for the democratic principles and human rights as proclaimed in the Universal Declaration of Human Rights and as defined in the Helsinki Final Act and the Charter of Paris for a New Europe, respect for international law principles and the rule of law as well as the principles of market economy as reflected in the Document of the CSCE Bonn Conference on Economic Cooperation, shall form the basis of the domestic and external policies of the Parties and constitute essential elements of this Agreement.'

[88] See Art. 2 SAA Croatia. The clause was originally applied in the Association Agreement with Bulgaria and is more generally known as the 'Bulgarian' clause.

In addition to the above-mentioned formal conditionality policies and criteria, as witnessed in the context of the ratification process of the SAA Croatia, some Member States have taken recourse to other forms of political pressure in order to stimulate compliance. For example, the United Kingdom persisted in requiring full cooperation with the ICTY as a condition for ratification of the SAA, and it was only on 19 April 2004 that it gave the green light to further progress, including the ratification of the SAA.[89]

More recent developments in relations between the European Union and Croatia follow the conditional open door policy. First, the Thessaloniki summit explicitly opened the door of the Union to all the countries of South-Eastern Europe. As stated in the Declaration of the 2003 EU-Western Balkans Summit, '... the EU reiterates its unequivocal support to the European perspective of the Western Balkan countries. The future of the Balkans is within the European Union.'[90] A similar wording is maintained in the Presidency Conclusions.[91] As far as conditionality is concerned, its most recent expression can be found in the so-called *safeguard clauses* that make progress towards EU membership contingent on the fulfilment of political criteria. These newly introduced safety valves apply not only to Croatia, which still has to negotiate its way into the European Union, but also to Bulgaria and Romania – countries that have completed the negotiations and signed their Accession Treaties.[92] In the case of Croatia, Article 2 of the SAA provides that

> the Commission will recommend the suspension of negotiations in the case of a serious and persistent breach of the principles of liberty, democracy, respect for human rights and fundamental freedoms and the rule of law on which the Union is founded. The Council should be able to decide on such recommendation by a qualified majority of Member States.

3.2 Regional cooperation conditionality

Regional cooperation conditionality is one of the core policies of the Union towards Croatia and the other states of South-Eastern Europe and was originally formulated by the European Commission in 1996.[93] It not only antedates the SAAs but serves as an underlying policy for their interpretation. It can therefore be said that the SAAs with Macedonia and Croatia integrate regional cooperation

89 As reported by *The Guardian* on 20 April 2004. 'The British government hopes to see Croatia as a member of the EU before the decade is out,' said Denis MacShane, the Minister for Europe.

90 Thessaloniki, 21 June 2003 10229/03 (Presse 163).

91 See n. 81 *supra*.

92 See chapters 7 and 8 in this volume.

93 See n. 11 *supra*.

conditionality in a contractual form.[94] The main principles of this policy are cooperation, conditionality, an individual approach and flexibility.

The principle of *cooperation* aims at promoting the development of cooperation and good neighbourly relations between the countries concerned. The principle of *conditionality* makes the development of relations with the European Union dependent on their willingness and readiness to cooperate and develop good neighbourly relations with the other states, and the same holds for compliance with human rights requirements. In both cases, a lack of compliance is threatened by the possible inclusion of suspension clauses into legal and political instruments. The principle of *individual approach* specifies that one state must not be made to suffer as a result of another state's lack of commitment or refusal to cooperate, and the principle of *flexibility* allows for a differential approach in the negotiation process and framing of the SAAs.

In pursuance of this policy, the SAA Croatia introduced two regional cooperation commitments. The first and possibly easiest commitment is to inform and consult the Community and its Member States about potential reinforcement of their cooperation with one of the SAP countries, countries concerned with the SAP or EU candidate countries. This should take place at the appropriate level, at regular intervals, and when circumstances require. The above-mentioned commitment represents a limitation on state sovereignty in external relations and forms a good example of how the gravitational field of the European Union affects relations between third countries. It also provides clear evidence of the specific nature of SAAs as opposed to 'ordinary' international agreements concluded with third states. Such a limitation of sovereignty can already have constitutional implications at this early stage of rapprochement since it may require a constitutional redefinition of the concept of national sovereignty.

The second commitment concerns negotiations and the eventual conclusion of a convention on regional cooperation. According to Article 12 SAA Croatia, which provides for cooperation with other countries that have signed an SAA, such a convention, which could take the form of a bilateral treaty, is to be concluded within two years after the entry into force of an SAA. It follows from the nature of such a convention that at least two SAAs have to be signed and in force

---

[94] See Council conclusions on the principle of conditionality governing the development of the European Union's relations with certain countries of south-east Europe of 29 April 1997, *Bull. EU* 4-1997, point 2.2.1. For a discussion of this topic, see B. Brandtner and A. Rosas, 'Trade Preferences and Human Rights', in Alston, op. cit. n. 80, at pp. 699 et seq. See also S. Rodin and M. Šarolić, *New Generation of Association Treaties for South-East Europe: Case for Croatia*, Proceedings of the III International Conference on the Economic System of the European Union and the Accession of the Republic of Croatia, University of Rijeka, University of Trieste and University of Antwerp, 2001. For a more recent contribution, see K.E. Smith, 'The Evolution and Application of EU Membership Conditionality', in M. Cremona, ed., *The Enlargement of the European Union* (Oxford, Oxford University Press 2003) p. 105 et seq. See also chapter 3 in this volume.

prior to the start of the negotiations. So far, Croatia has signed such bilateral agreements with Macedonia and Bulgaria.[95] Both agreements reiterate the ambition of the parties to become members of the European Union. They provide for a political dialogue, the establishment of free trade areas, mutual cooperation in the harmonisation of laws with the EU *acquis*, as well as for cooperation in the field of justice and home affairs. The free movement of workers, services and capital and the freedom of establishment are subject to separate agreements. Croatia has also entered into bilateral commitments with other SAP countries, regardless of whether or not they have actually signed an SAA.[96] This shows that, while the absence of readiness of any SAP country to conclude such a convention or bilateral treaty would prevent further development of the relations between European Union and the country concerned, regional cooperation is viable regardless of the existence of effective SAAs in all countries. In fact, regional cooperation policy does not exclude but stands side-by-side with cooperation with other countries, notably those concerned with the SAP and EU candidate countries.

4. BETWEEN REALISM AND FUNCTIONALISM

Both human rights and regional cooperation conditionality are based on certain realist and functionalist assumptions that originate from European integration theory.[97] The realist position assumes that states, being autonomous and rational subjects, by necessity have and represent certain interests. Since they are the main actors in the international arena, the structure of international politics is determined by their actions.[98] So the Union's conditionality approach is based on the

[95] The Croatian Government decided on 13 March 2005 to forward this agreement to the Parliament for ratification. The treaty has been ratified and published. See Zakon o potvrđivanju Sporazuma o suradnji između Republike Hrvatske i Republike Makedonije u okviru približavanja i pristupanja Europskoj uniji [Law on the Ratification of the Agreement on Cooperation between the Republic of Croatia and the Republic of Macedonia within the Framework of Approach and Accession to the European Union], *Narodne novine - Međunarodni ugovori* No. 2/2005 of 18 February 2005. See ibid. for the agreement with Bulgaria.

[96] See, e.g., the free trade agreement between Croatia and Bosnia Herzegovina [Zakon o potvrđivanju ugovora o slobodnoj trgovini između Republike Hrvatske i Bosne i Hercegovine], *Narodne novine - Međunarodni ugovori* No. 9/2001. Art. 2 of the agreement refers to European integration. For Serbia and Montenegro, see Zakon o potvrđivanju ugovora između Republike Hrvatske i Srbije i Crne gore o izmjenama i dopunama ugovora o slobodnoj trgovini između Republike Hrvatske i Savezne Republike Jugoslavije [Law on Ratification of the Agreement between the Republic of Croatia and Serbia and Montenegro on Amendments and Supplements to the Free Trade Agreement between the Republic of Croatia and the Federal Republic of Yugoslavia], *Narodne novine - Međunarodni ugovori* No. 4/2004.

[97] For a recent overview of European integration theory, see, e.g., A. Wiener and T. Diez, *European Integration Theory* (Oxford, Oxford University Press 2004).

[98] See, e.g., F. Laursen, 'Explaining the Intergovernmental Conference on Political Union', in F. Laursen and S. Vanhoonacker, eds., *The Intergovernmental Conference on Political Union: Institutional*

realist assumption and tailored towards motivating the SAP states to engage – or not engage – in certain courses of action. Another important consideration is exerting political and economic pressure on national elites and strengthening pro-European political options at national level.

At the same time, the SAAs, and in particular their *mirror requirements*, that is to say, provisions the wording of which is identical or substantially similar to provisions of the EC Treaty,[99] attempt to integrate national policies and regulations into the functional matrix of the European Union and serve as a harmonisation track in the pre-accession period. The functional approach employed by the Union reaches beyond the mirror requirements of the SAAs. In addition, there are external policy actions that can be characterised as both realist and functional. A good example of such mixity can be found in the gradual inclusion of Croatia in the European political dialogue, including the Common Foreign and Security Policy of the Union (CFSP).

4.1 Political dialogue between realism and functionalism

Political dialogue, as envisaged by the SAAs, can be understood as both a realist and a functional component of the Union's regional policy. Its realist aspect lies in the fact that the dialogue is contingent on compliance with political criteria and that its forms may vary. It *may* take place within a multilateral framework such as a regional dialogue.[100] When compared to earlier Association Agreements, the Union's commitment is weaker, which is understandable taking into account the uncertain development of the situation in the region, which at the time was threatening to reduce the possibilities for political dialogue. For example, the commitment to provide regular information on CFSP activities that was envisaged by Europe Agreements is softened in the SAAs to 'promoting the common views'. The participation of Croatia in the CFSP is described in Article 7 SAA Croatia, which specifies that the political dialogue is intended to promote, in particular, '... common views on security and stability in Europe, including

Reforms, New Policies and International Identity of the European Community (Maastricht, European Institute of Public Administration 1992) pp. 230-231. See also K.N. Waltz, *Theory of International Politics* (Reading, Mass., Addison-Wesley 1979).

[99] Examples of this include the free movement and competition provisions. The expression is used by the Commission in its communication to identify requirements that are phrased in substantially similar language to those applicable pursuant to the EC Treaty. However, the ECJ noted earlier that '... similarity of terms is not a sufficient reason for transposing to the provisions of the agreement (with Portugal) the above-mentioned case-law, which determines in the context of the Community the relationship between the protection of industrial and commercial property rights and the rules on the free movement of goods.' See ECJ, Case 270/80 *Polydor Limited and RSO Records Inc.* v. *Harlequin Records Shops Limited and Simons Records Limited* [1982] *ECR* 329.

[100] Art. 8 SAA Croatia.

cooperation in the areas covered by the Common Foreign and Security Policy of the European Union.' This provision took effect on the entry into force of the SAA on 1 February 2005, within the framework of the activities of the SAC. In the meantime, political dialogue was taking place in a traditional international relations format, on the basis of a joint declaration adopted by the European Union and Croatia on the occasion of the signing of the SAA.

Following the publication of the Thessaloniki Presidency Conclusions in June 2003, a new mechanism for cooperation in the field of foreign policy between the European Union and the states of South-Eastern Europe was instituted. Since then, the European Union has committed to invite, '... as appropriate, the SAP countries to align themselves with EU demarches, declarations and common positions on CFSP issues', without the possibility to take part in their adoption.[101] Since then, endorsing common positions has become regular practice in Croatia.[102] Although endorsing common positions has great political significance, they need to be implemented in national law in order to take legal effect, in spite of their mandatory language.[103] As compliance with and implementation of common positions has become a benchmark for measuring compliance with the political criteria for accession, their implementation in Croatia has been subject to the provisions of the International Restrictive Measures Act since December 2004.[104]

As one can see, provisions on political dialogue cannot be understood exclusively as an instrument of the Union's conditionality policy. Their functional component lies in the gradual inclusion of the SAP countries in CFSP actions, which arguably has two functional dimensions. While the rational dimension contributes to the achievement of the Union's foreign policy objectives, the experiential dimension contributes to the gradual inclusion of the political elites in SAP countries in the institutional framework of the Union and to burden sharing in the implementation of foreign policy goals.

---

[101] Council Conclusions of 16 June 2003 on the Western Balkans, Annex: 'The Thessaloniki Agenda for the Western Balkans: moving towards European integration'. In addition, a forum comprising the Foreign Ministers of the EU Member States and the states of South-Eastern Europe created additional space for the participation of these countries in European foreign policy. The forum held its first meeting in Brussels on 9 December 2003.

[102] See, e.g., Common Position 2004/694/CFSP of 11 October 2004 on further measures in support of the effective implementation of the mandate of the International Criminal Tribunal for the former Yugoslavia (ICTY), *OJ* 2004 L 315/52. As reported by the Council, Croatia and other countries declared that they share the objectives of the above-mentioned common position.

[103] The language of common positions sometimes includes clearly defined obligations for the Member States, for example: 'All funds and economic resources belonging to the natural persons listed in the Annex, who have been indicted by the ICTY, shall be frozen.' However, due to their legal nature, which is based in the CFSP, these obligations need to be implemented in national law.

[104] Zakon o međunarodnim restriktivnim mjerama [International Restrictive Measures Act], *Narodne novine* No. 178/2004.

4.2 Functional spill-over

An entirely new development in the European Union's contractual relationship with South-Eastern Europe started to unfold in late 2002, when the Athens Memorandum of Understanding launched an initiative for the creation of a regional energy market with a clear attempt to repeat the success of the functional spill-over that characterised the three original European Communities.[105] This led to the initiation of negotiations for the establishment of the Energy Community Treaty for South-Eastern Europe. The treaty was initialled on 22 March 2005 by the states concerned and by the European Commission. On 17 October 2005, the Council adopted a decision on its signature.[106] This paved the way for the official signature ceremony that took place in Athens on 25 October 2005.[107] Long kept away from the eyes of the public, the initialled version of the treaty was published by the European Federation of Public Services Unions[108] and was severely criticised for its lack of transparency, the undemocratic nature of the institutions and the disregard for the social dimension.[109] The disclosed version also revealed the change of the original name to the Treaty Establishing an Energy Community.[110]

The main aims of the Treaty, which brings together European Community, Albania, Bulgaria, Bosnia-Herzegovina, the Former Yugoslav Republic of Macedonia, Croatia, Serbia, Montenegro, Romania and UNMIK-Kosovo, are to create a regionally integrated energy market for electricity and natural gas networks and to integrate that market into the wider EU market. To this end, the parties have decided to establish common rules for the generation, transmission and distribution of electricity; to establish common rules for the transmission, distribution, supply and storage of natural gas; to establish state-level national energy authorities, regulators and transmission system operators; to establish compatible state and regional electricity and natural gas market action plans and embryonic regional level dispute resolution mechanism; to open the markets in line with the EU *acquis* in accordance with the transitional periods. It is interesting to note that several pieces of the EC *acquis* listed in the annexes to the agreement will be

105 Memorandum of Understanding on the Regional Electricity Market in South East Europe and its Integration into the European Union Internal Electricity Market ('The Athens Memorandum – 2002'), available at: <http://www.seerecon.org/infrastructure/documents/mou-rem-see.pdf>.

106 Council Decision 2005/905/EC of 17 October 2005 on the signing by the European Community of the Energy Community Treaty, *OJ* 2005 L 329/30.

107 The European Union and South-Eastern Europe sign a historic treaty to boost energy integration, Brussels, 25 October 2005, IP/05/1346.

108 See <http://www.epsu.org/a/871>.

109 'Unions condemn lack of social dimension of South East European Energy Treaty Energy Conference', Sarajevo, Bosnia-Herzegovina, 10-11 December 2004, Press Release, 10 December 2004.

110 Draft Energy Community Treaty, Version IV.5, Brussels, 3 December 2004, TREN/C2/EC/BD/kb-D(2004).

applicable between the parties. This includes, *inter alia*, the framework legislation on the internal market in electricity and gas,[111] as well as the legislation on environmental protection.[112]

The Treaty is undoubtedly building on the positive experiences of European integration, and neo-functionalist hopes of a functional spill-over and its importance have been explicitly compared to the ECSC Treaty.[113] Moreover, the motive behind the idea to create functional spill-over effects in South-Eastern Europe seems to be an attempt to integrate those states in the region that do not meet the Luxembourg criteria and do not qualify for the conclusion of an SAA[114] into a legal framework that would have a significant functional and meta-functional impact.[115] It could be inferred that the Union's choice between realism and functionalism is informed and motivated by the wish to speed up and facilitate structural reforms in and reconciliation among states in South-Eastern Europe.

On the other hand, it may be argued that the mechanism that the European Union is employing in an attempt to encourage Croatia to embark on higher levels of integration is a gradual replacement of the international law method with a tailor-made Community method. As can be seen from the example of political dialogue,

---

111 Directive 2003/54/EC of the European Parliament and of the Council of 26 June 2003 concerning common rules for the internal market in electricity, *OJ* 2003 L 176/37; Directive 2003/55/EC of the European Parliament and of the Council of 26 June 2003 concerning common rules for the internal market in natural gas, *OJ* 2003 L 176/57.

112 For example, Council Directive 85/337/EEC of 27 June 1985 on the assessment of the effects of certain public and private projects on the environment, *OJ* 1985 L 175/40 (as amended).

113 In a speech delivered in Vienna on 15 July 2004, Mr Erhard Busek compared the proposed treaty to the ECSC Treaty: 'However the originality of the ECSEE is that it substitutes to the vertical country by country approach, which could still take many years, a horizontal sectoral approach, which provides to most of you a unique opportunity to become much sooner part of the EU single market as far as the crucial energy sector is concerned. As I have said before, the proposed treaty is a unique political chance for the region. In the same way the European Coal and Steel Community, launched by Robert Schumann and Jean Monnet in 1950, cemented the reconciliation between France and Germany and was a prelude to the Treaty of Rome of 1957 establishing the European Economic Community, the proposed treaty establishing the ECSEE could consolidate reconciliation in the region and provide a powerful driver towards a more comprehensive economic and political integration of the whole of SEE into the European Union.' Available at: <http://www.stabilitypact.org/pages/speeches/detail.asp?y=2004&p=12>.

114 See n. 94 *supra*.

115 The dual nature of the Treaty has been emphasised by the European Commissioner for Energy, Mr Andris Piebalgs: 'The political objective is clear: an enhanced cooperation among the countries in this region will foster the conditions for peace, stability and growth. Experience in Western Europe has shown that, by working together, people can become more familiar with one another and make conflicts impossible, if not unthinkable. The economic objective is the establishment of an integrated market in natural gas and electricity, based on common solidarity. As it was already pointed out, this region suffers from a number of deficiencies: lack of energy sources, inadequate infrastructure for transporting energy, disruption of electricity supply, absence of competition, and serious environmental problems, to name only a few.' 'Energy Community is a key to the stabilisation and development of South East Europe', High Level EBRD Southeast Europe Regional Energy Seminar, Tirana, 10 February 2005, Reference: SPEECH/05/83.

the external relations voice of Croatia is maximised when exercised within the European framework and minimised when it is exercised individually. This is arguably a strong argument against proponents of unilateralism and an additional motive to proceed on the European track. Whether this effect was intended by the European Union or whether it is merely incidental can only be speculated.

5. IMPACT OF ENLARGEMENT AND THE TREATY ESTABLISHING A CONSTITUTION FOR EUROPE

Since the emergence of the regional approach policy in 1996, it is possible to identify several trends in the European Union's external relations with Croatia. Those trends can be described as:

- shifting from legal commitments to political assessment;
- the expansion of the conditionality approach;
- a combination of realism (conditionality) and functionalism; and
- a combination of regional and individual approach.

Two events that forever marked the history of Europe in 2004, namely the 'big bang' enlargement and the signing of the Treaty establishing a Constitution for Europe (TCE)[116] carry significant consequences for the relationship of the Union with Croatia.

5.1 Impact of enlargement

The entry of the ten new Member States that took place on 1 May 2004 postponed the entry into force of the SAA Croatia until 1 February 2005. As explained before, in order to become effective, the new Member States needed to accede to the agreement. The new Member States had a choice between ratification by individual states and the procedure laid down in Article 6 of the Act of Accession, which provides for a simplified procedure for the accession of new Member States to agreements and conventions concluded or provisionally applied by the Community.[117] The 'big bang' enlargement created a situation in which being outside the Union was becoming increasingly difficult, both economically and politically, amounting to exclusion from the European mainstream.[118] Admittedly,

---

[116] *OJ* 2004 C 310.

[117] See nn. 33 and 34 *supra* and accompanying text.

[118] An example of the disparate impact of the EU enlargement of 2004 is the application of existing Community legislation in new Member States that has proven to be more restrictive. See Commission Regulation (EEC) No. 2454/93 of 2 July 1993 laying down provisions for the implementation of

the change is in degree rather than in the kind of relationship. Nevertheless, it raises the motivation for joining the European Union and contributes to the arguments of the pro-European political actors in Croatia.

On the Union's side, the 'big bang' enlargement released a huge administrative burden from the Union and facilitated a shift of the political, administrative and economic focus to South-Eastern Europe and Croatia in particular. An understanding of the problems of transition in post-Communist Member States allows better tailoring to Croatia's needs. In terms of financial assistance, there is a clear trend towards the transition from humanitarian aid, which amounted to almost €205 million in 1994, to support for democracy and human rights, as well as other specific projects, in the amount of €62 million in 2003. As a candidate country, Croatia has become eligible for pre-accession financial instruments: Phare for institution building and economic and social cohesion, ISPA for environment and transport and SAPARD for rural development.[119] The Commission recommended the allocation to Croatia of €105 million (€80 million for Phare and €25 million for ISPA) in 2005 and €140 million (€80 million for Phare, €35 million for ISPA and €25 million for SAPARD) in 2006. These amounts will be financed out of the pre-accession funds. The Commission also proposed that the Council establish a new financial pre-accession instrument (IPA) applicable from 2007.[120] Following the 'big bang' enlargement, its recognition as a candidate country, and the decision by the Council to open accession negotiations, Croatia's European future is becoming more certain.

5.2 Impact of the Constitutional Treaty

Following the French and Dutch 'no' to the Constitutional Treaty it is becoming increasingly difficult to predict whether Croatia will accede to the Union under the terms of the Constitutional Treaty or under the present 'constitutional' framework. In any case, accession negotiations will be based on the current status of the EU law.[121] On the Union's side, the accession of Croatia under the terms of

Council Regulation (EEC) No. 2913/92 establishing the Community Customs Code, *OJ* 1993 L 253/1. In practice, the transit of Croatian trucks was restricted in Slovenia by the mere application of the above-mentioned regulation.

[119] See Council Regulation (EC) No. 2257/2004 amending Regulations (EEC) No. 3906/89, (EC) No. 1267/1999, (EC) No. 1268/1999 and (EC) No. 2666/2000, to take account of Croatia's candidate status, *OJ* 2004 L 389/1. See also Framework Agreement between the European Community and the Republic of Croatia on the general principles for the participation of the Republic of Croatia in Community programmes, *OJ* 2005 L 192/16.

[120] See chapter 19 in this volume.

[121] However, the Commission has said that it would be taking the Constitutional Treaty into account. It has emphasised that: 'In line with the Treaty on European Union and the Constitution for Europe, the Commission will recommend the suspension of negotiations in the case of a serious and persistent breach of the principles of liberty, democracy, respect for human rights and fundamental

the Treaty of Nice would require the amendment of carefully negotiated majorities and institutional structures. On the other hand, accession under the terms of the Constitutional Treaty would not require substantial adjustment, as the treaty envisages a flexible solution that can easily accommodate new Member States. A good example of such flexibility is Article I-25 TCE, which provides for a qualified majority of 55 per cent of the members of the Council comprising 65 per cent of the population of the Member States. Therefore, accession under the terms of the Constitutional Treaty would entail less bargaining and more consideration of what the new membership would mean in terms of the voice of the incumbent Member States.

The impact of the Constitutional Treaty on the Croatian side does not seem to be significant. The process of harmonisation has just entered the screening phase, and public opinion is not yet sensitive to potential differences. In either case, accession to the European Union will require a referendum, although it is not clear whether the Constitutional Treaty would be subject to a referendum in the case of accession under the terms of the Treaty of Nice. For the time being, public debate in Croatia is focused on the impact of accession on national sovereignty and the voluntary withdrawal clause envisaged by Article I-60 TCE seems to have been well received. In any case, both Croatian public opinion and the political elite support membership of the European Union, at least in general, as witnessed by the recent political alliance of the two largest political parties.[122]

6. CONCLUDING REMARKS

Croatia's relationship with the European Union has developed from almost complete isolation to the opening of membership negotiations. During this process, the European Union has developed several benchmarking instruments that control the dynamics of integration and link it to progress in meeting European criteria. There is a clear trend towards the expansion of conditionality policy from a political to a contractual form, and from human rights conditionality to other areas, such as regional cooperation. In addition, the national enforcement of conditionality, such as making the ratification of the SAA contingent on compliance with political criteria is accepted by the Union insofar as it furthers the common interests of the Union.[123] Although this approach has often proven to be

---

freedoms and the rule of law on which the Union is founded.' See Commission Communication, loc. cit. n. 39, at p. 6.

122 See *Jutarnji List*, 29 January 2005, p. 3. The Social Democrats and the HDZ entered into an 'Alliance for Europe'.

123 This is concluded from the reaction of the Commission in two cases concerning the national enforcement of conditionality. While the United Kingdom successfully insisted on cooperation with

effective, the effectiveness of the conditionality approach depends largely on acceptance by the associated states of the overarching political goal of joining the European Union. The persistence of the associated states in the pursuit of this goal affects the direction of legislative reform, the intensity of the impetus for legal harmonisation[124] and compliance with other requirements, such as cooperation with the ICTY. The mechanisms of conditionality, as can be seen from the Croatian example, can take the form of joint action, as in the case of CFSP actions,[125] or individual action by Member States that is made possible due to the fact that unanimity is required at each step towards the European Union. However, it should also be noted that conditionality policy has its limits. Croatian public opinion increasingly views it as an expression of the negative sentiment of the European Union towards the country, which creates a danger of political saturation concerning and increasing indifference or even hostility towards the integration process.[126]

In the broader context, the European Union's relationship with Croatia has two distinct –though closely related – dimensions: regional and individual (or country-specific). These dimensions may take the form of policy or legal instruments. After an initial period of incoherent reactions to developments in the region, the Union developed the SAP as a central policy framework that can be differentiated into a number of conditionality policies on, e.g., human rights or regional cooperation.

When they are transformed into legal instruments, these policies become more country-specific, while retaining their inherent regional dimension. The application of conditionality to contractual relations must be seen as an evolutionary process, where a lower level of compliance with EU benchmarks is required in the early stages, gradually increasing in the more advanced ones.[127] Compliance and progress are to be closely monitored and conditioned by the possible suspension of the relationship in case of 'serious non-compliance'.[128]

---

the ICTY, Slovenia was dismissed by the Commission and the Council when it threatened to withdraw support for Croatia's membership due to a minor border dispute.

124 See A. Evans, 'Voluntary Harmonisation in Integration between the European Community and Eastern Europe', 22 *ELR* (1997) pp. 207-208; see also Albi, loc. cit. n. 79, at pp. 198-199.

125 See, e.g., Common Position 2004/694/CFSP of 11 October 2004 on further measures in support of the effective implementation of the mandate of the International Criminal Tribunal for the former Yugoslavia (ICTY), *OJ* 2004 L 315/52 (as amended).

126 As reported by a prominent daily newspaper, *Večernji List*, on 28 February 2005, support for EU membership in Croatia dropped to 47 per cent due to the insistence that the requirement of full cooperation with the ICTY will be satisfied only if a single remaining fugitive is handed over to the ICTY. The Croatian Government insists he is not within the reach of the Croatian authorities, and this is considered to be the only outstanding issue of cooperation.

127 See chapter 3 in this volume.

128 Cf., Council conclusions on the principle of conditionality governing the development of the European Union's relations with certain countries of south-east Europe, *Bull. EU* 4-1997, point 2.2.1.

Table 1: Participation of Croatia in the European Union's external relations and the CFSP

Legal Basis	Format	Model	Form of participation	National sovereignty	Voice
Actual					
Joint Declaration	Diplomacy	International relations	Exchange of information	Formally intact	None
SAA	S&A Council	Transitional model	Possibility to block decisions adopted by unanimity	Formally intact	Low
Thessaloniki Agenda	Diplomacy	International relations	Joining common positions of the EU in the CFSP	Formally intact	Low
Potential					
TEU and TEC (Nice)	Council of Ministers and Commission	Art. 3 TEU; Art. 23 TEC Unanimity/QMV	Place at the table	Shared	Moderate to high
Constitutional Treaty	Council of Ministers, Minister of Foreign Affairs and Commission	Art. III-201 Unanimity/QMV	Place at the table	Shared	Moderate to high

It may also be observed that EU policy towards Croatia and the other states of South-Eastern Europe envisages their gradual inclusion in EU policies as a reward for compliance. As can be seen from the example of external relations and the CFSP, the voice of the SAP countries is minimised at the lower stages of integration and gradually increases in parallel with the progress of integration. This is the opposite of what advocates of national sovereignty in Croatia claim when they argue that EU membership will adversely affect Croatia's national sovereignty.

In conclusion, the SAAs represent the contractual component of the SAP. They build on various aspects and components of EU policy and integrate conditionality in relation to both human rights and regional cooperation. This approach has facilitated a necessary degree of flexibility while subjecting the target states to the same standards of scrutiny. It should be noted that the transition from the policy stage to a contractual relationship is governed by the political assessment of the Commission and the Council and, no less importantly, the Member States, due to unanimity principle. The same holds for progress towards membership of the European Union. As Cremona has noted, the criteria for differentiating between the countries in South-Eastern Europe were based 'entirely on the Community's own assessments', but with reference to individual economic and political progress and compliance with explicit conditions.[129] It appears that Croatia's progress towards possible membership depends on the country's own achievements, but judged by the strict didactic mechanisms of conditionality.

---

[129] See M. Cremona, 'External Policy and the European Economic Constitution', in G. de Búrca and J. Scott, eds., *Constitutional Change in the EU, From Uniformity to Flexibility* (Oxford and Portland, Hart Publishing 2000) pp. 64-65.

CHAPTER 12

THE MEDITERRANEAN COUNTRIES (MOROCCO, ALGERIA, TUNISIA, LIBYA, EGYPT, JORDAN, SYRIA AND LEBANON)

Karolien Pieters*

Relevant legal documents:

Morocco
- Euro-Mediterranean Agreement establishing an association between the European Communities and their Member States, of the one part, and the Kingdom of Morocco, of the other part, *OJ* 2000 L 70/2.

Algeria
- Euro-Mediterranean Agreement establishing an association between the EC and their Member States, of the one part, and the People's Democratic Republic of Algeria, of the other part, *OJ* 2005 L 265/2.

Tunisia
- Euro-Mediterranean Agreement establishing an association between the European Communities and their Member States, of the one part, and the Republic of Tunisia, of the other part, *OJ* 1998 L 97/2.

Libya
- Common Position 1999/261/CFSP of 16 April 1999 defined by the Council on the basis of Article J.2 of the Treaty on European Union concerning Libya, *OJ* 1999 L 103/1.
- Council Common Position 2004/698/CFSP of 14 October 2004 concerning the lifting of restrictive measures against Libya, *OJ* 2004 L 317/40.
- Council Regulation (EC) No. 1786/2004 of 14 October 2004 repealing Regulation (EC) No. 3274/93 preventing the supply of certain goods and services to Libya, *OJ* 2004 L 317/7.

* Researcher, T.M.C. Asser Instituut, The Hague.

S. Blockmans and A. Łazowski (eds.), The European Union and Its Neighbours

Egypt

- Euro-Mediterranean Agreement establishing an association between the European Communities and their Member States, of the one part, and the Arab Republic of Egypt, of the other part, *OJ* 2004 L 304/39.

Jordan

- Euro-Mediterranean Agreement establishing an association between the European Communities and their Member States, of the one part, and the Hashemite Kingdom of Jordan, of the other part, *OJ* 2002 L 129/3.

Syria

Euro-Mediterranean Association Agreement: negotiations concluded, Council to decide on signature.

Lebanon

- Euro-Mediterranean Agreement establishing an association between the European Community and its Member States, of the one part, and the Republic of Lebanon, of the other part, COM (2002) 170 final.
- Interim Agreement on trade and trade-related matters between the European Community, of the one part, and the Republic of Lebanon, of the other part, *OJ* 2002 L 262/2.

1. AN INTRODUCTION TO EURO-MEDITERRANEAN RELATIONS

1.1 Geopolitical characteristics

The Mediterranean region is divided into two subregional groups: the Northern Mediterranean, on the one hand, and the Eastern and Southern Mediterranean on the other. The Northern Mediterranean includes Malta, Cyprus and Turkey. The Eastern and Southern Mediterranean includes the Maghreb countries (Morocco, Algeria, Tunisia and Libya) and the Mashreq countries (Egypt, Jordan, Lebanon, Syria and the Palestinian Authority).[1] The most prominent international region that geographically abuts the Mediterranean region borders the north-western sector of the Mediterranean and is called the European Union.[2]

The close relationship between 'Europe' and the Mediterranean dates back to the days of the Roman Empire, when the *Mare Nostrum* was one functional and

[1] The European Union's relations with Israel and the Palestinian Authority are discussed in the next chapter in this volume.

[2] S.C. Calleya, 'Political and Economic Perceptions in the Euro Mediterranean Area', *The Southeast European Yearbook: 1997-1998* (Athens, EILIAMEP 1998) pp. 147-148.

administrative unit. Since then, both regions have been politically, commercially and culturally linked together. More recent ties are rooted in the colonial era of the 19th and early 20th centuries.[3] Algeria, Tunisia and Syria were occupied by France; Egypt, Cyprus, Gibraltar, Malta and Palestine by Britain; and Libya by Italy. European countries were interested in the Mediterranean countries during the colonial period due to the Mediterranean's position at the crossroads of three continents, where much world trade meets. The Mediterranean countries have been important suppliers to the EU market of natural resources such as gas and petroleum and are key markets for EU exports. Since the beginning of the European integration process, the European Community has played an essential role in the economic development of the Mediterranean countries. Many of the Mediterranean countries have embarked upon a process of economic reform to progressively open their economies. This has led their economies to be further integrated into the international economy. Tunisia, for example, already launched efforts towards promoting a growth strategy based on exports on investments in 1986. Syria, on the contrary, showed little interest in developing a competitive private sector and integration into international trade. An economic reform orientation became more perceptible with the installation of the new Syrian president, Bashar Al-Assad, in 2000.

In contrast, political reforms have lagged behind the economic reforms and it appears that they have also fallen behind political reforms in other regions of the world.[4] A stable and secure Mediterranean region would be in the best interests of Europe, but until today the situation in the region remains unstable and sometimes even volatile. Conflicts in the Mediterranean region have direct consequences for political and social stability in the European Union. Instability in the Mediterranean region has, for example, led to mass migration, fundamentalist extremism, terrorism, drugs and organised crime, which is harmful to the area itself as well as to the European Union. The European Union also fears the spill-over effect of national and interregional conflicts in the Mediterranean region.[5] At present, no Mediterranean country can be regarded as a military threat to Europe, but nearly every Mediterranean country has been involved in some form of military or political conflict with one or more of its neighbours since 1945.[6]

---

[3] R.H. Ginsberg, 'The European Community and the Mediterranean', in J. Lodge, ed., *Institutions and Policies of the European Community* (London, Frances Pinter 1994) pp. 154-160.

[4] R. Pace, 'Democracy, Economic Development and Regional Stability in the Mediterranean region', in P.G. Xuereb, ed., *Euro-Med Integration and the 'Ring of Friends': The Mediterranean's European Challenge*, Vol. IV (Malta, University of Malta, European Documentation and Research Centre 2003) pp. 101-134.

[5] For more information, see R. Aliboni, 'The Geopolitical Implications of the European Neighbourhood Policy', 10 *EFA Rev.* (2005) pp. 1-16.

[6] See Common Strategy 2000/458/CFSP of the European Council of 19 June 2000 on the Mediterranean region, *OJ* 2000 L 183/5. See n. 23 *infra*.

Syria maintained 14,000 troops in Lebanon after the country's civil war (1975-1990). In September 2004, the UN Security Council adopted a resolution in which the United Nations call for the withdrawal of all foreign forces from Lebanon and for free and fair elections in Lebanon without foreign interference. Syria only pulled out its troops in reaction to the killing of former Prime Minister Rafik Hariri on 14 February 2005 and subsequent international pressure. The ensuing political turmoil led to the organisation of free elections, which were won by anti-Syrian coalition led by his son, Sa'ad Hariri. Syria has also been at conflict with Israel ever since the latter occupied the Golan Heights in the Six-Day War of 1967.

Southern Lebanon was occupied by Israel for several years. Israeli forces withdrew from Southern Lebanon in May 2000. The Muslim militant group Hezbollah is still engaged in a conflict with Israel along the Israeli-Lebanese border, concentrated mainly at the Israeli-occupied Sheba Farms. A priority issue in Lebanon is the resettlement of 387,000 UNRWA[7] registered Palestinian refugees, most of whom fled to Lebanon as a result of the 1948 Arab-Israel war.

Egypt carefully monitors the Sinai, the border with Israel and the Gaza Strip and has increased its surveillance drastically since the attack on Taba and other Egyptian resorts in 2004. More bombings struck the Egyptian resort of Sharm-el-Sheikh on 23 July 2005.[8]

Algeria's border with Morocco remains an irritant to bilateral relations as each nation has accused the other of harbouring militants and arms smuggling. In an attempt to improve relations after unilaterally imposing a visa requirement on Algerians in the early 1990s, Morocco lifted the requirement in mid-2004 – a gesture not reciprocated by Algeria. Algeria has suffered primarily from internal conflicts, such as the *coup d'état* in 1992.

Jordan and Tunisia are the only Mediterranean countries that are not involved in neighbouring conflicts but on the contrary are trying to enhance interregional cooperation. Jordan, for example, has signed an economic and trade cooperation agreement and a scientific cooperation agreement with Israel. In Tunisia, the political situation is stable, but human rights organisations criticise a failure to respect the rule of law and fundamental freedoms, including the freedom of association and the freedom of expression.[9]

---

7 United Nations Relief and Works Agency for Palestine Refugees in the Near East.

8 A group citing ties to Al Qaeda issued a claim on an Islamic website.

9 The European Parliament adopted on 29 September 2005 a resolution on Tunisia in which it welcomed the significant economic and social progress made, but expressed its concern regarding the lack of progress on projects related to human rights, women issues, health and justice, ref. P6_TA(2005)0368, available at: <http://www.europarl.europa.eu/registre/seance_pleniere/textes_adoptes/definitif/2005/09-29/0368/P6_TA(2005)0368_EN.doc >.

Table I: Facts and figures regarding the Mediterranean countries (June 2005)

	Area (sq. km)	Population (mln)	Independence	Regime	Head of State
Morocco	446,550	32.7	2 March 1956	Monarchy	King Mohammed II
Algeria	2,381,740	32.5	5 July 1962	Republic	President Bouteflika
Tunisia	163,610	10.1	20 March 1956	Republic	President Ben Ali
Libya	1,759,540	5.76	24 December 1951	Republic	Colonel Al-Qaddafi
Egypt	1,001,450	77.5	22 February 1922	Republic	President Mubarak
Jordan	92,300	5.75	25 May 1946	Monarchy	King Abdallah II
Syria	185,180	18.4	17 April 1946	Republic	President Al-Assad
Lebanon	10,400	3.8	22 November 1943	Republic	President Lahoud

Libya, the only Mediterranean country without formal relations with the European Union, claims more than 32,000 sq km in south-eastern Algeria. Libya's international isolation and its refusal to join the Euro-Mediterranean Partnership (EMP) is an important weakness in the security relations between the Mediterranean region and the European Union. However, Libya recently expressed its desire to join the EMP, but no agreements have been concluded yet.

The Israeli-Palestinian conflict is obviously one of the main threats to security in the Middle East and the Mediterranean region. This key issue will be addressed in the next chapter of this book.

1.2 EC/EU policies and strategies towards the Mediterranean region

The first general European Economic Community (EEC) policy for the region came with the establishment of the Global Mediterranean Policy (GMP), involving all the Mediterranean countries, except Libya, and covering the period from 1976 to 1990.[10] The central pillar of the GMP was free access of manufactured goods from the Mediterranean countries to the European market. In 1976, the EEC concluded bilateral economic protocols with the Maghreb states. Jordan, Syria, Lebanon and Egypt signed similar protocols in 1977. The impact of the GMP was quite modest, due to a crisis in the European textile industry, the enlargement of the EEC to include Spain and Portugal in 1986 and the lack of regional integration. The enlargement of the EEC had negative consequences for the Maghreb countries, since the export patterns of these two groups of countries were quite similar. As a result, the Maghreb countries suffered a significant decline in their European market share. The application of Morocco to join the European Community in 1987 illustrated the Arab's frustration with the lack of regional integration.

The European Community subsequently took a more Mediterranean turn. The New Mediterranean Policy (NMP) was launched in 1992, increasing the amount of development aid and extending trade preferences.[11] By offering equal economic benefits, the European Community hoped that the Mediterranean countries would be too involved in the growing regional prosperity to jeopardise peace. For example, by balancing trade-and-aid benefits between Israel and the Mashreq countries, the European Community believed that a form of peaceful coexistence would develop between the states as a step towards political conciliation.[12] But the NMP did not bring the expected economic growth and development to the Mediterranean region. It did, however, mark two important changes in the European

---

[10] *Bull. EEC* 10-1972, points 151 and 152.

[11] General Report 1992, No. 829 referring back to General Report 1990, No. 718-719.

[12] Ginsberg, loc. cit. n. 3, at p. 162.

approach towards its southern neighbours. Firstly, the European Community's economically oriented cooperation with the Mediterranean countries started to give way to a more political approach. The NMP began to stress the importance of the social and economic development of the region for the security of the Member States in the broadest sense. The Commission also emphasised the importance of regional economic cooperation as a powerful tool in reducing the level of conflict, making peace irreversible and encouraging the people of the region to learn to live in peace. Secondly, the NMP placed a greater emphasis on horizontal south-south cooperation.

In April 1992, the Commission proposed a new regional framework that would gradually lead to a Euro-Maghreb partnership and the creation of a Mediterranean free trade area.[13] Negotiations were started, but the problems in EU-Libya relations and the crisis in Algeria prevented this regional initiative from being successful.

The completion of the Single Market, the creation of the World Trade Organisation (WTO) and concerns about European enlargement towards the East led to the general belief that Europe once again needed a new economic strategy towards the Mediterranean region. In 1994, the Commission sent a Communication to the Council and the European Parliament proposing its policy towards the Mediterranean region.[14] This document proposed an ambitious programme, building on existing economic and political relations between the European Union and the Mediterranean countries. According to this programme, further strengthening of the relations between the European Union and the Mediterranean countries should be achieved through a progressive establishment of a Euro-Mediterranean Economic Area (EMEA), a comprehensive political dialogue and Community-financed activities.[15] This document led to the Barcelona Conference in 1995, where the Barcelona Declaration was adopted, inaugurating the Euro-Mediterranean Partnership (EMP).[16] The EMP is intended, among other things, to establish a Euro-Mediterranean zone of peace and stability, based on respect for democracy, good governance and human rights. The Barcelona Conference took place on 27-28 November 1995 and included the fifteen EU Member States and twelve Mediterranean countries.[17] The countries adopted a Work Programme

---

13 Commission Communication on the future of the relations between the Community and the Maghreb countries, SEC (1992) 401; R. Weltner-Puig, 'Common Foreign and Security Policy in the EU and the Mediterranean Region', Working Paper No. 10, available at: <http://selene.uab.es/_cs_iuee/catala/obs/Working%20Papers/wp102001.html#_ftn14>.

14 Communication from the Commission of 19 October 1994 – Strengthening the Euro-Mediterranean Policy: Establishing a Euro-Mediterranean Partnership, COM (1994) 427 final.

15 F.S. Hakura, 'The Euro-Mediterranean Policy: The Implications of the Barcelona Declaration', 34 *CMLR* (1997) pp. 337-366.

16 *Bull. EU* 11-1995, point 1.3.166; C.M. Salama, 'The Euro-Mediterranean Partnership: Political and Economic Aspects', available at: <http://www.edpsg.org/Documents/Dp23.doc>.

17 Algeria, Cyprus, Egypt, Israel, Jordan, Lebanon, Malta, Morocco, Syria, Tunisia, Turkey and the West Bank and Gaza Strip.

launching a triple partnership: (i) a political and security partnership aiming to establish a common area of peace and stability; (ii) an economic and financial partnership aiming at creating an aria of shared prosperity, mainly through the establishment of a free trade area; and (iii) a social and cultural partnership seeking at a better understanding between cultures and an exchange between civil societies.[18]

Under the EMP, the Mediterranean region stretches from the Atlantic coast of Morocco in the Maghreb, through the Mashreq countries of the Middle East, to Turkey. It includes a country with no Mediterranean border – Jordan – and excludes the Arab country with the longest Mediterranean coastline of all – Libya.[19] In 2004, Cyprus and Malta joined the European Union, and Turkey started accession negotiations shortly after. As a result, the EMP now covers Morocco, Algeria, Tunisia, Egypt, Jordan, Israel, Syria, Lebanon and the Palestinian Authority. The EMP is supervised by the Euro-Mediterranean Conference of Ministers of Foreign Affairs (Euro-Med Conference) and the Euro-Mediterranean Committee for the Barcelona process (Euro-Med Committee).

The seventh Euro-Med Conference was held in Luxembourg on 30-31 May 2005. The Ministers assessed what had been achieved so far and prepared the way for the Extraordinary High Level Meeting that was held in Barcelona on 27-28 November 2005 in order to celebrate the tenth anniversary of the EMP. The Euro-Mediterranean Summit in Barcelona reached agreement on a Five-Year Work Programme for the further development of the partnership as well as on a Code of Conduct on Countering Terrorism. The Work Programme will allow work in the regional, Euro-Med framework to progress in full synergy and complementarity with the bilateral Action Plans developed under the European Neighbourhood Policy. The Code of Conduct, bringing Europeans, Arabs and Israelis together, highlights the common commitment to fighting terrorism in all its dimensions.[20]

The Euro-Med Committee consists of the EU troika and a representative from each of the MED partners. The Committee mainly discusses the agenda and work programme of the EMP. The different activities listed in the work programme are followed up by *ad hoc* sectoral meetings of ministers, senior officials and experts.

The parliamentary dimension of the EMP is well developed ever since the establishment of a Euro-Mediterranean Parliamentary Assembly (EMPA). The Euro-Mediterranean Parliamentary Forum for parliamentarians, which was set up

---

[18] For an assessment of the EMP, see F. Attina, 'The Euro-Mediterranean Partnership Assessed: The Realist and Liberal views', 8 *EFA Rev.* (2003) pp. 181-199; and E. Philippart, 'The Euro-Mediterranean Partnership: A Critical Evaluation of an Ambitious Scheme', 8 *EFA Rev.* (2003) pp. 201-220.

[19] J. Marks, 'High Hopes and Low Motives: The New Euro-Mediterranean Partnership Initiative', 1 *Mediterranean Politics* (1996) p. 1.

[20] *Euromed Report* (2005) pp. 1-17.

in 1998, declared in 2002 that the forum should become a parliamentary assembly. This proposal was accepted during the 6th Euro-Med Conference on 2-3 December 2003 in Naples and resulted in the creation of EMPA, which is meant to meet at least once a year to deliberate on developments in the Barcelona process. Three committees, focusing on politics and security, economic and financial affairs and culture carry out the preparatory work for the plenary sessions. A bureau, of which chairmanship rotates annually, supervises the plenary. The first plenary session of EMPA was held from 12 to 15 March 2005 in Cairo. Delegations from the thirty-five Euro-Mediterranean partner states' parliaments and the European Parliament attended and adopted various resolutions. During the last week of March 2006, the EMPA met again in Brussels. MPs from thirty-five countries discussed issues of common concern to people from both shores of the Mediterranean: the Israeli-Palestinian peace process, freedom of speech due to the cartoon crisis, respect for religious beliefs and development. At the meeting, EP President Josep Borrell said he was 'more convinced than ever that Europe's relations with the Muslim world will be the major challenge facing Europe in the years ahead', explaining that the Mediterranean region is on the one hand 'extremely dynamic' and on the other hand 'becoming increasingly fragile'.

Besides this multilateral framework, the European Union is also tied to the Mediterranean countries at bilateral level, via Association Agreements (AAs).[21] These AAs are first and foremost a tool for reforming the economic systems of the Mediterranean countries and aim to create a Euro-Med free trade area by 2010. The establishment of a Euro-Med free trade area not only entails a bilateral vertical trade liberalisation with Europe, but also a horizontal trade liberalisation between the Mediterranean countries themselves.[22] Therefore, the conclusion of bilateral AAs between the European Community and the Mediterranean countries in order to create a free trade zone by 2010 is not sufficient. In addition, free trade agreements between the Mediterranean countries themselves are required to exploit the region's potential for economic growth. The Barcelona Declaration also strongly supports the South-South dimension, as the integration of Mediterranean economies may lead to peace and stability in the region. The EU emphasises the achievement of economic integration in order to inhibit future wars in the Mediterranean. The obvious example here is the creation of the EEC as a way to discourage conflict between France and Germany after World War II.

---

21 For a legal overview of the Euro-Med AAs, see *infra* section 2.

22 Barcelona Declaration, adopted at the Euro-Mediterranean Conference of 27-28 November 1995, available at: <http://europa.eu.int/comm/external_relations/euromed/bd.htm#5>. In addition, all AAs stress the importance of regional cooperation. Art. 50 AA Algeria, for example, stipulates as follows: 'In order to maximise the impact of this Agreement *vis-à-vis* the development of the Euro-Mediterranean partnership and within the countries of the Maghreb, the Parties shall foster all activities which have a regional impact or involve third countries …'.

Since 1995, a number of actions have been taken to intensify the South-South dimension of the Barcelona process. Several free trade agreements have been signed between Mediterranean countries. For example, the Agadir Initiative, which was launched in May 2001, is a regional free trade agreement including Egypt, Jordan, Morocco and Tunisia.

The European Union reaffirmed the EMP and the Barcelona Declaration of 1995 in its Common Strategy towards the Mediterranean Region (CS), which was adopted at the Feira European Council in June 2000.[23] The CS built further on the existing framework of the EMP. It covered all EU relations with all its partners in the Barcelona process, as well as Libya, but excluding Cyprus and Malta, which joined the European Union in May 2004, and Turkey, since these relations were covered by the accession process. The CS complemented the EMP and the bilateral relations between the European Community and the Mediterranean countries. The broad scope of this document is surprising: as an instrument of the CFSP it would have been reasonable to find in it only the political and security aspects of the EMP, but it went beyond these limits. The CS also covered economic and social measures and even measures in the field of justice and home affairs. A similar approach appears to have been taken in the European Union's dealings with Ukraine and Russia. According to the CS, the European Union had the following goals in its policy towards the Mediterranean region: (1) to make significant and measurable progress towards achieving the objectives of the Barcelona Declaration; (2) to make use of the evolving common European policy on security and defence to strengthen, together with its Mediterranean partners, cooperative security in the region; (3) to contribute to peace in the Middle East region and develop the basis for a good neighbourly relationship between the parties; and (4) to increase the effectiveness, impact and visibility of EU actions and initiatives in the region. Part IV of the CS mentions all the instruments and means for implementing the CS. The CS was not only meant to be implemented by EU institutions, but also the Member States themselves were meant to contribute to the objectives of the CS by making use of all their relevant instruments and means. The European Parliament has been very critical of the CS. It regretted the fact that it was not involved in the drafting of the document and that it was offered no role. It also considered that the instruments and means for implementing

[23] Common Strategy 2000/458/CFSP of the European Council of 19 June 2000 on the Mediterranean region, *OJ* 2000 L 183/5. The application of the Common Strategy, which was applied for an initial period of four years, was prolonged for eighteen months until 23 January 2006 by Decision 2004/763/CFSP of the European Council of 5 November 2004 amending Common Strategy 2000/458/CFSP on the Mediterranean region in order to extend the period of its application, *OJ* 2004 L 337/72. No new decisions have been adopted to extend the Common Strategy's period of application, so it must be assumed that it has been silently replaced by the ENP. See section 5 *infra* and also chapter 19 in this volume.

the CS were vague and criticised the absence of a budgetary framework for financing the CS. Most significantly it regretted the exclusion of the free movement of persons and of agricultural products from the partnership.[24]

The EU enlargement process, the accession of Malta and Cyprus and the 'waiting room' position of Turkey have incited the European Union to reassess its relations with the countries on its southern and eastern borders that will not be joining the European Union in the near future.[25] Accordingly, the new European Neighbourhood Policy (ENP) was launched in 2002.[26] The ENP does not aim to replace the existing framework of the EMP, but intends to supplement and revitalise it.[27] The ENP includes individual action plans that aim to help promote democracy, good governance, the rule of law and human rights as well as to provide support for economic modernisation in the neighbouring countries. These plans, which build on the existing AAs, provide an agenda for working with the European Union for the next three to five years. The implementation of the plans will be taken forward to a large extent by the subcommittees set up in the framework of each AA. Following this, the European Union will examine the scope for new Neighbourhood Agreements, which will not replace the existing AAs, but will supplement and build on existing contractual relations.[28] Consultations with Morocco, Tunisia, Jordan, Israel and the Palestinian Authority concerning action plans were finalised in December 2004. The first action plans under the ENP (Israel, Jordan, Morocco, the Palestinian Authority and Tunisia) were approved by the Commission on 9 December 2004.[29]

---

24 Committee on Foreign Affairs, Human Rights, Common Security and Defence Policy, Report on the Common Strategy of the EU on the Mediterranean Region, 22 January 2001; Salama, loc. cit. n. 16.

25 R.A. Del Sarto and T. Schumacher, 'From EMP to ENP: What's at Stake with the European Neighbourhood Policy towards the Southern Mediterranean?', 10 *EFA Rev.* (2005) pp. 17-38. The enlargement of the European Union is the proximate motivation for the ENP, but the European Security Strategy document points out that it is in the European interest that countries on our borders are well-governed, see also Aliboni, loc. cit. n. 5, at pp. 1-16. The Mediterranean countries that fall under the scope of the ENP are Morocco, Algeria, Jordan, Egypt, Tunisia, Lebanon, Syria, Israel and the West Bank and Gaza Strip. Libya is not a member of the ENP, but was invited to become a full member of the EMP. Libya did not accept membership, in particular because of the disagreement over the position of Israel and the Palestinian Authority, and has at present an observer status with regard to the Barcelona process. Libya has recently announced that it has begun working towards full entry into the EMP.

26 Communication from the Commission of 11 March 2003 on a Wider Europe – Neighbourhood: A Framework for Relations with our Eastern and Southern Neighbours, COM (2003) 104 final; Communication from the Commission – European Neighbourhood Policy – Strategy Paper of 12 May 2004, COM (2004) 373 final. For further information, see section 5.

27 Conclusions for the 7th Euro-Mediterranean Conference of Ministers of Foreign Affairs, Luxembourg, 30-31 May 2005, p. 15.

28 COM (2003) 104 final.

29 Communication from the Commission to the Council of 9 December 2004 on the Commission proposals for Action Plans under the European Neighbourhood Policy, COM (2004) 795 final.

The CFSP was lacking strategic clarity, a clear definition of its interests and long-term policy objectives. In 2003, therefore, the European Union released a European Security Strategy (ESS), the first ever comprehensive strategic vision of the Member States.[30] The ESS was mainly drafted as a response to the attack on the World Trade Centre on 11 September 2001 and the deadly Madrid rail bombings on 11 March 2004, but also with a view to the approaching enlargement of the European Union in May 2004. The integration of acceding states was expected to increase security in Europe but also bring the European Union closer to trouble areas. The ESS therefore aimed to promote a ring of well-governed countries to the east of the European Union and on the borders of the Mediterranean. In the ESS, the European Union sums up the new global threats that Europe faces, some of which emerge from the Mediterranean region: (1) Europe is both a target and base for terrorism linked to violent religious regimes; (2) Proliferation of weapons of mass destruction is potentially the greatest threat to EU security. The possibility of a WMD arms race is growing, especially in the Middle East. Advances in the biological sciences may increase the potency of biological weapons in the coming years, and there is also a serious possibility of chemical or radiological attacks; (3) Regional conflicts, such as in the Middle East, impact directly and indirectly on European interests; (4) State failure, such as the collapse of state institutions in Somalia and Liberia, just to the south of the Mediterranean, is alarming and adds to regional instability; and (5) Europe is also a prime target for organised crime, such as cross-border trafficking in drugs, women, illegal migrants and weapons. In Part II, the ESS mentions three actions which the European Union will take to defend its security. Firstly, it will address these threats and will, for example, continue taking measures to tighten export controls and deal with illegal shipments and illicit procurement. Secondly, the European Union will build security in its neighbourhood. The resolution of the Arab-Israeli conflict, for example, is a strategic priority for Europe. The European Union must also continue its engagement with the Mediterranean countries through more effective economic, security and cultural cooperation, since the Mediterranean area continues to experience serious problems of economic stagnation, social unrest and unresolved conflicts. Thirdly, the European Union must establish an international order based on effective multilateralism. In this context, the EU requests countries that have placed themselves outside the bounds of international society and have sought isolation, such as Libya, to join the international community.

In 2003, the EU Member States requested a strengthening of the partnership between the European Union and the Arab world. A note, entitled 'Reinforcing the partnership between the EU and the Arab World', was issued by Javier Solana,

---

30 *Bull. EU* 12-2003, point 1.32.83 and 84.

Chris Patten and Romano Prodi in December 2003.[31] The note concluded that this strategy would complement the EMP and the ENP. The partnership will build on tested instruments such as the EMP and the European Union's work with the Gulf Cooperation Council (GCC). It will also serve as a complementary EU contribution to match the Greater Middle East Initiative launched by the United States under G-8 auspices. After intensive consultations with the regional partners, the European Strategic Partnership document was adopted by the EU Council on 18 June 2004.[32] It sets out a concrete policy agenda under which, through partnership and dialogue, and by recognising diversities, the Union will seek to: (i) promote political reform, good governance, democracy and human rights; (ii) stimulate trade and economic cooperation, economic liberalisation and people-to-people contacts; and (iii) promote conflict prevention and resolution in the Mediterranean and the Middle East as well as measures to combat terrorism, proliferation of weapons of mass destruction and illegal immigration. The strategy will take into account the differentiation requirements of individual countries in the region – it is not a 'one size fits all' approach. Furthermore, it is stated that the EMP and the ENP will remain the cornerstones of Euro-Mediterranean relations.

2. LEGAL ANALYSIS OF THE ASSOCIATION AGREEMENTS

All the Mediterranean countries have concluded AAs with the European Community that are based on Article 310 TEC.[33] They cover trade in industrial and agricultural goods, trade in services and the right of establishment, payments and capital movements, competition, intellectual property rights, financial cooperation, economic cooperation, agriculture and investments, transportation, telecommunications and energy, science and technology, environment and tourism, statistics and the fight against illegal drugs. Before the Barcelona process started, the European Community and its Member States had already signed an AA with Tunisia on 17 July 1995, which came into force on 1 March 1998 after being ratified by all fifteen EU Member States. In the framework of the Barcelona process, the European Community and its Member States signed an AA with Morocco on 26 February 1996, which entered in force on 1 March 2000, with Jordan on 24 November 1997, which came into force on 1 May 2002, with Egypt

[31] Reinforcing the partnership between the EU and the Arab World, 9 December 2003, CFSP 791, Press Release, Brussels, 9 December 2003, No. 15945/03.

[32] EU Strategic Partnership with the Mediterranean and the Middle East, June 2004.

[33] Art. 310 TEC: 'The Community may conclude with one or more States or international organisations agreements establishing an association involving reciprocal rights and obligations, common action and special procedure.' See also R. Leal-Arcas, 'The European Community and Mixed Agreements', 6 *EFA Rev.* (2001) pp. 483-513.

on 25 June 2001, which came into force on 1 June 2004, with Algeria on 22 April 2002, which came into force on 1 September 2005, and with Lebanon on 17 June 2002, which entered into force on 1 April 2006. The European Community signed an interim agreement on trade and trade-related matters with Lebanon, which entered into force on 1 March 2003, for the early implementation of trade measures.[34] The negotiations with Syria started in 1998. In 2002, after four years of negotiations, a compromise was reached on all topics except on the provisions concerning the non-proliferation of weapons of mass destruction. This issue was discussed again during the negotiations in 2003. Finally, an agreement on the text for these provisions was agreed in September 2004. At the end of 2004, the AA Syria was submitted to the political authorities on both sides for final approval and signature.

2.1 Institutional provisions

All AAs establish an Association Council and an Association Committee. The Council consists of the EU Council, members of the European Commission and members of the government of the Mediterranean country in question. The Council shall try to settle all disputes relating to the application or interpretation of the AA. The AAs establish an *ad hoc* dispute settlement body if the Council fails to settle the dispute. Each party[35] may notify the other of the appointment of an arbiter. The other party must then appoint another arbiter. The Council itself shall appoint a third arbiter. The arbiter's decision shall be taken by majority vote. The Council shall also examine any major issue arising from the AA and any other bilateral or international issue of interest; it may decide to set up any working group necessary for the implementation of the AA;[36] and it may delegate all its power to the Committee. The Council may take decisions that are binding upon the parties and make appropriate recommendations.[37]

The Committee consists of representatives of EU Member States and the European Commission, on the one hand, and representatives of the Mediterranean country in question, on the other. The Committee is responsible for the implementation of the AA. The Committee also has the power to take decisions relating

---

[34] *OJ* 2000 L 262/02.

[35] The European Community and the Member States count as one party to a dispute.

[36] See, for example, Proposal for a Council Decision of 15 May 2005 on a Community position in the Association Council on the implementation of Art. 67 and Art. 80 of the Euro-Mediterranean Agreement establishing an association between the EC and their Member States, of the one part, and the Arab Republic of Egypt, of the other part, COM (2005) 188 final. This proposal sets up a working group on migration, social and consular affairs and subcommittees attached to the Association Committee.

[37] The Council shall, for example, take appropriate measures to facilitate the cooperation and contacts between the European Parliament and the parliament of the Mediterranean country.

to the management of the agreement, as well as in those areas in which the Association Council has delegated its powers. The decisions will be binding upon the parties. The Council and the Committee meet on a regular basis and the technical subcommittees guarantee practical implementation.

In its Communication of 12 April 2005, the Commission announced that substantial progress had been made at the institutional level of the EMP in comparison to the sporadic contacts at the time of the launch of the EMP in 1995.[38] The Commission is also of the opinion that the EMP's institutional structure will provide a solid basis for the ENP. The Ministers of Foreign Affairs of the EU Member States and the Mediterranean countries shared exactly the same opinion as the Commission during the 7th Euro-Med Conference in Luxemburg on 30-31 May 2005.[39] The Commission and the Ministers seem satisfied with the current institutional structure of the partnership. They do not question the functioning of the Euro-Med institutions nor have they put it on their agenda for the near future. These opinions are not shared by all. Sharon Pardo and Lior Zemer argue that the current institutions do not reflect the objectives of the EMP and stress that the EMP needs to be institutionally restructured to meet the challenges of the EMP and the ENP. They design a new institutional mechanism for the ENP and declare that all institutions should be based in Valetta, since Malta is located at the heart of the European Neighbourhood Space.[40]

2.2 Political provisions

2.2.1 *Human rights*

All AAs provide that the relations between the parties, as well as all the provisions of the AA itself, shall be based on respect of democratic principles and fundamental human rights as set out in the Universal Declaration on Human Rights. Respect for democracy and human rights constitutes an 'essential element' of all AAs.[41] This 'essential element' clause, along with an addition article on action to be taken in the event of non-compliance with an obligation under the AA,[42] allows each party to take measures in response to a failure on the part of the other to respect democratic principles and human rights.

---

[38] COM (2005) 139/18.

[39] Conclusions of the 7th Euro-Mediterranean Conference of Ministers of Foreign Affairs, Luxembourg, 30-31 May 2005, p. 2.

[40] S. Pardo and L. Zemer, 'Towards a New Euro-Mediterranean Neighbourhood Space', 10 *EFA Rev.* (2005) pp. 39-77.

[41] A. Ward, 'Frameworks for Cooperation between the European Union and Third States: A Viable Matrix for Uniform Human Rights Standards?', 3 *EFA Rev.* (1998) pp. 505-507.

[42] The non-compliance clause is generally worded as follows: 'if either party considers that the other party has failed to fulfil an obligation under the Agreement, it may take appropriate measures.

The Commission's Communication of May 2001 placed the promotion of democracy, the rule of law and respect for human rights in the context of the Commission's overall strategic approach to external relations.[43] The Commission also invited the European Union to place a higher premium on human rights and democratisation in its relations with third countries and to take a more proactive approach. The Commission's Communication of May 2003, specifically aimed at the Mediterranean countries, stresses the importance of cooperation in the field of human rights and democratisation.[44] In its most recent Communication of 2005, which is also related to human rights, the Commission proposes to hold a Euro-Med Conference at subregional level on human rights and democratisation in 2006.[45] The Commission also proposed a 'Democracy Facility' that will serve to promote, support and reward those Mediterranean countries that show a clear commitment to common values and to agreed political reform priorities. This facility would go beyond the specific support that may be mobilised under regional or national action plans and should enter into force in 2007.

2.2.2 *Political dialogue*

All AAs contain a political chapter.[46] The political dialogue between the parties aims to (1) develop a better mutual understanding and an increasing convergence of positions on international issues, in particular those issues likely to have substantial effects on the parties; (2) enable each party to consider the position and interest of the other; (3) enhance regional security and stability; (4) contribute to consolidation security and stability in the Euro-Mediterranean region; and (5) promote common initiatives. The dialogue shall be established at ministerial level or at the level of senior officials and shall take place at regular intervals and whenever necessary.

Before so doing, except in case of special urgency, it shall supply the Association Council with all relevant information required for a thorough examination of the situation with a view to seeking a solution acceptable for the parties. In the selection of measures, priority must be given to those which least disturb the functioning of the Agreement. These measures shall be notified immediately to the Association Council and shall be subject of consultations within the Association Council and shall be the subject of consultations within the Association Council if the other party so requests.'

43 Communication from the Commission of 8 May 2001 on the European Union's Role in Promoting Human Rights and Democratisation in Third Countries, COM (2001) 252 final.

44 Communication from the Commission of 21 May 2003 on Reinvigorating EU actions on Human Rights and Democratisation with the Mediterranean Partners, COM (2003) 294 final.

45 Communication from the Commission to the Council and the European Parliament, 10th Anniversary of the Euro-Mediterranean Partnership: A work programme to meet the challenges of the next five years, COM (2005) 139/5.

46 M. Fouwels, 'The European Union's Common Foreign and Security Policy and Human Rights', 34 *Netherlands Quarterly of Human Rights* (1997) p. 291 at pp. 296-301.

2.3 The establishment of a Euro-Med free trade area

All AAs provide that the European Community and the Mediterranean country shall gradually establish a free trade area over a transitional period lasting a maximum of twelve years, starting from the date of entry into force of the agreement.[47] The free trade area shall be based on the provisions of the AA itself, as well as on the provisions of the General Agreement on Tariffs and Trade (GATT), the General Agreement on Services (GATS) and the provisions of the annexes to the WTO Agreement.[48] The free trade area will be gradually established through the free movement of goods, services and capital.

2.3.1 *Free movement of goods, services and capital*

2.3.1.1 The 'goods provision' in the Association Agreements[49]

All AAs ensure the free movement of goods.[50] Without prejudice to the provisions of the GATT: (i) no new quantitative restrictions on imports and measures having equivalent effect shall be introduced in trade between the European Community

---

47 Art. 6 of the AAs.

48 Except for Syria which is not a member of the WTO.

49 Rules of origin are specific provisions in the AAs created to determine the country where the goods are made. Only goods made in the Mediterranean country or the European Union enjoy the preferential trade regime of the free trade area. The European Union has decided to extend the system of pan-European cumulation of origin (also called diagonal cumulation) to the Mediterranean countries, provided that these countries have initiated negotiations among themselves to set up free trade areas and have harmonised their rules of origin with those of the European Union. Diagonal cumulation allows for materials supplied by specific countries which are not parties to the AA to be counted as 'domestic'. Therefore, a 'pan-Euro-Mediterranean' protocol on rules of origin was developed in a working group with the European Community and all the Mediterranean countries. This protocol was endorsed by the Euro-Med Trade Ministerial Meeting in Palermo on 7 July 2003.

50 The AA Algeria shall serve as an example. Art. 8 provides: 'Products originating in Algeria shall be imported into the Community free of customs duties and charges having equivalent effect.' Art. 9(1) provides: 'Custom duties and charges having equivalent effect applicable on import into Algeria of products originating in the Community listed in Annex 2 shall be abolished upon the entry into force of this Agreement.' Art. 9(2) provides: 'Custom duties and charges having equivalent effect applicable on import into Algeria of products originating in the Community shall be progressively abolished in accordance with the following timetable: ...'. Art. 9(3) provides: 'Custom duties and charges having equivalent effect applicable on import into Algeria of products originating in the Community other than those listed in Annexes 2 and 3 shall be progressively abolished in accordance with the following timetable: ...'. Art. 17(1), (2) and (3) provides: 'No new customs duties on imports or exports or charges having equivalent effect shall be introduced in trade between the Community and Algeria, nor shall those already applied upon entry into force of this Agreement be increased. No new quantitative restrictions on imports or exports or measure having the equivalent effect shall be introduced in trade between the Community and Algeria. Quantitative restrictions on imports or exports and measures having equivalent effect in trade between Algeria and the Community shall be abolished upon entry into force of this Agreement.'

and the Mediterranean country; (ii) quantitative restrictions on imports and measures having equivalent effect in trade between the Mediterranean country and the European Community shall be abolished progressively upon entry into force of the agreement; (iii) neither the European Community nor the Mediterranean country shall apply to the other's exports customs duties or charges having equivalent effect or measures of equivalent effect. The provisions concerning the abolition of customs duties on imports shall also apply to customs duties of a fiscal nature. Similar to Article 30 TEC,[51] the parties to the AAs may derogate from the principle of free movement of goods on the grounds of:[52] (i) public morality, public policy or public security; (ii) the protection of the life and health of humans, animals or plants; (iii) the protection of national treasures possessing artistic, historic or architectural value; (iv) the protection of intellectual, industrial or commercial property; and (v) rules related to gold and silver and the conservation of exhaustible natural resources.[53] The Mediterranean region is sensitive to religion and culture. When the Mediterranean countries believe that religion or culture are undermined by certain trading activities, they are likely to impose trade restrictions, especially on the grounds of public morality and public policy, and are given wide liberty by the European Community for doing so.[54] The derogations, however, must not constitute a means of arbitrary discrimination or disguised restriction on trade between the parties.

The free trade area in *industrial goods* between Europe and the Mediterranean countries is of an asymmetrical nature. This means that the European markets will be opened more rapidly to traders from the Mediterranean countries than the Mediterranean markets to the European traders. Imports into the European Union are free of all customs duties and equivalent charges upon the entry into force of the AAs. The Mediterranean countries, on the other hand, will gradually abolish customs duties on industrial goods in accordance to a timetable that is different for each category of product. Some products will enter the Mediterranean countries without customs duties upon the entry into force of the AA, others will enter the Mediterranean countries without custom duties only several years after the entry into force of the AA and some will only be liberalised at the moment of the

51 According to established case law, a mere similarity in the wording of a provision of the EC Treaty and an international agreement between the European Community and a non-member country is not sufficient to give to the wording of that agreement the same meaning as it has in the EC Treaty, see ECJ, Case 270/80 *Polydor and RSO* [1982] *ECR* 329, paras. 14 to 21; Case 104/81 *Kupferberg* [1982] *ECR* 3641, paras. 29 to 31; and Case C-312/91 *Metalsa* [1993] *ECR* I-3751, paras. 11 to 20.

52 Art. 27 AA Algeria; Art. 28 AA Morocco; Art. 28 AA Tunisia; Art. 26 AA Egypt; Art. 27 AA Jordan; Art. 27 AA Lebanon.

53 The derogation for the conservation of the exhaustible natural resources is only provided for in the AA with Lebanon (Art. 27 AA Lebanon).

54 F.S. Hakura, *EU-Mediterranean and Gulf Trade Agreements* (Isle of Wight, Palladian Law Publishing 1999).

establishment of the free trade zone. All AAs contain an 'infant industry clause' or safeguard clause.[55] This means that the Mediterranean countries may take exceptional measures which derogate from the general provisions on the liberalisation of industrial imports. The Mediterranean countries are allowed to increase or reintroduce customs duties under certain conditions.[56] The insertion of the 'infant industry clause' is another example of the asymmetric nature of the liberalisation of industrial goods between the European Community and the Mediterranean countries. The European Community and all Mediterranean countries provide that they shall progressively establish a greater liberalisation of their trade in *agricultural, fisheries and processed agricultural products*.[57] The Mediterranean countries will liberalise trade in agricultural products, fisheries products and industrial products with an agricultural component according to agreed schedules in the relevant Mediterranean country. Some of these products therefore remain subject to custom charges and quotas.[58]

All AAs have a similar provision concerning quantitative restrictions and measures having equivalent effect.[59] The provision forbids 'direct' and 'indirect' restrictions to trade between the European Community and the Mediterranean country in question. 'Direct' restrictions concern quotas or other bans related to the quantity of trade in industrial goods between the European Community and the country concerned. 'Indirect' restrictions or 'measures having the same effect as quantitative restrictions' are less clear and thus more controversial.[60] In the

---

55 'Anti-dumping and Safeguards in the Euro-Mediterranean Association Agreements', study carried out by Driessen, Vermulst and Waer in collaboration with UNCTAD Technical Cooperation Project on Trade Relations and Economic Cooperation in the Mediterranean Region (INT/93/A34), April 1998.

56 (i) The exceptional measures are intended for new and infant industries, or sectors undergoing restructuring or facing serious difficulties, particularly where these difficulties entail major social problems; (ii) these duties may not exceed 25 per cent of the value of the product and an element of preference for the products of EU origin must be contained; and (iii) the duties must be temporary and cannot be introduced in respect of a product if more than three years have elapsed since the elimination of all duties and quantitative restrictions or charges or measures having equivalent effect concerning that product.

57 See, for example, Art. 13 AA Lebanon.

58 The Commission's Communication on its new neighbourhood policy in an enlarged Europe also points out that there is still room to deepen the Euro-Mediterranean AAs in the domain of trade in agricultural products.

59 See, for example, Art. 18(1), (2) and (3) AA Jordan: 'No new quantitative restrictions on imports and measures having equivalent effect shall be introduced in trade between the Community and Jordan. Quantitative restrictions on imports and measures having equivalent effect on trade between the Community and Jordan shall be abolished upon entry into force of this Agreement. The Community and Jordan shall not apply to exports between themselves either customs duties or charges having equivalent effect, or quantitative restrictions or measures having equivalent effect.'

60 The abolition of measures having equivalent effect to quantitative restrictions has proved to be one main barriers to the implementation of the principle of free movement of goods between the Member States of the European Union. Due to the specific aims of the Association Agreements

Polydor case,[61] the ECJ ruled that the provision for the unconditional abolition of certain restrictions, such as quantitative restrictions and measures having the equivalent effect in the AA, does not have the same purpose as the similar provision in the EC Treaty.[62] The ECJ has given a more restrictive interpretation to the provision in the AA than to the similar provision in the EC Treaty. This provision only applies to goods which are totally liberalised, such as industrial goods. Other goods, such as agricultural products, fisheries products and industrial products with an agricultural element, can still be subject to quantitative restrictions or measures having the same effect.

2.3.1.2 The 'services provision' and 'establishment rights' in the Association Agreements

All AAs include a 'services provision' and an 'establishment' provision.[63] The AAs contain provisions related to trade in services, such as the cross-border supply of services by European or Mediterranean companies, the temporal presence of European or Mediterranean natural persons, exceptions in the field of transport (air transport, inland waterways and maritime transport), the application of domestic regulation and a provision with an overview of all relevant definitions. The AAs also define the right of establishment and the supply of services. The provisions in the AAs with Morocco, Tunisia and Egypt differ from the provisions in the AAs with Algeria, Lebanon, Jordan,[64] as the former were members of the WTO at the time of the drafting of the AAs. These countries could basically refer to the services provisions as provided for in GATS. The other Mediterranean countries had to create a legal framework concerning the free movement of services and the right of establishment for themselves.

Pursuant to the services provision in the AAs with Morocco, Tunisia and Egypt, the Association Council will take the necessary steps to broaden the scope of the AA to free movement of services and establishment rights.[65] The Association

---

discussed here, it is questionable to what extent the case law of the European Court of Justice on Articles 28-30 of the EC Treaty may be of relevance for the interpretation of agreements.

61 ECJ, Case 270/80 *Polydor and RSO* [1982] *ECR* 329. The *Polydor* case concerned the import into the European Community of gramophone records from Portugal, where they had been purchased from the exclusive licensee for that country. They were then sold in the United Kingdom without the consent of the copyright holder or his exclusive licensee in the United Kingdom. At the time in question, Portugal was not a member of the EEC.

62 Ibid.

63 The Commission adopted a proposal to open negotiations on the liberalisation of services and investment with the Mediterranean countries on 23 June 2005 (SEC (2005) 787/F of 24 June 2005). This marks an important step towards the creation of the free trade area between Europe and the Mediterranean.

64 The official AA Syria has not been published yet.

65 Art. 30 AA Egypt, Art. 31 AA Morocco and Art. 31 AA Tunisia.

Council will take measures to grant service suppliers the right to supply services and establish firms under the same laws, rules and regulations accorded to national suppliers or firms. In doing this, the Association Council has to take into account all the relevant provisions of GATS, especially the provisions in Article V GATS.[66]

Algeria, Lebanon and Syria are not members of the WTO. Jordan was not a member of the WTO at the time of the signing of its AA with the European Community in 1997.[67] These Mediterranean countries inserted a different services provision in their AAs, since they could not simply refer to GATS, in general, and MFN treatment, in particular. Algeria and Jordan drafted a similar legal framework to the services provisions provided for in GATS. The AA Jordan provides that the European Community and its Member States shall grant for the establishment of Jordanian companies, subsidiaries and branches a treatment no less favourable than that accorded to like companies, subsidiaries and branches of any third country. Jordan shall grant for the establishment of Community companies, subsidiaries and branches a treatment no less favourable than that accorded to its own companies or to companies of any third country, whichever is better.[68] The agreement includes reservation lists in which both Jordan and the European Community sum up the sectors that are not open for investment.[69] The AA Algeria contains similar provisions, but does not include reservation lists.[70] Lebanon only inserted a referral to the obligations under GATS which will take effect from the date of its accession to the WTO. For the time being, Lebanon and the European Community will refrain from taking measures that will render the conditions of supply of services more discriminatory that those existing on the date of entry into force of the AA Lebanon.[71]

The AAs with Morocco, Tunisia and Egypt do not include derogations from the free movement of services and the right of establishment, since it is the task of

---

[66] Art. V GATS allows members to enter into an agreement liberalising services, provided that the agreement has substantial sectoral coverage and provides for the elimination of substantially all discrimination in the sectors covered in paragraph (a) of Art. XVII GATS by prohibiting new discriminatory measures and elimination existing ones.

[67] Jordan has been a member of the WTO since 11 April 2000.

[68] Art. 30 AA Jordan.

[69] The European Community, for example, is not committed to granting national treatment conditions to subsidiaries of Jordanian companies in the field of mining, fishing, real estate purchase, audio-visual services including radio, telecommunications services including mobile and satellite services, agriculture and news agency services, see Annex V to the AA Jordan, *OJ* L 129/56.

[70] Arts. 30, 32 and 34 AA Algeria.

[71] Art. 30(1) and (5) AA Lebanon: 'Treatment by either Party to the other with respect to the rights of establishment and the supply of services shall be based on each Party's commitments and other obligations under GATS. This provision shall take effect from the date of the final accession of Lebanon to the WTO. … The Parties shall not, between the date of entry of into force of this agreement and Lebanon's accession to the WTO take any measures or actions which will render the conditions for the supply of services by the Community or Lebanese service suppliers more discriminatory than those existing on the date of entry into force of this Agreement.'

the Association Council to make all necessary recommendations, including provisions concerning the derogation from the basic principle of the free movement of services and the right of establishment.

2.3.1.3 The free movement of capital

All AAs provide for the free circulation of capital for direct investments.[72] In addition, current payments for current transactions may be made in freely convertible currency, for example, the euro. The European Community or the Mediterranean country may take restrictive measures with regard to current payments when one or several Member States or a Mediterranean country face or risk facing serious difficulties with regard to their balance of payments. These restrictions shall be limited in time and may not go beyond what is strictly necessary to remedy the balance of the payment situation.

Table II: The Euro-Med free trade zone in 2004

	Population (mln)	**GDP (PPP* bln)**	**GDP per capita (PPP bln)**
Mediterranean countries**			
Tunisia	10.1	$70.88	$7,100
Algeria	32.5	$212.3	$6,600
Lebanon	3.8	$18.83	$5,000
Jordan	5.7	$25.5	$4,500
Egypt	77.5	$316.3	$4,200
Morocco	32.7	$134.6	$4,200
Syria	18.4	$60.44	$3,400
TOTAL MC	180.7		**$5,000**
TOTAL NMS	74.1		**$16,170**
TOTAL EU 15	457.0		**$26,900**

* PPP = purchasing power parity

** Libya is not a member of the Euro-Med free trade area. Its oil revenues and small population (5.7 million) give Libya one of the highest GDPs per capita in Africa ($6,700).

72 Arts. 48-52 AA Jordan; Arts. 31-33 AA Egypt; Arts. 31-34 AA Lebanon; Arts. 38-40 AA Algeria; Arts. 33-35 AA Morocco and Arts. 31-34 AA Tunisia.

2.3.2 *Impact of the Euro-Med free trade area in the Mediterranean countries in 2005*

Ludvig Söderling analysed the trade potential of the Middle East and North Africa in relation to the European Union and came to the following conclusions:

> Ten years after the launch of the Barcelona process in 1995, it becomes clear that the Mediterranean integration efforts *vis-à-vis* the European Union, through the establishment of a Euro-Med free trade area, have yielded mixed results. Algeria and Syria both over-export to the European Union, but given the dominance of oil and gas exports, this can hardly be attributed to trade policy. In fact, the lack of growth in non-traditional exports from these countries suggests considerable scope for further integration. Meanwhile, Jordan and Lebanon under-export to all EU countries and Egypt has seen the degree of its integration into the European Union fall significantly over the past decade. Morocco's exports to the European Union are broadly on a par with predicted levels, while, on average, Tunisia over-exports to the European Union. Nevertheless, although the impact of the Barcelona process seems to have been modest in general, it appears to have had a significant effect in individual cases. This is most clearly observed in Tunisia, which has significantly improved its export performance *vis-à-vis* France, Italy, Belgium and Spain. Similarly, Morocco's export record to the United Kingdom and Spain has improved substantially since the beginning of the Barcelona process.[73]

Libya, which is not covered by the Euro-Med free trade zone, exports largely to the European Union. In 2004, its main export partners were Italy (37.7 per cent), Germany (16.7 per cent), Spain (11.6 per cent) and France (6.5 per cent). Its economy largely depends on revenues from the oil sector, but little of this income flows down to the lower orders of society. Since 2000, however, Libyan officials have made progress on economic reforms. These efforts increased after the UN sanctions were lifted in September 2003 and after the removal of almost all US sanctions against Libya in 2004. Libya now faces a long road to liberalise its economy, but initial steps such as applying for EMP and WTO membership are laying the groundwork for a more market-based economy.

---

[73] L. Söderling, 'Is the Middle East and North Africa reaching its trade potential?', International Monetary Fund Working Paper 2005, available at: <http://www.imf.org/external/pubs/ft/wp/2005/wp 0590.pdf>.

Table III: Trade, Industry and Labour in the Mediterranean countries (June 2005)

	Main natural resources	Main industry	Main EU export partners in 2004*	Population below poverty line	Unemployment rate
Morocco	phosphates	phosphate mining	France, Spain, UK, Italy, Germany	19% (est. 1999)	12.1%
Algeria	oil and gas	oil and gas	Italy, France, Spain, Belgium	23% (est. 1999)	25.4%
Tunisia	oil and phosphates	oil, mining and tourism	France, Italy, Germany, Spain, Belgium	7.6% (est. 2001)	13.8%
Libya	oil and gas	oil and gas	Italy, Germany, Spain, France	NA	30%
Egypt	oil and gas	terxtiles	Italy, UK, Germany, Spain, France	16.7% (est. 2000)	10.9%
Jordan	phisphates	phosphate mining	–	30% (est. 2001)	15%**
Syria	oil and phosphates	oil and textiles	Germany, Italy, France	20% (est. 2002)	20% (est. 2002)
Lebanon	lime stone and iron ore	banking, food processing and jewellery	France (5.1%)	28% (est. 1999)	18%

* Starting with the most important.
** Unofficially 30%.

2.4 Competition provisions

The extension of European competition rules to the Mediterranean countries is a key component which is required to establish a Euro-Med free trade area.[74] For example, the AAs contain provisions similar to the cartel prohibition in Article 81(1) TEC.[75] The following are incompatible with the proper functioning of the AAs, insofar as they may affect trade between the European Community and the Mediterranean countries: all agreements between undertakings, decisions by associations of undertakings and concerted practices between undertakings which have as their object or effect the prevention, restriction or distortion of competition, as defined in their respective legislation. In addition, the provisions in the AAs banning abuse of a dominant position by an undertaking are to a large extent drafted in a similar manner to Article 82 TEC.[76] Consequently, the abuse by one or more undertakings of a dominant position affecting the whole or a substantial part of the territory of the associated parties is incompatible with the proper functioning of the agreements.

The AAs with Tunisia, Algeria, Morocco and Jordan[77] provide that any practice contrary to the cartel provision and the dominant position provision shall be assessed on the basis of the criteria arising from the application of the rules contained in Article 85 TEC.[78] This means that the distorting practices will be determined in accordance with the decisions, notices and recommendations of the Commission and decisions of the European Courts.[79] The AAs with Lebanon and

---

[74] For more information, see F.S. Hakura, 'The Extension of EC Competition Law to the Mediterranean Region', 19 *European Competition Law Review* (1998) pp. 204-210 at p. 205; D. Geradin and N. Petit, 'Competition Policy and the Euro-Mediterranean Partnership', 8 *EFA Rev.* (2003) pp. 153-180; and D. Geradin and N. Petit, 'Competition Policy in the Southern Mediterranean Countries', 3 *Review of Networks Economics* (2004) pp. 65-82.

[75] Art. 41 AA Algeria; Art. 36 AA Morocco; Art. 36 AA Tunisia; Art. 34 AA Egypt; Art. 36 AA Jordan; Art. 35 AA Lebanon.

[76] Ibid.

[77] Art. 41 AA Algeria; Art. 36 AA Morocco; Art. 36 AA Tunisia and Art. 36 AA Jordan.

[78] With the entry into force of the Treaty of Amsterdam, Art. 85 TEC has been renumbered as Art. 81 TEC.

[79] This, for example, involves the claims for damages provided for in ECJ, Case C-453/99 *Courage* v. *Crehan* [2001] *ECR* I-6297. The ECJ ruled that it followed from the automatic nullity provision in Art. 85(2) and the fact that Art. 85(1) had direct effect that any individual, even a party to a contract that was liable to restrict or distort competition within Art. 85(1), could rely before a national court on that breach of that provision. Since it was the duty of national courts effectively to protect rights conferred on individuals by Community law, such a party could in principle claim damages for loss caused to him by the contract. However, in the light of the general principle that a litigant should not benefit from his own unlawful conduct, Community law did not prevent national law from refusing relief to a party who was found to have borne significant responsibility for the distortion of competition. Matters that were to be taken into account for that purpose included whether one party to the contract was in a markedly stronger position than the other, and so, *inter alia*, was in a position to impose terms on the other.

Egypt contain no similar provision. Lebanese and Egyptian judges will apply their respective national competition legislation. An infringement of a cartel prohibition and an abuse of dominant position will give rise to different judicial consequences in the European Community, on the one hand, and in Lebanon and Egypt, on the other, due to the lack of uniformity.

The AAs do not provide for an exemption procedure comparable to Article 81(3) TEC.[80] The question is whether an unlawful cartel can be exempted on other grounds than those provided for in Article 81(3) TEC, more specifically on the grounds provided for in the domestic legislation of the Mediterranean country. Furthermore, the question arises whether the national competition authorities are obliged to examine all four conditions of Article 81(3) TEC when they want to exempt an agreement. All AAs provide that the parties shall use their best endeavours to approximate their respective laws in order to facilitate the implementation of the AA. This 'best endeavours' clause contains no obligation for the Mediterranean country to adapt its legislation to EC legislation. This means that the Mediterranean country can apply its own competition legislation and that the domestic competition authorities of the Mediterranean countries are allowed to exempt anti-competitive agreements on other criteria than those provided for in Article 81(3) TEC.[81]

Other economic provisions in the AAs are the provisions relating to state aid,[82] state monopolies,[83] public enterprises,[84] and public procurement[85] and provisions relating to intellectual, industrial and commercial property matters.[86]

---

80 The AAs also do not deal with mergers. It is likely that the European Commission will apply its merger control rules to operations carried out by undertakings from associated countries which have an impact of the EC market.

81 Hakura, loc. cit. n. 74, at pp. 206-207.

82 Art. 41 AA Algeria; Art. 36 AA Morocco; Art. 36 AA Tunisia; Art. 34 AA Egypt; Art. 36 AA Jordan; Art. 35 AA Lebanon.

83 With regard to state monopolies, all AAs provide that the Member States and the Mediterranean country shall progressively adjust any state monopoly of a commercial character to ensure that, by the end of the fifth year following the entry into force of the agreement, no discrimination regarding the conditions under which goods are procured and marketed exists between nationals of the Member States and the Mediterranean country.

84 With regard to public enterprises and enterprises which have been granted special or exclusive rights, the Association Council shall ensure that no measure which disturbs trade between the Community and the Mediterranean country in a manner which runs counter to the interests of the parties is adopted or maintained.

85 All AAs provide that the parties shall set as their objective a reciprocal and gradual liberalisation of public procurement contracts. The Algerian AA also provides that parties shall adopt appropriate measures to ensure the protection of personal data in order to eliminate barriers to the free movement of such data between parties (Art. 45 Algeria AA).

86 All AAs provide that the parties shall provide suitable and effective protection of intellectual, industrial and commercial property, in line with the highest international standards.

2.5 Approximation of legislation

All AAs contain an 'approximation of laws' clause. The Maghreb AAs provide that Algeria, Tunisia and Morocco shall bring their legislation closer to that of the European Community in areas covered by the AA.[87] The other Mediterranean countries shall use their best endeavours to approximate their respective laws in order to facilitate the implementation of the AA.[88]

Besides these 'best endeavours' clauses, all AAs provide that the Mediterranean countries shall develop the use of EC rules in standardisation, metrology, quality control and conformity assessment.[89] The objective of this harmonisation is to promote trade by aligning standards and technical requirements, reducing costs related to duplicative testing and certification and thus facilitate market access. At present, a number of important steps towards eventual harmonisation and/or mutual recognition of trade-related standards across the Euro-Mediterranean region have been achieved.

The harmonisation of economic legislation has already started on the basis of the work programme adopted at the Euro-Med Trade Ministerial Conference of Palermo in July 2003. The Euro-Med Ministers instructed the existing working group on trade measures to begin to address the approximation of legislation in the field of standards, technical regulations and conformity assessment procedures.[90] At the 4th Euro-Med Trade Ministerial Conference in Istanbul in July 2004, the Ministers acknowledged the substantial progress made by the working group with regard to the approximation of legislation in the field of standards, technical regulations and conformity assessment procedures.[91] A number of Mediterranean countries have identified their priority sectors and all have started

[87] Art. 52 AA Morocco, for example, stipulates: 'Cooperation shall be aimed at helping Morocco to bring its legislation closer to that of the Community in areas covered by this Agreement.'

[88] Art. 48 AA Egypt, for example, stipulates: 'The Parties shall use their best endeavours to approximate respective laws in order to facilitate the implementation of this Agreement.'

[89] Art. 55 AA Algeria; Arts. 40 and 51 AA Morocco, Arts. 40 and 51 AA Tunisia, Art. 47 AA Egypt; Art. 48 AA Lebanon; Art. 68 AA Jordan.

[90] Conclusions of the Euromed Trade Ministerial Conference in Palermo of 7 July 2003, 64 *Euromed Report* (2003) para. 6. The Ministers instructed the working group to implement a six-point work programme that defines the steps required to approximate legislation in this field: (1) identification of priority sectors; (2) acquaintance with the applicable EC legislation and conduct a gap analysis on the basis of the existing legislation; (3) transposition of the necessary framework legislation and sectoral legislation; (4) creation/reformation of existing institutions; (5) set up necessary certification and conformity assessment bodies; (6) identification of technical assistance needs and make most of existing programmes.

[91] For an overview of the progress of approximation of legislation in the field of standards, technical regulations and conformity assessment procedures, see Annexes A, B and C of the Report on the Approximation of Legislation of 15 July 2004, available at: <http://europa.eu.int/comm/enterprise/enterprise_policy/ind_coop_programmes/med/doc/f1947_en.pdf>.

becoming acquainted with the EU legislative approach.[92] In May 2005, at the Luxemburg Euro-Med Conference, the Ministers of Foreign Affairs again stressed again the importance of the approximation of technical legislation in the area of standards and conformity assessment, since this harbours significant potential in terms of trade facilitation, investment attraction and, eventually, integration of economies.[93]

2.6 Justice and home affairs provisions

The AAs contain provisions on justice and home affairs. Among other things, they cover money laundering, the fight against drugs, organised crime and migration. All Mediterranean countries have promised to cooperate with the European Union in order to combat money laundering.[94] The Mediterranean countries, except for Jordan, agreed to insert a special provision against drugs use and trafficking in their AAs.[95] Only Algeria and Lebanon have committed to fight together with the Union against organised crimes such as human trafficking, exploitation for sexual purposes and corruption.[96] Algeria will combat racism, xenophobia and corruption.[97] Algeria and Egypt will cooperate with the European Union with a view to combating terrorism.[98] The AA Lebanon does not include cooperation on counter-terrorism, but this subject is covered by a separate exchange of letters between Lebanon and the European Union, which will enter into force at the same time as the agreement.[99]

---

[92] Conclusions of the 4th Euromed Trade Ministerial Conference in Istanbul of 21 July 2004, 81 *Euromed Report* (2004).

[93] Conclusions of the 7th Euro-Mediterranean Conference of the Ministers of Foreign Affairs, Luxembourg, 30-31 May, 90 *Euromed Report* (2005) para. 31.

[94] Art. 87 AA Algeria; Art. 61 AA Morocco; Art. 61 AA Tunisia; Art. 57 AA Egypt; Art. 78 AA Jordan and Art. 60 AA Lebanon.

[95] Art. 89 AA Algeria; Art. 62 AA Morocco; Art. 62 AA Tunisia; Art. 60 AA Lebanon and Art. 79 AA Egypt. Recently, the Council adopted Regulation (EC) No. 111/2005 of 22 December 2004 laying down the rules for the monitoring of trade between the Community and third countries in drug precursors, *OJ* 2005 L 22/1.

[96] Art. 86 AA Algeria and Art. 61 AA Lebanon.

[97] Art. 88 AA Algeria.

[98] Art. 59 AA Egypt and Art. 90 AA Algeria.

[99] On 12 October 2005, the Commission adopted a communication entitled 'A strategy on the external dimension of the area of freedom, security and justice', COM (2005) 491 final. The Communication identifies key areas for action with third countries, namely human rights, strengthening institutions and good governance, migration, asylum and border management, the fight against terrorism and organised crime, as well as principles to guide cooperation, such as geographic differentiation, partnership and flexibility. A broad range of instruments are identified to implement cooperation on justice, freedom and security issues with third countries, ranging from cooperation agreements and technical assistance to Europol and Eurojust.

2.7 Cooperation in other domains

All AAs contain a 'cultural cooperation' provision.[100] Cultural dialogue and cooperation are mainly focused on the conservation of heritage and audio-visual matters.[101] All AAs also contain 'financial cooperation' provisions relating to cooperation in the field of reforms, upgrading of the economic infrastructure, promoting private investment, repercussions of the introduction of a free trade area and accompanying social sector policies. All agreements contain an 'economic cooperation' provision which covers regular macroeconomic dialogue between parties; the exchange of information; the transfer of advice, expertise and training; joint ventures; and technical, administrative and regulatory assistance. The AA Tunisia acknowledges the importance of social development, which should go hand-in-hand with any economic development. Therefore, Tunisia and the European Community will give priority, for example, to the promotion of the equality of women, a balanced participation of women in the decision-making process in the economic and social spheres, the improvement of the social protection system, the development of family planning and the protection of mothers and children.[102]

The AAs also cover cooperation in other domains without defining exact objectives, including regional cooperation, scientific cooperation, education and training, environment, industrial cooperation, investments and promotion of investments, standardisation and conformity assessment, financial services, agriculture and fisheries, transport, information infrastructures and telecommunications, energy, tourism, customs, and statistics. Cooperation in consumer protection is only provided for in the AAs with Algeria, Lebanon and Egypt. These AAs provide that consumer protection systems in the European Community and in the Mediterranean countries in question should be made compatible.[103]

3. (FREE) MOVEMENT OF PERSONS AND EC MIGRATION POLICY TOWARDS THE MEDITERRANEAN COUNTRIES

In 1995, the European Community not only reviewed its policy towards the Mediterranean region in 1995 on economic grounds, but also because the EC

---

100 Art. 77 AA Algeria; Art. 74 AA Morocco; Art. 74 AA Tunisia; Art. 71 AA Egypt, Art. 85 AA Jordan and Art. 67 AA Lebanon.

101 ECJ, Case 293/83 *Françoise Gravier* v. *City of Liège* [1985] *ECR* 593, para. 24. The ECJ held that access to vocational training promotes freedom of movement of persons. The AAs touch upon vocational training when referring to cooperation in the field of education and training systems between the contracting parties.

102 Art. 45 AA Tunisia.

103 Art. 65 AA Algeria; Art. 58 AA Lebanon and Art. 61 AA Egypt.

feared a mass migration from the Mediterranean countries.[104] The Commission refused calls from the Mediterranean countries to ease migratory access and declared: 'If planned cooperation with the Mediterranean countries fails to produce a methodical way of tackling migratory pressures, friction could easily result.'[105] This fear resulted from the conviction that the Mediterranean region was a 'demographic time bomb'. According to forecasts, the population of the Mediterranean countries, which stood at 209 million in 1992, would reach 304 million in 2010. The World Bank suggests a 58 per cent increase in the population across the Mediterranean countries between 1990 and 2010.[106] The wealth gap between the European Union and the Mediterranean countries would increase from a level one to ten to a level one to twenty. As a consequence, migratory pressure and the risk of drug trafficking at the door of the European Union would increase in the future.[107]

All Mediterranean workers who reside legally in Europe enjoy limited rights under the European legislative framework and only Maghreb immigrants enjoy rights under their AAs.[108]

The main European legal instruments applicable to Mediterranean workers are Directive 2003/86/EC on family reunification and Directive 2003/109/EC on

---

[104] For an overview of the impact of the new Community immigration policy on the Euro-Mediterranean Partnership, see L. Hugelin, 'L'incidence d'une nouvelle politique communautaire de l'immigration sur le partenariat euro-mediterranéen', in Xuereb, op. cit. n. 4, at pp. 201-232.

[105] Communication from the Commission– Strengthening the Mediterranean Policy of the European Union: Proposals for Implementing a Euro-Mediterranean Partnership, COM (1995) 72 final, p. 6.

[106] 'Economic and Social Development in the Middle East and North Africa', Discussion Paper Series No. 3, October 1992, available at: <http://www.worldbank.org>.

[107] The countries of southern Europe do not receive the same types of immigrants, despite their common geographical position on the Mediterranean coast where the pressure of African migration is felt. Greece mainly receives citizens from Egypt, Bulgaria and Russia. Spain mainly receives flows of Moroccans. Italy receives Albanians, Moroccans and citizens from sub-Saharan Africa. Portugal remains attached to its former colonial empire (Cape Verde, Brazil and Angola). France and the United Kingdom, the two greatest colonial powers of the 20th century, receive citizens from Morocco and Algeria and Australia and New Zealand, respectively. The role of national histories, namely the ties with former colonial powers, the position with regard to the European Union's external borders, the different national migration policies and the needs of the national economy (skilled/unskilled) explain the national characteristics of migration. See Y. Breem and X. Thierry, 'Immigration in Europe and development levels of the source countries: what are the associations?', paper presented at the Second Conference of the EAPS Working Group on International Migration in Europe, Rome, 25-27 November 2004, available at: <http://www.irpps.cnr.it/ricmob/web_conf/download/_paper.pdf>.

[108] Mediterranean workers are in principle not covered by the Community *acquis* with regard to the free movement of workers. However, they may derive certain EC law based rights if they fall under one of the categories of family members of EU citizens. See Directive 2004/38/EC of the European Parliament and of the Council of 29 April 2004 on the right of citizens of the Union and their family members to move and reside freely within the territory of the Member States, amending Regulation (EEC) No. 1612/68 and repealing Directives 64/221/EEC, 68/360/EEC, 72/194/EEC, 73/148/EEC, 75/34/EEC, 75/35/EEC, 90/364/EEC, 90/365/EEC and 93/96/EEC, *OJ* 2004 L 158/77. See also ECJ, Case C-503/03 *Commission of the European Communities* v. *Spain* [2006] *ECR*, nyr.

long-term residence status.[109] In June 2003, the Thessaloniki European Council stressed the need for a further exploration of the legal means for third-country nationals to migrate to the Union, taking into account the reception capacity of the Member States. The Council therefore invited the Commission to present an annual report on migration and integration in Europe in order to map EU-wide migration data, immigration and integrations policies and practices.[110] Based on the results of this report, the Council and the European Parliament adopted Directive 2004/38/EC of 29 April 2004 on the right of citizens of the Union and their family members to move and reside freely within the territory of the Member States.[111] The Commission has also adopted a new proposal for a regulation on cross-border traffic by nationals of third countries who live in border areas and regularly travel for legitimate reasons to a Member State without constituting a threat to security.[112] The proposal creates the possibility of issuing a special visa to nationals of third countries who are subject to visa requirements and who reside in border areas[113] for the specific purpose of local border traffic.[114] This visa's territorial validity will be limited to the border area of the Member State concerned.

---

109 *OJ* 2003 L 251/12 and *OJ* 2004 L 16/44.

110 Presidency Conclusions, Thessaloniki European Council of 19-20 June 2005, available at: <http://ue.eu.int/ueDocs/cms_Data/docs/pressData/fr/ec/85324.pdf>.

111 European Parliament and Council Directive 2004/38/EC of 29 April 2004 on the right of citizens of the Union and their family members to move and reside freely within the territory of the Member States, amending Regulation (EEC) No. 1612/68 and repealing Directives 64/221/EEC, 68/360/EEC, 72/194/EEC, 73/148/EEC, 75/34/EEC, 75/35/EEC, 90/364/EEC, 90/365/EEC and 93/96/EEC, *OJ* 2004 L 158/77.

112 Proposal for a Council Regulation on the establishment of a regime of local border traffic at the external land borders of the Member States, COM (2003) 502 final. The Commission also proposed the establishment of an agency at the external borders, see Proposal for a Council Regulation establishing a European Agency for the Management of Operational Cooperation at the External Borders, COM (2003) 687 final. The agency will facilitate the application of Community measures concerning management of the European Union's external borders by coordinating Member States' actions to implement those measures. To that end, the agency will provide the necessary technical support and expertise. The proposal was adopted by means of Council Regulation (EC) No. 2007/2004 of 26 October 2004 establishing a European Agency for the Management of Operational Cooperation at the External Borders of the Member States of the European Union, *OJ* L 2004 349/1. The Council decided on 26 April 2005 that the agency shall have its seat in Warsaw. At the G-5 meeting in Evian on 4 July 2005, the Ministers of Interior recognised the importance of the European Border Agency in the coordinated EU fight against illegal immigration. The Ministers reaffirmed their commitment to ensuring the agency has a positive early effect and is able to begin its operational work as soon as possible. In this regard, they support the proposal to form a pool of operational experts in each member country who can take part in operations under the coordination of the agency.

113 Art. 3(b) of the Proposal defines 'border area' as 'an area which, as the crow flies, does not extend more than 50 kilometres from the frontier.'

114 Art. 3(c) of the Proposal explains 'local border traffic' as 'regular crossing of the external land border of a Member State by persons lawfully resident in the border area of a neighbouring country in order to stay in the border area of that Member State for a limited period of time provided for in the Regulation.'

In the AAs, the most restrictive provisions relate to the movement of persons. The Maghreb AAs, however, contain some liberal provisions. Algerian, Tunisian and Moroccan nationals who work and reside legally in Europe receive some social rights through their AAs. The Maghreb AAs contain a provision concerning equal treatment between workers from the countries in question and EU workers with regard to working conditions, remuneration and dismissal.[115] In the *El-Yassini* case, the ECJ found that this provision has direct effect.[116] The ECJ held that '[t]he provision in the field of working conditions and remuneration establishes a clear and unconditional principle which is sufficiently practical that it can be applied by national courts and is therefore capable of directly governing the legal situation of individuals.' This non-discrimination provision does not exist in the AAs with Egypt, Jordan and Lebanon. The Maghreb AAs also include social security provisions.[117] In the field of social security, workers of Algerian, Tunisian or Moroccan nationality, and any members of their families living with them, enjoy treatment free from any discrimination based on nationality relative to nationals of the Member States in which they are employed. This non-discrimination provision has also been granted direct effect by the ECJ in the *Kziber* case.[118] The Maghreb countries shall accord to workers of Member States and to their families residing in Tunisia, Algeria or Morocco a 'similar' treatment. The Association Council has to implement this provision and will have to determine what 'similar' means. In order to improve the movement of workers and the equal treatment conditions, and in order to achieve a better level of social integration, all AAs establish a regular dialogue procedure on social matters.[119] The AA

[115] Art. 52 AA Algeria; Art. 64 AA Tunisia and Art. 64 AA Morocco.

[116] ECJ, Case C-416/96 *El-Yassini* v. *UK Secretary of State of the Home Department* [1999] *ECR* I-1209, paras. 30-32.

[117] Arts 68-71 AA Algeria; Arts. 65-68 AA Tunisia and Arts. 65-68 AA Morocco. The social security field includes (i) sickness and maternity benefits, invalidity, old-age and survivors' benefits, industrial accident and occupational disease benefits and death, unemployment and family benefits; (ii) right of aggregation of periods of insurance, employment and residence completed in various Member States; (iii) family allowances for family members; and (iv) right to transfer pensions and other benefits. Under the AAs, the Association Councils receive competences to adopt provisions pertaining to the implementation of the equal treatment principle in the social security field.

[118] ECJ, Case C-18/90 *Office National de l'Emploi* v. *Kziber* [1999] *ECR* 199.

[119] For example, Art. 72 AA Algeria: 'The Parties shall conduct regular dialogue on any social matter which is of interest to them. Such dialogue shall be used to find ways to achieve progress in the field of movement of workers and equal treatment and social integration for Algerian and Community nationals residing legally in the territories of their host States. The dialogue shall cover, *inter alia*, all issues related to (a) the living and working conditions of workers and their dependants; (b) migration; (c) illegal immigration and the conditions governing the return of individuals who are in breach of their legislation dealing with the right to stay and the right of establishment in the host State; (d) schemes and programmes to encourage equal treatment between Algerian and Community nationals, mutual knowledge of cultures and civilisations, the furthering tolerance and the removal of discrimination.

Egypt also provides for a provision in which parties reaffirm the importance of the fair treatment of workers legally residing and employed in the territory of a party and agree to initiate talks on reciprocal bilateral agreements relating to the working conditions and social security rights of workers from Egypt and the Member States.[120]

The European Community and the Mediterranean countries also agreed to co-operate in the field of illegal immigration. Algeria, Egypt and Lebanon agreed to insert provisions about immigration in their AAs.[121] These countries and the European Community will exchange information on illegal immigration flows. They will readmit their nationals who are illegally present on the territory of the other party after the necessary identification formalities have been completed and will provide their nationals with the appropriate identity documents for this purpose. They shall also conclude bilateral agreements on combating illegal immigration and readmission. The Association Council shall examine the possibility of other forms of joint action for the prevention and control of illegal immigration, including ways of detecting forged documents. The only explicit provision on maintaining the visa requirements within a simplified and expeditious procedure appears in the AA Algeria.[122] Apart from these references, the AAs do not devote special attention to immigration issues.

Under the ENP, the Commission offered to grant all partner countries, including the Mediterranean countries, free movement of persons as the cornerstone of a wider Europe. The European Parliament, in its Napoletano Report of 5 November 2003, welcomed this idea and expressed its belief that the ENP should include a policy to facilitate the free movement of persons.[123] Some governments, however, fear an enormous increase of uncontrolled immigration once the free movement of persons regime is extended to the Mediterranean countries. Other governments are concerned about the entry of Islamist terrorists. These concerns incited strong reservations in the European Union towards the proposal under the ENP to extend the full EU *acquis*, including the free movement of persons, to the Mediterranean countries. It is to be expected that migratory access from Mediterranean nationals will continue to be restricted, judging by recent discussions about the establishment

[120] Art. 62 AA Egypt.

[121] Arts. 83-84 AA Algeria; Arts. 68-70 AA Egypt and Arts. 68-70 AA Lebanon.

[122] Art. 83 AA Algeria: 'Desirous of facilitating the movement of persons between them, the parties shall ensure, in accordance with relevant Community and national legislation in force, that the formalities for the issue of visas are carefully applied and executed and shall agree to examine, within the limits of their powers, ways of simplifying and speeding up the issue of visas to persons contributing to the implementation of the Agreements. The Association Committee shall periodically examine the implementation of this Article.'

[123] European Parliament, Report on 'Wider Europe-Neighbourhood: A Framework for Relations with our Eastern and Southern Neighbours, COM (2003) 104 – 2003/2018 (INI) (also known as the Napoletano Report).

of EU-financed camps in North Africa to control the arrival of potential immigrants during the Justice and Home Affairs Council of Ministers of Interior Affairs on 1 October 2004.[124] In June 2005, the European Parliament condemned the setting up in the Mediterranean countries, at the request of certain Member States, of 'preliminary reception centres' for immigrants heading for the European Union's territory, which do not offer minimum guarantees to the people concerned in terms of fundamental rights.[125]

During the 7th Euro-Med Conference in Luxembourg on 30-31 May 2005, the Ministers of Foreign Affairs stressed the need to intensify cooperation between the countries with potential migrants and the European Union. They pointed to the importance of the AAs and the neighbourhood actions plans that should help to promote joint management of the movement of persons as well as the integration of migrants. They also pushed for intensified cooperation between the European Union and the Mediterranean countries to address the negative affects of illegal immigration, including transit migration.[126] The Justice and Home Affairs Council pointed out the importance of cooperation with Libya on matters of migration during their meeting in Luxemburg on 3 June 2005. The Council urged the Union to engage in discussions with Libya as soon as possible on managing migratory flows between Africa and Europe on an *ad hoc* basis.[127]

On 4 July 2005, the G-5 Ministers of the Interior[128] met in Evian to set stricter immigration controls. The Ministers welcomed the proposals of Italy on immigration by sea from Africa. Italy proposed to set up joint patrols in the Mediterranean, to cooperate on repatriation, to jointly analyse migration flows from sub-Saharan Africa and to install joint investigation teams at the departure point for immigrants. They also agreed to develop joint group flights for the repatriation of irregular immigrants.[129] In September and October 2005, thousands of African migrants attempted to enter two Spanish exclaves in north-eastern Morocco (Ceuta and Melilla). These attempts to scale the fortified fences with wooden ladders led to deadly clashes between the migrants and the Spanish and Moroccan border guards. Ceuta and Melilla are seen by immigrants, notably from

---

124 Del Sarto and Schumacher, loc. cit. n. 25, at pp. 30-31.

125 European Parliament Resolution of 9 June 2005 on the links between legal and illegal migration and integration of migrants.

126 See Conclusions for the 7th Euro-Mediterranean Conference of Ministers of Foreign Affairs, Luxembourg, 30-31 May 2005, p. 13.

127 Conclusions of the JHA Council of Justice and Home Affairs, Luxembourg, 3 June 2005, available at: <http://www.eu2005.lu/en/actualites/conseil/index.html>.

128 United Kingdom, France, Italy, Spain and Germany.

129 Conclusions of the G-5 meeting in Evian on 4 July 2005, available at: <http://www.statewatch.org/ news/2005/jul/03eu-g5-meeting.htm>. The Euro-Mediterranean Consortium for Applied Research on International Migration (CARIM) published its first annual report in 2005: 'Mediterranean Migration 2005', available at: <http://www.carim.org/Publications/AR2005CARIM_lite01.pdf>.

sub-Saharan Africa, as a gateway to Spain, and hence the rest of Europe. It should be noted that at the present time, according to Spanish information sources, around 20,000 migrants in Algeria, in addition to approximately another 10,000 migrants in Morocco, are waiting to start their journey to reach Ceuta and Melilla. In response to these events, a Commission mission to Morocco and Ceuta and Melilla took place from 7 to 11 October 2005, with a view to assessing and better understanding the size and characteristics of illegal immigration from Africa to the European Union via Morocco. The mission report makes suggestions for intensifying the existing cooperation with Morocco on migration in the framework of the Association Agreement and the ENP Action Plan. It also calls on the Commission to initiate dialogue with Algeria on migration, given the recent entry into force of the Association Agreement.[130]

4. EU FINANCIAL AID TO THE MEDITERRANEAN COUNTRIES

The MEDA programme,[131] which was created in 1995, is the main financial instrument of the EMP. Under the MEDA programme, a broad range of programmes has been developed covering all aspects of the EMP. The MEDA programme provides support for economic transition, a better socio-economic balance and regional integration. The MEDA Regulation of 1996 forms the legal basis of the MEDA programme, and is usually referred to as MEDA I.[132] MEDA I was amended in 2000 and has since been referred to as MEDA II.[133] Through the MEDA I and MEDA II programmes, funding now stands at over €800 million per year. Based on strategy papers covering the 2000-2006 period, three-year national indicative programmes (NIPs) (Algeria, Egypt, Jordan, Lebanon, Morocco, Syria and Tunisia) are drawn up. MEDA funding is subject to the programming in these NIPs. Morocco is the leading beneficiary of community financial assistance among the Mediterranean countries.[134] Tunisia and Egypt are also major beneficiaries of

130 *Euromed Synopsis* No. 332 of 20 October 2005, p. 2. The mission report is available at: <http://europa.eu.int/rapid/pressReleasesAction.do?reference=MEMO/05/380&format=HTML&aged=0&language=EN&guiLanguage=en>.

131 MEDA stands for 'mesures d'accompagnement'.

132 The MEDA Regulation forms the legal basis that enables the European Union to provide financial and technical assistance to the Mediterranean countries with a view to realising the objectives of the EMP, see Council Regulation (EC) No. 1488/96 of 23 July 1996 on financial and technical measures to accompany (MEDA) the reform of economic and social structures in the framework of the Euro-Mediterranean partnership, *OJ* 1996 L 189, amended by Council Regulation (EC) No. 780/98 of 7 April 1998, *OJ* 1998 L 113.

133 Council Regulation (EC) No. 2698/2000 of 27 November 2000, *OJ* 2000 L 311/1.

134 Morocco was granted €1,005 million between the end of 1995 and 2003. For more information, see M. Boussetta, 'Processus de Barcelone et Partenariat Euro-Mediterraneen: Le Cas du Maroc avec l'Union Européenne', Working Paper, available at: <http://www.erf.org.eg/uploadpath/pdf/0110.pdf>.

EU financial assistance.[135] Algeria, in contrast, is a marginal beneficiary of community assistance.[136] Jordan is an excellent performer in terms of the use of MEDA funds, with up to 70 per cent of commitments disbursed. Lebanon received €150 million between 1996 and 2002 and an additional grant of €80 million for specific actions such as the reintegration of displaced persons and the fight against drugs. Following the withdrawal of Israel from Southern Lebanon in 2000, another €4 million was granted as well as €9.2 million for further rehabilitations projects in the southern region. For Syria, it will be important to use the MEDA funds for policy advice and institutional capacity building to facilitate necessary legislation and reforms.[137] Libya has not been granted financial benefits under the MEDA programme since it is not yet a member of the EMP.

In addition, the European Investment Bank (EIB) has played an important role in providing assistance to the Mediterranean countries since the mid-1970s. Its lending activities have been expanding continuously and stand at approximately €2 billion per year. In 2002, a new financing instrument was created at a meeting of the Finance Ministers of the fifteen Member States and the twelve Mediterranean countries in Barcelona. The EIB will grant loans to the Mediterranean countries via the Facility for Euro-Mediterranean Investment and Partnership (FEMIP).[138] The Ecofin Council agreed in November 2003 to review the FEMIP mandate before the end of 2006. The Mediterranean countries have recently underlined the importance of creating a Euro-Mediterranean Development Bank (EMDB). The possibility of establishing a EMDB should be carefully considered in the light of the FEMIP experience and an overall review of the EIB's external mandates.[139]

At first sight, the funding from the European Union to the Mediterranean countries seems to have increased between 1995 and the present. However, when comparing the financial allocation for MEDA I (1995-1999) and MEDA II (2000-2006), Eric Philippart reaches the opposite conclusion. According to the financial presentation of the European Union, it appears that €685 million was allocated

[135] Tunisia was granted €686 million between the end of 1995 and 2003. In the 1995-2003 period, major programmes were also funded in Egypt: Social Fund for Development (€155 million), Basic Education Programme (€100 million), Industrial Modernisation Programme (€250 million) and Health Sector Programme (€110 million).

[136] Algeria was granted €304.2 million between the end of 1995 and 2003.

[137] EIB Facility for the Euro-Mediterranean Investment and Partnership (FEMIP), Progress Report on the Implementation of FEMIP and Prospects for the Business Plan, 27 March 2003.

[138] In the Framework of FEMIP, the EIB announced its first loan to a Mediterranean country unsecured by a sovereign guarantee in September 2005. This is a €30 million loan to Banque Marocaine de Commerce Extérieur to assist in the medium-term financing of small and medium-sized enterprises.

[139] The Commission will submit an assessment in 2006 in this respect in consultation with the EIB, see Communication from the Commission to the Council and the European Parliament – Tenth Anniversary of the Euro-Mediterranean Partnership: A work programme to meet the challenges of the next five years, COM (2005) 139 final.

under MEDA I in comparison to €764 million under MEDA II. This financial presentation does not take into account that 1995 was only a marginal year for MEDA, since the programme officially started mid-November 1995. One should therefore take 1996-1999 as a more accurate basis of comparison for which the annual allocation for amounts to €812.8 million. MEDA II thus represents a financial decline and will most probably prove to be insufficient after the entry into force of all the AAs.[140]

Under the umbrella of the ENP, the Commission proposed other budgetary means.[141] Until 2007, MEDA will remain the main financial assistance instrument for the Mediterranean countries. MEDA will provide support for the ENP, in general, and for the implementation of the actions plans, in particular. Starting from 2007, another financial instrument will be launched, namely the European Neighbourhood and Partnership Instrument (ENPI). The ENPI will support cross-border cooperation as well as regional cooperation projects involving both EU Member States and all the ENP partner countries, including the Mediterranean countries.

Table IV: MEDA I & II (1995-2003)

Country	Payments (mln)
Morocco	€412.9
Tunisia	€411.7
Egypt	€366.6
Jordan	€300.4
Lebanon	€63.7
Algeria	€62.8
Syria	€20.8
TOTAL	**€1,638.9**

140 Philippart, loc. cit. n. 18, at pp. 210-211; For further evaluation of the MEDA programmes, see Evaluation Report of Economic Cooperation between the European Commission and Mediterranean countries, November 2003, available at: <http://europa.eu.int/comm/europeaid/evaluation/program/medrep.htm> (the countries examined in this study are Algeria, Egypt, Jordan, Lebanon, Morocco, Syria and Tunisia); E. Philippart, 'The MEDA Programme: Evaluation of the new design of EU assistance to the Mediterranean', in F. Attina and S. Stavridis, eds., *The Barcelona Process and Euro-Mediterranean Issues from Stuttgart to Marseille* (Milano, Giuffrè 2001) pp. 121-169.

141 Proposal of the Commission for a Regulation of the European Parliament and of the Council laying down general provisions establishing a European Neighbourhood and Partnership Instrument, COM (2004) 628 final; Communication from the Commission to the Council and the European Parliament: Building our common Future – Policy challenges and Budgetary means of the Enlarged Union 2007-2013, COM (2004) 101 final/2.

5. THE CREATION OF THE ENP AND ITS IMPACT ON THE MEDITERRANEAN COUNTRIES

The ENP is the result of the European Union's changed composition and geostrategic outlook in view of its enlargement of May 2004. Under the EMP, the Mediterranean region stretches from Morocco, through the Middle East to Turkey, but the new geopolitical vision under the ENP consists of creating a 'ring of friends', ranging from Morocco to Ukraine. The ENP is addressed to the European Union's existing neighbours and those that have drawn closer to the Union as a result of most recent enlargement. In Europe, this applies to Ukraine, Belarus and Moldova. In the Mediterranean region, the ENP concerns all the former Euro-Med countries, with the exception of Cyprus, Malta and Turkey, since Cyprus and Malta became members of the European Union in May 2004 and Turkey has started negotiations to become a member. In June 2004, the Council also decided, on the basis of a strategy paper by the Commission, to include Armenia, Azerbaijan and Georgia in the ENP.[142] The Commission stressed that the ENP will offer possibilities different from those available to European countries under Article 49 TEU.[143] Article 49 TEU stipulates that any European state may apply to become a member of the European Union. This means that accession is still ruled out for the non-European Mediterranean countries.[144] The European Parliament considered the scope of the ENP as a complex geopolitical area stretching from Ukraine to Morocco, which for historical and cultural reasons and on the basis of its geographical proximity may be defined as a 'Pan-European and Mediterranean region.[145]

At the launch of the ENP, a tendency towards expanding the geographic scope of the ENP became manifest. In June 2004, the European Council approved the EU Strategic Partnership with the Mediterranean and the Middle East.[146] This partnership will focus on the countries of North Africa and the Middle East, including the GCC,[147] Yemen, Iraq and Iran.[148] The European Union has contractual relations with the GCC and Yemen, but there is no contractual framework

---

142 Communication from the Commission – European Neighbourhood Policy – Strategy Paper, COM (2004) 373 final. However, Morocco, which already applied for EU membership in 1986, still has no perspective on EU membership.

143 COM (2004) 373 final, p. 3.

144 COM (2003) 104 final, p. 5.

145 European Parliament, Report on 'Wider Europe – Neighbourhood: A Framework for Relations with our Eastern and Southern Neighbours', COM (2003) 104 – 2003/2018 (INI) (also known as the Napoletano Report).

146 EU Strategic Partnership with the Mediterranean and the Middle East, June 2004, available at: <http://europa.eu.int/comm/external_relations/euromed/doc.htm>.

147 Saudi Arabia, Kuwait, Bahrain, Qatar, United Arab Emirates and Oman.

148 Aliboni, loc. cit. n. 5, at pp. 10-12.

with Iran and Iraq. The economic and social characteristics of these countries call for instruments different to the programmes within the EMP. Most Mediterranean Arab countries, in particular the Maghreb countries, are not eager to share their EU relations with the GCC and Iran. A shift towards these countries might be too premature for the Arab Mediterranean countries.

Since the ENP does not only reach out to the Mediterranean countries, but also to the other ENP partner countries, potential benefits will have to be allocated to a large number of countries which all have enormous capital demands. The Commission declared that the aim of the ENP is 'to share the benefits of the EU's 2004 enlargement with the neighbouring countries in strengthening stability, security and well-being.' Under the ENP, the Commission will distribute €955 million for the 2004-2006 period: €700 million under the INTERREG programme, €45 million under MEDA, €75 million under Tacis, €90 million under Phare and €45 million under CARDS.[149] As a consequence, the Mediterranean countries are put in one and the same basket as other countries, notwithstanding their extremely different political, cultural and historical backgrounds. It is possible that the Mediterranean countries will suffer financially as a result of the territorial overstretching of the ENP.[150] Erwan Lannon and Peter Van Elsuwege fear the concentration of the European Union's financial and economic aid towards its eastern periphery at the expense of the southern periphery, since the new financial initiatives under the ENP are already developed at the expense of the EMP.[151]

The Mediterranean countries are of the opinion that they did not derive sufficient economic benefits from the EMP. Therefore, the European Union should offer the Mediterranean countries real economic gains under the ENP.[152] The ENP should provide a further drive to economic reforms in the Mediterranean countries by opening up to agricultural exports and investment in major infrastructure projects. The Mediterranean countries are indeed suffering from the protectionist character of EU agricultural policy, but also from the restrictions imposed on the trade in textiles. The Mediterranean countries also feel resentment towards the European Union since they do not see direct investments in their countries by the European Union and its companies. Such investments could stimulate economic reorganisation in the Mediterranean countries, which is necessary for the establishment of a

149 COM (2004) 373 final, p. 24.

150 Del Sarto and Schumacher, loc. cit. n. 25, at pp. 30-33.

151 E. Lannon and P. Van Elsuwege, 'The EU's Emerging Neighbourhood Policy and its Potential Impact on the Euro-Mediterranean Partnership', in Xuereb, op. cit. n. 4, at pp. 60-61.

152 S. Biscop, 'The European Security Strategy and the Neighbourhood Policy: A New Starting Point for a Euro-Mediterranean Security Partnership?', paper presented at EUSA Ninth Biennial International Conference in Austin, Texas, 31 March-2 April 2005, available at: <http://aei.pitt.edu/archive/00002984/01/Paper_EUSA_ESS-EMP.txt>.

free trade area. Lannon and Van Elsuwege describe the lack of foreign direct investment in the Mediterranean countries as one of the most important failures of the EMP and its AAs.[153] The ENP should also support economic progress in the Mediterranean by offering to draw the Mediterranean countries deeper into the four freedoms of the single market. This will encourage regulatory reform, especially in the services sector, that could give a strong boost to economic growth and competitiveness.[154] The ENP should liberalise the movement of persons between the European Union and the Mediterranean countries.[155]

The ENP is not only determined to enhance the economic chapter of the Barcelona Declaration, but also intends to contribute to political-military cooperation between the European Union and the Mediterranean countries.[156] Under the EMP, the Mediterranean countries were reluctant to take part in discussions on political and security matters. Progress was made in strengthening dialogue and cooperation since the Council launched several proposals on 19 March 2003 to open up the European Security and Defence Policy (ESDP) to the Mediterranean countries. However, the Mediterranean countries remained extremely reluctant to engage in dialogue. Under the ENP, actual participation in the ESDP as a part of the European Union's CFSP is mentioned in the action plans for Jordan, Morocco and Tunisia. The mutual dialogue on the ESDP has been integrated into the EMP bodies since November 2004. Consequently, the Mediterranean countries seem to be willing to participate in the political and security debates, also because of the fear of terrorism and the spill-over effect of the Iraqi conflict.

6. CONCLUDING REMARKS

The Mediterranean region is characterised by an historical background of deadly conflicts between neighbouring Mediterranean countries and is today still far from being a homogeneous entity in political, economic and cultural terms. The

153 Lannon and Van Elsuwege, loc. cit. n. 151, at pp. 60-61.

154 Conclusions on the 7th meeting of Experts on Economic Transition, 23-24 April 2003, based on a 'The Economic Impact of the EU enlargement on the Mediterranean Partners', paper prepared by DG External Relations, available at: <http://europa.eu.int/comm/external_relations/euromed/etn/7mtg/agenda.htm>.

155 Immigrants of the Mediterranean countries who were already established in the European Union, however, do not have to fear increased competition from workers from the new Member States, since no significant changes in the Western European labour market are expected as a result of the European Union's enlargement, see B. Khader, 'Elargissement à l'Est et impact migratoire sur les pays arabes et méditerranéens', study in preparation for the 7th meeting of Experts on Economic Transition, 23-24 April 2003, available at: <http://europa.eu.int/comm/external_relations/euromed/etn/7mtg/kha.pdf>, p. 19.

156 S. Biscop, 'Opening up the ESDP to the South: A Comprehensive and Cooperative Approach to Euro-Mediterranean Security', 34 *Security Dialogue* (2003) pp. 183-197.

European Union has launched many initiatives to tackle the volatile and unpredictable situation in the Mediterranean region. At the Barcelona Conference in 1995, the European Union established an instrument known as the EMP in order to deal with instability in the Mediterranean region. At this conference, the European Union and the Mediterranean countries dealt with security, political, economic and cultural issues. The major aim of the conference was to establish a free trade area between the European Union and the Mediterranean countries, as economic integration at interregional and bilateral level (via the AAs) should prevent future wars between the Mediterranean countries, in the same way that the EEC prevented future wars between Germany and France after World War II. This partnership contributed to the development of the Mediterranean region, but also failed in many ways. The lack of foreign investment in the Mediterranean countries and the protectionist character of the agricultural sector in Europe, for example, did not bring the hoped-for result in the Mediterranean countries.

In 2002, the European Union established another new instrument known as the ENP, in response to the upcoming enlargement of 2004. The ENP is not only addressed to the Mediterranean countries, but also involves other countries that neighbour the enlarged European Union. With this initiative, the European Union not only aims to fill the gaps where the EMP failed and to further strengthening the Euro-Med relations, but also aims to cooperate more closely with other countries neighbouring the European Union. At present, Euro-Med relations are dealt with through two different – but overlapping – policies: the Euro-Mediterranean Partnership and the European Neighbourhood Policy. The EMP is considered to be too weak to tackle all the major problems confronting the Mediterranean region, and the answer to this weakness, the European Neighbourhood Policy, seems to be too ambitious to solve all the political and economic problems. Contrary to the EMP, the ENP rightly emphasises the importance of an individual approach towards each Mediterranean country, based on country reports and actions plans, but seems – due to its overstretching ambition – to neglect the importance of the integration of the Mediterranean countries themselves. The ENP should further stress the importance of the South-South dimension of Euro-Med relations. Interregional integration at both economic and cultural level and a mutual political understanding between the Mediterranean countries is a *condition sine qua non* for a profitable relationship between the European Union and the Mediterranean region.

The EMP and the ENP must focus on regional integration, such as, for example, political and economic cooperation between Syria and Lebanon and, first and foremost, the inconceivable but essential rapprochement between Israel and the Palestinian Authority. Peace and stability in the Mediterranean region would spare the European Union from major problems, such as terrorism and mass migration. The European Union is aware of this, judging by the importance it attaches to the security dimension of Euro-Med relations, through recent security and strategy papers. The ENP must not overlook the relations between the Mediterranean countries themselves in its ambition to address the Mediterranean and Eastern Europe as well as the South Caucasus. The unstable and unpredictable situation in the Mediterranean region is the source of mass migration and extreme fundamentalism; challenges to which the EMP and the ENP do not yet – but should – provide satisfying answers.

However, the Tenth Anniversary Euro-Mediterranean Summit of November 2005 highlighted the importance of migration, social integration, sustainable socio-economic development, justice and security as issues of common interest of the EMP. A Five-Year Work Programme, which was designed during the summit, promotes in a constructive way more regional integration, such as more regional agreements, regional transport networks and regional energy projects. A Code of Conduct on Countering Terrorism, also drafted during the summit, constitutes an ambitious agenda which should render the partnership more tangible, more politically relevant and more operational. For instance, the Code of Conduct proposes exchanging information on a voluntary basis on terrorists and their support networks, developing an effective and operational cooperation system to disrupt networks and bring individuals involved in terrorist acts to justice, coordinating work to identify the factors which contribute to the terrorist threat and sharing experiences and expertise on how to address them. It remains to be seen whether this Code of Conduct is not too ambitious in view of the difficulties within the European Union itself to exchange information between Member States on criminal acts and the reluctance of Member States to cooperate on criminal matters.

CHAPTER 13

ISRAEL AND THE PALESTINIAN AUTHORITY

Wybe Th. Douma*

Relevant legal documents:

- Council Joint Action 2006/119/CFSP of 20 February 2006 extending the mandate of the European Union Special Representative for the Middle East peace process, *OJ* 2006 L 49/8.
- Council Joint Action 2005/889/CFSP of 12 December 2005 on establishing a European Union Border Assistance Mission for the Rafah Crossing Point (EU BAM Rafah), *OJ* 2005 L 327/28.
- Council Joint Action 2005/797/CFSP of 14 November 2005 on the European Union Police Mission for the Palestinian Territories, *OJ* 2005 L 300/65.
- Agreement in the form of an Exchange of Letters between the European Community and the Palestine Liberation Organisation (PLO) for the benefit of the Palestinian Authority of the West Bank and the Gaza Strip concerning reciprocal liberalisation measures and the replacement of Protocols 1 and 2 to the EC-Palestinian Authority Interim Association Agreement, *OJ* 2005 L 2/6.
- Agreement on scientific and technical cooperation between the European Community and the State of Israel, *OJ* 2003 L 154/80.
- Convention between the European Community and the United Nations Relief and Works Agency for Palestine Refugees (UNRWA) concerning aid to refugees in the countries of the Near East (2002 to 2005), *OJ* 2002 L 281/12.
- Euro-Mediterranean Agreement establishing an association between the European Communities and their Member States, of the one part, and the State of Israel, of the other part, *OJ* 2000 L 147/3.
- Agreement on mutual recognition of OECD principles of good laboratory practice (GLP) and compliance monitoring programmes between the European Community and the State of Israel, *OJ* 1999 L 263/7.
- Agreement between the European Community and the State of Israel on government procurement, *OJ* L 1997 L 202/85.
- Agreement between the European Community and the State of Israel on procurement by telecommunications operators, *OJ* 1997 L 202/74.

* Senior Researcher in European Law and International Trade Law, T.M.C. Asser Instituut, The Hague.

- Euro-Mediterranean Interim Association Agreement on trade and cooperation between the European Community, of the one part, and the Palestine Liberation Organisation (PLO) for the benefit of the Palestinian Authority of the West Bank and the Gaza Strip, of the other part, *OJ* 1997 L 187/3.

1. INTRODUCTION

The history of EC/EU relations with Israel goes back to late 1950s, when Israel became the third country (after the United States and Greece) to establish diplomatic relations with the European Economic Community. These relations have been shaped by a multiplicity of economic and political factors connected not only with Israel as such but primarily with the Middle East conflict. It is indisputable that bilateral relations between the EC/EU and Israel have developed over the years and have extended beyond the original trade matters. In 2005, Israel is covered by both the Barcelona process and the developing European Neighbourhood Policy (ENP). The Euro-Mediterranean Agreement creating an association between the European Community and Israel remains the main legal instrument of this relationship. The European Union has not remained indifferent to the Middle East conflict and the gradual emergence of Palestinian Authority. Not only was it one of the drafters of the so-called Roadmap to Peace, but it has also used to a considerable extent the potential and instruments of the Common Foreign and Security Policy (CFSP) in order to advance its engagement in the region. In order to give its relations with the Palestinian Authority a legal framework, the European Community concluded an Interim Association Agreement with the PLO, on behalf of the Palestinian Authority. This chapter aims to analyse selected issues connected with the EC/EU's relationship with both Israel and the Palestinian Authority. It starts, however, with a general overview of the region's history providing the reader with a political background for further analysis.

2. THE CREATION OF THE STATE OF ISRAEL AND THE ROAD TOWARDS A PALESTINIAN STATE

2.1 General overview

At the beginning of the twentieth century, the Ottoman Empire encompassed much of the Middle East. As Turkey sided with Germany during World War I, the League of Nations granted the British a mandate over what has become today's Israel, the West Bank, the Gaza Strip and Jordan. After World War II, the British were unable to provide stability or a solution to the request for Jewish immigration, on the one hand, and Arab opposition to this immigration, on the other. They therefore indicated their intention to end the mandate.

A United Nations Special Committee on Palestine (UNSCOP) was appointed on 15 May 1947.[1] The Committee issued its report on 31 August of the same year.[2] The UN General Assembly followed the main recommendations made by the majority of the UNSCOP members and advised that the British mandate area (with the exception of Jordan, which had been assigned to the Arabs by the British in 1923) would be partitioned into independent Arab and Jewish states as of the moment that the British would withdraw.[3] The Arabs rejected the Partition Plan immediately and hostilities between Jews and Arabs grew.

On 14 May 1948, the British High Commissioner for Palestine and the last British soldiers left Palestine and the present-day State of Israel declared its independence.[4] Several neighbouring Arab nations immediately launched a war against the new state that lasted until January 1949. A large proportion of the Arab inhabitants fled or were chased away as a result of the hostilities. At the same time, many Jews living in Arab countries moved to Israel, often because they could no longer stay in their home countries. New wars took place in 1956-1957, 1967 and 1973. During the Six-Day War of 1967, Israel occupied the Gaza Strip, the West Bank, Jerusalem's Old City, the Golan Heights and the Sinai Peninsula. The Sinai Peninsula was returned to Egypt in 1982 in the framework of the Camp David Accords, in which peace between Israel and Egypt was negotiated with the help of the United States.

The occupation of the West Bank was declared illegal in UN Security Council resolution 446 of March 1979.[5] In the 1980s, the Palestinian Liberation Organisation (PLO) declared the State of Palestine and claimed the Gaza Strip and the West Bank as Palestinian territory. In December 1987, a popular Arab uprising began against Israeli rule and Israeli settlements in the occupied territories: the first *Intifada*. Violence continued until the signing of the Oslo Accords of 13 September 1993, in which an interim agreement between Israel and the Palestine

---

[1] UNSCOP consisted of representatives from Australia, Canada, Czechoslovakia, Guatemala, India, Iran, The Netherlands, Peru, Sweden, Uruguay and Yugoslavia.

[2] The majority of the nations represented in the committee (Canada, Czechoslovakia, Guatemala, The Netherlands, Peru, Sweden and Uruguay) recommended the creation of separate, independent Arab and Jewish states while preserving the economic unity of the country, with Jerusalem to be placed under international administration. The economic association proposed would encompass a treaty in which the two states agreed on a common customs system, a common currency and the maintenance of a country-wide system of transport and communications. A minority (India, Iran and Yugoslavia) supported the creation of a single federal state containing both Jewish and Arab constituent states. Australia abstained.

[3] Resolution 181of 29 November 1947. Voting in the UNGA was 33 to 13, with 10 abstentions, in favour of the Partition Plan. Both the United States and the USSR supported the resolution.

[4] For the text of Israel's Proclamation of Independence, see <http://www.knesset.gov.il/docs/eng/megilat_eng.htm>.

[5] Resolution 446 (1979) of 22 March 1979, text available in K.C. Wellens, ed., *Resolutions and Statements of the United Nations Security Council (1946-1992) – A Thematic Guide*, 2nd edn. (Dordrecht/Boston/London, T.M.C. Asser Instituut/Martinus Nijhoff Publishers 1993) p. 718.

Authority (PA) was signed.[6] The final status of the West Bank and Gaza was made dependent upon a future settlement between Israel and the Palestinians.

Despite various external efforts, tensions rose again and, in late September 2000, a second *Intifada* started. From that moment onwards, until the end of 2004, some 1,030 Israelis and 3,497 Palestinians were killed. In addition, 28,321 Palestinians and 6,964 Israelis were injured as a result of the conflict.[7]

The building of a separation barrier aimed at protecting Israel's citizens from Palestinian terrorism started in 2003. The construction was condemned by the European Union, notably because part of the barrier is constructed outside the territory of Israel and thus illegally cuts off Palestinians from their land and because it creates humanitarian problems.[8] A draft UN Security Council resolution declaring the construction of a wall departing from the armistice line of 1949 as illegal was vetoed by the United States in late 2003.[9] On 30 June 2004, Israel's Supreme Court ruled that the wall in itself was in conformity with the rules of international law, even in those places where it was situated inside the occupied territories, but held that parts of the separation fence were illegal because they imposed a disproportionate burden on the Palestinian population compared to the security benefits they provided, in violation of the proportionality principle.[10] Just nine days later, the International Court of Justice came to a different conclusion.[11]

---

[6] 'Israel-Palestine Liberation Organisation: Declaration of Principles of Interim Self-Government Arrangements', 32 *ILM* (1993) p. 1525.

[7] Economic and Social Council, Commission on Human Rights, Draft Report E/CN.4/2005/L.10/Add.8 of 14 April 2005, p. 4.

[8] Remarks of Javier Solana, EU High Representative for the CFSP, on the occasion of a meeting with Palestinian Prime Minister Ahmed Qurei, Ramallah, 13 July 2005.

[9] S/2003/980 of 14 October 2003. An adopted UN Security Council Resolution would have been binding for Israel.

[10] HCJ 2056/04 *Beit Sourik Village Council* v. *1. Government of Israel and 2. Commander of the IDF Forces in the West Bank.* In a more recent ruling, Israel's Supreme Court has ordered the dismantling of a section of the separation barrier that imposes a serious burden on the local Palestinian population. See HCJ 7957/04 *Zaharan Yunis Muhammad Mara'abe* v. *The Prime Minister of Israel.*

[11] ICJ, Advisory Opinion of 9 July 2004, Gen. List No. 131. The advice was requested by the UN General Assembly (GA resolution ES-10/14 (2003) of 8 December 2003). As their name indicates, advisory opinions lack binding effect. In response, Israel claimed that only the Israeli Supreme Court has the capacity to fully address all aspects of this matter, while stressing that every individual affected by the fence has the right to directly petition the Court, thus ensuring legal recourse without the need for outside involvement (Israel Ministry of Foreign Affairs, *Statement on ICJ Advisory Opinion*, 9 July 2004). As a result of a new Civil Torts (Liability of the State) Law passed by the Israeli Parliament (Knesset) on 27 July 2005, the latter argument might have become less valid. Under this law, the three and a half million Palestinians living in the West Bank and the Gaza Strip are considered 'residents of a conflict zone' and as such, they are denied the right to claim compensation for death, injury, or damage to property inflicted by Israeli forces. The law applies retroactively to incidents going back to September 2000. Source: Amnesty International, *Public Statement MDE 15/042/2005*, News Service No. 203, 28 July 2005. On 1 September 2005, nine human rights organisations in Israel and the occupied territories filed a petition to Israel's Supreme

It found that the construction of the wall was contrary to international law, notably because it was constructed inside the occupied territories and because of the regime associated with it.[12]

On 30 April 2003, the Roadmap to Peace was put on the table by the International Quartet, consisting of the United States, the Russian Federation, the United Nations and the European Union.[13] This three-phase plan aimed for a final and comprehensive settlement of the Israeli-Palestinian conflict by 2005, on the basis of a goal-driven and performance-based approach. For a long time, the results of the Roadmap remained very limited. In August 2005, the Israeli withdrawal from the Gaza Strip became a reality, although it also brought about new problems for the Palestinians, as will be discussed in the last section.

2.2 EC/EU position on the Middle East conflict

EC/EU positions on the Middle East conflict date back to 1970s. In 1973, the then nine Member States of the EEC affirmed their support for the 'legitimate rights of the Palestinians'.[14] The European Council's 'Venice Declaration' of 13 June 1980 affirmed the Community's support for the right to the existence and security of all states in the region, including Israel, and justice for all peoples, thus again stressing the recognition of the legitimate rights of the Palestinian people.[15] On 25 November 1996, on the basis of the Articles J.3 and J.11 TEU, Mr Miguel Angel Moratinos was appointed EU Special Envoy for the Middle East Peace Process, a function which he was to fulfil for over six years.[16] On 29 April 1997, an EU Advisor was appointed to oversee the implementation of the EU assistance programme to support the Palestinian Authority in its efforts to counter terrorist activities emanating from the territories under its control and to contribute to the Middle East peace process.[17] The 'Berlin Declaration' of 24 March 1999 introduced the notion

---

Court demanding that the Court declare void the above-mentioned amendments to the Civil Torts (Liability of the State) Law on the grounds that they are unconstitutional. Source: The Association for Civil Rights in Israel, Press Release, 1 September 2005.

12 For a comparison between the two cases, see Y. Shany, 'Capacities and inadequacies: a look at the two separation barriers cases', 38 *Israel Law Review* (2005) pp. 230-246. Also see S. Zunes, 'Implications of the U.S. reaction to the World Court Ruling against Israel's 'separation barrier'', *MIFTAH*, 18 January 2005, available at: <http://www.miftah.org>.

13 Joint Statement S0097/03, available at: <http://ue.eu.int/ueDocs/cms_Data/docs/pressdata/en/declarations/75591.pdf>.

14 Statement of the Nine Foreign Ministers on the Situation in the Middle East, 6 November 1973.

15 *Bull. EU* 6-1980, p. 7 et seq.

16 Joint Action 96/676/CFSP of 25 November 1996 adopted by the Council on the basis of Art. J.3 of the Treaty on European Union in relation to the nomination of an EU special envoy for the Middle East peace process, *OJ* 1996 L 315/1.

17 Joint Action 97/289/CFSP of 29 April 1997 adopted by the Council on the basis of Art. J.3 of the Treaty on European Union on the establishment of a European Union assistance programme to

of a viable Palestinian State by stating that the European Union is convinced that the creation of a democratic, viable and peaceful sovereign Palestinian State on the basis of existing agreements and through negotiations would be the best guarantee of Israel's security and Israel's acceptance as an equal partner in the region.[18] In the Common Strategy on the Mediterranean Region, adopted on 19 June 2000, the European Union outlines the steps it intends to take in order to secure peace in the region.[19] Among other things, it emphasises that bilateral and international actions need to be coordinated. Considering the enormous amounts of money being made available for projects, especially in Palestine (as explained in more detail in section 4 below), this seems a sensible idea. Finally, in the 'Seville Declaration' of 22 June 2002, the European Union stated that the objective should be an end to the occupation and the establishment of a democratic, viable, peaceful and sovereign State of Palestine, on the basis of the 1967 borders, if necessary with minor adjustments agreed by the parties. The end result should be two states living side by side within secure and recognised borders, enjoying normal relations with their neighbours. In this context, a fair solution should be found for the complex issue of Jerusalem and a just, viable and agreed solution to the problem of the Palestinian refugees.[20]

In spite of the EU role in the process of drafting the Roadmap, and in spite of the important role that the European Union plays as Israel's main trading partner[21] and as a major donor to the building up of a Palestinian State,[22] most commentators are of the opinion that a more substantial role in the peace process for the European Union is still lacking.[23]

---

support the Palestinian Authority in its efforts to counter terrorist activities emanating from the territories under its control, *OJ* 1997 L 120/2. The mandate was extended until 31 May 2002 by Council Decision 1999/440/CFSP of 6 July 1999 concerning the extension of joint action 97/289/CFSP on the establishment of a European Union assistance programme to support the Palestinian Authority in its efforts to counter terrorist activities emanating from the territories under its control, *OJ* 1999 L 171/1.

18 *Bull. EU* 3-1999, p. 7 et seq.

19 Common Strategy of the European Council of 19 June 2000 on the Mediterranean region, *OJ* 2000 L 183/5, extended until 23 January 2006 by Decision 2004/763/CFSP of the European Council of 5 November 2004 amending Common Strategy 2000/458/CFSP on the Mediterranean region in order to extend the period of its application, *OJ* 2004 L 337/72. No new decisions have been adopted to extend the Common Strategy's period of application, so it must be assumed that it has been silently replaced by the ENP. See section 7 below and also chapter 19 in this volume.

20 *Bull. EU* 6-2002, p. 8 et seq.

21 About 40 per cent of Israeli imports come from the European Union and about 30 per cent of Israeli exports are directed towards it. The European Union occupies first place in Israel's imports and second place in its exports. Source: <http://europa.eu.int/comm/external_relations/israel/intro/index.htm>.

22 See section 4 below on this issue.

23 B. Soetendorp, 'The EU's involvement in the Israeli-Palestinian Peace Process: the building of a visible international identity', 7 *EFA Rev.* (2002) pp. 283-295; E. Aoun, 'European Foreign Policy and the Arab-Israeli Dispute: Much ado about nothing?', 8 *European Foreign Affairs Review*

A new EU Special Representative for the Middle East Peace Process was appointed on 14 July 2003.[24] The mandate of the Special Representative, Marc Otte, is based on the European Union's policy objectives regarding the Middle East peace process, which include a two-state solution with Israel and a democratic, viable, peaceful and sovereign Palestinian State living side-by-side within secure and recognised borders enjoying normal relations with their neighbours in accordance with UN Security Council Resolutions 242, 338, 1397 and 1402 and the principles of the Madrid Conference. In June 2004, the Final Report on an EU Strategic Partnership with the Mediterranean and the Middle East[25] was approved by the Council, with the primary objective 'to promote the development, through partnership, of a common zone of peace, prosperity and progress in the Mediterranean and the Middle East.' This lucid objective 'will be developed mainly through existing instruments and mechanisms.' The report continues by outlining key principles and general approaches which the European Union intends to adopt to deal with different aspects of its relationship with the countries in this area. Apart from reaffirming the framework for action, the report seems to add little to earlier EU documents.

3. EC TRADE RELATIONS WITH ISRAEL AND THE PALESTINIAN AUTHORITY

3.1 **EC-Israel trade relations**

The first trade agreement between the European Economic Community and Israel dates back to 1964.[26] It provided for the temporary and partial suspension of the common external tariff duties on approximately twenty industrial and commercial products. Five years later, in 1970, a new five-year preferential agreement progressively reduced customs duties on Israeli goods and led to a staged reduction of Israeli import tariff barriers.[27]

(2003) pp. 289-312; N. Tocci, 'The widening gap between rhetoric and reality in EU policy towards the Israeli-Palestinian conflict', CEPS Working Document No. 217, January 2005, available at: <http://www.ceps.be>.

24 Council Joint Action 2003/537/CFSP of 21 July 2003 appointing the European Union Special Representative for the Middle East peace process and amending Joint Action 2002/965/CFSP, *OJ* 2003 L 184/45, as last amended by Joint Action 2006/119/CFSP of 20 February 2006 extending the mandate of the European Union Special Representative for the Middle East peace process, *OJ* 2006 L 49/8, until 28 February 2007 to include giving guidance to the heads of mission of EUPOL COPPS and EU BAM Rafah.

25 Available at: <http://ue.eu.int/uedocs/cmsUpload/Partnership%20Mediterranean%20and%20 Middle%20East.pdf>.

26 Trade Agreement between the European Economic Community and the State of Israel, *OJ* 1964 L 95/1571.

27 Accord entre la Communauté économique européenne et l'état d'Israël, signé à Luxembourg le 29 juin 1970, *JO* 1970 L 183/2.

In 1975, the first free trade area agreement was concluded, albeit of limited scope. Over time, several adaptations took place.[28] It has been described as a minimalist agreement, since it focused on trade relations and commercial cooperation, granting Israel a certain preferential status.[29] It sought the reciprocal abrogation of all custom duties and other quantitative import restraints on industrial goods and the establishment of a framework of cooperation, with the aid of additional protocols from 1977 in the areas of finance, agriculture and industry. The 1975 agreement did not stand in the way of the introduction of quantitative export restrictions by an EEC Member State, as these did not fall within its scope.[30] Where agricultural products were concerned, the 1975 agreement and the protocols from 1988 entitled Israel to concessions on approximately 70 per cent of its exports to the European Community. The latter received duty-free status for a number of its own products, subject to limited tariff quotas that applied during particular periods of the year. Still, many barriers to agricultural exports from Israel to the European Communities remained. Hence, the most important issue that delayed the signature of a new agreement was the negotiation of provisions on removing more of these agricultural trade barriers.[31] In addition, reluctance on the Israeli side to have Palestinians from outside the occupied territories included in the peace negotiations seems to have been a delaying factor.[32] Thus, it took until 20 November 1995 for a new Association Agreement to be signed, in other words, until just before the Barcelona Conference.[33] The agreement entered into force on 1 June 2000[34] and provides additional reciprocal trade concessions with the aim of 'the gradual establishment of a free trade area'. Although some argue

---

[28] P. Malanczuk, 'The legal framework of the economic relations between Israel and the European Union', in A.E. Kellermann, et al., eds., *Israel among the Nations* (The Hague, T.M.C. Asser Press 1998) pp. 263-279, provides an extensive overview of these developments.

[29] Zell, Goldberg & Co, 'Report on the Free Trade Agreement between Israel and the European Union', August 2001, available at: <http://www.fandz.com/hrtml/iseurft.html>.

[30] ECJ, Case 174/84 *Bulk Oil (Zug)* v. *Sun International Limited and Sun Oil Trading Company*, *ECR* [1986] 559.

[31] E. Lannon, 'The compatibility of the Euro-Mediterranean regional integration with the multilateral rules', in P. Demaret, J.-F. Bellis and G. García Jiménez, *Regionalism and multilateralism after the Uruguay Round* (Brussels, European Interuniversity Press 1997) pp. 771-802 at p. 792.

[32] R. Hollis, 'Europe and the Middle East: power by stealth?', 73 *International Affairs* (1997) pp. 15-29 at p. 20.

[33] The Euro-Mediterranean Conference of Ministers of Foreign Affairs, held in Barcelona on 27-28 November 1995, marked the starting point of the Euro-Mediterranean Partnership (Barcelona process), a wide framework of political, economic and social relations between the Member States of the European Union and partners of the Southern Mediterranean. See also n. 19 *supra*.

[34] Euro-Mediterranean Agreement establishing an association between the European Communities and their Member States, of the one part, and the State of Israel, of the other part, *OJ* 2000 L 147/3.

that Israel should become a member of the European Union,[35] the further establishment of a larger free trade area by the year 2010 is what is on the EU agenda for the time being, in accordance with the 1995 Barcelona Declaration.[36] Israel already has a free trade area relationship with the United States[37] and EFTA.[38] For agriculture, preferential treatment was extended and concessions were made by the Community on cut flowers and citrus fruits.

In July 2003, a new protocol on rules of origin was agreed upon, allowing for the extension of the pan-European system of cumulation of origin[39] to the Barcelona partners, which include Israel and the Palestinian Authority. The next stage aims at amending the protocols on origin in the relevant Euro-Mediterranean agreements, *inter alia*, the 1995 Association Agreement with Israel and in the 1997 Interim Association Agreement with the Palestinian Authority. This is necessary in order to insert the changes necessary for the application of diagonal cumulation,[40] which in its turn could help to foster economic integration and allow for a better use of the complementarities and the economics of scale in the Euro-Mediterranean area[41] and help to resolve the dispute on the preferential treatment of goods from disputed territories, a topic that will be dealt extensively below. Also in July 2003, agreement was reached on replacing the first two protocols to the Association Agreement with Israel as of 1 January 2004, further liberalising trade in agricultural products.

---

35 A. Tovias, 'Why should Israel become a member of the European Union? A strategic perspective', paper for the Conference on the full integration of Israel in the EU, European Parliament, Brussels, 4-6 March 2002.

36 In the Barcelona Declaration of 1995, the Euro-Mediterranean Partners (Israel, Morocco, Algeria, Tunisia, Egypt, Jordan, the Palestinian Authority, Lebanon, Syria, Turkey, Cyprus and Malta) and the European Union agreed on the establishment of a Euro-Mediterranean Free Trade Area (EMFTA) by 2010, by means of the Euro-Mediterranean Association Agreements between the European Union and the Mediterranean Partners, together with free trade agreements between the partners themselves. See also chapter 12 in this volume.

37 Agreement on the Establishment of a Free Trade Area between the Governments of Israel and the United States of America, 22 April 1985. This agreement provides for a gradual elimination of all tariffs between the two states during the 1985-1995 period.

38 Israel-EFTA Free Trade Agreement, 17 September 1992. This agreement eliminated all tariffs and other trade restrictions for industrial products and most tariffs for agricultural products as of 1 January 1993.

39 Cumulation allows originating products of country A to be further processed or added to products originating in country B, just as if they had originated in country B. The resulting product has the origin of country B. Source: <http://europa.eu.int/comm/taxation_customs/customs/customs_duties/rules_origin/preferential/article_774_en.htm>.

40 Diagonal cumulation operates between more than two countries provided they have free trade agreements containing identical rules of origin and provisions for cumulation between them. Products will have the origin of the country where the last working or processing operation took place, provided that it was more than a minimal operation.

41 Commission Staff Working Paper, ENP Country Report on the Palestinian Authority of the West Bank and Gaza Strip, COM (2004) 373 final, Brussels, 12 May 2004, p. 15.

3.2 EC-Palestinian Authority trade relations

The European Community first granted preferential access for products originating from the occupied territories through Regulation 3363/86.[42] This was a unilateral decision as the Community did not yet recognise any qualified Palestinian authority with which to conclude an agreement on this issue. As a consequence, the Community granted the Palestine Chambers of Commerce in the West Bank and the Gaza Strip the right to certify the origin of products from these territories. In April 1991, the 1986 regulation was replaced by Regulation 1134/91, which guaranteed improved access to the Community for a number of agricultural products.[43] This regulation was in turn replaced by Regulation 1981/94.[44] In 1997, a Euro-Mediterranean Interim Association Agreement on trade and cooperation[45] was concluded which is to guide the relationship with the territories and to provide a more stable legal, political and economic framework for EU-Palestinian relations. The Interim Agreement will be examined below.

3.3 Conclusions

Despite the existence of a legal framework, the provisions contained therein are not fully operational. As a matter of fact, two issues stood in the way of giving full effect to the Community agreements with Israel and the Palestinian Authority.

---

[42] Council Regulation (EEC) No. 3363/86 of 27 October 1986 on the tariff arrangements applicable to imports into the Community of products originating in the occupied territories, *OJ* 1986 L 306/103. The Israeli opposition to the implementation of this regulation stood in the way of signature and ratification of three Additional Protocols to the 1975 Agreement between Israel and the EEC for some time. See I. Greilsammer, 'The non-ratification of the EEC-Israel Protocols by the European Parliament (1988)', 27 *Middle Eastern Studies* (1991) pp. 303-321.

[43] Council Regulation (EC) No. 1134/91 of 29 April 1991 on the tariff arrangements applicable to imports into the Community of products originating in the occupied territories and repealing Regulation (EEC) No. 3363/86, *OJ* 1991 L 112/1. Amended by Council Regulation (EC) No. 539/96 of 25 March 1996 amending Regulations (EEC) No. 1134/91, (EEC) No. 4088/87 and (EC) No. 1981/94 with regard to the tariff arrangements applicable to imports into the Community of products originating in the West Bank and the Gaza Strip, *OJ* 1996 L 79/6.

[44] Council Regulation (EC) No. 1981/94 of 25 July 1994 opening and providing for the administration of Community tariff quotas for certain products originating in Algeria, Cyprus, Egypt, Israel, Jordan, Malta, Morocco, the Occupied Territories, Tunisia and Turkey, and providing detailed rules for extending and adapting these tariff quotas. Amended by Council Regulation (EC) No. 539/96 of 25 March 1996 amending Regulations (EEC) No. 1134/91, (EEC) No. 4088/87 and (EC) No. 1981/94 with regard to the tariff arrangements applicable to imports into the Community of products originating in the West Bank and the Gaza Strip, *OJ* 1996 L 79/6. The amendment raised the annual Community tariff quota for cut flowers from the West Bank and Gaza strip to 1,500 tonnes.

[45] Euro-Mediterranean Interim Association Agreement on trade and cooperation between the EC, of the one part, and the Palestine Liberation Organisation (PLO) for the benefit of the Palestinian Authority of the West Bank and the Gaza Strip, of the other part, *OJ* 1997 L 187/3. The agreement entered into force on 1 July 1997.

The first issue was the fact that, in practice, the Palestinian exporters could use only a fraction (estimated at an average of 5 per cent) of the possibilities offered to them by the Community's preferential trade schemes. Among the reasons mentioned for this were the *Intifada*, the cordoning off of the Palestinian territories, obstacles put in place by the Israeli customs authorities and the monopoly situation of Israeli operators. Looking at the example of exports of Palestinian strawberries to the Community, it may be noted that although the annual tariff quota was set at 1,200 tonnes, only 10 tonnes of strawberries from the West Bank and the Gaza Strip were exported directly to the Community market, while 203 tonnes transited through an Israeli company in 1993-1994.[46]

The second issue is related to the first. In some trade-related aspects, Israel treated the West Bank and the Gaza Strip as part of the State of Israel. The European Union insists on regarding them as occupied territories to which the EC-Israel Association Agreement does not apply, notably where the preferential treatment of exports to the European Union is concerned. A dispute about the export of goods from these territories to the European Union took years to solve.

4. EURO-MEDITERRANEAN AGREEMENT WITH ISRAEL

4.1 Preamble and joint declaration

The Euro-Mediterranean Agreement creates an association between the European Communities and their Member States, of the one part, and Israel, of the other part. It is based on Article 310 TEC, in conjunction with the second sentence of the first subparagraph of Article 300(2) TEC, and the second subparagraph of Article 310(3) TEC, as well as Article 95 ECSC.[47] In line with the new generation of Association Agreements between the European Community an its Mediterranean partners, the preamble to the agreement emphasises the importance of the UN Charter, and in particular the observance of human rights, democratic principles and economic freedom; the need to strengthen the political stability and economic development of the region through the encouragement of regional cooperation; the need to open a regular political dialogue in bilateral and international contexts on issues of common interest; and the need to maintain a dialogue

46 European Institute for Research on Mediterranean and Euro-Arab Cooperation (Medea), 'EU-Palestine exports, preferential arrangement granted unilaterally by the EC', Medea information file, April 1997, available at: <http://www.medea.be>. Hollis, loc. cit. n. 32, at p. 19 also stresses the logistical difficulties standing in the way of exporting Palestinian goods to Europe.

47 Decision (2000/384/EC, ECSC) of the Council and the Commission of 19 April 2000 on the conclusion of a Euro-Mediterranean Agreement establishing an association between the European Communities and their Member States, of the one part, and the State of Israel, of the other part, *OJ* 2000 L 147/1.

on scientific, technological, cultural, audio-visual and social matters. Respect for human rights and democratic principles is meant to guide the internal and international policy of both Israel and the European Community and is described as constituting an essential element of the agreement.[48] At the request of Israel, a joint declaration on the importance both parties attach to the struggle against xenophobia, anti-Semitism and racism was adopted.

4.2 Overview of the agreement

The agreement forms a legal basis for political dialogue as well as trade relations. It deals, *inter alia*, with the free movement of goods (Arts. 6-28); the right of establishment and supply of services (Arts. 29-30); capital movements, public procurement, competition and intellectual property (Arts. 31-39); scientific and technological cooperation (Art. 40);[49] economic cooperation (Arts. 41-57); cooperation on audiovisual, cultural, information and communication matters (Arts. 58-62); and cooperation on social matters (Arts. 63-66).

4.3 Free movement of goods

According to Article 6, a free trade area between the Community and Israel is to be reinforced in accordance with the modalities laid down in the Association Agreement and in conformity with the provisions of GATT 1994 and other multilateral agreements on trade in goods annexed to the WTO Agreement. The free trade area for industrial products is regulated in Articles 7, 8 and 9. Article 8 provides that customs duties on imports and exports (including those of a fiscal nature), and any charges having equivalent effect, are prohibited between the Community and Israel. Article 7 exempts two categories of goods. Where the

---

[48] R.A. Del Sarto and T. Schumacher, 'From EMP to ENP: What's at stake with the European Neighbourhood Policy towards the Southern Mediterranean?', 10 *EFA Rev.* (2005) pp. 17-38 at p. 22, point out that the European Union seems to lack the will and/or capacity to effectively follow up on human rights issues although the Association Agreements with Arab countries and Israel would offer possibilities to do so. The latest reports of the special rapporteur on the situation of human rights in the Palestinian territories occupied by Israel since 1967, John Dugard, (E/CN.4/2005/29 of 7 December 2004 and Add.1 of 3 March 2005) demonstrates the existence of numerous human rights violations by Israel (notably the continued existence of over 100 settlements in the West Bank and Gaza, inhabited by a rapidly growing number of settlers, contrary to Art. 49 of the Fourth Geneva Convention of 12 August 1949 and the wall being constructed within Palestinian territory, causing some 10 per cent of Palestinian land to be included in Israel and enclosing some 49,400 Palestinians). Israel claims Dugard's reports are one-sided, prejudiced and full of distortions of both fact and law (Letter from the Permanent Representative of Israel to the United Nations addressed to the Secretary-General, 25 October 2004).

[49] Art. 40 envisages the conclusion of separate agreements on scientific and technological cooperation. See, for instance, Agreement on scientific and technical cooperation between the European Community and the State of Israel, *OJ* 2003 L 154/80.

European Union is concerned, the provisions of Chapter 2 of the 1995 Agreement do not apply to those EU goods produced in overseas countries and territories listed in Annex II to the EC Treaty. As for products originating in Israel, one specific group of industrial products[50] is excluded. Article 9 allows for the retention of custom duties or charges for certain goods with an agricultural component. As far as agricultural products are concerned, the 1995 Agreement contains a lot more exemptions in Article 10 et seq.

How serious does the exclusion of agricultural products affect Israel? The country has a comparative advantage due to its climate when it comes to the production of fruit and vegetables, notably citrus fruit. In 2003, agricultural exports only represented some 3 per cent of Israel's export. Over 75 per cent of this export was destined to the European Union. Almost 50 per cent of Israel's agricultural production ends up in the European Union. Some agricultural sub-sectors such as dairy products and cereals are heavily protected nowadays.[51]

Protocols 1 and 2 to the 1995 Agreement were replaced as of 1 January 2004.[52] According to one EU publication, 'most of the agricultural trade in both directions is to be liberalised, covering a wide range of products, from meat and oil to vegetables and wine.'[53] However, a short comparison of the old and new rules reveals that, for several agricultural products, no changes occur where export from Israel to the European Union is concerned.[54]

The 2004 Protocols are to be replaced again via a protocol that takes account of the accession of the new Member States. The most important aspects of this adaptation are provision for the accession of the new Member States to the EC-Israel Association Agreement, adaptation of the protocol on agricultural products[55] and inclusion of the new official languages of the European Union. On 10 February 2004, the Council approved a mandate for the Commission to negotiate a protocol with the State of Israel. The text of the protocol was initialled by the Commission and the Israeli authorities on 29 April 2004 and amended on 19 May 2004 in Brussels. A Commission proposal[56] was issued on 18 November 2004,

---

50 Albumins, albuminates and other albumin derivates listed in Annex I to the Agreement.

51 A. Tovias, 'Mapping Israel's policy options regarding its future institutionalised relations with the European Union', CEPS Working Paper No. 3, January 2003, p. 6.

52 Agreement in the form of an Exchange of Letters between the European Community and the State of Israel concerning reciprocal liberalisation measures and the replacement of Protocols 1 and 2 to the EC-Israel Association Agreement, *OJ* 2003 L 346/67.

53 *Euromed Synopsis*, No. 245, 9 January 2004.

54 For instance, for fresh cut flowers the maximum of 19,500 tonnes that can be exported duty free stayed the same, as did the rules for strawberries (a maximum of 2,600 tonnes duty free during the November-March period).

55 Raising the tariff quota for fresh cut flowers from 19,500 to 19,800 tonnes, but again sticking to the maximum of 2,600 tonnes of strawberries.

56 Proposal for a Council Decision on the signature and provisional application of a Protocol to the Euro-Mediterranean Agreement between the European Communities and their Member States, of

and on 31 January 2006 the Council adopted a decision authorising the signing of a new Protocol. Meanwhile, in accordance with Article 13 of the Protocol, its provisions are to be applied provisionally as of 1 May 2004.

4.4 Products from the post-1967 territories

For both industrial and agricultural goods, the Association Agreement applies only to products originating in the Community and Israel. Article 83 specifies that the agreement applies to 'the territory of the State of Israel', without offering any further definition. The European Union claims that, under international law, the territorial definition of the State of Israel excludes the territories under Israel's administration since 1967 (West Bank, Gaza Strip, East Jerusalem and Golan Heights).[57] Israel regards some of these territories as a part of the State of Israel and issues certificates of origin accordingly.[58] Although the goods produced in these territories make up only a part of the Israeli exports to the European Union,[59] the Community demanded that Israel would label such products appropriately.

The export from the contested territories was not the only issue worrying the Community. In the mid-1990s, a multi-year fraud came to light (1991-1995) involving the export of Brazilian orange juice from Israel to the European Community under preferences. After unsuccessful demands to Israeli customs, which had certified these goods as originating in Israel, the Commission issued a notice in which operators were informed that there were grounds for doubts about the

---

the one part, and the State of Israel, of the other part, to take account of the accession of the Czech Republic, the Republic of Estonia, the Republic of Cyprus, the Republic of Hungary, the Republic of Latvia, the Republic of Lithuania, the Republic of Malta, the Republic of Poland, the Republic of Slovenia and the Slovak Republic to the European Union, COM (2004) 754 final.

[57] Commission Communication to the Council and the European Parliament on the implementation of the Interim Agreement between the EC and Israel, SEC (1998) 695 final.

[58] Israel also claimed that the Israel-Palestinian Protocol on Economic Relations (Paris Protocol) to the Interim Agreement between Israel and the Palestinians amounts to a customs union with the Palestinian authority, allowing it to export goods from the occupied territories. EU diplomats responded that the 'customs envelope' was not an exclusive arrangement since the Palestinians have the right to trade with other partners under Art. 9 of the Interim Agreement. Source: *Financial Times*, 24 April 1998.

[59] According to some sources, it might be a considerable part: 'In meetings with European negotiators, Israeli officials have said that as much as US$2 billion of Israel's annual US$7 billion exports to Europe could be penalised by a policy change, as many Israeli manufactured goods incorporate some materials from settlement communities.' W.A. Orme Jr., 'EU Targets Goods Made in Israeli Settlements', *New York Times*, 22 May 2001. The Commission did stress that this statement was never made to the Commission by Israeli officials. Answer given by Mr Patten on behalf of the Commission to written MEP question P-4072/03. According to others, it concerns only a fraction of the total. Zell, Goldberg & Co, Report on the Free Trade Agreement between Israel and the European Union, August 2001, available at: <http://www.fandz.com/hrtml/iseurft.html>. Israel's then Foreign Minister Simon Peres declared that the 'question is of minimal economic importance but of great political importance' (*Bulletin Quotidien Europe*, 8323, 10, 21-22 October 2002).

validity of so-called 'EUR.1 certificates'[60] submitted to the Community for the importation of orange juice from Israel, that there was a lack of effective administrative cooperation as foreseen in the different preferential agreements signed between the Community and Israel and that there were certain substantial errors in the application of the agreements, to the extent that the validity of all preferential certificates issued by Israel were put in doubt.[61]

By 2001, a new notice replaced the earlier one.[62] It stated that the certificates for orange juice that had been found to be invalid were withdrawn by Israel and that the necessary measures had been taken to allow administrative cooperation as foreseen in the agreements. As to the substantial errors in the application of the agreements, operators were informed that the results of the verification procedures confirmed that Israel issues proofs of origin for products coming from places brought under Israeli administration since 1967, which, according to the Community, are not entitled to benefit from preferential treatment under the agreements. Community operators presenting documentary evidence of origin with a view to securing preferential treatment for products originating from the territories were informed that they must take all the necessary precautions and that putting the goods in free circulation may give rise to a customs debt.

The Israelis were not very receptive to the Community's point of view on withholding trade privileges for goods produced in the occupied territories. A director-general of the Ministry of Agriculture threatened to cancel the benefits and advantages for Palestinian agricultural products under the Paris Agreement, describing the Community's steps as 'sanctions' and as 'defining for us the borders of the State of Israel'.[63] It was also pointed out by others that the 1975 Agreement had *de facto* been applied to products from the occupied territories since the start.[64] EU sources were said to indicate that if Israel would allow Palestinians to export directly to Europe, then the European Union would probably be able to reach an agreement with Israel allowing 'settler' products to come into Europe duty-free, as long as Israel would not mark these products as 'Made in Israel'.[65] The Commission stressed that it was merely demanding a correct application of an existing agreement and that this did not pre-judge final status negotiations between Israel and the Palestinians as regards borders.[66] A fact-finding mission

60 This certificate is described in Annex III to the 1995 Agreement. It is a form in which the details of exported goods and the applicable preferences are to be given. The form is to be endorsed by the customs offices of the state from which the exports takes place. The certificate indicates, *inter alia*, the 'country ... or territory in which the products are considered as originating'.

61 Notice to Importers – Importations from Israel into the Community, *OJ* 1997 C 338/13.

62 Notice to Importers – Imports from Israel into the Community, *OJ* 2001 C 328/6.

63 Danny Krichman, quoted in *Ha'aretz*, 15 May 1998.

64 Head of the Manufacturers Association, quoted in *Ha'aretz*, 22 May 1998.

65 *The Jerusalem Post*, 22 May 1998.

66 Answer to oral question H-0522/98 of MEP Mary Banotti.

took place, which concluded that 'the rules of origin contained in the EC/Israel and the EC/PLO agreements were clearly not respected and that *de facto* accumulation of rules of origin was a common practice for all kinds of goods.'[67] In spite of this report and a multitude of investigations in the EU Member States, by the year 2000 it was not possible to determine with certitude the origin of products suspected of having entered the European Union as Israeli products although they were in fact produced in the contested territories.[68]

For a long time, legal, practical and political aspects of the issue stood in the way of finding an acceptable solution for the parties involved. In July 2003, at the third Euro-Med Trade Ministerial Meeting, ministers endorsed a new protocol on rules of origin that allows the extension of the pan-European system of cumulation of origin to the Mediterranean countries. The next stage, it was reported, would be the amendment of the protocols on the origin of goods in the current bilateral Association Agreements in order to insert the changes necessary for the application of diagonal cumulation.[69] The European Union noted Israel's support for this project and stressed the importance of solving the bilateral issue of rules of origin before the origin protocol was amended. On 13 July 2003, the Commission announced that Commissioner Bolkestein and Israel's Deputy Prime Minister Ehud Olmert had 'agreed to solve the rules of origin problem between the two sides by distinguishing between goods from Israeli settlements and Israeli goods sent to the European Union under the Association Agreement.'[70]

According to APRODEV,[71] the solution aimed at would encompass Israel's disclosing of the name of the locality in which the products covered by all proofs of origin have undergone their final substantial transformation prior to being exported under the agreement. The initialled text also made reference to the Community's proceeding with the amendment of the agreement's protocol on origin to apply diagonal cumulation of origin in the context of the satisfactory implementation of the envisaged arrangement. In APRODEV's view, this would enable Israel to continue to determine the origin of the products it exports in a manner that does not distinguish between production carried out in the State of Israel and production carried out in the territories, since proofs of origin could be issued to ineligible products coming from the territories based on the cumulation of settlement materials, working and processing with Israeli materials, and working and processing within Israel. This would run counter to the Community's

---

67 Mission Report of 30 September 1998.

68 Answer to oral question No. 68 H-0018/00 by Ms Morgantini.

69 According to a Declaration made at the Fourth EU-Israel Association Council of 17-18 November 2003.

70 *Euromed Synopsis*, No. 279, 15 July 2004.

71 Association of World Council of Churches related Development Organisations in Europe (APRODEV), letter of 20 October 2004 to Romano Prodi, President of the European Commission.

objective of preferential treatment only for products from within the State of Israel's pre-1967 borders, would void the Community's right to partially suspend the agreement in response to Israel's continued application of the agreement to the territories and would undermine the position in international law on which the Community can now rely to obtain an end to Israel's application of the agreement to the occupied territories should the Community ever find it necessary to invoke the arbitration mechanism provided under the agreement.[72]

According to the Dutch Minister of Foreign Affairs in June 2004, Israel's promise to start indicating where products were produced was not yet effectuated. He did explain that, in practice, if doubts arise about the certificates of origin issued by Israel, the control mechanism of Article 32 of the protocol was used. Certificates were then sent back to the Israeli customs authorities. A very interesting further explanation by the Minister revealed that the Israeli authorities had only recently started to reply in such a manner that it was possible to establish the actual origin of the products and thus whether or not preferential treatment should be given.[73] In other words: many years after the European Community started complaining about this issue, the origin certificates still were of no help in establishing whether the products stemmed from Israel or the territories, and the Israeli authorities had not been cooperating in establishing exactly where products were produced.

In December 2004, it was reported that the EU-Israel Customs Cooperation Committee had given the green light to adopt a technical arrangement for identifying goods exported to the Union from settlements in the occupied territories. As a result of the arrangement, proposed earlier this year by Israel's Deputy Prime Minister Ehud Olmert, Israel will specify the place of production, thus allowing EU customs officials to identify which goods come from Israel proper (within its 1967 borders) and which from the settlements in the West Bank, the Golan Heights, East Jerusalem and the Gaza Strip. Products from the latter are subject to full customs duties. EU representatives underlined that this was purely a customs measure to allow the EU customs authorities to impose duties in accordance with the EC-Israel Association Agreement and that it was not a solution to the disagreement with Israel over the geographical applicability of the agreement.[74]

On 1 February 2005, a new notice was issued, replacing the one from 2001.[75] Operators were informed that the European Union and Israel had arrived at an

---

72 APRODEV reasons that the Community's acquiescence to Israel's malpractice is established in this case by its failure to take the opportunity to end Israel's malpractice under the agreement while choosing to enact a technical arrangement by agreement with Israel that would serve no purpose if the malpractice were to be discontinued, and is therefore predicated on its continuation.

73 Answers to questions of MPs Koenders and Wilders, TK 2003-2004, Aanhangsel van de Handelingen, 3507-3508. The Minister did add that since most Israeli goods could be assumed to stem from Israel itself, not all certificates of origin violated the agreement.

74 *Euromed Synopsis*, No. 296, 16 December 2004.

75 Notice to importers – Imports from Israel into the Community, *OJ* 2005 C 20/2.

arrangement for the implementation of Protocol 4 of the agreement.[76] As a result, as from 1 February 2005, all EUR.1 movement certificates and invoice declarations made out in Israel will bear the name of the city, village or industrial zone where production conferring originating status has taken place, be it in the territories or within Israel's pre-1967 borders. Operators presenting preferential proofs of origin under the EC-Israel Association Agreement were informed that the preferential treatment will be refused to the goods for which the proof of origin indicates that the production conferring originating status has taken place in a city, village or industrial zone which was brought under Israeli administration after 1967. The end result of this lengthy struggle thus enabled Israel to make its point by continuing to use the word 'Israel' to describe the location of the settlements and the European Union to make its point by charging a tariff on goods produced beyond the pre-1967 borders.

4.5 Institutional framework

The institutional arrangements are similar to the other Euro-Mediterranean Agreements.[77] They include an Association Council and an Association Committee. The creation of subcommittees is also envisaged.[78] The Council is equipped with decision and dispute settlement powers, while the Committee is responsible for the implementation of the agreement. It also has decision-making authority for the management of the agreement. Cooperation between the Knesset and the European Parliament is envisaged in Article 74.[79]

5. INTERIM ASSOCIATION AGREEMENT WITH THE PALESTINIAN AUTHORITY

5.1 Introduction

The 1997 Interim Agreement integrated the Palestinians into the Barcelona process. Its primary aim is to establish the conditions for increased liberalisation of trade and to provide an appropriate framework for a comprehensive dialogue

---

[76] This annex specifies the declaration referred to in Art. 22(4): the exporter of goods covered by this document declares that except where otherwise indicated, the goods meet the conditions to obtain originating status in preferential trade with the EC (or with Israel) and that the country of origin of the goods is Israel (or the EC).

[77] See chapter 12 in this volume.

[78] Decision No. 1/2005 of the EU-Israel Association Council of 29 August 2005 setting up Association Committee subcommittees (2005/640/EC), *OJ* 2005 L 233/34.

[79] It also extends to the European Union's Economic and Social Committee and Israel's Economic and Social Council.

between the European Union and the Palestinian Authority. Article 1 of the agreement adds as objectives contributing to the social and economic development of the West Bank and the Gaza Strip, the encouragement of regional cooperation with a view to the consolidation of peaceful coexistence, and economic and political stability, and the promotion of cooperation in other areas which are of reciprocal interest.

The Interim Agreement provides for a Joint Committee for EC-PA trade and cooperation, which is meant to meet once a year. The Commission, assisted by the EU Member States, represents the Community. Furthermore, the Interim Agreement provides for regular economic dialogue meetings between the parties covering all areas of macro-economic policy, budgetary policy, balance of payments and monetary policy. The first Joint Committee meeting took place on 23 May 2000. Due to the outbreak of the second *Intifada* in late September 2000, the second meeting was held much later than planned, namely on 26 June 2003. Facilitating trade between the European Union and the West Bank and the Gaza Strip were discussed, as were means to fully implement the Interim Agreement. Furthermore, an exchange of views took place on PA efforts to strengthen the rule of law, combat incitement to violence, stabilise public finances and prepare for elections.

A separate joint statement by the European Union and the PLO of the same date as the Interim Agreement established a regular political dialogue intended to help strengthen relations by developing better mutual understanding and regular coordination on issues of common interest. The aim of the joint statement was also to enhance regional stability and security, in particular as regards the Middle East peace process and the Euro-Mediterranean Partnership.

5.2 Free trade area

The 1997 Interim Agreement calls for the progressive establishment of a free trade area over a transitional period not extending beyond 31 December 2001.[80] Article 5 prohibits the introduction of new custom duties on imports, or any other charge having equivalent effect, on trade in industrial products between the Community and the West Bank and the Gaza Strip. Article 6 allows for the export of industrial products from these territories to the Community without any financial and quantitative restrictions. In return, customs duties, and charges having equivalent effect, applicable to the import of products originating in the Community into the West Bank and the Gaza Strip shall be abolished when the agreement enters into force, with the exception of a limited number of products.[81] Where

[80] Art. 3 of the Interim Association Agreement.

[81] Namely those listed in Annexes 2 (pasta and couscous, waffles and wafers, rusks and other bakers' wares) and 3 (candies, lollipops, chocolate, biscuits, chips and snacks, terry bath robes, towels).

agricultural products are concerned, Article 12 et seq. of the Interim Agreement merely lay down that the Community and the Palestinian Authority 'shall progressively establish a greater liberalisation of their trade in agricultural and fishery products of interest to both Parties.' The initial regime for these products was laid down in Article 13 and Protocols 1 (imports into the Community) and 2 (imports into the West Bank and the Gaza Strip) and allowed the European Community to maintain limitations, for example, on the amount of strawberries and cut flowers that could be imported duty free from these territories.[82]

5.3 Latest developments

Agricultural trade between the European Union and the West Bank and the Gaza Strip has been liberalised a bit further since 1 January 2005, following a decision by the EU Council of Ministers on 22 December 2004 amending the Interim Agreement.[83] This decision, implemented by a Commission regulation,[84] was described as a sign of the importance the European Union attaches to the Interim Association Agreement with the Palestinian Authority. It was also pointed out that it should also be seen in the context of the European Neighbourhood Policy (ENP), shortly after the adoption of a Neighbourhood Action Plan with the Palestinian Authority.[85] Palestinian products set to benefit from the new regime include flowers, tomatoes, grapes, strawberries and olive oil.[86] Although a step in the right direction if the European Union intends to stimulate the fragile Palestine economy, the agricultural trade benefits for the West Bank and the Gaza Strip seem to be modest, also in the light of the large amounts of money that the European Union is providing in the form of grants and loans to the Palestinians. This topic will be examined in more detail in the following section.

---

[82] Between 1 November and 31 March (i.e., the period in which it is too cold for most of the EC countries to grow their own strawberries), a maximum of 1,200 tonnes of strawberries could be exported to the EC free of custom duties. Likewise, for cut flowers and fresh flower buds, a maximum of 1,500 tonnes maximum applied.

[83] Agreement in the form of an Exchange of Letters between the European Community and the Palestine Liberation Organisation (PLO) for the benefit of the Palestinian Authority of the West Bank and the Gaza Strip concerning reciprocal liberalisation measures and the replacement of Protocols 1 and 2 to the EC-Palestinian Authority Interim Association Agreement, *OJ* 2005 L 2/6.

[84] Commission Regulation No. 2279/2004 of 30 December 2004 amending Council Regulation No. 747/2001 as regards the Community tariff quotas and reference quantities for certain agricultural products originating in the West Bank and the Gaza Strip, *OJ* 2004 L 396/38.

[85] *Euromed Synopsis*, No. 298 of 6 January 2005, p. 1.

[86] The new quota volumes for fresh cut flowers were set at 2,000 tonnes in 2005, 2,250 tonnes in 2006 and 2,500 tonnes as of 2007. For fresh strawberries, the 1 November to 31 March quota volumes will rise to 1,680 tonnes in 2005, 2,500 tonnes in 2006 and 3,000 tonnes in 2007.

6. FINANCIAL AND TECHNICAL ASSISTANCE

As the State of Israel is a fairly wealthy country, most of the financial and technical assistance of the European Community flows to the Palestinian Authority. Assistance to the Palestinians[87] began in 1971, when the first contribution was made to the regular budget of the United Nations Relief and Works Agency for Palestine Refugees in the Near East (UNRWA). Since then, an expanding number of financial assistance programmes have been supported. From 1994 to the end of 2002, the European Union committed approximately €1 billion in grants and loans and a further €500 million in contributions to UNRWA. On top of that, bilateral EU Member State assistance is estimated to have amounted to €2.5 billion over the same period.[88] The following overview for the period 2000-2003[89] shows where the money was sent in those years:

Community assistance 2000-2003				
	Commitment appropriations (miilion €)			
Budget heading	**2000**	**2001**	**2002**	**2003**
MEDA	119.60	0.00	104.5	92.75
Community operations in connection with the Peace Agreement	20.40	43.05	87.75	47.00
Contribution to the UNRWA	40.24	57.25	55.00	57.75
Humanitarian aid (ECHO)	18.20	26.26	35.00	38.00
Food aid/Food security	16.06	17.10	35.00	20.28
Total	**214.50**	**143.66**	**317.25**	**255.78**

In 2004, just as in 2003, EU aid amounted to over €250 million. It targeted two main objectives: addressing urgent needs caused by the severe economic recession and creating a viable and democratic Palestinian State. The European Union continued to cooperate with other donors, notably via the Reform Trust Fund established by the World Bank in April 2004. The objective of this fund is to improve the management of public finances and to support the viability of PA institutions. The initiative broadens the conditionality that the European Union

---

87 According to a 2002 estimate, approximately 3.2 million Palestinian reside in the West Bank and the Gaza Strip (source: <http://europa.eu.int/comm/world/enp/partners/palestinian_auth_en.htm>).

88 Source: 'The EU's relations with West Bank and Gaza Strip', available at: <http://europa.eu.int/comm/external_relations>.

89 Source: Commission Staff Working Paper, ENP Country Report on the Palestinian Authority of the West Bank and Gaza Strip, Brussels 12 May 2005, SEC (2004) 565.

has always applied to its own assistance to the Palestinian Authority to a wider group of donors and reflects the recognition in the international donor community of the value of the EU approach. The European Union contributed €65 million to this fund in 2004.

For emergency support to social services, €22.75 million was allocated in 2004. The objective of this programme was to mitigate the deterioration of health and higher education services resulting from the ongoing conflict. Following the implementation of the first and second Emergency Services Support Programmes, the Commission has approved €22.75 million for a third programme to be implemented through the World Bank.

As for the Middle East Peace Process (MEPP), some €7.5 million was made available under the European Partnership for Peace Programme for projects conducted with a range of partners that aim to provide support for initiatives that combat violence and strengthen civil society in the Middle East, in particular with groups in both Israeli and Palestinian society that seek a dialogue across cultures.

For the implementation of the Palestinian Authority's reform agenda, €5 million was made available in 2004. Technical assistance continued to be provided in key areas of the Palestinian reform agenda, building on previous support provided by the Commission to advance reforms in key areas of the Palestinian administration, such as financial control and good governance.

For the reinforcement of the Tempus programme, a further €1 million was made available in 2004. This programme, which started in 2003, supports the reform and modernisation of higher education in the Palestinian territories by developing inter-university cooperation with EU universities.

These packages came on top of around €128 million already earmarked through other programmes in 2004, notably €89 million through UNRWA (of which €8 million from ECHO), €37.35 million for humanitarian aid through the ECHO Humanitarian Aid Office and around €10 million for food aid/food security through the World Food Programme and various NGOs and for the European Initiative for Democracy and Human Rights (EIDHR).

Two political hot potatoes continued to pop up where EU funds in this region are concerned: the damage inflicted by the Israeli army on EU-funded projects and the use of these funds for terrorist activities. As for the first issue, upon the request of the EU presidency, a list of projects funded by the European Union and its Member States that were damaged or destroyed by Israeli armed forces was compiled. The damage was estimated at €17 million. The General Affairs Council discussed this list on 28 and 29 January 2002 and stated that the European Union was seriously concerned about the destruction of Palestinian infrastructure and other facilities that help Palestinians in their economic, social and humanitarian development and are financed by the European Union and other donors. The Israeli Government was urged to put an end to this practice. At this point in time, the European Union reserved 'the right to claim reparation in the appropriate fora.'[90] Strangely enough, less than one and a half months later, the Commission indicated, with regard to claims for compensation, that 'property and equipment funded by the Community budget belongs to the beneficiary. Therefore, in strict legal terms, it would be up to the beneficiary (which is in most cases the Palestinian Authority) to take legal recourse.' The Commission did add that '[o]n the political level, in accordance with the General Affairs Council conclusions, the Union has reserved the right to claim reparation in the appropriate fora.'[91] As far as the author could find out, neither the European Union nor the Palestinian Authority have submitted claims against Israel.

As for the second issue, the European Anti-Fraud Office (OLAF) started an investigation on 6 February 2003 in order to examine alleged irregularities concerning European Commission budget assistance provided to the Palestinian Authority under different instruments since 1997. This investigation was closed on 12 March 2005, and its results were communicated to the European Commission together with a number of recommendations on how to further improve safeguards and controls. On the basis of the information available, the investigation 'found no conclusive evidence of support of armed attacks or unlawful activities financed by EC contributions to the PA budget.' OLAF did note that 'there are consistent indications to support the hypothesis that it cannot be excluded that some of the assets of the PA may have been used by some individuals for other than the intended purposes' and that 'the possibility of misuse of the Palestinian Authority's budget and other resources cannot be excluded, due to the fact that the internal and external audit capacity in the Palestinian Authority is still underdeveloped.' Furthermore, it was underlined that 'some of the practices of the past, such as the payment of salaries to convicted persons or the financial aid given to families of "martyrs" as well as the Fatah contributions by PA staff, are liable to be misunderstood and so to lead to allegations that the PA is supporting terrorism.'[92] The misunderstanding seems to be more on the side of the investigators if EU funds were indeed used to support the Fatah movement and families of 'martyrs'.

It may be added that an application for damages based on the alleged liability of the European Commission for the harm suffered by the applicants as a result of the terrorist attack of 27 March 2002 on the Park Hotel in Netanya (Israel), in which thirty people were killed and 140 injured, based on Article 288 TEC was dismissed by both the Court of First Instance and the Court of Justice. It had been

---

90 Answer by the Commission of 25 February 2002 to written question E-0284/02 by Eluned Morgan (PSE), *OJ* 2002 C 277E/29.

91 Answer by the Commission of 8 April 2002 to written question E-0348/02 by Nelly Maes (Verts/ALE) to the Commission, *OJ* 2002 C 277E/35.

92 Source: <http://europa.eu.int/comm/external_relations/gaza/news/olaf05_03.htm>.

claimed that the attack was a result of the educational materials used in Palestinian schools, funded with the help of the European Union.[93]

7. EUROPEAN NEIGHBOURHOOD POLICY

7.1 Introduction

Although the enlarged Union is an economic world power, it is still in the process of shaping a more effective foreign and security policy. The Barcelona process tried to follow a regional approach, which turned out to be hard or even impossible where Israel and the Palestinians were concerned, notably because most of the Arab Mediterranean partners of the European Union are not willing to enter into regional cooperation agreements with Israel. The European Neighbourhood Policy (ENP) operates from a more bilateral perspective than the Barcelona process. Still, the question arises whether the ENP system – even when it is tailor-made for individual countries – is really designed to deal with such volatile issues as the ones existing between Israel and the Palestinians.

The general objective of the ENP is to share the European Union's stability, security and prosperity with neighbouring countries in a way that is distinct from EU membership.[94] In the special case of Israel and Palestine, turning such objectives into reality forms a formidable challenge for the European Union, to say the least. ENP Action Plans, adopted jointly by the European Union and Israel and by the European Union and the Palestinians, can structure the cooperation and can contribute to making progress. However, realising the objectives of stability and security is only feasible if a solution to the severe tensions between Israel and the Palestinians is found. On its own, the European Union can stimulate improvements, but real influence can only be exerted by cooperating with others, notably the United States. Prosperity is an issue that is relevant only to a limited extend to Israel, as its economy is one of the most successful in the Middle East. The same definitely does not apply to the Palestinians. The Palestinian economy was not flourishing in the past, and the current conflict has only worsened the situation. As a large donor, the European Union is making a real difference in this respect

---

93 CFI, Case T-73/03 *Bernard Zaoui and Others* v. *Commission of the European Communities*, not reported; ECJ, Case C-288/03P *Bernard Zaoui and Others* v. *Commission of the European Communities*, not reported.

94 European Neighbourhood Policy: the next steps, Brussels, 2 March 2005, IP/05/236. The Commission repeatedly stressed – for instance in COM (2003) 104 final, p. 15 – that the ENP is compatible with and complementary to the Barcelona process. Del Sarto and Schumacher, loc. cit. n. 48, at p. 21, point out that the ENP does abandon the prevalence of the principle of regionality, after noting that regional cooperation between Israel and the Arab Mediterranean partners of the European Union is almost non-existent (p. 19).

by supporting the Palestinian Authority, its civil servants and police. But here, also, coordination with other actors in the region is of the utmost importance.

7.2 The ENP Action Plans for Israel and the Palestinian Authority

Together with Israel and representatives of the Palestinian Authority, a set of priorities was defined and incorporated in jointly agreed Action Plans, covering a number of key areas for specific action. The EU Council meeting on 13 and 14 December 2004 in Brussels endorsed the ENP Action Plans for Israel and the Palestinian Authority,[95] and adopted conclusions on the ENP. The Council 'emphasised that the intensity and level of ambition of relations with each ENP partner will be differentiated, reflecting the degree to which common values are effectively shared, the existing state of relations with each country, its needs and capacities, as well as common interests'. The Council also noted that the Association Agreements concluded in the context of the Barcelona process 'provide the framework for pursuing the implementation and monitoring of the Action Plans'.[96]

In the Action Plan for Israel,[97] a three-year time frame is set out for helping to fulfil the provisions of the Association Agreement, build ties in new areas and encourage and support Israel's objectives for further integration into European economic and social structures. The document stresses that the ENP regarding Israel intends to move beyond cooperation to a significant degree of integration, including through a stake in the European Union's internal market and the possibility for Israel of participating progressively in key aspects of EU policies and programmes. For the time being, the Association Agreement remains the framework for cooperation. The action plan represents 'a declaration of mutual objectives and commitments.' Most of the described 'actions' in Part 2 of the document are little more than declarations, intentions and so forth and lack concreteness (e.g., 'Work together to promote the shared value of democracy, rule of law and respect for human rights and international humanitarian law' under section 2.1). It will thus be difficult to measure progress[98] in meeting the priorities outlined in the action plan.

---

[95] As well as others for Jordan, Morocco, Tunisia and for the European Union's Eastern neighbourhood. The Action Plan will be submitted for formal adoption within the framework of the EU-Israel Association Council.

[96] Diagonal cumulation operates between more than two countries provided they have free trade agreements containing identical rules of origin and provisions for cumulation between them. Products will have the origin of the country where the last working or processing operation took place, provided that it was more than a minimal operation.

[97] Available at: <http://europa.eu.int/comm/world/enp/pdf/action_plans/Proposed_Action_Plan_EU-Israel.pdf>.

[98] A task that falls upon the joint bodies established under the Association Agreement.

The Action Plan for the Palestinian Authority[99] covers a time frame of three to five years. Its implementation is intended to help fulfil the provisions of the interim Association Agreement and to encourage and support the Palestinian Authority's national reform objectives and further integration into European economic and social structures. Implementation of the action plan is also intended to significantly advance the approximation of Palestinian legislation, norms and standards to those of the European Union and to help to devise and implement policies and measures to promote economic growth, employment and social cohesion, to reduce poverty and to protect the environment, thereby contributing to the long-term objective of sustainable development. Contrary to the EU-Israel Action Plan, the one for the Palestinian Authority contains many concrete actions (e.g., 'Ensure effective implementation of the Basic Law…' and 'Develop sufficient administrative capacity to prevent and fight against fraud and other irregularities affecting national and international funds…' under section 2.1 subsections (3) and (10) respectively). One of the concrete steps taken under this action plan was the establishment of the EU Coordinating Office for Palestinian Police Support (EU COPPS).[100] At the start, the office consisted of four EU police experts and a local team handling administrative tasks.[101] After noting that, in spite of these efforts, violence in Israel and the occupied territories had started to escalate again, the Council agreed in principle on 18 July 2005 that EU support to the Palestinian civil police should take the form of an European Security and Defence Policy (ESDP) mission building on the work of the EU COPPS in cooperation with all parties concerned.[102] On 7 November 2005, in the light of the continued terrorist attacks on Israel after its withdrawal from the Gaza Strip, the Council indeed decided to launch a three-year ESDP Police Mission in the Palestinian Territories (EUPOL COPPS).[103] The aim of the mission is to contribute to the establishment of sustainable and effective policing arrangements under Palestinian ownership in accordance with the best international standards.[104]

The differences between the two action plans are large, notably where their concreteness is concerned. The main reason for this is the economic and security

---

[99] Available at: <http://europa.eu.int/comm/world/enp/pdf/action_plans/Proposed_Action_Plan_EU-Palestinian_Authority.pdf>.

[100] A name that begs the question whether the European Union has a special office for inventing catchy acronyms.

[101] Announcement by J. Solana, EU High Representative for the CFSP, of 20 April 2005, S 163/05.

[102] 2675th Council Meeting, External Relations, Brussels, 18 July 2005, 10815/05 (Presse 178) p. 17.

[103] 2687th Council Meeting, External Relations, Brussels, 7 November 2005, 13622/05 (Presse 274) p. 11.

[104] Council Joint Action 2005/797/CFSP of 14 November 2005 on the European Union Police Mission for the Palestinian Territories, *OJ* 2005 L 300/65.

situation in which the Palestinians find themselves, making it imperative to take concrete steps forward in order to improve their situation. The realisation of both of the action plans depends to a large degree on the progress that can be made in securing a solution to the Israeli-Palestinian conflict. In this respect, in spite of the numerous declarations and missions of special envoys, special representatives, advisors and experts, and in spite of the large amounts of money made available to the Palestinians, in particular, the European Union has until now only been able to play a limited role in the peace process.

8. LATEST DEVELOPMENTS: A WINDOW OF OPPORTUNITY?

After the death of Yasser Arafat on 11 November 2004, Mahmoud Abbas was elected as the new leader of the PLO. On Sunday 9 January 2005, elections for the Palestinian presidency took place. Some 45 per cent of the electorate went to vote, despite the call by radical Palestinian movements to boycott the elections. As expected, Mr Abbas won the elections, obtaining some 62 per cent of the vote. Mr Abbas is regarded as a moderate who has condemned the armed Palestinian uprising and favours resumption of negotiations with Israel. At the same time, he has pledged to be as unyielding as Yasser Arafat on the Palestinians' minimum conditions for peace: Israeli withdrawal from all the West Bank and the Gaza Strip, equating to 22 per cent of Palestine before the creation of Israel in 1948; East Jerusalem to be the capital of the new Palestinian State and a negotiated resolution for Palestinian refugees based on their right of return to homes in what is now Israel.

In February 2005, a summit took place in the Egyptian town Sharm El-Sheikh at the end of which a truce was announced by Israel and the Palestinian Authority, represented by Mr Abbas. He stated that 'the calm which will prevail in our lands starting from today is the beginning of a new era', and vowed to spare no effort 'to protect this emerging opportunity for peace.' Unfortunately, a spokesmen of the radical Hamas movement insisted that Mr Abbas's declaration of a truce was not binding on them, but a unilateral declaration of the Palestinian Authority.[105]

By October 2005, the Israeli withdrawal from the Gaza Strip had been achieved. The European Union has pushed for a two-state solution for a long time. The fact that Israel has now finally made a first step in this direction may mean that EU pressure has had some effect. However, it seems unlikely that without the support of the other countries in the Quartet the same progress would have been achieved. Israel's disengagement from the Gaza Strip is also just a first step. The European Union would like to see Israel withdrawing from the entire

---

105 *The New York Times*, 8 February 2005.

West Bank as well. The United States appears to accept the continued presence of Jewish settlers in the West Bank in certain settlement blocs. Without the United States changing its position in this respect, and given the strong opposition in Israel to withdrawing only a couple of thousand Jewish settlers from the Gaza Strip compared to the large numbers of settlers in the West Bank, the European Union faces an almost insurmountable task of realising its policy aims, given the fact that it might have become an economic world power but still lacks the coherency and instruments needed to also play a decisive role where foreign and security policy are concerned.

As for the economic aspects of the latest developments, the European Union did urge that one trade-related aspect would need to be taken into account, namely that Israel should not cancel free trade arrangements when withdrawing from the territories.[106] Commissioner Verheugen, meanwhile, has spoken out in favour of stronger ties between the European Union and Israel, saying that he could imagine Israel being widely integrated into the European economic structures and being a full participant in the internal market.[107]

On 5 October 2005, the Commission presented a Communication that sketches a vision of the road ahead.[108] Among other things, resources for infrastructure which could be used for sea or airports were mentioned. Such resources would be vital indeed. In order for Palestine to become a viable economic unit, it will need an airport[109] and a seaport.[110] Even if the European Union and other donors would be able to help in securing the (re)construction of such facilities, agreement with Israel on the operation and control will need to be reached before the Palestinians could profit from this infrastructure. Israel has agreed in principle with the construction of the seaport, but the tense security situation that emerged after the Israeli withdrawal from the Gaza Strip stands in the way of agreement on the airport. Meanwhile, an even more pressing transport issue has arisen. Regular means of moving goods and people to and from the Gaza Strip have been severely

---

106 'Mandelson urges Israel to retain Gaza free trade deal', *Financial Times*, 21/22 May 2005.

107 *Euobserver.com*, 11 January 2005.

108 Communication from the Commission to the Council and the European Parliament, EU-Palestinian cooperation beyond disengagement – towards a two-state solution, COM (2005) 458 final.

109 An international airport was inaugurated on 24 November 1998 as part of agreements stipulated in the September 1995 Oslo II Accord and the 23 October 1998 Wye River Memorandum. It has been largely closed since October 2000 by Israeli orders and its runway was destroyed by the Israeli Defence Forces between December 2001 and January 2002. Israel has indicated that it will allow the Palestinian Authority to rebuild the airport but it has not yet provided answers as to whether it will allow the Palestinian Authority to operate the airport following the evacuation. Under the terms of the 'Disengagement Plan', Israel will retain complete control over Palestinian airspace.

110 In 1999, in the Sharm el-Sheikh Agreement between the PLO and Israel, it was agreed that a seaport would be opened in Gaza. In July 2000, construction began on the seaport. This construction was halted by Israel in October 2000.

hindered and have at times come to a complete standstill after the withdrawal, basically isolating the Gaza Strip from the outside world and causing serious damage to the Palestinian economy. On top of this, the elections that brought a victory to Hamas[111] – an organisation aimed at the destruction of Israel – has lead Israel to postpone the transfer to the Palestinian Authority of tax revenues that Israel collects on behalf of the Palestinians. The European Union also has a problem with Hamas: it designated this group as a terrorist organisation.[112]

The current paradoxical situation is that the Palestinian Authority only stands a chance of getting a grip on the situation if the economy improves, but in order for the economy to improve a firmer grip on the situation in the Gaza Strip is necessary. The help of the European Union and of others should prevent extremists on both sides from further frustrating the peace process. In this respect, the External Relations Council's decision of 7 November 2005 to accept a third party monitoring role for the European Union at the Rafah crossing point on the Gaza-Egypt border,[113] together with the decision to launch an ESDP Police Mission,[114] both form examples of ways in which the European Union is trying to contribute to maintaining momentum towards full implementation of the Roadmap to Peace. Unfortunately, recent events only seem to be leading further away from peace.

---

111 The militant group – considered a terrorist organisation by the European Union and the United States – won 74 of the 132 seats contested in the Palestinian Legislative Council elections in January 2006.

112 Decision 2005/221/CFSP, *OJ* 2005 L 69/64.

113 2687th Council Meeting, External Relations, Brussels, 7 November 2005, 13622/05 (Presse 274) p. 10. The EU monitors at Rafah have been the object of Palestinian anger in a series of protests (e.g., by Palestinian police officers and most recently in connection with the publication of cartoons satirising the prophet Mohammed), causing EU personnel to leave their posts. See A. Rettman, 'EU election monitors face risks in Palestine', *EUObserver.com*, 3 January 2006.

114 Council Joint Action 2005/889/CFSP of 12 December 2005 on establishing a European Union Border Assistance Mission for the Rafah Crossing Point (EU BAM Rafah), *OJ* 2005 L 327/28.

CHAPTER 14

RUSSIAN FEDERATION (INCLUDING KALININGRAD)

Christophe Hillion*

Relevant legal documents:

- Joint Declaration on the establishment of official relations between the European Economic Community and the Council for Mutual Economic Assistance, *OJ* 1988 L 157/34.
- Council Decision 90/116/EEC of 26 February 1990 on the conclusion of an Agreement between the EEC, Euratom and the USSR, *OJ* 1990 L 68/1.
- Guidelines on the recognition of new States in Eastern Europe and the Soviet Union, *Bull. EC* 12-1991, points 1.4.5. and 1.4.6.
- Council and Commission Decision on the conclusion of a Partnership and Cooperation Agreement between the EC and their Member States, of the one part, and the Russian Federation, of the other part, *OJ* 1997 L 327/1.
- Protocol to the Partnership and Cooperation Agreement establishing a partnership between the European Communities and their Member States, of the one part, and the Russian Federation, of the other part, *OJ* 2000 L 283/19.
- Agreement on cooperation in science and technology between the European Community and the Government of the Russian Federation, *OJ* 2000 L 299/15, renewed in 2003 for a period of five years by a Council Decision concerning the conclusion of an Agreement aimed at renewing the Agreement on cooperation in science and technology between the European Community and the Government of the Russian Federation, *OJ* 2003 L 299/20.
- Agreement between the European Community and the Russian Federation on trade in textile products, *OJ* 1998 L 222/2.
- Agreement between the European Coal and Steel Community and the Government of the Russian Federation on trade in certain steel products, *OJ* 2002 L 195/55, amended by Council Regulation 1386/2004/EC, *OJ* 2004 L 255/1.
- Council Regulation (EEC, Euratom) No. 2157/91 of 15 July 1991 concerning the provision of technical assistance to economic reform and recovery in the Union of Soviet Socialist Republics, *OJ* 1991 L 201/2.

* Europa Institute, University of Leiden. The author thanks Anne Myrjord for her invaluable remarks and suggestions. The usual disclaimer applies.

- Council Regulation (Euratom, EEC) No. 2053/93 of 19 July 1993 concerning the provision of technical assistance to economic reform and recovery in the independent States of the former Soviet Union and Mongolia, *OJ* 1993 L 187/1.
- Council Regulation (Euratom, EC) No. 1279/96 of 25 June 1996 concerning the provision of assistance to economic reform and recovery in the New Independent States and Mongolia, *OJ* 1996 L 165/1.
- Council Regulation (EC, Euratom) No. 99/2000 of 29 December 1999 concerning the provision of assistance to the partner States in Eastern Europe and Central Asia, *OJ* 2000 L 12/1.
- Common Strategy 1999/414/CFSP of the European Union of 4 June 1999 on Russia, *OJ* 1999 L 157/1.
- Council Joint Action 1999/878/CFSP establishing an EU cooperation programme for non-proliferation and disarmament in the Russian Federation, *OJ* 1999 L 331/11.
- European Union action plan on common action for the Russian Federation on combating organised crime, *OJ* 2000 C 106/5.
- Common Strategy 2003/471/CFSP of the European Council of 20 June 2003 amending Common Strategy 1999/414/CFSP on Russia in order to extend the period of its application, *OJ* 2003 L 157/68.
- Protocol to the Partnership and Cooperation Agreement establishing a partnership between the European Communities and their Member States, of the one part, and the Russian Federation, of the other part, to take account of the accession of the Czech Republic, the Republic of Estonia, the Republic of Cyprus, the Republic of Latvia, the Republic of Lithuania, the Republic of Hungary, the Republic of Malta, the Republic of Poland, the Republic of Slovenia and the Slovak Republic to the European Union, 27 April 2004, available at: <http://www.europa.eu.int/comm/external_relations/ russia/russia_docs/protocol_0404.htm>.
- Joint Statement of the EU and the Russian Federation on transit between the Kaliningrad region and the rest of the Russian Federation, EU-Russia Summit, 11 November 2002, Brussels, available at: <http://www.europa.eu.int/comm/external_relations/russia/summit_11_02/js_kalin.htm>.
- EU-Russia Roadmap for the 4 Common Spaces, available at: <http://www.eu2005.lu/en/actualites/documents_travail/2005/05/10-4spaces/index.html>.

1. THE LARGEST NEIGHBOUR OF THE EUROPEAN UNION

The Russian Federation is by far the largest neighbour of the European Union. Its vast landmass (16,995,800 sq. km) is bounded, on its western flank, by several EU Member States (Estonia 294 km, Finland 1,340 km, Latvia 217 km, Lithuania (Kaliningrad Oblast) 227 km and Poland (Kaliningrad Oblast) 206 km). It is the most populated European country with nearly 144 million inhabitants. About a million of them live in the exclave of Kaliningrad. Russia is also a chief trading partner of the European Union, particularly as a major supplier of energy products, notably oil and natural gas, for which there is high demand in the Union. As main beneficiary of the Soviet Union's strategic and diplomatic legacy, Russia inherited, *inter alia*, a seat on the United Nations Security Council and large military assets, including a massive although partly deliquescing nuclear arsenal. It also plays a considerable role in the post-Soviet area, which is characterised by several 'frozen conflicts', such as in Transnistria and Nagorno-Karabakh, as well as peaceful revolutions, such as in Georgia and Ukraine.

In view of this non-exhaustive list of geopolitical and economic traits, Russia is not an EU neighbour *comme les autres*. Indeed, it excluded itself from the ambit of the specific European Neighbourhood Policy (ENP) developed by the Union in view of its 2004 enlargement,[1] to address the external implications of its expansion. Keen on being treated as a great power, Russia has instead favoured the development of a 'strategic partnership' with the Union, modelled on EU-US relations. Member States concur in supporting the principle of a close EU-Russia relationship, based on 'common values', as a means of ensuring the stability and prosperity of the European continent.[2] At the same time, they have often differed in their attitude towards Russia, a tendency which was accentuated with the 2004 EU enlargement. In short, the Russian Federation has been, and will continue to be, a challenging European partner for the Union,[3] if not the most testing one for its emerging foreign policy.

The establishment and development of the EU-Russia relationship is relatively new given the recent appearance of these two actors on the international stage.

---

1 See chapters 1 and 2 in this volume.

2 The connection between the EU-Russia relationship and the future of the continent is conspicuous in several EU documents. In 1995, the Commission emphasised that 'it is time that the European Union and Russia recognized their historical vocation as the two principal European powers and, in the common interest, sought to develop the close and enriching partnership'. Communication of the Commission on the European Union and Russia: the future relationship, COM (1995) 223 final, pp. 1-2. The 2003 European Security Strategy, upheld by the European Council, also points out, albeit in remarkably brief terms that: '[the EU] should continue to work for closer relations with Russia, a major factor in our security and prosperity'. *A secure Europe in a better world – The European Security Strategy*, approved by the Brussels European Council on 12 December 2003 and drafted under the responsibility of the EU High Representative for the CFSP, Javier Solana, available at: <http://ue.eu.int/uedocs/cmsUpload/78367.pdf>. See also European Parliament, Committee on Foreign Affairs, *Final Report on EU-Russia relations* (Rapporteur: Cecilia Malmström), 4 May 2005, A6-0135/2005.

3 The Russian Federation has joined the activities of several organisations in Europe. Russia was admitted to the Council of Europe on 28 February 1996. It ratified the European Convention on Human Rights and recognised the right of individual petition on 5 May 1998. As regards the Conference/Organisation for Security and Cooperation in Europe (C/OSCE), Russia took over from the Soviet Union (the USSR signed the Helsinki Final Act in 1975 and the Charter of Paris in 1990). After its independence, Russia became involved in the activities of the North Atlantic Treaty Organisation (NATO) with the establishment of the North Atlantic Cooperation Council (later renamed the Euro-Atlantic Partnership Council). In 1994, it joined the 'Partnership for Peace' programme and in 2002 the NATO-Russia Council was established. Russia applied for membership of the WTO in June 1993 and accession negotiations are still underway.

Russia emerged as a sovereign and independent state[4] from the collapse of the Soviet Union in 1991.[5] It was recognised as a 'new independent state' on 31 December 1991 by the European Community and its Member States.[6] At that time, the EC Member States were in the process of signing the Treaty on European Union that established the Union, with the aim to 'assert [its] identity on the international stage',[7] notably through a Common Foreign and Security Policy.[8] Crafted in this context, the EU-Russia relationship was formalised in a Partnership and Cooperation Agreement (PCA), signed in 1994. Part of the emerging eastern policy of the Union, this agreement was conceived as an alternative to its approach towards the Central and Eastern European countries (CEECs) embodied in the Europe Agreements that became a stepping stone to EU membership.[9]

The PCA was supplemented by several sectoral agreements and by all-encompassing instruments based on the evolving EU Treaty. The partnership has thus been given an increasingly wide scope embracing the different dimensions of the Union, thereby acquiring a complex legal nature. Indeed, it has often been used as a testing ground for new instruments of EU external relations. The common strategy, introduced by the Treaty of Amsterdam as a new instrument of the CFSP, is a case in point. More generally, the multifaceted EU-Russia partnership in many ways typifies the development of a complex system of EU external relations.

---

[4] Russia became the 'Russian Federation' on the basis of the Federation Treaty and Regional Power of March 1992.

[5] The Soviet Union was dissolved on 8 December 1991 by the Presidents of Byelorussia, Russia and Ukraine respectively. The next day, they announced the creation of the Commonwealth of Independent States (CIS), joined later by most other former Soviet republics on a voluntary basis. The CIS is a loose regional organisation dispossessed of any supranational powers, as set out by Art. 1 of the Charter of the CIS adopted on 22 January 1993 at a session of the CIS Council of Heads of States at Minsk. The text is available in 34 *ILM* (1995) p. 1282.

[6] On 16 December 1991, an extraordinary ministerial meeting was organised within the framework of the European Political Cooperation. Ministers adopted *guidelines on the recognition of new States in Eastern Europe and in the Soviet Union.* According to the resulting declaration, the process of recognition of the new states required: respect for the provisions of the Charter of the United Nations and the commitments subscribed to in the Final Act of Helsinki and in the Charter of Paris, especially with regard to the rule of law, democracy and human rights; guarantees for the rights of ethnic and national groups and minorities in accordance with the commitments subscribed to in the framework of the CSCE; respect for the inviolability of all frontiers which can only be changed by peaceful means and by common agreement; acceptance of all relevant commitments with regard to disarmament and nuclear non-proliferation as well as to security and regional stability; commitment to settle by agreement, including where appropriate by recourse to arbitration, all questions concerning state succession and regional disputes. For the text of the declaration, see *Bull. EC* 12-1991, points 1.4.5. and 1.4.6.

[7] Art. 2 TEU.

[8] Title V TEU.

[9] See further M. Maresceau and E. Montaguti, 'The relations between the European Union and central and eastern Europe: a legal appraisal', 32 *CMLRev.* (1995) p. 1327; M. Maresceau, 'On association, partnership, pre-accession and accession', in M. Maresceau, ed., *Enlarging the European Union* (London, Longman 1997) p. 3; K. Inglis, 'The Europe Agreements compared in the light of their pre-accession reorientation', 37 *CMLRev.* (2000) p. 1173.

This chapter seeks to give an overview of the key elements of this multifaceted partnership. It first examines its legal foundation, namely the PCA. It then looks at the continuous elaboration of the relationship, notably through the common strategy. The chapter finally gleans some insight into the EU enlargement's implications on the partnership, including a brief analysis of the four EU-Russia 'common spaces' which are being gradually established in the framework of the PCA.

2. THE LEGAL FOUNDATION OF THE EU-RUSSIA PARTNERSHIP

The EU-Russia partnership was established by the Partnership and Cooperation Agreement concluded in 1994 between the European Communities and their Member States of the one part, and the Russian Federation, of the other part.[10] It entered into force in 1997 for a period of ten years.[11] This section looks at the objectives and legal bases of the agreement (2.1). It then examines some its key substantive (2.2) and institutional (2.3) provisions and finally evokes the agreement's originality from the point of view of the law of EU external relations (2.4).

2.1 The objectives and legal bases of the PCA

Article 1 PCA sets out a long list of ambitious objectives. The partnership between the EU and Russia aims

- to provide an appropriate framework for the political dialogue between the Parties allowing the development of close relations between them in this field;
- to promote trade and investment and harmonious economic relations between the Parties based on the principles of market economy and so to foster sustainable development in the Parties;

10 It is sometimes referred to as a *'partenariat maximal'*. See M. Maresceau, 'Les relations entre l'Union européenne et la Russie à un tournant de leur histoire', in J. Raux and V. Korovkine, eds., *Le partenariat entre l'Union européenne et la Fédération de Russie* (Rennes, Apogée 1998). See further, e.g., Y. Borko, 'Russia and the EU in the 21st century: Four possible scenarios', 2 *The European Union Review* (1997) p. 91; V. Shemiatenkov, 'The relations between Russia and the EU', *RAE-LEA* (1997) p. 277. This novel type of agreement was also concluded with several other newly independent states (NIS) which emerged from the dissolution of the Soviet Union. See further, e.g., C. Hillion, 'Partnership and Cooperation Agreements between the EU and the NIS of the ex-Soviet Union', 3 *EFA Rev.* (1998) p. 399.

11 At their summit in May 2005, the leaders 'briefly discussed the future of EU-Russia relations after the expiry of the *first period of validity* of the [PCA] in 2007.' [emphasis added] The reference to the 'first period of validity' could suggest that the application of the PCA might be prolonged. The June 2006 European Council, however, referred to the 'successor to the Partnership and Cooperation Agreement' (see point 24 of the Presidency conclusions), suggesting that the PCA might soon be replaced by a new type of agreement.

- to strengthen political and economic freedoms;
- to support Russian efforts to consolidate its democracy and to develop its economy and to complete the transition to market economy;
- to provide a basis for economic, social, financial, and cultural cooperation founded on the principles of mutual advantage, mutual responsibility and mutual support;
- to promote activities of joint interest;
- to provide an appropriate framework for the gradual integration between Russia and a wider area of cooperation in Europe;
- to create the necessary conditions for the future establishment of a free trade area between the Community and Russia covering substantially all trade in goods between them, as well as conditions for bringing about freedom of establishment of companies, of cross-border trade in services and of capital movements.

These objectives surpass the aim of 'normalisation' of the 1989 Trade and Cooperation Agreement concluded between the EC and the Soviet Union, and which the PCA replaces.[12] The upgrading of the relationship to a 'partnership' takes account of the political and economic transformation embarked upon by the Russian authorities in the aftermath of the disintegration of the Soviet Union.[13] At the same time, the *rapprochement* envisaged by the PCA contrasts with that foreseen by the Association Agreements concluded with the CEECs during the same period (Europe Agreements – EAs), and later, with the Western Balkans (Stabilisation and Association Agreements – SAAs).[14] In particular, the PCA does not evoke the prospect of Union membership.[15] Instead, the preamble of the

---

[12] See Council Decision 90/116/EEC of 26 February 1990 on the conclusion of an Agreement between the EEC, Euratom and the USSR; *OJ* 1990 L 68/1. The agreement was concluded in the aftermath of the mutual recognition between EEC and Comecon of June 1988 (see Council Decision of 22 June 1988 on the conclusion of the Joint Declaration on the Establishment of official relations between the European Economic Community and the Council for Mutual Economic Assistance, *OJ* 1988 L 157/34). See further A. Toledano Laredo, 'L'Union Européenne, l'ex-Union Soviétique et les pays de l'Europe centrale et orientale: un aperçu de leurs accords', 30 *Cahiers de Droit Européen* (1994) p. 543; Borko, loc. cit. n. 10, at p. 91; Shemiatenkov, loc. cit. n. 10, at p. 277; J.-C. Gautron, 'Les relations entre l'union européenne et la Russie: un cadre historique et théorique', available at: <http://www.edc.spb.ru/publications/june/gautron.htmle>.

[13] On the objectives of the PCA, see further J. Raux 'Un partenariat aux finalités spécifiques', in Raux and Korovkine, op. cit. n. 10, p. 163 at p. 171.

[14] The SAA FYROM entered into force on 1 April 2004 (*OJ* 2004 L 84/13). The SAA Croatia entered into force on 1 February 2005 (*OJ* 2005 L 26/3). The conclusion of SAAs is still foreseen for Albania, Bosnia-Herzegovina and Serbia and Montenegro. See further chapter 10 in this volume.

[15] However, the reference to membership in the EA was ambiguous. The last indent of the preamble of the EA Poland read as follows: '[r]ecognizing the fact that the final objective of Poland is to become a member of the Community and that this association, in the view of the Parties, will help to achieve this objective'. Indeed, the initial proposal of the Commission concerning the establishment

agreement with Russia refers to 'a gradual rapprochement between Russia and *a wider area of cooperation in Europe and neighbouring regions*' [emphasis added].[16] This distinction between a 'wider area of cooperation in Europe', on the one hand, and the perspective of membership, on the other, is echoed by the provisions of the respective agreements. For instance, Article 1 EA Romania provides, *inter alia*, that the association establishes 'an appropriate framework for [its] gradual integration into the Community'.[17] By contrast, the first article of the PCA refers again, more modestly, to a 'gradual integration between Russia and a wider area of cooperation in Europe'. From the outset, therefore, the EU policy towards the Eastern European states embodied a differentiation between *partners* and *associated states*. The distinction with respect to the nature and ultimate goals of the respective relationships[18] was later confirmed by the *formal* acknowledgment, by the European Union, that associated countries in Central and Eastern Europe were eligible for membership.[19]

The difference of objectives is epitomised by the choice of legal bases of the respective agreements. While the EAs and the SAAs are based on Article 310 TEC, the PCA is founded partly on the classical legal basis of EC trade and cooperation agreements, namely Articles 133 and 308 TEC.[20] Not being an Association Agreement, the PCA does not create 'special, privileged' links between

---

of EAs with the CEECs emphasised that the question of membership should be dealt with separately. See Communication from the Commission to the Council and the Parliament – Association Agreements with the Countries of Central and Eastern Europe: A General Outline, COM (1990) 398 final. See further Maresceau, loc. cit. n. 9, at p. 9; P.-C. Müller-Graff, 'Legal framework for relations between the European and central and eastern Europe: general aspects', in Maresceau, op. cit. n. 9, p. 27 at p. 34. See also the Court's understanding of the EAs reference to membership in Case C-63/99 *The Queen* v. *Secretary of State for the Home Department, ex parte Wieslaw Gloszczuk and Elzbieta Gloszczuk* [2001] *ECR* I-6369; Case C-235/99 *The Queen* v. *Secretary of State for the Home Department, ex parte Eleanora Ivanova Kondova* [2001] *ECR* I-6427; Case C-257/99 *The Queen* v. *Secretary of State for the Home Department, ex parte Julius Barkoci and Marcel Malik* [2001] *ECR* I-6557; Case C-268/99 *Aldona Malgorzata Jany and Others* v. *Staatssecretaris van Justitie* [2001] *ECR* I-8615; and case note, 40 *CMLRev.* (2003) p. 465 at p. 489 et seq. The SAAs also aim to prepare the associated countries to enter the European Union. The preamble of the SAAs is more explicit in this respect than that of the EAs. See further chapter 10 in this volume.

16 This formulation prefigures the Wider Europe/European Neighbourhood Policy of the European Union towards the neighbours of the enlarged Union.

17 *OJ* 1994 L 357/2. For an interpretation of this EA objective, see the Opinion of Jacobs AG in Case C-162/00 *Land Nordrhein-Westfalen* v. *Beata Pokrzeptowicz-Meyer* [2002] *ECR* I-1049.

18 This was indeed emphasised during the negotiations of the PCAs by the representative of the Council before the European Parliament. See the response to Written Question E-2997/93 to the Council on the relations between the Community, Eastern Europe and the Commonwealth of Independent States, *OJ* 1993 C 35/46.

19 Presidency conclusions, Copenhagen European Council, June 1993, *Bull. EU* 6-1993, point 7.

20 See further S. Peers, 'EC frameworks of international relations: co-operation, partnership and association', in A.A. Dashwood and C. Hillion, eds., *The general law of EC external relations* (London, Sweet & Maxwell 2000) p. 160.

the parties to the agreement.[21] The initial legal basis of the PCA was later supplemented by additional provisions in the light of the European Court of Justice's conclusions in Opinion 1/94 on the WTO Agreement,[22] and given the wide scope of the trade and economic provisions of the agreement.[23]

2.2 Selected substantive aspects of the PCA

2.2.1 *Trade*

The PCA covers trade in goods and services and contains provisions on establishment and the movement of workers. With respect to trade in goods, the agreement anticipates Russia's accession to the WTO, in the sense that the trade regime it establishes is directly inspired by key GATT principles. For instance, the PCA foresees the application of the most favoured nation (MFN) principle to trade in industrial goods by reference to Article I(1) GATT. It also refers to the derogations to the MFN principle, foreseen in Article XXIV GATT.[24] Hence, the Community may maintain the free trade arrangements with its partners, and so can Russia, without the PCA trade regime being infringed. The MFN principle foreseen in the PCA is supplemented notably by the freedom of transit of goods (Art. V GATT) and the principle of non-discrimination in internal taxes, charges and regulations by reference to Article III(2) GATT. The extensive reference to the cardinal rules of GATT gives the PCA a flavour of '[WTO] pre-accession strategy',[25] particularly in view of the authority the parties have granted to the GATT *acquis*.[26]

---

[21] Interpreting the provisions of Art. 310 TEC, the Court refers, in para. 9 of the *Demirel* case, to 'special, privileged links with a non-member country which must, at least to a certain extent, take part in the Community system'. ECJ, Case 12/86 *Meryem Demirel* v. *Stadt Schwäbisch Gmünd* [1987] *ECR* 3719.

[22] ECJ, Opinion 1/94 *Competence of the Community to conclude international agreements concerning services and the protection of intellectual property* [1994] *ECR* I-5267.

[23] See further C. Flaesch-Mougin, 'Quel partenaire européen pour la Fédération de Russie? Union européenne, Communautés, Etats membres?', in Raux and Korovkine, op. cit. n. 10, at p. 57.

[24] As already envisaged in Art. 3 PCA. The draft PCA did not contain the reference to GATT, which appeared in the course of the negotiations. See European Commission, *A short guide to the Agreement on Partnership and Cooperation between the European Union and its Member States and the Russian Federation* (DG I, External Economic Relations, November 1994).

[25] See further J. Lebullenger, 'Un Accord de partenariat confronté aux règles du GATT et de l'OMC', in Raux and Korovkine, op. cit. n. 10, at p. 199.

[26] The inclusion of GATT entails that the relevant GATT practice is directly taken into account in the interpretation of the PCA provisions concerned, as indeed confirmed by Art. 94 PCA Russia. It states that '[w]hen examining an issue arising within the framework of the [PCA] in relation to a provision referring to an Article of the GATT, the Cooperation Council shall take into account *to the greatest extent possible* the interpretation that is generally given to the Article of the GATT in question by the Contracting Parties to the GATT'. [emphasis added] The legal effect granted to the

Unlike the EAs and the SAAs,[27] the PCA does not establish a free trade area between the parties, but rather mentioned it as a long-term objective. According to Article 3 PCA:

> The Parties undertake to consider development of the relevant titles of this Agreement, in particular Title III ['Trade in goods'] and Article 53 ['competition'], as circumstances allow, with a view to the establishment of a free trade area between them... Such development shall only be put into effect by virtue of an agreement between the Parties in accordance with their respective procedures.

The feasibility of the FTA is closely linked to the evolution of Russia's economic situation,[28] and implicitly to its accession to the WTO.[29] It should be recalled that, at the time of the signature of the agreement in 1994, Russia was not regarded as a market economy but as an 'economy in transition',[30] a concept which does not correspond to any particular Community commercial policy regime.[31] Until the Community's eventual recognition of Russia as a market economy in 2002,[32]

GATT/WTO *acquis* is noticeable given the Court's case law on GATT/WTO law. See, e.g., Case C-377/02 *Léon Van Parys NV v Belgisch Interventie- en Restitutiebureau (BIRB)* [2005] *ECR* I-1465. Maresceau and Montaguti, loc. cit. n. 9, at p. 1327.

27 In Title III on 'Free movement of goods', the EAs provide for the progressive establishment of a free trade area covering 'all industrial goods'. See for instance Art. 8 EA Bulgaria, where a specific regime concerns textiles, ECSC and agricultural products. See further, e.g., M. Cremona, 'Community relations with the Visegrád Group', 18 *ELR* (1993) p. 345; S. Norberg, 'The movement of goods in EU-CEECs relations in the light of the EEA experiences', in Maresceau, op. cit. n. 9, at p. 75. As regards SAAs, see, e.g., Art. 15 SAA Croatia.

28 The PCA's reference to the establishment of an FTA with Russia stems from the latter's insistence on having a trade regime that is as close as possible to that foreseen by the EAs. The European Parliament had unsuccessfully insisted on the establishment of free trade area between the Community and the NIS, notably in its Resolution of 17 September 1992 on relations with the CIS, *OJ* 1992 C 284/145. It criticised the restrictive trade regime envisaged by the Community towards the NIS on several occasions. See Report of the European Parliament Committee for External Economic Relations on the future agreements between the Community and the Newly Independent States of the former Soviet Union, A-30073/93); see also the Opinion of the Economic and Social Committee on the relations between the European Union and Russia, Ukraine and Belarus, *OJ* 1995 C 102/40.

29 European Commission, op. cit. n. 24. On 21 May 2004, then EC Trade Commissioner Pascal Lamy and Russian Economic Development and Trade Minister German Gref signed the agreement concluding the bilateral market access negotiations for the accession of the Russian Federation to the WTO.

30 See preamble of the PCA. See further Borko, loc. cit. n. 10.

31 J.-P. De Laet, 'L'accord de partenariat et de coopération entre l'Union européenne, ses Etats Membres et la Russie', in *Annales des mines. Réalités Industrielles* (Saint-Etienne, GEDIM 1995).

32 On 7 November 2002, the European Union formalised the recognition of Russia as a market economy in the context of trade defence by amending the EC's anti-dumping and anti-subsidy laws, see: <http://trade-info.cec.eu.int/doclib/cfm/doclib_results.cfm?action=results1>. However, market economy treatment had been granted to Russian companies on a case-by-case basis since 2000.

specific EC rules on trade defence mechanisms applied to Russia, notably Community anti-dumping regulations in relation to non-market economies.[33]

2.2.2 *Approximation of legislation*

The evolution of the economic situation to which the PCA refers also relates to the *legal* development of Russia. The agreement provides that an important condition for strengthening the economic links between Russia and the Community is the *approximation of legislation*. Under the PCA, Russia endeavours to ensure that its legislation is gradually made compatible with that of the Community.[34] This 'legislative cooperation' thus establishes a correlation between Russia's ability to take on EC rules in the fields of, *inter alia*, company law, banking law and the environment,[35] and the strengthening of their economic links, which includes the creation of an FTA.[36] Indeed, legal approximation has become increasingly prominent in the partnership, particularly in the context of the establishment of a common economic space between the Union and Russia.[37]

2.2.3 *Rights of workers*

As far as the PCA provisions on workers are concerned, Article 23, included in Chapter I on 'labour conditions', provides that '[s]ubject to the laws, conditions and procedures applicable in each Member State' the Community and its Member States 'shall ensure' that the treatment accorded to Russian nationals legally employed in an EU Member State is not discriminatory.[38] Although drafted differently, the proviso '[s]ubject to the conditions and modalities applicable in each Member State' included in a similar EA non-discrimination provision could not, according to the Court of Justice's judgment in the *Pokrzeptowicz-Meyer* case, 'be interpreted in such a way as to allow the Member States to subject the

[33] See further F.G. Jacobs, 'Anti-dumping procedures with regard to imports from eastern Europe', in M. Maresceau, ed., *The political and legal framework of trade relations between the European Community and Eastern Europe* (Dordrecht, Martinus Nijhoff Publishers 1989) p. 291.

[34] Art. 55 PCA.

[35] Art. 55(2) PCA establishes a non-exhaustive list of areas where approximation should take place. It includes company accounts and taxes, protection of workers in the workplace, financial services, rules on competition, public procurement, protection of the health and life of humans, animals and plants, consumer protection, indirect taxation, customs law, technical rules and standards, nuclear laws and regulation, and transport.

[36] See further C. Hillion, 'Approximation of law in the context of the EU-NIS Partnership', in L. Ficzere and A.E. Nikodém, eds., *Perspectives of the legal approximation process in Central Eastern Europe* (Budapest, Academy of European Law 2001) p. 78.

[37] See further section 4.3 below.

[38] At the start of negotiations, only a 'best endeavour' clause was foreseen by the Community. See European Commission, op. cit. n. 24, at p. 9.

principle of non-discrimination ... to conditions or discretionary limitations'.[39] Such an interpretation, said the Court, would render that provision 'meaningless and deprive it of any practical effect'.[40] In the *Simutenkov* case, which concerned a Russian football player employed by Club Deportivo Tenerife on the basis of an alleged discriminatory contract, the Court extended its *Pokrzeptowicz-Meyer* approach to the PCA labour provisions. It held that the latter establish an *obligation of result* on the parties.[41] The caveat contained in the PCA does not make the application of the non-discrimination principle dependent on further implementing measures to be taken by Member States[42] or by the Cooperation Council.[43] The PCA non-discrimination principle could thus be invoked by a legally employed Russian national, both against the authorities of a Member State and against a private employer.

It should be noted that, according to the Court, the 'finding that the principle of non-discrimination set out [in the PCA with Russia] is directly effective is not ... gainsaid by its purpose and nature':[44]

> The fact that the Agreement is thus limited to establishing a partnership between the parties, without providing for an association or future accession of the Russian Federation to the Communities, is not such as to prevent certain of its provisions from having direct effect. It is clear from the Court's case-law that when an agreement establishes cooperation between the parties, some of the provisions of that agreement may, under the conditions set out in paragraph 21 of the present judgment, directly govern the legal position of individuals...

39 ECJ, Case C-162/00 *Pokrzeptowicz-Meyer* [2002] *ECR* I-1049, para. 30. See also ECJ, Case 438/00 *Deutscher Handballbund* [2003] *ECR* I-4135.

40 ECJ, Case C-162/00 *Pokrzeptowicz-Meyer* [2002] *ECR* I-1049, para. 24. See also the Opinion of Jacobs AG, loc. cit. n. 17, at paras. 32-44. On the Member States' residual powers as regards immigration rules, see also the judgment of the ECJ in Case C-327/02 *Panayotova et al.* v *Minister voor Vreemdelingenzaken en Integratie*, judgment of 16 November 2004, and the Opinion of Maduro AG of 19 February 2004; Case C-63/99 *Głoszczuk* [2001] *ECR* I-6369; Case C-235/99 *Kondova* [2001] *ECR* I-6427; Case C-257/99 *Barkoci and Malik* [2001] *ECR* I-6557; Case C-268/99 *Jany and Others* [2001] *ECR* I-8615; and case note, 40 *CMLRev.* (2003) p. 465.

41 In this regard, see also ECJ, Case C-265/03 *Igor Sumitenkov* v. *Ministerio de Educación y Cultura and Real Federación Española de Fútbol* [2005] *ECR* I-2579.

42 Para. 23. See also the Opinion of Stix-Hackl AG. It should be recalled that a Spanish court had already allowed a Russian football player, Valery Karpin, to invoke the principle of non-discrimination of the PCA Russia against his club, before the ECJ acknowledged the direct effect of the relevant PCA provisions (Juzgado de lo social No 15 de Madrid, *Valeri Karpin / Liga nacional de Fútbol Profesional*, Sentencia 478/2000).

43 Para. 25.

44 ECJ, Case C-162/00 *Pokrzeptowicz-Meyer* [2002] *ECR* I-1049, para. 25. See also ECJ, Case C-312/91 *Procedural issue relating to a seizure of goods belonging to Metalsa Srl.* [1993] *ECR* 3751; Case C-63/99 *Głoszczuk* [2001] *ECR* I-6369; Case C-235/99 *Kondova* [2001] *ECR* I-6427; Case C-257/99 *Barkoci and Malik* [2001] *ECR* I-6557. On this point, see further R. Petrov, 'Rights of third country/Newly Independent States' nationals to pursue economic activity in the EU', 4 *EFA Rev.* (1999) p. 235.

It thus appears that the distinct purpose and legal nature of the PCA were only of reduced relevance in the Court's determination of the direct effect of the non-discrimination principle. This suggests more generally that the initial differentiation between *partners* and *associated* states is in effect of limited significance, at least with respect to the legal effect of certain provisions of the Association Agreements and Partnership and Cooperation Agreements, respectively. Indeed, the Court held that the *scope* of the PCA non-discrimination principle and that of the EAs were the same. It transposed its EA interpretations,[45] and indeed its EC interpretations,[46] to the equal treatment provisions of the Community-Russia partnership.[47] The Court reiterated that the difference in context or purpose of the PCA was not intended to give the prohibition of discrimination 'any meaning other than which follows from the ordinary sense of these words'.[48]

Differences nonetheless remain as regards the labour provisions of the respective agreements. While the PCA non-discrimination principle has the same legal implications as the EA principle, it should be pointed out that in contrast to the latter agreement the labour provisions of the former do not cover the situation of the spouse or children of the legally employed worker. Neither the spouse nor the children of a Russian worker in an EU Member State have access to the latter's labour market, contrary to the spouse and children of an 'EA worker'.[49] Furthermore, the PCA provisions on the coordination of social security require the parties to conclude further agreements on the matter,[50] whereas the EAs endow the Association Council with the power to take measures to ensure such coordination.[51]

2.2.4 *Right of establishment*

With regard to establishment, the PCA makes several distinctions between the establishment of companies, on the one hand, and the operation of subsidiaries and branches, on the other. Insofar as the establishment of Russian companies in the EU Member States is concerned, the PCA only provides for the MFN principle.[52] The operation of Community subsidiaries of Russian companies, however, is governed by national treatment, or MFN treatment, 'whichever is better'.[53] As

45 As articulated in ECJ, Case 438/00 *Deutscher Handballbund* [2003] *ECR* I-4135.

46 E.g., ECJ, Case 415/93 *Bosman* [1995] *ECR* I-4921.

47 Para. 34.

48 Paras. 35-36.

49 E.g., Art. 38 EA Romania.

50 Art. 24 PCA Russia.

51 E.g., Arts. 39 and 40 EA Romania.

52 Art. 28(1) PCA. The establishment of Community companies in Russia is also governed by the MFN principle.

53 Art. 28(2) PCA. The operation of Russian subsidiaries of Community companies enjoys national or MFN treatment, whichever is better (Art. 28(3) PCA).

to the operation of branches of Russian companies in the EU Member States, the PCA foresees the application of the MFN principle.[54] The agreement thus establishes a complex legal regime for Russian business operations in the Community,[55] which includes a distinction between *establishment* and *operation*, which is at odds with the notion of 'establishment' envisaged in the EA and EC contexts.[56] For instance, the EAs provide for national treatment with respect to the establishment and operation of companies but also of *nationals* from the other party.[57] Indeed, the EA right of establishment means setting up and managing subsidiaries, branches and agencies, and the right to take up and pursue economic activities as self-employed persons.[58] In the PCA, however, natural persons do not have a right of establishment of their own, and the right of entry and residence in relation to establishment is limited to 'key personnel'.[59] Clearly, the Member States wanted to maintain a strict control on the movement of persons coming from Russia, which ultimately limits the rapprochement between the parties. As far as trade in services is concerned, the PCA provides for the application of the MFN principle with regard to an exhaustive list of services annexed to the agreement.[60] Specific rules apply to sectors not mentioned therein,[61] such as transport, space launches and mobile satellite communications.

---

54 Art. 28(4) PCA. The operation of Russian branches of Community companies is governed by MFN treatment (Art. 28(4) PCA).

55 It could be added that the Community made a number of reservations concerning the operation of subsidiaries of Russian companies (Annex 3 of the PCA). Russia did the same with respect to the operation of subsidiaries of Community companies (Annex 4 of the PCA). In addition, the PCA contains various exceptions to the application of the MFN principle on establishment and national treatment in the sectors of Russian banking and insurance services (Art. 29 and Annexes 6 and 7 of the PCA). One may add that various sectors are not covered by the establishment provisions of the PCA, namely air, inland waterways and maritime transport (Art. 35(1) PCA), although an exception to the exception concerns shipping agencies involved in international maritime transport (Art. 35(2) and (3) PCA).

56 Art. 43 TEC. As regards the EA context, see ECJ, Case C-268/99 *Jany and Others* [2001] *ECR* I-8615.

57 E.g., Art. 45 EA Bulgaria. See further E. Guild, *A guide to the right of establishment under the Europe Agreements* (London, Baileys Shaw & Gillett 1996).

58 Art. 45(5) EA Bulgaria. These provisions have been interpreted widely by the ECJ in various cases dealing particularly with self-employed persons. It notably gave a wide scope to the EA right of establishment by acknowledging that rights of entry and residence are conferred, as 'corollaries', to self-employed persons (Case C-63/99 *Głoszczuk* [2001] *ECR* I-6369; Case C-235/99 *Kondova* [2001] *ECR* I-6427; Case C-257/99 *Barkoci and Malik* [2001] *ECR* I-6557). It also interpreted the EA notion of 'economic activities as self-employed persons' in terms that are similar to the EC notion of 'activities of self-employed persons' (Art. 43 TEC) (Case C-268/99 *Jany and Others* [2001] *ECR* I-8615).

59 Art. 32(2) PCA. See also the Joint Declaration in relation to Arts. 26, 32 and 37.

60 Art. 36 and Annex 5 of the PCA. The initial draft only foresaw a 'best endeavour' clause. See European Commission, op. cit. n. 24, at p. 14.

61 Arts. 39-43 PCA.

2.2.5 *Cooperation in specific policy fields*

In addition to trade provisions, the PCA encourages the parties to cooperate in several policy areas. The agreement contains titles on economic,[62] cultural[63] and financial cooperation.[64] In the economic sphere, the parties 'shall foster … cooperation … to contribute to the expansion of their respective economies, to the creation of a supportive international economic environment and to the integration between Russia and a wider area of cooperation in Europe.'[65] The economic cooperation foreseen by the parties notably covers science and technology (Art. 62), education and training (Art. 63), energy (Art. 65), the nuclear sector (Art. 66), the environment (Art. 69), transport (Art. 70) and small and medium-sized enterprises (Art. 76). However, the language used by the PCA is prudent and largely non-committal, and the provisions on cooperation generally foresee measures such as the exchange of information and know-how between the parties. As to cultural cooperation, the agreement modestly, but importantly, stipulates that such cooperation shall be geared towards reinforcing the existing links between Russian and EU citizens and 'to encourage the mutual knowledge of their respective languages and cultures while respecting creative freedom and reciprocal access of cultural values.'[66]

2.2.6 *Financial and technical assistance*

Under the PCA heading on financial cooperation, Russia benefits from temporary financial assistance to achieve the objectives of the agreement, particularly as regards economic and legislative cooperation. In practice, the multidimensional cooperation foreseen by the PCA has been made more tangible through projects supported technically and financially by the Community's Tacis programme.[67]

---

62 Title VII, Arts. 56-83 PCA.

63 Title IX, Art. 85 PCA.

64 Title X, Arts. 86-89 PCA.

65 Art. 56 PCA.

66 Art. 85(1) PCA.

67 Tacis is the acronym for Technical Assistance to the Commonwealth of Independent States, established by Council Regulation (Euratom, EEC) No. 2053/93 of 19 July 1993 concerning the provision of technical assistance to economic reform and recovery in the independent States of the former Soviet Union and Mongolia, *OJ* 1993 L 187/1, which replaced previous Council Regulation (EEC, Euratom) No. 2157/91 of 15 July 1991 concerning the provision of technical assistance to economic reform and recovery in the Union of Soviet Socialist Republics, *OJ* 1991 L 201/2. On the Tacis programme, see further, e.g., L. Delcour, *La politique de l'Union européenne en Russie (1990-2000)* (Paris, L'Harmattan 2002).

The current programme covers the 2000-2006 period.[68] Its priorities are to support institutional, legal and administrative reform; to support the private sector and assist economic development; to help address the social consequences of transition; to develop infrastructure networks; to promote environmental protection and management of natural resources; to develop the rural economy; and to support nuclear safety.[69] By 2006, the European Union will have committed €7,600 million through this programme. Russia is the largest beneficiary of all the countries covered, receiving about half of all funding under the programme (on average €200 million annually). This makes Tacis the largest provider of technical assistance to the Russian Federation.

Annual action programmes are defined jointly by the Commission and the Russian Government. These programmes list projects eligible for assistance. Below is an overview of the distribution of funds in these action programmes for the period 1991-2001.

2.3 The institutional set up of the PCA

The PCA establishes a multilevel institutional framework.[70] At the top of this framework, the EU-Russia summit gathers once or twice a year, at the level of the Presidency of the Council, together with the President of the Commission and the High Representative (HR) for the CFSP, on the one hand, and the President of the Russian Federation, on the other.[71] A Cooperation Council, subsequently renamed the Permanent Partnership Council (PPC) meets once a

---

[68] It is based on Council Regulation (EC, Euratom) No. 99/2000 of 29 December 1999 concerning the provision of assistance to the partner States in Eastern Europe and Central Asia, *OJ* 2000 L 12/1. The Commission services have been preparing a new Tacis concept and regulation through a process of consultation. See: <http://www.europa.eu.int/comm/external_relations/consultations/cswp_tacis.htm>. The Commission published two communications proposing the establishment of a new financial instrument concerning both Russia and the states covered by the ENP. The European Partnership and Neighbourhood Instrument should replace Tacis from 2007 (Communication from the Commission, Paving the way for a New Neighbourhood Instrument, COM (2003) 393 final; Commission's Proposal for a Regulation of the European Parliament and of the Council laying down general provisions establishing a European Neighbourhood and Partnership Instrument, COM (2004) 628 final).

[69] On Russia more specifically, see the 'Country Strategy Paper 2002-2006' for Russia, adopted by the Commission on 27 December 2001, available at: <http://www.europa.eu.int/comm/external_relations/russia/csp/02-06_en.pdf> and the 'National Indicative Programme' for Russia adopted by the Commission on 21 May 2003, available at: <http://www.europa.eu.int/comm/external_relations/russia/csp/04-06_en.pdf>.

[70] Title XI, Arts. 90-97 PCA.

[71] Art. 6 PCA, included in Title II on 'Political dialogue'. This article does not mention the HR for the CFSP, given that this new entity was established after the signature of the PCA by the Treaty of Amsterdam (Art. 26 TEU).

Tacis Action Programmes – Funds allocated to the Russian Federation (in € millions)

	1995	1996	1997	1998	1999	2000	2001	1991-2001
Support for institutional, legal and administrative reform	46	24	16	30	15	28	28	280
Support to the private sector and assistance for economic development	41	31	29	31	18	14	19	334
Support in addressing the social consequences of transition	7	10	11	3	7	6	16	95
Development and infra-structure networks	35	23	24	20	14	0	3	305
Environmental protection, management of natural resources	0	6	5	10	8	4	0	46
Rural economic development	17	10	13	9	5	0	0	153
Policy advice, Small Projects Programme, Bistro and reserves	4	21	27	24	20	35	20	183
Tempus	11	8	8	13	11	11	10	87
Total	161	133	133	140	98	98	96	1,483

Source: European Commission

Tacis funds are also allocated through programmes other than the annual action programmes:

	1995	1996	1997	1998	1999	2000	2001	1991-2001
Regional and other programmes	27	31	27	27	21	17	23	274
Nuclear Safety	30	40	34	17	12	33	19	319
Donor Coordination	20	25	27	28	28	32	30	238
Programme Implementation Support	12	19	18	16	17	18	18	150
Total	89	115	106	88	78	100	90	981

Source: European Commission

year at ministerial level.[72] It monitors the implementation of the agreement and examines any bilateral or international issues of mutual interest. In contrast to the EAs and SAAs which specifically endow the (Stabilisation and) Association Council with the power to take *binding decisions*,[73] the PPC only has the ability, in strict legal terms, to make *non-binding recommendations*. Therefore, any improvement in the PCA legal regime is in principle subject to a new agreement between the parties, with the intricate ratification process that this entails.[74] In other words, the EAs and the SAAs contain a mechanism to further the rapprochement between parties which the PCA does not include, with the effect of potentially deepening the gap between association and partnership.

It should also be noted that the PCA establishes a Parliamentary Cooperation Committee which consists of members of the European Parliament, on the one hand, and members of the Federal Assembly of the Russian Federation, on the other. It meets at intervals which it determines. The Committee may request relevant information regarding the implementation of the agreement from the Cooperation Council, which is obliged to supply the requested information. The parliamentarians shall also be informed of the recommendations of the Cooperation Council and may itself make recommendations to the latter.[75]

---

[72] The decision to re-brand the Cooperation Council was taken at the EU-Russia summit of Saint-Petersburg in May 2003. According to the Joint Statement, the name change was motivated by the parties' willingness to '[enhance] the efficiency of EU-Russia co-operation', adding that '[s]trong and efficient bodies dealing with all areas of co-operation are essential in this context. To this end we decided to strengthen the existing Co-operation Council as a Permanent Partnership Council. It should act as a clearing house for all issues of our co-operation. It should meet more frequently and in different formats, backed up by thorough preparation and policy co-ordination on both sides.' See: <http://ue.eu.int/ueDocs/cms_Data/docs/pressdata/en/er/75969.pdf>. The inaugural meeting of the PPC took place on 27 April 2004 in Luxembourg. See: <http://ue.eu.int/ueDocs/cms_Data/docs/pressData/en/er/80067.pdf>. On this occasion, the parties pointed out that the inauguration of the Permanent Partnership Council 'clearly signals a further intensification of positive relations between the EU and the Russian Federation. The PPC operates within the framework of the Partnership and Co-operation Agreement… While today's meeting took place in its regular Foreign Ministers' formation, the PPC may also meet in other formations, such as Justice and Home Affairs and Environment'. This was the case in the field of JHA and energy (see below).

[73] For instance, Art. 108 EA Romania, Art. 112 SAA Croatia.

[74] Art. 3 PCA stipulates that the 'Parties undertake to consider development of the relevant Titles of this Agreement… The Cooperation Council may make recommendations on such development to the Parties. Such development *shall only be put into effect by virtue of an agreement between the Parties* in accordance with their respective procedures…'. [emphasis added] In all areas falling outside the exclusive competence of the Community and involving specific obligations (either *a priori* or following the so-called *ERTA* effect), the Member States will have to ratify the new agreement, which is increasingly cumbersome in a Union of twenty-five or more members.

[75] Arts. 95-97 PCA. See also the website of the EU delegation to the EU-Russia Parliamentary Committee, at: <http://www.europarl.eu.int/intcoop/euro/pcc/d_ru/default_en.htm>.

2.4 The PCA as an original formula of EU external relations

Notwithstanding the lack of EU legal personality at the time the PCA was concluded, the latter touches upon the different facets of the Union. In that, the PCA constituted, at least at the outset, an original formula of *EU* external relations.

To start with, the PCA establishes a political dialogue between the parties. The inclusion of such a dialogue illustrates the contribution of the non-EC sub-orders of the Union to the development of the partnership. The relevant provisions add up to an entire title (Title II) placed at the very beginning of the agreement, following the title on 'General principles' and preceding that on 'Trade in Goods'. The political dialogue is thereby given a prominent place in the system of the agreement. The objective of the dialogue, which the parties intend to develop and intensify,[76] is to accompany and consolidate their rapprochement. More particularly, it seeks to support the political and economic changes underway in Russia and should contribute to the establishment of new forms of cooperation between the two partners. Indeed, novel forms of cooperation have been launched in the context of this dialogue, notably in the field of political and security matters in Europe,[77] energy[78] and justice and home affairs,[79] particularly as regards the fight against terrorism.[80] It is also in the context of the political dialogue that the parties endeavoured to address the implications of the Union's eastward expansion, *inter alia*, the transit by land of persons and goods between Kaliningrad and other parts of Russia.[81]

---

[76] The PCA stipulates that the political dialogue takes place twice a year at presidential level (Art. 7(1)), at ministerial level within the Cooperation Council/Permanent Partnership Council (Art. 7(2)) and at parliamentary level within the framework of the Parliamentary Cooperation Committee (Art. 9). The PCA also foresees that other mechanisms for political dialogue shall be set up by the parties at senior official level in Troika format or in the context of experts meetings (Art. 8).

[77] At their summit in Paris in 2000, the parties agreed to institute specific consultations on security and defence matters at the appropriate level and in the appropriate format; to develop strategic dialogue on matters, particularly in regard to security, which have implications for the Russian Federation and the European Union; to extend the scope of regular consultations at expert level on the issues of disarmament, arms control and non-proliferation; and to promote cooperation in operational crisis management. See Joint Declaration on strengthening dialogue and cooperation on political and security matters in Europe, EU-Russia summit, 30 October 2000, Paris.

[78] EU-Russia summit, 30 October 2000, Paris. Since then, a Permanent Partnership Council on energy has been set up, which met for the first time in London on 3 October 2005. The agenda of the meeting included security of energy supply, energy sector investments, infrastructure, trade, energy efficiency, climate change, Kyoto, the Energy Charter Treaty and the International Atomic Energy Agency, see: <http://www.eu2005.gov.uk/servlet/Front?pagename=OpenMarket/Xcelerate/ShowPage&c=Page&cid=1107293561746&a=KArticle&aid=1128331749219> (last visited on 6 November 2005).

[79] At their Moscow summit, the parties decided to convene specific ministerial meetings on justice and home affairs between the EU Troika and the Russian Federation. It gathered for the first time on 6 April 2001 in Stockholm. These meetings 'intend to develop a reinforced dialogue on these important issues between the European Union and Russia'. See Joint Statement, EU-Russia summit, 17 May 2001, Moscow.

[80] Joint Statement on the fight against terrorism, EU-Russia summit, 11 November 2002, Brussels.

[81] See further below.

Moreover, the political dialogue aims at fostering the convergence of the parties' positions on international issues, thereby attempting to enhance security and stability. The parties have thus discussed issues such as 'frozen conflicts' in the post-Soviet area (e.g., Transnistria, Abkhazia, South Ossetia and Nagorno-Karabakh).[82] The Middle East is also a recurring theme, particularly in view of the parties' participation in the so-called Middle East 'Quartet'.[83] Finally, the political dialogue shall 'foresee that the Parties endeavour to cooperate on matters pertaining to the observance of the principle of democracy and human rights, and hold consultations, if necessary, on matters related to their due implementation'.[84] In this regard, a specific human rights dialogue was set up in March 2005, following The Hague Summit of November 2004.[85]

The political dialogue thus appears to introduce flexibility and dynamism in the partnership, which partly compensates for the otherwise limited leeway for developing the relationship in legal terms, as pointed out above. On certain issues, however, the political dialogue has been a *dialogue de sourds*, the conflict in Chechnya and the situation of Russian minorities in the Baltic States being cases in point.

In legal terms, the political dialogue falls outside the competence of the Community and partly explains the mixity of the agreement.[86] It represents an instrument of 'EU foreign policy'[87] that corresponds to the objectives of the Union's Common Foreign and Security Policy set out in Article 11 TEU,[88] *inter alia*,

- to strengthen the security of the Union in all ways;
- to preserve peace and strengthen international security, in accordance with the principles of the United Nations Charter, as well as the principles of the Helsinki Final Act and the objectives of the Paris Charter;
- to promote international cooperation;
- to develop and consolidate democracy and the rule of law, and respect for human rights and fundamental freedoms.

---

82 See, e.g., Joint statement, EU-Russia summit, 10 May 2005, Moscow.

83 Joint Statement on the Middle East, EU-Russia summit, 11 November 2002, Brussels, available at: <http://ue.eu.int/ueDocs/cms_Data/docs/pressData/en/er/73188.pdf>.

84 Art. 6 PCA Russia.

85 A first EU-Russia human rights consultation took place at senior official level under the Luxembourg Presidency of the European Union, see: <http://ue.eu.int/ueDocs/cms_Data/docs/pressData/en/misc/83921.pdf>. A second round of human rights consultations was held on 8 September 2005, see: <http://ue.eu.int/ueDocs/cms_Data/docs/pressData/en/misc/86164.pdf>.

86 ECJ, Case 124/95 *Centro-com* [1997] *ECR* I-81, paras. 24-25. See further A. Rosas, 'Mixed Union – Mixed Agreements', in M. Koskenniemi, ed., *International law aspects of the European Union* (The Hague, Kluwer Law International 1998) p. 125.

87 M. Fouwels, 'The European Union's Common Foreign and Security Policy and Human Rights', 3 *NQHR* (1997) p. 291 at p. 301.

88 R.A. Wessel, *The European Union's foreign and security policy – A legal institutional perspective* (The Hague, Kluwer Law International 1999) at p. 114.

Alongside the political dialogue, the agreement includes a strong political conditionality whereby '[r]espect for democratic principles and human rights as defined in the Helsinki Final Act and the Charter of Paris for a New Europe, underpins the internal and external policies of the Parties and constitutes an *essential element* of partnership and of this Agreement' [emphasis added].[89] This provision relates to a 'non-execution clause', according to which violation of the 'essential element' by any of the parties represents a 'material breach of the Agreement'.[90] As such, it is a 'case of special urgency' which, in derogation from the rules attached to the dispute settlement mechanism set out by the agreement,[91] allows the party affected to suspend unilaterally the implementation of the PCA.[92] This procedure is not only exceptional from the point of view of the PCA dispute settlement mechanism,[93] it also derogates from the rules of public international law.[94]

---

89 See further M. Cremona, 'Human rights and democracy clauses in the EC's trade agreements', in N. Emiliou and D. O'Keeffe, eds., *The European Union and world trade law* (Chichester, Wiley 1996) p. 62; E. Riebel and M. Will, 'Human rights clauses in external agreements of the EC', in P. Alston, ed., *The EU and human rights* (Oxford, Oxford University Press 1999) p. 723; E. Fierro, 'Legal basis and scope of the human rights clauses in EC bilateral agreements: any room for positive interpretation?', 7 *ELJ* (2001) p. 41; M. Bulterman, *Human Rights in the Treaty Relations of the European Union – Real Virtues or Virtual Reality* (Antwerp, Intersentia 2001) p. 94; D.-C. Horng, 'The human rights clause in the European Union's external trade and development agreements', 9 *ELJ* (2003) p. 677.

90 A Joint Declaration on Art. 107, annexed to the PCA, defines the expression 'material breach', by reference to Art. 60(3) of the Vienna Convention on the Law of Treaties of 1969, as either a repudiation of the agreement not sanctioned by the general rules of international law or a violation of the essential elements of the agreement.

91 This dispute settlement mechanism is set out in Art. 107(2) PCA. The provision reads as follows: 'If either Party considers that the other Party has failed to fulfil an obligation under the Agreement, it may take appropriate measures. Before so doing, except in cases of special urgency, it shall supply the Cooperation Council with all relevant information required for a thorough examination of the situation with a view to seeking a solution acceptable to the Parties.'

92 Such a clause has been referred to as the 'Bulgarian clause', as it first appeared in the EA Bulgaria. See Arts. 6 and 118(2) EA Bulgaria, *OJ* 1994 L 358/3. This expression was used by the Commission in its Communication on the inclusion of respect for democratic principles and human rights in agreements between the Community and third countries (COM (1995) 216). The 'Bulgarian clause' contrasts with the 'Baltic clause', which refers to a specific suspension provision according to which 'the parties reserve the right to suspend this agreement in whole or in part with immediate effect if a serious violation occurs in the essential provisions of the present agreement'. See, e.g., Trade and Commercial and Economic Cooperation Agreement with Estonia, *OJ* 1992 L 403/1.

93 The PCA dispute settlement mechanism normally requires that before a party retaliates in response to the other party's non-compliance with its obligations, the former supplies the Cooperation Council with all the relevant information required for a thorough examination of the situation with a view to seeking a solution acceptable to the parties. Hence, dialogue is sought until the last moment.

94 Art. 61(1) of the Vienna Convention provides that a 'material breach' by one party allows the other party to terminate the agreement or suspend, partly or wholly, its implementation, in observance of the procedure set out in Art. 65 which requires three months between the notification and the suspension (International Law Commission, 1969). The 'case of special urgency' allows derogation from the obligations set out in Art. 65 of the Vienna Convention. See further Riebel and Will, loc. cit. n. 89, at p. 723.

The human rights dimension of the PCA transcends the embryonic competence of the Community in the field of human rights protection.[95] Straddling the pillars, it also relates to the CFSP provisions, such as Article 11 TEU,[96] and more globally to the general provisions of the EU Treaty, notably its Article 6.[97] The cross-pillar character of the PCA provisions on human rights is typified by the regular human rights consultations held between Russia and the European Union represented by the Troika.[98]

The PCA also covers areas of cooperation which can be related to Title VI on justice and home affairs, as originally established by the EU Treaty signed in Maastricht.[99] Notably, the agreement contains provisions on cooperation to combat drugs[100] and a title on 'Cooperation on prevention of illegal activities'. These

---

95 Consider in this regard the Court's Opinion 2/94 *Accession by the Community to the European Convention for the Protection of Human Rights and Fundamental Freedoms* [1996] *ECR* I-1759. On EC competence, see further, e.g., A. Rosas, 'The European Union and mixed agreements', in Dashwood and Hillion, op. cit. n. 20, at p. 200. It should be noted that the Treaty of Nice introduced a specific legal basis for 'Economic, financial and technical cooperation with third countries', namely Art. 181A TEC which, like Art. 181 TEC on development cooperation, refers to the objective of respecting human rights and fundamental freedoms. On this objective, see Case C-268/94 *Portuguese Republic* v. *Council of the European Union* [1996] *ECR* I-6177. The EC Treaty thereby establishes an express legal basis for introducing human rights clauses in cooperation agreements other than development agreements, such as the PCA, as indeed suggested by the Commission (Communication from the Commission to the European Parliament and the Council – Effects of the entry into force of the Nice Treaty on current legislative procedures, COM (2003) 61). It remains the case, in this author's view, that the human rights dimension of the PCA goes beyond the provisions of Art. 181A TEC. See further C. Hillion, 'The evolving system of European external relations as evidenced in the EU Partnerships with Russia and Ukraine', PhD thesis (Leiden 2005) p. 80 et seq.; C. Hillion, 'Introduction to the Partnership and Cooperation Agreements', in A.E. Kellermann, J.W. de Zwaan and J. Czuczai, eds., *EU enlargement – The Constitutional Impact at EU and National Level* (The Hague, T.M.C. Asser Press 2001) p. 215.

96 The latter states that the European Union has among its foreign policy objectives 'to develop and consolidate democracy and the rule of law'.

97 Art. 6(2) TEU stipulates that 'the Union shall respect fundamental rights, as guaranteed by the European Convention for the Protection of Human Rights and Fundamental Freedoms…'. The third paragraph of the same article then points out that the Union 'shall provide itself with means necessary to attain its objectives and carry through its policies'.

98 At the first of such consultations, the Troika was led by diplomats from the Member State holding the EU presidency, see: <http://ue.eu.int/ueDocs/cms_Data/docs/pressData/en/misc/83921.pdf> (Luxembourg) and <http://ue.eu.int/ueDocs/cms_Data/docs/pressData/en/misc/86164.pdf> (United Kingdom). It should also be pointed out that the Brussels European Council of 16-17 December 2004 'welcomed the decision to appoint a Personal Representative of the SG/HR on Human Rights in the area of CFSP as a contribution to the coherence and continuity of the EU Human Rights policy, with due regard to the responsibilities of the Commission.' See para. 52 of the Presidency conclusions.

99 Title VI was partly communitarised by the Treaty of Amsterdam, which re-branded it 'Police and Judicial Cooperation in Criminal Matters'. See further, e.g., D. O'Keeffe, 'Can the leopard change its spots? Visas, immigration and asylum following Amsterdam', in D. O'Keeffe and P. Twomey, eds., *Legal issues of the Amsterdam Treaty* (Oxford, Hart Publishing 1999) p. 271.

100 Art. 82 PCA.

two sets of provisions relate to the subject matters referred to in ex-Article K.1 TEU, which was in force when the PCA was concluded. This article provided that combating drug addiction and fraud on an international scale, as well as police cooperation for the purposes of preventing and combating, *inter alia*, unlawful drug trafficking and other forms of international crime, constitute matters of 'common interest' for the Member States.[101] As such, they could be the subject of Council joint positions or joint actions, which indeed, they were.[102] In legal terms, however, the JHA-inspired cooperation foreseen in the PCA is *ancillary* to the main objectives of the agreement, which means that the relevant provisions do not alter the legal basis of the PCA.[103]

The foregoing suggests that the agreement establishing the partnership between the European Union and Russia represented an original formula of EU external relations at the beginning of the 1990s. Despite the modesty of the parties' commitments, its scope is noteworthy as it includes provisions related to the three sub-orders of the Union. The connection between the PCA and the non-EC aspects of the European Union was made possible particularly through the subterfuge of mixity. Indeed, the agreement was concluded by the Member States 'acting in the framework of the European Union',[104] a formula which typifies the presence of the *Union* in the EU-Russia partnership. In the absence of EU legal personality, the mixity of the agreement has been conducive to the progressive projection of the Union in its various facets, thereby remedying its inability, in the mid-1990s, to conclude external agreements itself.

3. CONSOLIDATING THE HORIZONTAL DIMENSION OF THE PARTNERSHIP

The tendency to involve the Union as such in the partnership has developed ever since the PCA was signed in 1994, and particularly after the entry into force of the Treaty of Amsterdam, which introduced significant changes to the functioning of the EU system of external relations.[105] Alongside several specific Community

---

101 On the external dimensions of the third pillar, see further, e.g., E. Denza, *The Intergovernmental pillars of the European Union* (Oxford, Oxford University Press 2002) p. 63 et seq.; J. Monar, 'The EU as an international actor in the domain of justice and home affairs', 9 *EFA Rev.* (2004) p. 395.

102 The JHA dimension of the partnership has steadily increased since the signature of the PCA. See further: <http://www.europa.eu.int/comm/justice_home/fsj/external/russia/fsj_external_russia_en.htm>.

103 In this regard, see ECJ, Case C-268/94 *Portuguese Republic* v. *Council of the European Union* [1996] *ECR* I-6177.

104 Preamble, 3rd indent.

105 See further A. Dashwood, 'External relations provisions of the Amsterdam Treaty', in O'Keeffe and Twomey, op. cit. n. 99, at p. 201.

agreements adopted to supplement the trade and economic provisions of the PCA,[106] complementary measures were formulated by the EU institutions with the effect of embedding the PCA in the broader EU external policy towards Russia. A case in point is the Common Strategy (CS)[107] on Russia adopted by the European Council meeting in Cologne in 1999.[108]

The CS was conceived, first and foremost, as a means of strengthening the Union's 'strategic partnership' with Russia,[109] seen as 'crucial to maintain peace and security in Europe and beyond'.[110] The strategy is based on the European Union's 'vision of the partnership', namely 'a stable, democratic and prosperous Russia, firmly anchored in a united Europe free of new dividing lines', through an almost Schumanian 'ever closer cooperation' between Russia and the European Union.

More specifically, the CS is determined by the European Union's strategic goal to see 'a stable, open and pluralistic democracy in Russia, governed by the rule of law and underpinning a prosperous market economy benefiting alike all the people of Russia and of the EU'. On the basis of its 'vision of the partnership', the European Union enounces four 'principal objectives', namely the 'consolidation of democracy, the rule of law and public institutions in Russia', the

---

106 In particular, the Community and Russia concluded an agreement on cooperation in science and technology (*OJ* 2000 L 299/15), which was renewed in 2003 for a period of five years (*OJ* 2003 L 299/20). The Community and Russia also concluded an agreement on trade in textile products (*OJ* 1998 L 222/2). Finally, the European Coal and Steel Community and Russia concluded an agreement on trade in certain steel products (*OJ* 2002 L 195/55), amended by Council Regulation 1386/2004 (*OJ* 2004 L 255/1).

107 The common strategy was one of the novel instruments brought about by the Treaty of Amsterdam in the field of EU external relations. It is a new instrument of the CFSP set out in Art. 13 TEU.

108 Presidency conclusions, Cologne European Council, June 1999, pt. 78. Common Strategy 1999/414/CFSP of the European Union of 4 June 1999 on Russia, *OJ* 1999 L 157/1. Established for an initial duration of four years, it was prolonged until 24 June 2004 by the European Council, on the recommendation of the Council, in Common Strategy 2003/471/CFSP of the European Council of 20 June 2003 amending Common Strategy 1999/414/CFSP on Russia in order to extend the period of its application, *OJ* 2003 L 157/68. No new measures have been adopted to extend the Common Strategy's period of application, so it must be assumed that it has silently passed away and has been *de facto* replaced by the 'Common Spaces', although none of the policy papers behind the latter mention the Common Strategy, and *a fortiori* that they intend to replace them. See section 4.3 below and also chapter 19 in this volume. On the CS Russia, see further H. Haukkala, and S. Medvedev, eds., *The EU Common Strategy on Russia – Learning the Grammar of CFSP* (Helsinki, Finnish Institute of International Affairs/Berlin, Institut für Europäische Politik 2001); H. Haukkala, 'The EU Common Strategy on Russia: In search of the foundations of European foreign policy', *The Yearbook of Finnish Foreign Policy* (2002) p. 54; M. Maresceau, 'EU enlargement and the EU common strategies on Russia and Ukraine: an ambiguous yet unavoidable connection', in C. Hillion, ed., *EU enlargement: a legal approach* (Oxford, Hart Publishing 2004) p. 181.

109 Para. 4 of Part I: 'Vision of the EU for its partnership with Russia'.

110 Presidency conclusions, Cologne European Council, June 1999, pt. 78, available at: <http://ue.eu.int/ueDocs/cms_Data/docs/pressData/en/ec/kolnen.htm>.

'integration of Russia into a common European economic and social space', 'cooperation to strengthen stability and security in Europe and beyond' and finding common responses to 'common challenges on the European continent'.

The EU strategy is therefore all-encompassing, covering both the economic and political dimensions of the partnership. The increasing geographical proximity between the two partners, pointed out by the CS, may explain the Union's increasingly global approach towards Russia. Indeed, the 1998 Vienna European Council invited the Council, following the latter's recommendations,[111] to prepare common strategies on Russia, Ukraine and the Mediterranean region, as well as on the Western Balkans, on the understanding that the first CS would be on Russia.[112] The Council's recommendations underlined that the first common strategies 'should focus on the *neighbouring regions of the EU*. Not least in the context of enlargement and the development of the *acquis*; it is there that the EU has the greatest long term common interests and the greatest need for coherence and effectiveness' [emphasis added].[113] The CS may thus be regarded as the first instrument of the Union towards its immediate neighbourhood. Indeed, it followed earlier attempts to develop the cross-pillar dimension of the partnership towards Russia. For instance, an EU Action Plan (AP) for Russia was adopted by the Council on 13 May 1996,[114] following the Commission's draft of a 'Common Position on European Union-Russia relations' which was included in a communication 'on the future relations between the European Union and Russia'.[115] The AP established a long list of measures and initiatives under five themes that clearly transcend the scope of the Community competence and touch upon the other EU sub-orders.[116]

---

[111] Document submitted to the Vienna European Council, December 1998, available at: <http://ue.eu.int/ueDocs/cms_Data/docs/pressData/en/ec/00300-R1.EN8.htm>.

[112] Presidency conclusions, Vienna European Council, December 1998, pt. 74, available at: <http://ue.eu.int/ueDocs/cms_Data/docs/pressData/en/ec/00300-R1.EN8.htm> pt. 74.

[113] Document submitted to the Vienna European Council, December 1998.

[114] EU Action Plan for Russia, General Affairs Council, 1996, Press release No. 7073/96, 6 December 1996.

[115] Communication of the Commission on the European Union and Russia: the future relationship, COM (1995) 223 final.

[116] The first foresees measures that underpin the EU 'contribution to Russia's democratic reforms', mentioning in particular election monitoring, support for contacts between parliaments, support for the development of regional and local administration and legal training. The second, entitled 'economic cooperation', is itself divided into subsections on 'development of trade relations and integration of Russia into the international economy', 'regional cooperation', 'nuclear energy and nuclear safety', 'environment', 'modernisation of the production system' and 'humanitarian aid', all foreseeing measures of support and encouragement. The third focuses on 'cooperation in the field of justice and home affairs', and foresees actions to combat organised crime, particularly drug-related crime, money laundering, terrorism, actions to combat illegal immigration and cooperation on asylum and readmission policy. The fourth deals with 'security in Europe', underlining initiatives to develop contacts within the framework of existing mechanisms to exchange expertise on disarmament, non-

The implementation of the CS also involves the Union in its different facets. The strategy stipulates that 'appropriate use [shall be made] of all relevant instruments and means available to *the Union, the Community and the Member States*' [emphasis added].[117] Moreover, the CS calls on the Council, the Commission and the Member States to review existing action, programmes, instruments and policies to ensure their consistency with the strategy. The fulfilment of the objectives set out in the CS thus implies a trilateral cooperation between the European Union, the European Community and its Member States, a cooperation which at times has proved difficult.[118]

Indeed, the CS has been criticised for its lack of added value and follow up,[119] and has progressively been overtaken by new instruments, particularly in the context of the European Union's eastern enlargement, as will be seen below. It remains that both its adoption and further implementation consolidate the cross-pillar nature of the EU-Russia partnership established by the PCA. In that the partnership prefigures the development of the *Union* as an international actor, as foreseen in its objectives (Art. 2 TEU). This development appears to be furthered by the perceptions of the Union's partner: Russia responded to the CS by adopting its own 'Medium Term Strategy for the Development of Relations between the Russian Federation and the *European Union* (2000-2010)' [emphasis added].[120]

---

proliferation, arms export controls, conflict prevention and management and the 'continued promotion of information activities'. The fifth theme, finally, deals with 'foreign policy', recommending, *inter alia*, the strengthening of the political dialogue with Russia, 'in accordance with the provisions of the PCA'.

117 See the section on 'Instruments and means', together with the European Council Declaration, attached to the CS. The CS was followed by implementing measures in non-EC spheres. First, the Council adopted Joint Action 1999/878/CFSP of 17 December 1999 establishing an EU cooperation programme for non-proliferation and disarmament in the Russian Federation, *OJ* 1999 L 331/11. Second, the Council adopted an EU Action Plan on Common Action for the Russian Federation on combating organised crime, *OJ* 2000 C 106/5.

118 The paucity of the Presidency reports on the implementation of the CS testifies the lack of enthusiasm in carrying the CS forward. See further Maresceau, loc. cit. n. 108, at p. 208. On the institutional dimension of the CS, see C. Hillion, 'Institutional aspects of the partnership between the EU and the newly independent states of the former Soviet Union – case studies of Russia and Ukraine', 37 *CMLRev.* (2000) p. 1211.

119 In this regard, see High Representative for the CFSP, Common Strategies Report, 21 December 2000, Doc. 14871/00 CAB. See also the first report of 2005-2006 of the European Scrutiny Select Committee, p. 25, available at: <http://www.publications.parliament.uk/pa/cm200506/cmselect/cmeuleg/34-i/34i.pdf>; and Maresceau, loc. cit. n. 108.

120 The text is available at: <http://www.delrus.cec.eu.int/en/p_242.htm>. On Russia's approach to the European Union, see further I. Leshukov, 'Beyond satisfaction: Russia's perspectives on European Integration', ZEI Discussion Paper C26 (Bonn, Zentrum für Europäische Integrationsforschung 1998).

4. THE IMPACT OF ENLARGEMENT ON THE EU-RUSSIA PARTNERSHIP

The 2004 enlargement, and particularly the adoption by the acceding States of the EU *acquis*, had a direct impact on the partnership.[121] The PCA had to be extended to the new Member States through the signature of a protocol to the agreement, which proved to be difficult (4.1). Moreover, the eastward geographical shift of the Union had particular implications for the movement of people and goods between Kaliningrad and other parts of Russia, as well as between Russia and its western neighbours (4.2). Enlargement also had the effect of catalysing new initiatives, formalised in particular in the establishment of four 'common spaces' between Russia and the European Union (4.3).

4.1 **PCA protocol**

As a condition for their entry, the ten acceding States had to take up the EU *acquis*, particularly in the field of external relations.[122] In this context, a protocol to the PCA had to be signed by all the parties in order to extend the agreement's application to the new Member States. For several months, Russia delayed the signature of such a protocol, using it as leverage to make the European Union address the negative economic and geopolitical implications of its expansion.[123] The Russian authorities argued that, *inter alia*, enlargement would significantly reduce Russia's exports towards new Member States of Central and Eastern Europe, and thus sought compensation. They also expressed concerns regarding the situation of Russian minorities in Estonia and Latvia,[124] and the absence of agreements on borders with these two Baltic States. In response, the European Union maintained that the signature of the protocol ought to be a mere formality and suggested that Russian concerns should be discussed in a different context. It

---

[121] See further P. Van Elsuwege, 'EU enlargement and its consequences for EU-Russia relations: the limits of the "fair weather strategy"', Chair Baillet Latour Working Paper No. 14 (K.U. Leuven 2002); V. Shemiatenkov, 'Russia – Neighbour, Partner and Enigma', *The European Policy Centre* (2000).

[122] Art. 6 of the Act of Accession, *OJ* 2003 L 236/33. See further, e.g., M. Cremona, 'The impact of enlargement: external policy and external relations', in M. Cremona, ed., *The enlargement of the European Union* (Oxford, Oxford University Press 2003) p. 161.

[123] On the reluctance of the European Union to do so, see further, e.g., Maresceau, loc. cit. n. 108.

[124] 'The fate of all our compatriots, wherever they live, concerns us equally.' Interview with Russian First Deputy Foreign Minister Mitrofanova, Interfax News Agency, 5 January 2004; 'Russia to raise language concerns', BBC News, 10 March 2004; 'Russia warns of "vacuum" after enlargement', *EUobserver*, 4 February 2004.

also recalled that, as a non-WTO member, Russia was not *entitled* to any compensation for loss of market access.[125]

After long and sometimes acrimonious discussions, a deal was eventually struck in Brussels on 27 April 2004. The protocol was signed allowing the extension of the PCA to the new Member States. It has applied provisionally pending the parties' ratification.[126] In exchange, Russia obtained various, although limited, concessions from the European Union in a Joint Statement on EU enlargement and EU-Russia relations.[127] In particular, the European Union agreed to increase its imports of Russian steel and to adopt 'special measures concerning the most significant' existing EU anti-dumping measures on Russian exports. With regard to minorities, the joint statement simply mentioned that 'the Parties welcome membership as a firm guarantee for the protection of human rights and the protection of persons belonging to minorities' and recalled 'their commitment' in this regard.[128]

4.2 Kaliningrad

Because of their accession to the Union, Poland and Lithuania, as other new Member States, have had to apply EU rules on visa and border controls.[129] Transit by land from mainland Russia to Kaliningrad Oblast is thus subject to visa requirement, which has been another matter of concern for the Russian authorities.

The European Union and Russia found an arrangement at their tenth summit in November 2002. In a Joint Statement on Transit between the Kaliningrad Region

---

125 In principle, under WTO rules (notably Art. XXIV(6) GATT), WTO members are entitled to such compensation. See further J.-P. Puissochet, *L'élargissement des Communautés européennes* (Paris, Editions Techniques et Economiques 1974) pp. 26-27; Cremona, loc. cit. n. 122, at pp. 192-193.

126 Available at: <http://www.europa.eu.int/comm/external_relations/russia/russia_docs/protocol_0404.htm>.

127 Available at: <http://www.europa.eu.int/comm/external_relations/russia/russia_docs/js_elarg_270404.htm>.

128 Russia unsuccessfully proposed a different formula stating that the Commission would continue to provide assistance to intensify the social integration of minorities in the new Member States (*Le Monde*, 27 April 2004). Border agreements between Russia and the Baltic States have proved to be difficult to conclude. In the case of Estonia, Russia signed an agreement in May 2005 (*EUobserver*, 2 May 2005), but decided to remove its signature at the end of June 2005 (*EUobserver*, 28 June 2005).

129 Art. 3 of the Act of Accession 2003. See further G. Gromadzki, et al., eds., *More than Neighbours: The Enlarged European Union and Ukraine – Final Report* (Warsaw, Batory Foundation 2004) p. 78, available at: <http://www.batory.org.pl/doc/final_rep.pdf>; L. Fairlie and A. Sergounin, *Are borders barriers? EU enlargement and the Russian Region of Kaliningrad* (Helsinki, The Finnish Institute of International Affairs/Berlin, Institut für Europäische Politik 2001); S. Arnswald and M. Jopp, *The Implications of Baltic States' EU Membership* (Helsinki, The Finnish Institute of International Affairs/Berlin, Institut für Europäische Politik 2001) especially pp. 60-97.

and the rest of the Russian Federation,[130] the parties acknowledged the 'unique situation' of Kaliningrad and agreed to make 'special efforts to accommodate the concerns on both sides' in relation to the transit of people and goods,[131] 'and to intensify their cooperation to promote the social and economic development of the region as a whole'. The Joint Statement on Transit followed an earlier proposal made by the Commission at the request of the European Council, based on the principle that the arrangement should comply with the EU *acquis*.[132]

In the Joint Statement, the parties agreed to establish a Facilitated Transit Document (FTD) scheme that applies for the transit of Russian citizens between Kaliningrad and other parts of Russia by land. The FTD is valid for *direct* transit within a limited period of time, and is issued 'at a low cost'.[133] The scheme allows for two types of FTD to be issued. For multiple entry direct transit via all forms of transport by land to and from Kaliningrad, an FTD is obtainable on the basis of an application to a Lithuanian consulate, and subject to necessary checks and controls. In addition, for those Russian citizens intending to make single return trips by train through Lithuania, a Facilitated Rail Transit Document (FRTD) is obtainable at the time of ticket purchase, on the basis of personal data.[134] The European Union has provided assistance to Lithuania to cover the additional costs of this scheme.[135] It also committed itself to review its operation no later than

---

130 Joint Statement of the European Union and the Russian Federation on transit between the Kaliningrad region and the rest of the Russian Federation, EU-Russia summit, 11 November 2002, Brussels, available at: <http://www.europa.eu.int/comm/external_relations/russia/summit_11_02/js_kalin.htm>.

131 The Joint Statement on EU enlargement and EU-Russia relations already stated that goods in transit between Kaliningrad and the rest of Russia should not be subject to 'unnecessary delays'.

132 The Commission initially published its Communication to the Council: The EU and Kaliningrad, COM (2001) 26 final, in 2001. However, the Seville European Council invited the Commission to submit an 'additional study on the possibilities for an effective and flexible solution to the question of the transit of persons and goods to and from the Kaliningrad *oblast,* in compliance with the *acquis* and in agreement with the candidate countries concerned.' See Communication from the Commission to the Council: Kaliningrad: Transit, COM (2002) 510 final.

133 According the European Commission's website, Lithuania charges $15 for a regular visa, $8 for a transit visa, $25 for a multiple entry visa and $18 for a multiple entry transit visa. Poland charges $5 for single entry and $14 for multiple entry visas. Fees for future transit visas have not been set yet. Russia is reported to charge $15 for a regular visa for Lithuanian citizens and $35 for Polish citizens. The figures for multiple entry visas are $25 and $120 respectively. Source: <http://www.europa.eu.int/comm/external_relations/north_dim/news/mem02_192.htm>.

134 Tickets are not issued by the Russian authorities to those Russian citizens in cases where Lithuania has objections to their transit via its territory. An FRTD is delivered by the competent Lithuanian authorities to the passenger at, or before, the Lithuanian border once Lithuania has checked that the travel documentation carried by the passenger is in order. Bearers of an FRTD would not alight in Lithuania and the time allotted for each transit is limited.

135 The European Union has also allocated funds for the economic development of Kaliningrad through various channels, e.g., the Tacis programme, and through the Northern Dimension initiative. See: <http://www.europa.eu.int/comm/external_relations/north_dim/news/mem02_192.htm>; on the Northern Dimension, see H. Ojanen, ed., *The Northern Dimension: Fuel for the EU* ((Helsinki, The Finnish Institute of International Affairs/Berlin, Institut für Europäische Politik 2001).

2005. As to Russia, it made a proposal for visa-free transit by high speed non-stop train, and more generally aims at obtaining a visa-free arrangement with the European Union, which the latter is only ready to consider as a long-term perspective,[136] and provided Russia concludes a readmission agreement with the Community, which it did in October 2005.[137]

The scheme was consolidated by Protocol 5 of the 2003 Act of Accession on the 'transit of persons by land between the region of Kaliningrad and other parts of the Russian Federation'. Also, Article 3 of the Protocol states that any further decision on this issue will be adopted by the Council, acting by unanimity, on a proposal from the Commission, after the accession of Lithuania.[138]

4.3 The establishment of four common spaces

The 2004 enlargement of the Union catalysed new initiatives between the European Union and its Eastern European neighbours,[139] as epitomised by the European Neighbourhood Policy. While it is the largest neighbour of the enlarged Union, Russia willingly remains outside the group of countries covered by the ENP. Instead, a new approach was articulated by the two partners at their 2003 summit in Saint Petersburg,[140] in the form of four 'common spaces'. In addition to a planned common European economic space (CEES), the European Union and Russia decided to establish a common space of freedom, security and justice (CSFSJ), a common space of external security (CSES), and a common space on research and education (CSRE), including cultural aspects. These spaces, conceived primarily to give new momentum to the partnership in the post-enlargement context, should be developed gradually 'in the framework of the PCA',[141] which is still regarded as the cornerstone of EU-Russia relations. In

---

[136] In this regard, see Communication from the Commission to the Council and to the European Parliament on relations with Russia, COM (2004) 106.

[137] On the margins of the EU-Russia Permanent Partnership Council (JHA) which met in Luxembourg on 13 October 2005, the Commission and Russia initialled two bilateral agreements on the facilitation of visa procedures and on readmission, see: <http://www.europa.eu.int/comm/external_relations/russia/intro/ip05_1263.htm> (*EUobserver*, 5 October 2005). See also the conclusions of the 16th EU-Russia Summit of 4 October 2005, available at: <http://www.europa.eu.int/comm/external_relations/russia/intro/ip05_1263.htm>.

[138] On these issues, see further O. Potemkina, 'Some ramifications of enlargement on the EU-Russia relations and the Schengen regime', 5 *European Journal of Migration and Law* (2003) p. 229; Maresceau, loc. cit. n. 108, at p. 181.

[139] In this regard, see Presidency conclusions, Copenhagen European Council, December 2002, pt. 24.

[140] EU-Russia summit, 31 May 2003, St. Petersburg, Joint Statement, Press release No. 9937/03.

[141] The idea was further worked out at the EU-Russia summit in Rome in November 2003. The Joint Statement mentions each of the four spaces. Under the CEES, the Joint Statement includes the parties' discussions on Kaliningrad, Russia's accession to the WTO, the energy dialogue, transport networks and environmental challenges. The CSFSJ covers discussions on visa-free travel, an EU-Russia readmission agreement and an action plan on organised crime, as well as the signature of the

other words, they do not aim at replacing the agreement.[142] Indeed, the new initiative aims at furthering its implementation, which at times has been considered unsatisfactory.[143]

Since the launch of this new initiative, four 'road maps' were adopted at the EU-Russia summit in Moscow on 10 May 2005.[144] These road maps aim at furthering the establishment of the common spaces by establishing a long list of actions which could underpin their respective development. It would be beyond the scope of the present discussion to analyse these documents in detail. The following will be restricted to a few remarks on each of these common spaces as articulated in the road maps.

The first road map, entitled 'building blocks for sustained economic growth', concerns the common economic space (CES), the term 'European' having been dropped. It establishes a list of several hundreds of actions that ought to be taken to establish the CES. To a great extent, such actions revolve around dialogue, exchange of information and approximation. Their scope covers a wide range of issues such as trade and investment, competition, public procurement, intellectual property, financial services, industrial products, energy, transport and agriculture.

Hitherto, the CES has been the most elaborated of the four spaces, at least in conceptual terms. In a so-called concept paper, submitted to the Rome EU-Russia summit of November 2003,[145] a joint high-level group (HLG) established to elaborate the CES concept[146] defined it as

---

Europol-Russian Federation agreement. Under the CSES, the parties foresee the development of their dialogue and cooperation on political and security matters. They mention their ambition to explore possible cooperation in the field of civil protection and long-haul air transport for crisis management. Finally, under the heading of the CSRE, the Joint Statement covers the renewal of the Agreement on cooperation in science and technology, the accession of Russia to the Bologna process and the participation of Russia in the EU Erasmus Mundus programme. See EU-Russia summit, 6 November 2003, Rome, Joint Statement, Press release No. 13990/03.

142 However, the spaces *de facto* overtake the 1999 Common Strategy, whose application was extended only once and for a period of one year running until 24 June 2004 by Common Strategy 2003/471/CFSP of the European Council of 20 June 2003 amending Common Strategy 1999/414/CFSP on Russia in order to extend the period of its application, *OJ* 2003 L157/68.

143 See Communication from the Commission to the Council and to the European Parliament on relations with Russia, COM (2004) 106.

144 Available at: <http://ue.eu.int/ueDocs/cms_Data/docs/pressData/en/er/84815.pdf> and <http://www.europa.eu.int/comm/external_relations/russia/summit_05_05/index.htm>. The European Union had initially envisaged one Action Plan covering activity in the four spaces; however, Russia indicated that it preferred four distinct road maps, each covering a specific common space (first report of 2005-2006 of the European Scrutiny Select Committee, p. 26, available at: <http://www.publications.parliament.uk/pa/cm200506/cmselect/cmeuleg/34-i/34i.pdf>).

145 EU-Russia summit, 6 November 2003, Rome, Joint Statement, Press release No. 13990/03. See further, e.g., E. Vinokurov, 'The making of the concept of the EU-Russia Common Economic Space', Chair Interbrew/Baillet Latour Working Paper No. 22 (K.U. Leuven, 2004), available at: <http://www.soc.kuleuven.ac.be/pol/docs/docs_ibl/WP22-Vinokurov.pdf>.

146 The HLG was established by the Brussels EU-Russia summit of October 2001 (EU-Russia Summit, Joint statement. Brussels, 3 October 2001. Press release No. 12423/01) in accordance with

> an open and integrated market between the EU and Russia, based on implementation of common and compatible rules and regulations, including compatible administrative practices, as a basis for synergies and economies of scale associated with a higher degree of competition in bigger markets. It shall ultimately cover substantially all sectors of the economy.[147]

In particular, the HLG foresaw that the framework for cross-border trade in goods, covering substantially all industrial and agricultural goods, should include

> the necessary rules – whether set by standards, technical specifications or other regulatory and legal requirements – organisational structures and procedures; while ensuring that these do not create unnecessary obstacles to trade, and promoting equivalent levels of the protection of safety, health and the environment.[148]

The HLG's report also stated that 'Cooperation ... particularly *with regard to legislative approximation is an essential element* in order to promote trade and investment between the EU and Russia'.[149] Both the HLG documents and the road map thus emphasise the pivotal role that legislative approximation, already evoked in the PCA, should play in establishing the CES. Such approximation is, however, equivocal in both documents. The language used therein carefully refrains from making any connection between approximation and EU standards, thereby avoiding the impression that the Union is imposing its norms on Russia.[150] In this sense, the HLG reports cautiously chose references to concepts such as 'convergence' or 'compatibility'.[151] Equally, the road map refers, for example,

Art. 93 PCA. Meeting twice a year, the HLG was co-chaired by representatives of the Russian Federation and of the European Union. In practice, vice-Prime Minister Khristenko and External Relations Commissioner Patten, later replaced by Enlargement Commissioner Verheugen, chaired the HLG. The decision to establish the HLG was taken by the Russia-EU summit meeting in Moscow in May 2001 (EU-Russia Summit, Joint statement. Moscow, 17 May 2001. Press release No. 8853/01) following a meeting in Stockholm in March 2001 between the Heads of State and Government of the European Union and the President of the Russian Federation, where the idea of the CEES was reinvigorated.

147 In its second report, presented at the EU-Russia summit in November 2002, the HLG had already emphasised that the overall aim of the CEES is 'to link the EU and Russia in a privileged relationship, *focusing on regulatory and legislative convergence* and trade and investment facilitation' [emphasis added]. See: <http://ue.eu.int/ueDocs/cms_Data/docs/pressData/en/er/74449.pdf>.

148 EU-Russia High Level Group, *The Common European Economic Space (CEES) – Concept Paper*, submitted to the EU-Russia summit in Rome, 6 November 2003, Press release No. 13990/03, pt. 18.

149 Ibid., pt. 19.

150 C. Pursiainen, 'The Ambiguity of the Common European Economic Space: a Strength or a Weakness?', Russian-European Centre for Economic Policy (RECEP) (July 2004), available at: <http://www.recep.ru/files/documents/04_07_26_Economic_Space_En.pdf>.

151 A speech given by (then) External Relations Commissioner Patten uses language that is even weaker, pointing out that 'co-operation with Russia should promote *coherence* between our *respective*

to 'gradual approximation of relevant legislation and practices', 'harmonisation' and 'alignment of standards' in the general context of a 'regulatory dialogue'. No catalogue of precise norms or standards is evoked,[152] in contrast to the documents which elaborate the European Neighbourhood Policy, and *a fortiori* the instruments of 'pre-accession'.[153]

Despite this equivocal rhetoric, however, the legal convergence underpinning the establishment of the CES arguably implies that the burden of adaptation falls essentially on Russia.[154] Indeed, it is unlikely that the Union officials seriously consider revising the EU *acquis*, which they so vehemently protected and promoted in the pre-accession context, so as to ensure convergence with Russian rules. Support for this view can be found in the concept paper itself, whose section on 'guiding principles' (of the CES) establishes that the latter should be based on existing and future commitments of the parties *in the PCA* and WTO. One may recall, in this respect, that the provisions of the PCA, in the context of which the CES is to be established, include a specific article on legislative cooperation whereby Russia endeavours to ensure that its future legislation is compatible with Community law.[155] Nowhere is it envisaged in the agreement that the European Union should do the same with respect to Russia's legislation. It appears therefore that the legal approximation envisaged by the CES implicitly involves a projection of EU norms and standards towards Russia, on the basis of the PCA.[156] It remains to

---

legislative standards based on studies of the likely benefits for Russian industries' [emphasis added]. See C. Patten, 'EU-Russia Summit and Hoff Report on Kaliningrad', speech to the Plenary Session of the European Parliament, Strasbourg, 14 May 2002, SPEECH/02/201, available at: <http://europa.eu.int/comm/external_relations/news/patten/sp02_201.htm>.

152 In this regard, see M. Emerson, 'EU-Russia: four common spaces and the proliferation of the fuzzy', CEPS Policy Brief No. 71 (2005).

153 On the legal aspects of the ENP, see further M. Cremona, 'The European Neighbourhood Policy: legal and institutional issues', Stanford Institute for International Studies CDDRL Working Paper (Stanford 2004); C. Hillion, '"Thou shalt love thy neighbour": the draft European Neighbourhood Policy Action Plan between the EU and Ukraine', in A. Mayhew and N. Copsey, eds., *Ukraine and European Neighbourhood Policy* (Brighton, University of Sussex, Sussex European Institute 2005) p. 17.

154 See further V. Shemiatenkov, 'EU-Russia: the sociology of approximation', speech to the Sixth ECSA-World Conference: Peace, Security and Stability – International Dialogue and the Role of the European Union, Brussels, 5-6 December 2002, available at: <http://europa.eu.int/rapid/pressReleasesAction.do?reference=SPEECH/02/619&format=HTML&aged=0&language=EN&guiLanguage=en>.

155 Art. 55 of the PCA contains provisions on legislative cooperation by reference to the *acquis*, in the particular fields of company law, banking law, company accounts and taxes, protection of workers in the work place, financial services, rules on competition, public procurement, protection of the health and life of humans, animals and plants, the environment, consumer protection, indirect taxation, customs law, technical rules and standards, nuclear laws and regulation, and transport.

156 Indeed, the concept paper mentions the elaboration of action plans to make the CEES concept operational and, in particular, to transform the objectives of the CEES into specific goals and actions. See EU-Russia High Level Group, *The Common European Economic Space (CEES) –*

be seen whether the Russian authorities will in practice identify with this interpretation.[157]

As regards the CSFSJ, the relevant road map stipulates in its preamble that it shall be aimed at building 'a new Europe without dividing lines, thus facilitating travel between all Europeans', a theme close to home for the Russians. This second space should, also according to the preamble of the road map, be based on 'common values', such as democracy and the rule of law and respect for human rights, including 'the rights of persons belonging to minorities', terminology which echoes the draft Treaty establishing a Constitution for Europe.[158] In the light of these principles, which are only mentioned in the preamble, the road map envisages, in its first section on 'freedom', a list of actions to 'facilitate' legal cross-border movement and stay on the partners' territories. In this context, the parties undertake to conclude 'parallel' negotiations on an agreement on visa facilitation and an agreement on readmission, whereby Russia should accept to take back persons who have entered illegally into the EU from its territory, which has been the subject of difficult negotiations for a long time.[159] The partners also pledge to continue and intensify the visa dialogue, to examine the conditions for a mutual visa-free regime, 'as a long term perspective', to promote the better use of 'existing flexibilities under Schengen' and to cooperate on border management. In real terms, therefore, the 'freedom' dimension of the CSFSJ appears to be understood as the *control* of movement and efficacy of borders. The road map also contains a section on 'security', which establishes ways to tackle terrorism, all forms of organised crime and illegal activities, such as human and drug trafficking. Finally, the section on 'justice' suggests measures to foster the efficiency of the judicial system and enhance cooperation in civil and criminal matters. On the whole, the text is detailed, structured and seemingly more operational than the road map for the CES. It establishes a long, but not entirely new, list of objectives and actions to be taken by the parties, for example the signature and implementation of international and regional instruments, such as Council of Europe and UN conventions and protocols. The road map also evokes agreements and cooperation between EU agencies such as Europol and Eurojust, on the one hand, and the

Concept Paper, submitted to the EU-Russia summit in Rome, 6 November 2003, Press release No. 13990/03, pt. 22.

157 In this regard, it is worth pointing out President Putin's remarks at the Kremlin on 21 May 2004, on the occasion of the Russia-EU summit: 'We would very much like this joint work to be constructive, to reflect the interests of one and the other side so that our work proceeds in parallel, so that we identify common priorities and try to achieve common goals. I am convinced that there should be no leaders and the led [sic] in our dialogue.' Information and Press Department, Ministry of Foreign Affairs, 21 May 2004, Moscow.

158 See Art. I-3 TCE, *OJ* 2004 C 310/1.

159 *EUobserver*, 24 January 2003.

appropriate Russian authorities, on the other.[160] Finally, the JHA road map includes a specific paragraph on *monitoring* of the development of the CSFSJ which should be ensured by existing mechanisms such as the PPC and sectoral JHA ministerial meetings.

The common space of external security (CSES) is also elaborated in a specific road map, which starts off by emphasising the partners' shared responsibility for an international order based on 'effective multilateralism'. Echoing the European Security Strategy, the document emphasises the need for the partners to promote regional and international organisations, the OSCE and the Council of Europe being singled out as contributing to 'a more just and secure world'. It contains a list of actions to develop cooperation in, and dialogue on, *inter alia*, crisis management, the fight against terrorism, non-proliferation of weapons of mass destruction, civil protection and existing and potential regional and local conflicts,[161] with particular focus on the 'regions adjacent to the EU and Russian borders'.[162]

In several areas, the CSES is likely to overlap with the CSFSJ, particularly with regard to the fight against terrorism. Internal coordination between the EU actors involved in the respective frameworks is thus critical. In this regard, the CSES road map points out that the objectives of the common space are to be monitored 'within existing formats at the meeting of the PSC Troika at ambassadors' level and at political directors' consultations'. Reports on the implementation should be made to the specific PPC ministerial meetings and/or at ministerial EU/Troika-Russia meetings.

The CSRE, including cultural aspects, is the last of the four spaces and probably the most promising.[163] It aims at enhancing 'people-to-people' contacts in the fields of education, youth and culture. It also seeks to 'promote common values' and to contribute to the increase of the competitiveness of the partners' economies. The road map on the CSRE recalls that Russia already participates in the EU Tempus programme and in the Bologna process, illustrating Russia's increasing

---

[160] The EU-Russia Permanent Partnership Council on Justice and Home Affairs that met in Luxembourg in October 2005 also mentioned potential cooperation between the new European Border Agency (FRONTEX) and the Federal Border Security Service of Russia, see: <http://ue.eu.int/ueDocs/cms_Data/docs/pressData/en/er/86596.pdf>.

[161] At the 16th EU-Russia summit meeting in London, the European Union thus briefed Russia on its plans for a border assistance mission in Moldova. In addition, it expressed concern about the situation in Belarus and Uzbekistan, following the continued Uzbek refusal to allow an inquiry about the massacre in Andijan.

[162] Here, again, the terminology is cautious. As pointed out by Emerson, the text does not refer to the phrase 'common neighbourhood' which has been used by the European Union, e.g., in the Communication from the Commission to the Council and to the European Parliament on relations with Russia, COM (2004) 106.

[163] T. Gomart, 'Les trois enjeux du partenariat entre l'Union européenne et la Russie', 2 *Politique étrangère* (2004).

'integration into the European Higher Education Area'. The document also contains a long list of initiatives aimed at intensifying links and exchanges between universities, students, researchers and artists, including harmonisation of standards in the fields of research and education. This list of actions further recommends a more effective use of available mechanisms of interaction such as the PCA. Financial support and flexibility with respect to the application of Schengen rules will also be needed for this common space, based on people-to-people contacts, to become tangible. In this respect, the conclusion of the visa facilitation agreement initialled in October 2005 is to be welcomed.

The foregoing remarks suggest that four spaces appear to *integrate* the existing strands of the multifaceted partnership.[164] To an extent, the creation of the common spaces appears to be a 'tidying-up' and 'repackaging' exercise, at a time when the partners feel that there is a need for new momentum in their relationship. It relies heavily on the existing structures and provisions of the PCA, but uses new and promising concepts. Time will tell whether this new initiative brings added value to the relationship. In this respect, there is a need for a clearer, concrete and shared understanding of the tasks to be fulfilled by each partner, approximation being a case in point. Indeed, elaborated and potentially monitored by several actors, the development of the common spaces will require strong and efficient coordination within the European Union.

5. CONCLUDING REMARKS

The development of the EU-Russia relationship is a story with several twists. Used as a laboratory for the emerging EU foreign policy, the 'partnership' was articulated through many EU instruments of a different legal nature. Based on the modest and yet novel PCA, it was notably elaborated in a common strategy and is now being revamped through the creation of four 'common spaces'. The inflation of EU initiatives towards Russia is indicative of the continuous profound interest the Union has in its largest neighbour. It also tellingly suggests that the Union remains powerless 'in asserting its identity' towards Russia. Substantive clarity and institutional efficacy have often lacked in EU-Russia relations and, with twenty-five Member States having quite different perceptions of Russia, addressing these shortcomings is likely to be an uphill battle.

---

164 The combination of the common spaces has indeed been characterised as a 'comprehensive' initiative by the parties, the four spaces forming part of a 'single package', which integrates the different facets of the partnership with Russia. See, e.g., EU-Russia summit, 25 November 2004, The Hague, Press release No. 15061/04; and EU-Russia summit, 10 May 2005, Moscow, Press release No. 8799/05.

CHAPTER 15

UKRAINE

Eugeniusz Piontek*

Relevant legal documents:
- Partnership and Cooperation Agreement between the European Communities and their Member States, of the one part, and the Republic of Ukraine, of the other part, *OJ* 1998 L 49/3.
- Protocol to the Partnership and Cooperation Agreement establishing a partnership between the European Communities and their Member States, of the one part, and Ukraine, of the other part, *OJ* 2000 L 283/28.
- Proposal for a Council and Commission Decision on the conclusion of the Protocol to the Partnership and Cooperation Agreement between the European Communities and their Member States, of the one part, and Ukraine, of the other part, to take account of the accession of the Czech Republic, the Republic of Estonia, the Republic of Cyprus, the Republic of Latvia, the Republic of Lithuania, the Republic of Hungary, the Republic of Malta, the Republic of Poland, the Republic of Slovenia and the Slovak Republic to the European Union, COM (2004) 251 final.
- European Council Common Strategy 1999/877/CFSP of 11 December 1999 on Ukraine, *OJ* 1999 L 331/1.
- Common Strategy 2003/897/CFSP of the European Council of 12 December 2003 amending Common Strategy 1999/877/CFSP on Ukraine in order to extend the period of its application, *OJ* 2003 L 333/96.
- Agreement between the European Economic Community and Ukraine on trade in textile products *OJ* 1994 L 123/718 (as amended).
- Exchange of Letters between the Community and Ukraine in relation to the establishment of companies, *OJ* 1998 L 49/47.
- Agreement for Cooperation between the European Atomic Energy Community and the Cabinet of Ministers of Ukraine in the field of nuclear safety, *OJ* 2002 L 322/33.
- Agreement for Cooperation between the European Atomic Energy Community and the Cabinet of Ministers of Ukraine in the field of controlled nuclear fusion, *OJ* 2002 L 322/40.
- Agreement on cooperation in science and technology between the European Community and Ukraine, *OJ* 2003 L 36/32.

* Director of the Department of European Law, Faculty of Law and Administration, University of Warsaw.

- Agreement between the European Union and Ukraine on the participation of Ukraine in the European Union Police Mission (EUPM) in Bosnia and Herzegovina (BiH), *OJ* 2003 L 239/38.
- Agreement between the European Union and Ukraine on the participation of Ukraine in the European Union Police Mission in the former Yugoslav Republic of Macedonia (EUPOL 'Proxima'), *OJ* 2004 L 354/82.
- Agreement between the European Union and Ukraine establishing a framework for the participation of Ukraine in the European Union crisis management operations, *OJ* 2005 L 182/29.
- Agreement between Ukraine and the European Union on security procedures for the exchange of classified information, *OJ* 2005 L 172/84.
- Agreement between the European Community and the Government of Ukraine on trade in certain steel products, *OJ* 2005 L 232/42.

1. IMPACT OF UKRAINE'S POLITICAL EVOLUTION ON ITS RELATIONS WITH THE EUROPEAN UNION

Following the accession to the European Union of eight countries from Central and Eastern Europe, Ukraine became one of the biggest and strategically most important neighbours of the enlarged European Union. Ukraine occupies the unique geopolitical position of an independent state established on the ashes of the former Soviet Union and located in the buffer zone between Poland, Russia and Belarus. This factor in itself requires a clear and coherent policy from the European Union. The 2004 enlargement has further increased the need for a reformulated and sophisticated policy. It should aim to secure the European Union's interests in the region without at the same time undermining official relations with Russia. In that respect, it would be wise to take on board the experiences of the European Union's new Member States, in particular the countries neighbouring Ukraine. The aim of this analysis is to take a closer look at relations between the European Union and Ukraine over the last decade. It will lead to a number of policy recommendations formulated in the final sections of this chapter.

The relations between the European Union and Ukraine have been naturally determined by a variety of political and economic factors. It should also be stressed that they have been heavily influenced by political developments in Ukraine itself. The contemporary history of Ukraine started with its proclamation of independence from the Soviet Union on 24 August 1991. It functions as a constitutional democracy, led by a President and ruled by a unicameral assembly of 450 deputies (*Verkhovna Rada*).[1] Leonid Kravchuk won the first presidential

[1] Конституція України від 28 червня 1996 [Constitution of Ukraine of 28 June 1996], 30 *Vidomosti Verkhovnoi Rady (BBP)* [Information Bulletin of the Ukrainian Parliament] (1996) p. 141.

elections in 1991, but his presidency was troubled by soaring inflation and so much public unrest that elections were brought forward and Leonid Kuchma was voted in as the new President in 1994. Initially, Kuchma's presidency saw some improvements in the domestic economy, but the strongest reformers were dismissed before long and the government recoiled into an oligarchic regime fraught with serious corruption scandals. In 1999, Kuchma was re-elected for a second five-year term. With an approval rating of less than 15 per cent, Kuchma decided not to run for a third term in the presidential elections of November 2004. These were filled with irregularities that eventually led to the so-called 'Orange Revolution' and the election of Viktor Yushchenko as the new President.[2] The events of late 2004 and 2005 are generally considered to have been of pivotal importance for the determination of Ukraine's future and the reorientation of its foreign policy. At this stage, it remains to be seen what will be the impact on EU-Ukraine relations of the decreasing popularity of the presidential administration and the political set-up following the parliamentary elections in March 2006.

In geographic terms, Ukraine is one of the biggest countries on the continent, with a territory of 603,700 sq. km.[3] In 2003, it had 48.4 million inhabitants of which almost 30 per cent lived below the poverty line. Per capita income is less than €65 per month, with per capita GDP at just €1,080 in 2004. Society is dominated by Ukrainians, who constitute 77.8 per cent of the population.[4] In general, Ukraine is a Christian Orthodox country.[5] Food processing is an important part of

---

2 Kuchma rallied the oligarchs behind his last Prime Minister, Viktor Yanukovich, a former regional governor with a broad popular base in his native Donetsk region. Russia's President Putin also endorsed Yanukovich. The western and central regions, where identification with the Ukrainian nationality and language is stronger, rallied behind Yushchenko. The middle class and the moderately wealthy also mostly backed the former central banker. These groups poured into central Kiev after Yanukovich was declared the winner of a run-off in November 2004 amid clear evidence of fraud. The campaign inflamed Ukraine's historically rooted East-West divide to sometimes hysterical extremes. During the protests, Yanukovich led a meeting of local councillors from the southern and eastern regions where threats were made to formally split the country. Attempts to secure a peaceful settlement of the dispute were made by Poland (represented by President Aleksander Kwaśniewski as well as ex-President and Solidarity leader Lech Wałęsa), Lithuania (President Valdas Adamkus) and the European Union itself (CFSP High Representative Javier Solana). Ukraine's Supreme Court defused the crisis with a ruling that fully backed Yushchenko's complaint and ordered a repeat election in December 2004, which he won. It took Yanukovich a few weeks to accept his defeat and assume the role of main opposition leader. See A. Krushelnycky, *An Orange Revolution. A Personal Journey Through Ukrainian History* (London, Harvill Secker 2006).

3 Ukraine data profile on the website of the World Bank, available at: <https://www.worldbank.org>.

4 The other nationalities include: Russian 17.3 per cent, Belarusian 0.6 per cent, Moldovan 0.5 per cent, Crimean Tatar 0.5 per cent, Bulgarian 0.4 per cent, Hungarian 0.3 per cent, Romanian 0.3 per cent, Polish 0.3 per cent, Jewish 0.2 per cent, other 1.8 per cent. Source: CIA World Factbook, available at: <http://www.cia.gov/cia/publications/factbook/index.html>.

5 Ukrainian Orthodox-Kiev Patriarchate 19 per cent, Orthodox (no particular jurisdiction) 16 per cent, Ukrainian Orthodox-Moscow Patriarchate 9 per cent, Ukrainian Greek Catholic 6 per cent,

the economy. Ukraine is rich in mineral resources, but historically imported all its oil from Russia and is now suffering from energy shortages. Industry is dominated by extensive mining, steel production, machine building, engineering and chemicals. Most of the heavy industry is located in the pro-Russian Donetsk region in the south-east of the country.[6]

In legal terms, the EU-Ukraine relations are based on the Partnership and Cooperation Agreement (PCA) signed on 16 June 1994.[7] It entered into force almost four years later (on 1 March 1998), although its trade section has been in operation since 1996, under an Interim Agreement.[8] In accordance with Article 101 PCA Ukraine, the agreement is concluded for an initial period of ten years and 'shall be automatically renewed year-by-year provided that neither Party gives the other Party written notice of denunciation.' It is generally considered that the delay in ratification reflected the low priority placed on Kuchma's Ukraine by the European Union and its Member States. Consecutive declarations by Ukraine regarding its intention to seek EU membership were ignored.[9] In the period from the signing of the PCA through much of 2003, not a single EU Member State, perhaps with the exception of Greece, took into account the possibility of Ukraine being invited to join the European Union, even in the distant future. The European Union traditionally took a very restrained approach to the 'European choice' declared by Ukraine, avoiding any meaningful declarations on this issue on its own part. This is well illustrated by the language of a communiqué from the EU-Ukraine summit held in Copenhagen on 4 July 2002, where the European Union reconfirmed that 'it welcomes Ukraine's European aspirations'.[10] It noted the address of President Kuchma of 18 June to the European Parliament on the 'European Choice Strategy of economic and social development in Ukraine till the year 2011', with all its implications for the further development of EU-Ukraine relations. The Union also noted the relevant Parliamentary resolution following this address. Furthermore, the President of Ukraine underlined the desire of Ukraine to bring the EU partnership to a qualitatively new level. Full implementation of the relevant PCA provisions and WTO accession would be the

---

Ukrainian Autocephalous Orthodox 1.7 per cent, Protestant/Jewish/none 48 per cent. Source: CIA World Factbook, available at: <http://www.cia.gov/cia/publications/factbook/index.html>.

[6] See CIA World Factbook, available at: <http://www.cia.gov/cia/publications/factbook/index.html>.

[7] Partnership and Cooperation Agreement between the European Communities and their Member States, of the one part, and the Republic of Ukraine, of the other part, *OJ* 1998 L 49/3.

[8] Interim Agreement on trade and trade-related matters between the European Community, the European Coal and Steel Community and the European Atomic Energy Community, of the one part, and Ukraine, of the other part, *OJ* 1995 L 311/2.

[9] See, e.g., the declarations by the Minister of Foreign Affairs of Ukraine, as reported by ITAS-TASS on 27 April 1998 and by Holos Ukrayiny on 26 March 1999.

[10] EU-Ukraine Summit, Copenhagen, 4 July 2002, Joint Statement, 10607/02 (Presse 195).

best for eventually establishing the free trade area foreseen in the PCA. Thus, the European Union restricted itself only to 'welcoming' and 'noting' desires expressed and steps taken by Ukraine, leaving unanswered the latter's insistence on the need to bring mutual relations 'to a qualitatively new level'. On the other hand, the European Council recommended in Copenhagen that progress on the implementation of the PCA be reviewed for the five-year period since 1998. The joint review report, issued in March 2003, concluded that:

- political dialogue had been largely achieved, with the agenda becoming 'progressively more substantial and operational' and that the future of EU-Ukraine relations should be intensified within the framework of the 'Wider Europe' initiative;
- the implementation of the promotion of trade and investment and harmonious economic relations was mixed;
- there had been progress in financial, scientific and technological cooperation but that social and cultural cooperation had 'scope to be developed further';
- support for the consolidation of democracy had been undertaken through the political dialogue, although the report stated that 'the achievement of this goal is the responsibility of Ukraine' and that Ukraine had 'progressively developed democratic principles and human rights and the rule of law' since 1992 and the entry into force of the PCA. However, the European Union had concerns regarding 'judicial reform and implementation of legislation' and with regard to the 'rights and freedoms of journalists';
- negotiations on accession to the WTO had supported transition to a market economy;
- the dialogue on Ukraine's participation in crisis management, such as with Moldova concerning the border region of Transnistria, should continue;
- there should be an intensification of legislative approximation;
- cooperation in the realm of justice and home affairs should be intensified under the Action Plan;
- cooperation on the transit of energy, energy sector reform and efficiency should be developed.[11]

The conclusions of the report reflected in a diplomatic manner the state of mutual relations between the European Union and Ukraine at the time. The unwillingness of the Ukrainian authorities to go beyond the mere technical implementation of the PCA, their lack of respect for certain contractual obligations due to misapplication,

---

[11] Joint Report on the Implementation of the Partnership and Cooperation Agreement between the EU and Ukraine, text available at: <http://europa.eu.int/comm/external_relations/ukraine/intro/pcarep2.pdf>.

protectionism or bureaucratic disdain, and the ensuing refusal by the European Union to meet Ukraine's expectations regarding the implementation of the PCA caused the relations to run out of steam. The unresolved murder of the *Ukrainska Pravda* journalist Georgy Gongadze in 2000, the Kolchuga scandal in the autumn of 2002,[12] and the gradual reversion of President Kuchma to a neo-Soviet political culture, combined with his new political orientation expressed in the slogan 'to Europe with Russia', gradually brought EU-Ukraine relations to a standstill. Although not stated publicly, there was little desire among European leaders to be seen as rewarding Kuchma. As Romano Prodi, former President of the European Commission, put it in the fifth year of the PCA's operation: 'The fact that Ukrainians or Armenians feel European means nothing to me.'[13] For Jean-Luc Dehaene, at the time vice-chairman of the European Convention, there was also no place for Ukraine in the European Union. In his view, the eastern borders of the European Union that would be reached after the enlargement of May 2004 should remain fixed for good.[14] From the Union's perspective, relations were therefore kept at a minimum until the moment that President Kuchma would leave office.[15] However, what might have been the right reaction under normal circumstances was not necessarily the best one with regard to a country desperately looking for a safe harbour while sailing through the stormy waters of domestic conflicts and external pressures.

In this context, it is worth recalling that during the presidential term of Leonid Kravchuk (1991-1994) and Kuchma's first tenure (1994-1999), the main issue that dominated Kiev's policy was that of Russia coming to terms with Ukrainian independence and Ukrainian sovereignty over the Crimean peninsula and the city of Sevastopol. During Kuchma's second term (1999-2004), President Vladimir Putin's Russia eventually accepted and officially recognised Ukraine's statehood, while at the same time seeking to draw Ukraine into its own sphere of influence. Lack of tangible progress in EU-Ukraine relations led to a situation in which, from 2001 onwards, President Putin became Kuchma's main external ally. In late 2002, Russia proposed to Ukraine, Belarus and Kazakhstan to establish a free trade area, labelled the 'Single Economic Zone'. On 22 May 2003, the Ukrainian Parliament, by a narrow majority of 266 deputies, backed its creation. The other three potential participants did not. Shortly before speaking on Europe Day in May 2003, President Kuchma referred to the past to highlight Ukraine's long-lasting links to Europe,

---

[12] The scandal erupted when the news of Ukraine selling 'Kolchuga' radar systems to Iraq was revealed.

[13] See the interview with Prodi in *De Volkskrant*, as quoted by Reuters on 27 November 2003.

[14] As quoted by Taras Kuzío in 'EU and Ukraine: a turning point in 2004?', EU-ISS Occasional Paper No. 47 (Paris, European Union Institute for Security Studies 2003).

[15] Ibid., at p. 19.

stretching back to the medieval state of Kyiv Rus. Such a topsy-turvy policy prevailed until the end of Kuchma's second term. The European Union also adopted an incoherent policy towards Ukraine, made even more confusing by Ukraine itself, as noted by one analyst.[16]

As pointed out above, the 'big bang' enlargement of the European Union and the so-called 'Orange Revolution' in Ukraine have brought about a shift in EU-Ukraine relations in geographic, political and economic terms. Since 1 May 2004, Ukraine shares a direct border with the European Union (Poland, Slovakia and Hungary), which will be extended even further when Romania joins the European Union in 2007 or 2008.[17] As direct neighbours, the European Union and Ukraine were already set to reinforce their political and economic interdependence under Kuchma's rule, but the implementation of these aims was precipitated by the democratic transition process set in motion after the second round of presidential elections in December 2004. The Orange Revolution and the elevation of Viktor Yushchenko to the presidency in January 2005 marked a turning point in EU-Ukraine relations. By establishing a Western-type democracy in Ukraine, the new authorities of the country firmly confirmed their determination to accelerate reforms to bring Ukraine closer to EU standards. 'Our road to the future is that of a united Europe... We are part of the same civilisation and we share the same values. ... Our place is in the European Union. My goal is a Ukraine in a United Europe,' stated the new Ukrainian President in his inaugural speech on 23 January 2005.[18]

Thus, the 2004 EU enlargement and Ukraine's democratic 'awakening' at the end of that year have created the opportunity for the European Union and Ukraine to develop an increasingly close relationship, going beyond cooperation to gradual economic integration and a deepening of political cooperation. But a closer relationship with the Union will depend on the sustainability of the reform process in Ukraine. Due to shortcomings and failures in implementing the reform agenda and intense external pressure from Russia, President Yushchenko did not achieve significant successes in his first year in office. The consistency of the reform process suffered from a lack of clarity regarding the distribution of competences in the government and between the President and the star-like Prime Minister, Yulia Tymoshenko. The latter somewhat improved following the surprise appointment of the new government under Prime Minister Yuri Yekhanurov in September 2005. At first, this new government seemed to follow a more technocratic and

---

16 Ibid., at p. 10.

17 See chapter 8 in this volume.

18 The full text of the address is available on the official website of Viktor Yushchenko, at: <http://www.yuschenko.com.ua/eng/Press_centre/168/2167>.

business-friendly approach, but its wings were clipped after it was sacked by the Parliament over its handling of the gas dispute with Russia, a move declared unconstitutional by the President. Fortunately, the stand-off did not reverse the consolidation of democratic standards. The March 2006 parliamentary elections were generally considered to be free and fair. But the mid and long-term prospects for the reform process in Ukraine strongly depend on the follow-up given to these elections and on the steps taken in implementing the constitutional reform. At the time of writing, the chances for success appear to outweigh the inevitable risks.

Membership of the European Union is a goal desired by many parts of Ukrainian society and the political establishment. NATO membership is more controversial, for this issue is mired in the Cold War stereotype of NATO as the enemy.[19] Nonetheless, the post-revolution Ukrainian Government has clearly stated that it aspires to full membership of both international organisations.[20] This was not an obvious action. In its Orange Revolution, Ukraine rid itself from the monopoly and sole influence of Russia. Seeking another influence was therefore not necessarily an immediate objective, but the new leadership understood that it was too dangerous for Ukraine to remain unaligned between the two power blocs, effectively in a security vacuum. Indeed, Ukraine has few options in its foreign policy at present: it is still establishing itself as a new state, focusing on institution building and policy development. In the meantime, the reality of existing between two powerful zones is pressing, especially for a country which is dependent on Russian imports despite its access to Caspian oil and gas and has to deal with vast Soviet-era heavy weapons dumps across the country and the frozen conflict of Transnistria next door.[21] A commitment to the West as a balancing solution was therefore logical. Yushchenko has won recognition and support from both EU leaders and the US Congress, but his popularity at home has diminished. Ukraine now hopes for membership of the World Trade Organisation in the near future.[22]

---

[19] Also, many Ukrainians still remember the military action NATO took against Serbia in 1999 in response to the crisis in Kosovo: it bombed and ruined bridges, hospitals and Orthodox churches.

[20] See the documents available at the website of Ukrainian mission to the European Union, at: <http://ukraine-eu.mfa.gov.ua>. See also BBC Report 'Nato chief in Ukraine bid talks' of 27 June 2005, available at: <http://news.bbc.co.uk/1/hi/world/europe/4626121.stm>.

[21] Transnistria has become a regional centre for international arms dealers and human traffickers since it declared independence from neighbouring Moldova in 1992. See chapter 17 in this volume.

[22] It should be noted that Ukraine has been a member of the Council of Europe since 1995 and of the OSCE since 1992.

2. LEGAL RELATIONS BETWEEN THE EUROPEAN UNION AND UKRAINE

2.1 Partnership and Cooperation Agreement

The PCA with Ukraine was tailored to the state of the European Union's policy at the time of its conclusion. Its aims are specified in Article 1 and have not lost their relevance since then. They are fourfold:

1. to provide a framework for political dialogue;
2. to promote trade, investment and economic relations;
3. to support the consolidation of democracy and transition to a market economy; and
4. to enhance cultural, economic, social, financial, civil, scientific and technological cooperation.

Like all other PCAs, the PCA Ukraine belongs to the category of mixed agreements and represents a sub-group among the 'association', 'stabilisation' and 'development' agreements, categories which are very well known in the practice of the European Communities. The PCA can be classified as an entry-level agreement that does not envisage membership of the European Union but endorses a potential interest in developing closer mutual cooperation between the parties.[23] At the same time, however, the PCA Ukraine goes beyond the proper scope of the European Community: it has a clear cross-pillar dimension. Its institutional framework covers the Common Foreign and Security Policy (CFSP) and Justice and Home Affairs (JHA). As Petrov notes, the PCA aims towards the development of closer political relations, the promotion of trade, investment and harmonious economic relations between the European Community and Ukraine and the latter's completion of the transition to a market economy, while holding the country at a controllable distance from closer access to the EC single market.[24]

The PCA Ukraine covers a wide range of issues, including, *inter alia*, political dialogue (Arts. 6-9), trade in goods (Arts. 10-23),[25] business and investment (Arts.

---

[23] See D. McGoldrick, *International Relations Law of the European Union* (Longman, London 1997) pp. 116-137; C. Hillion, 'Institutional Aspects of the Partnership Between the European Union and the Newly Independent States of the Former Soviet Union: Case Studies of Russia and Ukraine', 37 *CMLRev.* (2000) pp. 1211-1235.

[24] See R. Petrov, 'The Partnership and Cooperation Agreements with the Newly Independent States', in A. Ott and K. Inglis, eds. *Handbook on European Enlargement. A Commentary on the Enlargement Process* (The Hague, T.M.C. Asser Press 2002) pp. 175-194.

[25] One should remember that trade in goods is also covered in sectoral agreements on textiles and steel products. See Agreement between the European Economic Community and Ukraine on

24-48), competition (Arts. 49-51), economic cooperation (Arts. 52-79), cultural cooperation (Art. 80) and financial cooperation (Arts. 81-84).

The PCA Ukraine places emphasis on the approximation of Ukrainian law to EC law, and to this end Article 51 articulates the priority areas for approximation. It provides that

> The Parties recognise that an important condition for strengthening the economic links between the Ukraine and the Community is the approximation of Ukraine's existing and future legislation to that of the Community. Ukraine shall endeavour to ensure that its legislation will be gradually made compatible with that of the Community.

The priority areas include customs law, company law, banking law, intellectual property law, legal protection of workers in the work place, rules on financial services, competition, public procurement, protection of the life and health of humans, animal and plants, the environment, consumer protection, indirect taxation, technical rules and standards, nuclear energy law and regulations on transport. The extent of the approximation priorities provided for under the PCA Ukraine is therefore very similar to that envisaged under the Europe Agreements with the countries of Central and Eastern Europe that acceded to the Union on 1 May 2004.[26] On the other hand, the PCA Ukraine avoids any reference to the possibility of future membership of the European Union and instead provides only for an examination of the circumstances which might allow for the establishment in the future of a EU-Ukraine free trade area. This has an impact on the interpretation of the best endeavours clause contained in the agreement.[27] In addition, Annex III emphasises the necessity of the application by Ukraine, prior to obtaining WTO membership, of a number of specific international trade rules and international agreements while trading with the EC Member States. A scoreboard is tracking progress in the field of legislative approximation. The Commission's conclusions in its March 2003 review of the bilateral negotiations on market access aimed at Ukraine's accession to the WTO are an important part of Ukraine's progress towards the achievement of 'market economy' status. Thus, as far as the first pillar of the European Union is concerned, the aims of the PCA do not, as a matter of principle, go beyond the facilitation of trade relations between the parties.

---

trade in textile products, *OJ* 1994 L 123/718 (as amended); Agreement between the European Community and the Government of Ukraine on trade in steel products, *OJ* 2005 L 232/42.

[26] See A. Łazowski, 'Approximation of Laws', in Ott and Inglis, op. cit. n. 24, at pp. 631-639.

[27] For an analysis of the changing interpretation of the similarly constructed Art. 68 EA Poland, see E. Piontek, 'Central and Eastern European Countries in Preparation for Membership in the European Union – A Polish Perspective', 1 *YPES* (1997) pp. 73-87.

As far as the third pillar of the European Union is concerned, the EU Action Plan of 10 December 2001 on cooperation in the field of justice and home affairs is operational and progress is being monitored, also by way of a scoreboard.[28]

It is hard to suppress the feeling that the European Community's formula for the PCA with Ukraine is less beneficial than the formula of the PCA with Russia.[29] Thus, for example, the preamble of the PCA Russia explicitly contains the objective 'to create the necessary conditions for the future establishment of a free trade area between the Community and Russia'.[30] As indicated earlier, the creation of a free trade area between the Community and Ukraine was treated only as a possibility to be considered in the future. At the same time, however, consecutive EU-Ukraine summits consistently emphasised the need for approximation of Ukrainian legislation to EU legal standards, and Ukraine has repeatedly been urged to accelerate its approximation process as a condition of further *rapprochement* with the European Union. In contrast, EU-Russia legislative cooperation lacks the intensity and momentum inherent in EU-Ukrainian relations. This did not prevent the European Union from already placing the possibility of establishing a 'common European economic space' with Russia on the agenda in 2002.[31] At the same time, the European Union minimised Ukraine's record on approximation, even though its achievements were significant,[32] and not much worse than those of Romania, an acceding country. Such an approach to Ukraine's European aspirations was detrimental. In contrast to the policy of openness and tolerance toward Russia, the policy of the European Union toward Ukraine was – until the end of 2004 – characterised by a reproachful tone. In practice, this was a policy which discouraged integration, evoking in Ukrainian society a sense of rejection by the unifying Europe. Many Ukrainians are of the view that the Union actually supports Ukraine's economic integration into the CIS precisely so that it can forget about the country. These suspicions are not necessarily unfounded.

In short, the PCA has exhausted its potential. Formulating various and often far-reaching obligations, although without a precise description of their binding power and without describing specific deadlines or the effects of their implementation, creates more problems in the mutual relations than it solves. In this

---

[28] See <http://europa.eu.int/comm/externalrelations/ceeca/pca/pcaukraine.pdf>.

[29] See chapter 14 in this volume.

[30] Agreement on partnership and cooperation establishing a partnership between the European Communities and their Member States, of one part, and the Russian Federation, of the other part, *OJ* 1997 L 327/3.

[31] Report to the EU-Russia Summit of 29 May 2002 of the High-Level Group on the common European economic space, available at: <http://www.europa.eu.int/comm/external_relations/russia/summit_05_02/rep.htm>.

[32] See R. Petrov, 'Recent Development in the Adaptation of Ukrainian Legislation to EU Law', 8 *EFA Rev.* (2003) pp. 125-141.

situation, the replacement of the PCA with a new agreement has become necessary. If this does not happen, strengthening the 'European orientation' of Ukraine will become increasingly difficult or even impossible.

2.2 The EU Common Strategy on Ukraine

The EU Common Strategy on Ukraine (CSU),[33] like all other EU common strategies, does not contain strict instructions or operational legal provisions for the Union, but rather 'calls' on the Council, the Commission and the Member States to review, each according to their own competencies and capacities, existing actions, programmes, instruments and policies to ensure their consistency with the strategy.[34] It is further worth noting that the CSU follows rather than precedes Community policies and instruments.[35] Javier Solana once characterised common strategies 'as rhetorical and descriptive of existing instruments'.[36] Some commentators, however, are of the opinion that they offer an overview of existing and projected programmes that is helpful for the country or region concerned as well as for those working in a narrow subject area of the Council or the Commission. By formulating objectives and policies unanimously agreed to by the Member States, they open the way for the adoption of implementing decisions (joint actions and common positions).[37]

The CSU complements the PCA, thereby outlining the skeleton of contractual relations between the European Union and Ukraine. The PCA occupies the upper level.[38] According to paragraph 5 of the CSU, the European Union has the following strategic goals with regard to Ukraine:

---

[33] European Council Common Strategy 1999/877/CFSP of 11 December 1999 on Ukraine, *OJ* 1999 L 331/1, extended until 23 December 2004 by Common Strategy 2003/897/CFSP of the European Council amending Common Strategy 1999/877/CFSP on Ukraine in order to extend the period of its application, *OJ* 2003 L 333/96. No new measures have been adopted to extend the Common Strategy's period of application, so it must be assumed that it has silently passed away and has been *de facto* replaced by the ENP, although none of the policy papers behind the latter mention the Common Strategy, and *a fortiori* that they intend to replace them.

[34] The Common Strategy was preceded by the Common Position 94/779/CFSP defined by the Council on the basis of Article J.2 of the Treaty on European Union on the objectives and priorities of the European Union towards Ukraine, *OJ* 1994 L 313/1.

[35] See P. Eeckhout, *External Relations of the European Union. Legal and Constitutional Foundations* (Oxford, Oxford University Press 2004) pp. 405-407.

[36] See Report by the Secretary-General/High Representative, *Common Strategies*, Council of the European Union, Doc. No. 1487/100, 21 December 2000 (declassified 30 January 2001).

[37] See E. Denza, *The Intergovernmental Pillars of the European Union* (Oxford, Oxford University Press 2002) p. 292; Eeckhout, op. cit. n. 35, at p. 407.

[38] For an overview of its implementation, see Council report to the European Council on the implementation of the Common Strategy of the European Union on Ukraine, Doc. No. 15516/02; Draft Council report to the European Council on the implementation of the Common Strategy of the European Union on Ukraine, Doc. No. 15989/04.

- to contribute to the emergence of a stable, open and pluralistic democracy in Ukraine, governed by the rule of law and underpinning a stable functioning market economy which will benefit all the people of Ukraine;
- to cooperate with Ukraine in the maintenance of stability and security in Europe and the wider world, and in finding effective responses to common challenges facing the continent;
- to increase economic, political and cultural cooperation with Ukraine as well as cooperation in the field of justice and home affairs.

Among the 'instruments and means' which are to be employed in fulfilment of these goals, the CSU mentions efforts aimed at the coordination of the Member States' actions *vis-à-vis* Ukraine in regional and other international organisations, considering extending technical assistance in support of Ukraine's economic and social reform, supporting the development of a transparent and stable legal, regulatory and institutional framework in Ukraine designed to promote increased economic activity and domestic and foreign investment, as well as promoting the progressive approximation of Ukrainian legislation to that of the European Union (paras. 51-53). The CSU also provides for initiatives serving closer collaboration with Ukraine in justice and home affairs (paras. 63-64) and in the performance of the 'Petersberg Tasks' and other security activities (paras. 54-55). It also declares the European Union's readiness to support Ukraine's efforts to meet the requirements of WTO accession (paras. 60-62) and to examine 'the circumstances which might ... allow for the future establishment of an EU-Ukraine Free Trade Area as provided in Article 4 of the PCA' (paras. 32-33). Regional and cross-border cooperation with neighbouring countries, in particular on border management issues, including the technical modernisation of border crossing points with Hungary, Poland, Romania and Slovakia are also listed amongst the tasks (para. 65). Cooperation in the field of environment, energy and nuclear safety, as well as in the field of culture, twinning and educational and scientific programmes, closes the list of 'specific initiatives' provided for the European Union under the CSU (paras. 63-64 and 66 respectively). As regards nuclear energy, a framework for mutual relations in this domain was set up in the Agreement for cooperation in the field of nuclear safety, which was signed in Kiev on 23 July 1999.[39]

While accepting a generally positive evaluation of common strategies as a starting point, it is difficult – like in the case of the PCA – to resist the impression that its formula in respect to Ukraine is less beneficial than the formula of the

[39] Agreement for Cooperation between the European Atomic Energy Community and the Cabinet of Ministers of Ukraine in the field of nuclear safety, *OJ* 2002 L 322/33, actualised operationally for 2004-2006 by the Nuclear Safety Indicative Programme, adopted by the European Commission on 7 November 2003 in line with proposals and conclusions contained in the Nuclear Safety Strategy Paper 2002-2006.

Common Strategy on Russia.[40] Throughout the 1990s and the early years of the new millennium, Russia has in fact been perceived by France and other influential EU Member States as a valuable counterweight to US 'unilateralism' and thus an as essential ally in their pursuit of the so-called 'new multi-polar world'. These Member States did not wish to undermine their good relations with Russia by fully supporting Ukraine's European choice.[41] Until the withdrawal of its troops in 2005, the participation of Ukraine in the Polish zone of the US-led coalition forces in Iraq seemed for some EU Members States to serve as yet another argument to keep Ukraine at arm's length. Such a lopsided policy suited Russia, which was seeking to develop a strategic partnership with the Union as a whole, or with some of its Member States, but not Ukraine, for which only being inside the Union would serve as an accomplishment of its 'European choice'.

2.3 Institutional framework for bilateral relations

The bilateral dialogue between the European Union and Ukraine is conducted at various levels and consequently within differentiated institutional frameworks. In political terms, the annual EU-Ukraine summits are undoubtedly of pivotal importance. For example, during the Ninth Summit held on 1 December 2005, it was confirmed that Ukraine is expected to be granted a market economy status paving the way for further enhancement of trade relations and its membership in the WTO.[42] Another forum for bilateral cooperation are the so-called Ukraine-EU Troika meetings. A considerable number of these meetings concentrate on justice and home affairs.[43] In common with other PCAs, the one between the European Communities and Ukraine also creates a special institutional framework. Under Article 85 PCA Ukraine, the Cooperation Council is empowered to supervise the implementation of the agreement. It is composed of representatives of the Council of the European Union and European Commission, on the one hand, and members of the Ukrainian Government, on the other (Art. 86). The Cooperation Council meets annually. It is worth noting that, at its eighth meeting, the EU-

---

40 European Council Common Strategy 1999/414/CFSP on Russia, *OJ* 1999 L 157/1, extended by Common Strategy 2003/471/CFSP of the European Council amending Common Strategy 1999/414/CFSP on Russia in order to extend the period of its application, *OJ* 2003 L 157/68. See chapter 14 in this volume.

41 As Dov Lynch diplomatically observed: 'Moscow values relations with Paris for the similarity in Russian and French views on international relations', in 'Russia Faces Europe', Chaillot Papers No. 60 (Paris, EU Institute for Security Studies 2003) p. 50.

42 EU-Ukraine Summit, 1 December 2005, Joint Statement, Council Doc. No. 15222/05 (Presse 337).

43 See, *inter alia*, Conclusions of the meeting on Justice and Home Affairs between the European Union and Ukraine held in Brussels on 11 November 2002, Doc. No. 14433/02; Conclusions of the Ministerial Troika meeting on Justice and Home Affairs between the EU and Ukraine held in Brussels on 29 March 2004.

Ukraine Cooperation Council endorsed the Ukraine Action Plan.[44] The Cooperation Council is supported in its activities by a Cooperation Committee (Art. 87). The PCA Ukraine also provides for a Parliamentary Cooperation Committee (Arts. 90-92).

2.4 Financial and technical assistance: Tacis and related programmes

Despite all the weaknesses of the existing PCA and CSU, the European Union and Ukraine managed to strengthen the basis and the instruments of cooperation in a number of fields already identified for support in the framework of the Technical Assistance to the Commonwealth of Independent States (Tacis) programme, thereby reconfirming the agreed priorities. Tacis, which was established in 1991, is currently based on a Council Regulation of 29 December 1999.[45] The programme concentrates on seven main areas of cooperation, which are listed in Annex II of the regulation. They are:

1. support for institutional, legal and administrative reform;[46]
2. support to the private sector and assistance for economic development;[47]
3. support in addressing the social consequences of transition;[48]
4. development of infrastructure networks;[49]
5. promotion of environmental protection and management of natural resources;[50]
6. development of the rural economy;[51] and
7. support for nuclear safety.

---

44 See EU-Ukraine Cooperation Council, Eight Meeting, Brussels, 21 February 2005, Press Release 6428/05.

45 Council Regulation (EC, Euratom) No. 99/2000 concerning the provision of assistance to the partner States in Eastern Europe and Central Asia, *OJ* 2000 L 12/1.

46 Development of the rule of law; support for effective policy making; reform of public administration at national, regional and local level; support for executive and legislative bodies (national, regional, local); support for justice and home affairs activities; reinforcement of the legal and regulatory framework; support for the implementation of international commitments; support for the civil society; and support for education and training.

47 Promotion of small and medium-sized enterprises; development of the banking and financial services systems; promotion of private entrepreneurship including joint ventures; industrial cooperation, including research; privatisation; enterprise restructuring; and promotion of market-orientated framework for trade and investment.

48 Reform of the health, pension, social protection and insurance systems; assistance to alleviate the social impact of industrial restructuring; assistance for social reconstruction; and development of employment services, including re-training.

49 Transport networks; telecommunication networks; energy pipelines and transmission networks; and border-crossings.

50 Development of sustainable environmental policies and practices; promotion of harmonisation of environmental standards with European Union norms; improvement of energy technologies in supply and end use; and promotion of sustainable use and management of natural resources, including energy, saving, efficient energy usage and improvement of environmental infrastructure.

51 Legal and regulatory framework, including land privatisation; increasing access to finance and promotion of training; and improvement of distribution and access to markets.

Over time, the European Union has become the largest donor to Ukraine. Total assistance since 1991 amounts to more than €1 billion. In the wake of the nuclear power disaster at Chernobyl on 26 April 1986, Tacis assistance in the area of nuclear safety alone has amounted to almost €260 million from 1991 to 2003. Assistance also includes the Fuel Gap programme and a major contribution to the Chernobyl Shelter Fund managed by the European Bank for Reconstruction and Development (€100 million for 2001-2004). Euratom loans may be made available for the modernisation of two nuclear power stations at Khmelnitsky and Rivne ('K2R4') in conjunction with a loan agreement to be coordinated by the EBRD.

Table 1: Financial Assistance to Ukraine (in € millions)[52]

	1998	1999	2000	2001	2002	2003	2004	Total
Tacis National Programme	44	46.5	48	48	47	50	70	353.5
Tacis Nuclear Safety**	7.7	8.4	5.5	32.4	23.9	27	25	129.9
Tacis Cross-border Cooperation*	10.3	5.2	1	5.5	0.5	3	3	28.5
Tacis Regional Programme*	4.8	3.7	6	9.1	10.5	6	4	44.1
Fuel Gap	-	-	25	20	20			65.0
Chernobyl Shelter Fund	50	40.5	-	40	20	18	22	190.5
Contribution to STCU	3	3	4.5	4	4	4	4	26.5
Total	119.8	107.3	90	159	125.9	108	128	838.0

* Estimated pro-rata share for Ukraine in regional programmes.
** Includes both national projects and estimated share of multi-country projects.

The current programming of Tacis assistance is guided by the Country Strategy Paper (CSP) of December 2001 for the 2002-2006 period, the multi-annual National Indicative Programme (NIP) and the annual (sometimes biennial) Action Programme (AP). The first NIP (2002-2003) was divided into three sections, all of which were heavily oriented towards economics and trade, namely (i) institutional, legal and administrative reform; (ii) support to the private sector and assistance for economic development; and (iii) addressing the social consequences of transition. The current NIP for Ukraine, adopted by the European Commission on 4 August 2003, covers the 2004-2006 period and focuses on five priority areas: (i) legal, judicial and administrative reform; (ii) border management; (iii) business, trade and investment promotion; (iv) civil society, training

52 Source: <http://europa.eu.int/comm/external_relations/ukraine/intro/index.htm>.

and education; and (v) social reform.[53] The overall amount provided under these programmes for the 2004-2006 period is forecast to be €212 million. Under the NIP for 2004-2006, a number of important recommendations have been formulated, including stronger and more flexible input in supporting PCA implementation, institution building (i.e., through judicial reform), improvement of the business environment and access to credit for SMEs, the strengthening of local/municipal governance and development, in particular with regard to SME promotion and the environment sector, the continuation of programmes in the energy sector to enhance energy efficiency, and the strengthening of NGO programmes, in particular those providing social assistance to vulnerable groups.

A new Country Strategy Paper will cover the 2007-2013 period. Assistance to Ukraine over that period will primarily be covered under the new European Neighbourhood and Partnership Instrument (ENPI). This instrument will be established to provide assistance for the development of an area of prosperity and good neighbourliness involving the European Union and the ENP countries. Funding levels for Ukraine under the ENPI are estimated at €865 million, which would represent a 72.7% increase compared to 2006 levels. Ukraine's nuclear energy sector will also benefit from assistance under the new Nuclear Safety Instrument. In addition, certain measures in the area of conflict prevention and crisis management may be supported under the future Stability Instrument.

2.5 Towards a new form of contractual relations

The advantages derived by Ukraine from the implementation of the PCA and CSP are quite marginal. They barely provide any perspective for an enhanced association of Ukraine with the European Union. Ukraine is too large a country with too great a developmental potential and strategic significance for the balance of power in Europe as a whole to feel satisfied with the current nature of its relations with the European Union. Continuous reliance on existing schemes would be detrimental to the Union and, in particular, the neighbouring Member States of Poland, Slovakia and Hungary. That is why these states are set on supporting ever stronger relations between Ukraine and the European Union. Strong ties between Ukraine and the European Union also form a guarantee of Ukraine's continued unity and independence. Objectively speaking, close ties between Ukraine and the European Union, capped by membership of the Union, lies within the vital interest of both sides. That is why EU-Ukraine relations should, sooner rather than later, be based on new and more dynamic principles of cooperation. Fortunately,

---

[53] Text available on the European Commission website, at: <http://europa.eu.int/comm/external_relations/ukraine/csp/index.htm>.

both sides agree on the latter.[54] The agreement that will replace the current PCA and CSP should be modelled on elements of the Europe Agreements and the Stabilisation and Association Agreements, as well as on the EEA Agreement.[55] Vividly and unambiguously defined goals of the new agreement on EU-Ukraine cooperation should be:

- building the free trade area in stages, followed by full implementation;
- proceeding towards the creation of common economic area;
- gradual inclusion of Ukraine in the cooperation in the framework of the Area of Freedom, Security and Justice (AFSJ); and
- further alignment with the Common Foreign and Security Policy (CFSP) and continued cooperation in the framework of the European Security and Defence Policy (ESDP).

Each of the above-mentioned programmes for cooperation should be broken down into concrete tasks to be accomplished within specified periods of time. They should be accompanied by a description of the methods and means for their implementation, the rights and obligations of each side and the consequences of the implementation of the undertaken obligations. This should be an organically and institutionally organised cooperation.

The European Union should undertake to support Ukraine's own activities in the above-mentioned areas and to actively support the country in its negotiations for membership of the WTO at the earliest possible opportunity. This is already part of the implementation of the ENP Action Plan. In the initial phase, the European Union should unilaterally grant Ukraine privileged treatment in the field of trade that is no less favourable than the treatment accorded to the Western Balkan countries. The starting point for the programme concerning the gradual inclusion of Ukraine in the Schengen system should be the agreement providing for the removal of Ukraine from the EU visa regime, along with the determination of implementation deadlines for the entire programme subject to the fulfilment of the necessary conditions.

Considering all the above-mentioned circumstances, the new agreement on EU-Ukraine relations should state that it is the concerted will of the parties to work towards the integration of Ukraine in the structures of the European Union

---

[54] See EU-Ukraine Cooperation Council, Eight Meeting, Brussels, 21 February 2005, Press Release 6428/05. See also EU-Ukraine Summit, 1 December 2005, Joint Statement, Council Doc. No. 15222/05 (Presse 337).

[55] For the time being, both parties are enhancing their relations by means of sectoral agreements. To this end, the EC-Ukraine Aviation Agreement and a memorandum of understanding on the Galileo satellite radionavigation programme were signed during the EU-Ukraine Summit on 1 December 2005.

once all the action programmes have been fully implemented. Thus, the EU-Ukraine strategic partnership should be afforded a special character that is on a par with the privileges granted to the countries of the Western Balkans. The perspective of EU membership and privileged conditions should be accompanied by EU assistance to Ukraine for education, scientific work and building civil society. These are areas in which a community of thought, intellect and habits arises, on which success in other areas of cooperation depends. This is the kind of assistance that is needed in Ukraine and will also serve the European Union's interests. The proposed agreement should have a long-term character (i.e., it should be concluded for a period of fifteen to twenty years), but with a possibility of shortening the duration if its action points are fully accomplished before then. In such a case, the proposed agreement should be replaced with a successive agreement whose contents corresponds to the new conditions and identifies new requirements in the field of cooperation. This process would have to be repeated until the accession of Ukraine to the European Union.

3. IMPACT OF EU ENLARGEMENT ON EU-UKRAINE RELATIONS

3.1 The Polish contribution

Poland, traditionally a staunch promoter of Ukraine's 'European choice', already produced a 'non-paper' and a 'paper' in support of an Eastern dimension for the European Union in April and May 2003, calling for new action plans for Ukraine and Moldova that would prepare both countries for an enhanced association with the European Union by the time the present PCAs expire in 2008.[56] Both documents of the Polish Ministry of Foreign Affairs made a number of recommendations, in particular:

- to upgrade EU-Ukraine relations to those of Russia, starting with granting market economy status to Ukraine, as granted to Russia in 2002 mainly on political grounds;
- to provide targeted assistance to NGOs as well as to SMEs through a 'European Democracy Fund' or a 'European Neighbourhood Society Fund';
- to intensify assistance towards the effective implementation by Ukraine of the *acquis communautaire* in the field of economic policy and justice and home affairs, together with the necessary adjustment of the structures and functioning of public administration and the judiciary;

---

56 See Ministry of Foreign Affairs, 'The New Neighbours – A Framework for Relations. Proposals from Poland' (Warsaw, Ministry of Foreign Affairs 2003).

- to enhance the political and security dialogue as part of the elaboration of a common European political and economic space. Coupled with an 'open doors' policy, this would untie the notions of the European Union and 'Europe' by including countries, such as Ukraine, as potential future members, as they would be then considered 'European';
- to ensure a balance between the tight border controls needed to combat soft security threats and less restrictive border controls that will not halt cross-border trade, and academic, cultural and official cooperation;
- to expand military cooperation, as agreed at the Seville European Council of June 2002, and to use Ukrainian troops in a broad array of crisis management operations undertaken by the European Union; and
- to undertake joint infrastructure projects in the fields of energy, transportation and communications.

These policy recommendations coincided with the publication of a 'road-map' for EU-Ukraine relations developed by experts from the Stefan Batory Foundation in Warsaw, the Centre for Peace, Conversion and Ukrainian Foreign Policy in Kiev, the Centre for European Policy Studies in Brussels and Birmingham University.[57] Moderate in character, they could serve as a good starting point for building strategic long-term cooperation between the Union and Ukraine. Some of them are outlined in the following sections of this chapter.

3.2 Policy recommendations in selected areas

3.2.1 *Economy*

The latest enlargement round of the European Union has substantially influenced growth in Ukrainian foreign trade. The European Union's share of Ukrainian exports currently stands at 40 per cent. But Ukraine's exports to Russia have also grown, reaching 18.1 per cent in the first quarter of 2005. Ukraine's main import partner is the CIS, mainly because of the country's dependence on the import of Russian energy carriers, oil and gas. Ukraine's gas pipelines carry more than 80 per cent of Russia's gas exports to Europe, which gives Ukraine an important bargaining chip. In order to strengthen economic relations with the Union, the priority of Ukrainian policy for the near future should be building an effective market economy and membership of the WTO. Joining the WTO is a prerequisite

[57] G. Gromadzki, A. Sushko, M. Vahl and K. Wolczuk, eds., *More than a Neighbour – proposals for the EU's future policy towards Ukraine* (Warsaw, Stefan Batory Foundation 2003); G. Gromadzki, A. Sushko, M. Vahl and K. Wolczuk, eds., *More than Neighbours. The Enlarged European Union and Ukraine – New Relations. Final Report* (Warsaw and Kiev, Stefan Batory Foundation, International Renaissance Foundation 2004).

for the further liberalisation of trade. A swift completion of the negotiations with this organisation is in the interests of both Ukraine (quantitative restrictions on its steel exports will be removed) and the European Union (for anti-dumping purposes).

However, the process of liberalisation in EU-Ukraine relations should remain asymmetrical, because the entire Ukrainian economy, in particular such sectors as steel, machine building and agriculture, will otherwise not be capable of resisting the pressure of European competition. A quick and complete opening of Ukraine's market would risk producing a complete economic breakdown and result in mass unemployment. From a somewhat more long-term perspective, the asymmetry in trade relations should be gradually removed as part of the establishment of a free trade area. The creation of the foundations for an EU-Ukraine free trade area should be one of the priorities in the economic policies of both parties.

One of the ways to change the structure of trade is to increase the share of services in Ukraine's exports to the European Union. There is significant development potential in this sphere, especially when it comes to the Ukrainian tourist industry, transport, building and services in the field of information technology. An additional benefit lies in the fact that the above-mentioned economic activities are less susceptible to anti-dumping limitations and other types of restrictive procedures. Closer cooperation between the EU and Ukrainian aviation industries and R&D centres in this domain should also be considered.

Ukraine should develop a cohesive and consistently applied strategy of investment promotion. This strategy should be based on a precise evaluation of the state of the Ukrainian economy and international investment tendencies. It should encompass the development of a cohesive strategy for investment promotion supported by all the Ukrainian authorities, as well as facilitating contacts between foreign investors and these authorities. This could be achieved, for example, through the establishment of a 'one-stop shop' mechanism, whereby foreign investors could obtain all the required licenses, consents and permits from the relevant authorities. It could also include assistance for foreign investors that encounter difficulties with the Ukrainian authorities. All this would facilitate and enliven a regular dialogue between foreign investors and Ukrainian decision makers in the sphere of investment policy.

In the energy sector, relations between Ukraine and the European Union should be based on the provisions of the Energy Charter, which delineates relations on the basis of the principle of non-discrimination. Ukraine could play a key role in the delivery of hydrocarbon fuels to the European Union. Upon the completion of the Odessa-Brody-Płock pipeline, Ukraine will have the necessary infrastructure to transport significant amounts of Caspian oil to Europe. It is expected that the European Union will be the most important recipient of Caspian oil. Not by chance, the European Commission recognised just this pipeline as an undertaking of general European significance.[58] An additional advantage connected to the start-up of the Odessa-Brody-Płock pipeline lies in the fact that it is not only one of the shortest routes leading from the Caspian Sea basin to Europe but also that it offers EU countries – and Ukraine – a diversification of deliveries away from Russian supplies, thereby increasing their energy security. Recently, however, the construction of the Brody-Płock section of the pipeline running through the territory of Poland was stopped. Without the Union's clear standpoint and financial support, it will not be possible to resolve these matters propitiously.

As noted earlier, a significant proportion of the gas that the European Union receives from Russia is sent through Ukrainian territory. The creation in Ukraine of an international consortium involved in the forwarding of natural gas would therefore be in the interests of all parties (i.e., the European Union, Ukraine and Russia). It is absolutely necessary that the process of creating such a consortium is transparent, because Western investors will otherwise be reluctant to engage in it. Their engagement is vital for guaranteeing sufficient funds and also assuring consumers that one can depend on gas from the CIS countries.

Only two multifunctional trans-European transport corridors run through the territory of Ukraine, and the country has been included in one of the three Trans-European transport areas. Only three of the ten existing corridors connect between Western and Eastern Europe, while the remaining seven are intended to improve North-South connections. In order to achieve greater *rapprochement* between Ukraine and the enlarged European Union, the latter should place a greater emphasis on the development of the East-West connections, in general, and those linking Ukraine directly to the European Union, in particular.

3.2.2 *Free movement of people*

Collaboration in building an AFSJ plays an ever more important role in relations between the European Union and Ukraine, especially since the two countries share a border since May 2004. They should coordinate an entire range of legal, administrative and technical instruments as part of the creation of a friendly border policy. The purpose of such a policy would be to strengthen the ties between the European Union and Ukraine, *inter alia*, by eliminating barriers to the movement of people while simultaneously raising border security levels. The abolition of the visa requirement in respect of Ukrainian citizens should become one of the main goals of long-term European policy in respect of Ukraine.[59] In the

---

58 See, for instance, 'The Commission and Ukraine strengthen energy cooperation in the framework of the EU-Ukraine Neighbourhood Action Plan', Press Release IP/05/504 of 28 April 2005.

59 On 7 November 2005, the Council authorised the Commission to negotiate a visa facilitation agreement between the European Union and Ukraine. See Council Conclusions of 7 November 2005, Press Release No. 13621/05 (Presse 273).

near future, however, it is of essential importance that visas be easily available to citizens on both sides of the border. The introduction of alleviations in the small border traffic between the European Union and Ukraine should not only become a practical tool that will make life easier for people living near the border but would also constitute an important political gesture, which would be a positive contribution to relations between the European Union and Ukraine. When it comes to future EU-Ukraine relations, the definition of border regions should not end at 50 kilometres from the border, but should coincide with the borders of administrative units. Such a solution could meet important needs and minimise the risk of abuses.

As a result of EU enlargement, the consular network of EU Member States has also been expanded. At the same time, due to new visa procedures, the Ukrainian demand for EU visas has grown significantly. It seems that, in the context of the 'Wider Europe' initiative, both old and new Member States should think in terms of an integrated consular infrastructure concentrated along the European Union's external border. Technological and organisational advancements will make it possible, within a short time, to improve the quality of information within the Schengen Information System (SIS), thanks to the extensive use of transferable terminals with immediate access to SIS, easy to use readers for passports with a magnetic code and the technical capacity for printing visa stickers within the passport control procedure.

Easier access to visas, which would bring about policy and institutional modifications in the European Union, will require positive action on the part of Ukraine. As a sign of good will, Ukraine has extended visa-free travel for EU citizens indefinitely (originally from 1 May to 1 September 2005).[60] Ukrainian politicians should appreciate that in this case there is no room for traditional reciprocity in relations with the European Union and should make Ukraine's citizens aware of this matter.

Access to the EU labour market for citizens of third states is possible, albeit limited. When it comes to employment for a limited time, many precedents exist in the relations between the European Union and various non-Member States.[61] Ukraine and the European Union should pass regulations reflecting both the difficult economic situation of Ukraine and the state of European labour markets. The two sides should then sign an agreement pertaining to the mutual protection of labour markets. It would be good if this agreement provided transparent and constant possibilities of legal employment for Ukrainian citizens, as well as assuming responsibility for providing assistance to seasonal workers temporarily returning to Ukraine and the fulfilment of all contractual provisions. For its part,

---

60 Presidential Order 569/2005 of 31 March 2005.

61 See chapter 2 in this volume.

Ukraine should facilitate access to its labour market for EU citizens, and in particular for managerial personnel, by simplifying bureaucratic procedures such as the registration requirement and so forth.

3.2.3 *Common Foreign and Security Policy*

Ukraine is partly aligned with the European Union's CFSP. For now, it has shown that it is willing to participate in non-military operations conducted in the framework of the European Security and Defence Policy (ESDP): EUPOL 'Proxima' in Macedonia[62] and the ongoing EUPM in Bosnia-Herzegovina.[63] Ukraine has abundant experience in international peace operations (under the NATO flag in Kosovo and Afghanistan and in the US-led coalition in Iraq). It is obvious that the potential for cooperation in this field would increase significantly in the case of a swift transformation and modernisation of the Ukrainian armed forces. Ukraine should be more firmly included in the European Union's structures for dialogue with third countries to enable it to participate more fully in so-called Petersberg operations. In this context, it should be noted that Ukraine already cooperates with two EU Member States. A Ukrainian-Polish battalion with a force of 750 soldiers took part in peace missions in Bosnia and Kosovo (UKRPOLBAT). There also is a Ukrainian-Hungarian battalion known as 'Cisa'.

As a direct neighbour of Moldova and a mediator, along with the OSCE and the Russian Federation, in the five-party mediation process, Ukraine has a major role in the efforts to find a solution to the Transnistrian issue in the Republic of Moldova.[64] An estimated 26 per cent of the total population of 740,000 in the Transnistrian region are originally Ukrainian. Over the past three years, the European Union and Ukraine have intensified their exchange of information and dialogue on the Transnistrian conflict, including in the OSCE framework. Ukraine now plays an active role in the implementation of the Joint Declaration on customs issues of the Ukrainian and Moldovan Prime Ministers. In preventing smuggling, trafficking and customs fraud, Ukrainian (and Moldovan) border and customs officials are assisted by officials from sixteen Member States working for the EU Border Assistance Mission to Moldova and Ukraine.[65]

---

[62] Agreement between the European Union and Ukraine on the participation of Ukraine in the European Union Police Mission in the former Yugoslav Republic of Macedonia (EUPOL 'Proxima'), *OJ* 2004 L 354/82.

[63] Agreement between the European Union and Ukraine on the participation of Ukraine in the European Union Police Mission (EUPM) in Bosnia and Herzegovina (BiH), *OJ* 2003 L 239/38.

[64] See further chapter 17 in this volume.

[65] Only Council Joint Action 2005/776/CFSP amending the mandate of the European Union Special Representative for Moldova, *OJ* 2005 L 292/13, refers in the fourth recital of the preamble to an agreement reached within the Political and Security Committee of the Council on 22 September 2005 on the establishment of the border mission.

3.2.4 *Civil society*

International cooperation with Ukrainian non-governmental organisations should be increased. Many of the projects carried out by Ukrainian NGOs in recent years thanks to support from US institutions are in line with European priorities for Ukraine (protection of human rights, freedom of speech and supervision of electoral procedures). These projects should continue to be supported under the European Initiative for Democracy and Human Rights (EIDHR). In order to facilitate access to EU assistance and increase the capacity of Ukrainian NGOs for receiving it, the EU representation in Ukraine should provide the fullest possible information regarding the capacity for receiving such assistance in an ordered and transparent manner. Member State representations should also be engaged in this process. It is essential to disseminate information about programmes organised by various European funds and organisations operating in Ukraine. They should cooperate in publicising European programmes and the results of projects conducted in Ukraine with the assistance of the European Union.

It is necessary to coordinate the actions of government bodies and non-governmental organisations assisting Ukraine. Transparent and coordinated information pertaining to all possibilities offered by a given country to NGOs, the media, academic institutions and specific persons is needed. Support by local Ukrainian sponsors is a long-term goal. The presence of Ukrainian NGOs in international projects will be greater if the capacity for their financial input into joint projects is increased.

Support for education should be provided through the expansion of European educational programmes – Socrates and Erasmus – to Ukraine, facilitating exchanges between universities, promoting short-term specialised training programmes that are not conducive to emigration of the intellectual elite, offering small grants in support of educational initiatives by non-government organisations (innovations in education, distance or on-line education, operating schools in small localities, multicultural education in near-border regions) and supporting European studies centres. These goals could be served, *inter alia*, by the establishment in eastern Poland, in Lublin, for example, of a European university for students from Ukraine and eventually also from Belarus, co-financed by the Union.

3.2.5 *Trans-border cooperation*

The enlargement of the European Union and the full implementation of the Schengen principles will have the greatest influence on the regions on both sides of the European Union's new eastern border. Unfortunately, a lack of awareness of the possibilities resulting from EU enlargement can be observed on both sides of this new border. In order to overcome this phenomenon and increase the engagement of people in these regions, the European Union should create regional offices situated along its external border in the new Member States and in Ukraine.

The 'Euroregions' did not fulfil the expectations placed upon them, despite some achievements, mainly due to improper financing, hesitation and lack of experience on the part of local and regional authorities. They do remain, however, the main tool of cooperation in the near-border regions of Ukraine and the enlarged European Union. They promote dialogue between local political elites, create possibilities for the exchange of know-how, which can lead to an increase in institutional efficiency, promote development and help to improve the situation of regions that have had to overcome the effects of social and economic underdevelopment and political marginalisation. Nonetheless, the full potential of the Euroregions in these key areas still needs to be realised. The European Union should take advantage of the potential of the Euroregions situated along its eastern border by providing assistance to states interested in creating local and regional organisational structures capable of maintaining and managing trans-border cooperation, creating respective service bodies, which would support the Euroregions in coordinating various EU activities, creating programmes and possibilities within near-neighbour programmes and promoting the establishment of multicultural education programmes for inhabitants of near-border areas.

4. UKRAINE IN THE EUROPEAN NEIGHBOURHOOD POLICY

The Commission's Communication of 11 March 2003 on the wider European neighbourhood[66] opened the way towards closer economic cooperation and deepening political relations.[67] Short of any form of membership perspective, it does not mention the possibility of the extension of the four freedoms to Ukraine, or any other participating country either. Nonetheless it creates, *inter alia*:

- the perspective of moving beyond cooperation to a significant degree of integration, including through a stake in the European Union's Internal Market, and the possibility for Ukraine to participate progressively in key aspects of EU policies and programmes;
- the opportunity for convergence of economic legislation, the opening of economies to each other, and the continued reduction of trade barriers, which will stimulate investment and growth; …

[66] Communication from the Commission to the Council and the European Parliament, Wider Europe – Neighbourhood: A New Framework for Relations with our Eastern and Southern Neighbours, COM (2003) 104 final.

[67] Communication from the Commission, European Neighbourhood Policy – Strategy Paper, COM (2004) 373 final.

- wider access to financial assistance for Ukraine for a number of projects involving infrastructure investment; and
- possibilities of the gradual opening of, or reinforced participation in, certain Community programmes promoting cultural, educational, environmental, technical and scientific links.

A joint EU-Ukraine Action Plan, adopted by the Commission on 9 December 2004 for a period of three years, was endorsed by the EU-Ukraine Cooperation Council on 21 February 2005.[68] It sets out a comprehensive set of priorities in areas within and beyond the scope of the PCA Ukraine. Among these priorities, particular attention has been given to:

- strengthening the stability and effectiveness of institutions guaranteeing democracy and the rule of law;
- ensuring respect for and freedom of the media and freedom of expression;
- ensuring the democratic conduct of presidential elections in 2004 and parliamentary elections scheduled for 2006 in accordance with OSCE standards;
- developing possibilities for enhancing EU-Ukrainian consultations on crisis management;
- enhanced cooperation in the common neighbourhood and regional security, in particular working towards a viable solution to the Transnistria conflict in Moldova, including addressing border issues;
- enhanced cooperation in the field of disarmament and non-proliferation;
- accession to the WTO;
- gradual removal of restrictions and non-tariff barriers that impede bilateral trade and implementation of the necessary regulatory reforms;
- improving the investment climate, through non-discriminatory, transparent and predictable business conditions, simplified administrative procedures and by the fight against corruption;
- tax reform, including improved tax administration and sound management of public finances;
- establishing a constructive dialogue on visa facilitation between the Union and Ukraine, with a view to preparing for future negotiations on a visa facilitation agreement, taking account of the need for progress on the ongoing negotiations for an EC-Ukraine readmission agreement;
- gradual approximation of Ukrainian legislation in the field of norms and standards with those of the European Union;
- further reinforcing administrative and judicial capacity;

68 See EU-Ukraine Cooperation Council, Eight Meeting, Brussels, 21 February 2005, Press Release 6428/05.

- encouraging dialogue on employment issues and best endeavours, in accordance with the PCA, to ensure that treatment of migrant workers does not discriminate on grounds of nationality.

Ukraine is considered a 'priority partner' country within the European Neighbourhood Policy.[69] Although the new Action Plan continues to refrain from any reference to the prospects of Ukrainian membership of – or even association with – the Union, the EU Ministers of Foreign Affairs agreed in a joint statement of the same day to a number of important steps aimed at strengthening EU relations with Ukraine. These are summarised as follows:

- to initiate early consultations on an enhanced agreement between the European Union and Ukraine, to replace the existing PCA at the end of its initial ten-year period, as soon as the political priorities of the ENP Action Plan have been addressed;
- to explore possibilities for closer cooperation in the area of foreign and security policy, including European Security and Defence Policy;
- to deepen trade and economic relations between the European Union and Ukraine;
- to lend further support to Ukraine's WTO accession;
- to grant 'market economy status' to Ukraine, as soon as the 'limited remaining issues' have been satisfactorily resolved;
- to consider options for possible facilitation of procedures for granting visas;
- to enhance cooperation in key sectors, including energy, transport, environment and health as well as in private sector development and treating Ukraine as a priority country in the ongoing preparations for the extension of trans-European networks;
- to step up support for legislative approximation;
- to welcome and increase people-to-people contacts, including in the key areas of youth and education;
- to maximise access to funding from the European Investment Bank (EIB), the European Union's chief lending arm. After final endorsement of the ENP Action Plan, up to €250 million of EIB lending could be made available to Ukraine; and
- to provide increased assistance to Ukraine to help it to pursue the reform process.[70]

---

[69] See the Commission's official website on EU-Ukraine relations, at: <http://www.europa.eu.int/comm/external_relations/ukraine/intro/index.htm>.

[70] See EU-Ukraine Cooperation Council Eight Meeting, Brussels, 21 February 2005, Press Release 6428/05.

Progress in meeting these priorities is to be monitored in the bodies established by the PCA. At first glance, all these priorities may seem very impressive, but in fact the 'Wider Europe' Communication and the flanking documents put Ukraine in the same category as the Southern Mediterranean countries and those of the Middle East, and therefore well below the treatment extended by the European Union to the countries of the Western Balkans. This provoked previous Ukrainian authorities to critically assess the whole programme as 'one more blunder for Ukraine'.[71] Although the stance of the post-Orange Revolution authorities is much softer, the truth is still that it would be difficult if not impossible to find a substantive justification for the adoption by the European Union of such double standards. Both Ukraine and the Western Balkans belong to Europe geographically, and the latter have not provided proof of a higher commitment to 'common values' than the former.[72] Quite the contrary: Ukraine has not experienced the type of conflicts characterising the experience of several countries in the Western Balkans, and in many other domains Ukraine's record is also more encouraging than that of, say, Albania or Bosnia-Herzegovina. Taking all this into account, it becomes evident that the European Union needs a new 'Eastern Dimension' framework programme. The 'Eastern Dimension' could serve as a coordination mechanism for actions, a kind of 'toolbox of instruments' that would pave the way for the gradual upgrading of EU-Ukraine relations to that of association status.[73]

5. CONCLUDING REMARKS

Current relations between the European Union and Ukraine are covered by the European Neighbourhood Policy (ENP). The ENP is an initiative that seeks to boost the European Union's relations with its post-enlargement neighbours to the east and south, without even purporting to say anything either way about whether countries in Eastern Europe such as Moldova and Ukraine could ultimately have a perspective of EU membership. However, this old-fashioned approach is gradually disappearing.

When questioned on 25 January 2005 by members of the European Parliament's Foreign Affairs Committee, Benita Ferrero-Waldner, Commissioner for External Relations and European Neighbourhood Policy, said that the European

71 See Kuzío, op. cit. n. 14, at p. 21.

72 See Commission Staff Working Paper, European Neighbourhood Policy, Country Report Ukraine, SEC (2004) 566.

73 See the Polish view articulated at a round-table at the European Union Institute for Security Studies (EU-ISS) on 3 June 2003.

Union 'which has already just digested ten new countries' must be 'pragmatic'.[74] She went on to say that 'it would be a pity to drop the neighbourhood policy just as it has been set up.' At the same time, however, the Commissioner acknowledged that any European country which meets the 'Copenhagen criteria' is entitled to apply for membership, but there is one criterion which must not be forgotten: 'the European Union's absorption capacity'.[75] When asked by Ukraine's representatives about the usefulness of a new action plan for bringing their country closer to the Union, she replied: 'Please use it to get closer to the EU step-by-step'. To her own question on the future for EU-Ukraine relations – 'what lies beyond the horizon?' – the answer was even more elusive: 'I cannot say today.'[76]

There is no doubt that further enlargements of the Union will need time, and no one may reasonably expect this to happen soon. Nonetheless, the door should be opened. In the Joint Declaration of February 2004, MEPs and Ukrainian MPs already stated that the European Neighbourhood Policy must 'constitute an important instrument enabling those countries neighbouring the EU to move towards the stage at which they are in a position to apply for association' and that 'the enlarged EU must not have closed external borders'.[77] In its resolution of 13 January 2005,[78] the European Parliament pledged 'continuing support, assistance and commitment to the Ukrainian people's establishment of a free and open democratic system, their creation of a prosperous market economy and their country's assumption of its rightful place in the community of democratic nations.'[79] And, above all, MEPs called on 'the Council, the Commission and the Member States to consider, besides the measures of the Action Plan within the framework of the European Neighbourhood Policy, other forms of association with Ukraine, giving a clear European perspective for the country and responding to the demonstrated aspirations of the vast majority of the Ukrainian people,

---

74 See EP - The European Parliament and Ukraine, Summary, 26 January 2005, The European Parliament and Ukraine (Brussels), Ref. EPO5-014EN; B. Ferrero-Waldner, Commissioner for External Relations and European Neighbourhood Policy, Remarks to the Foreign Affairs Committee, Speech 05/41, European Parliament Brussels, 25 January 2005, section 3: 'European Neighbourhood Policy and Ukraine', available at: <http://europa.eu.int/comm/external_relations/news/ferrero/2005/ip05_41.htm>.

75 See chapter 3 in this volume.

76 B. Ferrero-Waldner, 'The EU and Ukraine – what lies beyond the horizon?', Speech to the Mardi de l'Europe luncheon, Brussels, 26 April 2005, available at: <http://www.europa.eu.int/comm/external_relations/news/ferrero/2005/sp05_257.htm>.

77 See EU-Ukraine Parliamentary Cooperation Committee, Seventh Meeting, 16-17 February 2004, Brussels, Final Statement and Recommendation, 25 February 2004, Ref. PCC/TB/ES (DV/526086EN.doc).

78 European Parliament resolution on the results of the Ukraine elections, 13 January 2005, P6_TA(2005)0009.

79 Ibid., at para. 9.

possibly leading ultimately to the country's accession to the EU.'[80] Thus, the negative taboo of keeping Ukraine outside the Union has finally been broken at the EU level and the door towards the gradual inclusion of this country in the Union opened.

In contrast to former President Kuchma, who was also ostensibly in favour of eventual accession to the European Union, the push towards EU membership has become credible under Viktor Yushchenko, as it is accompanied by economic and political reform. As Prime Minister in 1999-2001, Yushchenko pushed vigorously for economic reforms. Indeed, the threat such reforms posed to powerful oligarchs closely associated with the former President was the reason he was dismissed. If the reform agenda is pushed forward rapidly after the March 2006 parliamentary elections, the European Union will find it increasingly difficult to continue its current policy of 'welcoming Ukraine's aspirations' without acknowledging Ukraine as a (potential) candidate for EU membership.

Ukraine is *de facto* treated as a peripheral country without great strategic significance by the European Union. This approach has worsened since the French and Dutch rejection of the Constitutional Treaty. The current perception of Ukraine and its problems is a grave mistake with potentially dangerous consequences for the entire system of relations in Europe. The gas dispute with Russia, which erupted in early 2006, only proves that relations with Ukraine are of pivotal economic and political importance for the entire European Union.[81] The Member States on the Union's eastern border are aware of this. It is high time that it is also understood by the other Members States and by the Union as a whole.

---

80 Ibid., at para. 14.

81 See chapter 19 in this volume.

CHAPTER 16

BELARUS

Eugeniusz Piontek*

Relevant legal documents:
- Proposal for a Council and Commission Decision on the conclusion of the Partnership and Cooperation Agreement between the European Communities and their Member States, of the one part, and Belarus, of the other part, COM (1995) 44 [ratification has been suspended].
- Proposal for a Council Decision on the Interim Agreement on Trade and Trade-Related Matters between the European Community, the European Coal and Steel Community and the European Atomic Energy Community, of the one part, and the Republic of Belarus, of the other part, COM (1995) 245 [ratification procedure has been suspended].
- Draft Commission Decision concerning the conclusion on behalf of the European Coal and Steel Community of the Interim Agreement between the European Community, the European Coal and Steel Community and the European Atomic Energy Community, of the one part, and the Republic of Belarus, of the other part, on trade and trade-related matters, COM (1995) 245 [ratification procedure has been suspended].
- Council Common Position 2004/661/CFSP of 24 September 2004 concerning restrictive measures against certain officials of Belarus, *OJ* 2004 L 301/67.
- Council Common Position 2004/848/CFSP of 13 December 2004 amending Common Position 2004/661/CFSP concerning restrictive measures against certain officials of Belarus, *OJ* 2004 L 367/35.
- Agreement in the Form of an Exchange of Letters between the European Community and the Republic of Belarus amending the Agreement between the European Community and the Republic of Belarus on trade in textile products, *OJ* 2005 L 72/19.
- Agreement in the form of an Exchange of Letters between the European Community and the Republic of Belarus amending the agreement between the European Community and the Republic of Belarus on trade in textile products, *OJ* 2005 L 345/23.

* Director of the Department of European Law, Faculty of Law and Administration, University of Warsaw.

1. INTRODUCTION

A Partnership and Cooperation Agreement (PCA) between the European Communities and their Member States, of the one part, and Belarus, of the other part, was signed in March 1995, confirming the commitment of both parties to collaborate in a broad range of policy fields.[1] However, it has not yet entered into force, effectively leaving the parties without a proper treaty framework or a forum for bilateral dialogue. Along with Turkmenistan, Belarus is the only successor state of the former Soviet Union without a PCA. For the time being, an agreement on trade in textiles remains the main legal instrument binding both parties.[2] Progress in bilateral relations stalled in 1996-1997 as a consequence of what the European Union saw as serious setbacks to the development of democracy in Belarus, notably the 1996 reform of the Constitution and repression of the opposition and the independent media, as well as interference with the judiciary. Whereas the European Union was probably too late in showing an interest in young Belarusian statehood, its reaction to the emerging difficulties in the country was definitely not sophisticated enough.

Belarus has not been included in significant political or academic discussions or debates in Europe. This is illustrated by the very short list of books specifically devoted to current developments and politics in the country. Very few academics focus their attention on Belarus, the most noteworthy being David Marples, Jan Zaprudnik and Ann Lewis.[3] For the majority of Western observers, Belarus is a kind of enigma perceived as a part of Greater Russia rather than as a distinctive nation-state.[4]

2. THE HISTORY OF BELARUS

2.1 Introduction

As Ramunas Davidonis has noted:

---

[1] Proposal for a Council and Commission Decision on the conclusion of the Partnership and Cooperation Agreement between the European Communities and their Member States, of the one part, and Belarus, of the other part, COM (1995) 44.

[2] Agreement between the European Economic Community and the Republic of Belarus on trade in textile products, *OJ* 1994 L 123/120 (as amended).

[3] D.R. Marples, *Belarus: A Denationalized Nation* (Amsterdam, Harwood Academic Publishers 1999); D.R. Marples, *Belarus: From Soviet Rule to Nuclear Catastrophe* (New York, St. Martin's Press 1996); Jan Zaprudnik, *Belarus at the Crossroads* (Moscow, Carnegie Endowment for International Peace 1998); Ann Lewis, ed., *The EU and Belarus: Between Moscow and Brussels* (London, The Federal Trust 2002).

[4] H. Timmermann, 'The Union of Belarus and Russia in the European Context', in Lewis, op. cit. n. 3, at p. 277.

> The question of where Europe ends in the East is very appropriate when trying to get a perspective of Belarus' place in Europe. The country is in a crucial strategic location as it borders Russia, Ukraine, Poland, Lithuania and Latvia. Throughout its history, due to peculiar historical circumstances and lack of natural resources, Belarus has never been a destination but rather a transit point to Moscow and other points further East, or from there to Western Europe. In terms of geography, there is no doubt that Belarus belongs to Europe.[5]

The population living within the territory of modern Belarus ('White Rus') was originally organised within the loose structure of a cluster of city-states known under the common name of Kievan Rus. Established in mid-ninth century it soon became the dominant political factor in Eastern Europe. At its peak in the early thirteenth century, Kievan Rus stretched from Moscow in the north-east, to San River in the west and to the Black Sea in the south. When Kievan Rus was destroyed in 1240 by the Mongol invaders, the north-eastern principalities of Moscow and Suzdal fell under the conquerors' rule for a period of over two centuries, while the principalities of Polotsk, Pinsk, Minsk and the rest of contemporary Belarus found refuge in an alliance with the Grand Duchy of Lithuania. In 1389, Poland and Lithuania set up a dynastic union later transformed into the Commonwealth of Both Nations – the Kingdom of Poland and the Grand Duchy of Lithuania ('Rzeczpospolita Obojga Narodów') which endured until the end of the eighteenth century, with Belarusian people and territory forming an integral part of it. Worth mentioning is the fact that between the mid-thirteenth and late sixteenth centuries the Belarusian language persisted as an official medium of written communication throughout the Grand Duchy of Lithuania and that the Lithuanian legal codes, the so-called 'Lithuanian Statutes', were accordingly written in the Belarusian language. A high point of Belarusian cultural development occurred in 1517, when Francis Skoryna, a scholar from Polotsk, translated the Bible into Belarusian for the first time and published it in his printing house in Vilnius. In 1569, however, the Parliament declared Polish as the official language of the entire Commonwealth, thus initiating a gradual decline of the Belarusian language.

The organised russification of Belarus commenced after 1794, when all its territory was annexed by the Russian Empire. However, instead of being deterred, Belarusians once again began to think and feel like a distinct nation. Despite the severity with which the Russians crushed consecutive uprisings in 1830 and 1863, the first modern dictionary of the Belarusian language was published in 1870, while the literary language of the nation was boosted by the publication of writings by

---

[5] R. Davidonis, 'The Challenge of Belarus, and European Responses', ISS-EU Occasional Paper 29 (July 2001) p. 2.

poets such as Janko Kupala, Jakub Kolas and Maxim Bohdanovic in the then influential journal *Our Cornfield.*

2.2 Turbulent twentieth century

When Russia, engulfed in the Bolshevik Revolution of 1917, made its separate peace with Germany in March 1918, the Belarusian National Republic was proclaimed. It enjoyed only nine months of independence before it was deposed by Bolshevik forces. In its place, the Belarusian Soviet Socialist Republic was established in January 1919, only to be routed later the same year by the Polish army. At that time, Poland endeavoured to reinvigorate an independent Belarus within a framework of wider confederation comprising Finland, Estonia, Latvia, Belarus, Ukraine and Poland, which was also open to Lithuania, as endorsed under the 1919 Treaty of Bulduri (Latvia). After this concept had failed to materialise, the territory of Belarus was divided, under the Treaty of Riga, between Poland and Russia. In the eastern part of the country under the Russian control, the Soviet Belarusian Republic was re-established, becoming one of the founding members of the USSR in 1922. In September 1939, as a result of a joint invasion of Poland by Germany and the USSR, the whole territory of Belarus was incorporated into the USSR.

The Soviet rule over Belarus was a mix of intense modernisation and denationalisation.[6] The country's infrastructure and large machinery industry were developed, accompanied by a mass transfer of the population from the countryside to cities and the widespread settlement of ethnic Russians. There was a sharp decline in the official use of the Belarusian language, which was no longer taught in schools and gradually receded into the shadow of the Russian language.

Starting in the early 1930s, Soviet Belarusian society experienced the systematic extermination of the national elite. After World War II, hundreds of thousands of people were deported to Siberia. Mass graves of Stalin's victims at Kuropaty near Minsk reflect this policy of genocide. The Communists did their utmost to deprive Belarusians of their sense of national identity. This was the price paid by Belarus for becoming one of the most prosperous republics of the USSR in the early 1970s.

2.3 Revival of national identity

The Chernobyl nuclear disaster of April 1998 in northern Ukraine, which hit Belarus the hardest with some 70 per cent of the radioactive fall-out, led to the emergence of political opposition in the country. The Belarusian Popular Front

---

[6] Marples (1999), op. cit. n. 3.

was established under the leadership of an archaeologist named Zenon Pozniak and an academic physicist named Stanislav Shushkevich. Eventually, under the umbrella of Gorbachev's *Perestroika*, the Belarusian Supreme Soviet responded to a virtual explosion of national sentiment by proclaiming its sovereignty on 27 July 1990. Belarusian was declared the Republic's official language. With the backing of the Popular Front, Shushkevich was elected to the Belarusian Supreme Soviet when the country held its first multi-candidate election in 1990. The following year, he was elected Speaker of the Supreme Soviet, at that time the highest post in the country.[7] On 25 August 1991, a declaration of national independence was issued, and one month later the country's name was changed to the Republic of Belarus, in place of the Russified 'Belarussia' that had been used until then. Belarus's traditional flag of red, white and red horizontal stripes was also introduced. One of the main themes of the speeches of Belarusian leaders at that time was the need for Belarus to 'return to Europe'.[8] Some government officials even openly considered the possibility of Belarus becoming a member of the European Union in ten years' time. On 4 March 1994, Piotr Kravchenka, the then Foreign Minister of Belarus, stated during an official visit to Germany that by 2005 the country would fulfil the Maastricht criteria.[9]

Belarus became a member of the IMF, the World Bank, the EBRD and the CSCE (later OSCE) in 1992. In 1993, Belarus applied for membership of the Council of Europe. Due to political reasons, this application remains in a limbo, but the Belarusian Parliament was granted special guest status to the Parliamentary Assembly of the Council of Europe in 1992-1997.[10] Since 1995, Belarus has participated in the NATO Partnership for Peace programme. The country also accepted and complied with the START and CFE Treaties signed by the USSR and took on all the obligations associated with these agreements. The disarmament process actually went fairly smoothly. Belarus also signed an interim agreement and a Partnership and Cooperation Agreement with the European Communities.[11]

---

[7] See E. Teague, 'Belarus: A Brief History', in Lewis, op. cit. n. 3.

[8] See J. Zaprudnik, 'Development of Belarusian National Identity and Its Influence on Belarus's Foreign Policy Orientation', in Roman Szporluk, ed., *National Identity and Ethnicity in Russia and the New States of Eurasia* (New York, M.E. Sharp Inc. 1994).

[9] Cited in Davidonis, loc. cit. n. 5, at p. 23.

[10] Following political developments in Belarus it was suspended by the Bureau of the Assembly. Subsequent requests for restoration have been rejected. In the meantime, Belarus ratified a small number of Council of Europe Conventions, including the European Cultural Convention, the European Convention on Information on Foreign Law (with Additional Protocol) and the Convention on the Recognition of Qualifications concerning Higher Education in the European Region. It has also signed the Anti-Doping Convention, the Criminal Law Convention on Corruption and the Civil Law Convention on Corruption. In all three cases, signature has not been followed by ratification.

[11] Proposal for a Council Decision on the Interim Agreement on Trade and Trade-related Matters between the European Community, the European Coal and Steel Community and the European

2.4 Forward march into the past

Soon, Shushkevich and his followers found themselves in a political vacuum. Members of the old Communist political, economic, military and security establishment consolidated their control over all branches of the state authorities. All attempts by a tiny reformist group to embark on marketisation were turned down. Only a small fraction of state-owned enterprises were privatised, while the collective farm sector remained intact. This was presented as a safeguard against mass unemployment and national patrimony being sold off to domestic or foreign profiteers.

Against this background, and on the wave of promises to clamp down on the spreading corruption, Aleksander Lukashenko, a former KGB border guard and a collective poultry farm manager convincingly won the presidential elections in July 1994. One year later, in a national referendum, President Lukashenko was granted the power to dissolve Parliament. The Russian language was upgraded to the status of a second official language, National Day was changed from the anniversary of the 1918 declaration of independence to the date commemorating the recapture of Minsk by the Red Army from the Nazis in 1944 and the national symbols and the flag were replaced by new ones that were near replicas of their Soviet versions.

By the end of 1995, Russian security guards were once again permitted to police the Belarusian border with Poland at Brest, and elsewhere together with Belarusian guards. President Lukashenko began to reassert Belarus's 'traditional links' with Russia and, at the same time, to progressively impose growing constraints on the independent media and the political opposition. After a short-lived upheaval in his rule – from which he was bailed out by diplomatic intervention, presented as 'mediation' by the then Prime Minister of the Russian Federation, Viktor Chernomyrdin – President Lukashenko held another successful referendum on 24 November 1996. Unconcerned by the criticism of EU, Council of Europe and OSCE observers of the undemocratic practices of the authorities that pervaded the entire referendum process, President Lukashenko went ahead with the implementation of institutional reforms that granted him almost unrestrained

Atomic Energy Community, of the one part, and the Republic of Belarus, of the other part, COM (1995) 245; Draft Commission Decision concerning the conclusion on behalf of the European Coal and Steel Community of the Interim Agreement between the European Community, the European Coal and Steel Community and the European Atomic Energy Community, of the one part, and the Republic of Belarus, of the other part, on trade and trade-related matters, COM (1995) 245; Proposal for a Council and Commission Decision on the conclusion of the Partnership and Cooperation Agreement between the European Communities and their Member States, of the one part, and Belarus, of the other part, COM (1995) 44.

power.[12] This was sympathetically described by his fellow countrymen as a 'paternalistic presidency'. In the space of two years, he successfully managed to change the country.

On 30 March 1994, a new Constitution was adopted. It provided for a President, a Parliament and a judicial system. Central to the judicial system was a Constitutional Court with the authority to determine the conformity with the Constitution of laws passed by the Parliament, decrees of the President, rules and regulations of the public administration and actions of officials. In the late summer of 1996, the President and the Parliament entered into open warfare. In line with his powers, President Lukashenko called for a nationwide referendum on proposals amending the 1994 Constitution. The Parliament also put forth amendments. A referendum was scheduled for 26 November 1996.

On 4 November 1996, the Constitutional Court, after a contested hearing, held:

1. that both proposals were not amendments but represented entirely new Constitutions, fundamentally changing the structure of the authorities;
2. that while amendments could be adopted by referendum, new Constitutions could only be adopted by Parliament; and
3. that the referendum could proceed, but would have no binding force.

The referendum did indeed proceed, and Lukashenko controlled the printing, distribution and counting of the ballots as well as all significant media outlets. After the referendum, he disregarded the decision of the Court and declared the results binding. He then proceeded to oust the existing Parliament and Constitutional Court and established an entirely new regime – assuring himself the start of a new five-year term of office. Acting under his concept of a new Constitution, he acquired almost total control over all state institutions.

President Lukashenko took actual control of the judiciary via his authority to appoint and dismiss judges at will without any parliamentary check. He also controlled the Constitutional Court, appointing six of the twelve judges, including the President of the Court, and the Lower House of Parliament, personally selecting the current members and having the power to appoint one-third of the members of the Upper House of Parliament at all times. Organised opposition

---

[12] D.R. Marples, 'Belarus: The Last European Dictatorship?', in Lewis, op. cit. n. 3, at pp. 31-49; M. Hawkes, 'Republic of Belarus: An Elegant Dictatorship?', in Lewis, op. cit. n. 3, at pp. 75-88; S. Eke, 'With the State or Against the State: The Media in Belarus', in Lewis, op. cit. n. 3, at pp. 89-102.

was successfully silenced by administrative and judicial measures.[13] The forward march back into the semi-Soviet past had commenced.[14]

On 2 April 1996, a 'Russian-Belarusian Community' was proclaimed. It is based on a bilateral treaty concluded by the two countries and ratified by Belarus on 10 July 1997.[15] This was not done without widespread social support. A large number of the country's ordinary citizens felt that a union with Russia would bring back the 'good-old Soviet times' of relative prosperity, in contrast to the dire economic situation prevailing in Belarus after it declared independence and society began to suffer the difficulties of transformation. They hoped that a union with Russia would be economically beneficial. President Lukashenko strongly relied on these illusions while tightening the links of his country with Russia. The fact that these illusions have not materialised is another matter. However, this development significantly strengthened the geopolitical position of Russia. It provided direct access to the borders of the European Union and facilitated mainland ties with the Russian enclave of Kaliningrad as well as undermining the so-called Baltic-Black Sea 'belt' on the western borders of the Russian Federation. Taking all these factors into consideration, Moscow certainly benefited from the creation of the Russian-Belarusian Community. For the same reasons, Russia is not the least bit interested in democratisation in Belarus, because this could lead to a pro-Western switch in the latter's political orientation and weaken its dependence on the former.

3. THE POLICY OF THE EUROPEAN UNION TOWARDS BELARUS

The European Community recognised the independence of Belarus in December 1991. Until 1994, relations between the European Communities and Belarus were based on the Trade and Cooperation Agreement concluded with the USSR in 1989.[16] In 1995, as already mentioned earlier, the European Communities and Belarus signed a separate Partnership and Cooperation Agreement (PCA) that was meant to build on the 1989 agreement. Until Lukashenko took over, the relations between the European Union and the Republic of Belarus were developing in a very

[13] See E. Korosteleva, 'Political Leadership and Public Support in Belarus: Forward to the Past', in Lewis, op. cit. n. 3, at pp. 51-69.

[14] See G. Drakokhrust, 'Referendum: New Era Begins', *Minsk Economic News* No. 23 (December 1996) p. 2; S.N. Martynov, 'The EU and Belarus: Time for a Fresh Start', in Lewis, op. cit. n. 3, at pp. 303-316.

[15] See D.R. Marples, 'Belarusian-Russian Treaty: An Analysis', 8(1) *Belarusian Review* (1996).

[16] Agreement between the European Economic Community and the European Atomic Energy Community and the Union of Soviet Socialist Republics on trade and commercial and economic cooperation, *OJ* 1990 L 68/2.

constructive manner. There were no indications that these relations might become confrontational.

A negative turning point was marked by the outcome of the November 1996 referendum in Belarus. Almost one year later, on 15 September 1997, the conclusions and recommendations of international observers prompted the Council to suspend the process of ratification of the PCA with Belarus and freeze the Interim Trade Agreement, which was meant to cover the long drawn-out process of ratification of the PCA by all EU Member States. The 1997 decisions also restricted contacts between the European Union and Belarus to below ministerial level and virtually ended all technical assistance and cooperation programmes except those that were regionally based.

With the passing of time, respect for human rights and the democratic process deteriorated in Belarus, and EU-Belarus relations therefore evolved from bad to worse. The so-called 'Drozdy conflict' of 1998, in which the Belarusian authorities evicted foreign diplomats from their residences in a suburb of Minsk on the pretext of repairing water and sewage pipes, led the European Union and the United States to retaliate by imposing a visa ban on the President of Belarus, the head of the presidential administration and other high-ranking officials.[17] Finally, after fifteen months of confrontation and impasse, Belarus decided to improve relations with the relevant Western countries and agreed to pay compensation. As a result, the Common Position was repealed.[18]

Then, in early 2002, the Belarusian authorities decided not to renew the visa of the acting head of the OSCE Advisory and Monitoring Group (AMG) in Minsk. On 15 April 2002, the Council of the European Union expressed its great concern regarding this decision and its support for the OSCE Chairman-in-Office in order to overcome the crisis.[19] On 21 October of the same year, the Council of the European Union adopted an eight-point declaration in which it reiterated the hope that Belarus would eventually take its place among Europe's democratic countries, not least because Belarus would become a direct neighbour of the European Union after its enlargement.[20] The Council emphasised the importance that the European Union attaches to respect for human rights and fundamental freedoms as guaranteed by the UN Charter and embodied in the Helsinki Final Act. It also emphasised that it might not accept the position of the Belarusian authorities that the OSCE's AMG in Minsk should be formally closed before negotiations on a

---

17 Common Position 98/448/CFSP of 9 July 1998 defined by the Council on the basis of Article J.2 of the Treaty on European Union, concerning Belarus, *OJ* 1998 L 195/1.

18 Council Decision 1999/156/CFSP of 22 February 1999 repealing Common Position 98/448/CFSP concerning Belarus, *OJ* 1999 L 52/1.

19 A selection of Council Conclusions on Belarus is available at: <http://europa.eu.int/comm/external_relations/belarus/intro/gac.htm#b211002>.

20 Ibid.

new OSCE presence had begun. The Council of the European Union expressed its readiness to continue working closely with the Chairman-in-Office of the OSCE to ensure that the organisation could contribute to the development of genuine democracy and broad respect for human rights in Belarus, including via an active OSCE presence. In its statement of 14 April 2003, the Council of the European Union expressed its great concern regarding the flawed conduct of the local elections held in March 2003 and the arrest and imprisonment of a number of the participants in peaceful demonstrations in Minsk.[21] At the same time, however, the Council declared its intention to lift the visa ban in recognition of the constructive cooperation of Belarus with regard to the re-establishment of an OSCE office in Minsk.

In 2002-2004, after noting with regret that the state of law and respect for human rights were deteriorating in Belarus, various EU institutions repeatedly called on the Belarusian authorities to establish a fair dialogue with the opposition, to reform electoral laws in line with democratic standards and to give the Parliament a real power. In spite of this, Belarus was included by the European Commission in its European Neighbourhood Policy. The Commission declared that

> Belarus and the EU will be able to develop contractual links when Belarus has established a democratic form of government, following free and fair elections. It will then be possible to extend the full benefits of the European Neighbourhood Policy to Belarus. [22]

It ought to be noted that the political developments in Belarus drew the attention of the European Parliament.[23] Moreover, subsequent EU Presidencies[24] and the Council have dealt with Belarus to some extent. In its Conclusions of 13 September 2004, the Council expressed concern about the lack of democratic guarantees surrounding the upcoming referendum, which would allow a president to run without limitation in future presidential elections. Following the Council of

---

[21] Ibid.

[22] Communication from the Commission to the Council and the European Parliament, Wider Europe – Neighbourhood: A New Framework for Relations with our Eastern and Southern Neighbours, COM (2003) 104 final. The citation is from the Communication from the Commission, European Neighbourhood Policy Strategy Paper, COM (2004) 373 final.

[23] See Report on relations between the European Union and Belarus: towards a future partnership, A-5-0024/2003.

[24] See, for example, Declaration by the Presidency on behalf of the European Union on Belarus, 27 September 2004, 12735/04; Declaration by the Presidency on behalf of the European Union on the parliamentary elections and the referendum of 17 October 2004 in Belarus, 20 October 2004, 13728/04; Declaration by the Presidency on behalf of the European Union regarding the cases of Mr Marinich and Mr Bandazhevsky, 4 April 2005, 7731/05; Declaration by the Presidency on behalf of the European Union concerning the closure of the Independent Institute of Socio-Economic and Political Studies (IISEPS), 29 April 2005, 8556/05.

Europe's Pourgourides Report,[25] the Council of the European Union adopted Common Position 2004/661/CFSP preventing entry into the European Union of four Belarusian officials responsible for the disappearance of well-known persons in 1999-2000 and 'subsequent obstruction of justice'.[26] Following this, in its Conclusions of 22 November 2004, the Council underlined that Belarus, as a direct neighbour of the European Union, had an opportunity to become an active partner of the European Union in the framework of the European Neighbourhood Policy. It called upon President Lukashenko and his government to reverse their existing policies and embark on fundamental democratic and economic reforms to bring the country closer to European values. The Council also noted with great concern that the parliamentary elections and referendum of 17 October 2004 in Belarus were not conducted in a free and fair manner and condemned attacks on peaceful demonstrators, individual opposition leaders and journalists. As a result, the Council decided to impose restrictions on persons mainly responsible for fraud during the electoral process.[27] The Presidency has described the presidential elections of 2006 as 'fundamentally flawed'.[28] In this context, the European Council decided to introduce yet another set of restrictive measures covering persons responsible for the election frauds, including President Lukashenko.[29]

Current Belarusian policy toward the European Union could be defined as a mixture of isolationism and confrontation. According to President Lukashenko's vision, the world is divided into 'us' and 'them', 'allies' and 'enemies', and he himself decides who belongs to which category. Thus, democrats were classified as 'domestic enemies', whereas the European Union and the West in general were classified as 'outside enemies', all of them allegedly trying their utmost to destabilise the country and deprive it of its identity.[30] Under such circumstances, it is

---

[25] Parliamentary Assembly of the Council of Europe, 'Report on Disappeared Persons in Belarus', Doc. 10062, 28 April 2004.

[26] Council Common Position 2004/661/CFSP of 24 September 2004 concerning restrictive measures against certain officials of Belarus, *OJ* 2004 L 310/67, as extended by Council Common Position 2005/666/CFSP of 20 September 2005, *OJ* 2005 L 247/40.

[27] Council Common Position 2004/848/CFSP of 13 December 2004 amending Common Position 2004/661/CFSP concerning restrictive measures against certain officials of Belarus, *OJ* 2004 L 367/35. The annex lists the head of the Central Electoral Commission as well as the commander of the OMON special forces. Surprisingly enough, President Lukashenko is not on the list.

[28] Declaration by the Presidency on behalf of the European Union on the presidential elections in Belarus, 22 March 2006, 7682/06.

[29] Declaration on Belarus, Presidency Conclusions, Brussels European Council 23-24 March 2006, 7775/06, p. 35. See also Council Common Position 2006/362/CFSP of 18 May 2006 amending Common Position 2006/276/CFSP concerning restrictive measures against certain officials of Belarus, *OJ* 2006 L 134/45; Council Regulation (EC) No. 765/2006 of 18 May 2006 concerning restrictive measures against President Lukashenko and certain officials of Belarus, *OJ* 2006 L 134/1.

[30] See O. Manaer, 'Po Tonkom Ldu – sociologiceskij portret elektorata Aleksandra Lukashenko', 3(5) *Novosti NISEPI* (1997) p. 270; see also V. Cernov, 'Avtoritarnij Razim v Belarusi: Charakter, Zapas Procnosti, Varianti Transformacji', 4(106) *Adkrytae Gramatsva* (1998) p. 1, available at: <http://www.data.minsk.by/opensociety/106/2.html>.

very difficult for the European Union to develop any positive or effective policies towards Belarus. On the one hand, as Davidonis correctly observes, it would be possible to resort to negative diplomacy, namely to freeze all forms of contact and cooperation and cut aid and assistance programmes. By doing so, however, the European Union would completely lose what little means of influence it still has on Belarus.[31] There would be no channels of communication left, and the relationship would deteriorate even further, eventually leading to a situation that is wholly unacceptable in relations with a country that borders the European Union. Therefore, the European Union should deal with Belarus with patience and at the same time show evidence of good will and a real interest in the development of a constructive neighbourhood policy while insisting on the necessity of respect for human rights in the country.

Against the background of these development, and building on previously established EU policy, the Council of the European Union in November 2004 decided on the following actions:

- The EU remains open for a dialogue with Belarus on gradual development of bilateral relations, as soon as the Belarus authorities demonstrate by concrete actions a sincere willingness to re-engage;
- The EU will introduce a visa-ban against the officials directly responsible for the fraudulent elections and referendum and against those responsible for severe human rights violations in the repression of peaceful demonstrators;
- Bilateral ministerial contacts of the European Union and its Member States with President Lukashenko and his government will be established solely through the Presidency, SG/HR, the Commission and the Troika. Other contacts with President Lukashenko and the members of his government, including multilateral contacts and contracts necessary for transborder relations, will be limited to a minimum;
- Community and Member States' assistance programmes will support the needs of the population and democratisation, notably by humanitarian, regional, and cross-border cooperation and by projects supporting directly and indirectly democratisation and democratic forces in Belarus. The Commission will continue and further intensify its efforts with regard to assistance to Belarus in order to meet the challenges arising from the self-isolation of Belarus. The Commission is invited to make proposals to this effect as soon as possible;
- The Council invites the Commission to organise a workshop with the participation of Member States, other interested countries, NGOs, and other relevant actors to co-ordinate assistance to democratisation and civil society in Belarus;

---

31 Davidonis, loc. cit. n. 5, at p. 23.

- The relevant bodies of the Council will closely follow Belarus' conduct with regard to arms trade and proliferation;
- The EU reiterates that it is willing to deepen its relationship with Belarus, including within the European Neighbourhood Policy (ENP), once the Belarusian authorities clearly demonstrate their willingness to respect democratic values and the rule of law. The EU will take steps to communicate and demonstrate the benefits of the ENP to the Belarusian population at large.[32]

Bearing in mind its eastward enlargement in 2004 and the adoption of the European Neighbourhood Policy, the long-term goals of the European Union are that Belarus be a democratic, stable, reliable and increasingly prosperous partner with which the enlarged Union will share not only common borders, but also a common agenda driven by shared values. The difficulty in achieving these goals is that the present Belarusian authorities show little practical interest in developing relations with the European Union based upon such principles.

In the late spring of 2004, Günter Verheugen, then Commissioner for Enlargement and Wider Europe, summing up the results of a meeting with Belarusian opposition leaders, made three points. First, he stressed that Belarus was considered part of the European Neighbourhood Policy (ENP) that looks to boost the European Union's relations with post-enlargement neighbours to the east and south. Second, however, Belarus would only be fully able to enjoy the benefits of the ENP once fundamental political reform had been carried out in areas such as democracy and human rights. Commissioner Verheugen made it clear that under the prevailing conditions it was not possible to offer Belarus an ENP action plan, as was being developed with Moldova and Ukraine. The Commissioner's third point was that Belarus would nevertheless be eligible for funding for cross-border and regional cooperation and funding under the new European Neighbourhood Policy Instrument from 2007 onwards.[33] Belarus is already eligible to participate in three of the neighbourhood programmes, namely the Baltic Sea programme, the Latvia/Lithuania/Belarus programme and the Poland/Ukraine/Belarus programme.

4. FINANCIAL ASSISTANCE OF THE EUROPEAN UNION TO BELARUS

The European Union thus continues to be engaged in Belarus, albeit on a limited scale. An overview of EU financial assistance to Belarus is presented in the table below.

---

32 Available at: <http://europa.eu.int/comm/external_relations/belarus/intro/gac.htm#b211002>.

33 See *Europe Information*, No. 2872, 29 May 2004, p. V-1.

EC Assistance to Belarus 1991-2005 (in € millions)

	1991	1992	1993	1994	1995	1996	1997	1998	1999	2000	2001	2002	2003	2004-2005	Total
Tacis National Programme	8.92	14.6	9	7	12	0	0	5	0	5	0	0	5	10	76.55
Tacis Nuclear Safety	0.3	0	1.5	0	0.6	0	1.1	0	0	0	0	1	2	0	6.5
Tacis CBC						1.34	2.8	4.7	2.31	8.15	0	11.2	n/a	6	36.5
Tacis SPF							0.6	0.2	0.4	0	0.9	0.2	0.44	0	2.74
Tacis Regional Programme	5.4	4.6	5.1	2.6	3.3	6.5	6.3	4.6	1.7	2	3.9	2.2	7.4	n/a	55.6
ECHO	0	0	0	0.56	2.73	1.73	0.95	0.34	1.99	0.69	0.2	0	0	0	9.19
INTAS	0	0.02	0.9	0.5	0.1	0.6	1.2	0	0.4	0.8	0.5	0	n/a	n/a	5.02
Macro financial assistance	0	0	0	0	0	30	0	0	0	0	0	0	0	0	30
Total															222.1

Source: <http://www.europe.eu.int/comm/external_relations/belarus/intro/index.htm#technical>.

Tacis	Technical Assistance for the Commonwealth of Independent States
CBC	Cross-Border Cooperation
SPF	Small Project Facility
ECHO	European Community Humanitarian Aid Department
INTAS	International Association for the Promotion of Cooperation with Scientists from the newly independent states of the former Soviet Union

It should be noted that the amount of aid has been significantly cut. From 1991 until 1995, within the framework of the Tacis programme, Belarus was given an average of more than €10 million annually. After 1996, EU assistance was for the most part suspended, including €37 million of aid that had already been allocated. On 11 December 1997, the Tacis office for assistance to CIS countries stated that the decision to suspend aid to Belarus would not be reviewed until 1999. In 1996-1999, Belarus received an average of €5 million to €10 million per year. A similar amount of financial assistance was allocated in 2000-2004.

However, in addition to the Tacis Programme, the European Union continues to provide financial assistance within the framework of the Interstate Programme on justice and home affairs. This programme, which tries to support NGOs in Belarus, was not affected by the European Union's disapproval of undemocratic developments in the country. The European Union's National Indicative Programme (NIP) for Belarus for 2005-2006 adopted by the European Commission on 28 May 2004 follows this direction.[34] It focuses on support for civil society and democratisation, education and training as well as Chernobyl-affected areas.

The NIP for 2004-2006 follows the guidelines set out in the Common Framework for Country Strategy Papers.[35] It is the first CSP for Belarus and builds on the NIP adopted in February 2001. A total allocation of €10 million is foreseen for 2005-2006, subject to the availability of funds.

5. CONCLUSIONS

Belarus's shift to authoritarianism was not anticipated by the European Union. In the political vacuum that occurred in recent years between Brussels and Minsk, the lack of new policy conceptions comes harshly into focus. The 'reactive approach' has been dominant in the European Union's policy towards Belarus. It was based on the false assumption that President Lukashenko's regime is interested in goods and privileges, which the Union was refusing him. In reality, this strategy pushed the Belarusian authorities to make internal policy more stringent by limiting democratic freedoms. This helps to kindle anti-European Union and anti-Western feelings in society and pushes Belarus into the sphere of exclusive influence of and dependency on Russia. The former brings to mind the words of Jerzy Urban, press spokesman for the Polish Government during the period of martial law in the 1980s, that 'the government will feed itself'.

Regardless of this, no strategy will bring positive results if no consideration is given to the active and authentic participation of those members of society that

34 Text available at: <http://europa.eu.int/comm/external_relations/belarus/csp/index.htm>.
35 SEC (2000) 1049.

are interested in it. That is why the greatest hope should be attached to programmes oriented towards support for local aspirations for reform, starting with the encouragement of constructive changes in the approach of Belarusian society to local living conditions by making it easier for Belarusian society to 'discover' values represented by the European Union.

An important component of such a strategy seems to be a gradual increase in the number of non-political economic, social, educational and cultural programmes. These should be implemented with the participation of different social and intellectual circles rising above divisions into 'opposition' and 'those in power'. The fundamental goal should be to assist Belarusians to acquire knowledge and capabilities that will facilitate effective self-help, in other words, 'capacity building'. The components of this include the development of intellectual and professional potential, including business, and exposure to the international environment in order to make it easier for the future elite and opinion-forming circles to build civil society and democratic order in Belarus. An important element of this strategy at the level of the masses might be to open, in one of the bordering Member States of the European Union (e.g., Poland, where a Belarusian minority lives), a permanent radio station broadcasting in the Belarusian language, modelled after Radio Free Europe, with extensive training programmes on subjects that are of particular importance for building civil society, as well as cultural programmes. In a similar vein, a satellite TV station broadcasting in the Belarusian language could also be established. Supporting projects to increase access in Belarus to independent sources of news and information is one way to enhance the knowledge of the Belarusian population about democracy, pluralism, the rule of law, freedom of the press and human rights.[36] Another way is to support higher education activities. To this end, the European Commission decided in March 2006 to financially support the Belarusian University in exile (operating in Vilnius).[37]

Until the time that democratic institutions arise in Belarus, the European Union should in particular support the development of civil society structures. Above all, it should maintain and strengthen various scientific, cultural and educational contacts, as well as interpersonal contacts between Belarusians and non-governmental institutions in the European Union.

To secure his grip on Belarus, President Lukashenko is doing his best to deepen the isolation of the country from the European Union and from Western

---

[36] Further to a €138,000 contract already granted to Deutsche Welle Radio, which began broadcasting via radio and internet on 1 November 2005, the Commission prepared a €2 million project for co-production and broadcasting on TV and radio in Belarusian and Russian over a period of two years starting on 1 January 2006. See 'Commission launches further support for independent broadcasting in Belarus', Press release IP/05/1121, Brussels, 9 September 2005.

[37] Midday Express of 24 March 2006, MEX/06/0324.

democracies in general. At the end of November 2005, he managed to secure preliminary parliamentary backing for a draft bill amending the penal code aimed at reinforcing his defences against any attempt to stage a Ukrainian-style popular revolution ahead of the 2006 presidential elections. While the European Union is right to take further restrictive measures against the individuals responsible for the frauds during those elections, it should refrain from taking steps that might ultimately be harmful to the ordinary citizens of the country. It should instead focus on initiatives demonstrating the benefits that would materialise if Belarus opened up towards its western neighbours. In order to achieve this goal, the European Union should maintain a (limited) dialogue with Minsk. On the whole, relations with Belarus should be subordinate to pragmatic concerns.

It is thus in the interest of the European Union to strengthen Belarus's independence and help it to build a democratic order and a market economy. That is why an important element of an improved EU strategy towards Belarus should be aimed at gradually building foundations for establishing cooperation under the Area of Freedom, Security and Justice (AFSJ) programmes, supporting Belarus's membership of the WTO and facilitating the expansion of small border traffic and trade between Belarus and the European Union. In all these areas, Belarus should be treated as a sovereign partner, capable of making independent decisions regarding its own affairs. Above all, the European Union should make it easier for Belarus to speak with its own voice and demonstrate in practice that such behaviour will bring Belarus measurable benefits. Once this has been achieved and a democratic order has been built in Belarus, there will come a time for considering more advanced forms of mutual relations between Belarus and the European Union.

CHAPTER 17

MOLDOVA

Alla Skvortova*

Relevant legal documents:

- Partnership and Cooperation Agreement between the European Communities and their Member States, of the one part, and the Republic of Moldova, of the other part, *OJ* 1998 L 181/3.
- Protocol to the Partnership and Cooperation Agreement establishing a partnership between the European Communities and their Member States, of the one part, and the Republic of Moldova, of the other part, *OJ* 2000 L 283/37.
- Interim Agreement between the European Community, the European Coal and Steel Community and the European Atomic Energy Community, of the one part, and the Republic of Moldova, of the other, on trade and trade-related matters, *OJ* 1996 L 40/11.
- Agreement between the European Community and the Republic of Moldova on trade in textile products, *OJ* 1997 L 227/2.
- Agreement in the form of an Exchange of Letters between the European Community and the Republic of Moldova establishing a double-checking system without quantitative limits in respect of the export of certain steel products from the Republic of Moldova to the European Community, *OJ* 2004 L 315/33.
- Council Regulation (EC) No. 1762/2004 of 24 September 2004 on administering of the double-checking system without quantitative limits in respect of the export of certain steel products from the Republic of Moldova to the European Community, *OJ* 2004 L 315/1.
- Commission Regulation (EC) No. 1649/2000 of 25 July 2000 granting the Republic of Moldova the benefit of the special incentive arrangements concerning labour rights, *OJ* 2000 L 189/13.
- Council Common Position 2004/179/CFSP (as amended) concerning restrictive measures against the leadership of the Transnistrian region of the Moldovan Republic, *OJ* 2004 L 55/68.
- Council Joint Action 2005/265/CFSP appointing a Special Representative of the European Union for the Republic of Moldova, *OJ* 2005 L 81/50 (as amended).

* Doctor of History, Head of DFID Section in Moldova.

1. HISTORICAL AND POLITICAL ACCOUNT OF EU-MOLDOVA RELATIONS

1.1 Political situation in Moldova

The independence of the Republic of Moldova, which was declared in 1991, raised a great number of crucial questions for the future of the new country – problems that had to be solved without delay. One of them was the orientation of its foreign policy and external allies. Moldova is literally situated on the border between East and West or between the countries that have chosen a 'Euro-Asian' way (Ukraine, Russia and Belarus) and the countries of Eastern Europe that, after the revolutions of the late 1980s, made a decisive choice in favour of the alignment to European standards. Unlike the Baltic countries, Moldova lost the momentum on its path towards Europe after independence for a number of reasons. Firstly, the only available external market for the goods that the country produced (predominantly wine and agricultural products) was in the East. Also in the East was the only available source of energy (gas, electricity, coal and oil products). Thus, Moldova remained oriented towards the East by the virtue of economic factors. Secondly, the outbreak of a secessionist conflict compromised the public support that initially was given to the pro-Western political elite, and it was substituted in the Parliament by pro-Russian groups that were more likely to solve the conflict in which Russian interests were so obvious. Thirdly, even in the view of the most advanced pro-reformist politicians, the West for Moldova was only Bucharest. They did not think of the possibility of entering Europe without joining Romania, while the majority of the population at the time was against unification.

After declaring independence in 1991, the Republic of Moldova actively aspired to membership in different international organisations. In 1992, it was accepted into the OSCE and the United Nations, and in 1994 it became a member of the Council of Europe and adhered to the NATO 'Partnership for Peace' programme. Moldova has been a *de facto* member of the CIS since 1991, but *de jure* adhesion happened only after its Parliament ratified the constituent agreements in 1994. Moldova has limited its participation in the CIS to economic cooperation and did not sign the military-political agreement. The economic and political failure of the CIS, acknowledged even in its official documents and reports, is confirmed indirectly by the re-groupings that have occurred lately within the organisation: the Russian-Belarus Union, the Eurasian Economic Community (*ЕврАзЭС*), GUUAM (Georgia, Ukraine, Uzbekistan, Azerbaijan and Moldova) and the Common Economic Space between Russia, Belarus, Ukraine and Kazakhstan. The CIS's role was diluted in Moldova's Foreign Policy Concept of 2002 by the importance given to European integration.

The Moldovan Constitution was approved in 1994 and modified by the Parliament in 2000.[1] The legislative power of the State lies with the Parliament, which consists of one chamber of 101 deputies elected for a four-year term. The President of the Republic is elected by Parliament for a four-year mandate. The Prime Minister is designated by the President, in consultation with the Parliament. Within fifteen days of his or her designation, the Prime Minister designate must request a vote of confidence from the Parliament regarding his or her work programme and cabinet.

Moldova's legal framework provides a basis for democratic elections. The 2001 parliamentary and 2003 local elections were assessed by the OSCE as free and fair. However, in recent years, the OSCE and the Council of Europe have expressed increasing concerns about the practical implementation of basic democratic principles in Moldova.[2] The judicial system comprises the Supreme Court of Justice, courts of appeal and courts of first instance, as well as a system of economic courts including an Economic Court of Appeal. Both the Constitution and the Law on the Court System stipulate that the judicial system is independent from the executive and legislative powers. Judges are appointed by the President of the Republic on a proposal from the Superior Council of Magistracy, except for judges of the Supreme Court of Justice, who are appointed by the Parliament.

In spite of many attempts and changes in the public administration system, the public administration reform has not been completed and institutional capacity in the public sector remains weak. The government institutions are not able to perform efficiently due to inconsistencies in their functional and institutional frameworks. At the same time, public opinion polls rank corruption as the second most pressing problem in Moldova after poverty. In 2001, the Government established a coordination council to fight corruption, and in 2004 the Parliament approved the Strategy on Fighting Corruption.

Numerous civil society organisations can act freely in Moldova, but their internal capacity is rather low, while financing from abroad is decisive for their very existence.

All in all, although democracy has been established in Moldova, further progress is needed to consolidate civil society, public governance and the rule of law.[3]

---

1 Constitution of the Republic of Moldova (Chisinau, Moldpres 1994 and 2001).

2 Committee for the Honouring of Obligations and Commitments by Member States of the Council of Europe, *Moldova Report: Functioning of Democratic Institutions in Moldova*, Rapporteurs: Josette Durrieu (France) and Lauri Vahtre (Estonia), Doc. 9418 (Strasbourg, 23 April 2002), available at: <http://www.coe.int>.

3 European Union, *Country Strategy Paper 2002-2006, National Indicative Programme 2002-2003, Moldova* (Brussels, 27 December 2001) p. 3, available at: <http://europa.eu.int/comm/external_ relations/moldova/csp/index/htm>.

Both the political and economic stability of the country are seriously threatened by the so-called Transnistrian conflict. Transnistria, situated east of the river Nistru, has since 1991 tried to become an independent state and fought a short war with Moldova in 1992. After establishing a ceasefire, the two sides have faced each other along a separation line guarded by a peacekeeping force consisting of Russian troops and troops from the two sides. The self-proclaimed 'Transnistrian Moldovan Republic' is not internationally recognised. Since 1993, the OSCE has been active in trying to reach a settlement of the conflict without any significant progress. The situation has economic implications, since most of the industrial structure of Moldova is located in Transnistria, together with important power plants. This disruption is causing a shortfall in revenues and customs duties accruing to the Moldovan budget. It facilitates contraband, illegal migration, trafficking in human beings and, reportedly, in drugs and arms, due to the fact that the border between Transnistria and Ukraine remains uncontrolled by Moldova. Additionally, Russian troops, military equipment and large amounts of ammunition are stationed in Transnistria in spite of Russia's commitment at the OSCE Istanbul summit to complete the withdrawal by the end of 2002. If the situation is not resolved, it will directly affect the security and stability of the European Union's border after Romania's accession.[4]

1.2 Establishment of EU-Moldova relations

Unlike the countries of the Central and Eastern Europe, Moldova had received a rather limited amount of attention from the European Union. The differentiated EU approach towards Eastern Europe and the Baltic States and the lack of interest towards Moldova were already evident in the first Stability Pact proposed by the French Prime Minister, Édouard Balladur, in 1993.[5] The Pact promoted over 100 bilateral agreements between the countries of Central and Eastern Europe. Although Moldova participated in the Pact, no significant agreements between Moldova and its neighbours were concluded. The relations between Moldova and its neighbours, Romania and Ukraine, have been more conflictual than between other CEECs.[6] In addition, the 'silent' division of the CEECs between the European Union's and Russia's spheres of interests probably played a role in the arrangements.

---

[4] A detailed account of the development of the conflict and its implications for the European Union can be found in V. Solonari, 'Transdniestria: Old Problems, New Developments', in Iris Kempe, ed., *Prospects and Risks Beyond EU Enlargement. Eastern Europe: Challenges of a Pan-European Policy* (Leverkusen, Leske + Budrich 2003) pp. 195-216.

[5] M. Vahl, 'The EU and Moldova: A Neglected Relationship', in Ann Lewis, ed., *The EU and Moldova: On a Fault-line of Europe*, Europe's Eastern Borders Series (London, The Federal Trust 2004) p. 172.

[6] Ibid.

Moldova only addressed the European Union with a request to start negotiations for a Partnership and Cooperation Agreement (PCA) in 1994. The agreement was signed at the end of the same year, when the majority of Eastern European countries had already been associated with the European Communities. While the Foreign Strategy, approved by the Moldovan Parliament in 1995, stated that the PCA was the first step in the country's integration into the European Union, neither the political elite nor the general population believed that there was a real opportunity for Moldova to become a member of the European Union. The Union itself did not even perceive Moldova as a potential candidate for accession. The PCA reflected the commitment of the two sides to democratic values and demonstrated the European Union's commitment to support Moldova in its democratisation process and its transition to a market economy.

The ratification process of the PCA Moldova took three and a half years, and the agreement came into force on 1 July 1998. This was the third PCA between the European Communities, their Member States and a CIS country to become operational, following those with Russia in December 1997 and Ukraine in March 1998.[7] The agreement is valid for ten years, or until 2008, and sets out the general framework for EU-Moldova cooperation, covering the development of a political dialogue; the promotion of long-term investment and economic links; economic, commercial, social, cultural and scientific cooperation; and support for Moldova's efforts to strengthen democracy and complete the transition to a market economy. The PCA established the usual set of institutions, with a ministerial-level Cooperation Council, a Cooperation Committee of senior officials assisted by a number of expert working groups, as well as a consultative Parliamentary Committee for Cooperation, including members of the European and Moldovan Parliaments.

Since 1991, the European Union has provided assistance to Moldova totalling €253 million. This assistance had been channelled through the Tacis programmes, macro-financial aid in loans and grants, assistance through the Food Security Programme and humanitarian assistance. It should be mentioned that the macro-financial assistance and the assistance under the Food Security Programme are conditional on the implementation of the IMF programme. Since the Moldovan IMF programme went off track in the spring of 2003, this support has been halted.

However, the Tacis programmes, which were not bound to IMF conditionalities, were aimed at support for the transition process in the governance, economic and social spheres. Since 1991, they were implemented in such areas as food production, private sector establishment and the development of human resources. Since 1999, Tacis has further adjusted the focus of its programmes to the country's

7 Ibid., at p. 174.

Table: European Union assistance to Moldova since 1991 (in € millions)[8]

	1991	1992-3	1994	1995	1996-7	1998-9	2000-1	2002-3	Total
Tacis Action Programme	1.0	9.0	10.0	9.0	13.1	14.7	16.2	25.0	98.1
Small Projects Programme					4.9	4.8	4.7		14.4
CBC Programme					4.7	2.0	7.0	3.7	17.4
Macro-financial assistance		27.0*	25.0	20.0	15.0			15.0	102.0
Food Security Programme							5.5	10.4	15.9
Humanitarian Assistance						3.9	1.6		5.5
Total	1.0	36.0	35.0	64.0	37.7	25.4	35.1	54.1	253.3

* Grant

needs and to other donors' interventions. The Tacis Indicative Programme for 2002-2003 was concentrated on the achievement of goals established by the PCA, that is to say, on three priority areas: support for institutional, administrative and legal reforms; promotion of private sector and economic development; and addressing the social consequences of transition. In this framework, a number of projects are being implemented: strengthening the judicial system in the area of civic and commercial law; *rapprochement* of standards and norms; strengthening customs and border infrastructures; improvement of the statistics service; promotion of cross-border cooperation; development of higher education; development of small and medium business; support for the health services; social reforms with a focus on child protection; and projects in the field of energy and environment. What differentiated this programme from previous assistance was the emphasis on the investment component for the development of infrastructure.

One of the key activities is the project on the 'Implementation of the Partnership and Cooperation Agreement between the European Union and the Republic of Moldova' (PCA Implementation). It contributed to the elaboration of the Guide for PCA Implementation, to the analysis of and comments concerning existing legislation, to the development of materials for the EU-Moldova Cooperation

[8] Commission Staff Working Paper, *European Neighbourhood Policy, Moldova Country Report*, SEC (2004) 567 (COM (2004) 373 final) p. 4, available at: <http://europa.eu.int/comm/trade/issues/bilateral/countries/moldova/index_en.htm>.

Council and its working groups, to the creation of the Centre of European Legislation and to the harmonisation of Moldovan legislation with European standards.[9] Some visible progress has been made in such areas as trade liberalisation, investments and current capital flows. At the same time, many areas of Moldovan legislation are still in the initial phases of harmonisation with EU law, since the Tacis projects have frequently stopped at the information stage, having not gone beyond comparative analyses of EU and Moldovan legislation.[10]

The above-mentioned projects were significantly supported by the EBRD's initiatives included in its Strategy for Moldova: support for small and medium-sized enterprises (SMEs), privatisation, investment in the agribusiness and infrastructure, and support for and development of the banking sector. Twenty-three EBRD projects have an investment character.[11] In general, over thirty EU projects are currently being implemented in Moldova.

Other donors are also present in Moldova (e.g., the IMF, the World Bank, the United Nations and a few bilaterals), but the level of assistance is still limited. The European Union's Country Strategy Paper 2002-2006 for Moldova gloomily asserted that

> for the international community Moldova is in a relatively marginal geographical position. This, together with its small size and lack of resources, may explain why there has been relatively little interest shown by the international community in Moldova, despite the country's burning problems.

The fact that Moldova remains a CIS member, and the country's former close links to Russia, do affect the attitude of the Western world. Although Moldovan leaders have on a few occasions expressed their pessimism concerning the viability of the CIS, and although Moldova's relations with Russia deteriorated significantly after the failure of the Kozak Memorandum[12] and as the result of Moldova's new course towards European integration, it is evident that in the European Union's understanding Moldova still remains within the Russian sphere of influence.

---

[9] A. Gudym, *Respublica Moldova i Evropeiskii Soiuz kak partnery* [The Republic of Moldova and the European Union as Partners] (Kishinev, TACIS-CISR 2002) pp. 36, 39.

[10] V. Chirila, 'The Relations between the Republic of Moldova and the European Union', in *The Republic of Moldova and European Integration* (Chisinau, Institute of Public Policy 2002) pp. 58-59.

[11] EBRD, *Strategy for Moldova* (London, 2001).

[12] The pro-Western policy of the Moldovan Government and its position on the Transnistrian issue expressed in official statements made at the OSCE summit in November 2004 in Sofia, which contained strong criticism of the Russian policy on the issue, entailed a series of mutual accusations at the level of the foreign ministries (*Nezavisimaia Moldova*, 16 December 2004; 10 February 2005; *Ekonomicheskoie obozrenie*, 17 December 2004). In February 2005, Russian State Duma discussed an initiative to introduce a visa regime for Moldovan citizens, to raise the price of gas exported to Moldova and to introduce limitations on Moldovan exports to Russia (*Infotag*, 17 February 2005).

As a form of compensation for the lack of attention to Moldova some observers qualified its inclusion into the Stability Pact,[13] which the country had been requesting since 1999 in the context of its new strategy of European integration, including requests for a Stabilisation and Association Agreement, as a route to being considered a potential candidate for EU accession. The interest of the Republic of Moldova in the Stability Pact was determined, first of all, by the advantages offered by the Pact in solving stringent problems faced by the country. In Chisinau, the Stability Pact was viewed as a means to leave the 'turbid waters' of the CIS and direct the country towards Brussels, even if it would have to take a roundabout route through the Balkans.[14] Moldova was accepted into the Stability Pact on 28 June 2001. However, the momentum was lost, and the country was late to benefit to a full extent from the opportunities offered by the Pact to its members, since many programmes had already been started and the finance committed. On the other hand, unlike other members of the Pact, Moldova is not a member of the Stabilisation and Association Process.

Moldova associated itself with the Memorandum of Understanding on Trade Liberalisation and Facilitation (2001), which was signed under the Stability Pact between Albania, Bosnia-Herzegovina, Bulgaria, Croatia, FYROM, Romania and Serbia and Montenegro.[15] Each country has to conclude bilateral FTAs with the other signatories before 2008. By 2004, Moldova had succeeded in concluding free trade agreements with the other Stability Pact members, had joined the Athens Process on the regional energy market, obtaining observer status, and the Educational Memorandum for South-Eastern Europe and had actively entered the work of the Border Anti-Criminal Centre and a number of other initiatives in the field of democracy and security.[16] In 2004, Moldova co-chaired the Third Working Table of the Stability Pact (security, justice and home affairs).

The Moldovan authorities believe that participation in the Stability Pact for South-Eastern Europe will permit the country's natural and progressive integration into the South-East European area, which will in the future become a part of the European Union.[17] At the same time, the EU policy in this respect is not clear, since it keeps Moldova in two different groups of countries to which different types of policies are applied and different perspectives are designed: the Stability

---

[13] J.M. Wiersma, 'Moldova and the European Union: A Missed Opportunity?', in Lewis, op. cit. n. 5, at p. 198.

[14] O. Ungureanu, 'Stability Pact for South-Eastern Europe and Perspectives for the Republic of Moldova's Inclusion', in *The Republic of Moldova and European Integration*, op. cit. n. 10, at p. 69.

[15] Available at: <http://europa.eu.int/comm/trade/issues/bilateral/countries/moldova/index_en.htm>.

[16] I. Severin, 'Stability Pact expects Moldovan initiatives', in *Kishinevskii obozrevatel* [Chisinau Observer], 4 March 2004.

[17] Interview with Andrei Stratan, Minister of Foreign Affairs of Moldova, on the occasion of the fifth anniversary of the Stability Pact, *Moldova suverana* [Sovereign Moldova], 30 July 2004.

Pact and the European Neighbourhood Policy (ENP). This situation could be interpreted as the absence of a common approach of the European Union towards Moldova. From the point of view of the stability and security for the European Union itself, acceptance of Moldova into the Stabilisation and Association Process would be beneficial, and it would be logical from a geopolitical and geographical perspective. At the same time, the level of economic development of the Republic might impose an additional financial burden on the European Union. On the other hand, the economic situation in some Balkan countries is not much better than the one in Moldova, while the relatively small size of the country requires less effort and resources for reform. The major factor in this discussion is the reduced economic and strategic interest that the European Union has in Moldova,[18] although this has changed somewhat since the Orange Revolution in Ukraine.

2. EC-MOLDOVA PARTNERSHIP AND COOPERATION AGREEMENT

The most important document among those that form the legal framework for the relationship between the Republic of Moldova and the European Union is the PCA. However, the problem is that, despite the advantages of the PCA, it is far less generous than the agreements signed by Brussels with the CEECs, which expected to join the European Union at some stage. The PCA does not offer EU-Moldova relations a clear finality concerning gradual integration. In addition, the Republic of Moldova is located in a regional area in which the European Union is not ready to broach an integration strategy. In this way, the PCA represents Moldova as a component of the former Soviet space, which does not correspond to its aspired geopolitical identity as a Southern European state.

Though the PCA takes its inspiration from the Europe Agreements in terms of structure and even content, it reflects a different approach by the European Union regarding both final goals and territorial limits. The first and foremost difference is that, while the Europe Agreements offered the real prospect of EU membership, the PCA does not. In addition, the financial assistance offered in the context of the Europe Agreements (Phare) was far more substantial than the one offered through the PCA (Tacis). Additionally, the PCA does not make any differentiation in the European Union's policy towards different countries in the CIS, which Moldova had joined in the meantime. However, the PCA does not exclude the

---

[18] K. Neukirh, 'Integration of the Republic of Moldova in European Structures from the Western Point of View', in *Moldova, Romania, Ukraine: Integration into the European Structures* (Chisinau, Perspectiva 2000) p. 65.

prospects of the potential evolution of the European Union's relations with Moldova. Article 5 of the PCA, for example, contains the clause for modification of the agreement in the case that circumstances change, especially in the context of the adherence of the Republic of Moldova to the WTO.[19] Furthermore, this article stipulates that the parties would proceed to a first examination of the PCA three years after its entry into force, a term that expired on 1 July 2001. Since the European Union persists in emphasising the integral implementation of the PCA, the above-mentioned article offers Moldova the opportunity to propose some factors that would open the possibility of a progressive evolution of its contractual relations with the European Union.[20] Since Article 50 of the PCA imposes on Moldova an obligation to take the necessary measures to gradually increase the compatibility of its legislation with the legislation of the European Union, it also provides for legislative compatibility of the country with EU requirements. All in all, the objectives of the PCA fully meet the criteria for acceding to the European Union declared in Copenhagen in 1993.[21]

The PCA gives a political dimension to EU-Moldova relations. In order to give substance to political cooperation, both parties took on the obligation to promote political dialogue bringing the Republic of Moldova and the European Union closer together, to support the economic and political changes in Moldova, to contribute to a larger positional convergence in international problems of common interest and to encourage the mutual cooperation on problems connected with the observance of democratic principles and the consolidation of stability and security in Europe.

The PCA also institutionalises the relations between the Republic of Moldova and the European Union for the first time. The PCA stipulates the creation of a hierarchical institutional scheme divided into three levels: the Cooperation Council at the ministerial level (Arts. 82-83), the Cooperation Committee at senior-official level (Arts. 84-85) and the Parliamentary Committee for Cooperation, including members of the European and Moldovan Parliaments (Arts. 87-88). The official implementation of the PCA in the political, economic, legal, financial, social and cultural spheres. as well as the promotion of political dialogue, are the highest purposes of these institutions.

The PCA reflects the commitment of the two sides to democratic values and demonstrates the European Union's wish to support Moldova in its democratisation process and its transition to a market economy. Furthermore, the PCA introduces a political dimension to the EU-Moldova relationship, going beyond purely economic objectives. The establishment of economic links was not really

---

[19] Although Moldova became a WTO member in 2001, it did not modify the PCA Moldova, as it had promised to. See Gudym, op. cit. n. 9, at p. 31.

[20] *The Republic of Moldova and European Integration*, op. cit. n. 10, at p. 6.

[21] Available at: <http://europa.eu.int/comm/enlargement/intro.criteria.htm>.

at the heart of the document, but rather a way to bring symmetry to all the fields of interaction between the European Union and Moldova.

The first meeting of the EU-Moldova Cooperation Committee took place on 14 July 1998 and then continued to take place on an annual basis for the evaluation of progress on the implementation of the agreement and for the identification of areas that require the special attention of the both parties or additional assistance from the European Union. Disregarding some problems and delays, the experience of the first years of EU-Moldova cooperation in the framework of the PCA demonstrates that it had a significant positive influence on the harmonisation of Moldovan legislation, the liberalisation of trade, the development of the private sector and the amelioration of the social consequences of transition.

In the beginning, the emphasis was put on strengthening democracy, establishing the rule of law, reforms in agriculture, restructuring industrial enterprises and developing human resources. This approach was considered a less productive one, and in 2001 the European part of the Cooperation Council suggested a more pragmatic approach of prioritising issues and concentrating efforts on harmonising legislation, customs and border cooperation, fighting crime and finalising the study on the possibility of creating a free trade zone, the conclusion of a Free Trade Agreement (FTA) between the European Community and Moldova and the latter's entry into EFTA.[22] The parties also agreed upon the progressive liberalisation of cross-border services, for the purpose of developing a range of services oriented towards the market.

The modernisation and Europeanisation of the Moldovan law has stumbled on obstacles greater than initially expected. The new Civil Code was elaborated over a period of eight years and was supported by expertise and funds provided by Tacis, GTZ and USAID. It entered into force on 1 January 2003 and implemented a number of standards and principles that are guaranteed under international treaties or traditionally inform the legislation of European countries. It provided for the inviolability of property rights, freedom of agreements, judicial protection of civil rights and other measures.[23]

According to the PCA, the Republic of Moldova and the European Union have offered to each other the status of most favoured nation (Art. 10) and have established the principle of free transit for domestic commodities or goods destined for the territory of the other party and the principle of free circulation for certain types of the capital (Art. 11). At the same time, the real potential of the PCA in the sphere of economic cooperation has to be realised through the creation of a free trade zone between the parties (Art. 48) and also through the harmonisation of the Moldovan legislation with the standards and norms of the Community (Art. 50).

---

22 EU-Moldova Cooperation Council, Minutes, Brussels, May 2001, April 2002; Chirila, loc. cit. n. 10, at p. 64.

23 Gudym, op. cit. n. 9, at p. 45.

Under Article 4 of the PCA, the European Union and Moldova are engaged to develop provisions of the PCA, especially those regarding commodity trade and competition in order to establish a free trade zone. The negotiations in this sphere are conditioned by the progress achieved by Moldova in the establishment of a viable free market economy. Moldova has to take concrete steps in the following areas: (1) the growth of effective national authority in the sphere of competition and in response to changing attitudes concerning the rules regarding competition; (2) the adoption of international standards and an efficient application of the certificate system; (3) the foundation of companies; (4) the beginning of the efficient implementation of existing rules and regulations in the sphere of intellectual property rights; and (5) the improvement of the taxation system.[24]

In the meantime, the European Union has become an increasingly important economic partner for Moldova. The Russian financial crisis of 1998 and the energy crisis in the spring of 2000 stimulated Moldovan efforts to identify new opportunities that would boost its trade with the European Union. The effects of these efforts were: (1) negotiations with the European Union concerning a number of agricultural products that could be commercialised on the Community's market through ECHO; (2) obtaining authorisation from the European Commission to export wine made from two types of grape (January 2000); (3) obtaining supplementary facilities in the General System of Preferences (GSP); (4) an extension of the validity of the agreement regarding trade in textile products (January 2000); and (5) the launch of a Tacis project involving a study on the feasibility of establishing a free trade zone between the Republic of Moldova and the European Union.[25]

As a result, the European Union has become Moldova's most important trading partner, with a share of 36 per cent of the country's total bilateral trade (€1 billion in 2003). In 2003, imports from the European Union constituted 37.1 per cent of the total, while exports to the European Union made up 33.8 per cent of the total exports from Moldova. Moldova mainly exports agricultural and food products, textiles, base metals and articles of base metal to the European Union. Its main imports from the European Union are machinery and electrical products, agricultural products, textiles and clothing.[26] Moldova benefits from EU GSP preferences, including the GSP social incentive scheme. In 2000, Moldova was the first country to be granted additional reductions of customs duties under the special protection scheme for the promotion of labour rights. Preferential imports from Moldova under the GSP have steadily increased from €77 million in 2000 to

---

24 *Study of the economic feasibility of an EU-Moldova Free Trade Area* (Brussels 1999) pp. 3-5 quoted in Chirila, loc. cit. n. 10, at pp. 63-64.

25 Chirila, loc. cit. n. 10, at pp. 61-62.

26 Available at: <http://europa.eu.int/comm/trade/issues/bilateral/countries/moldova/index_en.htm>.

€110 million in 2002, with exports of clothing and footwear playing an important role. Moldova now ranks thirty-third out of 178 beneficiaries of the European Union's GSP.[27]

Following the EU enlargement of 1 May 2004, the Moldovan Parliament ratified the Additional Protocol to the PCA that starts the accession process of the ten new EU members to the agreement between Moldova and the European Communities.[28]

3. THE TRANSNISTRIAN ISSUE AS A SECURITY THREAT FOR THE EUROPEAN UNION

Moldova is distinct from the European Union's other neighbouring countries, in terms of the Transnistrian conflict. It started in 1989-1990, in the context of the declaration of Moldovan as the official state language, the movement for Moldova's independence from the USSR and the increasing pro-Romanian rhetoric of the Moldovan Popular Front that guided these processes. The Russians who in 1989 formed 25 per cent of the population of the territory currently known as 'Transnistria', the Ukrainians who formed another 28 per cent and the largely Russified Moldovans (40 per cent, predominantly rural dwellers) did not want to accept the changes. Their fears of the possible unification of Moldova with Romania, linguistic and ethnic discrimination, as well as the anti-Soviet, anti-Russian and pro-Romanian decisions and acts on the part of the Moldovan Parliament, which was still called the Supreme Soviet although it had been elected in 1990 in the country's first competitive ballot, had been used by the local (Transnistrian) elite to mobilise popular support for the secession of the region from Moldova. This fuelled 'anti-separatist' sentiments in Chisinau, resulting in nationalistic violence and the 'de-Russification' of power structures.[29] Escalation led to the secession of Transnistria in September 1990. The Moldovan authorities responded with attempts to forcefully suppress the Transnistrian rebellion, which led to armed conflict and bloodshed in the fall of 1991 and the spring and summer of 1992.[30] The XIVth Russian Army stationed in Tiraspol (the capital of Transnistria) intervened in the armed conflict on behalf of the separatist authorities, which

---

27 Commission Staff Working Paper, *European Neighbourhood Policy, Moldova Country Report*, COM (2004) 373 final.

28 *Nezavisimaia Moldova* [Independent Moldova], 31 December 2004.

29 By 1991, ethnic Moldovans occupied nearly 90 per cent of leadership positions within the government and state administration. See 'Moldova: No Quick Fix', 147 *ICG Europe Report* (2003) p. 3.

30 The analysis of those events is to be found in C. King, *The Moldovans: Romania, Russia and the Politics of Culture* (Stanford, CA, Hoover Institution Press 2000) pp. 120-142; and P. Kolstoe and A. Malgin, 'The Transnistrian Republic: A Case of Politicized Regionalism', 26 *Nationalities Papers* (1998) pp. 524-552.

led to the defeat of the Chisinau Government in June and July 1992. The latter had to conclude an agreement with Moscow and Tiraspol based on the disengagement of the belligerent forces and the introduction of Russian peacekeeping troops in the region. Tiraspol, which benefited from the direct and indirect support of Russia and Ukraine, continued the process of consolidating the independence of Transnistria with all the usual state attributes (a president, a parliament, a government, a police force, an army, a currency, a flag, an emblem, and an anthem), while Chisinau persistently searched for a way to reunify the territory of Moldova.

The continuation of the Transnistrian conflict, as well as the lack of reform in Moldova, not only reduces the credibility of the country's aspirations for EU membership but also creates security risks on the Union's future border. Visible progress was achieved in 2002 and 2003, with the creation of a common Moldovan-Transnistrian working group for the elaboration of a new Constitution and the mutual concessions made by the Transnistrian authorities and by Chisinau on the nature of the future common state. This success could be attributed partially to the more active involvement of the European Union: a number of proposals for an EU role in peacekeeping emerged in 2003 from the Dutch OSCE Chair and have been discussed internally by the European Union. The High Representative for the Common Foreign and Security Policy (CFSP), Javier Solana, has committed EU support for political settlement efforts in Transnistria.[31]

The increased EU focus on Transnistria has been accompanied, and indeed caused by, a growing awareness of the linkages between the unresolved conflict and Moldova's difficult economic and political situation. Concerns about the impact of the Transnistrian 'black hole' of smuggling and transnational crime on the European Union itself rose as enlargement brought the European Union closer to Moldova.[32] An attempt to put pressure on the Tiraspol administration to cooperate in finding a compromise by imposing a limited visa ban for a number of representatives of the Transnistrian administration was an important step.[33] The European Union also used its position to persuade Ukraine to strengthen its customs regime along the Transnistrian border.

However, the negotiation process was interrupted after Moldova refused to sign the Memorandum on Federalisation suggested by Russia (known as the Kozak Memorandum), because its stipulations seriously undermined the sovereignty of the Moldovan State. Moldova then asked the international community, and in particular the European Union, to interfere more actively in the resolution

---

31 Brussels, 15 September 2003, S0182/03, available at: <http://ue.eu.int/newsroom>.

32 Vahl, loc. cit. n. 5, at p. 180.

33 Council Common Position 2004/179/CFSP of 23 February 2004 concerning restrictive measures against the leadership of the Transnistrian region of the Moldovan Republic, *OJ* 2004 L 55/68, extended and amended by Council Common Position 2005/147/CFSP, *OJ* 2005 L 49/31.

of the conflict. The increasingly comprehensive set of instruments available to the European Union makes it better equipped – perhaps better than any of the other international organisations and actors that are present in Moldova today – to play a leading role in finding a settlement in the Transnistrian conflict. The European Union's opportunities for playing a more prominent and effective role in the eventual settlement are enhanced by the widening of EU competencies, particularly in the field of justice and home affairs (for instance in relation to visas and asylum) and foreign security and defence policy (most notably the establishment of an EU peacekeeping force).[34] The European Union has repeated its commitment to attach great importance to the settlement of the Transnistria issue by employing the full range of instruments and policy tools at its disposal to support Moldova in achieving the settlement. At the same time, the European Union has encouraged Moldova to take advantage of cooperation in the field of justice and home affairs, by establishing a comprehensive anti-money laundering regime, as well as a balanced and integrated national drug strategy, and by improving border management and customs controls.[35]

Meanwhile, the conflict has developed further as a result of the ban placed by the Transnistrian administration on Romanian schools under Moldovan Government administration in the territory of Transnistria. In response to this, the EU Council adopted Common Position 2004/622/CFSP on 24 August 2004 imposing further restrictive measures against the leadership of the Transnistrian region, denying them entry to or transit through the territories of the EU Member States.[36]

On 16 March 2005, the Council created the position of EU Special Representative (EUSR) for Moldova and appointed Adriaan Jacobovits de Szeged in this position.[37] The mandate of the EUSR is mainly to strengthen the European Union's contribution to the resolution of the Transnistrian conflict in accordance with agreed EU policy objectives and in close coordination with the OSCE, Moldova and other domestic actors, and to assist in the further development of the European Union's policy towards Moldova and the region, in particular regarding conflict prevention and conflict resolution. At the request of President Yushchenko of Ukraine and President Voronin of Moldova in June 2005, a fact-finding mission headed by the EUSR in the Moldova-Ukraine frontier region in August 2005 led to the signing on 7 October 2005 of a Memorandum of Understanding between

---

34 Vahl, loc. cit. n. 5, at p. 181; Solonari, loc. cit. n. 4, at pp. 212-213.

35 EU Council press release, 'Sixth Meeting of the Cooperation Council between the European Union and the Republic of Moldova', Brussels, 24 February 2004, 6295/04 (Presse 50), available at: <http://eurojournal.org/files/79153.pdf>.

36 *OJ* 2004 L 279/47.

37 Council Joint Action 2005/265/CFSP appointing a Special Representative of the European Union for the Republic of Moldova, *OJ* 2005 L 81/50. The mandate was extended on 28 February 2007 by Council Joint Action 2006/210/CFSP, *OJ* 2006 L 49/11.

the European Commission, Moldova and Ukraine, paving the way for the launch of an EU Border Assistance Mission.[38] The Border Assistance Mission was launched on 1 December 2005. It has a two-year mandate, which can be extended if necessary, and will cost €7 million. This mission, comprising 50 EU customs officials and border guards mostly seconded from EU Member States, plus a core team of fifteen, will help prevent cross-border crime by providing advice and training to improve the capacity of the Moldovan and Ukrainian border and customs services to prevent trafficking in people, smuggling of goods and the proliferation of weapons. It is hoped that improving cooperation between the two countries on border issues can also help to create the right climate for settlement of the conflict in Transnistria.

The invitation extended to the European Union and the United States to participate as observers in the so-called 'five-sided talks' between Moldova, Transnistria, Ukraine, Russia and the OSCE on the resolution of the Transnistrian conflict also signals the deepening of relations between the European Union and Moldova.[39]

4. 'WIDER EUROPE' INITIATIVE

Before the Chisinau authorities managed to finalise a European Strategy of their own, Brussels introduced its 'Wider Europe' concept for neighbours without an EU perspective.[40] The Chisinau Government was the first to reject the 'Wider Europe' concept and the inclusion of Moldova in it.[41] An official document reflecting the opinion of the 'Moldovan authorities' was published on the website of the Ministry of Foreign Affairs.[42] It welcomed the declaration of the European Commission, stating that the enlargement process must avoid drawing new dividing lines in Europe and that the new framework for EU relations with its present and future neighbours should establish conditions for stability, security and sustainable development within and beyond the enlarged European Union. At the same time, this opinion was aimed at building on the idea of a differentiated approach by the European Union towards its future neighbours, in order to interpret it as the perspective of joining the European Union in case Moldova would

---

[38] Council Joint Action 2005/776/CFSP amending the mandate of the European Union Special Representative for Moldova, *OJ* 2005 L 292/13.

[39] Draft European Union Statement on Moldova, Permanent Council No. 571, 6 October 2005, available at the UK EU Presidency's website: <http://www.eu2005.gov.uk>.

[40] European Commission, *Wider Europe – Neighbourhood: A New Framework for Relations with our Eastern and Southern Neighbours*, COM (2003) 104 final, 11 March 2003.

[41] See W. Van Meurs, 'Moldova *ante portas*: The EU Agendas of Conflict Management and "Wider Europe"', available at: <http://www.cap-lmu.de/aktuell/positionen/2004/moldova.php>.

[42] On file with author.

meet the accession criteria. The document stated the firm willingness of the Moldovan authorities to take an active part in all EU initiatives related to the 'Wider Europe' initiative:

> to enjoy the free movement of persons, goods, services and capital, and to integrate into European interconnected transport, energy and telecommunications networks … to benefit from credits offered by the European Investment Bank in order to realise common project on environment protection … to be included in the EU programmes in the fields of education, culture and scientific research … to participate in promoting cross-border cooperation aimed at preventing and combating with joint efforts common threats – terrorism, organised crime, corruption, money laundering, smuggling, trafficking in arms, drugs and human beings, illegal migration, etc. – and to contribute to the stability and security of the country, the region and the whole continent.[43]

At the same time, the document requested the European Commission to play a more active role in solving the Transnistrian problem and to initiate a stabilisation and reconstruction programme ensuring EU participation in the post-conflict security arrangements.

The main concern stated in the document, however, was related to the fact that Moldova would become an immediate neighbour of the European Union only in 2007, and thus would be able to access the benefits of the New Neighbourhood much later than other neighbours, which would enjoy preferential treatment from 2004. As compensation for this, the Moldovan authorities requested the European Union to include the country in the group of South-East European countries rather than in the group of CIS neighbours and apply to Moldova the relevant treatment for this region, such as an asymmetric trade regime. Further on, in order to avoid 'a negative impact on political, economical, social and security situation in the country' that could result from Romania's accession to the European Union in 2007, the document suggested the inclusion of provisions in the future EU-Moldova Action Plan that would grant the Republic the status of an associate member no later than the moment at which Romania would become a member of the European Union.

It was revealing that the whole document consisted of requests addressed to the European Union and that it did not reflect an understanding by the Moldovan authorities of the fact that the country should match the EU criteria in order to receive a desirable status in relation to the European Union, which was clearly stated in the 'Wider Europe' Communication. The European Neighbourhood Policy aims for considerable integration and cooperation across all policy areas

---

43 Ibid.

between the European Union and its neighbours, but indeed falls short with regard to the prospect of EU membership. The 'Wider Europe' Communication did quote Article 49 TEU, which grants any European country the right to apply for membership. Prospective candidates must meet the criteria for membership: democracy, the rule of law, human rights, respect for minorities, a functioning market economy and the capacity to cope with competitive pressures, and the ability to take on the obligations of membership.[44]

The EC Communication on 'Wider Europe' established a new differentiated approach towards each of the new neighbours of the enlarged European Union. The extent of EU assistance to its neighbours would depend on the progress of political and economic reform at the domestic level. But some observers consider that the differentiated approach to the neighbours was more of a declaratory character than real. They think that the lack of a differentiated approach is one of the main weaknesses of the new policy, because it places Moldova in the same category with Belarus, Ukraine and, eventually, Armenia, Azerbaijan and Georgia, which could all be included in the 'Wider Europe' framework.[45] In addition, it is not clear how the 'Wider Europe' framework could accommodate Moldova's participation in cooperative arrangements in South-Eastern Europe, including the Stability Pact.

The concept of Moldova's European integration, presented in September 2003 in Brussels,[46] stressed the importance of the principle of differentiation. Some of the Western observers also suggested separation of two categories – 'Wider Europe' and 'Neighbourhood'. According to them, the former should cover the map of the Council of Europe and the states included in it should have the perspective of joining the European Union at some point in the future. The latter would exclude Southern Mediterranean countries.[47] Such a separation would correspond to Moldova's interests. Moreover, Moldova would prefer a further differentiation between the Western NIS countries that do and do not have European aspirations, which could ultimately lead to a preferential status for Moldova's intention to become a candidate country.

The European Union, however, did not see enough justification for a different treatment of Moldova. The assessment undertaken within the framework of the

---

44 Ibid.

45 'Moldova pe calea spre Uniunea Europeana' [Moldova on the Road towards European Integration], International Conference, 13-14 October 2003, available at: <http://www.ipp.md/Comments/moldova_pe_calea_UE>; N. Popescu, 'Moldova's European Policy Options', available at: <http://www.azi.md/investigation?ID=27683>.

46 Commission Staff Working Paper, *European Neighbourhood Policy, Moldova Country Report*, SEC (2004) 567 (COM (2004) 373 final). The text of the document was never published in Moldova, though different versions were circulated.

47 M. Emerson, 'The shaping of a policy framework for the Wider Europe', *39 CEPS Policy Brief* (2003), available at: <http://www.ceps.be>.

ENP had shown that the country is still far away from European standards and stated that the main instrument for the development of bilateral relations would be the PCA.[48] This conclusion was brought to the Moldovan leadership's attention by European Commissioner Günter Verheugen. He stated that the 'New Neighbourhood' initiative was an ambitious and realistic framework for further reinforcing EU-Moldova relations, allowing Moldova to benefit fully from EU enlargement. He invited Moldova to cooperate in the preparation of the Action Plan implementing the objectives of the European Neighbourhood Policy and also confirmed that this policy and accession are separate policies, while recalling that the latter was not on the agenda for Moldova.[49]

The objective of the ENP is to share the benefits of the European Union's 2004 enlargement with neighbouring countries and, at the same time, to strengthen stability, security and well-being along its borders. The policy was designed to prevent a new dividing line between the European Union and its neighbours and to offer them a chance to participate in various EU activities through greater political, economic, security and cultural cooperation.

One of the elements of the 'Wider Europe' Communication was the specific possibility of creating a new neighbourhood instrument, 'which builds on the experience of promoting cross-border cooperation within the Phare, Tacis and INTERREG programmes' and which could focus on ensuring the smooth functioning and secure management of the future borders, promoting sustainable economic and social development of the border regions and pursuing regional and transnational cooperation. The Commission's Communication 'Paving the Way for a New Neighbourhood Instrument' immediately followed the 'Wider Europe' Communication in July 2003.[50] It expands on the creation of a new instrument to develop cross-border cooperation and to promote stability and prosperity within and beyond the new EU borders. It will build on the experience to date of coordinating the Phare, Tacis and INTERREG programmes. The Communication states that the instrument should complement and be coherent with other relevant EU policies and instruments, including national financial assistance programmes, as well as specific sectoral policies and instruments. The first phase of the neighbourhood programmes covers 2004-2006. Taking into consideration that Romania will become part of the European Union no earlier than 2007, but most probably in 2008, Moldova does not become a direct neighbour of the European Union until then, and it would be only logical if the new instrument would not cover Moldova. However, the Communication stipulated that, for the Bulgarian

48 Commission Staff Working Paper, *European Neighbourhood Policy, Moldova Country Report*, SEC (2004) 567 (COM (2004) 373 final) p. 3.

49 Available at: <http://europa.eu.int/comm/world/enp/news/06122003_en.htm>.

50 European Commission, *Paving the Way for a New Neighbourhood Instrument*, COM (2003) 393 final, 1 July 2003.

and Romanian borders with the Western NIS countries and the Western Balkans (future external borders of the European Union), Phare cross-border cooperation programmes would be established to cover the 2004-2006 period and would provide a useful basis for the neighbourhood programmes.

The Commission presented a strategy paper and country reports in May 2004. The strategy paper sets out how the Union can work more closely with its neighbours and extend some benefits of the enlargement. In addition, it sets out the principles, geographical scope and implementation methodology of the ENP and issues related to regional cooperation.[51]

The substance of this policy was developed through bilateral action plans setting out common objectives and the timetable for their achievement. According to the ENP, neighbouring countries have to formulate the action plans, which take the form of political documents drawing together existing and future work in the full range of the European Union's relations with its neighbours, setting out clearly the overarching strategic policy targets and benchmarks by which progress can be judged over several years. The action plans have to serve the principles of differentiation and progressivity. The implementation of the action plans is reviewed annually, which reflects the enhanced political interest of the European Union and provides governments with the opportunity to receive credit from the European Union for their political and economic reform efforts. At the same time, contractual relations will be developed through new 'neighbourhood agreements', which move beyond the existing Association Agreements and Partnership and Cooperation Agreements.

This instrument, which is supposed to replace the common strategy, can reverse one element of the relative marginalisation of Moldova – one of the few non-EU, non-candidate countries in Europe not covered by a common strategy.[52] Although the ENP does not provide for the prospective EU membership in the medium term, it does not exclude this for Moldova in a long run, a position reiterated by Enlargement Commissioner Günter Verheugen. At the same time, this issue depends not so much on the wishes and plans of the European Union itself as on Moldova's foreign and domestic affairs and on the extent to which the political leadership in Chisinau can attract EU support.

The Republic of Moldova was in the first wave of ENP countries, for which action plans were approved by the European Union in December 2004. The Action Plan for Moldova covers a three-year timeframe and is designed to help the country fulfil the PCA's provisions and, in this way, to advance the approximation of Moldovan legislation, norms and standards to those of the European Union. The implementation of the Action Plan creates new – although quite

---

51 Available at: <http://europa.eu.int/comm/world/enp/policy_en.htm>.

52 Vahl, loc. cit. n. 5, at p. 179.

vague – perspectives for Moldova in its relations with the European Union. The document states that, after three years, the Commission will issue a report on the progress achieved, and on this basis decisions may be taken on the next step in the development of bilateral relations, including the possibility of new contractual links. Additionally, as a part of the ENP, the Action Plan opens up the perspective of moving beyond cooperation to a significant degree of integration, including a stake in the European Union's internal market and the possibility for Moldova to participate progressively in key aspects of EU policies and programmes. The plan also foresaw the opening of a full EU delegation in Chisinau for facilitating cooperation and support during the implementation of the Action Plan. The Moldovan Government adopted a decree on the establishment of a Moldovan diplomatic mission to the European Union at the end of 2004,[53] and the Ambassador of Moldova to the European Commission was appointed in early 2005.[54] A delegation of the European Commission to Moldova was opened by the European Commissioner for External Relations and the ENP, Benita Ferrero-Walder, on 6 October 2005.[55]

It is an important characteristic of the Action Plan that it is not only Moldova's responsibility to implement it but that the European Union in its turn has also made some commitments:

- to support the settlement of the Transnistria conflict, drawing on the instruments at the European Union's disposal, and to consider ways to further strengthen its engagement;
- to mutually open its economy and to reduce trade barriers, which will stimulate investment and growth;
- to increase the financial assistance to Moldova through the European Neighbourhood and Partnership Instrument (ENPI) starting in 2007;
- to gradually open or reinforce participation of Moldova in certain Community programmes promoting cultural, educational, environmental, technical and scientific links;
- to provide technical assistance and twinning to meet European norms and standards, including legislative approximation through a mechanism such as TAIEX;
- to establish a constructive dialogue on visa cooperation, etc.

Inclusion of the EU commitment for more active involvement in the settlement of the Transnistrian conflict is one of the most important provisions of the Action

53 Reported in 'European Strategy of the Republic of Moldova', p. 17, available at: <http://www.ipp.md/public/biblioteca/89/en/SE-Intr.doc>.

54 Reported at: <http://www.newsmoldova.md/news.html?nws_id=395975>.

55 European Commission, Press Release No. IP/05/1221, 4 October 2005.

Plan for Moldova. Indeed, while the implementation of PCA provisions more or less depends on state policies and their implementation, the Transnistrian conflict cannot be solved by Moldova alone, without the active involvement of international organisations. At the same time, the European Union is currently the dominant player on the European political scene, and there is no substitute for its active role in European security issues. No other international organisation carries an economic, moral and political weight that is even remotely comparable to that of the European Union. The EU strategy in dealing with the Transnistrian conflict has been formulated for the first time in the Action Plan. It foresees stepping up EU involvement in supporting the OSCE and mediators in the settlement process and preparing for engagement in the post-settlement scenario; continuing efforts to ensure the fulfilment by Russia of the Istanbul commitments with regard to Moldova; furthering progress with Ukraine on pending border questions along the Transnistrian border and engaging in the trilateral Moldova-Ukraine-EC talks to ensure proper management and control of the entire Moldovan border with Ukraine; and supporting the active involvement of the civil society.[56]

While Moldovan officials expected that the implementation of the Action Plan and the accession of Romania in 2007 would present the necessary conditions for starting the negotiations between Moldova and the European Union on association,[57] the European officials were far less optimistic. At a press conference held in Chisinau after the signing of the EU-Moldova Action Plan, the head of the EU delegation to Ukraine, Belarus and Moldova, Ian Boag, noted that 'it would be too optimistic' for Moldova to become an associated country by 2008. He did not exclude the possibility that a successful implementation of the Action Plan would allow Moldova to build relations with the European Union that would go beyond the PCA and to create a new quality of relations with the European Union, but this would not mean integration.[58]

The ENP involves both advantages and disadvantages for Moldova. On the one hand, it provides better-structured EU assistance for the implementation of the PCA and could provide Moldova with greater access to the European market and, as noted by Romano Prodi, the spreading of the four freedoms: movement of goods, services, capital and people. However, the Moldovan authorities realised that the ENP is a much longer way to the European Union. While working on the Action Plan in parallel, they repeated Moldova's aspiration to become part of the Stabilisation and Association Process, which clearly opens the door to the European Union. The agreement of Chisinau to concentrate on the implementation of

---

[56] See *supra* section 3.

[57] 'Individual nyi plan deistvii dlia Moldovy' [Individual Action Plan for Moldova], *Ekonomicheskoie obozrenie* [Economic Review], 27 February 2004.

[58] D. Lungu, 'Planul de Actiuni UE-RM va exporta stabilitate catre Moldova' [EU-RM Action Plan will export stability to Moldova], in *Moldova suverana*, 16 December 2004.

the EU-Moldova Action Plan was a sign of its commitment to a *rapprochement* with the European Union, but at the same time Moldova continues to promote the idea that the country belongs to the South-East European region and should be treated on a par with the members of the Stabilisation and Association Process.

5. THE FUTURE OF EU-MOLDOVA RELATIONS

The idea of the desirability of Moldova joining the European Union and the need to start the preparation procedures for this purpose were formulated for the first time after the presidential elections of 1996. This development was supported by a number of EU Member States and candidate countries. However, the general conclusion regarding Moldova's European future was formulated in March 1998, and it clearly stated that the country should pass through the first step – implementation of the PCA.[59]

Successive Moldovan government programmes reiterated the importance of Moldova's movement towards Europe and formulated the steps that were to be undertaken: the development of a national strategy of European integration, implementation of the PCA, intensification of the political and diplomatic efforts, etc. However, the institutional structures were not established, the strategy was not finalised and its drafts were not made public, and many of the reforms required by the PCA were either not introduced or remained unimplemented. In this context, the frustration of the Moldovan leadership after the Helsinki European Council summit of 1999, which decided on starting accession negotiations with six more countries, but not with Moldova, looked very inappropriate.[60]

After the first 'shock' reaction to the decisions of the Helsinki summit, Moldovan state officials started to adjust their rhetoric to reality. They admitted that it was a mistake to expect an invitation from the European Union when Moldova was neither economically nor politically ready. The Government expressed its sincere commitment to taking all the necessary steps and to instigate reforms to meet EU conditions: to sign the bilateral Basic Treaties with Romania, Ukraine and Russia and to implement the PCA. European integration began to be understood more and more as the essential element for ensuring the country's security, stability and prosperity.

As a result, the 1999-2002 government programme put an emphasis on European integration as the primary goal of Moldova's foreign policy. The programme called for the creation of institutional structures to administer a more pro-active

---

59 Gudym, op. cit. n. 9, at p. 20.

60 See A. Skvortova, 'Moldova and the EU: Direct Neighbourhood and Security Issues', in Iris Kempe, ed., *Beyond EU Enlargement*, Vol. 1: The Agenda of Direct Neighbourhood for Eastern Europe (Gutersloh, Bertelsmann Foundation Publishers 2001) p. 106.

policy geared towards eventual EU accession, the elaboration and putting into practice of the national strategy of integration in the European Union, the implementation of the provisions of the PCA and the intensification of the political and diplomatic solicitations to start the association of the Republic of Moldova to the European Union.[61]

A majority of external observers and many internal observers and politicians interpreted the decision of the Helsinki summit as a sign that Moldova would never even become a candidate for EU membership, regardless of the pro-European declarations of successive Moldovan governments. However, quite unexpectedly, the Communist government appointed after the parliamentary elections of 2001 gave a new impetus to EU-Moldova relations. The Communists gradually mitigated their pro-Russian rhetoric and made some real progress, on the international scene, towards closer cooperation with the European Union. In January 2002, the Government adopted the programme for the social and economic development of Moldova until 2005, which gave highest priority to the country's participation in the European integration process. European integration was included as a long-term goal into the economic growth and poverty reduction strategy adopted by the Moldovan Parliament at the end of 2004.

In September 2002, President Voronin launched the process of establishing political and administrative structures to coordinate efforts towards integration in the European Union. As a result, the National Commission for European Integration was already established by the end of the year. Its tasks included developing a European integration strategy and coordinating the cooperation between various government institutions in this area (with interministerial groups responsible for each of the thirty-one chapters in the accession negotiations). A Parliamentary Commission for European Integration was also formed to be responsible for the harmonisation of national legislation with the basic law of the Union.[62] At the same time, a Department for European Integration was created within the Ministry of Foreign Affairs. Its task was to consolidate national institutional capacity to promote the strategic priorities for Moldova's European integration and make Moldova's participation in the Stability Pact more effective. The department consists of three directorates: the Directorate for Political Relations with the European Union, the Directorate for Economic Cooperation with the European Union and the National Bureau for the Stability Pact for South-Eastern Europe.[63]

The institutionalised multi-level dialogue between the European Union and Moldova in the framework of the existing cooperation structures subsequently

---

[61] I. Klipii, 'Evolution of Political Framework of the European Integration Problem', in *The Republic of Moldova and European Integration* (Chisinau, Institute of Public Policy 2002) pp. 20-21.

[62] A. Neguta and A. Simionov, 'Moldova and the EU: A View from Chisinau', in Lewis, op. cit. n. 5, at p. 194.

[63] *Nezavisimaia Moldova*, 7 August 2003.

became intensive and regular. Subcommittees were established to assist the Cooperation Committee, reflecting the emphasis on economic issues in the PCA. Their work was accompanied by increasing amounts of economic assistance from the European Union. At the same time, non-economic issues had gradually become more prominent in the overall relationship. This was particularly true of justice and home affairs (mainly money laundering, illegal migration and customs cooperation against drugs and arms trafficking, trafficking in human beings, smuggling of goods and the fight against terrorism), which received growing attention. The increased activity and the gradual broadening of the scope of cooperation could be interpreted as reflecting a readiness for deeper engagement on the part of the European Union and as a response to the 'European choice' made by the Moldovan Government.

At the same time, Moldova's CIS membership is still used freely by the political opposition within the country as a tool for criticising the government. The opposition claim that relations with the CIS make European integration impossible for Moldova, since membership of the European Union is presumably closed to countries that are members of this multilateral agreement. However, this argument belongs to political rhetoric and emotions rather than forming a real obstacle to the integration process. It seems that even the officials in Brussels realise that until Moldova obtains a visible presence on the European market and alternative energy resources, and until the Transnistrian conflict is definitely resolved, the country will be bound to Russia and, consequently, to the CIS.[64]

The official position in Chisinau in this respect is as follows. European integration is a medium to long-term goal, an inevitable process, which is being embraced slowly due to local opposition and traditional inertia. In the short term, Moldova will remain in the CIS, given its lack of room for manoeuvre, based on the understanding that this will preserve stable relations with its main economic and political partner, the Russian Federation. Any precipitate exit from CIS would probably have negative consequences for Moldova. This policy does not exclude but combines with the long-term option of a Western orientation. According to President Voronin, European integration should no longer be viewed as the alternative to CIS membership. He has also reiterated on numerous occasions that Moldova is the first CIS country to have expressed the initiative of a programmatic and consistent *rapprochement* of the legal, social and economic standards of the CIS with those of the European Union.[65]

Indeed, the European Union has not asked Moldova or other EU neighbours to leave other multilateral organisations such as the CIS. The official position of the

---

[64] I. Stavila, 'Moldova between East and West: a Paradigm of Foreign Affairs', in Lewis, op. cit. n. 5, at p. 131.

[65] *Ekonomicheskoie obozrenie*, 7 June 2002; *Nezavisimaia Moldova*, 17 July 2002.

Union was repeated by Ian Boag: Moldova can build cooperative relations with its strategic partners as long as these relations do not interfere with other commitments.[66]

Despite the firm European orientation and vocation of Moldova, only the European Union has the ultimate say concerning when a new member can be accepted. Moldova has already achieved some results as regards the Copenhagen criteria. It has made considerable progress in creating democratic institutions and consolidating the rule of law, in enforcing respect for fundamental human rights, including national minority rights, and in the approximation of the legislation to the European standards. According to the conclusions of international organisations, structural reforms have been undertaken in the economy, a programme of privatisation has been implemented with the support of the international financial institutions, some steps have been taken to improve the climate for the private sector, impressive budgetary and tax reforms have been undertaken and the state has limited its interference in the economy.[67]

However, Chisinau's ambitious integration plans are hardly realistic as far as Moldova's accession is concerned. On the one hand, the country does not have the capacity to implement the requirements set forth by the European Union for prospective candidates fully and in a short period of time. On the other hand, the European Union has made it very clear that it views Moldova as a member of the ENP for the longer term, while the EU-Moldova Action Plan, complemented by regional cooperation in the Stability Pact framework, is implemented. It will allow the country to develop further relations with the European Union, that is to say, to gradually and consequently progress in different areas – economic, political, social and cultural – and to become a prosperous and secure EU neighbour that will eventually be offered the most important benefits that are enjoyed by the EU members: free movement of goods, services, capital and people.

---

[66] Lungu, loc. cit. n. 58.

[67] *Moldova suverana*, 16 February 2005.

CHAPTER 18

THE SOUTHERN CAUCASUS (ARMENIA, AZERBAIJAN AND GEORGIA)

Anna Łabędzka*

Relevant legal documents:

- Partnership and Cooperation Agreement between the European Communities and their Member States, of the one part, and the Republic of Armenia, of the other, *OJ* 1999 L 239/3 (with 2004 Protocol extending the agreement to the new EU Member States, *OJ* 2004 L 300/44).
- Partnership and Cooperation Agreement between the European Communities and their Member States, of the one part, and the Republic of Azerbaijan, of the other, *OJ* 1999 L 246/3 (with 2004 Protocol extending the agreement to the new EU Member States, COM (2004) 267 final).
- Partnership and Cooperation Agreement between the European Communities and their Member States, of the one part, and the Republic of Georgia, of the other, *OJ* 1999 L 205/3 (with 2004 Protocol extending the agreement to the new EU Member States, COM (2004) 268 final).
- Council Joint Action 2004/523/CFSP of 28 June 2004 on the European Union Rule of Law Mission in Georgia, EUJUST THEMIS, *OJ* 2004 L 228/21.
- Council Decision 2004/924/CFSP of 22 November 2004 concerning the conclusion of the Agreement between the European Union and Georgia on the status and activities of the European Union Rule of Law Mission in Georgia, EUJUST THEMIS, *OJ* 2004 L 389/41.
- Agreement between the European Union and Georgia on status and activities of the European Union Rule of Law Mission in Georgia, EUJUST THEMIS, *OJ* 2004 L 389/42.
- Agreement between the European Economic Community and the Republic of Georgia on trade in textile products, *OJ* 1994 L 123/250 (as amended and extended by subsequent agreements).
- Agreement between the European Economic Community and the Republic of Azerbaijan on trade in textile products, *OJ* 1994 L 123/92 (as amended and extended by subsequent agreements).

* Graduate of Institute of International Relations, University of Warsaw; Diploma in Contemporary European Studies SEI, University of Sussex; 2000-2004 Secretary of the Sejm and Senate Delegation to the OSCE Parliamentary Assembly.

S. Blockmans and A. Łazowski (eds.), The European Union and Its Neighbours

- Agreement between the European Economic Community and the Republic of Armenia on trade in textile products, *OJ* 1994 L 123/64 (as amended and extended by subsequent agreements).

1. DISTANT NEIGHBOURS

1.1 The characteristics of the region

With the development of European integration and changes in the EU membership, new factors occur in the formulation of its external policy. The countries of the Southern Caucasus are no longer distant neighbours: they are about to become the European Union's next-door neighbours. Upon the accession of Bulgaria and Romania (2007 or 2008), the European Union will have a maritime border with Georgia. If and when Turkey accedes, the European Union will have a direct land border with Armenia, Azerbaijan and Georgia. EU policy towards the Southern Caucasus is the result of the ever-present factors of the region's geostrategic location, oil reserves and conflicts emerging in parallel to the struggle of building new democracies on the debris of the Soviet Union. Often, the European Union is exposed to a clash of interests. To start with, it is important to outline the major characteristics of the region. The analysis of the European Union's relations with the Southern Caucasus is preceded by a section devoted to a brief analysis of the region's history, specific data on the countries of the Southern Caucasus, the location of the region on the map of interests of international actors and, based on this background, the evolution of EU policy towards the region. The complexity of factors shaping the situation of the South Caucasian countries implies a lengthy introduction. This will help to avoid omissions that could lead to a misunderstanding of the region. It is worth pointing out at this introductory stage that only an in-depth analysis provides a basis for well-structured policy. Therefore, EU policy towards the region, like all areas of European foreign policy, should be visionary, well-balanced and prepared for rapid adaptation to new developments.

The dissolution of USSR brought to the international stage a number of fragile states that needed to rapidly make the transition from a centrally planned Soviet economy to a market economy.[1] These new states with a limited record of political independence had to open up to the outside world while rapidly formulating

[1] 'In the case of the Caucasus today, there is an altogether new reality. We're dealing with historic nations which are now independent. These countries have deep roots and a deep sense of their identity. And yet, paradoxically, they are just now engaged in the process of modern nation-building. The creation of the Soviet Union delayed that process for them.' Z. Brzeziński, 'The Caucasus and the New Geo-Political Realities', 5(2) *Azerbaijan International* (1997), available at: <http://www.azer.com/aiweb/categories/magazine/52_folder/52_articles/52_caucasus.html>.

their foreign policies and building up new judicial and administrative structures. At the same time, the Southern Caucasus, as well as other newly independent states (NIS), had to develop their identity. The analysis of the relations of the European Union with the three republics of the Southern Caucasus – Armenia, Azerbaijan and Georgia – would not be complete without underlining the unique nature of the Caucasus.[2] At this point, it is necessary to stress the fact that the northern part of Caucasus is home to even more conflicts, flammable situations, shortages and ethnic problems.[3] Therefore, the influence of the northern part of the Caucasus on the southern part's development is strong.[4] However, this chapter only reviews the state of the relations between the European Union, on the one hand, and Armenia, Azerbaijan and Georgia, on the other, with an emphasis on the issues that are characteristic of the region. At this point, it should be stressed that although the Southern Caucasus is often approached as a whole, the three states – Armenia, Azerbaijan and Georgia – require an individual approach. There are reasons to treat the Southern Caucasus as a region, but there are also issues that are specific only to a particular state.

Although the three countries share a common geographic position, there are many factors that are specific to each one of them. Moreover, the region is inhabited by numerous ethnic groups representing different religions, making the Southern Caucasus a real meeting point of different worlds. The difficulties inherited from the Soviet era are putting these young democracies to the test as regards their statehood and responsibility. The relations among Armenia, Azerbaijan and Georgia, as well as their differences and disputes, are also being tested in a different manner, as their prosperity depends on cooperation and joint efforts towards the development of the exploitation of energy resources and transportation.

Other issues common to all three South Caucasian countries include:

---

2 'Caucasus – one of the regions of the Eurasian continent most affected by what in the last decade has come to be called the "new world disorder". Together with the former Yugoslavia, it is the area of Eurasia most gravely hit by ethno-political conflict and warfare. … Most of the armed civil conflicts that have occurred on the territory of the former Soviet Union have taken place in the Caucasus (Nagorno-Karabakh, South Ossetia, the Prigorodny Rayon of North Ossetia and Chechnya).' See S.E. Cornell, *Small Nations and Great Powers. A Study of Ethnopolitical Conflict in the Caucasus* (Richmond, Curzon Press 2001) p. 17.

3 Immigrants in the Caucasus (northern and southern parts) include ethnic Russians, Armenians, Azeris, Georgians, Abkhazians and other indigenous residents of the Southern Caucasus (initially coming from areas of military conflict like Nagorno-Karabakh, Abkhazia and South Ossetia, followed by economic immigrants), Chechens, Dagestanis and other North Caucasian autochthons, as well as Tajiks and Uzbeks. See: <http://www.osw.waw.pl>.

4 Next to the Southern Caucasus is the Northern Caucasus where the following republics and *krais* are located: Dagestan, Chechnya, Ingushetia, North Ossetia, Kabardino-Balkiria, Karachay-Cherkessia, Adygeya, Kalmykia, Stavrol and Krasnodar Krais. See M. Falkowski, 'North Caucasus: the Russian Gordian knot', CES Studies No. 16 (Warsaw, Centre for Eastern Studies 2004) p. 44 and annex, available at: <http://www.osw.waw.pl>.

(a) Internally displaced persons: Due to the conflicts in the region (Nagorno-Karabakh, Abkhazia and South Ossetia) civilians have been forced from their homes. The figures still remain high as the conflicts remain unresolved. The estimated number of displaced persons varies depending on the source of the information. The latest estimates show that:

- in Armenia approximately 72,000 persons are internally displaced (according to government sources);
- in Azerbaijan approximately 575,000 persons are internally displaced (according to the government sources);
- in Georgia approximately 240,000 persons are internally displaced (according to the government sources).[5]

(b) Organised crime: The Southern Caucasus is highly exposed to the activities of organised crime and is regarded, next to the Balkans, as an international centre of drugs and arms trafficking. Once again, the unresolved conflicts lead to instability and corruption and crime therefore gets a rich harvest.[6] Moreover, the fact that considerable areas are outside the control of the countries' authorities makes these territories even more vulnerable to criminal activities. The parties involved in the conflicts are often providers and suppliers of arms.

(c) Corruption: Corruption is at a high level in all three South Caucasian countries.[7] However, in accordance with their international obligations, the countries[8] are taking measures to introduce new legislation to strengthen the fight against corruption-related crimes.[9]

---

5 See also the country reports of the Global IDP Project at: <http://www.db.idpproject.org>.

6 Drugs and arms smuggling takes place from Iran to Russia and Western Europe via Armenia's territory, while Azerbaijan is a vital point on the Balkan and northern trafficking route and Georgia is a vital point on the drugs smuggling route to Russia and Western Europe. See also: <http://www.unodc.org/unodc/index.html>.

7 Transparency International ranked Armenia in 82nd place, Azerbaijan in 140th place and Georgia in 133rd place in its 2004 Corruption Perceptions Index, available at: <http://www.transparency.org>.

8 Armenia signed the Council of Europe Criminal Law Convention on Corruption in May 2003 and ratified the UN Convention against Transnational Organised Crime in May 2003 (source: *Global Corruption Report 2004*). Azerbaijan ratified the Council of Europe Civil Law Convention on Corruption in February 2004, ratified the Council of Europe Criminal Law Convention on Corruption in February 2004, signed but did not yet ratify the UN Convention against Corruption in February 2004 and ratified the UN Convention against Transnational Organised Crime in October 2003. Georgia ratified the Council of Europe Civil Law Convention on Corruption in May 2003, signed but did not yet ratify the Council of Europe Criminal Law Convention on Corruption in January 1999 and signed but did not yet ratify the UN Convention against Transnational Organised Crime in December 2000 (source: *The Global Corruption Report 2005*).

9 See A. Saribekyan, 'Country Reports – Armenia', in *Global Corruption Report 2004* (London, Transparency International 2004) p. 150; R. Safaralieva, 'Country Reports – Azerbaijan', in *Global*

1.2 Country-specific data

1.2.1 *Armenia*

Armenia[10] is a presidential republic with a unicameral parliament (*Azgayin Zhoghov*, 131 seats).[11] It is a nation with centuries of history.[12] It is a landlocked country, bordering Azerbaijan, Georgia, Turkey and Iran. Since 1991, Armenia is building a new economy based on small-scale agriculture (which currently accounts for 20 per cent of the country's GDP),[13] which still requires investment and technology updating. Of the three countries, Armenia is the one with no significant natural resources (having only limited deposits of gold, copper, zinc and alumina). Armenia has resolved its energy shortages with the nuclear power plant at Metsamor. However, Armenia is under strong pressure from the international community to close it.

The conflict of Nagorno-Karabakh has significantly influenced the economic decline experienced by Armenia at the beginning of its independence. Although the conflict is still unresolved, the Armenian authorities have managed, with assistance of international bodies, to introduce reforms aimed at liberalisation, privatisation and stabilisation of the currency.

The European Union is Armenia's biggest import and export partner (its biggest European partners in 2004 were Belgium, Germany, the Netherlands and France). The exchange is limited: the European Union mainly imports precious and semi-precious stones (imported to Armenia, cut there and re-exported to the European Union) and aluminium. Armenia imports machinery equipment and vehicles from the European Union.[14]

Corruption Report 2005 (London, Transparency International 2005) p. 100; J. Dadiani, 'Country Reports – Georgia', in *Global Corruption Report 2005* (London, Transparency International 2005) p. 147.

10 Declaration of Sovereignty on 23 August 1990; Declaration of Independence on 23 September 1991; member of the United Nations, the Council of Europe, the OSCE, EAPC, FAO, CIS, BSEC, IMF, World Bank, EBRD, WTO, IAEA, Interpol and WHO; population 3,344,000; ethnic groups: 93 per cent Armenian, 1.5 per cent Russian, 5.5 per cent other; religions: 90 per cent Armenian Orthodox, 9 per cent Catholic, 1 per cent other (Russian Orthodox, Jewish).

11 The latest presidential and parliamentary elections took place in March and May 2003. They fell short of international standards. See also Republic of Armenia Presidential Elections of 19 February and 5 March 2003, Final Report, ODIHR, Warsaw, 28 April 2003. Republic of Armenia Parliamentary Elections of 25 May 2003, Final Report, ODIHR, Warsaw, 31 July 2003. The next parliamentary elections are expected to take place during the first half of 2007.

12 Armenia adopted Christianity in the fourth century. It enjoyed periods of autonomy but was also under the rule of various empires (Roman, Byzantine, Arab, Persian and Ottoman). It was incorporated into Russia in 1828 and the USSR in 1920. See V.M. Kurkjian, 'A History of Armenia', available at: <http://penelope.uchicago.edu/Thayer/E/Gazetteer/Places/Asia/Armenia/_Texts/KURARM/home.html>.

13 European Neighbourhood Policy, Country Report Armenia, COM (2005) 72 final, p. 21.

14 Ibid., p. 20. See also <http://www.bsec-business.org>.

Still, it is Russia that remains Armenia's strongest partner, especially since the latter depends on Russian energy supplies. Armenia also has the strongest ties with Russia in the field of defence of the South Caucasian countries.[15] In recent years, however, Armenia's foreign policy orientation has changed in favour of Euro-Atlantic structures, although there are factors that are making the relations with the European and American partners more difficult, namely the country's close relations with Iran. However, the fact that there is a sizeable and active Armenian community in the United States means the country receives adequate attention, *inter alia*, in the form of financial assistance. Post 9/11 developments have strengthened the Armenian position even more.[16]

In the close neighbourhood, Armenia has poor relations with Turkey. The countries present extremely different interpretations of the events in 1915. Armenia seeks Turkish acknowledgement of the genocide.[17] When Turkey took the side of Azerbaijan in the dispute over Nagorno-Karabakh, diplomatic relations between Armenia and Turkey were suspended and the borders were closed.

1.2.2 *Azerbaijan*

Azerbaijan[18] is a presidential republic with unicameral national assembly (*Milli Mejlis*, 125 seats).[19] It has a majority Muslim population. It has borders with

---

[15] In 1997, Armenia signed a Friendship, Cooperation and Mutual Assistance Treaty with Russia, as the basis for a twenty-five year military alliance, which includes a mutual assistance clause in case of a military attack on either party. In addition, in 2003, the parties signed a Military and Technical Agreement. Within Armenian's territory there is a Russian military base (in Gyumri). Armenia is also the only South Caucasian country that is a member of the CIS Collective Security Treaty Organisation.

[16] T. Gabelnick, 'Security Assistance After September 11', 7(4) *Foreign Policy in Focus* (2002), available at: <http://www.fpif.org/pdf/vol7/04ifpost911.pdf>. For more information, see <http://www.csis.org>.

[17] In 1915, over a million Armenians were killed by the Ottoman Empire. See T. Akçam, *From Empire to Republic. Turkish Nationalism and the Armenian Genocide* (London and New York, Zeb Books 2004).

[18] Declaration of Sovereignty on 23 September 1989; Declaration of Independence on 18 September 1991; member of the United Nations, the Council of Europe, OSCE, OIC, CIS, BSEC, GUUAM, IMF, World Bank, EBRD and observer at the WTO; population: 7,750,000; ethnic groups: 74 per cent Azeri, 11 per cent Talish, 2.5 per cent Russian, 4 per cent Lezgi, 3.2 per cent Dagestani, 5.3 per cent other; religions: 93.5 per cent Muslim, 6.5 per cent other (Russian Orthodox, Jewish, Buddhist).

[19] The most recent presidential election took place in October 2003. International observers pointed out numerous violent incidents and a failure to meet international standards. The ODIHR's Final Report expressed serious concerns regarding the election process. For more information, see Republic of Azerbaijan, Presidential Elections of 15 October 2003, OSCE/ODIHR Election Observation Mission Report, ODIHR, Warsaw, 12 November 2003. According to the ODIHR Election Observation Mission the parliamentary elections of 6 November 2005, the first elections held under the amended Constitution did not meet a number of OSCE commitments and other international standards for democratic elections. The ODIHR established a Limited Election Observation Mission

Armenia, Georgia, Iran, Russia and Turkey. Like all post Soviet countries, it suffers from the problems associated with the transition to a market economy, although it has a strong advantage – natural resources (petroleum, natural gas, iron ore, nonferrous metals and aluminium). Oil exports grant Azerbaijan good economic prospects, especially since the opening of the Baku-Tbilisi-Ceyhan (BTC) pipeline on 25 May 2005.[20] There is also a visible shift of economic ties with Russia and the NIS in favour of trade with Turkey and European countries, which is a result of the strengthening of the country's pro-Western orientation. In 2004, Azerbaijan's main European import and export partners were the Czech Republic, Germany, France and the Netherlands.[21] The development of industries in the fields of petroleum, natural gas, petroleum products and chemicals will never be achieved in full and produce prosperity for the country as long as stability is not achieved in the region. The lack of visible progress in the Nagorno-Karabakh conflict weakens the development opportunities. Azerbaijan also has to deal with the consequences of being exposed to the Islamic radicalism and radical movements. The foreign policy of Azerbaijan has a European orientation. The country has good relations with the United States, which puts additional tension on Azeri-Iranian relations. Although the economic ties between them are deepening, the efforts of the Iranian mullahs to spread their vision of Islam to Azerbaijan, as well as to millions of Azeris (estimated at 16 million) living in Iran, make these relations tense.[22]

1.2.3 *Georgia*

Georgia[23] is a presidential republic with a unicameral supreme council (*Umaghiesi Sabcho*, 235 seats). It has borders with Armenia,[24] Azerbaijan, Russia and

---

in Baku in advance of the repeat parliamentary election in ten of the 125 parliamentary constituencies on 13 May 2006.

20 The Baku-Tbilisi-Ceyhan (BTC) pipeline, built by a consortium led by British Petroleum, is considered to become the primary export route to the Mediterranean for oil from the Azeri-Chirag-Guneshli (ACG) off-shore oil fields located in the Azeri section of the Caspian Sea. See: <http://www.eurasianet.org/departments/business/articles/eav052505.shtml> and *infra* n. 50.

21 See: <http://www.bsec-business.org>.

22 Stability and security in the South Caucasus, WEU Assembly Document A/1879, Paris, 2004, p. 15.

23 Declaration of Sovereignty on 9 August 1990; Declaration of Independence on 9 April 1991; member of the United Nations, the Council of Europe, OSCE, CIS, BSEC, GUUAM, IMF, World Bank, EBRD and WTO; population: 5,411,000; ethnic groups: 71 per cent Georgian, 8 per cent Armenian, 6.3 per cent Russian, 5.7 per cent Azeri, 3 per cent Ossetian, 1.9 per cent Greek, 1.8 per cent Abkhazian, 2.3 per cent other; religions: 75 per cent Orthodox (65 per cent Georgian Orthodox, 10 per cent Russian Orthodox), 11 per cent Muslim, 8 per cent Armenian Orthodox, 6 per cent other.

24 Armenia and Georgia have good relations. However, there is the matter of the Armenian minority in Abkhazia that took the Abkhazian side in the conflict.

Turkey. In 1991, Georgia regained its independence[25] and started the necessary reforms. In the autumn of 2003, a protest against the manipulation of the elections – *the Rose Revolution* – led to the resignation of President Shevardnadze (who had held the presidential functions since 1995). New presidential and parliamentary elections brought Mikhail Saakashvili and the National Movement Party to power.[26]

Georgia has limited natural resources, including manganese deposits, iron ore, copper and minor coal and oil deposits. However, it has the advantage of having the suitable soils and climate for tea and citrus growth. Georgia's main economic activities therefore concentrate on agriculture (the cultivation of citrus fruits, tea and grapes). There is also production of alcoholic and non-alcoholic beverages, metals, machinery and chemicals. The country is dependent on energy imports (including natural gas and oil products) as its only energy source is hydropower. Despite the difficulties, Georgia, with the help of international bodies, has made substantial economic gains since 1995, achieving positive growth and curtailing inflation. Georgia has linked its long-term prosperity to its involvement with transit pipelines and trade. The construction on the BTC oil pipeline and the Baku-Tbilisi-Erzerum gas pipeline are attracting investments. Like Armenia, Georgia cannot rely on its own energy resources. However, their geographic position makes them an important part of the Eurasian transport corridor.[27] However, the economic prosperity and integrity of the country depend on the resolution of conflicts.

Georgia's foreign policy is based on a strong European orientation, also in its economic relations. The country's main EU import and export partners in 2004 were Spain, Greece, Germany and the United Kingdom.[28] Georgian-Russian relations are tense as a result of Georgia's geographic position.[29] The future of

---

[25] Georgia covers the ancient kingdoms of Colchis and Kartli-Iberia. The area came under Roman influence in the first centuries AD and Christianity became the state religion in the 330s. The country underwent domination by Persians, Arabs and Turks. The golden age of Georgia took place between the 11th and 13th centuries. It was subsequently invaded again by Mongols, Ottomans and Persians. In the 19th century, the Russian Empire took over. Georgia had three years of independence after World War I and was then incorporated into the Soviet Union until its independence in 1991.

[26] Presidential elections last took place in January 2004 and parliamentary elections in March 2004. The ODIHR noted that the elections 'demonstrated notable progress over previous elections and in several respects brought the country closer to meeting OSCE commitments and other international standards'. For more information, see Georgia Extraordinary Presidential Elections of 4 January 2004, OSCE/ODIHR Election Observation Mission Report, ODIHR, Warsaw, 28 February 2004; Georgia Partial Repeat Parliamentary Elections of 28 March 2004, OSCE/ODIHR Election Observation Mission Report, Part 2, ODIHR, Warsaw, 23 June 2004.

[27] K. Raptis, 'Nagorno Karabakh and the Eurasian Transport Corridor', ELIAMEP Occasional Paper No. 98/03, p. 1.

[28] See: <http://www.bsec-business.org>.

[29] Russia claims that terrorists prepare actions conducted in Russia (i.e., Chechnya) within Georgian territory, in the Pankisi Gorge.

Russian bases within Georgian territory strengthens the differences.[30] Tensions are also heightened by good relations between Georgia and the United States, as well as Georgia's aspirations regarding NATO membership. In addition, Georgia's energy shortages make the country vulnerable to Russian expansionist policy in the energy sector executed by the company Gazprom.[31]

1.3 Regional conflicts and their impact on regional cooperation

Although the establishment of modern state structures is in itself a tremendous task to be dealing with, Armenia, Azerbaijan and Georgia have had to face yet another challenge – emerging conflicts. Often described as 'frozen' conflicts,[32] their influence on the situation in the region is tremendous. They form the major obstacle on the region's path towards stability and prosperity.

1.3.1 *The Abkhazian conflict*

Abkhazia was incorporated into Georgia as an autonomous region (with the status of a republic) in 1931. In 1988, it demanded reinstitution within the Soviet Union. In 1991, Georgia proclaimed its independence without autonomous regions. This decision induced Abkhazia to reinstate the 1925 Constitution, which granted Abkhazia the status of an independent state united with Georgia on the basis of a union treaty.[33] The conflict escalated, putting Georgia in a deep crisis at the same time as the South Ossetia conflict erupted (in the autumn of 1990). Abkhazia received support from Chechen fighters as well as from Russia. The 1993 cease-fire was broken and Abkhazia took control of the capital Sukhumi. Although international efforts are being made to resolve the situation, progress will depend on the improvement of relations with Russia.

---

30 Although Russia committed itself to reducing its military presence in Georgia at the 1999 OSCE Summit in Istanbul, the progress of the implementation of this commitment has been slow. Russia has bases in Vaziani and Gaudata (Abkhazia), Batumi (Ajara) and Alhalkalaki (Samtskhe-Javakheti), as well as other facilities like military camps and warehouses.

31 'The resource wealth burden – oil and gas sectors in the former USSR', CES Studies No. 12 (Warsaw, Centre for Eastern Studies 2003) p. 22.

32 At this point, it is worth recalling the opinion of David Bakradze (Georgian MP) that 'frozen' conflicts is a better description of the process of conflict resolution than just conflicts, as they are indeed developing. See 'Regional preconditions for the development of an integrated European policy towards the South Caucasus', Documentation of the Conference at the H. Böll Foundation (Tbilisi 1-2 June 2004) p. 9.

33 N. Sabanadze, 'International Involvement in the South Caucasus', ECMI Working Paper No. 15 (Flensburg, European Centre for Minority Issues 2002) p. 12.

1.3.2 *The Adjara conflict*

Adjara enjoyed autonomous status within the independent state of Georgia, although it did not declare its independence. The situation changed in 1992. Aslan Abashidze formed a separatist army, created separate political institutions and refused to pay taxes to the Georgian authorities. In 2003, he declared himself president of Adjara. The year 2004 brought a breakthrough, and Adjara was taken back under Georgian control. The Council of Europe mission to monitor the June 2004 elections to the regional Supreme Council found that the electoral process fell short of certain international standards.[34] The Council of Europe also issued a critical opinion on the Status of the Autonomous Republic Act adopted two days before the elections on 18 June 2004.[35]

1.3.3 *Tensions in Javakheti*

Javakheti (Djavakhetia) is a region within the borders of Georgia, on the border with Armenia and Turkey, with a population that consists for almost 90 per cent of ethnic Armenians. Georgia refuses to grant administrative autonomy to the region. Tension is growing, as parties of Javakheti Armenians, like *Dashnak-tsutiun*, are expressing radical demands and anti-Georgian statements. The situation is also fuelled by the fear that the closure of the Russian military base (located in the town of Akhalkalaki) would leave almost 10,000 people unemployed.[36]

1.3.4 *The Nagorno-Karabakh conflict*

Nagorno-Karabakh is a region populated by Armenians in the western part of Azerbaijan.[37] The dissolution of the Soviet Union brought a wave of escalation of the conflict. In 1991, a new wave of clashes occurred. By the next year, with the support of Armenia, the Armenians of Nagorno-Karabakh took control of the region and beyond, ending up with control of almost 20 per cent of Azerbaijan's territory. The effects of the conflict are worrying, as thousands of people have

---

[34] 'Compliance with commitments and obligations: the situation in Georgia', six-monthly report prepared by the Directorate of Strategic Planning (DSP), February-June 2004, SG/Inf (2004) 19, Council of Europe, Strasbourg, 28 June 2004.

[35] Venice Commission, Opinion No. 291/2004 on the Draft Constitutional Law of Georgia on the Status of the Autonomous Republic of Adjara, 59th Plenary Session, Venice, 18-19 June 2004.

[36] See: <http://www.jamestown.org/publications.php>.

[37] It was a Soviet decision to locate Nagorno-Karabakh within the borders of Soviet Azerbaijan. There is a theory that Stalin decided to place the Armenian-populated region within the borders of Azerbaijan to strengthen Moscow's position. See Sabanadze, loc. cit. n. 33, at p. 12. The conflict already erupted in 1988, but strengthened after the collapse of the Soviet Union.

been driven from their homes, both Azeris (over 800,000 people from territories occupied by Armenia) and Armenians (230,000 ethnic Armenians forced out of Azerbaijan).

The conflict of Nagorno-Karabakh forms an obstacle to the development of the states involved,[38] but also to that of the whole Southern Caucasus region. The effects of the conflict are worrying, as it creates room for the transitional crimes of trafficking in drugs, arms and people, due to its location on the route from Afghanistan to Western Europe. It is a source of destabilisation for the region. Moreover, there is no visible means for positive developments. Recent years have shown that although attempts at negotiations are taking place and a certain level of stability has been achieved, there has been no significant improvement.[39] Some observers point out that at least there is no new armed conflict.[40]

1.3.5 *The South Ossetia conflict*

South Ossetia, which is inhabited by a majority population of Ossetians (66 per cent of the population in 1989), declared its demand for unification with North Ossetia (a republic in the Russian Federation) in 1989. This was followed by Georgia's decision in 1990 to abolish the region's autonomous status. The situation became tense with fighting by 1991, followed by the exodus of Ossetians leaving for North Ossetia and Georgians leaving for Georgia. The year 1992 brought a ceasefire, which is monitored by the OSCE and a Joint Peacekeeping Force composed of Georgians, Ossetians and Russians. The situation remains tense. Russia provides support to South Ossetia in the form of military equipment and also leads the policy of encouraging the South Ossetians to acquire Russian citizenship, which makes a settlement even more difficult.

The state of limbo in South Ossetia results in an increased level of smuggling and other unlawful activities within the region.

1.3.6 *Regional cooperation*

Unresolved conflicts also form a direct barrier to the development of regional cooperation. It should be noted that cooperation between the South Caucasian

---

38 The Nagorno-Karabakh conflict became a tool in the internal politics of Armenia and Azerbaijan.

39 There is no prospect of a solution to the conflict in the near future, despite the efforts of the OSCE and the Prague Process. The latter was initiated in 2004 to reinvigorate the dialogue between the parties to the conflict. For more information, see E. Mehtiyev, *Armenia-Azerbaijan Prague Process: Road Map to Peace or Stalemate for Uncertainty?* (Camberley, Conflict Studies Research Centre May 2005).

40 Foreign Affairs Committee of the Sejm (Lower Chamber of Polish Parliament), Bulletin 4465/IV 20 April 2005, available at: <http://www.sejm.gov.pl>.

countries is rather poor and unsatisfactory. There are numerous opinions stating that regional cooperation and the establishment of strong regional ties would strengthen the position of individual countries as well as the position of the region in the world.[41] There is no institutional forum for the three South Caucasian countries.[42] The Black Sea Economic Cooperation Organisation (BSEC) and GUUAM should be treated as a good starting point for the political dialogue between Armenia, Azerbaijan and Georgia to develop a framework for their cooperation.

1.3.6.1 BSEC

The end of the bipolar division of the world brought into the limelight the idea of creating a framework for cooperation among the countries gathered on the shores of the Black Sea. In 1992, the leaders of Albania, Azerbaijan, Armenia, Bulgaria, Romania, Georgia, Greece, Moldova, Russia, Ukraine and Turkey signed the Istanbul Declaration on Black Sea Economic Cooperation, which provided the basis for cooperation towards the creation of an area of peace and prosperity.[43] The process was institutionally enriched in 1995 by the decision to establish a Secretariat based in Istanbul.[44] The BSEC Charter was signed in 1998 and ratified a year later.[45] The BSEC thus became an organisation with members committed to the development of cooperation. The organisation deals with the main aspects of the relations between its members: trade and economic development, communication, environmental protection, agriculture, energy, transport and tourism. It has created means of cooperation on different levels (platforms): governmental, parliamentary, entrepreneurial, financial and scientific.[46] The effectiveness of the organisation is rather modest, due to the fact that its members are diverse and have different needs.

---

41 R. Motika, 'New Context for Regional Cooperation in Southern Caucasus', XXXII *The Turkish Yearbook of International Relations* (2001) p. 299.

42 D. Lynch, 'A regional insecurity dynamic', in P. Baev and D. Lynch, eds., *The South Caucasus: a challenge for the EU*, Chaillot Papers No. 65 (Paris, Institute for Security Studies, European Union 2003) p. 9.

43 Istanbul Declaration on Black Sea Economic Cooperation, 25 June 1992, available at: <http://www.mfa.gov.tr>.

44 Statement of the High Level Meeting of the BSEC Participating States, Bucharest, 30 June 1995, available at: <http://www.bsec.gov.tr>.

45 BSEC Charter, Yalta, 5 June 1998, available at: <http://www.bsec.gov.tr>.

46 See: <http://www.bsec.gov.tr>.

1.3.6.2 GUUAM

GUUAM (Georgia, Ukraine, Uzbekistan,[47] Azerbaijan and Moldova) was established[48] in the aftermath of the Soviet Union's collapse as a political and economic alliance, but also as a counterbalance to Russia's position in the CIS area.[49] GUUAM aims to encourage cooperation at the regional level. It is involved in the development of TRACECA (Transport Corridor Europe-Caucasus-Asia) as part of the region's path towards prosperity and stability. In practice, however, the impact of the organisation has been weak, although political changes in Ukraine and Georgia may have a positive impact on cooperation within the alliance. The pro-Western orientation of the GUUAM members should enhance their will to prove, both to themselves and to partners like the European Union, their capability of developing effective regional cooperation.

1.4 **International players in the region**

In the past, interest in the region was shown by the Russian, Persian and Ottoman Empires. At present, Russia, the United States, Turkey and Iran are paying interest to the South Caucasian countries. It is also worth pointing out that these interests are expressed at different levels – from the governmental to the company level.[50] The reason for this lies in the location of energy resources. Energy resources and their attractiveness to external parties is another factor hampering regional cooperation.

---

[47] The 2002 declaration suspending Uzbekistan' membership of GUUAM was followed by a decision of 5 May 2005 on withdrawal from the organisation. The move is regarded as a presidential measure against criticism of the country's failure to implement protection of human rights and democratisation. See *EurActiv*, 12 May 2005.

[48] In 1997, during the Council of Europe meeting, the leaders of Azerbaijan, Georgia, Moldova and Ukraine issued a joint statement expressing their interest in the development of regional cooperation. See Joint Communiqué of the Presidents of Azerbaijan, Georgia, Moldova and Ukraine, 10 October 1997. In 1999, Uzbekistan joined the original members of the group. A year later, a framework of regular meetings and channels for information exchanges were agreed to strengthen the cooperation. See: <http://www.guuam.org>.

[49] CES Comments, 28 April 2005.

[50] Many companies from the energy sector saw the potential of the region, including ENI, BP, TotalFinalElf, Shell, Chevron, Texaco, Statoil, LUKoil. For example, BP has been in Azerbaijan since 1992. It concentrates on 'offshore oil and gas exploration and production in the Caspian Sea and the development and operation of export pipelines'. BP is leading the Baku-Tbilisi-Ceyhan (BTC) pipeline project. It has production and development contracts: Azeris, Chirag and Deepwater Gunashli (ACG), the Shah Deniz, as well as exploration contracts: Inam and Araz-Alov-Sharg. For more information, see: <http://www.bp.com>. 'In October 2001, Eni acquired a 5 per cent interest in the consortium to build and manage the Baku-Tbilisi-Ceyhan oil pipeline. This 1740 km long pipeline transports oil from the Caspian Sea region towards the Mediterranean, from Baku to the Turkish port of Ceyhan, crossing Georgia. In the oilfield services, construction and engineering sector, Saipem has installed the offshore infrastructures for the development of the Azeri-Chirag-Gunashi fields.' For more information, see: <http://www.eni.it>.

1.4.1 *Evolution of EU policy towards the region*

The formulation of EU policy towards the Southern Caucasus is carried out by a wide spectrum of actors that are involved and interested in the region. The development of the policy has undergone necessary adaptations to the changing situation and the emergence of new demands. Some of the decisions were taken too late, however, resulting in a loss of the position that could have been achieved by the European Union.

The European Union was present in the region from the early stages of the establishment of the NIS following the collapse of the Soviet Union. Although the European Union has been aiming to become a fully fledged international key player, in reality until the signing of the PCAs its activities were limited to technical and humanitarian assistance supporting poverty reduction and sustainable growth, which it provided through ECHO[51] and Tacis.[52] Later, the regional approach was applied through the establishment of the SCAD, INOGATE and TRACECA programmes. The European Union's ambitions in the field of peacekeeping and conflict resolution require close cooperation with other actors present in the region.[53]

The European Union also has to face another sensitive matter when addressing the region. As Russia is a strategic EU partner, any measures taken in relation to the Southern Caucasus require consideration of Russia's reaction to them. As the European Union develops the CFSP and, moreover, the ESDP, the sensitivity of this matter is growing.

1.4.2 *Russia*

Next to Iran and Turkey, Russia is the regional hegemon and approaches the region as its very own sphere of influence. However, it does not have sufficient means to keep the region under its control.[54] As Russia's security depends on the development of the situation in the Northern Caucasus, its position towards the Southern Caucasus strongly depends on the evolution of events in the Federation's Caucasian republics.[55] Russia follows a policy of emergency response

---

[51] Council Regulation (EC) No. 1257/96 of 20 June 1996 concerning humanitarian aid, *OJ* 1996 L 163/1.

[52] Council Regulation (EC, Euratom) No. 99/2000 of 29 December 1999 concerning the provision of assistance to the partner States in Eastern Europe and Central Asia, *OJ* 2000 L 12/1.

[53] For further information, see section 4 of this chapter.

[54] M.-R. Djalili, 'New Foreign Policies for New States: Transcaucasia and Central Asia in the International Arena', in R. Sabahi and D. Warner, eds., *The OCSE and the Multiple Challenges of Transition: the Caucasus and Central Asia* (Aldershot, Ashgate 2004) p. 14.

[55] Falkowski, loc. cit. n. 4, at p. 44.

instead of addressing the causes of conflicts in the Caucasus.[56] Its involvement in the regions of Abkhazia and South Ossetia increases tensions between Georgia and Russia. The new political forces in Georgia have pushed for a more efficient policy towards Russia.[57] The countries also face the issue of the withdrawal of Russian troops from Georgia. In 1999, the OSCE Istanbul summit saw the Joint Statement on the withdrawal of the Russian troops.[58] However, there has not been much progress since then. The declaration of the Russian Minister of Foreign Affairs, who, on 30 May 2005, after talks with his Georgian counterpart, confirmed that 'the final withdrawal will be completed by 2008', is regarded as a breakthrough.[59]

Russia looks at the pro-Euro-Atlantic aspirations of the Southern Caucasus with anxiety and regards them as a threat to its position in the region. However, since it holds the economic and energy advantage, its presence in the region remains significant.

1.4.3 *United States*

The Southern Caucasus and Central Asia are important parts of the United States' global strategy. The location close to Russia, China, India and Pakistan – all nuclear powers – makes this a strategic place.[60] The United States encouraged the construction of the BTC pipeline. American aid to the region not only has economic aspects but also, more importantly, a political one. The assistance of the United States in restructuring and training the armed forces in Georgia helped to create a counterbalance to Russia's aspiration for hegemony in the region. Armenia also receives a lot of attention from the United States, as the active Armenian community in America is a strong ally of its fatherland.

The attacks of 9/11 deepened US interest in the Caucasus as an alternative source of oil to the Middle East,[61] but also as an important element of its security strategy.[62] In fact, the use of Azerbaijan's military bases and the right to fly over its territory have been crucial for US operations against terrorism.[63]

---

56 Ibid.

57 S. Freizer, 'It's dangerous to tease a bear', *International Herald Tribune*, 10 May 2005.

58 Joint Statement of the Russian Federation and Georgia of 17 November 1999, Istanbul Summit Documents, Annex 14, Istanbul, 1999, p. 252.

59 *MosNews*, 30 May 2005. The declaration was welcomed by the European Union, Statement of the High Representative for the CFSP, Brussels 31, May 2005.

60 Djalili, loc. cit. n. 54, at p. 27.

61 J. Gault, 'Caspian Oil: Did America Really Win?', in Sabahi and Warner, loc. cit. n. 54, at p. 121.

62 D. Lynch, 'The EU: towards a strategy', in Baev and Lynch, loc. cit. n. 42, at p. 175.

63 The pro-Western orientation of Azerbaijan was expressed again during the Iraq war, where the only Muslim country in the coalition was Azerbaijan.

1.4.4 *Turkey*

Being a regional power, Turkey has used the changes in the region as a way to strengthen its position.[64] The history of its foreign relations still weakens its position, especially in relation to Armenia, as Turkey is not willing to admit to the 1915 genocide of Armenians. Efforts are being made to resolve this obstacle in the bilateral relations, as there are other issues causing hostility. The Nagorno-Karabakh conflict made relations with Armenia tense, as Turkey took the side of Azerbaijan. However, awareness of the fact that only an improvement in their relations will bring an economic advantage to Turkey and the whole region is a driving force behind their reconciliation. It is also an answer to the European Union's recommendation to Turkey to improve its relations with its neighbours in preparation for EU accession.[65]

1.4.5 *Iran*

Iran has a direct border with Azerbaijan and Armenia. It has therefore seen an opportunity emerging from the changes that occurred in 1991. Iran is using its activity in the Southern Caucasus as a way of signalling its importance to the Western world.[66] The sizeable Azeri community in Iran (estimates vary from 16 to over 20 million) adds a dose of hostility to the bilateral relations. Azerbaijan's deepening relations with the United States add to the discontent expressed by Iran. However, Iran could use its religious influence on Azerbaijan, a possibility which is regarded as a threat to democracy and civil society in this Southern Caucasus republic by other actors in the region.

In case of Armenia, the ties have an economic and military character, as a vast amount of the Armenian army's military supplies come from Iran. These ties will be even stronger following the completion of the gas pipeline from Iran to Armenia, which should be done by 2007.

1.4.6 *International organisations*

Mediation efforts to resolve the aforementioned ethno-political conflicts have been undertaken by various international organisations, in particular by the United Nations and the OSCE.[67]

---

[64] It plays the card of linguistic connections – successfully in the case of Azerbaijan – to return to the pan-Turkism idea. See Djalili, loc. cit. n. 54, at p. 23.

[65] Communication from the Commission to the Council and the European Parliament, COM (2004) 656 final, 6 October 2004; Commission Staff Working Paper, Issues arising from Turkey's membership perspective, SEC (2004) 1202, 6 October 2004.

[66] Djalili, loc. cit. n. 54, at p. 20.

[67] Sabanadze, loc. cit. n. 33, at p. 5.

1.4.6.1 United Nations

The United Nations leads the efforts to resolve the Abkhazian conflict. The United Nations Observer Mission in Georgia (UNOMIG)[68] was established in 1993[69] to monitor compliance with the ceasefire agreement between the Georgian Government and the Abkhazian authorities (with a special focus on the situation in Sukhumi). Its mandate was modified in 1994. The scope of its activities include monitoring the implementation of the Ceasefire and Separation of Forces Agreement (Moscow, 14 May 1994), observing the operation of the peacekeeping forces of the CIS, patrolling and observing the troops of the parties (with a particular focus on possible attempts to reintroduce weapons into the security zone), patrolling the Kodori Valley and reporting regularly to the UN Secretary General.[70]

In 1996, an additional component was added to the UNOMIG structure, when the Security Council adopted a resolution establishing a United Nations office for the protection and promotion of human rights in Abkhazia.[71] The Human Rights Office is jointly staffed by the Office of the High Commissioner for Human Rights and the OSCE. Its mandate is to monitor the human rights situation in Abkhazia, promote respect for human rights and contribute to the safe return of internally displaced persons (IDPs) and refugees, and advise the authorities on the best way of improving the human rights situation. In 2003, the Security Council adopted decisions adding a civilian police component to UNOMIG, in particular to contribute to the safe return of IDPs and refugees.[72]

1.4.6.2 OSCE

The OSCE devotes a lot of attention to the region by conducting a wide range of activities. It is involved in wide-ranging assistance measures in the fields of conflict prevention, border management, democratisation (including election assistance), human rights, military reform and the preservation of the rule of law. The OSCE's Chairman-in-Office (CiO) requested the development of tools necessary for enhancing the organisation's activities in this field. The OSCE's achievements are closely followed by other organisations. The OSCE itself continues its work through close cooperation with other parties involved in the stabilisation process of the Southern Caucasus.

---

[68] UNOMIG is composed of a total of 130 uniformed personnel, including 119 military observers and 11 civilian police, supported by 99 international civilian personnel and 181 local civilian staff. For more details, see: <http://www.un.org/Depts/dpko/missions/unomig/index.html>.

[69] Security Council resolution No. 858, 24 August 1993.

[70] See 'United Nations Observer Mission in Georgia (UNOMIG)', in *The Blue Helmets: A Review of United Nations Peacekeeping*, 3rd edn. (New York, UNDPI 1996) pp. 569-588.

[71] Security Council resolution No. 1077, 22 October 1996.

[72] Security Council resolution No. 1494, 30 July 2003.

The OSCE has offices in Yerevan and Baku, as well as a mission to Georgia. The OSCE Office in Yerevan[73] was established in 1999[74] and started its activities in 2000. It works on a wide range of issues, stressing the importance of legislative reform, especially in the fields of freedom of assembly, mass media, the fight against corruption and armed forces reform. It also conducts various projects, from the elimination of rocket fuel component (melange) disposal to support for the ombudsperson's office. The OSCE Office in Baku[75] was established in 1999[76] and started its activities in 2000. Within the scope of its mandate, the Baku Office promotes the OSCE's principles and commitments. A particular emphasis is placed on legislative reform in the fields of elections, mass media and civil society. The Baku Office also addresses the issues of national minorities, trafficking in human beings, IDPs and refugees.

The establishment of the Mission to Georgia in 1992[77] was a response to the emerging Georgian-Ossetian and later Georgian-Abkhazian conflicts. Since then, the prime objective of the mission 'to promote negotiations ... which are aimed at reaching a peaceful political settlement' was extended.[78] This broad mandate includes facilitating the creation of the political framework for achieving a lasting settlement in the Georgian-Ossetian conflict, monitoring events and liaising with the UN operation[79] in the Georgian-Abkhazian conflict. In Georgia, the mission works towards the development of respect for human rights and fundamental freedoms and the development of legal and democratic institutions.

Since 1999, the OSCE Mission to Georgia includes conducting a border monitoring operation on the border between Georgia and Chechnya.[80] In 2001, the mission was given a new task: conducting a border monitoring operation on the border between Georgia and Ingushetia.[81] Since 2003, the mission's border monitoring operations also include monitoring the border between Georgia and Dagestan.[82]

---

73 See: <http://www.osce.org/yerevan>.

74 OSCE Permanent Council Decision No. 314 of 22 July 1999.

75 See: <http://www.osce.org/baku>.

76 OSCE Permanent Council Decision No. 318 of 16 November 1999.

77 17th CSO Meeting, 6 November 1992, Journal No. 2, Annex 2.

78 The first decision on extending the mandate was taken by 14th Permanent Committee Meeting, 24 March 1994, Journal 14/Revised, Annex 1.

79 The mission's cooperation with the United Nations is based on a Memorandum of Understanding (1997) which enables one (at certain times two) OSCE officer(s) to work at the UN Human Rights Office in Abkhazia and monitor closely the human rights situation in the region. Survey of OSCE Long-Term Missions and other OSCE Field Activities, SEC.INF/115/04, Vienna, 2 June 2004, p. 13.

80 Permanent Council Decision No. 334 of 15 December 1999.

81 Permanent Council Decision No. 450 of 3 December 2001.

82 Permanent Council Decision No. 523 of 19 December 2003.

Another important aspect of the OSCE's activities in the region is the so-called Minsk Process. In 1992, the CiO requested the creation of a forum for negotiations leading to the peaceful settlement of the Nagorno-Karabakh conflict. Although the planned conference (in Minsk) did not take place, the initiative led to the establishment within the OSCE structure of a group willing to work towards a peaceful solution. The Budapest Summit (December 1994) adopted the decision to establish a co-chairmanship for the process, which was implemented in March 1995.[83] The process is aimed at obtaining an agreement on the cessation of the armed conflict, providing a framework for conflict resolution and promoting the peace process by deploying OCSE multinational peacekeeping forces. The Co-Chairmen pay visits to the region, consult with the parties to the conflict and hold meetings with the OSCE CiO. The CiO appointed a Personal Representative of the OSCE CiO on the conflict dealt with by the OSCE Minsk Conference in 1995. Since then, the Personal Representative (with five field assistants) has fulfilled a wide range of duties, including representing the OSCE CiO on issues related to the Nagorno-Karabakh conflict and assisting parties to develop and implement confidence-building measures.

The Budapest Summit of 1994 laid the basis for the establishment of the High-Level Planning Group (HLPG). Its aim is to intensify the process related to the conflict dealt with by the Minsk Conference. It is composed of eight military and one non-military staff members seconded by the OSCE Participating States.[84]

1.4.6.3 Council of Europe

As the Iron Curtain fell, the Council of Europe became an attractive proposition for the Central and Eastern European countries. Since the Statute of the Council of Europe grants the perspective of membership to any European state that is willing to uphold the principles of the rule of law, human rights and fundamental freedoms, the new democracies commenced their quest for membership of the organisation.

The interest paid by this new group of countries[85] represented a two-way advantage, as the new Member States not only gained recognition through membership but the organisation itself also enjoyed a revival. The self-described

[83] *OSCE Journal* No. 106 (March 1995). The co-chairmanship of the Minsk Group consists of France, Russia and the United States. Other members include the parties to the conflict – Armenia and Azerbaijan – as well as Bulgaria, Germany, Italy, Slovenia, the Netherlands, Sweden and Finland.

[84] Survey of OSCE Long-Term Missions and other OSCE Field Activities, SEC.INF/115/04, Vienna, 2 June 2004, p. 62.

[85] The collapse of the Soviet Union and its sphere of influence added seventeen new Member States to the Council of Europe.

new role of the Council of Europe includes assistance to post-Communist democracies with political, legal and economic reforms. Moreover, as the Council of Europe's achievements, especially in the field of the protection of human rights, are incomparable to those of any other organisation, the fulfilment of the organisation's requirements has a strong influence on the members' relations with other institutions of international relations, for example, the European Union.[86]

In the case of the South Caucasian countries, the process of gaining membership was a lengthy one. Georgia acquired member status in April 1999, while Armenia and Azerbaijan joined in January 2001. The organisation's assistance has a sustained character, which has enabled it to monitor (e.g., through election monitoring missions) and assist with the further reforms in the South Caucasian countries. The cooperation programmes are devoted to helping the new members with their institutional, legislative and administrative reforms, as well as the establishment of an independent media.

Alongside individual programmes, the Council of Europe also has close relations with other organisations that are active in the region. Examples of this include the cooperation between the Council of Europe's Venice Commission and the OSCE's Office for Democratic Institutions and Human Rights (ODIHR) on the revision of Armenia's electoral legislation, in the framework of which they issue joint recommendations.[87]

1.4.6.4 NATO

As the political map of Europe changed dramatically and new security threats started to emerge, the Alliance commenced the process of adapting to the new security requirements. The Rome Declaration on Peace and Cooperation issued by the Heads of State and Government participating in the meeting of the North Atlantic Council (Rome, 8 November 1991) laid the foundations for the institutionalisation of the relations between NATO and Central and Eastern European countries (former Warsaw Pact members).[88] In 1991, the North Atlantic Cooperation Council (NACC) held its inaugural meeting and became a consultation forum. In response to the events resulting from the dissolution of the Soviet Union, all members of the CIS were invited to join the NACC in 1992. The further development of relations took place in the deteriorating context of regional conflicts and the crisis in the former Yugoslavia.

---

[86] M. Rantala, 'The Council of Europe', in A. Ott and K. Inglis, eds., *Handbook on European Enlargement. A Commentary on the Enlargement Process* (The Hague, T.M.C. Asser Press 2002) pp. 72-74.

[87] For more information, see: <http://venice.coe.int>.

[88] Declaration on Peace and Cooperation, Rome, 8 November 1991, available at: <http://www.nato.int/docu/comm/49-95/c911108a.htm>.

In 1997, the Euro-Atlantic Partnership Council (EAPC) was established as the successor of the NACC. It is a forum for consultation and political negotiations on aspects of cooperation between NATO members and partners (among them Armenia, Azerbaijan and Georgia). The meetings are conducted at the level of ambassadors[89] (once a month) and at the level of foreign and defence ministers (once a year). The EAPC complements the Partnership for Peace.

The Partnership for Peace (PfP) created the framework for involving non-NATO members in the process of building European security.[90] It enables defence cooperation and contributes to a reduction in the risk of conflict. Efforts are concentrated on developing the capabilities of the partner countries for joint operations with NATO forces. The South Caucasian countries became members of the PfP in 1994.[91] Special recognition of the region was granted by the North Atlantic Council in 2004.[92] During the process of the implementation of this decision, NATO's Deputy Assistant Secretary General for Security Cooperation and Partnership was handed the responsibility of Special Representative for the Caucasus and Central Asia.[93] His duties include making contacts with senior officials in the Southern Caucasus (and Central Asia) to support the best use of partnership measures.

Broadly speaking, NATO serves as a forum to consult on security concerns. Its knowledge and expertise in the defence field enables the Alliance to assist partner countries in their efforts to reform and adapt their armed forces. NATO aims for the interoperability of the partner countries' armed forces, which allows them to take part in NATO missions.

---

89 All three countries of the Southern Caucasus have diplomatic missions accredited to NATO.

90 Partnership for Peace: Framework Document, North Atlantic Cooperation Council, Brussels, 10-11 January 1994.

91 Armenia signed the PfP Framework Document on 5 October 1994, Azerbaijan on 4 May 1994 and Georgia on 23 March 1994.

92 'In enhancing the Euro-Atlantic Partnership, we will put special focus on engaging with our Partners in the strategically important regions of the Caucasus and Central Asia. Towards that end, NATO has agreed on improved liaison arrangements, including the assignment of two liaison officers, as well as a special representative for the two regions from within the International Staff. We welcome the decision by Georgia, Azerbaijan and Uzbekistan to develop Individual Partnership Action Plans with NATO. This constitutes a significant step in these countries' efforts to develop closer Partnership relations with the Alliance. We welcome the commitment of the new government of Georgia to reform.' Istanbul Summit Communiqué, 28 June 2004.

93 The Special Representative operates from the HQ in Brussels and plans to make three to four trips a year to the capitals of the partner countries.

2. LEGAL FOUNDATIONS OF THE EU-SOUTHERN CAUCASUS PARTNERSHIPS

2.1 Partnership and Cooperation Agreements

In response to the dissolution of the Soviet Union, the European Union formulated a new type of external agreement that provided a legal basis for cooperation with the NIS – the Partnership and Cooperation Agreements (PCAs)[94] between the European Communities and the Member States, on the one hand, and Armenia,[95] Azerbaijan[96] and Georgia,[97] on the other, were signed in 1996. They entered into force on 1 July 1999.[98] In 2004, the protocols[99] extending the agreements to the new EU Member States were signed. As a new generation of bilateral agreements, the PCAs created the framework for EU relations with the South Caucasian countries.[100] The objectives of the partnership are laid down in common Article 1 of the PCAs:

---

94 On PCAs with Central Asian countries, see B. Berdiyev, 'The EU and Former Soviet Central Asia: An Analysis of the Partnership and Cooperation Agreements', 22 *YEL* (2003) pp. 463-481.

95 Partnership and Cooperation Agreement between the European Communities and their Member States, of the one part, and the Republic of Armenia, of the other, *OJ* 1999 L 239/3.

96 Partnership and Cooperation Agreement between the European Communities and their Member States, of the one part, and the Republic of Azerbaijan, of the other, *OJ* 1999 L 246/3.

97 Partnership and Cooperation Agreement between the European Communities and their Member States, of the one part, and the Republic of Georgia, of the other, *OJ* 1999 L 205/3.

98 As stated in Art. 94 PCA Armenia and Art. 97 PCA Azerbaijan and PCA Georgia, the agreements are concluded for ten years with the possibility of prolongation on a year by year basis.

99 Protocol to the Partnership and Cooperation Agreement between the European Communities and their Member States, of the one part, and the Republic of Armenia, of the other part, to take account of the accession of the Czech Republic, the Republic of Estonia, the Republic of Cyprus, the Republic of Latvia, the Republic of Lithuania, the Republic of Hungary, the Republic of Malta, the Republic of Poland, the Republic of Slovenia and the Slovak Republic to the European Union, *OJ* 2004 L 300/44; Protocol to the Partnership and Cooperation Agreement between the European Communities and their Member States, of the one part, and the Republic of Azerbaijan, of the other part, to take account of the accession of the Czech Republic, the Republic of Estonia, the Republic of Cyprus, the Republic of Latvia, the Republic of Lithuania, the Republic of Hungary, the Republic of Malta, the Republic of Poland, the Republic of Slovenia and the Slovak Republic to the European Union, COM (2004) 267 final; Protocol to the Partnership and Cooperation Agreement between the European Communities and their Member States, of the one part, and the Republic of Georgia, of the other part, to take account of the accession of the Czech Republic, the Republic of Estonia, the Republic of Cyprus, the Republic of Latvia, the Republic of Lithuania, the Republic of Hungary, the Republic of Malta, the Republic of Poland, the Republic of Slovenia and the Slovak Republic to the European Union, COM (2004) 268 final.

100 Due to their contents, the PCAs have been concluded on a combination of legal bases, including Art. 44(2), the last sentence of Art. 47(2), Arts. 55, 57(2), 71, 80(2), 93, 94, 133, 308 TEC, in conjunction with second sentence of Art. 300(2) as well as the second subparagraph of Art. 300(3) TEC. Additional legal bases include Art. 95 ECSC and Art. 101 Euratom. The PCAs are mixed agreements with the EC and its Member States on one side and the three South Caucasian countries on the other.

- to provide an appropriate framework for the political dialogue between the Parties allowing them the development of political relations;
- to support [the South Caucasian states'] efforts to consolidate [their] democrac[ies] and to develop [their] econom[ies] and to complete the transition into market econom[ies];
- to promote trade and investment and harmonious economic relations between the Parties and to foster their sustainable development;
- to provide basis for legislative, economic, social, financial, civil scientific, technological and cultural cooperation.

2.1.1 *Selected elements of the PCAs*

The PCAs are based on the common values shared by the parties, which are referred to at the beginning of the preamble and then laid down in detail in Title I. These general principles include respect for democracy, principles of international law, human rights and market economy rules.

As stated in Article 3 of the PCAs, cooperation between the South Caucasian countries is regarded as essential for their future prosperity and stability. The main aim of the PCAs is to assist them in their efforts towards establishing strong ties with the European structures. There is clarity in the message that this can only be achieved if the condition of the peaceful resolution of regional conflicts is met.

The PCAs offer a platform for potentially wide-ranging political, economic and cultural cooperation.[101] All three agreements cover political dialogue (Arts. 5-8), trade in goods (Arts. 9-19) and provisions on business and investment, including labour conditions,[102] supply of services, current payments and capital, intellectual property and legislative and economic cooperation (Arts. 20-67 PCA Armenia and Arts. 20-70 PCA Azerbaijan and PCA Georgia). Separate titles are devoted to cooperation in the field of democracy and human rights (Art. 68 PCA Armenia and Art. 71 PCA Azerbaijan and PCA Georgia), as well as to the prevention of illegal activities and immigration (Arts. 69-72 PCA Armenia and Arts. 72-75 PCA Azerbaijan and PCA Georgia). The PCAs also cover cultural cooperation (Art. 73 PCA Armenia and Art. 76 PCA Azerbaijan and PCA Georgia) and financial cooperation in the field of technical assistance (Arts. 74-77 PCA Armenia and Arts. 77-80 PCA Azerbaijan and PCA Georgia).

---

101 PCAs do not cover defence issues.

102 The obligation of non-discrimination in the work place is drafted differently in the PCA Russia and contains only a best endeavours clause. It justifies the argument that the potential effects of the ECJ's judgment in Case C-265/03 *Igor Simutenkov* v. *Ministerio de Educación y Cultura, Real Federación Española de Fútbol* will be limited. See chapter 14 on Russia in this volume.

Unlike the Europe Agreements, the PCAs concluded with the South Caucasian countries do not envisage the creation of a free trade area between the parties. Common Article 9 states that the parties shall accord to one another most-favoured-nation treatment in all areas in respect of:

- customs duties and charges applied to imports and exports, including the method of collecting such duties and charges,
- provisions relating to customs clearance, transit, warehouses and trans-shipment,
- taxes and other internal charges of any kind applied directly or indirectly to imported goods,
- methods of payment and the transfer of such payments,
- the rules relating to the sale, purchase, transport, distribution and use of goods on the domestic market.

The import of goods originating from the South Caucasian countries shall be free of quantitative restrictions, while goods originating from the European Union imported into those countries must be free of both quantitative restrictions and measures having an equivalent effect. It is worth noting that the PCAs do not apply to trade in textiles, which is governed by a separate regime.[103] Finally, Georgia is covered by the tariff preferences established under Council Regulation 980/2005/EC.[104]

In accordance with the provisions of common Article 43 of the PCAs, the South Caucasian countries have committed themselves to endeavour to approximate their legislation to EC law.[105] The approximation process covers laws and regulations governing investments by companies; customs law; company law; banking law; company accounts and taxes; intellectual property; protection of workers in the workplace; financial services; competition; public procurement; protection of the health and life of humans, animals and plants; the environment; consumer protection; indirect taxation; technical rules and standards; nuclear laws and regulations; and transport.

---

103 Agreement between the European Economic Community and the Republic of Georgia on trade in textile products, *OJ* 1994 L 123/250 (as amended and extended by subsequent agreements); Agreement between the European Economic Community and the Republic of Azerbaijan on trade in textile products, *OJ* 1994 L 123/92 (as amended and extended by subsequent agreements); Agreement between the European Economic Community and the Republic of Armenia on trade in textile products, *OJ* 1994 L 123/64 (as amended and extended by subsequent agreements).

104 Council Regulation (EC) No. 980/2005 of 27 June 2005 applying a scheme of generalised tariff preferences, *OJ* 2005 L 169/1.

105 Like in the case of the Europe Agreements, it can be argued that this is a matter of 'voluntary harmonisation'. See A. Evans, 'Voluntary Harmonisation in Integration between the European Community and Eastern Europe', 22 *ELRev.* (1997) p. 201. See also A. Łazowski, 'Approximation of law', in Ott and Inglis, op. cit. n. 86, at pp. 631-639.

Article 95(1) PCA Armenia and Article 98(1) PCA Azerbaijan and PCA Georgia state the obligation of parties to take all measures necessary to fulfil their obligations under the agreements.

2.2 Institutional framework for EU-Southern Caucasus relations

The bilateral relations between the European Union and the South Caucasian countries are conducted mainly within the framework of the PCAs. Unlike the relations with Ukraine and Russia, there is no tradition of bilateral summits. The agreements lay the foundations for establishing a regular political dialogue (Title II of the agreements). The institutional structure offered by the three PCAs is fairly standard and includes Cooperation Councils, Cooperation Committees and Parliamentary Cooperation Committees (Title XI PCA Armenia and PCA Azerbaijan and Title IX PCA Georgia).[106] The agreements offer the possibility of extending the institutional framework if this is required in the framework of the progress in the implementation of the agreements.

Cooperation Councils[107] meet at least once a year and are composed of members of the Council of Ministers, members of the European Commission and members of the Governments of Armenia, Azerbaijan or Georgia. They guard the implementation of the agreements. Their other powers include the discussion of any subject of common interest, dispute settlement, reviewing major issues arising from the agreements and making recommendations. The Cooperation Councils adopt their own rules of procedures.[108]

The composition of the Cooperation Committees[109] is the same as that of the Cooperation Councils but at the senior civil servant level. The duties of the Committees are laid down by the Cooperation Councils and include, *inter alia*, the preparation of Cooperation Council meetings. It is also the Councils that decide on the organisation of the Committees' activities. If necessary, sub-committees may be established.

Parliamentary Cooperation Committees[110] were established within the framework of the PCAs to lay the foundations for cooperation between the European

---

106 Since 1999, there have been six meetings of the Cooperation Councils and six meetings of the Parliamentary Cooperation Committees.

107 Arts. 78-82 PCA Armenia and Arts. 81-85 PCA Azerbaijan and PCA Georgia.

108 Rules of procedure of the Cooperation Council between the European Communities and their Member States, of the one part, and the Republic of Armenia, of the other part, of 12 October 1999 – Rules of procedure of the Cooperation Committee, *OJ* 1999 L 297/24; Rules of procedure of the Cooperation Council between the European Communities and their Member States, of the one part, and the Republic of Azerbaijan, of the other part, of 12 October 1999 – Rules of procedure of the Cooperation Committee, *OJ* 1999 L 297/29; Rules of procedure of the Cooperation Council between the European Communities and their Member States, of the one part, and Georgia, of the other part, of 12 October 1999 – Rules of procedure of the Cooperation Committee, *OJ* 1999 L 297/34.

109 Art. 80 PCA Armenia and Art. 83 PCA Azerbaijan and PCA Georgia.

110 Arts. 83-85 PCA Armenia and Arts. 86-88 PCA Azerbaijan and PCA Georgia.

Parliament and the national parliaments of the South Caucasian countries.[111] There is a separate Parliamentary Cooperation Committee for each of the three South Caucasian countries. The representation of the European Parliament on the Parliamentary Cooperation Committees is composed of members of the delegation to the Southern Caucasus. The Committees provide a forum for debate and permit parliamentary oversight over the implementation of the agreements. They have the right to receive information from the Cooperation Councils and the Cooperation Committees. They can submit recommendations to the Cooperation Councils. The European Parliament pays attention to developments in the region. This is reflected in the resolutions it has adopted on this issue. It should be stressed that the European Parliament often voices a forward-looking approach to relations with the region.[112]

3. FINANCIAL AND TECHNICAL ASSISTANCE

It should be stressed that the economic and financial assistance to the South Caucasian countries commenced in 1991, in other words from an early stage of the transition process. EU resources are used for a wide spectrum of issues, from developing and strengthening democracy, the rule of law and respect of human rights to establishing a functioning market economy.

Tacis is the main instrument for assisting the South Caucasian countries in the implementation process of the PCAs.[113]

Tacis assistance granted to Armenia,[114] Azerbaijan and Georgia comes from EU resources as well as from international donor organisations. Its action programmes concentrate on the following:

---

[111] Before the entry into force of the PCAs, parliamentary relations were conducted until 1994 by the EP Delegation for relations with the Republics of the Commonwealth of Independent States and during the 1994-1999 period by the EP Delegation for relations with the South Caucasian Republics.

[112] As an example, one can point to the fact that it has been the European Parliament that has advocated a better position for the South Caucasian countries within the foreign policy of the European Union. In a report adopted on 5 November 2003, it strongly argued the case of the South Caucasian countries: 'The southern Caucasus has been left outside the WE-NNI by the Commission. This should be changed, and the strategy should be extended to Georgia, Armenia and Azerbaijan. The three countries are members of the Council of Europe and the OSCE. Conflict prevention needs to give the EU every reason to enhance its role in the region.' P. Napoletano, Report on 'Wider Europe-Neighbourhood: A Framework for Relations with our Eastern and Southern Neighbours', COM (2003) 104-2003/2018(INI) p. 17.

[113] Council Regulation (EC, Euratom) No. 99/2000 of 29 December 1999 concerning the provision of assistance to the Partner states in Eastern Europe and Central Asia, *OJ* 2000 L 12/1.

[114] The biggest contributor is USAID, with a main focus on employment creation. Armenia has also received considerable international support in various forms from the Armenian Diaspora.

- support for institutional, legal and administrative reform (support for the Armenian-European Policy and Legal Advice Centre (AEPLAC) which strengthens the effectiveness of the implementation of Armenia's international obligations; support for the National Assembly of the Republic of Armenia to support effective management of the legislative process; the Georgian-European Policy and Legal Advice Centre (GEPLAC));
- support for the private sector and assistance for economic development (establishment of credit guarantee funds for small enterprises);
- the development of infrastructure networks (in Armenia special attention is given to the energy sector and the development of alternative sources of energy to the Metsamor nuclear power plant).

The European Union is also very interested in the resolution of internal conflicts, which is a vital condition of sustainable economic and social development.[115] Under the PCAs, Tacis assistance is also granted in the field of small-scale rehabilitation projects in South Ossetia and Azerbaijani regions liberated from Armenian occupation, such as the restoration of a hydroelectric plant in Inguri (close to Abkhazia). As the conflicts remain unresolved, assistance through other channels, such as TEMPUS, TRACECA (Transport Corridor Europe-Caucasus-Asia) and INOGATE (Interstate Oil and Gas Transport to Europe), is losing the momentum.

As the political changes in Georgia were welcomed by the international community, support was also expressed through an understanding of the financial needs of the country. In June 2004, the international donors of thirty-one countries and twelve international organisations met at the Joint European Commission and World Bank Conference to coordinate the financial support to Georgia for the 2004-2006 period. It was decided to provide Georgia with €850 million to support urgent budgetary and investment needs.[116]

Since 1991, the European Union has provided a total of over €1 billion in aid to Armenia, Azerbaijan and Georgia from Community funds, with a comparable amount of assistance granted by the individual EU Member States. The assistance in 2005-2006 will continue to be distributed through Tacis. A new framework of assistance under the ENP will be introduced in 2007. Although the amount of resources flowing to the Southern Caucasus is high, the outcome is often seen as far from satisfactory.[117]

---

115 Country Strategy Paper 2003-2006, Tacis National Indicative Programme 2004-2006, Georgia, Brussels, 2003, p. 4.

116 European Commission, World Bank Press Release, 16 June 2004.

117 B. Coppieters, 'An EU Representative to a new periphery', in Baev and Lynch, op. cit. n. 42, at p. 161.

Table 1: Total EC grants to Armenia since 1991 (in € millions)

	1991-1993	1994	1995	1996	1997	1998	1999	2000	2001	2002-2003	2004-2006	Total
Tacis national allocations	28.90	-	6.00	14.00	-	10.00	-	10.00	-	10.00	20.00	98.90
Nuclear safety	-	-	-	10.00	1.00	-	-	11.00	-	-	7.00	29.00
Humanitarian	10.40	19.90	23.96	4.97	1.96	1.60	2.30	1.10	2.10	0.5	-	68.79
EAGGF	-	-	34.00	13.20	-	-	-	3.00	-	-	-	50.20
FSP	-	-	-	13.00	6.00	12.00	10.00	10.00	10.00	20.30	21.00	102.30
Macro financial assistance	-	5.70	-	-	-	8.00	4.00	-	-	11.00	7.00	35.70
Aid against effects of Russian financial crisis	-	-	-	-	-	-	1.50	-	-	-	-	1.50
Total	38.30	25.60	63.96	55.17	8.96	31.60	17.80	35.10	12.10	41.80	55.00	386.39

Source: Commission Staff Working Paper, Annex to European Neighbourhood Policy Country Report Armenia, COM (2005) 72 final, p. 7.

Table 2: Total EC grants to Azerbaijan since 1992 (in € millions)

	1992-1994	1995	1996	1997	1998	1999	2000	2001	2002-2003	2004-2006	Total
Tacis national allocations	20.50	6.00	8.00	8.00	8.00	8.00	7.00	7.00	14.00	30.00	116.50
Exceptional macro financial assistance	-	-	-	-	10.00	10.00	10.00	-	-	-	30.00
Humanitarian	31.10	-	-	28.82	9.69	6.10	9.66	5.15	1.57	-	92.09
FEOGA	-	43.00	22.70	-	-	-	-	-	-	-	65.70
Food security	-	-	15.00	16.00	14.00	12.00	-	-	20.00	-	77.00
Rehabilitation	-	-	3.00	4.00	4.50	3.20	3.67	-	-	-	18.37
Exceptional humanitarian aid	-	8.00	-	-	-	-	-	1.50	-	-	9.50
Total	51.60	57.00	48.70	56.82	46.19	39.30	30.33	13.65	35.37	30.00	409.16

Source: Commission Staff Working Paper, Annex to European Neighbourhood Policy Country Report Azerbaijan, COM (2005) 72 final, p. 5.

Table 3: Total EC grants to Georgia in 1992-2004 (in € millions)

	1992	1993	1994	1995	1996	1997	1998	1999	2000	2001	2002	2003	2004	Total
Humanitarian aid	-	11.78	17.81	27.45	10.20	5.80	6.41	6.93	2.62	1.05	2.00	2.20	4.00	98.25
EAGGF	-	-	-	41.00	21.55	-	-	-	-	-	-	-	-	62.55
Exceptional humanitarian aid	-	6.00	-	-	-	-	-	-	-	-	-	-	-	6.00
Aid against effects of Russian financial crisis	-	-	-	-	-	-	-	4.00	-	-	-	-	-	4.00
Food security programme	-	-	-	-	18.25	16.00	-	12.00	-	-	-	13.00*	12.00*	71.25
Tacis national allocations	9.00	4.00	4.00	6.00	8.00	8.00	8.00	8.00	11.00	4.00	14.00*	-	27.00**	111.00
Rehabilitation in conflict zones	-	-	-	-	-	3.50	6.50	7.50	-	-	-	-	2.00	19.50
Macro financial assistance (disbursed)	-	-	-	-	-	-	10.00	9.00	-	6.00	-	-	6.50	31.50
CFSP***	-	-	-	-	-	-	-	-	1.09	0.25	0.10	0.16	-	1.60
EIDHR	-	-	-	-	-	-	-	-	-	0.23	2.50	2.82	2.00	7.55
RRM	-	-	-	-	-	-	-	-	-	-	-	2.00	4.65	6.65
Total	9.00	21.78	21.81	74.45	58.00	33.30	30.91	47.43	14.71	11.53	18.60	20.18	58.15	419.85

Source: Commission Staff Working Paper, Annex to European Neighbourhood Policy Country Report Georgia, COM (2005) 72 final, p. 7.

* Disbursed

** Two-year allocations

*** The CFSP budget is also used to finance the activities of the EU Special Representative for the Southern Caucasus and the rule of law mission in Georgia (EUJUST THEMIS).

4. MEASURES WITHIN THE FRAMEWORK OF THE CFSP

4.1 EU support for border control

4.1.1 *Georgian border with Chechnya and Ingushetia*

The European Union took measures to prevent the spill-over of the Chechen conflict into Georgia. Under Joint Action 2000/456/CFSP,[118] it provided assistance to the Georgian authorities to support the OSCE Observer Mission on the Georgian-Chechen border during the second half of 2000. This assistance, valued at €1 million, was provided in the form of equipment for the Georgian border guards. The Commission guarded the implementation of the Joint Action as well as the effectiveness of the delivery.

Based on the assessment mission of the relevant EU experts and the OSCE decision to expand the OSCE Mission to Georgia, the Council adopted Joint Action 2002/373/CFSP[119] to assist the Georgian authorities in support of the OSCE Observer Mission on the Georgian-Ingush border as well as to continue its assistance in relation to the Georgian-Chechen border.

4.1.2 *Georgian border with South Ossetia*

Following the declaration regarding its willingness to play a more active role in the Southern Caucasus (February 2001), the European Union joined the OSCE mechanisms for the settlement of the Ossetian conflict. Council Joint Action 2001/759/CFSP[120] laid down the European Union's commitment to participate in covering the costs of the meetings of the bodies entrusted with the settlement of the conflict, namely, the Joint Control Commission and the Experts' Group. The Commission's Delegation in Tbilisi liaises with the OSCE to monitor and evaluate the progress of the mission.

4.2 The EU Special Representative for the Southern Caucasus

The first proposal for appointing an EU Special Representative for the Southern Caucasus occurred in 2001, when Germany voiced such proposal. However, it

---

[118] *OJ* 2000 L 183/3, as amended on 26 July 2001, *OJ* 2001 L 202/2.

[119] Council Joint Action 2002/323/CFSP of 21 May 2002 regarding a contribution of the European Union towards reinforcing the capacity of the Georgian authorities to support and protect the OSCE observer mission on the border of Georgia with the Ingush and Chechen Republics of the Russian Federation, *OJ* 2002 L 134/1.

[120] Council Joint Action 2001/759/CFSP of 29 October 2001 regarding a contribution from the European Union to the conflict settlement process in South Ossetia, *OJ* 2001 L 286/4; Council Joint Action 2003/473/CFSP of 25 June 2003 regarding a contribution of the European Union to the conflict settlement process in Georgia/South Ossetia, *OJ* 2003 L 157/72.

was Greece that took a firm step towards the creation of such a post during its EU Presidency (in the first half of 2003). On 7 July 2003, the Council adopted Joint Action 2003/496/CFSP, appointing Heikki Talvitie (Finland) as EU Special Representative for the Southern Caucasus. His mandate was extended in July 2005 until 28 February 2006.[121] He supports the High Representative's work in the region through his duties contributing to the implementation of the policy objectives of the European Union in the Southern Caucasus:

- assistance to the South Caucasian countries in leading political and economic reforms (with a special emphasis on the rule of law, democratisation, human rights, good governance, development and poverty reduction);
- conflict prevention in the region, assistance with conflict resolution and promotion of the return of refugees and internally displaced persons;
- cooperation with the main national actors in the region;
- encouraging cooperation between the South Caucasian countries;
- enhancing the European Union's presence in the region.

The appointment of the Special Representative for the Southern Caucasus is part of a wider process of adapting the CFSP to new needs.[122] However, the mandate of the Special Representative should be wider, while greater clarity in the division of duties with other EU bodies would make his role more efficient.[123] There are critical opinions that the Special Representative's involvement in conflict resolution is limited.[124] However, as the creation of the position came at a time when there were already numerous actors involved in the region, the implementation of the Special Representative's mandate started with the provision of assistance to other international bodies.[125] Such a starting point provides limited scope for effective conflict resolution.

4.3 The EU Rule of Law Mission in Georgia, EUJUST THEMIS

The EU Rule of Law Mission in Georgia was the first rule of law mission launched in the ESDP context, established for the purpose of providing 'support

[121] Council Joint Action 2003/496/CFSP of 7 July 2003 concerning the appointment of an EU Special Representative for the South Caucasus, *OJ* 2003 L 169/74. Extensions and amendments of the mandate took place with the adoption of Council Joint Action 2003/872/CFSP of 8 December 2003, *OJ* 2003 L 326/44; Council Joint Action 2004/532/CFSP of 28 June 2004, *OJ* 2004 L 234/16; Council Joint Action 2005/100/CFSP of 2 February 2005, *OJ* 2005 L 31/74; and Council Joint Action 2005/582/CFSP of 28 July 2005, *OJ* 2005 L 199/92.

[122] See chapter 1 in this volume.

[123] S. Cornell, 'Europe and the Caucasus: in search of a purpose', available at: <http://www.cacianalyst.org>.

[124] *European Voice*, 19-26 May 2004.

[125] See: <http://www.eurasianet.org>.

to the Georgian authority in addressing urgent challenges in the criminal justice system'.[126] It was the Georgian Prime Minister, Zurab Zhvania, who invited the European Union to deploy this mission. The European Union expressed its will to assist Georgia in its efforts to introduce international rule of law standards into the local framework.[127] It reacted very quickly to the request for assistance: on 6 April 2004, the President of Georgia expressed the wish to receive support in the area of the rule of law, on 3 June 2004, the Prime Minister sent a letter with such request to the European Union, and on 28 June 2004 the Council adopted Joint Action 2004/523/CFSP[128] on the European Union Rule of Law Mission in Georgia, EUJUST THEMIS.

The scope of the mission's activities were laid down in Article 2 of the Joint Action. It was obliged to work in coordination with EC programmes as well as other donors' programmes dedicated to the development of the reform process within criminal justice system. Based on Art. 2(2) of the Joint Action, the main activities of the mission were to:

- Provide urgent guidance for the new criminal justice reform strategy;
- Support the overall coordinating role of the relevant Georgian authorities in the field of judicial reform and anti-corruption;
- Support the planning for new legislation as necessary, e.g., Criminal Procedure Code;

  secondarily:
- Support the development of international as well as regional cooperation in the area of criminal justice.

The mission was established for a period of twelve months (as stated in Art. 13 of the Joint Action with a budget of €2,050,000. The Head of Mission led EUJUST THEMIS and was responsible for the management of the mission. Sylvia Pantz (France) was appointed as Head of Mission on 30 June 2004.[129] There was a direct link between the mission and the EU Special Representative for the Southern Caucasus, who gave guidance to the Secretary General/High Representative and to the Head of Mission and was also a recipient of the Head of Mission's reports to the Secretary General/High Representative.[130]

---

126 Press Release, 2591st Council Meeting (GAERC), 14 June 2004, 10191/04 (Presse 196) p. 2; *Bull. EU* 6-2004.

127 See: <http://www.ceis.ge/publi0107.html>.

128 *OJ* 2004 L 228/21.

129 Political and Security Committee Decision THEMIS/1/2004 of 30 June 2004 concerning the appointment of the Head of Mission of the EU Rule of Law Mission in Georgia, in the context of ESDP, EUJUST THEMIS (2004/540/CFSP), *OJ* 2004 L 239/35.

130 Art. 8 of the Joint Action.

The mission was launched on 16 July 2004. The personnel of the mission were composed of experts seconded by the EU Member States and EU institutions.[131] The mission achieved its main aims and completed its tasks on 14 July 2005.

EUJUST THEMIS was the very first rule of law mission launched under the ESDP and, as such, is seen as a proof of the development of the civilian aspects of the ESDP. It may also be stressed that it is a way of executing the European Council decision on establishing EU missions to strengthen the rule of law.[132]

5. THE EUROPEAN NEIGHBOURHOOD POLICY (ENP)

The development of EU policy towards the Southern Caucasus was signalled right after the EU Troika visited the region, with the statement that 'the EU is willing to play a more active role in the region'.[133] However, this statement did not produce any instant and new measures for EU relations with Armenia, Azerbaijan and Georgia. For the first results, the region had to wait until 2003.

On 11 March 2003, a Communication from the Commission to the Council and the European Parliament, entitled 'Wider Europe-Neighbourhood: A New Framework for Relations with our Eastern and Southern Neighbours',[134] was released. This document is seen as a development which was necessary for the European Union to settle into its full-scale international role. It was supposed to work as a proof of EU interests, but without giving the countries EU membership as a short-term perspective.[135] However, the Southern Caucasus was only mentioned in a footnote of the document.[136] The absence of the three countries of the Southern Caucasus from the list of countries involved in the European Neighbourhood Policy (in March 2003) proved that the European Union was missing an in-depth strategy towards the region. The exclusion of the Southern Caucasus from the circle of the European Union's neighbours[137] was seen as even more wasteful given the level of aid and assistance provided to the region by the European Union and its Member States. The absence of the Southern Caucasus from the list was also seen as a result of the lack of an EU Member State that would strongly advocate the Caucasian case.[138] Although certain EU countries

---

131 See: <http://ue.eu.int/uedocs/cmsUpload/Factsheet%20THEMIS%20041026.pdf>.

132 Presidency Conclusions, Santa Maria Da Feira European Council, 19-20 June 2000, available at: <http://ue.eu.int/ueDocs/cms_Data/docs/pressData/en/ec/00200-r1.en0.htm>.

133 2331st Council Meeting (GAERC), Brussels, 26 February 2001.

134 COM (2003) 104 final, Brussels, 11 March 2003.

135 Lynch, loc. cit. n. 62, at p. 174.

136 Ibid., at p. 171.

137 As stated in footnote 4 of the document: 'Given the location, the South Caucasus therefore also falls outside the geographical scope of this initiative for the time being.'

138 Cornell, loc. cit. n. 123.

were indeed paying interest to the region – Finland, Sweden and Greece made the Southern Caucasus one of priorities of their Presidency agendas – EU policy towards the region still lacked coherence.

The first radical improvement came with the European Security Strategy adopted by the European Council in December 2003.

> It is not in our interest that enlargement should create new dividing lines in Europe. We need to extend the benefits of economic and political cooperation to our neighbours in the East while tackling political problems there. We should take a stronger and more active interest in the problems of the Southern Caucasus, which will in due course also be a neighbouring region.[139]

The idea, which started to take shape in 2003, is aimed at creating a circle of countries around the European Union that obtain a stake in the internal market: 'something more than association, but less than membership – everything but institutions'.[140]

The initial version of ENP showed the European Union's lack of consistence and coherency. This omission was noticed and the conclusion was drawn that the European Union should find a way to acknowledge the region's importance and position. A Special Representative for the Southern Caucasus was therefore appointed in July 2003. However, the fact remains that the European Union's aspirations to become an international actor require a well-structured policy with a long-term vision.

On 14 June 2004, the Council (GAERC) adopted a decision in Luxembourg to include the three countries of the Southern Caucasus in the European Union's European Neighbourhood Initiative.[141] This was followed by the visit of Commissioner Janez Potočnik to the South Caucasian countries.[142] During his talks in the

139 A Secure Europe in a Better World – European Security Strategy, Brussels, 12 December 2003, p. 13.

140 *EUobserver*, 26 January 2004.

141 'Concerning the Southern Caucasus, the Council recalled its conclusions of 16 June 2003 and of 26 January 2004 and its continuing interest in promoting stability, democracy and prosperity in this region. The Council noted the recommendations of the European Parliament, the Commission, SG/HR and the EU Special Representative for the Southern Caucasus and decided to include Armenia, Azerbaijan and Georgia in the European Neighbourhood Policy. This marks a significant step forward in the Union's engagement with this region. Each country will be given the same possibility to develop its links with the EU, including through action plans, and will be treated on its individual merits in line with the general policy of the European Neighbourhood Policy. The Council also invited the Commission, and the SG/HR for issues related to political cooperation and the CFSP, to report on progress made by each country with regard to political and economic reforms.' 2590th Council Meeting, Luxembourg, 14 June 2004, 10189/04 (Presse 195) p. 13.

142 Georgia, 5-6 July 2004; Azerbaijan, 6-7 July 2004; Armenia, 7-8 July 2004; IP/04/848, Brussels, 5 July 2004.

three capitals, he stressed the importance of the ENP as a tool to promote reform. The step of including the South Caucasian countries in the ENP provides a framework for preparing actions plans for each country. On 2 March 2005, as it published the relevant country reports, European Commission recommended the intensification of relations with Armenia, Azerbaijan and Georgia.[143]

In setting the recommendations[144] for the action plans for the South Caucasian countries, the difficulties of the humanitarian situation resulting from the collapse of the Soviet Union were stressed as a factor that makes the countries' efforts towards building a democratic and stable statehood a difficult task. The objectives for the Action Plan for Armenia include:

- strengthening the rule of law, including the reform of electoral law;
- strengthening respect for human rights;
- effective combating of corruption;
- reform of tax and customs legislation and administration;
- decommissioning of the Metsamor nuclear power plant;
- further support for the economic rehabilitation of conflict zones.[145]

The objectives for the Action Plan for Azerbaijan include:

- strengthening the rule of law, including democratic structures and pluralism;
- enhanced protection of human rights;
- improvement of the business climate;
- reform of tax and customs legislation and administration;
- WTO accession;
- combating of corruption;
- further support for the economic rehabilitation of conflict zones.[146]

The objectives for the Action Plan for Georgia include:

- strengthening respect for the rule of law, including reform of the judiciary and public services;
- strengthening democratic checks and balances, in line with obligations of OSCE and Council of Europe membership;

---

143 Commission Staff Working Paper, Annex to European Neighbourhood Policy, Country Report Armenia, SEC (2005) 285; Commission Staff Working Paper, Annex to European Neighbourhood Policy, Country Report Azerbaijan, SEC (2005) 286; Commission Staff Working Paper, Annex to European Neighbourhood Policy, Country Report Georgia, SEC (2005) 287.

144 European Neighbourhood Policy Recommendations for Armenia, Azerbaijan, Georgia and for Egypt and Lebanon, COM (2005) 72 final.

145 Ibid., at p. 3.

146 Ibid., at p. 4.

- effective combating of corruption;
- further improvement of the investment climate.[147]

The Commission recommended the action plans as a useful means of strengthening relations with Armenia, Azerbaijan and Georgia, and consultations on those documents should therefore start as soon as possible.[148] It is now up to the Council to decide on the development of action plans for the South Caucasian countries under the ENP.

The preparation of action plans proves that the South Caucasian countries still face challenges while establishing a framework for stability and require persistent and well-coordinated assistance.

6. CONCLUDING REMARKS

Due to the complexity of the situation, the European Union's presence in the region requires strategic planning carefully drafted on the basis of in-depth knowledge and understanding of the region. It is in the best interests of the European Union and its Member States that the process of transition towards democracy, the rule of law and a functioning market economy will be successfully completed by the three South Caucasian countries. The Southern Caucasus is an important part of the energy supply scheme for the European Union. The economies and energy supply of the South Caucasian countries depend directly on conflict prevention and conflict resolution. It is therefore also in the European Union's best interests to make efforts towards peace and reconciliation in the region. Conflict resolution would allow all the interested parties to make full use of the profits of energy resources and their transport.

The European Union has a unique chance to become a major player in the Southern Caucasus. However, success requires an articulate and complex long-term policy towards the region. The European Union should rely on its high status among the South Caucasian countries[149] and offer a formula that proves that EU membership is not necessary for stability, prosperity and strength.

The European Union's success also depends on the efforts made by the South Caucasian countries themselves. It is their challenge to overcome their differences and see the value of establishing stronger mutual ties.

---

147 Ibid., at p. 5.

148 Ibid., at p. 7.

149 The expectations of the South Caucasian countries towards the European Union are high. It should be noted that opinion polls show how much the citizens of these three countries tie their future and prosperity to the European Union. For example, a strong majority of Georgians (80 per cent) expressed their vision of their state within the European Union. See *EUobserver*, 19 May 2005.

The best position and role for the European Union in the Southern Caucasus would be to coordinate the efforts of the international community to contribute to ongoing reform efforts. The European Union is looking for a specific role in a space already crowded by international actors. The case of the Southern Caucasus shows the importance of coordinating actions with others, such as the OSCE, NATO and the United Nations.[150]

The Southern Caucasus forms an integral part of EU security. It is therefore in the European Union's strongest interest to work for the stability of the Southern Caucasus as well as for the elimination of other security threats (conflicts, organised crime and trafficking). Although the PCAs are long-term instruments[151] and the ENP shifts the relationship to a new level, the European Union lacks a long-term vision of its relations with the Southern Caucasus. The main effort should now focus on formulating a broad concept while avoiding situations like the omission of the Southern Caucasus in the initial formulation of the ENP. A common strategy towards the Southern Caucasus, together with an internal driving force, perhaps embodied by a new EU Member State, would contribute to the establishment of a complex and well-functioning external policy of the European Union and raise its credibility on the international scene. Such a move would leave the European Union better prepared to deal with diverse matters in the region – a credible leader.

The EU enlargement of 2004 brought the Southern Caucasus closer to the European Union. This shift is not so much a geographic one as it is a matter of awareness. The European Union should use the experience and knowledge of its new Member States in the formulation of its external policy. There is no doubt that the European Union should expand its zone of security towards the strategically important Black Sea region.[152] The control and early prevention of conflicts in the EU neighbourhood is a vital condition of EU stability, as security is not dividable.

---

[150] N. Burgess, 'The Council's Early Warning Process', in V. Kronenberger and J. Wouters, eds., *The European Union and Conflict Prevention. Policy and Legal Aspects* (The Hague, T.M.C. Asser Press 2004) p. 22 at p. 26.

[151] R. Petrov, 'The Partnership and Cooperation Agreement with the Newly Independent States', in Ott and Inglis, op. cit. n. 86, at p. 193.

[152] Conclusion by the editors in Kronenberger and Wouters, loc. cit. n. 150, at p. 583.

CHAPTER 19

CONCLUSIONS: SQUARING THE RING OF FRIENDS

Steven Blockmans* and Adam Łazowski**

1. INTRODUCTION: THE EUROPEAN UNION AND ITS NEIGHBOURS AFTER THE 2004 ENLARGEMENT

It almost amounts to a *cliché* to start with the claim that the recent enlargement of the European Union has been an unprecedented and multidimensional exercise.[1] It is beyond doubt that the EU enlargement has had far-reaching political, economic and legal consequences for the European Union. It has led to the reformulation of many of its internal and external policies, including a redesign of the relations with its neighbouring countries. One has to remember that, in purely geographical terms, the European Union finds itself in a rather new environment. With its own borders moved further to the east and south of Europe, it has spread throughout most of the continent, with all the political and legal consequences resulting from this major development. On the one hand, EU enlargement has lead to the extension of the area of peace and stability to the countries that less then two decades ago had been directly or indirectly part of the Soviet Union's ruthless empire. On the other hand, this strategic decision has brought the European Union closer to troublesome areas, which require a fair degree of political finesse to be dealt with on a regular basis. It has often been claimed that enlargement has been one of the biggest achievements of the European Union's external policy.[2] Even if one

* Researcher in European Union Law, T.M.C. Asser Institute, The Hague.
** Senior Lecturer in Law, School of Law, University of Westminster, London.

The authors wish to thank Anna Łabędzka for her useful comments on earlier versions of this chapter. The usual disclaimer applies.

[1] See, *inter alia*, A. Mayhew, *Recreating Europe. The European Union's Policy towards Central and Eastern Europe* (Cambridge, Cambridge University Press 1998); A. Ott and K. Inglis, eds., *Handbook on European Enlargement. A Commentary on the Enlargement Process* (The Hague, T.M.C. Asser Press 2002); M. Cremona, ed., *The Enlargement of the European Union* (Oxford, Oxford University Press 2003); Ch. Hillion, ed., *EU Enlargement. A Legal Approach* (Oxford/Portland, Oregon, Hart Publishing 2004); E. Brimmer and S. Fröhlich, eds., *The Strategic Implications of European Union Enlargement* (Washington, Centre for Transatlantic Relations 2005).

[2] See M. Cremona, 'Enlargement: A Successful Instrument of EU Foreign Policy?', in T. Tridimas and P. Nebbia, eds., *EU Law for the Twenty-First Century: Volume I* (Oxford/Portland, Oregon, Hart Publishing 2004) p. 397.

S. Blockmans and A. Łazowski (eds.), The European Union and Its Neighbours

shares this approach, one has to accept that the enlargement has at the same time been one of the biggest challenges to the Union's functioning and effectiveness (not to mention its absorption capacity).[3]

Over the past couple of years, the nature of the debate on EU enlargement has gradually shifted from one driven by external relations motives, that is to say, the eradication of dividing lines in Europe, to a major internal policy discussion about the developing character of the European Union and its potential and future status. The last enlargement round coincided with the most comprehensive 'constitutional' reform of the European Union to date. Two years after the big bang enlargement, the situation gives some reasons for satisfaction and some reasons for concern. On the positive side, the European Union is still functioning, despite the fact that its twenty-five Member States do not always speak with one voice. It still has the capacity to deal with new challenges. Those first two years have served as an eye-opener, showing clearly the scale, breadth and consequences of the enlargement. This book shows how the accession of ten new Member States in 2004 has influenced the European Union's policies towards its neighbours. Being only one of many dimensions of the enlargement, it serves as a perfect laboratory for an evaluation of the Union's developing policies and its adjustments to the new geopolitical position in which it finds itself in the wake of the enlargement.

2. COMPETENCES, INSTRUMENTS AND INTERESTS

Following the recent revisions of the Treaty framework, there is no doubt that, in legal terms, both the European Communities and the European Union are well equipped to be important actors on the international stage, especially in the immediate neighbourhood.[4] To this end, they have the necessary powers as well as a wide range of legal and political instruments to serve their needs. For a number of years, the formal division of powers between the European Community and its Member States has been a matter of concern and, in some cases, litigation.[5] The recent disputes over the civil air transport agreements with the United States[6] and the follow-up agreement to the Lugano Convention only serve

---

[3] This is the so-called fourth accession criterion established by the Copenhagen European Council in 1993. See chapter 3 in this volume. For an analysis of the accession criteria and their evolution, see, *inter alia*, Ch. Hillion, 'The Copenhagen Criteria and Their Progeny', in Hillion, op. cit. n. 1, at p. 1.

[4] See E. Cannizzaro, ed., *The European Union as an Actor in International Relations* (The Hague/London/New York, Kluwer Law International 2002); P. Koutrakos, *EU International Relations Law* (Oxford/Portland, Oregon, Hart Publishing 2006); M. Cremona, 'The Union as a Global Actor: Roles, Models and Identity', 41 *CMLRev.* (2004) p. 553.

[5] See chapter 2 in this volume as well as the ECJ's case law and the literature referred to therein.

[6] See, *inter alia*, L. Heffernan and C. McAuliffe, 'External Relations in the Air Transport Sector: The Court of Justice and the Open Skies Agreements', 28 *ELR* (2003) p. 601.

to prove this point and show that the debate is far from over.[7] If and when it enters into force, the Treaty establishing a Constitution for Europe will be a major step forward, as it provides for a variety of changes that may potentially lead to the strengthening and consolidation of the European Union's external activities.[8]

Fresh tensions between some of the new Member States, on the one hand, and Russia as well as Belarus, on the other, combined with high hopes vested by the newcomers in the European Union's intervention, show that not only the formal but also the real division of competences between the European Union and its Member States is of the highest concern.[9] This is where the question of interplay between interests of the European Union and its members comes to the surface. This book shows that the external relations are one of those areas of EU law where law and politics not only meet but in fact are bound by an unbreakable chain. Legal developments are usually based on complex and sophisticated compromises balancing the varying interests of the Member States and the interests of the European Union.

From a legal perspective, it appears that there is no common template for the European Union's engagement with all of its neighbours. It is characterised by a multiplicity of models and instruments. The levels of intensity vary and characterise the nature of the relationship between the European Union and its neighbours (stabilisation, partnership, association or integration). While a number of neighbours have been given more or less firm commitments that their integration will be next, others are looking for various other forms of cooperation. The diversity of the relations of the European Union with neighbouring countries like Albania, Iceland, Morocco, Romania and Russia attests to this fact. While countries are grouped together in various initiatives, relations are in most cases governed by bilateral dealings between the European Union and the individual states. With the exception of the EEA and the Energy Community there is no multilateral framework, and it seems that the patchwork of relations will simply continue to exist. Although the European Commission set out a multilateral framework for relations over the coming decade with the eastern and southern

[7] ECJ, Opinion 1/03 *Competence of the Community to conclude the new Lugano Convention on jurisdiction and the recognition and enforcement of judgments in civil and commercial matters* [2006] *ECR*, nyr.

[8] M. Cremona, 'The Draft Constitutional Treaty: External Relations and External Action', 40 *CMLRev.* (2003) p. 1347; J. Wouters, 'The Union Minister for Foreign Affairs: Europe's Single Voice or Trojan Horse?', in J. de Zwaan, et al., eds., *The European Union: An Ongoing Process of Integration* (The Hague, T.M.C. Asser Press 2004) p. 77; and R. Wessel, 'Fragmentation in the Governance of EU External Relations: Legal Institutional Dilemmas and the New Constitution for Europe', in ibid., p. 123.

[9] The role played by the European Union during the Orange Revolution in Ukraine serves as another very good example. For a general overview of these events, see A. Krushelnycky, *An Orange Revolution. A Personal Journey Through Ukrainian History* (London, Harvill Secker 2006).

neighbouring countries that do not currently have a perspective of EU membership, there is no single model or template, as plans are tailored to the specific circumstances and the European Union's expectations of each partner.

For the purposes of this chapter, it is worth paying particular attention to Article I-57 TCE, which sets forth the general principles on the European Union's relations with its neighbouring countries. The first paragraph reads as follows:

> The Union shall develop a special relationship with neighbouring countries, aiming to establish an area of prosperity and good neighbourliness, founded on the values of the Union and characterised by close and peaceful relations based on cooperation.

Although this provision speaks for itself, it is worth taking a closer look at some of its elements. First off all, it creates an explicit obligation for the European Union to develop a special kind of relationship with its neighbours. This is not limited to countries covered by the existing European Neighbourhood Policy but implicitly extends to all present and future geographical neighbours. Such an enhanced relationship shall be tailored to create an area of prosperity and good neighbourliness. Some elements of conditionality are visible at the outset, given that this cooperation shall be founded on the values of the European Union. Those are clearly defined in Article I-2 TCE and include, *inter alia*, 'respect for human dignity, freedom, democracy, equality, the rule of law and respect for human rights'. Although the Treaty establishing a Constitution for Europe has not yet entered into force and its future is rather uncertain, this principle deserves closer attention. To some extent, it reflects the existing reality and policies undertaken by the European Union. It also reflects the political need to establish friendly relations with neighbouring countries. In short, the principle already serves as the backbone of EU actions towards its neighbours. It has already been argued that differences between the neighbours of the European Union preclude a single and uniform neighbourhood policy. Countries like Switzerland, the Holy See, Georgia, Morocco and Iceland are not only geographically but also politically, economically and culturally miles apart. All deserve the European Union's close attention, although the relevant policies should be tailored to serve the interests of the European Union itself, its Member States and the neighbouring countries. In some cases, good neighbourly relations may lead to EU membership; in others, they may lead to a long-term partnership that is of a mutual benefit to the parties concerned.

As this book shows, conditionality plays a central role in the formulation of the European Union's policies towards most of its neighbouring countries and regions.[10] This includes countries which are on the path to integration as well as

---

[10] See chapter 3 in this volume. See also L. Bartels, *Human Rights Conditionality in the EU's International Agreements* (Oxford, Oxford University Press 2005).

those whose membership is either excluded for geographical reasons or impossible in political terms. The emerging problem is the use of different standards towards particular neighbouring countries or groups of countries, partly ignoring the will of the new Member States and their vital national interests. The morally doubtful human rights conditionality applied *vis-à-vis* Russia may serve as an excellent example of such *'real politik'*. On the one hand, breaches of fundamental rights led to the freezing of relations with Belarus.[11] On the other hand, the atrocities of the war in Chechnya,[12] a very doubtful democracy and human rights record and the recent threats to cut the supply of gas to the European Union have not stopped the Union from offering the Russian Federation a free trade agreement and relations based on a partnership.[13] This is all happening at a time when Estonia, one of the European Union's new Member States, has not yet been able to fix its final borders with the Russian Federation. This is only a snapshot of what are very complex and sensitive relations. Nevertheless it clearly shows the multiplicity of problems and challenges emerging on the horizon. In this respect, one has to keep in mind that, based on a redefinition of interests and requirements, the relations between the European Union and its neighbours can be described as an equation with multiple variables: political, economic, cultural and other motives and realities are the determining factors.

The European Union's policies towards its neighbouring countries are in most cases based on networks of international treaties usually centred on an association or partnership agreement. There is a tendency to supplement them with bilateral or multilateral instruments and a large variety of policy documents. In the case of certain groups of countries, the basic treaty framework follows a particular pattern. To this end, treaties only marginally differ from one another in each given category. The Europe Agreements with Central and Eastern European countries,[14] the Stabilisation and Association Agreements with the countries of the Western

---

11 See chapter 16 in this volume.

12 See, *inter alia*, Parliamentary Assembly, Council of Europe, Recommendation 1733 (2006), Human rights violations in the Chechen Republic: the Committee of Ministers' responsibility *vis-à-vis* the Assembly's concerns, available at: <http://assembly.coe.int/Main.asp?link=/Documents/AdoptedText/ta06/EREC1733.htm>.

13 'European Commission approves terms for negotiating new EU-Russia agreement', Press Release IP/06/910, 3 July 2006.

14 Europe Agreement establishing an association between the European Communities and their Member States, of the one part, and the Republic of Bulgaria, of the other part, *OJ* 1994 L 358/3; Europe Agreement establishing an association between the European Communities and their Member States, of the one part, and Romania, of the other part, *OJ* 1994 L 357/2. See, *inter alia*, M. Maresceau, '"Europe Agreements": A New Form of Cooperation between the European Community and Central and Eastern Europe', in P.-Ch. Müller-Graff, ed., *East Central European States and the European Communities: Legal Adaptation to the Market Economy* (Baden-Baden, Nomos 1993) p. 209; M. Maresceau and E. Montaguti, 'The Relations between the European Union and Central and Eastern Europe: A Legal Appraisal', 32 *CMLRev.* (1995) p. 1327.

Balkans[15] and the Partnership and Cooperation Agreements with the countries of the former Soviet Union serve as excellent examples.[16] The specificity of the EEA-EFTA countries, Turkey, Russia, Switzerland and the micro-states has required special, tailor-made arrangements that differ to a considerable degree from the ones mentioned above. In the case of each neighbouring country, there are always a number of flanking agreements extending the cooperation to other areas of mutual interest covering all three pillars of the European Union. This includes not only the countries of the former Soviet Union and the Western Balkans but also Iceland, Norway and Switzerland. Moreover, this area is filled with unilateral legal instruments originating in the European Union. These include not only first pillar regulations and decisions but also a variety of acts adopted in the framework of the Common Foreign and Security Policy. Although common strategies seem to have become redundant, other instruments like joint actions and common positions play an important role in the everyday functioning of the second pillar.[17]

Despite many differences between the above-mentioned 'backbone' agreements there are a number of common denominators. In most cases, they contain a selection of trade-oriented provisions, facilitating the liberalisation of trade or even the creation of free trade areas.[18] A degree of liberalisation is also provided for when it comes to freedom of establishment and the free movement of services. The free movement of workers is an exception, and most of the agreements only contain clauses on non-discrimination in the workplace.[19] Most of the agreements also contain clauses on competition and state aid.

---

[15] Stabilisation and Association Agreement between the European Communities and their Member States, of the one part, and the Republic of Croatia, of the other part, *OJ* 2005 L 26/3; Stabilisation and Association Agreement between the European Communities and their Member States, of the one part, and the former Yugoslav Republic of Macedonia, of the other part, *OJ* 2004 L 84/13. For an academic appraisal, see D. Phinnemore, 'Stabilisation and Association Agreements: Europe Agreements for the Western Balkans?', 8 *EFA Rev.* (2003) p. 77.

[16] See, *inter alia*, Agreement on partnership and cooperation establishing a partnership between the European Communities and their Member States, of one part, and the Russian Federation, of the other part, *OJ* 1997 L 327/3; Partnership and Cooperation Agreement between the European Communities and their Member States, of the one part, and the Republic of Ukraine, of the other part, *OJ* 1998 L 49/3. See, *inter alia*, R. Petrov, 'The Partnership and Cooperation Agreements with the Newly Independent States', in Ott and Inglis, op. cit. n. 1, at pp. 175-194.

[17] See Art. 12 TEU.

[18] Partnership and Cooperation Agreements with countries of the former Soviet Union provide only for the liberalisation of bilateral trade. Europe Agreements and Stabilisation and Association Agreements have fixed legal frameworks for the creation of free trade areas. The same goes for the FTA between the EEC and Switzerland. The Turkish example of a customs union with the European Communities is very unique. So is the EEA Agreement, which sets forth rules on the free movement of goods without at the same time creating a customs union.

[19] See Art. 23 PCA Russia. See also ECJ, Case C-265/03 *Igor Simutenkov* v. *Ministerio de Educación y Cultura and Real Federación Española de Fútbol* [2005] *ECR* I-2579.

In most cases, detailed arrangements are made in order to allow a political dialogue between parties. Depending on the needs of bilateral cooperation, the institutional dialogue takes place at different levels. With major partners like Russia and Ukraine, summits of Heads of State and Government are quite regular events.[20] At lower levels, cooperation is usually effected within joint committees established by the parties.

One of the key elements of these agreements consists of clauses on the approximation of laws. The character of the obligation and its reading differs depending on the type of relationship that a third country has with the European Union. Such clauses are flexible and facilitate different readings depending on the development of the bilateral relationship. The approximation clauses in the Europe Agreements with Bulgaria and Romania may serve as excellent examples.[21] The original interpretation of those provisions highlighted the softness of the obligation based on the 'best endeavours clause'. Following the applications of both countries for membership of the European Union, the interpretation has evolved into an obligation to implement the entire *acquis* into their national legal systems. Approximation clauses have also been inserted in Association Agreements with countries that, due to their geographical position, will never become members of the European Union. This shows the importance of legal approximation in the European Union's attempts to square the ring of friends. However, the interpretation of these clauses will not be as far-reaching as in the case of the acceding countries. It has to reflect the nature and aims of the agreement and the relationship between the European Union and its neighbour.

The relations with the EEA-EFTA countries, as well as with Switzerland and the countries participating in the Energy Community, are a real step further, as the parties are formally obliged to exhaustively apply specific elements of EU legislation. Moreover, they are obliged to interpret this legislation in a manner consistent with the case law of the European Court of Justice. This inevitably adds integration flavours to the European Union's relationship with these neighbours.[22]

Financial assistance provided by the European Union is definitely one of the tools used to support its policies towards the neighbouring countries. Over the years, the Union has developed a system of different aid programmes addressing, *inter alia*, the candidate countries of Central and Eastern Europe (Phare, SAPARD, ISPA and the Turkish pre-accession instrument), the potential candidate countries of the Western Balkans (CARDS), the neighbouring countries bordering the Mediterranean Sea (MEDA) and those built on the ashes of the

---

20 See chapters 14 and 15 in this volume.

21 Art. 69 EA Bulgaria, Art. 69 EA Romania. For an academic appraisal, see, *inter alia*, A. Łazowski, 'Approximation of Laws', in Ott and Inglis, op. cit. n. 1, at pp. 631-639.

22 See chapters 4 and 5 in this volume.

Soviet Union (Tacis).[23] In the context of recent reforms, the European Commission has presented plans to harmonise (insofar as possible) the existing aid programmes. This includes aid to the future Member States of the European Union as well as to the countries covered by the ENP. With regard to the former, the Council has adopted a regulation establishing a single Instrument for Pre-Accession Assistance (IPA), thereby replacing the five existing instruments, for the period covered by the next financial perspectives (2007-2013).[24] The IPA will provide an envelope of €11.5 billion over the next seven years for the countries with candidate status (currently Croatia, Macedonia and Turkey) or potential candidate status (Albania, Bosnia-Herzegovina, Montenegro and Serbia, including Kosovo according to UNSCR 1244 (1999)).[25] The European Commission has also presented a proposal for a European Neighbourhood and Partnership Instrument (ENPI).[26] The rationale behind the proposal is to replace existing geographical and thematic programmes covering the countries concerned, namely MEDA and Tacis. The proposed budget of the ENPI is roughly €15 billion for the 2007-2013 period. Compared with a combined total of €8.5 billion Euro for Tacis and MEDA for the 2000-2006 period, this constitutes a significant increase in available resources.

---

[23] Interestingly enough, following the recent enlargement, some of the closest neighbours are also financing projects in the new Member States of the European Union. This includes the EEA grants as well as Swiss funds.

[24] Council Regulation (EC) No. 1085/2006 of 17 July 2006 establishing an Instrument for Pre-Accession Assistance (IPA), *OJ* 2006 L 210/82.

[25] The final envelope is even less than the €14.65 billion proposed by the Commission in its Proposal for a Council Regulation establishing an Instrument for Pre-Accession Assistance (IPA), COM (2004) 627 final. Section 5.1.1 of the Explanatory Memorandum to the Draft Regulation stated the principles according to which funds would be allocated to the official candidates: Croatia, Turkey and, in due course, Macedonia. The Draft Regulation read: 'The intention is that future candidate countries should be treated broadly the same as past candidate countries. As the countries of the Western Balkans become candidate countries it is proposed that they will receive per capita per year about the level of assistance established in the financial perspective 2000-2006 … for the 10 candidate countries in central and eastern Europe.' The European Stability Initiative, a non-profit research and policy institute with bases in Berlin, Brussels and Istanbul, heavily criticised the proposed envelope. The ESI calculated that, according to this formula, each of the candidates would receive around €27 per capita per year. For Croatia, this would boil down to €120 million per year, and for Macedonia around €54 million per year. In fact, all Western Balkan countries would receive less than they receive now (with the exception of Bosnia-Herzegovina, where CARDS funding has already fallen to this lower level). In Kosovo, the decline in EU assistance would be particularly steep. See ESI, *Breaking Out of the Balkan Ghetto: Why IPA Should Be Changed* (Berlin, ESI 2005). The envelope agreed to by the Council in July 2006 will no doubt make it even harder for some of the Western Balkan states to carry out the necessary reforms to 'break out of the ghetto'. See Council Regulation (EC) No. 1085/2006 of 17 July 2006 establishing an Instrument for Pre-Accession Assistance (IPA), *OJ* 2006 L 210/82.

[26] Proposal for a Regulation of the European Parliament and of the Council laying down general provisions establishing a European Neighbourhood and Partnership Instrument, COM (2004) 628 final.

The substantial volume of aid which has been granted to the beneficiary countries over the past decades has played an important role in the development of bilateral relations. For the European Union, it has been one of the tools used to support those countries and their political and economic reforms. From the perspective of the countries, it has been one of the incentives for those economic and legal changes. In the case of the new Member States of the European Union, it served as a prelude to EU structural funds and the potential benefits they bring to national economies.

As argued in this section, the European Union undoubtedly has powers and instruments to conduct effective policies towards its neighbours. The main issue remains whether it has the real will to do so. The big bang enlargement proves that finding a balance between the European Union's interests and the national interests of particular Member States may be quite difficult. It is clearly one of the major obstacles to a fully fledged foreign policy of a Union composed of twenty-five Member States. In the long term, it may weaken the European Union's position towards the outside world. The diversity of interests within the club has particularly far-reaching consequences for overall policy towards the neighbourhood. The recent newcomers from Central and Eastern Europe have little interest (if any) in EU policy towards most of the countries of the Mediterranean. At the same time, the eastern dimension and policies towards Russia, Belarus and Ukraine are of major importance for countries like Poland, Lithuania, Latvia and Estonia. The dispute with Russia about energy resources in 2006 only proves that reaching a consensus between the Member States of the European Union may be far from easy. At the same time, such a diverse environment gives the newcomers a chance to influence existing EU policies. Whether the actions of those countries are effective is a different matter, but they should be given the chance to contribute to the shaping of the European Union's relations with its immediate neighbourhood. By the same token, the old Member States should give themselves a chance to benefit from the experiences of those countries in handling troubled relations with some of their neighbours.

What are the interests of the European Union? The list is far too long to be included here, but they have been spelled out in the country and regional analyses in the second part of this volume. On a more general level, one can argue that, first and foremost, the European Union has a major interest in maintaining peace and stability in Europe. This relates in particular to the safety of its own Member States, both old and new, in the broadest sense. Friendly relations with its neighbours are thus a prerequisite for the European Union's own smooth and effective functioning. As highlighted in this book, recent and forthcoming enlargements (will) bring Europe closer to countries or regions with escalating ethnic and religious conflicts. The experiences of the last fifteen years prove that, on a human level, such conflicts lead to massive immigration, humanitarian disasters and the spread of various forms of organised and transnational crime.

The European Union cannot afford another failure of its policies comparable to the one dating back to civil war in Yugoslavia. That is why the European Union should formulate its policies in a more active way and not on an *ad hoc* basis in response to developments taking place in its immediate neighbourhood. As argued in chapter 7 of this volume, this was exactly the case when the Communist dictatorships collapsed in the early 1990s. It is in the European Union's own interest, and conducive to its safety, to formulate such policies in advance. The development of the European Neighbourhood Policy ahead of the big bang enlargement proves that there has been a change of attitude in this respect.

Article I-57 TCE makes it clear that the European Union shall spread the benefits of prosperity and good neighbourliness that are founded on respect for fundamental rights. To this end, it can be argued that the promotion of democracy, respect for fundamental rights and good governance should be at the top of the European Union's list of priorities.

3. EU MEMBERSHIP

3.1 Introduction

The pre-accession process is one of the most developed policies of the European Union towards its neighbours. As already mentioned, EU enlargement is often considered to be the biggest success of the Union's foreign policy. Not only did it bring an end to the division of Europe going back to the end of the Second World War, but it has also served as an incentive for unprecedented reforms in countries that have managed to put an end to totalitarian regimes and Soviet dominance in the region. Contrary to some general perceptions, the concept of integration must not be equated with EU membership. As the next section shows, integration can take on many faces. Various models have been developed in recent decades to bring neighbouring countries closer to the European Union by integrating them in certain common policies or by giving them a stake in the internal market.

3.2 Pre-accession process

Following the fall of Communism in Central and Eastern Europe, the European Communities/European Union have been faced with a constantly increasing interest in membership. The developments of the last two decades led to a doubling of the number of the Member States. All the countries that acceded in 2004 never expressed an interest in anything short of the membership. From the early days, they considered association as a mere transitional phase leading to the accession to the European Union. The path to integration of Bulgaria and Romania follows in the footsteps of the new EU Member States from Central and

Eastern Europe. One could even argue that they are part of the same enlargement exercise, though delayed for economic and legal reasons. Still, despite all the similarities, there are a number of factors that make the forthcoming sixth enlargement different from the previous one. The main difference lies in the enhanced conditionality applied towards Bulgaria and Romania.[27] It has been introduced in order to comfort the concerns connected with those countries' relatively poor performance in transposing the *acquis* and implementing the necessary legal and economic reforms. The Accession Treaty contains a set of safeguard clauses, some of which can be used in order to postpone the membership of one or both of these countries until 1 January 2008.[28] There is also a degree of differentiation between the two acceding countries themselves. The membership postponement clause puts Romania in a much more challenging position, as its list of pre-accession commitments is far broader that that of Bulgaria.[29] At the time of writing, it is still unclear whether the European Union will eventually decide to use this opportunity to delay the next wave of the enlargement. Although there may be a political rationale for such a move, it would certainly be doubtful in practical terms. Another twelve months in the waiting room will not solve the structural and legal problems of these countries. On the contrary, due to the potential sociological and political side-effects, they could make the accession even more problematic.

Notwithstanding all those factors, the expected membership of Bulgaria and Romania marks an important date in the contemporary history of the European Union. They are the last two countries that, following the fall of the Communist dictatorships, have gone all the way from association based on the Europe Agreements to membership of the European Union. They are also the last two countries envisaged for accession by the Treaty of Nice.[30] Moreover, as is clear from recent political developments, the European Union is going to apply modified rules to any future enlargements.

At the time of writing, accession negotiations have been opened with Turkey and Croatia. Both countries have very different histories of relations with the

---

[27] See chapters 3, 7, 8 in this volume.

[28] Treaty between the Kingdom of Belgium, the Czech Republic, the Kingdom of Denmark, the Federal Republic of Germany, the Republic of Estonia, the Hellenic Republic, the Kingdom of Spain, the French Republic, Ireland, the Italian Republic, the Republic of Cyprus, the Republic of Latvia, the Republic of Lithuania, the Grand Duchy of Luxembourg, the Republic of Hungary, the Republic of Malta, the Kingdom of the Netherlands, the Republic of Austria, the Republic of Poland, the Portuguese Republic, the Republic of Slovenia, the Slovak Republic, the Republic of Finland, the Kingdom of Sweden, the United Kingdom of Great Britain and Northern Ireland (Member States of the European Union) and the Republic of Bulgaria and Romania, concerning the accession of the Republic of Bulgaria and Romania to the European Union, *OJ* 2005 L 157/11.

[29] See Annex IX to the Act on Conditions of Accession.

[30] Treaty of Nice amending the Treaty on European Union, the Treaties establishing the European Communities and certain related acts, signed at Nice, 26 February 2001, *OJ* 2001 C 80/1.

European Communities/European Union, and their path towards membership also differs. Turkey has been associated with the European Community since the 1960s on the basis of the so-called Ankara Agreement.[31] It submitted its application for membership in 1987, but for a complex set of reasons accession negotiations only started in late 2005.[32] Notwithstanding this development, Turkey's potential accession to the European Union still remains uncertain. It is not only a question of when it could take place but primarily a question of whether it will take place at all. A growing concern among the existing Member States means that the European Union may be forced to look for other ways of creating a close relationship with Turkey. Croatia is one of the countries established on the ruins of the former Yugoslavia and has been covered by the Stabilisation and Association Process for a number of years.[33] Following the political developments of 2005, combined with its improved cooperation with the International Criminal Tribunal for the Former Yugoslavia, it has been given the green light for accession negotiations. However, the *modus operandi* in this respect has been modified.

At its summit in Brussels on 16-17 December 2004, the European Council agreed on a revised framework for every future round of accession negotiations, to be created 'according to own merits and specific situations and characteristics of each candidate state.'[34] It adopted this new approach to soothe worries in some Member States over its decision to open accession talks with Turkey (most notably France and Austria), and to a lesser extent with Croatia (the Netherlands, the United Kingdom and Italy). The European Council stressed, for instance, that long transition periods, derogations, specific arrangements or even permanent safeguard clauses (defined as 'clauses which are permanently available as a basis for safeguard measures') could in the future be imposed in areas such as freedom of movement of persons, structural policies and agriculture.[35] Although this approach seems to be reasonable from the point of view of some Member States, it is questionable as a permanent solution for a constitutional system like that of the European Union.[36]

[31] Agreement of 12 September 1963 establishing an Association between the European Economic Community and Turkey, *OJ* 1977 L 361/29.

[32] See chapter 9 in this volume.

[33] See chapter 11 in this volume.

[34] See *Bull. EU* 12-2004, point I.8.23.

[35] And all matters relating to freedom of movement of persons will allow 'a maximum role of [those] individual Member States' that are afraid that their labour market will be flooded with Turkish workers. The European Council emphasised that transitional arrangements or safeguards should be reviewed regarding their impact on competition or the functioning of the internal market.

[36] See U. Becker, 'EU-Enlargements and Limits to Amendments of the EC Treaty', Jean Monnet Working Paper No. 15 (2001), available at: <http://www.jeanmonnetprogram.org>; A. Bodnar, 'Transitional Periods for Employment – "Second Class" EU Citizenship?', in O. Zetterquist, ed., *Law and Modernity* (Kraków, Polpress 2004) p. 121; Ch. Hillion, 'The European Union is dead. Long live

As in previous pre-accession rounds, all Member States will take part in chapter-by-chapter negotiations with each candidate. But there will be more chapters to be negotiated by present and future candidate countries. This is the result of both a technical rearrangement – certain chapters were considered too big and were chopped up while smaller ones were merged[37] – and the introduction of a new package on judiciary and human rights.[38] The latter reflects a normative advancement in comparison with previous rounds of accession negotiations, as the political Copenhagen criteria on respect for democracy, human rights and the rule of law have now been incorporated into a so-called '*acquis* chapter'. From now on, candidate countries will have to show that they have the administrative capacity to effectively apply and implement the *acquis* on human rights and – crucially when dealing with the current and future candidate countries – minority rights.

Another novelty in the revised procedure agreed to by the December 2004 European Council concerns the right of the Council, acting by unanimity on a proposal by the Commission, to lay down benchmarks for the provisional closure and, where appropriate, the (re)opening of each chapter. Depending on the chapter concerned, these benchmarks will refer to legislative alignment and a satisfactory track record of implementation of the *acquis*, as well as obligations deriving from contractual relations with the European Union. Thus, after agreement has been reached between the European Union and the candidate country on an individual chapter of the negotiations, and once the benchmarks have been met, the chapter concerned is considered *temporarily* closed. The formal decision is made by the Intergovernmental Conference at ministerial level. If, before the Accession Treaty has been concluded, new elements of the *acquis* falling within the scope of a specific chapter are developed, or if the candidate country does not meet the benchmarks or obligations assumed under the chapter concerned, negotiations for that chapter can be reopened. The revised procedure thus provides for an extra 'stick behind the door' to make sure that candidate countries deliver on each of the chapters – something about which the Commission had become distrustful after the experiences of the fifth round of enlargement negotiations.

---

the European Union…', 29 *ELR* (2004) p. 583 at p. 593. For a more optimistic view, see D. Thym, *Ungleichzeitigkeit im Europäischen Verfassungsrecht* (Baden-Baden, Nomos 2002) p. 341.

[37] For example, the chapter on the free movement of persons was divided into a chapter on the free movement of workers and one dealing with the right of establishment and the free movement of services, and the chapter on agriculture was separated into a chapter on agriculture and rural development and one on food safety, veterinary and phytosanitary policy. On the other hand, the chapters on industrial policy and small and medium-enterprises were merged into one chapter on enterprise and industrial policy.

[38] Instead of the thirty-one chapters that Bulgaria and Romania had to negotiate, Croatia and Turkey are looking at thirty-five chapters.

In fact, the December 2004 European Council stated that the new frameworks for negotiations will be established by the Council on a proposal by the Commission, 'taking account of the experience of the fifth enlargement process and of the evolving *acquis*.' Under the terms of the frameworks, 'the shared objective of the negotiations is accession', but 'the outcome cannot be guaranteed beforehand.' In one way, the European Council merely stated the obvious: accession negotiations have – and have always had – an open-ended character. But the political signal towards new candidate countries cannot be underestimated. Where a candidate seriously and persistently breaches the principles of liberty, democracy, respect for human rights, fundamental freedoms and the rule of law, negotiations can be suspended.[39] If a candidate is not in a position to assume in full all the obligations of membership – diplomatic language for a failure in negotiating accession – the European Union will nevertheless ensure 'that the candidate state concerned is fully anchored in the European structures through the strongest possible bond.' Supposedly, the candidate would then fall back to its status as an associate.

4. ASSOCIATION, STABILISATION AND PARTNERSHIP

4.1 **Introduction**

As argued above, integration should not be equated with EU membership. There are other ways in which the integration of particular neighbouring countries or groups of countries into the political, economic and legal spheres of the European Union can be achieved. Of course, the breadth and level of such integration will be of a more limited scale when compared with accession to the European Union. Over the past decades, the European Union has successfully developed neighbourhood policies of association, partnership and stabilisation.

For the countries that joined the European Union on 1 May 2004, association served as a vehicle towards integration.[40] And so it has for Bulgaria and Romania, which are expected to accede shortly. Membership of the European Union is not always the ultimate goal of association. For some countries, which for one reason or another are not 'able or willing' to accede to the European Union, association

[39] In such a case, the European Commission will, on its own initiative or on the request of a third of the Member States, recommend the suspension of negotiations and propose conditions for their eventual resumption. The Council will decide by qualified majority on such a recommendation, after having heard the candidate state. The Member States will act in the IGC in accordance with the Council decision, without prejudice to the general requirement for unanimity in the IGC. The European Parliament will be informed.

[40] K. Inglis, 'The Europe Agreements Compared in the Light of their Pre-accession Reorientation', 37 *CMLRev.* (2000) p. 1173.

may serve as a satisfactory arrangement. Those 'unable' to accede include the non-European neighbours, which due to their place on the map cannot fulfil the conditions laid down in Article 49 TEU. Those 'unwilling' to accede include Norway, Iceland and Switzerland, which have found such association arrangements to meet their desires.

In reaction to the fall of the Soviet Union and the violent implosion of the Socialist Federal Republic of Yugoslavia, the European Union developed policies of partnership and stabilisation. While relations with the Western Balkans are slowly developing from stabilisation, via association, to pre-accession, the policies of partnership, cooperation and association towards the countries of the southern Mediterranean and the former Soviet Union have been reorganised to take account of the geopolitical changes resulting from the big bang enlargement. This extends to countries covered by the European Neighbourhood Policy as well as Russia, with which the European Union has an ambition of developing a special relationship.

Each of these forms of 'integration' will be briefly discussed below.

4.2 EEA-EFTA countries and Switzerland

There is no doubt that, in legal terms, the EEA-EFTA countries remain the most integrated neighbouring countries.[41] First and foremost, this is due to the Agreement on the European Economic Area, which, being a form of enhanced multilateralism, extends the four freedoms of the internal market, combined with some flanking policies, to Iceland, Liechtenstein and Norway.[42] Large chunks of the *acquis* are applicable to those countries; moreover, in accordance with the principle of homogeneity, they shall be interpreted in a fashion consistent with the relevant case law of the European Court of Justice.[43] This gives the relationship very strong integration flavours. Moreover, by means of additional agreements, cooperation with these countries also extends to aspects of the Common Foreign and Security Policy and Justice and Home Affairs. In the case of the latter, the association of Iceland and Norway with the Schengen *acquis* is of particular relevance.[44] Interestingly enough, all additional agreements are being adopted outside the EEA framework. So far, proposals for a revision of the Agreement have not been submitted.

---

41 On relations between the EEA and the European Union, see P-Ch. Müller-Graff and E. Selvig, eds., *EEA-EU Relations* (Berlin, Berlin Verlag & Arno Spitz GmbH 1999).

42 Agreement on the European Economic Area, *OJ* 1994 L 1/1.

43 See chapter 4 in this volume.

44 See N. Wichmann, 'The Participation of the Schengen Associates: Inside or Outside?', 11 *EFA Rev.* (2006) p. 87.

The evaluation of the EEA's functioning leads to a number of conclusions. The first decade of its functioning proves that, despite its complexities and Byzantine institutional structure, it is a well-functioning hybrid. The call for a closure of the business that followed the EU accession of Austria, Finland and Sweden has proved to be premature. However, with more countries joining the European Union, the question of the sustainability of the EEA will return like a boomerang. The ultimate question is whether the EEA has a future. It certainly has one, as long as Iceland and Norway remain members on the EFTA side. This does not exclude their potential membership of the European Union at some later stage. Another model that Norway and Iceland may find attractive in the years to come is enhanced bilateralism based on the EU-Swiss *modus operandi*. A decision in favour of such options would probably lead to the end of the EEA, unless it is revitalised by more accessions on the EFTA side.

In light of the recent attempts to enhance the European Union's relations with some of its members, the question is emerging whether the EEA can be revitalised or whether it is, at least, capable of serving as a model for rearranging relations with countries like Ukraine, Russia, Georgia and potentially even Turkey (as a less controversial alternative to EU membership). This argumentation has its roots in the school of thought, supporting EEA membership for the emerging democracies of Central and Eastern Europe as a prelude to EU accession,[45] that was prevalent in the 1990s. Contrary to common perception, EEA membership may potentially have considerable economic and political benefits. It would expand the internal market to those countries without the possibility of the EU membership in the long run. Participation in such an 'antechamber' would certainly lead to a high degree of legal approximation and economic integration. Implementation of the *acquis* would fall under the strict scrutiny of the EFTA Surveillance Authority and the EFTA Court. In practical terms this would allow the neighbouring countries to get acquainted not only with EU law as such but also with its application and its enforcement machinery on a daily basis. Such an arrangement would also have advantages for the European Union itself. It would allow it to pause for a break following the big bang enlargement and the accession of Bulgaria and Romania. It could facilitate the completion of the constitutional reform of the European Union and the further adaptation to the political, economic and legal reality of twenty-seven Member States (not to mention the improvement of the European Union's absorption capacity).

Of course, there are a number of reasons why such a *modus operandi* may not be the best way forward. The EEA-EFTA countries do not participate in EU decision-making procedures on an equal footing with the EU members. On the

[45] S. Peers, 'An ever closer waiting room?: The case for Eastern European accession to the European Economic Area', 32 *CMLRev.* (1995) p. 187.

contrary, they take part mainly in the pre-pipeline committee stages. In order to reflect the nature of this activity, it is usually referred to as 'decision shaping'. The Norwegian and Icelandic examples prove that, even with such limited access to decision making, there is an ample space for influencing EC legislation. Notwithstanding those limitations, the EEA-EFTA countries are obliged to swallow pieces of EC secondary legislation with EEA relevance. Not surprisingly, these factors make the option of the EEA membership not very attractive for the neighbouring countries. The list of such negative factors is much longer though. It includes the lack of a policy equivalent to the Common Agricultural Policy and the lack of a customs union between the EEA-EFTA and EEA-EU countries. Moreover, the levels of financial assistance are not comparable to any of the pre- or post-accession funds granted to the poorest Member States. All those factors may make the implementation of this scenario rather unacceptable for the neighbouring countries. Nevertheless, some key elements of the EEA framework may serve as models for the future development of some of the EU neighbourhood policies.

Following the entry into force of the two packages of bilateral treaties with Switzerland, we have witnessed the creation of a new model for the arrangement of the European Union's relations with its neighbours.[46] Because of its characteristics, this model can be referred to as enhanced bilateralism. Although some of the treaties between the parties are formally classified as Association Agreements, this relationship is full of integration flavours. The agreement on the association of Switzerland with the Schengen *acquis* serves as an excellent example in this respect. The Swiss Confederation is obliged to apply some pieces of EU law, and this obligation extends to the interpretation of those acts in accordance with the case law of the European Court of Justice.

The inevitable question is what comes next in European Union's relations with Switzerland. Membership of the European Union is still a long-term goal of the Swiss Confederation although it is a rather unlikely scenario in the current political environment. In the coming years, we are more likely to see the further enhancement of bilateral relations and the conclusion of an agreement on services.

Another question that pops up immediately is whether a similar model of enhanced bilateralism can potentially be used in relations with certain other EU neighbours. This may sound like a tempting scenario for some of the current EU neighbours, Russia in particular. Although beneficial for a third country, such *à la carte* integration may not be a desired option for the European Union, unless a guillotine clause is used again. On the one hand, it is certain that such tailor-made sectoral enhancement of bilateral relations may cover areas of mutual interest. On

46 See chapter 5 in this volume.

the other hand, different sets of agreements with specific neighbouring countries may create an incomprehensible and messy matrix of international treaties covering various aspects of EU law. One has to remember that an obligation to apply selected aspects of the *acquis* is one of the key features of enhanced bilateralism. A diversity of agreements combined with an ever-developing *acquis* and the necessity of adapting such agreements may seriously affect the coherence and effectiveness of such bilateral frameworks.

4.3 The Energy Community: a new model of 'enhanced multilateralism'

The creation of the Energy Community between the European Community and Albania, Bulgaria, Bosnia-Herzegovina, Croatia, FYROM, Montenegro, Romania, Serbia and the UN Mission in Kosovo shows yet another face of sectoral integration between the European Union and the group of the neighbouring countries and territories with a special status (Kosovo).[47] Due to its very strong integration factors, this framework may also be described as 'enhanced multilateralism'. In this case, it is limited to the creation of 'an integrated market in natural gas, and electricity, based on common interest and solidarity'.[48] The Treaty sets forth a legal framework for the creation of an Energy Community equipped with powers and instruments.[49] Despite its sectoral character, it may be regarded as a model for future arrangements with groups of EU neighbours.

4.4 Russia

Russia is definitely one of the most difficult EU neighbours to deal with, not only because Russia is a tough partner by nature but also because of the diverging interests among the Member States themselves.

One of the challenges is the fact that the Russian Federation, despite its crumbling and corrupted economy, very doubtful democracy and human rights record of the past ten years, still openly aspires to be a political superpower. Some of the Member States of the European Union still perceive Russia as a reliable partner that deserves a privileged partnership. EU-Russia relations have changed considerably over the past decade. Without a doubt, NATO and EU expansion have considerably reduced the Russian sphere of influence and pushed the Central and Eastern European countries towards the path of integration. The moving borders of Russia's spheres of influence are directly affecting the European Union's

47 The Energy Community Treaty, *OJ* 2006 L 198/18.
48 Seventh recital of the Energy Community Treaty.
49 See chapter 11 in this volume.

relations not only with Russia but also with all its eastern neighbours. This was more than apparent during the presidential elections in Ukraine in 2004 and the subsequent Orange Revolution.

The old and new Member States have dramatically different histories of relations with the Soviet Union/Russian Federation. This gives rise to misconceptions and misunderstandings, but at the same time it is a strong factor forcing the European Union of twenty-five Member States to look for compromises and arrangements that will be satisfactory for the entire block. The infamous German-Russian deal on the gas pipeline is an example of *'real politik'* conducted by Germany behind the backs of the other Member States that not only undermines the interests of its direct neighbours but also those of the European Union as such. The consequences of these charades became visible in early 2006, when the actions of the Russian administration and its dependent gas and oil companies threatened gas supplies to some of the EU Member States. One side-effect of these manoeuvres has been the reactivation of the EU debate on energy resources and the diversification of gas supplies.[50]

So far, legal relations between the European Communities/European Union and Russia have been based on the Partnership and Cooperation Agreement. In recent years, a number of attempts have been made to enhance the bilateral framework in order to create a partnership between the parties. To this end, proposals have been made to establish four common spaces and a free trade area. These options still remain open, but it is in the European Union's interest to seek a solution which is not only satisfactory for some of the old Member States but also for the newcomers, especially the ones that have vital interests in the region. This, as argued by Hillion, 'is likely to be an uphill battle'.[51] One thing is certain, though. The European Union is in great need of a coherent policy towards Russia. Any steps in this direction should be based on a detailed analysis of the potential benefits for the European Union and its Member States. Moreover, this arrangement must be based on the equality of rights and obligations between the parties. Any asymmetries in this respect would be less than welcome. From an EU perspective, such a relationship should have a cross-pillar dimension extending to issues of trade, environmental protection, energy supplies, nuclear safety and justice and home affairs. Bearing this in mind, one has to evaluate the idea of common spaces in a positive fashion. However, the success of this policy will strongly depend on the next steps taken by the parties.

---

[50] See, *inter alia*, Green Paper: A European Strategy for Sustainable, Competitive and Secure Energy, COM (2006) 105 final. See also European Commission, A European Strategy for Sustainable, Competitive and Secure Energy. What is at stake – Background document, COM (2006) 105 final.

[51] See chapter 14 in this volume.

4.5 ENP countries

Shortly before the big bang enlargement, the European Union made the decision to revamp its policies towards its eastern and southern neighbours. To this end, the European Neighbourhood Policy was launched in 2003, with the publication of the European Commission's 'Wider Europe' initiative.[52] A detailed plan was published a year later in a strategy paper on the European Neighbourhood Policy.[53] Shortly thereafter, the ENP entered into its first phase: the conclusion of action plans with the neighbouring countries.[54] The purpose of this exercise is to enhance relations with the neighbours and facilitate their further development. As explained by the European Commission, the policy objectives include the creation of 'an increasingly close relationship, going beyond cooperation to involve a significant measure of economic and political integration'.[55]

At the time of writing, the group of neighbours covered by the ENP includes Algeria, Armenia, Azerbaijan, Belarus, Egypt, Georgia, Israel, Jordan, Lebanon, Moldova, Morocco, the Palestinian Authority, Syria, Tunisia and Ukraine. Libya is formally not (yet) part of the process. The development of relations with Belarus depends on the political situation in the country. The choice of countries that have been offered enhanced relationships under the ENP umbrella includes countries that are not only geographically but also politically and economically miles apart. Moreover, due to their geographic position, some of them will never be eligible for membership of the European Union, while others could one day fulfil all the conditions set forth in Article 49 TEU.[56] This arrangement has already received a fair degree of criticism. Experience proves that gathering such a diversified set of countries under the umbrella of one policy may not be the best *modus operandi*. The interests of the European Union in the Mediterranean region and in Eastern Europe are simply to diverse.

Despite its *prima facie* multilateral character, the ENP aims to develop relations with particular countries on an individual basis. The intensity of those relations depends heavily on a variety of political and legal factors. In purely legal terms, the relations with the countries covered by the ENP are based on existing

---

52 Communication from the Commission to the Council and the European Parliament, Wider Europe-Neighbourhood: A New Framework for Relations with our Eastern and Southern Neighbours, COM (2003) 104 final.

53 Communication from the Commission, European Neighbourhood Policy, Strategy Paper, COM (2004) 373 final.

54 For a list of action plans, see: <http://ec.europa.eu/world/enp/documents_en.htm>.

55 Communication from the Commission, European Neighbourhood Policy, Strategy Paper, COM (2004) 373 final, p. 5.

56 It has been revealed that the separation of countries that are eligible and non-eligible for membership may be considered under the German Presidency in the first half of 2007. See *The Guardian*, 17 July 2006.

legal instruments. This includes Partnership and Cooperation Agreements with the countries of the former Soviet Union and Euro-Mediterranean Agreements with the southern neighbours. The ENP serves as the framework for the proper enforcement of those instruments. As explained by the European Commission, they 'define priorities and provide focus for the implementation of existing agreements.' Moreover, the action plans 'include "deliverables" of importance to the EU and the country concerned in various fields covered by the agreements'.[57] The country-specific action plans provide roadmaps for future action by the neighbouring countries. The added value of such an approach is the concept of 'shared ownership' and responsibility of both parties for its successful functioning. To this end, a monitoring role is played by joint bodies established on the basis of the PCAs and EMAs.

The ENP will enter into a new era with the adoption of the first European Neighbourhood Agreements. They will replace the existing legal framework and are expected to be the next generation of international agreements to be concluded by the European Communities/European Union with its neighbours. Their scope and breadth will be based on an evaluation of performance based on the action plans.

The experiences of the first two years lead to one major question: is the ENP the right response to the challenges posed by relations with the European Union's Mediterranean and eastern neighbourhood? Certainly it is an interesting attempt to lay the foundations for a modern and sophisticated foreign policy based on shared ownership and mutual trust. The diversity of the countries covered, as well as the diversified interests of the European Union in those regions, may prove to be an obstacle to the development of the ENP. Looking at the Mediterranean, the role of the European Union in the resolution of the conflict in the Middle East should be increased, although involvement in this region requires particular abilities. So does the eastern dimension, where the European Union is clearly stepping into territories generally considered to be within the Russian sphere of interest. Moreover, the European Union is getting much closer to areas of potentially violent conflicts.[58] For a number of reasons, the European Union should increase its presence in the region. This is in the interests of both the Union itself and its Member States (especially some of the newcomers). Is the ENP an adequate framework to cope with the challenges faced? Practice may prove that the European Union is more effective in the implementation of its policies in those regions on a purely bilateral basis.

---

[57] Communication from the Commission. European Neighbourhood Policy. Strategy Paper, COM (2004) 373 final, p. 9.

[58] See chapter 18 in this volume.

4.6 *Quo vadis?* The questionable concept of 'privileged partnership'

On several occasions since the big bang enlargement, a number of primarily French and German political leaders have insisted that the European Union should pause for breath, consolidate and grant a 'privileged partnership' instead of full EU membership to big neighbouring countries like Turkey and Ukraine.[59] From those statements, it is not clear what exactly is to be understood by the concept of 'privileged partnership', other than the creation of 'arrangements that would bring maximum benefits to all sides without endangering the EU itself.'[60] While one's initial thoughts immediately go in the direction of Article I-57 TCE and the partnership and 'privileges' offered by the European Union in the framework of the ENP, this is apparently not what the likes of Germany's Chancellor Angela Merkel and France's Minister of the Interior and a presidential hopeful in the election of 2007, Nicolas Sarkozy, have in mind. Turkey and Ukraine are too big and strategically important for the European Union, in both (geo)political and economic terms, to be placed in the same category as countries like Azerbaijan and Lebanon. The European Union cannot suffice by granting these countries enhanced trade relations and increased financial and technical assistance. Some sort of 'third way' is implied, whereby Turkey and Ukraine would be granted a special status in relation to the European Union which would go beyond a customs union but would not envisage any Turkish or Ukrainian participation in the Union's common policies (e.g., structural funds and agriculture), except – for obvious reasons – in the fields of security and defence. The free movement of goods, services and even capital would be guaranteed, but the EU labour market would remain closed. In legal terms, this situation could be created either by granting *full* membership to these countries, albeit with the permanent safeguard clauses proposed under the revised procedure for accession negotiations,[61] or by concluding an international agreement between the European Union and the countries concerned that is based on a customs union and otherwise comes as

[59] See, e.g., L. Harding and N. Watt, 'Turkey's EU dream dealt double blow as Chirac and Merkel raise doubts', *The Guardian*, 27 August 2005; L. Kubosova, 'Sarkozy calls for definition of "borders of Europe"', *EUObserver.com*, 31 March 2006; V. Giscard d'Estaing, 'A better European bridge to Turkey', *Financial Times*, 25 November 2004; and A. Leparmentier, 'UE: les turcosceptiques durcissent leurs positions', *Le Monde*, 16 November 2004. Austrian Chancellor Wolfgang Schüssel used the argument as *ultimum remedium* to block a unanimous decision on the opening of accession talks with Turkey until the other Member States agreed to do the same for Croatia. See A. Browne, 'Turkey left out in cold as Austria digs in heels over EU entry talks', *The Times*, 3 October 2005.

[60] A poor definition offered by Wolfgang Schäuble (then deputy head of Germany's CDU/CSU group which brought Angela Merkel to power after winning the parliamentary elections in 2005) in a response to an article by David Phillips in *Foreign Affairs*. See W. Schäuble, 'A Still-European Union', 83 *Foreign Affairs* (2004) p. 134.

[61] See *supra*.

close to the *acquis* as politically acceptable. While those options might seem attractive in legal terms, they represent a position which – politically speaking – it is unwise to adopt when one is concerned with the positioning of the European Union on the international scene. By abandoning its commitments towards Turkey, the European Union would create an image of itself as an unreliable negotiating partner, with all the imaginable consequences.

More troubling is the fact that German Chancellor Angela Merkel was the first head of government to publicly suggest a loose partnership option for the Western Balkans.[62] Merkel's statement came just days after EU Ministers of Foreign Affairs struggled to find a common wording for their aims towards the region after their (ultimately not so) informal meeting with leaders from the Western Balkans in Salzburg on 10-11 March 2006. A draft statement had avoided the term 'membership' while confirming the goal of EU accession in more general terms. After strong overnight pressure from the Balkan states, the final statement read:

> [T]he EU confirms that the future of the Western Balkans lies in the European Union. … All [Western Balkans states] have in the last year made significant steps along their road towards the EU, with EU membership as ultimate goal in conformity with the Thessaloniki Declaration.[63]

But diplomats from the Western Balkans lost the battle to remove the notion 'absorption capacity' from the final text. 'The EU also notes that its absorption capacity has to be taken into account,' the statement reads.[64] France and the Netherlands strongly insisted on keeping the absorption capacity paragraph, as they saw perceptions of uncontrolled enlargement as a key reason why their citizens voted down the Constitutional Treaty in their national referenda. The French Minister of Foreign Affairs Philippe Douste-Blazy was reported as having said: 'We cannot act as if the people do not exist. … We must not rush headlong into enlargement.'[65] His Dutch counterpart Bernard Bot indicated: 'We should not go too fast, we should pay attention to our public opinion,' adding that a 'very long process' lies ahead.[66] In spite of the more or less clear message sent by the

---

62 See E. Krasniqi and M. Beunderman, 'Merkel moots "privileged partnership" for Balkans', *EUObserver.com*, 17 March 2006.

63 Salzburg EU/Western Balkans Joint Press Statement of 11 March 2006, Press release No. 7283/06 (Presse 77).

64 Ibid. In a similar vein, see EP Committee on Foreign Affairs, Report on the Commission's 2005 enlargement strategy paper (2005/2206(INI)), No. A6-0025/2006 final, 3 February 2006, prepared by rapporteur Elmar Brok, and adopted by the EP on 16 March 2006, P6_TA-PROV(2006)0096.

65 See M. Beunderman, 'EU membership goal clarified under Balkan pressure', *EUObserver.com*, 11 March 2006.

66 Ibid.

French and Dutch voters on the future membership of Turkey,[67] it would be unwise, dangerous even, to renege on the commitments made *vis-à-vis* the countries of the Western Balkans, for it could disrupt a valuable process that is helping to build stable states in the region.[68] In the words of Olli Rehn in a speech before the European Parliament: 'If [the European Union] were to go wobbly about the Western Balkans' European perspective, [its] beneficial influence would be seriously eroded, just when the region enters a difficult period of talks on Kosovo's status.'[69] Thus, the opposition to EU enlargement, as expressed in the disruptive referenda in France and the Netherlands, has to give way to the responsibilities of the European Union in ensuring security and stability on the continent by continuing the process of enlargement.

4.7 Western Balkans

The relations between the European Union and the countries of the Western Balkans are built on a conundrum: how to effectively reconcile the regional approach that is essential for the stabilisation of the Western Balkans with the requirement of evaluating countries on the basis of their individual performances, a concept which lies at the heart of the pre-accession process? With the creation of the Stabilisation and Association Process (SAP), the European Union tried to answer this question by emphasising the central need for regional cooperation as part of the Stabilisation and Association Agreements. The past five years, however, have demonstrated that this works only to a limited extent. The laggards in the pre-accession process – Bosnia-Herzegovina, Montenegro and Serbia (including Kosovo) – no longer regard the SAP as a fast integration track. The lesson from this is that only real incentives can bring real reforms. Arguably, the creation of a free trade area in South-Eastern Europe could provide the missing incentives for regional cooperation.[70] After all, the economic interdependence of the countries of the Western Balkans is vital for the future of the region.[71] The economic sustainability of their small and unattractive markets depends on the creation of a common economic area that will attract foreign direct investment.

[67] For an analysis, see S. Blockmans, 'Reconciling widening and deepening: enlargement as a vehicle to break the Union's constitutional deadlock', in A. Albi and J. Ziller, eds., *The European Constitution and National Constitutions: Ratification and Beyond* (Dordrecht, Kluwer Law International 2006) forthcoming.

[68] See S. Blockmans, *Tough Love: the European Union's Relations with the Western Balkans* (The Hague, T.M.C. Asser Press 2006) forthcoming.

[69] See O. Rehn, 'Commission's Enlargement Strategy', Strasbourg, 15 March 2006, SPEECH/06/171.

[70] See chapters 10 and 11 in this volume.

[71] On the high levels of intra-regional trade, see European Commission, 'Trade in South-Eastern Europe', MEMO/06/155, Brussels, 5 April 2006.

Thus, in an economic sense, a regional approach is a necessary precondition for development. The Central European Free Trade Agreement (CEFTA) could provide the countries of the Western Balkans with a platform to realise their economic ambitions and meet two important requirements of EU (pre-)accession conditionality: regional cooperation and readiness for the competitive impact of participating in the single market. In view of the fact that Bulgaria and Romania will leave CEFTA when they accede to the European Union in 2007, the agreement may be preserved by extending it to cover the rest of the Western Balkan states, which have already completed a matrix of bilateral free trade agreements. This idea has only recently gained momentum. On 6 April 2006, nine heads of government and one Minister of Foreign Affairs from the Balkans, as well as the Special Representative of UNMIK, adopted a joint declaration underpinning their political commitment to starting negotiations on the enlargement and amendment of CEFTA.[72] The countries that are to be included in the enlarged CEFTA are Albania, Bosnia-Herzegovina, Moldova, Montenegro, Serbia and the United Nations Interim Administration Mission in Kosovo. The negotiations on the amendments to the agreement will focus on the promotion of simpler and less bureaucratic procedures and the introduction of modern trade provisions in areas such as harmonisation, competition, state aid, services and the protection of intellectual property rights.

More importantly, the European Union can render the SAP a much more credible framework by transcending the 'potential members' mindset and showing its commitment to the countries of the Western Balkans. The experience of the CEECs illustrates best how the institutionalisation of the EU integration perspective is the most efficient way to foster and accelerate the overall political, economic and administrative reforms in aspirant countries. To put an end to the growing fears of some countries in the Western Balkans that they might be left out of the process altogether, a so-called 'Helsinki moment' should be created for the region, in reference to the historic decision of the European Council gathered at Helsinki in December 1999 to grant candidate country status to Turkey.[73] In a similar historic spirit, the European Council should use one of its forthcoming summits to review the achievements of the Western Balkans in satisfying the Copenhagen 'plus' criteria and grant candidate country status to Albania, Bosnia-Herzegovina, Montenegro, Serbia and – if independent – Kosovo. These countries – plus Macedonia if accession negotiations have still not been opened – should then be presented with their accession road maps. The summit should be held

72 The text of the Joint Declaration by Prime Ministers, South-Eastern Europe Summit, Bucharest, 6 April 2006, is available at: <http://www.stabilitypact.org/trade/documents/tradeFINAL-joint%20 declaration.pdf>.

73 *Bull. EU* 12-1999, point I.3.2.

soon after the last Stabilisation and Association Agreement has entered into force. Working on the assumption that the European Commission will meet its ambition to conclude the remaining SAAs before the end of 2006, or soon thereafter, a new 'Helsinki moment' could come as early as in the first half of 2008. To that end, popular anxiety over any further enlargements, now very apparent in the internal politics of EU Member States, should be countered, for the European Union 'cannot take a sabbatical' from enlargement while it sorts out its internal rules.[74] Convincing the enlargement-wary citizens of the Union will not be an easy task, but it is necessary if the European Union wants to keep a firm grip on the most effective tool for dealing with its roughest neighbourhood. In this respect, the revised procedure for accession negotiations could take away some of the existing enlargement fears.

4.8 Micro-states

Last but not least, one has to mention the micro-states, namely Andorra, Monaco, San Marino and the Vatican City. Due to their special status and strong ties with some of the EU Member States there is clearly no need for a very rich and sophisticated EU policy. The tailor-made agreements signed with these countries have proved their usefulness and are an adequate response to the needs of both sides. This very unique kind of partnership will probably exist in the decades to come. As such it has not been significantly affected by enlargement.

5. CONCLUSIONS

This anthology proves that squaring the ring of friends is a very complex and sophisticated exercise. The diversity of the Member States and their interests, combined with a very heterogonous neighbourhood, requires not only powers and capacity but also a fair degree of flexibility and skill in order to achieve desirable effects. The former may be considered as a challenge to the assumption of a single position and voice of the European Union on the international plane. In order to secure a strong standing, the 'old' Member States need to take a broader look and acknowledge the presence of the 'new' Member States and their vital political and economic interests. Strengthening the links of the latter with the immediate neighbourhood would inevitably strengthen the European Union's position as an important international player. *Mutatis mutandis*, this would also support the neighbours themselves and serve as an encouragement for further internal reforms.

---

[74] Olli Rehn, quoted in G. Parker and C. Condon, 'Some Balkan states may find EU's door closed', *Financial Times*, 7 April 2006.

The European Union cannot ignore the membership aspirations of some of its neighbours. After all, the perspective of full membership is the most powerful incentive which the European Union can offer to (potential) candidate countries in return for reform. Of course, further enlargements cannot be self-defeating, in the sense that they would weaken the fabric of the Union to such an extent that they would threaten the very aims of peace, prosperity, stability and security on the European continent which they seek to achieve.[75] The best way forward for the European Union is to reconcile its widening and deepening agendas without creating second-class members. Full integration of some neighbouring countries is one of the options; others include association and partnership. All those policies are very dynamic and, as proved by recent experiences, flexible and adjustable. It is in the interest of the European Union, its Member States and the neighbours to develop them further in order to expand the area of peace, security and justice on the European continent and beyond.

75 A response to K. Inglis in chapter 3 of this volume.

BIOGRAPHIES

Steven Blockmans is a senior research fellow in EU law at the T.M.C. Asser Institute (The Hague). He combines his academic research with consultancy activities and training in EU law. His academic research focuses on EU external relations, enlargement and constitutional law. His PhD thesis, 'Tough Love: The European's Union relations with the Western Balkans', is forthcoming with T.M.C. Asser Press. With Professor Deirdre Curtin and Dr Alfred Kellermann, he co-edited a volume on the Treaty establishing a Constitution for Europe, entitled *The EU Constitution: The best way forward?* (The Hague, T.M.C. Asser Press 2005). His consultancy activities include research projects for the European Commission and various Dutch ministries and are usually concerned with the legal problems that Member States and/or (potential) candidate countries face in the implementation of the *acquis communautaire*. In addition, he serves as a short-term expert in projects sponsored by the European Union and the Dutch Government to train judges, court clerks, prosecutors and lawyers of new Member States and (potential) candidate countries in EU law matters. Before moving to the T.M.C. Asser Institute, Mr Blockmans worked as a lecturer on the law of international organisations at the Europa Institute of Leiden University (1998-2002).

Wybe Th. Douma studied law at the University of Groningen (The Netherlands) and the Eberhard Karls University, Tübingen (Germany) and wrote his doctoral thesis on 'The Precautionary Principle. Its application in International, European and Dutch Law'. After having worked at the Department of Administrative Law and Public Administration and the Department of European Law at the University of Groningen, he switched to the T.M.C. Asser Institute where at present he is Head of the Department of European Law and Head of Projects. He has lectured on institutional and substantive European law, international and European environmental law, administrative law, EU-Russia relations and WTO law at the Universities of Warsaw, Lublin and Krakow (Poland), the Chulalongkorn University in Bangkok (Thailand), the Moscow State Institute for International Relations (MGIMO), the Institute for State and Law (Moscow) and the Universities of Irkutsk and Kazan (Russia), as well as for civil servants, lawyers, judges and public prosecutors in Russia, Bosnia-Herzegovina, Slovenia, the Czech Republic, Romania, Bulgaria, Estonia, Germany, the Netherlands and Lithuania. Dr Douma has been the Team Leader and Senior Legal Expert in Dutch consultancy projects for several Dutch ministries and in numerous Phare and Tacis projects, notably on the issue of harmonising national law with EU legislation, *inter alia*, in Estonia, the Czech Republic, Bosnia-Herzegovina and Russia. He is the editor of and a contributor to several Dutch, English and German journals and editor-in-chief of the European Environmental Law website (<http://www.eel.nl>).

Christophe Hillion is Professor of European Institutional Law at the University of Leiden, and a visiting professor at the College of Europe (Bruges/Natolin-Warsaw). His research focuses on EU external relations, enlargement and constitutional law. He wrote his PhD thesis on the evolving system of EU external relations, taking the EU partnerships with Russia and Ukraine as case-studies. He is presently turning this study into a book. He also published an edited collection on the EU enlargement process, entitled *EU Enlargement: A Legal Approach* (Oxford, Hart Publishing 2004), and a volume on EC external relations, entitled *The General Law of EC External Relations* (London, Sweet & Maxwell 2000), which he edited with Professor Alan Dashwood. He is a member of the editorial board of the *European Foreign Affairs Review* (Kluwer Law International).

Kirstyn Inglis qualified as a Scottish solicitor in 1990 and has since built her career in EC law in Brussels. Currently, as senior legal researcher at the European Institute of the University of Ghent, she specialises in the legal aspects of enlargement of the European Union and in environment and food law in the context of enlargement. She has also acted as a legal consultant within specialised EU regulatory consultancies for private clients and trade federations and, independently, in projects for the European Commission, the UN Economic Commission for Europe and the World Bank and projects focusing on judicial and administrative capacity building in Central and Eastern Europe. At present, she is a consultant for Wragge & Co Solicitors. She will defend her PhD thesis, on the subject of EU enlargement: an analysis of pre-accession and transitional arrangements with case studies on agri-food and environment law, in Ghent in September 2006. Her latest book, co-edited with Dr Andrea Ott, is entitled *The Constitution for Europe and an Enlarging Union: Unity in Diversity?* (Groningen, Europa Law Publishing 2005).

Dr Mónika Józon is an associate professor at the School of Business Administration and Humanities of the Sapientia-Hungarian University of Transylvania (Romania) where she teaches European business law, international trade law, civil law and comparative competition law. She holds a PhD in international trade law (Adacemia de Studii Economice Romania, 2004), an LL.M in European Business Law (Amsterdam School of International Relations, 1998) and a master's degree in Advanced European Studies (Europa Institut Basel, 1997). Professor Józon's research activity focuses on the field of EU enlargement (law and economics of legal integration, unification of private law in Europe, product liability and environmental liability). During the past ten years, she has participated as legal expert in several EU-funded technical assistance projects aimed at the reform of the judiciary and the public administration (public utilities) in Romania. She has recently been involved in the ECTIL Project on Human Rights and Tort and in the Project on Personal Injuries of the Trento Group Project on the Common Core of European Private Law.

Edgar Lenski is a lecturer at the Faculty of Law of Humboldt-University Berlin. After obtaining a Diploma in French Law from the University of Trier (Germany) he graduated from Humboldt University Berlin with a degree in (German) law in 2000. Since then, he has been working at the Walter Hallstein Institute for European Constitutional Law of Humboldt University and has been giving lectures at the Humboldt Faculty of Law. He also teaches at the German-Polish Law School, a joint programme of Humboldt University and Wrocław University, and, as a visiting lecturer, at the Law Department of the University of Wales (Aberystwyth). Since 2000, he has been regularly teaching EU law and international law for practitioners. From 2004 to 2006, he pursued his *Referendariat* in Berlin and Brussels at, *inter alia*, the German Permanent Representation to the European Union. Edgar Lenski's research focuses on EU law and public international law, especially WTO law. He is the author of articles on EU law and international law and the co-author of a textbook on international law.

Anna Łabędzka is a graduate of the Institute of International Relations at the University of Warsaw. She has also completed postgraduate studies in contemporary European studies at the Sussex European Institute. In recent years, Ms Łabędzka worked as a civil servant at the Office of the Committee of European Integration in Warsaw and later in the Chancellery of *Sejm*, the lower chamber of the Polish Parliament. In the latter position, she served as a secretary to delegations to the parliamentary assemblies of the Western European Union and the Organisation for Security and Cooperation in Europe. Ms Łabędzka has successfully managed to combine her professional experience with academic research. Since 1999, she has regularly contributed to various publications in Poland and abroad. This includes a chapter on the EU institutional framework in a highly acclaimed practitioners guide to EU institutional and substantive law published by Wolters Kluwer Poland. Ms Łabędzka's academic interests include international security, human rights, the European Security and Defence Policy, the Common Foreign and Security Policy and the resolution of the conflict in Northern Ireland.

Adam Łazowski is a senior lecturer at the School of Law at the University of Westminster (London). He obtained a Master's Degree in 1999 and a PhD in 2001 from the Faculty of Law of the University of Warsaw. Between 1999 and 2003, he lectured at the University of Warsaw. During the next two years, he worked as a senior researcher in European law at the T.M.C. Asser Institute (The Hague). Dr Łazowski's scientific interests include the law of the European Union as well as public international law. His research has so far led to a number of books, articles, contributions to edited volumes and conference papers. In 2003, his monograph on non-judicial remedies in EU law received first prize in a nationwide competition for the best book on EU law organised in Poland by the

Foundation for the Promotion of European Law. Since 1999, Dr Łazowski has actively participated in various EU law training programmes for practitioners in Poland, Bulgaria, Romania, Slovakia and Estonia. In Estonia, he served as a mid-term expert in an EU-financed biannual project. In that capacity, he provided extensive training to national lawyers as well as co-writing a distance learning course combined with a series of case studies aimed at Estonian judges.

Fiona Murray trained as a barrister in London and has law degrees from Trinity College, Dublin (LL.B) and the Vrije Universiteit Brussel (LL.M), the latter in international and European law. Ms Murray has published various articles on EU law and policy and is the author of a book on relations between the European Union and Member State territories under the EC Treaty. She is currently studying for a PhD on the territorial scope of the EC Treaty at Erasmus University (Rotterdam). Ms Murray has worked as an EU lawyer and public affairs consultant in Brussels for over fifteen years, including with the law firms Freshfields and White & Case and with her own public affairs consultancy, Athrónan Associates. She now works with the EU policy and funding consultancy, Schuman Associates.

Andrea Ott has worked as a university lecturer on European law at Maastricht University (The Netherlands) since 2003. Previously, she was a researcher at the Chair of International and European Law at the University of Greifswald (Germany), where she obtained her PhD in 1996 on the integration of GATT/WTO law into the EC legal order. From 1998 to 2003, she was a senior research fellow in European law and international economic law at the T.M.C. Asser Institute (The Hague). In 2002-2003, she was also a Jean Monnet Fellow at the European University Institute in Florence (Italy). Dr Ott has extensive experience in legal consultancy for Dutch ministries and the European Commission on issues relating to Central and Eastern Europe and regularly teaches on European institutional law, external relations, enlargement and WTO law in the Netherlands, Central and Eastern Europe and Southeast Asia. Since 1999, she has been a visiting guest professor for international economic law for the MA in European Studies of the Chulalongkorn University in Bangkok (Thailand). Since 2005, she has taught a Jean Monnet Module on external relations at Maastricht University. Dr Ott has published widely in her fields of interest and has co-edited two books on EU enlargement with Kirstyn Inglis from the University of Ghent. She contributed to a commentary project on the accession treaties in 2006.

Karolien Pieters is currently working as a researcher in European Law at the T.M.C. Asser Institute (The Hague). She obtained her master's degree in law at the Catholic University of Leuven (Belgium) and specialised in European law at the European Institute of the University of Gent (Belgium). Her scientific interests include the study of the Euro-Mediterranean Association Agreements, on which she is currently writing her PhD thesis, and European competition law, on which she has published various articles.

Eugeniusz Piontek, Professor ordinarius Dr hab., is Head of the Chair of European Law at the Faculty of Law and Administration of the University of Warsaw. He was Vice-Director (1978-1982) and Director (1982-1986) of the Institute of International Law at the Faculty of Law and Administration of the University of Warsaw. In addition, he was Chairman of the Division of International Organisations (1978-1993) and Chairman of the Scientific Council (1986-2002) of the Institute of International Law at the Faculty of Law and Administration of the University of Warsaw. Since 1991, he has been a member of the Advisory Council on European Law at the Centre of European Law at King's College London. In 1992, he was a lecturer at the Hague Academy of International Law. He has been a guest professor at a number of US, Western European and Australian universities, and was a member of the Polish delegation to the Uruguay Round (1987-1991), responsible for legal coordination. Professor Piontek is the author of eight books on international and European Law and over 600 articles on international law and international relations. He is the chairman and co-author of the Phare-Sierra Reports on the adjustment of Polish law to the EU law in the fields of banking and currency regulations, energy law, customs law, free movement of goods, telecommunications and air law, and he is a specialist in comparative competition law. Professor Piontek is an advocate and managing partner at the law office of Piontek, Ślązak, Wiśniewski & Associates L.P., Warsaw (Poland).

Siniša Rodin is Professor of European Public Law at the University of Zagreb. He obtained his PhD from the Law Faculty of the University of Zagreb in 1995 and his LL.M. from the University of Michigan Law School in Ann Arbor, Michigan, in 1992. He specialised in European law at the European University Institute in Florence (Italy) and German constitutional law at the Max Planck Institut für ausländisches öffentliches Recht und Völkerrecht in Heidelberg (Germany). He is a recipient of the University of Michigan Law School Merit Award and the University of Zagreb Rector's Award. In 2001-2002, he was a Fulbright Fellow and Visiting Scholar at Harvard Law School. Professor Rodin is a member of the International Association of Constitutional Law and of the European Communities Studies Association. He is the author of two books and more then twenty research papers. His scientific interests include issues of constitutional interpretation, fundamental rights and constitutional aspects of European integration. As of the 2002 academic year, Professor Rodin teaches a Jean Monnet module on advanced issues of European law.

Alla Skvortova works for the British Department for International Development (DFID) as the Head of the DFID Section at the British Embassy in Moldova. She obtained her first doctoral degree in history (*Kandidat Nauk* – Candidate of Sciences) from the Institute of History of the Academy of Science of the USSR in 1984 and her second doctoral degree in history (*Doktor Nauk* – Doctor of Sciences) from the Institute of Slavic Studies of the Academy of Science of the Russian Federation in 2003. She worked as a researcher at the Institute of History and the Institute of National Minorities of the Moldavian Academy of Science and as a human rights expert for the UNDP. She did research on national minority issues as a visiting scholar at the Center for Russian and East European Studies of the University of Michigan in Ann Arbor, Michigan, in 1995-1996. She is a recipient of the Moldavian Academy of Science Award for Young Researchers and a US Government Fellowship for the Regional Scholars Exchange Programme administered by the International Research and Exchange Board (IREX). Dr Skvortova is the author of one book and more then thirty research papers and contributions to other books. Her scientific interests include the history of Moldova from 1917 to 1940, the history and current situation of national minorities and ethnic policy in Moldova, human rights, EU enlargement and the European Neighbourhood Policy.

Svetla Yosifova is an associate at PI Partners, a law firm, which is associated with Ernst & Young in the South-East European region. At present, she is also a contributing editor to *European Current Law*, a legal digest published by Thomson, Sweet & Maxwell in the United Kingdom. She specialises in company and commercial law and corporate governance. Prior to joining PI Partners, she was engaged in a project under the national Phare programme in the area of the judicial reform and training for the judiciary implemented by a consortium comprising the British Council (Bulgaria), T.M.C. Asser Institute (The Netherlands) and the College of Europe (Belgium) (2003-2004). In 2004, Svetla Yosifova was awarded an LL.M. by Sofia University 'St. Clement Ohridsky'. In 2005, she was a scholar at The Hague Academy of International Law for the summer session on private international law.

Ramses A. Wessel is Professor of the Law of the European Union and other International Organisations and Co-Director of the Centre for European Studies at the University of Twente (The Netherlands). He is the Director of the European Studies Programme and Senior Research Fellow of the University's Institute for Governance Studies. Ramses Wessel is a senior member of the Netherlands Institute of Government and an associate member of the Ius Commune Research School. His additional functions include: editor-in-chief and founder of *International Organizations Law Review* and editor-in-chief of the Dutch journal and yearbook on peace and security, *Vrede en Veiligheid*. Ramses Wessel graduated from the University of Groningen with a degree in international law and international relations in 1989 and subsequently worked as an assistant professor at the same university (1989-1991) and in the Department of the Law of International Organisations at Utrecht University (1991-2000). He is the author of *The European Union's Foreign and Security Policy: A Legal Institutional Perspective* (The Hague, Kluwer Law International 1999) and a number of other publications in the field of EU external relations. His general research interests lie in the field of international and European institutional law, with a focus on international organisations, peace and security and European foreign, security and defence policy.

INDEX

D

E

F

G

H

R

S

T

U

V

W